TRANSFORMING GENDER CITIZENSHIP

Gender quotas are a controversial policy measure. However, over the past twenty years they have been widely adopted around the world and especially in Europe. They are now used in politics, corporate boards, state and local public administration and even in civil society organizations. This book explores this unprecedented phenomenon, providing a unique comparative perspective on gender quotas' adoption across thirteen European countries. It also studies resistance to gender quotas by political parties and supreme courts. Providing up-to-date comprehensive data on gender quotas regulations, *Transforming Gender Citizenship* proposes a typology of countries, from those which have embraced gender quotas as a new way to promote gender equality in all spheres of social life, to those who have consistently refused gender quotas as a tool for gender equality. Reflecting on divergences and commonalities across Europe, the authors analyze how gender quotas may transform dominant conception of citizenship and gender equality.

ÉLÉONORE LÉPINARD is Associate Professor in Gender Studies at the Institute of Social Sciences, University of Lausanne.

RUTH RUBIO-MARÍN is Professor of Constitutional Law at the University of Seville, Spain, and a member of the Faculty of The Hauser Global Law School Program at New York University.

G000067942

CAMBRIDGE STUDIES IN LAW AND SOCIETY

Founded in 1997, Cambridge Studies in Law and Society is a hub for leading scholarship in socio-legal studies. Located at the intersection of law, the humanities, and the social sciences, it publishes empirically innovative and theoretically sophisticated work on law's manifestations in everyday life: from discourses to practices, and from institutions to cultures. The series editors have longstanding expertise in the interdisciplinary study of law, and welcome contributions that place legal phenomena in national, comparative, or international perspective. Series authors come from a range of disciplines, including anthropology, history, law, literature, political science, and sociology.

Series Editors

Mark Fathi Massoud, *University of California, Santa Cruz*

Jens Meierhenrich, *London School of Economics and Political Science*

Rachel E. Stern, *University of California, Berkeley*

A list of books in the series can be found at the back of this book.

TRANSFORMING GENDER CITIZENSHIP
The Irresistible Rise of Gender Quotas in Europe

Edited by

Éléonore Lépinard
University of Lausanne

Ruth Rubio-Marín
University of Seville

CAMBRIDGE
UNIVERSITY PRESS

CAMBRIDGE
UNIVERSITY PRESS

University Printing House, Cambridge CB2 8BS, United Kingdom

One Liberty Plaza, 20th Floor, New York, NY 10006, USA

477 Williamstown Road, Port Melbourne, VIC 3207, Australia

314–321, 3rd Floor, Plot 3, Splendor Forum, Jasola District Centre,
New Delhi – 110025, India

79 Anson Road, #06-04/06, Singapore 079906

Cambridge University Press is part of the University of Cambridge.

It furthers the University's mission by disseminating knowledge in the pursuit of
education, learning, and research at the highest international levels of excellence.

www.cambridge.org
Information on this title: www.cambridge.org/9781108429221
DOI: 10.1017/9781108636797

© Cambridge University Press 2018

First published 2018

Printed and bound in Great Britain by Clays Ltd, Elcograf S.p.A.

A catalogue record for this publication is available from the British Library.

Library of Congress Cataloging-in-Publication Data

Names: Lépinard, Éléonore, editor. | Rubio-Marín, Ruth, editor.
Title: Transforming gender citizenship : the irresistible rise of gender
    quotas in Europe / edited by Éléonore Lépinard, Universite de Lausanne,
    Switzerland, Ruth Rubio-Marín, University of Seville.
Description: Cambridge, United Kingdom ; New York, NY : Cambridge University
    Press, 2018. | Series: Cambridge studies in law and society.
Identifiers: LCCN 2018011050 | ISBN 9781108429221 (hardback : alk. paper) |
    ISBN 9781108453356 (pbk. : alk. paper)
Subjects: LCSH: Women—Political activity—Europe. | Sex
    discrimination—Government policy—Europe. | Women public
    officers—Europe. | Europe—Politics and government.
Classification: LCC HQ1236.5.E85 T728 2018 | DDC 320.082/094—dc23 LC record
    available at https://lccn.loc.gov/2018011050

ISBN 978-1-108-42922-1 Hardback

ISBN 978-1-108-45335-6 Paperback

CONTENTS

FIGURES

TABLES

ACKNOWLEDGMENTS

The editors of this volume would like to thank the European University Institute (Florence, Italy) and the Jean Monnet Lifelong Learning Program of the European Union for funding the workshop and research project leading to this book. We would also like to thank all the contributors for their patience in revising and updating their chapters. Many thanks to Miluska Kooij and Stefano Osella for helping setting up the workshop and tracking down the contributors for dates and data. Finally, many thanks to Madeleine Arenivar for her skillful editing job.

INTRODUCTION

Completing the Unfinished Task? Gender Quotas and the Ongoing Struggle for Women's Empowerment in Europe

Éléonore Lépinard and Ruth Rubio-Marín

A global conversation about women's participation in political and economic decision-making has been taking place for the past two decades. International organizations, European institutions, women's rights organizations, political parties, and femocrat bureaucracies have been engaging in the promotion, adoption and diffusion of a new conception of gender equality, which, beyond equal rights, requires women's equal presence in places such as elected political assemblies, political parties' internal bodies, corporate boards, public advisory boards, governmental commissions, the judiciary, and university juries and commissions. Different terms have been coined, including equal participation, gender-balanced representation, or parity, to describe this goal of equal presence in decision-making. More often than not, voluntary or compulsory gender quotas have become the preferred answer to women's long-lasting underrepresentation in many spheres of social, economic, and political life, providing an apparently simple and efficient solution to the complex problem of women's exclusion from active and full citizenship.

What we designate in this volume as the "gender quota revolution" was bolstered at the global level by the Beijing Declaration and Platform for Action, signed at the sixteenth plenary meeting of September 15, 1995 at the United Nations Fourth World Conference on Women. It was there that the principle of equal participation of women and gender balance of women and men in decision-making was established for the first time. The Beijing Platform for Action

1

came to epitomize a true breakthrough in its attempt to foreground women's inclusion in decision-making and empowerment as a democratic requirement, explicitly endorsing affirmative action and substantive or de facto equality not only as legitimate but also as a *necessary* remedy, linking women's access to decision-making to the notion of justice as well as democracy.[1] In doing so, the Platform built on the expansion in the Convention on the Elimination of All Forms of Discrimination against Women (CEDAW) of the identified domains of public participation and decision-making from which women are said to be problematically excluded, in ways that better exposed the sexed separation between the public and private spheres. The Platform indeed recognized that action should be taken to enable women to access *all* those avenues to power and authority that had been traditionally closed to them, in the domain of the state (including, for the first time, a reference to the judiciary)[2] but also in civil society, explicitly mentioning political parties, employer organizations, trade unions, research and academic institutions, as well as executive and managerial positions in corporations and institutions.[3]

I.1   SETTING THE EUROPEAN STAGE FOR THE GENDER QUOTA REVOLUTION

While it is a phenomenon with worldwide dimensions and promoted by international organizations, the gender quota revolution has a specific genealogy in Europe. It was in Europe that the democratic framing of the problem of women's underrepresentation became more relevant. In 1988, the Committee of Ministers of the Council of Europe adopted a "Declaration on equality of women and men,"[4] stating gender equality to be an integral part of human rights and a prerequisite for genuine democracy. This declaration was followed up by a seminar on "The democratic principle of equal representation" in 1989, where the concept of *parity* was first discussed. Inspired by the emerging discourse on parity democracy, fourteen high-ranking female elected officials

---

[1] Fourth World Conference on Women, "Beijing Declaration and Platform for Action," Strategic Objective G1: §181.

[2] "Beijing Declaration and Platform for Action," Strategic Objective G1: §190a.

[3] §§184 and 191a.

[4] "Declaration on Equality of Women and Men," Committee of Ministers of the Council of Europe, adopted on November 16, 1988 (Eighty-third Session).

attending the first European Summit of Women in Power, held in Athens in November 1992, signed the "Athens Declaration" supporting gender parity in the representation and administration of nation states on November 3, 1992. A "Declaration on Equality between women and men as a fundamental criterion of democracy" was subsequently adopted during the Fourth European Ministerial Conference on Equality between Women and Men, held in 1997 in Istanbul, which became a framework of reference for all those working to increase the participation of women in decision-making. Since the turn of the century, the balanced participation of women has remained a clear priority of the Council of Europe, with the Committee of Ministers adopting in 2003 a Recommendation on "The Balanced Participation of Women and Men in Political and Public Decision-Making,"[5] defining and endorsing balanced participation as a minimum of 40 percent of both sexes in all decision-making bodies in political or public life, and the Parliamentary Assembly similarly adopting several resolutions seeking to enhance women's political representation.[6]

At the level of the European Union (EU), although legally binding directives on gender quotas have not been adopted, the endorsement of positive actions in the Treaties, the development of soft policy measures, and provision of funding to actions targeting women's increased political representation have certainly contributed to promoting social learning and reciprocal influence processes among member states (Beveridge 2011). Since the 1990s, the EU, be it the Commission or the European Parliament, has promoted gender equality action programs, produced reports, created a database on women in decision-making, and convened conferences on parity democracy.[7]

The concern with the participation of women in decision-making was reflected for the first time in the Third European Commission's Pluriannual Action Program (1991–5), under a new chapter on the

[5] "On balanced participation of women and men in political and public decision making," Recommendation Rec(2003)3, Committee of Ministers of the Council of Europe, adopted on March 12, 2003 (831st Session).

[6] See, most recently, Resolution 2111 (2016) "Assessing the impact of measures to improve women's political representation," which restates the importance of gender balance and of quotas to achieve it (para. 2); Resolution 1898 (2012) Final version, "Political parties and women's political representation," which calls for party quotas (para. 6); and Resolution 1706 (2010), "Increasing women's representation in politics through the electoral system."

[7] These include Athens 1992, Rome 1996, and Paris 1999 (Lombardo 2008).

"status of women in society." The actions taken to implement the Program marked the beginning of a process now recognized to have been decisive in most member states, spawning an intensive follow-up process across Europe and culminating in a recommendation by the Council in 1996.[8] This recommendation invited the member states to adopt a comprehensive, integrated strategy to redress the under-representation of women in decision-making bodies, including, where necessary, through the introduction of legislative and/or regulatory measures and incentives. In the new century, the goal of balanced participation has also remained high on the EU agenda. It is an objective for which the European Parliament continues to press,[9] and a priority area under the Commission's Action Programs on Equality between Men and Women, including the latest one: Strategic Engagement for Gender Equality (2016–19).

This growing European awareness of the need to enhance women's political participation through the adoption of regulatory measures and incentives must be understood as a reaction against a simple historical fact: although women in European countries gained suffrage rights between the turn of the last century and the arrival or restoration of liberal democracy after WWII (Rodríguez Ruiz and Rubio-Marín 2012; Rubio-Marín 2014), for decades women's political participation in elected bodies has remained dismal. It is in this context – and with the exception of some early attempts (starting in the 1970s) to redress the situation through soft law measures and voluntary quotas, mostly undertaken by political parties – that we observe the adoption of gender quotas (both voluntary and legislated) to ensure the inclusion of women in decision-making bodies. Quotas have especially gained traction since the mid-1990s, mainly in the realm of political representation, a trend that has since become truly global. By 2012, gender quotas for elected offices had been adopted in more than a hundred countries, with the pace of adoption of these policy measures accelerating greatly over the last fifteen years. Specifically, by 2016, ten EU member states

[8] "Council Recommendation on the balanced participation of women and men in decision-making," 96/694/EC.
[9] See the European Parliament resolution of March 13, 2012 on equality between men and women in the EU, which calls for a better balance between work and family life (25); for legislation, including quotas, to increase female representation in corporate management bodies (28); and for measures to ensure the balanced presence of women and men in positions of responsibility in business, public administration, and political bodies (29).

implemented legislated quotas for their lower parliamentary chamber (Belgium, Croatia, Greece, France, Ireland, Italy, Poland, Portugal, Slovenia, and Spain), while in nineteen EU countries, at least one political party implements voluntary gender quotas.[10]

The first phase of adoption and diffusion of electoral gender quotas worldwide (1990s–2000s) has received much attention in the extensive literature on gender quotas, mainly situated in political science (Dahlerup 2006; Dahlerup and Freidenvall 2005; Dahlerup and Leyenaar 2013; Hughes, Krook, and Paxton 2015; Krook 2006; Praud 2012). Several authors have explored the origins, adoption, and impact of electoral gender quota reform (Baldez 2004; Celis, Krook, and Meier 2011; Dahlerup 2006; Krook 2007a, 2009, 2010; Krook, Lovendusky, and Squires 2009; Meier 2012; Murray, Krook, and Opello 2012). They have highlighted factors that may hinder or facilitate electoral reforms implementing gender quotas, and they have assessed quotas' efficiency in improving women's descriptive representation. Other studies have concentrated on the discursive, legal, and normative public debates surrounding quota reforms, a perspective we advance and develop in this volume (Baudino 2005; Bereni and Lépinard 2004; Freidenvall 2005; Holli, Luhtakallio, and Raevaara 2006; Lépinard 2007; Rodríguez Ruiz and Rubio-Marín 2008; Sgier 2004). These studies, often looking at a single country case, have focused on the normative and legal arguments developed to legitimize gender quotas, and their success in challenging well-entrenched conceptions of political representation and gender equality. In spite of this rich field of research, there is still a dearth of studies that look at a wide set of European cases, allowing for cross country comparisons and, possibly, identification of specific regional features.[11] Moreover, the adoption and diffusion of gender quotas in Europe is more complex than an analysis focused only on political representation may suggest. Electoral gender quotas have indeed expanded to additional countries beyond the initial Belgium, France, and Greece in the 2000s, and now include Italy, Poland, Portugal, Slovenia, and Spain. In the meantime, the quota mechanism has been applied to other domains of authority than

---

[10] "Global Database of Quotas for Women," International IDEA, Inter-Parliamentary Union, and Stockholm University, available at: www.quotaproject.org. Accessed November 11, 2016.

[11] Notable exceptions are Dahlerup (2006); Franceschet, Krook, and Piscopo (2012). On Europe see also Lovenduski (2005), and on Africa see Tripp and Kang (2008).

political representation, both inside and outside of the state apparatus – including public bodies, corporate boards, universities, unions, and other civil society institutions – both by countries that had already implemented electoral quotas, and those that had not taken this route (Lépinard 2016; Meier 2014). Furthermore, in several countries, including Belgium and Greece, quotas in public administration have preceded electoral gender quotas, giving to the adoption process of the latter a different timing and dynamic; and in Austria and Germany the adoption of those quotas in the administration has never spilled over into the realm of political representation. Finally, these recent developments show a progressive increase in the threshold of representation (from 30 to 40 percent or even 50 percent), often accompanied by a change of rhetoric (from "women's minimal representation thresholds," "temporary special measures," and "affirmative action," to "gender-balanced participation" or "parity"), raising interesting questions as to the scope and nature of this phenomenon in terms of new conceptualizations of gender equality, governance, and even democratic legitimacy (Table I.1) (Franceschet and Piscopo 2013; Piscopo 2016; Praud 2012).

Of particular regional significance seems to be the diffusion of gender quotas to the corporate domain, thus far a typically (and recent) European trend. Indeed, while women's participation in decision-making in general has been high on the agenda of several international and European organizations since the 1990s, the issue of women's presence in *economic* decision-making did not raise much attention before the mid-2000s, when Norway decided to act in this domain. Hence, while the glass ceiling in employment has been discussed since the 1980s in many European countries, it was only in 2010 that the European Commission adopted its new gender equality strategy for 2010–15, announcing it would consider "targeted initiatives to get more women into top jobs in decision making."[12] Following on this, in March 2011, Vivian Reding, then EU Justice commissioner, challenged publicly listed companies to voluntarily promote women's presence on their boards and launched the "Women on the board pledge for Europe."[13] A year later, she announced that the European Commission would explore the possibility of drafting a directive imposing gender quotas on the corporate boards of publicly listed companies. The issue

[12] http://ec.europa.eu/justice/gender-equality/document/index_en.htm
[13] http://ec.europa.eu/commission_2010-2014/reding/womenpledge/index_en.htm

TABLE I.1 Typology of gender quotas

Gender quota type	Domains of implementation	First introduced	Efficiency
Voluntary party quota (VPQ)	Political parties adopt voluntarily gender quotas (numbered targets) to increase the representation of women in their internal structures (committees, federations, etc.) and on their candidates' lists for elections.	In the 1970s in Nordic countries	Depends on the party's will
Legislated Electoral quotas (LEQ)	Legislatures adopt bills that impose a quota of women on candidate lists for various electoral levels. Quotas usually vary between 25 and 50%	In the 1990s in Latin American countries, then Western Europe	Depends on the sanctions established by the law. They can be financial or the nonregistration of the candidate lists for the elections. Some gender quota bills may not entail specific sanctions and be interpreted as only objectives to be promoted.
Public bodies quotas (PBQ)	Legislatures adopt bills that impose a quota of women at some echelons of the central or federal levels of the public administration or in independent public bodies or committees. Often linked to affirmative action measures in employment.	In the 1990s in Nordic countries, as well as in Germany, Greece, and Austria	Depends on the compulsory character of the law. Usually numbers are fixed targets to be reached in a defined time interval.
Corporate board quotas (CBQ)	Legislatures adopt bills that impose a quota of women on corporate boards of publicly and/or privately owned firms registered on the stock market and with specific features of capitalization.	In the 2000 by Norway, then other Western European Countries	Legislation can impose fix numbers of nomination of women on boards to be reached. Sanctions may be financial or the dissolution of the board. In Spain and Denmark those are only incentive numbers with no sanctions.

of women's presence on corporate boards, or what the European institutions have recently termed "gender diversity in corporate boards" is a central item in the Europe 2020 Strategy. Preceding or following these pronouncements, twelve EU member states have adopted legal measures to promote women to corporate boards (Fagan, González Menéndez, and Gómez Ansón 2012; Teigen 2012). While electoral quotas were justified in the name of improving democratic representation and women's political participation, the diffusion of the quota mechanism to the business sector, public service, universities, and so on leads to question the meaning of gender quotas and their role in contemporary modes of governance. In particular, we may ask ourselves whether we are witnessing a shift in conceptions of gender equality and democratic citizenship in ways that challenge the traditional separation of spheres in a comprehensive manner, something which was not realized by the simple granting of suffrage. This would explain the fact that women's underrepresentation in every domain of authority and decision-making, and not just in state institutions, is finally attracting attention. Moreover, while the demand for gender quotas is premised upon the idea that they will help overcome structural gender inequalities, it is still an open question as to whether they can transform the various gender regimes that are present in Europe, even as they expand into an ever-increasing number of domains. Only a comparative study of states which have either adopted the full range of these mechanisms, adopted only one, or resisted the tide of gender quotas can allow us to reflect on the meaning and the normative shift that gender quotas might be introducing to our conceptions of equality and citizenship.

I.2   GENDER QUOTAS IN EUROPE: NEW RESEARCH QUESTIONS

This book thus proposes a timely assessment of the adoption and diffusion of gender quotas in three main domains (elections, administrative bodies, corporate boards) and in thirteen European countries: Austria, Belgium, Denmark, France, Germany, Greece, Italy, Norway, Poland, Portugal, Slovenia, Spain, and Sweden. This selection covers eight of the ten EU-member countries implementing legislated electoral quotas. It represents a wide range of situations with respect to women's historical and actual participation to representative politics, and, beyond the realm of politics, with respect to the degree and nature of gender inequalities in each country. Indeed, our broad comparison aims at surveying the main gender regimes found in Europe and questioning the extent to which they have facilitated the adoption and spread of gender quotas and/or been affected by it. The purpose of this large comparison is to allow for a broader view of the "gender quota revolution": its genesis, its outcomes and its possible meanings in terms of conceptions of gender equality and women's citizenship in Europe.

Following Sylvia Walby, we consider that a gender regime is "a set of inter-related gendered social relations and gendered institutions that constitutes a system" (Walby 2009, 301).[14] Gender regimes vary along two axes: their placement of women on the public/private continuum, and the degree of gender inequalities that charaterizes the various domains of gender relations (such as the economy, politics, or civil society) (Walby 2004). Domestic gender regimes are characterized by a conservative and rigid dichotomy, which assigns women to the domestic sphere (focusing on care work, the informal economy, and social welfare benefits – depending on their family status), while public regimes have fostered the massive entrance of women into the labor market, independent welfare rights, women's participation in politics, and the collectivization of care work. Our sample therefore includes contrasting gender regimes: Nordic countries marked by a strong gender equality culture, Southern European countries often characterized by more traditional and domestic gender regimes, Eastern European countries that, arguably, have experienced the transition to liberal democracy with consequences in both directions for their national gender regimes, and Western European countries with both mixed gender regimes (such as Belgium, France, and Portugal, with a historically strong presence of women in the workforce but a weak presence in politics), and conservative ones (such as Austria and Germany).

In all these countries gender quotas have been proposed, discussed, contested, and often adopted. Our selection includes major European players in this field: France and Belgium, important cases of victories for legislated electoral gender quotas which have helped diffuse the trend, and Norway and Germany, important actors in the unfolding of the wave of corporate board quotas – Norway as a precursor, Germany as a site of resistance finally overcome. It includes cases in which quota laws were first constitutionally challenged but

[14] For an implementation of this framework on a country case see Lombardo (2017).

upheld (such as Spain); countries in which they were declared unconstitutional before being finally adopted after subsequent revision of the constitution (such as France and Italy); countries in which constitutional revisions were made before quotas could be adopted (such as Slovenia and Portugal); countries in which, despite the existence of enabling constitutional clauses, gender quotas were not adopted, or adopted only in very limited ways, excluding the paradigmatic parliamentary domain (such as Germany, Austria, and Norway), and countries that have long refused to take the mandatory quota path (such as Denmark and Sweden). While not exhaustive of the extreme diversity of cases within Europe, our selection provides a uniquely broad comparison within the borders of a common political entity, the EU, which has been instrumental in shaping the development of gender quotas. Our selection of case studies thus delivers ample material to identify patterns and divergences that illuminate the irresistible rise of gender quotas across Europe and its potentially transformative reach.

The chapters that follow analyze how, in the four corners of Europe, gender quota measures have been triggered by complex legal, social, and political dynamics involving political parties (with more or less active women's sections), women's movements, women's policy agencies, national and supranational courts, other supranational institutions, and cross-country fertilization. The chapters decipher the interactions, synergies, and alliances between these actors and their successful or failed attempts at challenging dominant norms of gender equality and exclusive conceptions of citizenship. We survey the various domains in which legislated quotas have been implemented – that is, electoral politics, public bodies, and corporate boards – and we also describe the emergence of a new sphere of quota implementation in the social domain (in higher education and research, sports institutions, labor unions, etc.).

Most of the gender quota literature so far has focused on electoral politics, policy processes, and institutional change, with most research focusing on gender quotas' impact on women's political representation (descriptive and substantive) (Childs and Krook 2009; Dahlerup 1988; Franceschet and Piscopo 2008), and in terms of political parties' strategies and practices (Meier 2008; Meryl and Verge 2016; Murray 2010; Opello 2006; Verge and De La Fuente 2014). Contrastingly, in this volume we place electoral gender quotas in a broader frame of analysis. Indeed, it is our contention that the processes of adoption, or rejection, of these various gender quota policies reveal continuities and changes in the ways in which women's citizenship – political, economic, social – is being reshaped in the twenty-first century. In particular, we ask: to what extent are gender quotas redrawing the boundaries of women's political inclusion and, more broadly speaking, of their belonging to the public sphere? To what extent is this revolution transforming the meaning of gender equality itself as a shared normative concept? Finally, does this trend reflect new configurations of actors within feminist politics in the twenty-first century? In answering these questions, we identify patterns of success and failure, of progression and resistance in the rise and diffusion of gender quotas, as well as the relative merit of new actors and geopolitical and legal contexts in the contemporary struggle for women's empowerment.

Precise causality mechanisms accounting for quota adoption and domain diffusion are difficult to identify. However, patterns may be delineated. Similar collective and institutional actors animate alternately or in combination the push for quotas. These include women's sections in political parties, autonomous women's movements, women's policy agencies, and international and regional organizations. Our sample of case studies in this volume largely confirms the existing literature on the adoption of electoral gender quotas (Hughes, Krook, and Paxton 2015; Krook 2009; detailed analysis below). In addition, our collection addresses an angle largely understudied so far, showing how, in each country, for each type of quota, a different set of actors combined its efforts, building on previous struggles and victories. Strikingly, our case studies also show that key individual actors in the political elite have often been instrumental, sometimes making up for the absence of visible mobilization from civil society – especially in the adoption of corporate board quotas. When members of right-wing political parties, these key players have also promoted quotas against the will of their own party. These actors have often relied on the networks and resources institutionalized in previous struggles for electoral gender quotas. In particular, legal victories enshrining substantive definitions of equality or even renewed understandings of representative democracy have proven crucial stepping-stones for the adoption of electoral quotas and their later diffusion to other spheres. Each case provides a rich account of how varying combinations of actors seized opportunities to push for reform, but also of how these reforms were sometimes fiercely resisted by opposing political parties – often, but not exclusively, right-wing – as well as, quite frequently, by supreme and constitutional courts defending opposing formalistic views of gender equality, political party autonomy, and/or competing and more procedural notions of democratic representation (Krook 2016). In all these instances, and just like in the struggle for suffrage, discourses to promote gender quotas have combined strategic and principled, equality and difference-based arguments connecting with each country's preexisting and idiosyncratic narrative of gender equality and gender roles.[15] Typically, formal equality notions, meritocracy, and entrepreneurial autonomy from the state's interference have been held up by opponents of gender quotas. However, unlike what happened in the fight for women's suffrage, almost no actor now openly suggests that minimal participation of women in the public sphere is sufficient (although opposing forces have often relied on supply factors, suggesting that women simply have less interest in decision-making). On this point, there now seems to be European consensus, for which the concept of formal equality as equality of rights, whatever its shortcomings, is to be thanked.

1.3 FACTORS AND TIMING OF QUOTA ADOPTION: ENLARGING THE SCOPE OF ANALYSIS

To this day, comparative work on gender quotas has tried to identify factors to explain the success, failure, and/or timing of quota adoption (Dahlerup and Leyenaar 2013; Krook 2009). We briefly review this scholarship to assess what our innovative perspective, which takes into account various types of gender quotas, adds to the existing literature.

Previous studies have mostly been limited to legislated electoral quotas (LEQs), leaving out of the analysis both public bodies quotas (PBQs) and corporate board quotas (CBQs). Yet the transformations that gender quotas bring to these various spheres of decision-making must be examined together if we want to make sense of the quota revolution. This broader framework reveals the importance of understudied precedents – such as the adoption of PBQs – on the development of gender quota policies; it reveals new dynamics between actors pushing for and against quota adoption, as well as unexpected successes (see Table 1.2).

---

[15] On Europe, see Rubio-Marín (2014, 9–17). On France's longue durée, see Scott (1996).

TABLE I.2 Overview of gender quotas implemented in thirteen European countries as of 2017

	Voluntary party quotas (candidate lists)	Legislated electoral quotas	Public bodies quotas or similar legislation	Corporate board quotas or similar legislation	Other domains (legislation)
Austria	SPÖ – 25% quota in 1985, 40% in 1993, alternate candidates in 2010. Green party – 50% in 1987. ÖVP – 30% in 1995, 40% in 2014 for all committees, and alternate lists for federal and provincial elections.	None	1993 Federal Equal Treatment Act – 40% quotas in federal administrative units where women are underrepresented; in 2012 raised to 50%. Provincial laws also implement quotas in the nine provincial bureaucracies.	2011 – 35% quota on supervisory boards of state-owned enterprises (state majority share-holder), until 2018.	2010 – 45% quota for some of Public Broadcasting Agency (ORF) positions. 2009 and 2015 – university law 50% quota in university organs and committees. 2007 – Austria Trade Union association voluntary quota proportional to female membership.

(cont.)

TABLE I.2 (cont.)

	Voluntary party quotas (candidate lists)	Legislated electoral quotas	Public bodies quotas or similar legislation	Corporate board quotas or similar legislation	Other domains (legislation)
Belgium	Flemish Christian democrats – 20% target on local lists in 1975. Flemish Greens – 50% quota in 1985. Flemish Social Democrats – 25% in 1992. Francophone social democrats – 50% quota in 2000.	1994 – Maximum 67% of candidates of the same sex. 2002 – 50% candidate quota 2011 – Maximum 2/3 of members of the same sex for candidates to Senate (article 67 of the Constitution).	1990 – Mandatory one male and one female candidate for all federal advisory committee positions. 1997 – Maximum 67% of members of the same sex on federal advisory committees; balance legislation at the regional level.	2011 – Boards of listed and state-owned companies must have 33% women members. Transition period of five years for large listed firms.	33% quota for the National railway company, Belgian agency for development and cooperation, High council of Justice, Flemish universities' bodies, Flemish research council. Constitutional Court, since 2014 every third appointment must be a member of the underrepresented sex (long-term goal 33%).
Denmark	Social Democrats and socialist People's party adopted quotas in the 1970s but quotas were abolished in 1996.	None	For each nomination on public boards and committees there must be one male and one female candidate.	None; only soft measures since 2012.	None

14

France	Socialist party – 30% quota for European elections in 1978.	2000 – parity (50%) implemented on candidate lists (zipper system) for all list elections. Financial sanctions for the election to the lower chamber, applies to the total number of candidates across the country.	2012 – 40% quota in high ranked public service.	2011 – gradual implementation of up to 40% quota for members of listed companies.	2013 – parity on electoral lists for universities' decision-making bodies. 2014 – parity in sport federations' decision-making bodies, agricultural, commercial, and industrial chambers, social security organs, professional orders.
Germany	Green Party – 50% quota in 1986. SPD – 33% quota in 1988 increased to 40% in 1996. CDU – 33% "quorum" in 1988. PDS (then, Die Linke) – 50% quota.	None	1984 – preferential treatment in sub-national administrational hires. 1994 – FG Women Equality Law encourages equal representation on boards in the federal administration. 2001 – Mandate to privilege equally qualified female candidates in areas where women are underrepresented. 2009 – One female and one male candidate for every nomination to federal administration.	2015 – 30% female members of corporate boards for listed companies.	Initiatives in professions (medicine and journalism) asking for quotas.

(cont.)

TABLE I.2 (cont.)

	Voluntary party quotas (candidate lists)	Legislated electoral quotas	Public bodies quotas or similar legislation	Corporate board quotas or similar legislation	Other domains (legislation)
Greece	PASOK – 20% quota in the party structure in 1999; raised to 30% in 2001. New Democracy – 20% quota in the party structure in 1994; raised to 30% in 2001. The Communist Party (KKE) and the European-oriented communists (SYN) have a similar commitment without specifying a percentage.	2001 – 33% quota in the party ballots for local and regional elections. Applies to the total number of party candidates across the country. 2006 – 33% quota on total number of party's candidates running for all local elections (reiterated in 2010). 2008 – one-third quota on total number of party's candidates in national elections. 2014 – one-third quota on candidates for European Parliament	1992 – One woman in each service council. 2000 – At least 1/3 of positions filled by each sex (service councils in public administration departments and in collective bodies appointed by the public administration). 2010 – one-third quota for high and mid-level public administration.	None	2008 – one-third quota in the National Council for Research and technology, sector-specific research councils, and evaluation committees for research project proposals.

| Italy | Democratic Party – 50% quota for women, with strict alternation on electoral lists in 2008. | 2004 – 33% quota for European Parliament elections. 2004–2005 – 33% quota in various regions. 2007 – 40–60% quota in Friuli Venezia Giulia Region. 2014 – No more than 50% of the same sex in European Parliament elections. 2015 – No more than 50% of MP candidates of the same sex and a zipped party list composition; 60% maximum of the same sex for head-of-list candidates. | None | 2011 – Maximum two-thirds members of the same sex on a board. 30% quota on the second renewal of a company board's mandate for stock market listed and state-controlled companies (temporary measure valid until the third renewal). | 1990s – 30% gender quota on the composition of selection committees in the civil service. |

(cont.)

TABLE I.2 (cont.)

	Voluntary party quotas (candidate lists)	Legislated electoral quotas	Public bodies quotas or similar legislation	Corporate board quotas or similar legislation	Other domains (legislation)
Norway	Liberal Party – 40% quota in 1974. Socialist left party – 40% quota in 1975 Labor Party – 40% quota in 1983. Center Party – 40% quota in 1989. Christian Democratic Party – 40% quota in 1993.	None	1981 – First regulation of the composition of public committees. 1988 – 40% quota on the composition of public committees.	2003 – 40% quota for listed and publicly owned companies, fully implemented in 2008.	None
Poland	Social Democratic Alliance, Liberty Union, and Labor Union – Voluntarily adopted a 30% quota on their candidate list in 2011.	2011 – 35% quota for each sex on candidates for the Sejm (lower house of Parliament). 2014 – 35% quota for each sex on candidates for local councils. 2014 – 35% quota for each sex on candidates to the European Parliament.	None	None; only soft measures since 2013.	The Law on Higher Education: statutory gender quotas on membership in the Polish Accreditation Committee; statutory requirement to respect the principle of gender parity in the appointment of the General Council of Science and Higher Education.

Portugal	Socialist Party – 25% quota for each sex in 1988, raised to 33% in 2003.	2006 – Parity law, 33% quota for each sex.	None	2017 – 33% quota for state-owned companies from 2018 onwards; 20% for listed companies (30% in 2020). Sanctions for listed companies are only symbolic.	None
Slovenia	Liberal Democracy of Slovenia (LDS) – 30% quota only on the nomination process in 1994. 25% quota in 2000, to be increased by 3% in every following election up to 40%. Social Democrats (ZLDS, now SD) – 40% quota in 1996.	2004 – 40% gender quota for candidate lists to European Parliament. 2005 – gradual quota for municipal elections (20% in 2006, 30% in 2010, 40% in 2014) 2006 – 35% quota for the National Assembly.	1970s – The Communist Party adopted (though never fully implemented) a policy to ensure women's representation in public bodies. 2004 – 40% representation of each sex by decree.	None	None

(cont.)

TABLE I.2 (cont.)

	Voluntary party quotas (candidate lists)	Legislated electoral quotas	Public bodies quotas or similar legislation	Corporate board quotas or similar legislation	Other domains (legislation)
Spain	Spanish Communist Party – 25% quota for women in 1988. Spanish Socialist Workers' Party (PSOE) – 25% quota for women in 1988; 40:60 gender-neutral proportion in 1997; zipping system in 2013. United Left (IU) – 25% quota for women in 1989; 40:60 gender-neutral proportion in 1997; zipping system in 2008.	2007 – Maximum of 60% of either sex; same proportion prescribed at the regional level. Regional quota laws (which establish a minimum of 50% quota for either sex or introduce zipping): Andalusia in 2005, Balearic Islands in 2002, Basque Country in 2005, and Castile La Mancha in 2002.	2007 – The statutory principle of gender balance also affects appointments made by the central government but no sanction or supervision is imposed.	2007 – The statutory principle of gender-balanced established in the Equality Law also applies (i.e. maximum of either sex). This legislation, which contains no sanction mechanism, has systematically been under enforced.	Some trade unions apply quotas to the composition of their executive bodies. Equality plans at universities mandate gender balance in the composition of governing bodies and selection committees but supervision is weak and gender balance is often not reached.

| Sweden | Liberal Party – 40% "soft" quota in 1974; zipped lists in 1984.

Green Party – 40% quota on internal boards and committees in 1981, extended to electoral lists in 1987.

Left Party – 50% quota in 1987.

Social Democratic Party – 40% recommendation in 1987, quota in 1993. | None | 1987 soft rule to promote gender balance in public boards and committees and state commissions of inquiry. No sanction for noncompliance. | None; only soft measures. | None |

I.3.1 Beyond the Fast-track–Incremental-track Dichotomy

While the literature has so far often contrasted an "incremental track" to gender equality in political representation, which characterizes Nordic countries and other "old democracies," often starting from voluntary party quotas, to a "fast track" based on legislated gender quotas and adopted in many countries in the Global south (Dahlerup and Freidenvall 2005; Dahlerup and Leyenaar 2013; Freidenvall, Dahlerup, and Skjeie 2006), our sample reveals that quotas voluntarily adopted by political parties are not so much an alternative to legislated electoral quotas, but rather their precursor in many cases. Indeed, more often than not, and with the exception of some Nordic countries, Germany, and Austria, countries where left-wing political parties adopted gender quotas in the 1970s and 1980s have adopted legislated gender quotas later on (e.g. Belgium, France, Portugal, Spain).[16] What is more, our study shows the comparable importance of public bodies quotas in paving the way or accompanying legislated electoral quotas or corporate board quotas in countries such as Austria, Belgium, Germany, Greece, and Norway, suggesting that beyond electoral politics, gender quota reforms in public administration in fact already implied a redefinition of the legal conception of gender equality (from a formal to substantive equality conception, often leaving constitutional traces) that opened the door to quota claims in other domains. Think of the example of Greece, where contestation on the meaning of gender equality was expressed through the judicial challenge of a (weak) quota, of at least one woman in every "service council" (commissions representing employees in public service), adopted in 1992. Only after the legal battle to accept substantive equality and authorize affirmative action in favor of women was won – and the victory constitutionally enshrined – did it become possible and legitimate to ask for gender quotas in electoral politics in Greece. Similarly, substantive notions of gender equality enshrined in Norwegian law in 1981, backing gender quotas for publicly appointed boards, councils, and committees, paved the way for the adoption of corporate board quotas almost two decades later. In a similar vein, countries traditionally exemplifying the rejection of legislated electoral quotas, such as Germany, appear in a new light when also taking into account PBQs and CBQs. While Germany has never

---

[16] On the historical relationship between party quotas and legislated quotas, see for example Verge (2012) on Spain, Verge and Espírito-Santo (2016) on Portugal and Spain, and Bereni (2015) on France.

adopted LEQs, it was in fact a pioneer in the field of affirmative action for women in public service, its policies generating some of the case law that shaped European jurisprudence early on, and it has recently adopted corporate board quotas.

In view of this data, we argue that while explanations identifying factors facilitating the adoption of LEQs are still adequate to understand the dynamics of adoption of electoral quotas in our sample of countries, this sequencing of the adoption – or rejection – of electoral quotas needs to be replaced by a broader framework which signals a country's path with respect to the three types of quotas that can be legislated. Only this broader scope of analysis is capable of revealing interactions and diffusion processes between different quota measures – highlighting the importance of previous if less visible legal battles around PBQs – and thus giving a fuller picture of both the factors that facilitate or hinder the development of gender quota policies, and of their potential to transform a country's gender regime, a point we will return to below.

I.3.2   Revisiting the Relevance of the Citizenship Model for Gender Quota Adoption

Comparative studies on the adoption of gender quotas so far have hypothesized that the dominant model of citizenship in a country is a factor predicting the adoption or rejection of gender quotas: while liberal and republican citizenship models are deemed to be, for different reasons, inimical to gender quotas, corporatist-consociational and hybrid (social-democratic) models are more favorable to the adoption of gender quotas (Krook, Lovendusky, and Squires 2009). The chapters in this volume confirm but add significant nuance to these claims. Indeed, in line with this hypothesis, the Belgian model of consensus democracy, which involves and integrates different linguistic groups into the bureaucracy and state institutions, offered a particularly propitious context in which to argue for specific tools for women's inclusion in political representation, as Petra Meier shows in her chapter. Contrarily, the French republican model based on abstract citizenship and universalism proved an important obstacle to gender quota claims in France, though clearly not an insurmountable one. In fact, France, which upheld the republican model of citizenship par excellence, has become a true land of gender quotas in many spheres of public life, and a European leader in domains of application and implementation thresholds, like its Belgian neighbor and despite radically different conceptions of citizenship in the two countries. The strong model of the participatory, democratic welfare state in Northern Europe also proved a favorable context in which to advance the goal of women's equal political participation, as the chapters on Norway, Sweden, and Denmark in this volume detail. However, in these three countries, which are often classified as hybrid/social-democratic models of citizenship, no legislated electoral quotas were ever adopted. Similarly, Austria's neo-corporatist system of social partnership paved the way for the adoption of voluntary but not legislated gender quotas.

The explanatory power of citizenship models for gender quota adoption is furthermore harder to pin down if one adds to the analysis corporate board quotas or public bodies quotas, both of which have naturally weaker links to political citizenship. Thus, taking all three into account, the picture becomes obviously much messier. Sharing a social-democratic citizenship model, Norway, Sweden, and Denmark nevertheless show different paths towards adoption or rejection of other types of quotas: while Norway did not adopt LEQs, it did legislate quotas for public committees and corporate boards; Denmark resisted quotas in all spheres; and Sweden used the threat of quotas but ultimately did not adopt any.[17] All in all, then, our comparative perspective shows that conceptions of citizenship may play an important role in *framing the debates* on quotas, more than in predicting if and what type of quota will be adopted.

I.3.3 Revisiting the Relevance of Women's Mobilization for Gender Quota Adoption

Another strand of comparative research on electoral gender quotas in comparative perspective has stressed a series of broad factors, or facilitating conditions, that explain the adoption of gender quotas across the globe. As Mona Lena Krook summarizes: "women mobilize for quotas to increase women's representation; political elites recognize strategic advantages for pursuing quotas; quotas are consistent with existing or emerging notions of equality and representation; and quotas are

---

[17] In 2016, the minority Social-democrat/Green government did present a bill imposing a 40 percent CBQ to be reached in 2019. However, in January 2017, the Swedish Parliament stated in its Committee report 2016/17:CU6 that the government should ensure that the gender distribution on company boards continued to be a matter for company owners to determine. The Government bill that had been prepared for submission to parliament was thus hindered from being submitted.

supported by international norms and spread through transnational sharing" (Krook 2007a, 369). As Krook argues, all of these factors might not be present at all times, scenarios of quota adoption vary, and the possibilities of combination between the actors identified – women's movements, political elites, international organizations, and transnational networks – and their possible motivations are endless (Krook 2009, 32). Despite this rich empirical variety, Krook identifies different types of coalitions instrumental in passing electoral gender quota reforms, based on alliances between women's organizations in civil society and various actors such as women's policy agencies (WPAs), male political elites, international organizations, or their transnational counterparts.

Our case studies once again both confirm these assertions, in particular the overall relevance of women's mobilizations for quota adoption in most countries (but not all), and yet provide important additional data suggesting new scenarios for quota adoption, especially for CBQs or PBQs. In particular we offer new insights through cases in which women's mobilization was missing but was successfully replaced by the lobbying of WPAs and key individual elite actors, sometimes under the influence of European political and normative forces.

Where legislated electoral gender quotas were adopted in our sample, they were generally advocated by a large constituency of women's groups within and outside political parties. Broad coalitions of women, cutting across the political spectrum, were in fact instrumental in promoting legislated electoral quotas in France, Belgium, Greece, Slovenia, and Poland. And women's groups allied primarily with left-wing political parties to achieve quotas, for example, in Spain. By contrast, in Germany and Denmark legislated electoral quotas were never high on the women's movement agenda and never adopted. However, it should be noted that in countries such as Portugal or Italy, where the women's movement was either weak, marginal, disempowered (in the sense of excluded from the decision-making process), or internally divided on the issue of quotas, and where broad cross-partisan coalitions of women were missing, top-down reforms in favor of electoral quotas were nevertheless implemented. In these cases the influence of European incentives and standards, the "critical acts" of key political figures (male and female),[18] and the lobbying of WPAs seem to have provided the necessary impetus for reform. As Ana Espírito-Santo underscores in her

---

[18] The concept was coined by Dahlerup (1988).

chapter, irrespective of the efforts undertaken by the Portuguese WPA and in particular by its NGO Section to pursue this agenda, they have been excluded from the decision-making process. Still, they had an instrumental role in promoting the importance of gender quotas among political agents and in sustaining the efforts of key female actors in left-wing parties to pass the parity law, finally adopted in 2006. In Italy, where the women's movement was particularly divided on the issue of quotas, the Minister for Equal Opportunity in the right-wing Berlusconi government, Stefania Prestigiacomo, was key – first in pushing through a constitutional revision and then in lobbying for an electoral reform introducing a one-third quota for European elections, against her own party and without support from left-wing female MPs or women's rights organizations. Interestingly, in both countries the electoral reforms resulted in less ambitious quota schemes, imposing only a one-third threshold. However, they proved no less efficient than electoral quotas legislated in Greece or Poland where, despite strong women's mobilization, the resistance of conservative political parties ensured that both the threshold and implementation of adopted quotas would remain low. Hence, while women's mobilization remains an important factor in most cases, it is in fact supplemented and can even be replaced by the support of key political actors and WPAs in some cases. These cases therefore suggest that scenarios without strong women's organizations' mobilizations may still lead to quota adoption, thereby expanding Krook's typology of actors' coalitions. What is more, as we will detail bellow, in contrast with Krook's scenarios for electoral gender quotas, when it comes to CBQs, women's mobilizations are, with only some exceptions, particularly weak, while WPAs' influence is instrumental.

I.3.4 Understanding the Forms and Impact of European and Transnational Influences on Gender Quota Adoption

The importance of international and European incentives has also been noted in the quota literature (Bereni and Lépinard 2004; Krook 2007b, 2009; Lépinard 2007). In all of our countries, mobilization in favor of quotas benefited from international and European norms – including hard law, soft law, policy documents, and funded action programs – pushing for affirmative action, substantive conceptions of gender equality and gender-balanced participation or parity. While both CEDAW's endorsement of temporary special measures to achieve de facto equality and, more importantly, the UN Beijing Platform for Action have often been relied upon in legitimation and justification strategies of quota proponents, the greatest supranational influence on European countries has come from within Europe itself.

Our broad comparative perspective provides new insights on the various forms that this influence can take, but also on the different impact it can have depending on the national context. Evidence of European influence can be found in all the countries that adopted LEQs: Belgium, France, Greece, Italy, Portugal, Spain, Slovenia, and Poland. Indeed, our cases show that more often than not the rhetorical use of European norms and incentives in the national debate aimed (and to some extent succeeded) at circumventing important national opposition, in spite of their nonlegally binding nature. These norms and standards were sometimes given particularly high visibility during campaigns organized around European Parliament elections. Indeed, in countries such as France, Spain, Portugal, and Italy,[19] in which quota reforms were first introduced in the realm of electoral politics, the rhetoric of "parity democracy" coined by the Council of Europe – successfully combining the notions of equality *and* democracy – as well as that of gender-balanced representation present in European Council Recommendation 96/694, had a particular impact (MacRae 2012). Indeed, it was the Council of Europe's seminar on "parity democracy," held in 1989, which catalyzed for many activists a new claim for women's political representation, by insisting that the fulfillment of the democratic ideal of political representation and participation required women's equal presence in elected assemblies.

At the same time, the "parity" rationale did not meet with the same success and was not translated in the same terms in all countries, depending on the national configuration of actors and the preexisting legal norms and citizenship model. In France, as Éléonore Lépinard details in her chapter, the parity rationale proved particularly important in framing a new principle, logically and necessarily implying a 50 percent threshold that would arguably improve and perfect democracy, ensuring the representation of both sexes while at the same time overcoming the preexisting constitutional ban on gender quotas by the Conseil Constitutionnel from 1982, in which quotas were seen as contrary to notions of equality and popular sovereignty. In Belgium on the other hand, the parity rationale was rhetorically endorsed but

---

[19] See Praud (2012), as well as: on Spain, Verge (2012), on Italy, Palici di Suni (2012), and on Belgium, Meier (2012). The parity rhetoric also had a strong impact in Belgium, despite the fact that it had already passed a PBQ law earlier on, in 1990.

translated into an initial one-third threshold quota (increased incrementally to 50 percent) – threshold quotas and parity quotas were not seen as responding to two conceptually different logics, as they were in France. This difference in the interpretation and incorporation of the same European concept and narrative is in part due to the fact that while the national French debate on electoral quotas revolved around a notion of universalism antithetical to any form of group representation, the Belgian debate, in line with the country's consociational model, revolved around the notion of different forms of "diversity" (other than language-based diversity) which could and should be represented. Still other countries, like Italy (33 percent), Portugal (33 percent), Poland (35 percent) and Greece (33 percent), have embraced the notion of parity even if the threshold required by the adopted quotas is far from full equality, raising the question as to whether, in some contexts, parity – as full equal representation – may constitute the desired normative end to be achieved progressively (especially in view of the lingering resistance of male political elites), or if it has become the more appealing term to push forward any kind of quota agenda. In Spain, on the other hand, gender-balanced representation was the term used – rather than parity – to minimize the rejection that parity might provoke among conservative opponents. Part of the appeal, both rhetoric and legal, seems to be that the notion of parity or even gender-balanced representation suggests a form of equal treatment or a new relationship between the sexes, and can thus be less divisive than minimum threshold quotas for the underrepresented sex, which is invariably women and presents the issue as an apparently zero sum game.

Not surprisingly, the European rhetoric on gender-balanced participation and the Council of Europe's "parity democracy" discourse were especially influential in countries facing major political change and seeking alternative conceptions of citizenship and democracy, because such contexts offered the best scenarios to articulate a new relationship between the sexes as part of the agenda of a "new," "more legitimate," and often, a "modernized democracy." Thus, in France the discourse on parity democracy appeared to be particularly suited to counter the democratic deficit that seemed to plague French political life in the 1990s. Similarly, the use of the parity rhetoric in Italy happened at a time when the old "partitocrazia" and the traditional political actors were collapsing, opening up new avenues for democratic change and linking the agenda of women's empowerment to the idea of "modernizing" the country. In Slovenia, the democratic transition and the need to show democratic credentials in the process of accession to the EU also opened venues to import the European discourse on the positive link between democracy and women's presence in decision-making bodies.

However, the use of European discursive and legal resources was not always met with success, and the nature of the European influence has varied, depending on the national constellation of issues and actors and their relationship to the European institutions. As Alessia Donà underscores in her chapter, under center-left governments between 1996 and 2001, Italian political elites were more receptive to European arguments about women's participation in decision-making, while in the following decade, under a center-right government, European discourses and incentives did not have a real impact on the conservative Italian gender regime. The influence of the European institutions on Eastern European countries in the process of accession to the EU is also specific and varied. In this volume, Milica Antić-Gaber and Irena Selišnik show how in Slovenia the process of EU accession boosted the push for electoral quota reform at the turn of the millennium through the adoption of a discourse about gender-balanced representation in politics in a country with gender equality featuring high in its self-representation. However, Anna Śledzińska-Simon notes that, in Poland, European rhetoric on gender equality proved inefficient beyond the domain of equal employment and services on which the EU has strict competences and had explicitly validated affirmative action. Indeed, despite a similar process of accession to the EU, Polish elites were not receptive to the European discourse stressing the importance of women's participation in decision-making bodies. Instead, the elites have engaged in a process of recovering a purely conservative gender regime, with nationalist and religious overtones, from precommunist times. Nevertheless, even in Poland the EU's agenda had some impact on the matter, as EU institutions contributed funding to the flourishing of women's rights groups and NGOs challenging the conservative status quo.

A further complexity for the assessment of the importance of European influence in the national adoption of gender quotas is the fact such influence obviously varies depending on the domain in which gender quotas are being explored and whether it falls more or less closely under the jurisdiction of European law. In the domain of quotas in the public administration, European influence has been very direct, as such quotas can be seen as compromising European antidiscrimination employment legislation. In this respect, the legal evolution of European law has clearly been in the direction of endorsing substantive equality and the legitimacy of affirmative action measures in favor of the underrepresented sex,[20] but the reach and limits of that endorsement have been subject to judicial scrutiny by the European Court of Justice (ECJ). Indeed, the ECJ's jurisprudence on affirmative action in public employment in the 1990s was key in defining the range of admissible forms of positive discrimination employment measures in European countries, starting with Germany, the country originating three out of the four first cases that reached the ECJ.

In her chapter in this book, Sabine Lang shows how these early decisions of the ECJ indeed shifted the grounds of the German quota debate. The first and most controversial decision on the matter was the Kalanke case, where a male job applicant sued the state of Bremen over its positive action law for women in underrepresented parts of its public administration. While not ruling out, in principle, the legitimacy of positive measures (affirming that formal equality could, in fact, help reproduce gender inequalities) the ECJ struck down the Bremen legislation arguing that automatic preference for women in case of equal qualification amounted to discrimination against men.[21] After German and European women's rights advocates blamed this ruling for initiating a backlash against positive-action plans in general and quotas

---

[20] As far as secondary legislation is concerned, already Council Directive 76/207 on the implementation of the principle of equal treatment for men and women regarding access to employment, vocational training and promotion, and working conditions confirmed the validity of positive measures, something which is reaffirmed under article 3 of the Directive 2006/54/EC on the implementation of the principle of equal opportunities and equal treatment of men and women in matters of employment and occupation (Gender Recast Directive). In terms of primary law, the Amsterdam Treaty in 1999 explicitly incorporated the competence of the EU, allowing the Council to undertake pro-active measures to combat discrimination based on sex (article 13.1 – the new article 19 after the Lisbon Treaty renumbering) and giving permission to Member States to adopt positive discrimination measures for the underrepresented sex with a view to ensure full equality in practice between men and women in working life (article 141 – the new article 157 TFEU). Similarly, article 23.2 of the Charter of Fundamental Rights of the European Union now provides that equality between men and women must be ensured in all areas, including employment, work, and pay but that the principle of equality shall not prevent the maintenance or adoption of measures providing for specific advantages in favor of the underrepresented sex.

[21] *Kalanke v. Freie Hansestadt Bremen*, Case C-450/93; 1995 ECR I-3078.

in particular,[22] the Court nuanced its position in the next decision, the Marschall case,[23] which set the litmus test for positive action plans and quota regulations across Germany and the EU by arguing that, as long as the decision to advance a woman is made on a single-case basis and considers the equal merits of each individual candidate, quotas are legal.[24] Also of direct relevance, as described by Lenita Freidenvall, was the European case-law in Sweden (a country which otherwise does not have a judicial review tradition inviting courts to strike down legislative measures based on rights review), by which the ECJ invalidated an earmarking procedure – that, by requiring only comparable qualification of candidates, sought to increase the number of women among research assistant university positions – for contravening the principle of equal treatment.[25] Contrastingly, positive influence of EU law on national case law, enabling forms of public bodies quotas, is to be found in Austria and Greece.

With the same goals of equal opportunities for women in employment, the marketplace, and the economy, European actors, legislative proposals, and narratives have had a somewhat reduced though still quite noticeable influence on national debates around the adoption of corporate board quotas. This has included provoking reactions of resistance in countries like Sweden, where European initiatives were seen as contradicting the principle of subsidiarity. In particular, Commissioner Vivian Reding's threat to legislate at the European level was often relied upon in legitimation and justification strategies, proving more or less effective in different European countries: while Denmark finally opted for soft measures (explicitly coining its model as the "Danish" model in opposition to the binding European Commission model), Portugal adopted a new law in 2017 with a 33-percent quota for state-owned companies and a 20-percent quota for listed companies, and German Chancellor Angela Merkel finally gave in after having openly challenged what she framed as an intrusion of the European Commission (EC) into national government prerogatives. However, as the chapter on Germany shows, even Merkel's change of heart, giving up the direct

---

[22] E.g. "Gender War," *Focus Magazine* 43, 1995.

[23] *Marschall v. Land Nordrhein-Westfalen*, Case C-409/95; 1997 ECR I-6363.

[24] In a third German case in 2000, the ECJ upheld the legality of decision quotas, goal quotas, and fixed quotas for training positions in a Hesse Statute, basically confirming its prior case law (see *Badeck v. Hessische Ministerpräsident*, Case C-158/97; 2000 ECR I-1875).

[25] *Abrahamsson and Anderson v. Fogelqvist* (2000) C-407/98.

challenge against European intrusion through mandatory legislation, was the result not only of avoiding stigmatization as a "backward oriented veto power in the EU" but also of pressures inside her own political camp, and the work of key actors advancing women's rights.

As is rightly claimed by Emanuela Lombardo and Tània Verge, in the Spanish case, Europeanization entails not only the downloading of EU legislation at the member state level and the discursive usage of the EU by national actors to legitimize gender change, but also horizontal cross-loading or policy transfer through learning from other member states. This is clearly shown in all the chapters in this volume. The relevance of transnational – and not only supranational – influences through isomorphism is exemplified by the case of voluntary political quotas adopted in all the Nordic countries, but also by the German precedent affecting Austria. As for legislated electoral quotas, their adoption in France had a clear effect in Italy, Belgium, Spain, Slovenia, and Portugal. The adoption of corporate board quotas in Norway also had an impact on France, Belgium, Sweden, Spain, Austria, and Denmark. Similarly, as described by Dia Anagnostou in her chapter on Greece, the precedent of constitutional amendments in some European countries was often rhetorically relied upon to support the convenience of similar domestic reforms. And while the notion of a shared constitutional culture among European countries did not directly support the spread of gender quotas – which have only been directly enshrined in the Belgian Constitution – in some countries (such as Slovenia, Poland, and Portugal) it clearly conditioned the general perception of the need to engage in constitutional amendment before quotas could be legislated, precisely to avoid the constitutional obstacles encountered in neighboring countries (like France or Italy).

The influence of transnational diffusion takes place through various mediums. Sometimes legislative delegations visited other countries to learn from their experience, as was the case with a French delegation visiting Norway to learn about their corporate board quota policy. In 1979, women in the French socialist party invited their Spanish counterparts to the launch of voluntary quotas on the candidate lists for the European elections that year. This experience proved crucial for Spanish socialist feminists, who then battled in their parties for similar measures. Also in Slovenia, the connection of women's groups with their sister women's and party organizations in Europe, especially Scandinavian countries, helped their mobilization. Sometimes transnational organizations were key diffusion instruments. Thus, the Socialist

International, and in particular its women's section, was instrumental in diffusing ideas of political parity between France, Spain, Italy, and Portugal in the 1990s. This is probably in no small part due to the leadership of Anita Gradin, a Swedish politician who chaired Socialist International Women in the 1980s. She was a promoter of the 40-percent rule at the level of the Socialist International, and a key actor in favor of gender quotas in Sweden as well as one of the "mothers" of the *varannan damernas* rule, which introduced zipping in many political parties' lists in 1993 in Sweden.[26] In general, participation in a European network of experts (like the EU-sponsored Expert Network on Women in Decision-Making) and associations (such as the European Women's Lobby or the European Women's Lawyers Associations) allowed exchange of information and experience and proved especially conducive when the national experts were also integrated into the country's WPA, political parties (as was the case in Belgium), or NGOs (as was the case in Portugal).

To summarize, broadening the scope of analysis to the entire range of gender quota policies reveals dynamics that have been overlooked so far, such as the influence of public bodies' quotas on the later adoption of electoral or corporate board quotas. It also nuances the role played by factors such as the citizenship regime when accounting for the entire gender quota revolution, and not only a part of it, and provides a fresh look at the role of actors such as women's coalitions and European supranational institutions in the adoption of gender quota policies across the board. This broader view also directs us towards the identification of new similarities and differences, and hence, new typologies, around the dynamics of adoption and diffusion of quotas in the three domains under investigation, that we explore in the concluding chapter of this volume. Indeed, in this concluding chapter we propose a typology of countries that analyzes the adoption and diffusion of gender quotas, as well as their transformative potential. We distinguish between four scenarios: the first scenario, typical of Nordic countries, is one in which gender quotas are *accessory measures*, often rejected in the name of gender equality, due to the already high proportion of women in politics in these countries. The second group includes countries characterized by mixed gender regimes with relatively high participation of women in the labor market, but low presence in politics up until the end of the 1990s. Here, gender quotas are the central tool

---

[26] See Lenita Freidenvall's chapter in this volume.

in a strategy of *transformative equality remedies*: they are often linked to a broader vision of making the democratic system more inclusive and/or disestablishing traditional gender roles. A third group comprises countries sharing a conservative domestic gender regime in which the adoption of gender quota schemes was particularly protracted, and which continue to display important sites of resistance by male incumbents to the potential for gender regime change brought by quotas. In this group, quotas can be better described as *symbolic equality remedies*. Finally, a last group includes Germany and Austria, countries also sharing features of conservative domestic gender regimes combined with the early adoption of public bodies quotas. In these countries, the early development of gender quota policies in public administration has so far not brought about the expected gains for women and gender quotas remain weak *corrective equality remedies*. The structure of this volume follows this typology, grouping together the countries that present similar features. These four different scenarios of quota adoption suggest that, in each set of countries, quota claims have faced different challenges and brought distinctive transformations for women's empowerment and citizenship. We examine these variations in the transformative potential of gender quotas, both in the political and the legal realms, in our conclusion.

References

Baldez, Lisa. 2004. "Elected Bodies: The Gender Quota Law for Legislative Candidates in Mexico." *Legislative Studies Quarterly* 24 (2): 231–58.

Baudino, Claudie. 2005. "Gendering the Republican System: Debates on Women's Political Representation in France." In *State Feminism and Political Representation*, edited by Joni Lovenduski, 85–105. Cambridge: Cambridge University Press.

Bereni, Laure. 2015. *La bataille de la parité. Mobilisations pour la féminisation du pouvoir*. Paris: Economica.

Bereni, Laure, and Éléonore Lépinard. 2004. "'Les femmes ne sont pas une catégorie': les stratégies de légitimation de la parité en France." *Revue française de science politique* 54 (1): 71–98.

Beveridge, Fiona. 2011. "'Going Soft'? Analysing the Contribution of Soft and Hard Measures in EU Gender Law and Policy." In *The Europeanization of Gender Equality Policies: a Discursive-Sociological Approach*, edited by Emanuela Lombardo and Maxime Forest, 28–48. Basingstoke: Palgrave.

Celis, Karen, Mona Lena Krook, and Petra Meier. 2011. "The Rise of Gender Quota Laws: Expanding the Spectrum of Determinants for Electoral Reform." *West European Politics* 34 (3): 514–30.

Childs, Sarah, and Mona Lena Krook. 2009. "Analyzing Women's Substantive Representation: From Critical Mass to Critical Actors." *Government and Opposition* 44 (2): 125–45.

Dahlerup, Drude. 1988. "From a Small to a Large Minority: Women in Scandinavian Politics." *Scandinavian Political Studies* 11 (4): 275–98.

  ed. 2006. *Women, Quotas and Politics*. London: Routledge.

Dahlerup, Drude, and Lenita Freidenvall. 2005. "Quotas as Fast track to Equal Representation for Women: Why Scandinavia Is No Longer the Model." *International Feminist Journal of Politics* 7 (1): 26–48.

Dahlerup, Drude and Monique Leyenaar. 2013. *Breaking Male Dominance in Old Democracies*. Oxford: Oxford University Press.

Fagan, Colette, Maria González Menéndez, and Silvia Gómez Ansón, eds. 2012. *Women on Corporate Boards and in Top Management: European Trends and Policy*. Basingstoke: Palgrave Macmillan.

Franceschet, Susan, Mona Lena Krook, and Jennifer Piscopo, eds. 2012. *The Impact of Gender Quotas*. New York: Oxford University Press.

Franceschet, Susan, and Jennifer M. Piscopo. 2008. "Gender Quotas and Women's Substantive Representation: Lessons from Argentina." *Politics & Gender* 4 (3): 393–425.

  2013. "Equality, Democracy and the Broadening and Deepening of Gender Quotas." *Politics & Gender* 9 (3): 310–16.

Freidenvall, Lenita. 2005. "A Discursive Struggle. The Swedish National Federation of Social Democratic Women and Gender Quotas." *NORA: Nordic Journal of Women's Studies* 13 (3): 175–86.

Freidenvall, Lenita, Drude Dahlerup, and Hege Skjeie. 2006. "The Nordic Countries: An Incremental Model." In *Women, Quotas and Politics*, edited by Drude Dahlerup, 55–82. London: Routledge.

Holli, Anne-Maria Eeva Luhtakallio, and Eeva Raevaara. 2006. "Quota Trouble: Talking About Gender Quotas in Finnish Local politics." *International Feminist Journal of Politics* 8 (2): 169–93.

Hughes, Melanie M., Mona Lena Krook, and Pamela Paxton. 2015. "Transnational Women's Activism and the Global Diffusion of Gender Quotas." *International Studies Quarterly* 59 (2): 357–72.

Krook, Mona Lena. 2006. "Reforming Representation: The Diffusion of Candidate Gender Quotas Worldwide." *Politics & Gender* 2 (3): 303–27.

  2007a. "Candidate Gender Quotas: A Framework for Analysis." *European Journal of Political Research* 46 (3): 367–94.

2007b. "National Solution or Model From Above? Analyzing International Influences on the Parity Movement in France." *French Politics* 5 (1): 3–19.

2009. *Quotas for Women in Politics. Gender and Candidate Selection. Reform Worldwide.* New York: Oxford University Press.

2010. "Beyond Supply and Demand: a Feminist Institutionalist Theory of Candidate Selection." *Political Research Quarterly* 63 (4): 707–20.

2016. "Contesting Gender Quotas: Dynamics of Resistance." *Politics, Groups, and Identities* 4 (2): 268–83.

Krook, Mona Lena, Joni Lovendusky, and Judith Squires. 2009. "Gender Quotas and Models of Political Citizenship." *British Journal of Political Science* 39 (4): 781–803.

Lépinard, Eléonore. 2007. *L'égalité introuvable. La parité, les féministes et la République.* Paris: Presses de Sciences Po.

2016. "From Breaking the Rule to Making the Rules: the Adoption, Entrenchment and Diffusion of Gender Quotas in France." *Politics, Groups and Identities* 4 (2): 231–45.

Lombardo, Emanuela. 2008. "Gender inequality in politics. Policy frames in Spain and the European Union." *International Feminist Journal of Politics* 10 (1): 78–96.

2017. "The Spanish Gender Regime in the EU Context: Changes and Struggles in the Wake of Austerity Policies." *Gender, Work and Organizations.* 24 (1): 20–33.

Lovenduski, Joni, ed. 2005. *State Feminism and Political Representation.* Cambridge: Cambridge University Press.

MacRae, Heather. 2012. "Double Speak: the European Union and Gender Parity." *West European Politics* 35 (2): 301–18.

Meier, Petra. 2008. "A Gender Gap Not Closed by Quotas. The Renegotiation of the Public Sphere." *International Feminist Journal of Politics* 10 (3): 329–47.

2012. "From Laggard to Leader: Explaining the Belgian Gender Quotas and Parity Clause." *West European Politics* 35 (2): 362–79.

2014. "Quotas for advisory committees, business and politics: Just more of the same?" *International Political Science Review* 35 (1): 106–18.

Meryl, Kenny and Tania Verge. 2016. "Opening Up the Black Box: Gender and Candidate Selection in a New Era." *Government and Opposition* 51 (3): 351–69.

Murray, Rainbow. 2010. *Parties, Gender Quotas and Candidate Selection in France.* Basingstoke: Palgrave Macmillan.

Murray, Rainbow, Mona Lena Krook, and Katherine A.R. Opello. 2012. "Why are Gender Quotas Adopted? Parity and Party Pragmatism in France." *Political Research Quarterly* 65 (3): 529–43.

Opello, Katherine A.R. 2006. *Gender Quotas, Parity Reform and Political Parties in France.* Lanham, MD: Lexington Books.

Palici di Suni, Elisabetta. 2012. "Gender Parity and Quotas in Italy: A Convoluted Reform Process." *West European Politics* 35 (2): 380–94.

Piscopo, Jennifer M. 2016. "Gender Balance as Democracy: The Shift from Quotas to Parity in Latin America." *Politics, Groups, and Identities* 4 (2): 214–30.

Praud, Jocelyne. 2012. "Introduction: Gender Parity and Quotas in European Politics." *West European Politics* 35 (2): 286–300.

Rodríguez Ruiz, Blanca, and Ruth Rubio-Marín. 2008. "The Gender of Representation: On Democracy, Equality and Parity." *International Journal of Constitutional Law* 6 (2): 287–316.

eds. 2012. *The Struggle for Female Suffrage in the EU: Voting to Become Citizens*. Leiden: Brill.

Rubio-Marín, Ruth. 2014. "The Achievement of Female Suffrage in Europe: On Women's Citizenship." *International Journal of Constitutional Law* 12: 4–34.

Scott, Joan W. 1996. *Only Paradoxes to Offer. French Feminists and the Rights of Man*. Cambridge, MA: Harvard University Press.

Sgier, Léa. 2004. "Discourses of Gender Quotas." *European Political Science* 3 (3): 67–72.

Teigen, Mari. 2012. "Gender Quotas on Corporate Boards: On the Diffusion of a Distinct National Policy Reform." In *Firms, Boards and Gender Quotas: Comparative Perspectives*, edited by Fredrik Engelstad and Mari Teigen. Bingley: Emerald, 115–146.

Tripp, Aili Mari, and Alice Kang. 2008. "The Global Impact of Quotas: On the Fast Track to Increased Female Legislative Representation." *Comparative Political Studies* 41: 338–61.

Verge, Tània. 2012. "Institutionalising Gender Equality in Spain: From Party Quotas to Electoral Gender Quotas." *West European Politics* 35 (2): 395–414.

Verge, Tània, and Maria de La Fuente. 2014. "Playing with Different Cards: Party Politics, Gender Quotas and Women's Empowerment." *International Political Science Review* 35 (1): 67–79.

Verge, Tània and Ana Espírito-Santo. 2016. "Interactions between Party and Legislative Quotas: Candidate Selection and Quota Compliance in Portugal and Spain." *Government and Opposition* 51 (3): 416–39.

Walby, Sylvia. 2004. "The European Union and Gender Equality: Emergent Varieties of Gender Regimes." *Social Politics* 11 (1): 4–29.

2009. *Globalization and Inequalities. Complexity and Contested Modernities*. London: Sage.

PART I

GENDER QUOTAS AS TRANSFORMATIVE EQUALITY REMEDIES

CHAPTER ONE

GENDER QUOTAS IN BELGIUM

Consolidating the Citizenship Model While
Challenging the Conception of Gender Equality

Petra Meier

Nowadays, Belgium, much like France, is a land of gender quotas (Lépinard 2016). At the outset this may seem surprising since Belgium has been known for being a laggard in granting women equality (Woodward 1998). Studies analysing this phenomenon have examined mainly party and legislated candidate quotas, more particularly their adoption (Meier 2000a, 2004b, 2005, 2012b), interaction with the electoral system and effects (Celis and Meier 2013; Celis, Erzeel, and Meier 2013; Meier 2004a; Meier and Verlet 2008; Sliwa, Meier, and Thijssen 2011), including an intersectional perspective (Celis et al. 2013), the way in which they have affected the recruitment procedures of political parties (Erzeel and Meier 2011; Moor, Marien, and Hooghe 2013; Wauters, Maddens, and Put 2014), and the perceived legitimacy of these measures (Erzeel and Caluwaerts 2013; Meier 2008, 2012a).

While some studies have analysed how the spectrum of gender quotas broadened over time (Meier 2013, 2014; Schandevyl et al. 2013), this chapter takes as its starting point a comparative approach between sectors of implementation. In line with the other chapters in this volume, it considers the gender quota laws adopted so far for different branches of government and other sectors of society,[1] focusing on three topics. The first topic analyses how the different gender quota laws relate to the Belgian understanding of citizenship. While this has already been discussed with respect to party and legislated

---

[1] The chapter does not include a discussion of voluntary party quotas, most of which were abandoned once legislated candidate quotas were introduced.

candidate quotas (Meier 2000b; Paye 1997), this chapter analyses how the different gender quota laws relate to the predominant conception of citizenship, democracy, and representation. The second topic looks into whether and how the various gender quota laws have challenged the dominant legal and political conceptions of gender equality. Finally, the third topic of this chapter seeks to understand the dynamic underlying the development of this panoply of gender quota laws. While this question has been amply addressed with respect to party and legislated candidate quotas (see for instance Dahlerup 2006; Krook 2007; Lovenduski 2005), an analysis comparing gender quota laws for the different branches of government and beyond is largely missing.

1.1 BELGIAN GENDER QUOTA LAWS AND DECREES

Since the early 1990s, an impressive array of gender quota legislation has come about in Belgium, which can be characterised in five points. First, it covers the three branches of government, though not equally. Second, it goes beyond these three branches of government to also cover other sectors of society. Third, the Belgian gender quota legislation is a mix of generic and particular rules, the first focusing on an entire sector, the latter a particular institution. Fourth, this legislation is issued by both the federal (through laws or constitutional provisions) and the regional (through decrees) governments. Finally, this gender quota legislation is regularly on the move, with newer, more far-reaching legislation replacing older measures. Let us now take a more detailed look at the Belgian landscape of gender quotas.

The first generic gender quota law ever adopted in Belgium dates from 1990 and it required that for each open seat in any public advisory committee providing the government with advice in particular policy fields, all nominating bodies would present a male and a female candidate.[2] However, no sanctions were applied and the law had no impact. There was no increase in the number of women on advisory committees, and the nomination of women candidates was not always handled with care. In 1997, a new law 'promoting the balanced presence of men and women on public advisory boards' was adopted.[3] It provided for a maximum of 67 percent of members of the same sex on federal advisory committees and it included sanctions. Posts would remain vacant

[2] Belgisch Staatsblad, 9 October 1990.
[3] Belgisch Staatsblad, 31 July 1997.

until they were filled with candidates of the required sex and committee decisions would lack binding force until the quota was met.

By 1997, Belgium was a fully fledged federal state and the public advisory bodies at the sub-state level no longer fell under the jurisdiction of the 1997 federal gender quota law. Since then, the various constituting entities of the Belgian federation have adopted similar rules by decree for their public advisory bodies. The Flemish authorities (Flemish Region and Community) adopted a first decree in 1997, which was fine-tuned in 2003 and again in 2007. The Brussels Capital Region followed in 2001, the Federation Wallonia-Brussels (French Community) in 2002, the Walloon region in 2003. All of them adopted a similar quota to that at the federal level, although the last Flemish government raised the minimum representation amongst members for each sex to 40 percent. The German Community is the only sub-state within the Belgian federation not to have adopted any gender quota for public advisory bodies.

The gender quota for which Belgium became known was its 1994 law 'promoting a balanced presence of men and women on lists of candidates' and which was first applied in the 1994 European and local elections.[4] In line with most of the quota laws to follow later on, the 1994 law imposed a 33 percent quota, stipulating that electoral lists must not comprise more than 67 percent of candidates of the same sex (although for the first elections after adoption, the law specified a temporary quota of 75 percent). In the event of non-compliance, the authorities would not accept the list, which is a de facto exclusion from elections. The law applied to elections for political office at all levels, from European elections down to local ones. From the beginning, this law was criticised because it did not insist on an equal number of women and men or impose a placement mandate to guarantee that women were given eligible positions on the parties' electoral lists. This criticism led to the 2002 law 'guaranteeing an equal presence of men and women on lists of candidates',[5] which compelled parties to put forward an equal number of female and male candidates, including for the top two positions of each list (at least one woman in the top three

---

[4] Belgisch Staatsblad, 1 July 1994. The Act applied to the 1994 elections and to all elections taking place from 1996 onwards (the 1995 federal and regional elections were deliberately exempted from the quota rules).
[5] Belgisch Staatsblad, 28 August 2002; Belgisch Staatsblad, 13 September 2002; Belgisch Staatsblad, 10 January 2003.

in the first election after coming into force). Non-compliance again would result in the list being rejected.

By 2002, responsibility for organising local and provincial elections had devolved to the regional authorities. All of the regions issued decrees copying the new federal gender quota legislation, except for Flanders. Under the Flemish rule, only one out of the top three positions of each electoral list had to go to a candidate of the underrepresented sex, instead of one out of the top two, as in the other regions. In 2012, Flanders changed their rule to agree with the other regions, mandating equality in the first two candidates on each electoral list.

In the wake of the sixth state reform of 2011, further federalising the Belgian state, the Senate was reformed. From this point onwards it would be composed of Senators appointed by the regions and communities. Given this indirect composition of the Senate, the laws on electoral gender quotas were no longer applicable. The new article 67 of the Belgian Constitution defines the precise composition of the Senate. In §3, it stipulates that the Senate may not be comprised of more than two-thirds of Senators of the same sex (Popelier 2014).

While not called a quota, article 11b of the Constitution targets gender parity in the executive branch of government. In the wake of the constitutional reform of February 2002, article 10 of the Constitution, which stipulates that all Belgians are equal before the law, was revised to add the sentence 'the equality of women and men is guaranteed'. Next to this clause, which is often referred to as the parity clause, article 11b was added, stipulating that no executive shall comprise only members of one sex.[6] The latter actually comes down to a constitutional gender quota for the executive branch of government, which applies to all political levels in Belgium, from the local to the federal level (Meier 2012a).

To a more modest extent, Belgian gender quota laws also touch the judicial branch of government, particularly the Belgian Constitutional Court. Since 2003 the Act organising the Belgian Constitutional Court has stipulated that it should be composed of judges of both sexes. In practice, this has meant the inclusion of one woman. The long-term aim is to achieve a 33 percent quota for the twelve judges composing the Constitutional Court: since 2014 every third appointment must be a member of the underrepresented sex until the 33 percent quota is reached (Remiche 2014). While gender quotas for women in the

---

[6] Belgisch Staatsblad, 26 February 2002.

judicial branch of government are under debate (Remiche 2013), gender quota provisions have not yet been adopted for other Belgian courts.
However, there is a gender quota rule for the members of the High
Council of Justice, where 33 percent of the magistrates and at least four
of the other members must be of the female sex (Popelier 2011).

In 2011, the spectrum of generic gender quota laws was broadened
with the adoption of a law imposing corporate board quotas. The boards
of listed and state-owned companies, including the national lottery,[7]
need to comprise at least 33 percent women members (formulated as
'being of a sex other than that of the serving members'). Companies
were given a transition period to comply with the law depending on
their size and status: large listed companies are entitled to a period of
five years; smaller ones eight. Companies not complying with the law
by that time are required to appoint only women until they meet the
gender quota. Otherwise, serving board members will lose the financial
and other advantages resulting from their mandate. In cases where the
gender quota is even then still not achieved, the general meeting must
appoint a new board. State-owned companies have to apply the gender
quota without delay, given their 'role model' function.

Next to such generic laws targeting entire sectors, other gender
quota laws have been adopted focusing on specific institutions and
bodies with a unique statute or position. One of these is the national
railway company (Popelier 2011), and another is the Belgian Technical
Cooperation, an institution of public law that manages Belgian development aid and cooperation.[8] A maximum of two-thirds of members
may be of the same sex, corresponding with the 2011 gender quota law,
but no sanctions have been defined. This quota is to be implemented
from the first renewal of the board onwards.

The federal government was the first to initiate gender quota legislation. Over the years, the different regions and communities (the
sub-state level within the Belgian federation) also adopted gender
quota decrees. In some cases, they copied the federal legislation for
institutions that were no longer under the jurisdiction of the federal
authorities and therefore were not covered by federal legislation, as is
the case of the legislated candidate quotas at the local and regional levels and for public advisory bodies at the sub-state level. In other cases
the regions or communities adopted decrees for institutions exclusively

---

[7] Belgisch Staatsblad, 14 September 2011.
[8] Belgisch Staatsblad, 6 July 2012.

falling under their remit, sectors in which the federal state has no say. The most notorious of these cases is the academic world.

In 2010, the French Community adopted a 33 percent gender quota for candidates put forward for decision-making bodies of institutions designated by the French Community.[9] If only two candidates are presented, they must be of different sexes. If three or more candidates are presented, at least one-third of them must be of each sex. This decree applies to a broad range of cultural institutions, and also to the Francophone Belgian universities, but it does not specify to which decision-making bodies within these institutions the quota applies. Nor does the decree impose sanctions in cases of non-compliance.

In 2012, the Flemish government adopted a 33 percent quota for women in all major decision-making bodies of the three Flemish universities (those of Antwerp,[10] Ghent,[11] and Hasselt)[12] and for the selection committees of the Flemish Research Council. Currently, only two publicly financed universities, those of Leuven and of Brussels, do not fall under a gender quota decree, due to their separate statutes. The decrees stipulate that a maximum of 67 percent of the members of all decision-making bodies can be of the same sex. The case of the Flemish Research Council is a particular one in that it actually falls under the scope of the Flemish decree for public advisory bodies. When the Flemish authorities adopted a first gender quota decree for public advisory bodies in 1997, the Flemish Research Council asked for an exemption, invoking the argument that scientific committees should not be submitted to gender quota rules given their exclusive focus on quality, which was argued to be a gender-neutral criterion. The more concrete argument was a lack of qualified (female) candidates (Cromboom, Samzelius, and Woodward 2001). The 2007 successor of the 1997 decree closed the door to such an exception for the Flemish Research Council, and led, among other consequences, to the adoption of new statutes for the Council including the obligation of a 67 percent quota for all its scientific committees, as well as a new open selection procedure for its scientific committees and new selection criteria for the committee members (Schandevyl et al. 2013).

Belgian gender quotas therefore cover a broad range of sectors, including to a certain extent all branches of government, through a

[9] Belgisch Staatsblad, 8 February 2011.
[10] Decreet van 13 juli 2012, Belgisch Staatsblad, 8 August 2012.
[11] Decreet van 13 juli 2012, Belgisch Staatsblad, 17 September 2012.
[12] Decreet van 13 juli 2012, Belgisch Staatsblad, 8 August 2012.

range of generic and particular gender quota provisions issued by both the federal and the regional governments. As has been described, this gender quota legislation is also regularly updated, as former gender quota legislation is replaced by more far-reaching measures. Three tendencies can be detected here. First, the gender quotas have evolved towards higher percentages, although the most frequently applied gender quotas stipulate a minimum of 33 percent and a maximum of 67 percent of one sex. Second, there is a shift from gender quotas applying to candidates to what the literature tends to call reserved seats: a fixed share of places reserved for members of either sex within the decision-making body itself. Third, there is a growing tendency for gender quota provisions to go hand in hand with sanctions, many of which safeguard against the circumvention of the gender quota provisions.

1.2 BELGIAN GENDER QUOTAS AND THE COMMON UNDERSTANDING OF CITIZENSHIP AND REPRESENTATIVE DEMOCRACY

As the overview in the previous section has shown, Belgium has implemented gender quotas applying to a broad range of sectors of society and often across different state levels. How do these different gender quotas relate to the predominant conception of citizenship and its related understanding of democracy and representation? The literature on the adoption of gender quotas underlines the importance of reconciling gender quotas with normative cornerstones of the political system in place. Gender quotas tend to be adopted in countries characterised by egalitarian political cultures (Lovenduski and Norris 1993) and consociational or corporatist notions of group representation, especially where such measures exist for other groups (Dahlerup 2006; Krook 2007; Leyenaar 2004; Meier 2000a). The Belgian concept of citizenship reflects the specific history of the Belgian state and is a good illustration of how the latter can pave the way for gender quotas.

Belgium is a consensus democracy à la Lijphart, integrating (the elites of) diverse social groups into all major processes of decision-making regarding public life and important decision-making bodies. Leading positions in politics, public administration, state companies, boards of companies comprising state capital, and cultural institutions, including universities and other institutions of higher education or research, are occupied by actors affiliated with specific political parties, and are often designated by political parties. Belgian public life is therefore characterised by a segmented pluralism, reflecting the basic social cleavages. Whereas the segmentation of political and civil society is decreasing, the balanced representation of key social groups continues to be seen as an essential legitimising feature of the political system (Paye 1997). Phillips (1993) considers consociationalism to be one of the 'mainstream' traditions dealing with a form of identity politics but suggests that this model of democracy only takes into account groups or segments of society that are embodied by political parties. Others are neglected because consociationalism mainly deals with accommodation between political elites and not with democracy itself. However, in the Belgian case, the consociational logic has undoubtedly helped the women's movement in making its claim for gender quotas politically plausible, as has also been underlined by Krook, Lovenduski and Squires (2006). While all the sectors in which gender quotas were introduced already contained forms of representation for the social groups located on different sides of various social cleavages, it was above all the increasingly salient linguistic cleavage and the development of assured representation for language groups that paved the way for gender quotas. The federalisation of the unitary Belgian state (1960–93), as well as the further fine-tuning of the federal institutions (2001–11), led to an institutionalisation of guarantees of representation for the main language groups in the European Parliament, in the federal Senate, and in the Parliament of the Brussels Capital Region. Similar arrangements were made for the federal government and for the government of the Brussels Capital Region (Pilet and Teuns 2010). The representation of linguistic groups is also required when it comes to public administration, public boards, and the courts (Uyttendaele and Sohier 1995).

Even though there was opposition to gender quotas, in the Belgian context there were simply no valid arguments against them from the 1990s onwards. The argument that sex was not grounds for quotas no longer held politically at a moment in time when gender equality was an internationally recognised topic and the underrepresentation of women in public life was a widely recognised fact. The recognition of the de facto inequality between men and women cleared the way for gender quotas in a context where quotas and reserved seats are a frequently – although in some cases only recently – applied tool. Typical arguments against gender quotas focusing on the legitimacy of the tool itself do not hold in the Belgian case, where this tool, including in particular reserved seats, is applied to many institutions in a wide range of sectors, including those seemingly founded on merit, such as academia. Arguments focusing on women's lack of interest in such positions were deemed weak and were not supported by the facts. In this context it is interesting to note that, as has been documented elsewhere (Meier 2013, 2014), the arguments invoked in favour of and against gender quotas were very similar across different cases and different sectors. The main argument in the debates in favour of legislated candidate quotas – which constructed gender quotas as a symbol of valuing the representation of diversity – can also be found in the debate on corporate board quotas. When it comes to the arguments against gender quotas, the debates on legislated candidate and corporate board quotas show even more similarity.

In this respect the Belgian case is different from others such as the French. The debates on gender quotas did not reshape concepts of citizenship or democracy, as was the case with the French parity debate. It is rather the conceptualisation of citizenship in Belgium that allowed for the adoption of gender quotas. The adoption of gender quotas for the legislative and executive branches of government can be seen as a logical extension of other quotas in use, and to a certain extent the same holds true for the judiciary branch of government. The judiciary is a sector where typically the argument of neutrality is used against the introduction of gender quotas. However, the Belgian Constitutional Court is politically composed and the presence of these social groups is deemed important for its functioning. Adding yet another criterion for quotas, namely sex, turns the composition of this institution into a more complicated exercise. However, it does not change the basic logic of how the institution is composed. This logic can also be extended to the cases of corporate board quotas and of the important decision-making institutions in academia. While quotas in these sectors might seem strange at the outset, they are plausible in Belgium given the fact that many decision-making bodies in these sectors do respect balances between social groups.

1.3 BELGIAN GENDER QUOTAS AND THE COMMON UNDERSTANDING OF EQUALITY

While the introduction of gender quotas did not really alter the predominant concepts of citizenship and representation, what about the concept of equality, and especially of gender equality? Throughout the development of gender quotas in Belgium, only in one instance was a proposed quota rejected on legal grounds. In 1980, the first bill on legislated candidate quotas was submitted to parliament, attempting to impose a maximum of 75 percent of candidates on local lists of the same sex. As all bills are, it was sent to the Council of State to review its legal grounds. The Council of State rejected the bill on the grounds that a gender quota would violate the constitutional principles of equality and non-discrimination. This decision put an end to the first attempt to introduce gender quotas. In one other case, that of the 1994 bill on legislated candidate quotas, the Council of State deemed the suggested sanctions to be disproportionate.[13] The Council no longer tackled the gender quotas on the grounds that they would violate the constitutional principles of equality and non-discrimination, though these principles had not been rephrased since 1980. The sanctions were changed to those figuring in the final law. In 2002, with respect to the preparation of the successor law to the 1994 legislated candidate quotas, the Council of State simply pleaded for a stronger legal basis for such measures.[14] This plea is very interesting, since it actually paved the way for the adoption of the so-called parity clause within the Constitution, and, in its wake, the constitutional requirement for all executives to contain members of both sexes. In this respect Belgium is an interesting case. Not only was there little resistance to gender quotas from the judiciary, but it is also the judiciary that paved the way for enshrining the legal grounds for gender quotas more explicitly in the constitution (Meier 2012b).

If we look back at the overview of Belgian gender quota provisions presented earlier in this chapter, it is interesting to see that the different gender quota rules do resemble each other across the various sectors and political levels. The quotas set are similar in all cases, with the exception of most gender quotas for elected political office, which are set at 50 percent, and those for the executive branch of government, imposing a minimum of one member of the underrepresented sex. All other gender quotas tend to impose a minimum of 33 percent of members of the underrepresented sex or a maximum of 67 percent of members of the overrepresented sex. The language in the gender quota provisions reflects this proportion, speaking of a *balanced* presence of men and women. Only the 2002 gender quota law applying a 50 percent gender quota to electoral lists speaks of an *equal* presence (Meier 2013, 2014). Hence, the formulation of the gender quota provisions addresses the fact that most gender quotas in Belgium do not stand for real equality, but rather for recognition of the need to provide

---

[13] House of Representatives, Parliamentary Documents 1316/1 (1993–4).
[14] See for instance Council of State L.29.910/2.

women with access to the functions of steering public life. They do not request an equal representation of both sexes, but merely a minimum representation of the underrepresented sex.

While the principle of the inclusion of women is thus relatively easily recognised in the Belgian conception of citizenship and representative democracy – in contrast to certain other countries – this does not automatically imply equal access of men and women to steering positions. This lack is all the more interesting since the mandated presence of social groups in Belgian public life is generally based on their numerical strength, with a minimal presence – and thus de facto overrepresentation – for very small minorities, especially when it comes to language groups. However when it comes to gender, this principle is not applied, as it would by definition imply a 50–50 repartition of positions among men and women. Although article 10 of the Belgian Constitution does contain the so-called parity clause, stipulating that 'the equality of women and men is guaranteed', this constitutional provision is not automatically translated into regulations mandating gender *equality* – which does not mean that the gender quota provisions do not to a certain extent further the level of gender equality. We will come back to this idea at the end of this section.

Also, and again with the exception of legislated candidate quotas (and the decree of the French Community targeting publicly-funded institutions), over time all Belgian gender quota provisions have begun to target the composition of the body concerned, not the mere number of candidates. This principle applies to the executive branch of government, the Constitutional Court, public advisory bodies, boards of listed and state-owned companies, Flemish decision-making bodies of universities, and particular institutions such as the national railway company and the Belgian Technical Cooperation, all of which comprise reserved seats for members of either sex. Therefore, while the Belgian gender quotas are not as far-reaching as in some other countries that mandate 50 percent, they may be more effective since they determine reserved seats (in most cases) and not just the number of candidates.

Legislated candidate quotas are an exception as compared to other gender quota provisions within Belgium, as they do translate a principle of equality into equal numbers. But they target the candidates and not the actual composition of the assembly, as the other gender quota provisions in Belgium do. However, since they impose a 50 percent gender quota and target the top positions of each list of candidates, in combination with efficient sanctions, these gender quota rules do attempt to ensure a real impact on the composition of the assembly. Since the 50 percent gender quota was applied, women have made up 35 percent (2003), 37 percent (2007), and 39 percent (2010, 2014) of the MPs in the House of Representatives.

Elected assemblies tend to use reserved seats stingily, using them in exceptional cases for small language, ethnic, or religious minorities (Reynolds 2006). Across the world, reserved seats for women are also less frequently found than gender quotas. However, three Belgian elected assemblies do have reserved seats for language groups: the Belgian delegation in the European Parliament, the federal Senate, and the Parliament of Brussels Capital Region. This tool for protection of social groups is thus used in Belgian electoral politics. Furthermore, the sixth State reform of 2011 introduced reserved seats for women in the Senate. The assemblies of the sub-states, when composing their delegations for the federal Senate, must make sure that overall not more than two-thirds of their Senators will be of the overrepresented sex, thus reserving at least one-third of the seats in the federal Senate for women. The gender quotas applying to the federal Senate are therefore very much in line with most of the other gender quotas applicable in Belgium. And while the powers of the Senate were further cut in the latest State reform – as its status has been decreasing over the last two decades, the introduction of reserved seats based on sex for a political assembly in Belgium should not be underestimated. In Belgium the only other indirectly composed political assembly, that of the French Community, is composed of members of the Walloon regional parliament and the Brussels regional parliament. No gender quota has ever applied to it since its members are indirectly elected. The federal Senate, remarkably, departs from this logic to adapt gender quota tools to its composition – namely, through the use of reserved seats. While the Senate reserves only one-third of seats – thus not mandating full gender equality, as the 50 percent legislated candidate quotas do – the new rule still recognises the importance of ensuring the presence of men and women, to an extent in line with the other gender quotas applicable in Belgium.

Gender quotas for the executive branch of government are also an exception, in that the limit set is far below the one-third rule applying to most bodies. However, while it does not at first sound far-reaching, the impact of article 11bis of the Belgian Constitution, stipulating that no executive branch of government in Belgium should contain members of only one sex, should again not be underestimated. First, similar to the Swiss case, the composition of the federal government is an important foundation of the Belgian political equilibrium. Therefore, both the number of ministers in the federal government and the language groups to which they belong are enshrined in the Constitution. Adding yet more criteria to this political equilibrium further complicates the puzzle of composing a federal coalition government. Bringing in a gender quota, no matter how weak, is therefore an important achievement for protagonists of equal rights for women and men. It reflects the fact that the issue of gender equality is no longer ignored, even in the cornerstones of the complex architecture of the Belgian federal State, and even when it requires a revision of the Constitution. Second, a number of executive branches of government are very small, such as the government of the German Community, which initially comprised only three members, or the local executive branch of government in small rural municipalities. At the time of the constitutional change about a quarter of the local governments had no woman mayor or alderman. The executive branch of government of the German Community had never had a female member before article 11bis. In all those cases, article 11bis made a huge difference at the next renewal of the executive branch, as women joined executive branches of government that for decades and even centuries had been exclusively composed of men.

What does this section tell us about gender equality in Belgium and the impact of gender quota provisions on this concept? As we saw in Section 1.1, gender quotas mainly confirmed the Belgian concept of citizenship, adding another layer to the existing compartmentalised citizenship and to the representation and presence of citizens. When it comes to the concept of equality, with some caution one could say that gender quotas challenged it, notwithstanding the numerical specifics of the provisions. Similar to other European countries, the Belgian concept of gender equality was very formalistic at the outset, merely providing for the principle of equality. From the 1980s onwards, the concept shifted to provision of equal opportunities. Most of the gender quotas initially adopted in Belgium fit that category. However, the latter generation of gender quotas moves the concept of gender equality into one of substantive equality: equality of outcome. While not imposing an equal number of reserved seats for men and women, they still focus on the composition of institutions and decision-making bodies. Also telling is the fact that most of the more recent gender quota provisions impose significant sanctions in cases of non-compliance. This inclusion reflects a shift from a permissive legislation to one that is meant to trigger change. Slowly but steadily Belgium is moving beyond equal rights and opportunities to equal governance, and without any significant challenges to this turn, through, for example, court rulings.

1.4 DYNAMICS UNDERLYING THE DEVELOPMENT OF THE BELGIAN GENDER QUOTA LANDSCAPE

Finally, the third topic of this chapter seeks to further understand the dynamics underlying the creation of this panoply of gender quotas, addressing who and what played a role in the debates over and adoption of gender quotas, with particular interest in possible differences between the gender quotas for different sectors of society. Krook (2007) distinguishes three types of important actors in the adoption of gender quotas: (women's) civil society organisations, the political elite, and international/transnational actors. In the Belgian case, gender quotas were mainly introduced top-down by the political elite, a statement requiring two qualifications. First, gender quotas were initially put on the agenda by segments of the women's movement close to the political establishment. Second, gender quotas would never have been adopted without the persistent lobbying of this segment of the women's movement. With the exception of the 2011 corporate board quotas, as well as the 2012 quota for the Belgian Technical Cooperation, all gender quota laws adopted have been introduced by the government – in fact, most Belgian legislation emanates from the government and not from parliament, and following this pattern guarantees a successful vote on the bill. Thus, the pressure of the women's movement – including members of the movement with close ties to political parties – was essential to put the issue on the political agenda.

At the forefront of this issue was – and still is – the women's branch of the Flemish Christian-Democrats. This organisation has always made a point of promoting gender quotas, first for candidates and public advisory bodies, then later for other sectors such as the judiciary and academia. All early attempts to enact gender quotas, going back as far as 1980, have been undertaken by MPs affiliated to the women's branch of the Flemish Christian-Democrats. The proactive attitude of this party on gender quotas does not fit with general findings, whereby left-wing parties are often more open to gender quotas than other parties (Kittilson 2006). The explanation for this atypical pattern resides in the fact that the women's branch of the Flemish Christian-Democrats is a well-organised movement and strongly integrated within the party's organisational structures, which makes it one of the strongest political women's organisations (Van Molle and Gubin 1998). Lobbying in favour of gender quotas by the women's branch takes place both within the party, so as to convince the party hierarchy to support gender quotas, as well as outside of it, even against the official line of the party – although the women's branch tries to find a balance, not opposing the party-line too much, without neglecting its own agenda and priorities. No other Belgian political party has such a strong women's branch, lobbying extensively for women's issues, both within the party and beyond it. This political organisation explains the Belgian exception to the rule that left-wing parties are more open to gender quotas, but it also shows that parties are not monolithic blocs.

While the women's branches of the Social-Democrats are also in favour of gender quotas, in the beginning they made less of an issue of the topic, although they caught up in the debates on the 2011 corporate board quotas. The women's branches of the Liberal parties are even less outspoken on gender quotas. The majority think that gender quotas do not fit with the party's ideology, but a number of women within those parties – including the current president of the Flemish Liberals – are openly in favour of such measures. When it comes to the Flemish and Francophone Green parties, the parties themselves support gender quotas, traditionally making an issue of presenting a balanced number of men and women candidates as well as supporting other gender quotas. The women's branches of these parties, often defending a broader set of interests and not only those of women, thus do not need to be as outspoken on gender quotas. Finally, the parties on the right side of the political spectrum, both the Flemish Nationalists and the Flemish Radical Right (there being no real Francophone counterpart), have no women's branch and take an outspoken stance against any form of gender quota. While not formally disapproving of gender equality, overall they prefer minimal state intervention and arguments relating to merit, at least in these matters (Meier 2013, 2014).

The women's branches of the parties played an important role in putting and keeping gender quotas on the agenda until the issue was picked up by the political elite. In Belgium, there is a pattern to how gender quotas are introduced and legislated, which reflects to what extent the issue is politically accepted. First, MPs affiliated to the women's branches of political parties put the issue on the agenda, but their attempts fail. In a later phase, the government itself introduces a bill on gender quotas, which is voted through, because by then the bill has the necessary support within the coalition to be accepted by the majority within parliament. For instance, in the case of the gender quotas for elected political office, several male MPs of the majority have openly admitted that they voted for the bill only because it emanated from the majority and not because they supported gender quotas; quite the contrary. In a number of cases, the gender quota bills have directly emanated from the political elite, although affiliated with the women's movement. For instance, this was the case with the 1990 and 1997 public advisory bodies quotas: both bills were drafted by the cabinet of the Secretary of State in charge of equal opportunities, who was a former president of the women's branch of the Flemish Christian-Democrats. Later, as an MP in the Flemish parliament, she also stirred up the debate on gender quotas for decision-making bodies of Flemish universities. The latter case is another illustration of the pattern described above: her initial attempts were unsuccessful, but the coalition in the next legislature supported the gender quota decree voted on in 2011. Only two of the gender quota laws put on the Parliamentary agenda by MPs were actually voted through: the 2011 corporate board quotas, and the 2012 quotas for the Belgian Technical Cooperation for Development. In the first case, there was less consensus within government about the measure, although there was enough support in parliament; in fact, the bill was put on the agenda by a coalition of individual MPs from different parties of both language groups. The second bill was of minor importance, as it simply copied the existing rules for a separate institution.

Notwithstanding the fact that resistance against gender quotas can be found in several parties, the parties do not necessarily constitute the main pockets of resistance against such measures. In each case, the sector being regulated showed the most resistance towards gender quotas, eventually backed up by some political parties defending its interests. In the case of gender quotas for public advisory bodies, resistance manifested in the non- or nonserious application of the first gender quota law of 1990. Even the second gender quota law was at first poorly implemented, and the same could be said of the decrees applying to public advisory bodies at the region and community levels. In other cases, resistance was stronger in parliament, during debate of the quota or even in the run-up to such debates. The first legislated candidate quotas in 1994 were based on a compromise negotiated by the party presidents of the coalition partners at the time, since no compromise could be reached within the government attempting to prepare the bill. Such a partitocratic initiative was no longer necessary for the 2002 successor law, but the debates in parliament were among the most intense of any parliamentary debates on gender quotas – notwithstanding the fact that by that time, three gender quota laws and a number of decrees had already been adopted. In the case of both corporate board quotas, and quotas for the important decision-making bodies within universities, a corporatist reflex of self-regulation was put forward in an attempt to avoid gender quotas imposed by law or decree, a reaction also found in the judiciary more recently when the issue of gender quotas was put on the table (Schandevyl et al. 2013). The underlying idea is that the state should not intervene in the composition of such institutions, which should be constituted on the basis of expertise and thus merit. The parliamentary debates on corporate board quotas were also very intense and – after those on the 2002 legislated candidate quotas – the most agitated ones, which is easily understandable if one considers that they are among the most far-reaching quotas in terms of both the standards imposed and the sanctions to be faced in cases of non-compliance.

Finally, while the creation of gender quotas in Belgium took place concurrently with similar developments in many other countries and with a growing interest by international organisations and institutions in the importance of the presence of women in political and public life, little reference was made in the Belgian struggle to these broader evolutions. Primarily in the cases of legislated candidate quotas, gender quotas for the executive branch of government, and corporate board quotas, some links to international developments can be seen, adding legitimacy to such measures. At the time of the discussions on legislated candidate quotas and those for the executive branch of government, actors within the Belgian women's movement were abreast of the international initiatives of the time. These included the Council of Europe's studies on parity democracy, the various EU Community action programmes on equal opportunities, the 1996 Council Recommendation on the balanced participation of women and men in the decision-making process, and the UN Beijing Platform for Action. Especially during the 1990s, a number of prominent feminists had intense contact with colleagues from abroad, particularly other EU member states and the European institutions themselves, partly within formalised networks such as the EU-sponsored Expert Network on Women in Decision-Making. The Expert Network was initiated and coordinated by a feminist Senator from the Flemish Christian-Democrats, Sabine de Bethune, at the time also presiding over the women's branch of that party. Such formalised networks also gave direct access to the European Commission's Directorate General in charge of gender equality and key actors such as Odile Quentin, Agnès Hubert, and Maria Stratigaki. Another notorious example is the late Eliane Vogel Polsky, a legal scholar from the Free University of Brussels, who had close ties with French scholars and activists in the parity movement. While not necessarily referred to in debates, these networks were a rich source of inspiration and encouragement in the struggle for gender quotas in politics.

The French parity debates of the 1990s were in fact mentioned in the discussion of the 2002 legislated candidate quotas. They were also extensively referred to when arguing for constitutional reform enshrining the principle of parity, as well as the measure implementing the gender quota for the executive at the local, provincial, regional, or federal level. The debates on the 2011 corporate board quotas referred most extensively to transnational evolutions. Reference was repeatedly made to Norwegian law from 2006 imposing similar quotas. Reference was also made to the debates taking place at the European level and Justice Commissioner Viviane Reding's open stance in favour of gender quotas and her attempts to introduce them.

1.5   CONCLUSION

Belgium applies gender quotas to a broad range of sectors. The adoption of these measures was mainly top-down but would have been impossible without the persistent agency of the women's movement, especially actors embedded within the women's branches of some political parties. They, and not the women's policy agencies (traditional players when it comes to gender equality policies), initially put the issue on the agenda. Courts and legal arguments were also of little significance in the Belgian case. This unique process can to a certain extent be explained by the fact that most gender quota laws emanated from the governing coalition, and that the necessary consensus and support had therefore already been gathered. Also, while inter- or supranational influences cannot be denied, domestic factors played the main role in the adoption of Belgian gender quotas. Important among these is the Belgian tradition of thinking in terms of social groups and their presence within important decision-making bodies, thus providing fertile ground for all types of gender quotas to mirror such measures. The Belgian gender quotas across various sectors are very similar, and can be seen to build upon each other. The adoption of gender quotas for different types of body was not simply about duplicating existing gender quotas in other sectors. New gender quotas built upon former ones and raised the standard each time. Once a norm has been established with respect to gender equality, it is difficult to set a completely different one, even in another sector. In this respect the Belgian gender quotas, while supporting the dominant concept of citizenship, tend to push the concept of gender equality towards an increased focus on equality of output.

References

Celis, Karen, and Petra Meier. 2013. 'Genderquota als een kieshervorming: terug naar de context, actoren en belangen'. *Res Publica* 55 (3): 287–301.

Celis, Karen, Silvia Erzeel, and Petra Meier. 2013. 'Twintig jaar quota en wat nu? Een empirische reflectie op de tijdelijkheid van genderquota in de lokale politiek'. In *Op zoek naar de kiezers. Lokale partijafdelingen en de gemeenteraadsverkiezingen van oktober 2012*, edited by Kris Deschouwer, Tom Verthé, and Benoit Rihoux, 123–46. Brussels: Academic & Scientific Publishers.

Celis, Karen, Silvia Erzeel, Liza Mügge, and Alyt Damstra. 2013. 'Quotas and intersectionality: ethnicity and gender in candidate selection'. *International Political Science Review* 35 (1): 41–54.

Cromboom, Sofie, Johanna Tove Samzelius, and Alison Woodward. 2001. *Toepassing van het quotadecreet van 1997 in de Vlaamse adviesraden*. Brussels: RHEA.

Dahlerup, Drude, ed. 2006. *Women, Quotas, Politics*. London: Routledge.

Erzeel, Silvia, and Didier Caluwaerts. 2013. 'Hoe parlementsleden denken over de legitimiteit van quota: een Europese vergelijking'. *Res Publica* 55 (3): 321–38.

Erzeel, Silvia, and Petra Meier. 2011. 'Is er iets veranderd? De rekrutering en selectie van kandidaten door Belgische partijen na de invoering van quotawetten'. *Tijdschrift voor Genderstudies* 14 (2): 6–19.

Kittilson, Miki Caul. 2006. *Challenging Parties, Changing Parliaments. Women and Elected Office in Contemporary Western Europe*. Columbus, OH: Ohio State University Press.

Krook, Mona Lena. 2007. 'Candidate gender quotas: a framework for analysis'. *European Journal of Political Research* 46 (3): 367–94.

Krook, Mona Lena, Joni Lovenduski, and Judith Squires. 2006. 'Western Europe, North America, Australia and New Zealand. Gender quotas in the context of citizenship models'. In *Women, Quotas and Politics*, edited by Drude Dahlerup, 194–221. London: Routledge.

Lépinard, Éléonore. 2016. 'From breaking the rule to making the rules: the adoption, entrenchment, and diffusion of gender quotas in France'. *Politics, Groups, and Identities* 4 (2): 231–45.

Leyenaar, Monique. 2004. *Political Empowerment of Women: The Netherlands and Other Countries*. Leiden: Martinus Nijhoff Publishers.

Lovenduski, Joni, ed. 2005. *State Feminism and Political Representation*. Cambridge: Cambridge University Press.

Lovenduski, Joni, and Pippa Norris, eds. 1993. *Gender and Party Politics*. London: Sage.

Meier, Petra. 2000a. 'From theory to practice and back again: gender quota and the politics of presence in Belgium'. In *Democratic Innovation*, edited by Michael Saward, 106–16. London: Routledge.

——— 2000b. 'The evidence of being present: guarantees of representation and the example of the Belgian case'. *Acta Politica* 35 (1): 64–85.

——— 2004a. 'De kracht van de definitie. Quotawetten in Argentinië, België en Frankrijk vergeleken'. *Res Publica* 46 (1): 80–100.

——— 2004b. 'The contagion effect of national gender quota on similar party measures in the Belgian electoral process'. *Party Politics* 10 (3): 583–600.

——— 2005. 'The Belgian paradox: inclusion and exclusion of gender issues'. In *State Feminism and Political Representation*, edited by Joni Lovenduski, 41–61. Cambridge: Cambridge University Press.

——— 2008. 'A gender gap not closed by quotas: the renegotiation of the public sphere'. *International Feminist Journal of Politics* 10 (3): 329–47.

——— 2012a. 'Paradoxes in the meaning of quotas in Belgium'. In *The Impact of Gender Quotas*, edited by Susan Franceschet, Mona Lena Krook, and Jennifer Piscopo, 157–72. New York, NY: Oxford University Press.

——— 2012b. 'Why the traditional laggard became a model student: explaining the Belgian gender quotas and parity clause'. *West European Politics* 35 (2): 362–79.

——— 2013. 'Quotas, quotas everywhere: from party regulations to gender quotas for corporate management boards. Another case of contagion'. *Representation* 49 (4): 453–66.

——— 2014. 'Quotas for advisory committees, business and politics: just more of the same?' *International Political Science Review* 35 (1): 106–18.

Meier, Petra, and Dries Verlet. 2008. 'La position des femmes en politique locale belge et l'impact des quotas'. *Swiss Political Science Review* 14 (4): 715–40.

Moor, de Joost, Sofie Marien, and Marc Hooghe. 2013. '"Won't You Be My Number Two?" De invloed van genderquota op het rekruteringsproces van vrouwelijke burgemeesters in het Vlaams Gewest van België (2012)'. *Res Publica* 55 (3): 303–20.

Paye, Olivier. 1997. 'Féminiser le politique: recitoyennisation ou tribalisation? Une réponse du monde politique belge'. *Sextant* 7: 139–61.

Phillips, Anne. 1993. *Democracy and Difference*. University Park, PA: Pennsylvania State University Press.

Pilet, Jean-Benoit, and Teun Pauwels. 2010. 'De vertegenwoordiging van taal-groepen in België: de weg naar een hyperinstitutionalisering'. In *Gezien, Gehoord, Vertegenwoordigd? Diversiteit in de Belgische Politiek*, edited by Karen Celis, Petra Meier, and Bram Wauters, 47–68. Gent: Academia Press.

Popelier, Patricia. 2011. 'Geslachtsquota in de besluitvormingsorganen van publieke instellingen vanuit juridisch perspectief'. In *Recht en Gender in België*, edited by Eva Brems and Liesbeth Stevens, 145–79. Brugge: Die Keure.

——— 2014. 'Het kaduke masker van de Senaat: tussen deelstaatfederalisme en multinational confederalisme'. In *De Zesde Staatshervorming. Instellingen, Bevoegdheden en Middelen*, edited by Jan Velaers et al., 53–90. Antwerp: Intersentia.

Remiche, Adélaïde. 2013. 'Le juge est une femme. Réalité, impact et justifica-tion de la presence des femmes dans la magistrature'. Paper presented at the conference 'Le juge est une femme', Brussels, 7–8 November 2013.

——— 2014. 'Belgian Parliament Introduces Sex Quota in Constitutional Court'. OxHRH-Blog, 21 April 2014, available at: http://humanrights.dev3 .oneltd.eu/?p=5385. Accessed 2 February 2016.

Reynolds, Andrew. 2006. *Electoral Systems and the Protection and Participation of Minorities*. London: Minority Rights Group International.

Schandevyl, Eva, Alison E. Woodward, Elke Valgaeren, and Machteld De Metsenaere. 2013. 'Genderquota in de wetenschap, het bedrijfsleven en de rechterlijke macht in België'. *Res Publica* 55 (3): 359–74.

Sliwa, Sandra, Petra Meier, and Peter Thijssen. 2011. 'De impact van party magnitude op het aantal vrouwelijke verkozenen. Gender quota in België kritisch bekeken'. *Res Publica* 53 (2): 141–65.

Uyttendaele, Mark, and Jérôme Sohier. 1995. 'Les quotas féminins en droit électoral ou les paradoxes de l'égalité'. *Journal des Tribunaux* 114 (5754): 249–56.

Van Molle, Leen and Eliane Gubin. 1998. *Vrouw en Politiek in België*. Tielt: Lannoo.

Wauters, Bram, Bart Maddens, and Gert-Jan Put. 2014. 'It takes time: the long-term effects of gender quota'. *Representation* 50 (2): 143–59.

Woodward, Alison. 1998. 'Politische partizipation von Frauen in Belgien: die gespaltene frau'. In *Handbuch Politische Partizipation von Frauen in Europa*, edited by Beate Hoecker, 17–39. Opladen: Leske und Budrich.

CHAPTER TWO

THE FRENCH PARITY REFORM

The Never-Ending Quest for A New Gender Equality Principle

Éléonore Lépinard

Geneviève Fraisse, a philosopher and historian of the French Revolution and long-time supporter of the French parity reform to introduce a 50-percent gender quota in political elected assemblies, often stated during the parity campaign that parity was "false in theory but true in practice" (Fraisse 2001). This statement was quite iconoclastic at a time when parity activists were, by contrast, trying to persuade power elites that parity was indeed a new normative principle that would bring about real gender equality and would renew French democracy. Almost two decades after parity reform was passed in 1999, it is opportune to ask if, in the end, parity has fulfilled its normative ambitions or if it has remained a pragmatic tool, albeit an efficient one. Indeed, the demand for parity has led to numerous legislative reforms, two constitutional revisions, and several decisions from the French Constitutional Council (CC) over more than fifteen years (1999–2015). In light of these numerous legal developments, one may question whether they reflect a deeper enshrinement of the parity principle in the French constitutional order, or the continuing – and continually resisted – expansion of a pragmatic tool to address persisting gender inequalities, or something in between.

The history of parity reform has been well documented (for detailed accounts see Scott 2005; Lépinard 2007; Bereni 2015) and is becoming more complex as what some have called the "parity reform matrix" (Roman and Hennette-Vauchez 2013, 882) takes hold of new spheres of social life, with gender quotas being implemented in public administration, universities, independent governmental bodies, agricultural chambers, publicly listed companies, and sports federations, to name but a few institutions.[1] The aim of this chapter is to retell this story with an eye to the tension between principle and pragmatism that lies at the heart of the parity claim and its subsequent institutionalization. While the French parity campaign, like the campaign for female suffrage decades earlier, has combined pragmatic and principled rationales, its victorious result is more ambiguous than that of the suffrage campaign. Indeed, the end result of the French campaign for suffrage, whatever its strategic combination of equality and difference, of pragmatism and principles, was the acquisition of a new right henceforth uncontested and guaranteeing women's political participation through voting (although not through election, as French history shows and as parity activists have denounced). Contrastingly, the end result of the parity campaign has been a heterogeneous mix including the legitimation of a new way of conceptualizing gender equality (Lépinard 2007; Rodriguez Ruiz and Rubio-Marín 2008), a constitutional amendment promoting equal access to elective functions and social and professional responsibilities, and the introduction of several legislative schemes to implement gender quotas. Contrary to the suffrage victory, these gains have a much more ambiguous status, especially in the legal order. Indeed, while parity activists aimed at no less than legally enshrining a new conception of equality to go beyond the aporia of formal equality, they have only partially achieved their goal.

Furthermore, parity activists aimed at directly challenging women's de facto exclusion from citizenship. They denounced the French republican gender regime as falsely universal and proposed to challenge the public/private dichotomy upon which it has historically been erected. Indeed, since the end of World War II, the French citizenship regime has been characterized as "republican" (Siim 2000) and "gender biased" (Mazur 1995): while a strong universalist (male) republican conception of citizenship has made it difficult for women to participate concretely in the political sphere because of their perceived "difference," their

---

[1] On women in French public administration, see Edel (2013); Jacquemart, Le Mancq, and Pochic (2016); on quotas in French universities, see Lemercier (2015); on quotas for French corporate boards see Bender, Dang, and Scotto (2016); and on the process of diffusion of gender quotas in France from political bodies to other spheres of social life, see Lépinard (2016).

socio-economic rights have often been justified in the name of this very difference, and women have received rights and benefits mostly as mothers (Jenson 1986; Commaille 1993). As Birte Siim summarizes, the "republican discourse has defended an active family policy, but the hypothesis is that it has at the same time served as an influential institutional and cultural barrier to women's equal integration as citizens" (Siim 2000, 20). Hence, simultaneously republican and familialist, promoting women's employment *and* women's primary role as mothers, the French gender regime has treated women differently depending on the sphere of activity that is being regulated, creating an "unending dilemma" for French women to present themselves as either similar to or different from men and effectively excluding them from active citizenship, i.e. political *participation* and *representation* (Jenson and Sineau 1994). The challenge mounted by parity activists to the French gender regime therefore implied redefining the relationship between equality and difference and opening new routes to include women in the political sphere.

In order to explore the complex heritage of the parity claim, this chapter focuses in particular on the legal controversies of the parity reforms. Struggles to redefine gender equality in the legal sphere, and subsequently to extend this redefinition beyond the original realm of politics, constitute a prime site to analyze the tension between pragmatism and principle and to investigate closely whether and how these struggles to legitimize gender parity have or have not brought about change in the French gender regime. I identify three phases during which the tension between principle and pragmatism has unfolded in distinct ways in the history of gender parity in France. First, from 1982 to 1999, from the first claims for quota mechanisms in political representation to the constitutional reform making them possible, parity activists deployed legal narratives that aimed at transforming parity into a normative principle. Second, from 2000 to 2014, the parity project is mostly developed in a pragmatic manner and extended to other spheres of social life. This period of extension is not without legal fights, however it marks the time of institutionalization and pragmatism. In a last section, I reflect on recent developments that exemplify the continuing resistance of the two highest French courts to recognizing parity as a legal norm. However, despite these ambivalences, the disruptions introduced by parity in the French gender regime are remarkable.

2.1 THE (HALF-)LOST STRUGGLE TO IMPOSE PARITY AS A NEW PRINCIPLE (1982–1999)

In 1999, the French Assembly and Senate, reunited in a Congress for the occasion, adopted a constitutional revision of art. 3 of the French Constitution. It stated that "the law *promotes* men and women's equal access to elected mandates and elective functions."[2] The revision also stated in art. 4 that political parties had to contribute to this goal. The reform was a large success if one judges by the vast majority of the – predominantly male – assembly that voted to adopt it: 741 deputies and senators said yes to the revision while only forty-two opposed the reform. However, from the point of view of the parity activists who had mobilized for almost a decade to achieve this reform, the outcome of the constitutional revision process was ambivalent. Indeed, while parity advocates had fought to define parity as a new legal norm of gender equality, the term itself was not included in the Constitution. Moreover, the new constitutional provision reframed parity, initially the objective of equal presence of women in elected assembly, into little more than an equal opportunity principle: the law now could facilitate (*favoriser*) women's access but did not have to impose it. This formulation was the result of a compromise between, essentially, left-wing parties such as the Greens and the Communists, and center and right-wing ones, which marked both the victory of the parity movement and its ultimate vexation (Lépinard 2007, ch. 4). To understand this mixed result, the widespread legitimation of a constitutional reform, and its disappointing content, it is worth looking back at the constitutional politics which presided over these developments: that is, how various collective and institutional actors shaped and reacted to different constitutional interpretations of the parity claim.

Before the parity claim emerged at the very beginning of the 1990s, gender quotas had already been put in place in various parties and trade unions, making the French case initially similar to other countries that experienced early gender quotas within political parties. However, the rapid failure of these schemes makes the French case unique. Indeed, as early as 1974 the French socialist party (PS) adopted a timid 10-percent quota for its various internal structures (Bereni 2015, ch. 1).

---

[2] Loi constitutionnelle 99-569, July 8, 1999. The history of the mobilization for the reform, and of the institutional and political factors presiding over its final legislative success are now well known, see Baudino (2005); Bereni and Lépinard (2004); Murray (2010); Rosenblum (2006); Scott (2005).

At that time women represented a mere 15 percent of party members and only one of them was an elected MP. This internal quota was progressively raised to 20 percent in 1979 and, under pressure from feminist figures in the party such as Marie-Thérèse Eyquem and Yvette Roudy, as well as a broader mobilization of women in 1978 demanding 50 percent of socialist candidates be female for the first European elections, a 30-percent quota was adopted for 1979 European elections. François Mitterand logically included the proposal of a 30-percent gender quota on electoral lists in his 1981 presidential candidate program. At the same moment, on the right-wing of the political spectrum, the women's section of the Rassemblement pour la République (RPR) asked for a 30-percent gender quota on candidate lists and in the party organization, to no avail (Opello 2006). However, the soft mobilization for gender quotas in various political parties at the time encouraged Monique Pelletier, right-wing delegate minister for the "feminine condition" to lobby the Council of ministers in 1979 to adopt a measure in favor of women: a 20-percent gender quota on candidate lists to be tested for the 1983 municipal elections. In 1982, the Confédération Française Démocratique du Travail (CFDT), an important center-left trade union, adopted the principle of proportionate representation of women on its executive board – at the time this meant a 30-percent quota for women.[3] As these soft commitments and declarations of intentions suggest, at the beginning of the 1980s, gender quotas were seen as a legitimate instrument to redress gender imbalance in decision-making, in particular in politics. At that time France was therefore not so different in its approach from some of its European neighbors.

However, the similarities with other countries end in 1982. Indeed, taking up Monique Pelletier's proposal of a gender quota on municipal electoral lists, newly elected socialist deputy – and historic figure of the second wave of the French feminist movement – Gisèle Halimi pressured her political group to sponsor an amendment to a pending electoral bill stating that there could be no more than 75 percent of candidates of the same sex on the candidate lists for municipal elections. Publicly criticized by prominent constitutional scholars, the bill was deferred to the Constitutional Council, which declared the

---

[3] Despite the increase in the number of women members of the CFDT the quota on the executive board did not exceed 30 percent until 2014, at which time women represented 47 percent of the members; see Guillaume, Pochic, and Silvera (2015).

gender quota amendment unconstitutional.[4] The CC argued its refusal of gender quotas on principled grounds invoking two constitutional provisions: the indivisibility of the sovereignty of the people affirmed in art. 3 of the Constitution, and the formal equality principle formulated in art. 6 of the 1789 Declaration of the Rights of Man and Citizen. The use of a quota was perceived as dividing the people into different groups (men and women) and therefore incompatible with the idea that the French people is undividable and exercises its sovereignty through its deputies who act as representatives of the whole nation rather than as representatives of a part of it or of their sole constituency. Second, the quota was perceived as opposing the principle of formal equality as applied to electoral candidates. This concise decision did not propose any discussion of what gender equality should mean with regard to other national or international legal texts and norms, despite the almost simultaneous ratification of the Convention on the Elimination of all Forms of Discrimination Against Women (CEDAW) a year later. However, it clearly ruled out the possibility of breaching temporarily – and pragmatically – the principle of formal equality in order to achieve substantive equality, which is one of the usual conditions for legitimizing quota mechanisms. From this perspective, the CC 1982 decision resembles opposition posed to female suffrage in France decades earlier. Indeed, Sylvie Chaperon notes that "the strongly universalistic French constitutional culture precluded partial suffrage. Not one of the numerous propositions for limited suffrage (for widows, for single women, at the local level) was adopted, so strong was the pull towards universalism" (Chaperon 2012, 314). With parity, a similar universalistic constitutional culture precluded an "incremental track" to improve women's political representation.[5] This decision thus shifted the ground upon which the battle for inclusion in political decision-making could be fought.

Indeed, this decision first stalled the claim for women's presence in politics: during the 1980s, gender quotas stagnated in the socialist party and were not respected for candidate lists despite the protests of feminists inside the party (Bereni 2015, 40–1). It took several years for feminists inside left-wing parties and in women's rights organizations to reorganize their struggle and to reformulate their claim.

[4] Decision n°1982-146 DC, November 18, 1982.
[5] The incremental track characterizes some Nordic countries, see Dahlerup and Freidenvall (2005).

On the movement front, a wide alliance comprising women from left-wing political parties and some from right-wing parties, traditional reformist women's rights organizations, and second-wave feminists with ties to academia and feminist organizations was formed at the end of the 1980s, thanks in part to those feminists who occupied multiple positions (in academia, in women's organizations, and in political parties) (Bereni 2015, 23), and in part to various initiatives at the European level. Indeed, as early as 1992 the Athens Declaration was signed by two prominent French female politicians, Simone Veil and Edith Cresson, under the auspices of the Council of Europe. It drew attention to women's underrepresentation in politics and invigorated French women's non-partisan "civic" organizations – born during the first (related to suffrage) and second waves of feminist activism – as relevant actors (particularly in view of the absence of women's sections in French political parties), putting this new demand on their agenda. As Laure Bereni notes, the networks that were forged during the 1990s were limited in number and heterogeneous. However, they proved efficient because they comprised women from the elites: women who had political experience (as elected representatives or party members) as well as strong ties with some political parties and the femocrat bureaucracy (Bereni 2015). Hence, when it finally emerged, the movement to improve women's political representation was a novel alliance, which called on the European level (through expertise networks on gender balance in political representation) and the 1995 Beijing UN conference proposal in favor of gender quotas to bypass a hostile national political arena (Bereni and Lépinard 2004).

When the demand for improving women's political representation reemerged at the beginning of the 1990s, it used a new motto: parité, a nice rhyme with liberté and égalité, coined in an essay by parity activists Claude Servan-Schreiber and Anne Le Gall with former socialist deputy Françoise Gaspard (Gaspard, Servan-Schreiber, and Le Gall 1992). Since public intellectuals and political elites expressed opposition to gender quotas in line with the CC's 1982 decision – in the name of preserving the integrity of Republican constitutional principles, including the principle of equality itself (Rodriguez Ruiz and Rubio-Marín 2008, 2009) – parity activists decided to take the higher normative ground (Lépinard 2016).

To do so, they first defined gender as a specific difference, different from other social differences such as ethnicity or language. For example,

Eliane Viennot, feminist historian and prominent advocate in favor of parity, stated:

> Women are not a social category or a community. They are one of the two genders which constitute humanity ... this is why quotas are not the right concept because they assimilate women to a minority ... [there is] a specificity to the sexual division, which is radically differ-ent from any other economic or ethnic division within humankind. (Viennot 1994)

This argument that sex is a more universal difference than any other social difference means that it can be legally recognized without endangering constitutional republican principles (or granting other groups similar rights to representation).[6] It opened the door to framing parity as a "principle" (rather than a tool) and imposed a threshold of at least 40 percent rather than lower quotas: a fifty/fifty gender balance is the only logical political claim that can follow the affirmation that sex difference is universal. Flirting with essentialism (and sometimes embracing it), parity activists emphasized women's different social experience to legitimize their participation in political decision-making. Rather than advocating for temporary measures in order to achieve a concrete pragmatic goal – women's access to politics – parity activists framed parity as a democratic normative principle that would ensure not only women's fair political representation but also a better and more modern democracy because both components of humankind, men and women, would be present (Rosenblum 2006; Lépinard 2007). This conception of a democratic representation that should embody sexual difference echoes differentialist arguments in favor of female suffrage and, strangely enough, two centuries later, it echoes the words of revolutionary feminist figure Olympe de Gouges for whom "the nation is nothing but the union of Woman and Man" (cited in Chaperon 2012).

Parity activists performed a second move to respond to the 1982 decision: they proposed redefining gender equality. Remarkably, they affirmed that parity could perfect gender equality, and therefore could act as a (better) substitute for it. Parity was indeed defined as "perfect equality" or "absolute equality" by parity advocates (Gaspard 1996). The ambition that parity should replace gender equality meant that

---

[6] For an analysis of the consequences of the parity reform from an intersectional perspective see Lépinard (2013).

parity needed a legal definition that differed from gender equality. Legal scholar Eliane Vogel-Polsky (1996) argued in this vein, stating that parity could overcome the opposition between formal equality and substantive equality because it affirmed the principle of gender equality and realized it at the same time. Parity activists thus offered a new legal and political horizon for gender equality: defined as the equal presence of women and men, parity could overcome the aporia of formal equality – always invoked and never realized. Thus, parity was not (like gender quotas) a means to achieve the end of gender equality, it was rather a new, and perfect, political and legal definition of gender equality. As French feminists discussed and critiqued the limited conception of gender equality based on the formal equality endorsed by the CC, the debate about what other measures, beyond equal presence, might be required to achieve substantive equality or equal opportunities for women became irrelevant.

While this clever parity rhetoric offered feminists a new way to critique the aporia of formal equality and to ask for more, it was not accepted as such in the French legal order. Indeed, the constitutional definition of gender equality remains formal equality: the new constitutional clause only suggests that the law "promotes" or "encourages" (favoriser) equal access; it does not guarantee the equal opportunities, equality of results or equal presence demanded by parity activists. What is more, while the legislature is free to promote or encourage equal access, in the dominant constitutional interpretation of the 1999 constitutional revision, it has no obligation to do so. In fact, legal scholar Danièle Lochak pointed out provocatively during the hearings of the legislative commission of the National Assembly that the constitutional clause was only proclaiming (again) formal equality.[7] However, the concrete legal dispositions adopted a year later that detail the implementation of this new constitutional clause did introduce, on the one hand, compulsory gender quotas in several elections – sometimes leading de facto to an almost equal presence of men and women in political bodies, and on the other hand, non-compulsory mechanisms such as financial sanctions for legislative elections – leading in sum to a very small and disappointing increase in the presence of women in the Parliament: from 10.9 percent in 1997 to 12.3 percent in 2002.[8]

---

[7] Rapport n°1240 Commission des Lois de l'Assemblée Nationale, December 1998.
[8] Loi n°2000-493, June 6, 2000.

In other words, the parity motto did not lead to the adoption of a new constitutional definition of gender equality, as formal equality remained the rule outside politics and the legislature still had no obligation to go further; but it troubled the legal definition of gender equality in a productive way. Compared to other European or Latin American countries who opted, during the same period, for incremental quotas starting at 30 percent, the parity claim opened the door to a bolder fifty/fifty demand, and prompted parity activists to place themselves on the terrain of democratic renewal and universalism. Hence the battle to win the normative ground was only half lost by parity activists: the new legal principle that emerged was limited to politics and not really enforceable, but a powerful new normative definition of gender equality as sharing power and equal presence took hold in the public sphere. This new conception relied at the same time on a powerful difference narrative and on the dominant universalist republicanism that had characterized the 1982 decision of the Constitutional Council. Parity activists had managed to turn republicanism upside down by introducing a universal difference. From this perspective, the parity constitutional reform was, symbolically at least, both a subversion of the exclusive republicanism that characterized the French gender regime (Lépinard and Mazur 2009) and its confirmation.

However, to assess the subsequent unfolding of parity reform, one needs to look beyond the legal battles and scrutinize institutional change as well. Indeed, parity activists succeeded as early as 1995 in introducing parity as a new principle inside the state bureaucracy with the creation of an Observatory for Parity (Observatoire de la parité) in charge of promoting parity and, later on, collecting data on its implementation. While the French femocrat bureaucracy had traditionally been divided between a stable administrative service in charge of women's rights (service aux droits des femmes) with few powers, and a more political and shifting bureaucracy attached to the women's rights ministries or state secretaries (when they existed), the Observatory was created as a stable independent administrative entity, attached to the Prime Minister, and less susceptible to being dismissed. It was a token of good faith given by recently elected President Jacques Chirac to parity activists who had lobbied for him during the presidential campaign. The mandate of the Observatory was to evaluate women's participation in the public sphere and to propose means for improving it. This institutionalization of parity inside the state bureaucracy proved crucial in the following decade.

2.2   THE TIME FOR PRAGMATISM (2000–2014)

While the debate on constitutional reform contributed to framing parity as a normative principle that should apply to the realm of democratic governance, the breach created in the constitutional order by the new art. 3 proved to be wider and more productive than expected, launching the "parity reform matrix." Indeed, in the following decades numerous new bills were adopted that extended quota mechanisms to various spheres of social life. However, the dynamics of the adoption of new gender quota schemes differed from the preceding phase of constitutional revision. Indeed, once the Constitution had been changed to promote parity in elected assemblies, the mobilization for parity – once a heterogeneous but powerful alliance between reformist feminists, female politicians, and second wave feminists – disbanded. This dissolution did not mean, however, that the mobilization for parity had ended. In fact, as a result of the creation of the Observatory as well as the two parliamentary committees for women's rights in 1999,[9] the struggle relocated: from mainly *outside* institutions to taking place mainly *inside* institutions, and therefore becoming less visible.[10] This relocation also meant that while during the first phase of mobilization activists had strong ties with European institutions and looked to European and international resources and narratives to build their case, in this second phase, the development of new legislation was centered on the French political system, now a pioneer in gender quotas: amendments adding parity clauses were added to pending legislations in piecemeal fashion with little reference to developments happening simultaneously at the European level or in other countries such as Belgium and Norway. During this period, the normative debate also evolved as it shifted to the more hushed universe of high courts. Indeed, champions of parity in the parliamentary arena relied now almost exclusively on pragmatist reasons rather than normative conceptions to justify the extension of parity to other spheres, bringing parity measures closer in line with

[9] The *délégations parlementaires aux droits des femmes*. France was a latecomer to the creation of parliamentary delegations for women's rights, a transnational development that characterized many parliamentary democracies under the impetus of the Interparliamentary Union, among other actors.

[10] While the opposition between outside and inside institutions is in part artificial since, as Bereni (2015) notes, many parity activists were both inside and outside institutions, there is a clear shift in the nature of the mobilization after 2000 to being more inside than outside.

gender quotas. At the same time, the legal debate on the nature of parity and its relationship with (formal) equality, which had had some resonance in the public debate and in the women's movement, was now confined to the Constitutional Council and the State Council (Conseil d'Etat, the highest administrative court) which maintained a fierce opposition to the diffusion of parity mechanisms to other spheres than politics.

The 2000s witnessed two main achievements on the parity front: the adoption of new legal mechanisms to improve the implementation of parity in the political sphere, and the adoption of gender quotas beyond politics – with corporate board quotas in 2011, quotas in higher public service in 2012, quotas in universities' decision-making bodies in 2013, and quotas in various private and semi-public decision-making bodies (boards of directors, supervisory boards etc.) in 2014. Neither of these developments went unchallenged, however, revealing unresolved tensions around the relationship between equality and parity. Moreover, the extension of quotas to new domains relied on a new set of actors and different political processes from the previous sequence, in which quotas had been adopted for political representation. I now detail these two policy developments.

2.2.1 Refining and Improving Parity in the Political Sphere[11]

The 2000 law defining the concrete parameters for the implementation of the new constitutional clause presented a Janus face. While it introduced a strict zipper system on candidate lists for European elections and elections to the Senate (both elections with a proportional list system), and a loose zipper system (three women in every six candidates) for regional elections and municipal elections in cities with over 3,500 inhabitants (also ruled with a proportional list system), it introduced only financial sanctions for legislative elections and no scheme at all for the local elections of Conseils Généraux (a political entity located at the department level, between cities and regions), arguing that the uninominal system used for both the National Assembly and the Conseils Généraux was inimical to implementing parity. The concrete results of these schemes were likewise contrasted (see Table 2.1). Where quotas on candidate lists were compulsory and used a zipper system, they proved efficient. For other elections they proved less reliable, with parties using the loopholes of the legislation to preserve male

---

[11] This section draws on Lépinard (2016).

TABLE 2.1   Percentage of women elected in all electoral mandates 2000–16

Mandates	Election periods			
	2001–4	2007–10		2012–17
Municipal councilors in cities where parity does not apply[a]	30.0	32.2	34.4	
Municipal councilors in cities where parity applies	47.4	48.5	48.2	
Municipal executive elected members in cities where parity does not apply[b]			30.2	
Municipal executive elected members in cities where parity does apply		48.2	47.5	
Departmental councilors[c]	9.2	13.9	49.5	
Regional councilors	47.6	48.0	47.8	
Deputies	12.3	18.5	26.9 (2012)	38.8 (2017)
Senators in constituencies where parity does not apply	7.1 (2001) 4.5 (2004)	9.5 (2008) 17.2 (2011)	8.3 (2014)	29 (2017)[d]
Senators in constituencies where parity applies	27.0 (2001) 34.9 (2004)	27.5 (2008) 34.8 (2011)	29.4 (2014)	
European MPs	43.6	44.4		

[a]From 2000, a loose zipper system applied to all cities of over 3,500 inhabitants; from 2007 a strict zipper system applied; since 2013 a strict zipper system has applied to all cities of over 1,000 inhabitants.
[b]A strict zipper system applied for the first time in 2007.
[c]Compulsory parity applied for the first time in 2015 with a binominal ballot.
[d]At the time of writing, the distribution of the seats in the two types of constituencies (where parity applies, where it does not apply) was not known
Source: Observatoire de la parité 2008 / Haut Conseil à l'Egalité entre les femmes et les hommes 2014

privilege.[12] In the following years, femocrats inside the Observatory for Parity and female politicians heading the parliamentary committees for women's rights created in 1999 mobilized to prevent setbacks and to improve the electoral schemes.

Indeed, as the right-wing majority came to power in 2002, it passed electoral reforms in 2003 with the direct effect of reducing the scope of the parity laws for senatorial, regional and European elections. While the new electoral bill introduced a strict zipper system for candidate lists for senators elected through a proportional representation system, it reduced the number of senators elected through such a system: the proportional election-with-list system which had previously applied to all départements with at least three senators would henceforth apply only to the (fewer in number) départements with four senators.[13] Similarly, the government and its parliamentary majority introduced smaller districts for both European and regional elections, with the predictable effect of limiting the impact of the parity requirement.[14] However, parity activists inside political institutions did not witness these attempts to curb parity reform and its disappointing implementation in the National Assembly without taking action. Quite the contrary: from 2002 to 2009 the Observatory, under the tenure of right-wing MP Marie-Jo Zimmermann and comprising mostly academic experts, femocrats, and independent political personalities, as well as a few permanent staff, helped craft legislation to improve the efficacy of the parity laws.

Hence, after this initial setback, parity advocates achieved some new gains. In 2007, Zimmermann fighting against some members of her own political party, helped pass a law to promote women's and men's equal access to electoral mandate and elective functions.[15] The law extended parity to executive functions in regional and municipal councils (in cities with over 3,500 inhabitants). Indeed, so far parity had applied only to candidate lists, leaving untouched executive functions. Traditionally the head of the list would designate a number of elected candidates to be part of the executive body of the city or the regional council, and the regional or municipal council would vote in

---

[12] For recent overviews of the electoral results of the parity reform as well as how parties used or abused it, see Southwell (2013, 2014); Verge and Troupel (2014).

[13] Loi n°2003-697, July 30, 2003.

[14] Loi n°2003-327, April 11, 2003.

[15] Loi n°2007-128, January 31, 2007.

favor of its executive body when meeting for the first time. Hence, there was no obligation to respect parity in allocating the crucial executive functions. The 2007 law imposed parity in executive functions and increased the financial penalty for political parties that would not apply parity for legislative elections. Finally, this law also imposed a "mixed ticket" for uninominal elections (legislative and département): the substitute should be of the opposite sex of the candidate (a rule which does not prevent women from being systematically placed as substitutes rather than as candidates).

A new round of legislative reforms to improve the implementation of political parity took place when the Left came back to power in 2012. In 2013, an electoral law[16] changed the way local councilors (*conseillers départementaux*) are elected in order to impose parity. It introduced a real "mixed ticket," with one man/one woman on the ballot (creating a "bi-nominal" electoral system) and coupled districts together in order to maintain the same number of representatives. This electoral reform also aligned cities with over 1,000 inhabitants on the same electoral system as cities with over 3,500 inhabitants (a proportional list system, allowing strict parity to be applied to candidate lists), a reform demanded by parity activists as early as 1999. Parity was also applied to EPCIs (*établissements publics de cooperation intercommunale*), an important type of indirectly elected local political institution reuniting several cities that had been thus far left out of the scope of parity reform, prompting local power, and local men, to relocate there. Subsequently, another electoral law re-introduced a proportional list system to elect senators in districts with three or more senators.[17] In 2014, a general law on "real gender equality" promoted by the Minister for women's rights Najat Vallaud-Belkacem introduced new provisions increasing the financial sanctions for political parties that would not respect parity on candidate lists for legislative elections. It was implemented for the first time in 2017, in the context of a very unusual electoral race that culminated in a landslide victory for a newcomer centrist party, La République en Marche (LRP), which had indeed respected parity for its candidates. Because the LRP had 50-percent women candidates and won an absolute majority of seats, the percentage of elected women MPs rose to 38.8. However, continuing resistance in the main right-wing party is evidenced by a relatively

---

[16] Loi n°2013-403, May 17, 2013.
[17] Loi n°2013-702, August 2, 2013.

higher percentage of female candidates than in previous elections (39 percent), but still only 23 percent of women elected MPs among its own ranks (against 14 percent in 2012). Hence, despite resistance from right-wing MPs in the first half of the decade, the implementation of parity was incrementally improved, and the numbers of women elected gradually went up.

2.2.2 Pragmatic Expansion Meets Stalwart Resistance: The Struggle Over the Legal Meaning of Parity

In parallel with these developments in the political sphere, several attempts to extend parity to other spheres than politics – mainly promoted by institutional actors inside the state bureaucracy and inside the executive and legislative powers – met with enduring resistance from high courts and momentary defeats. However, these initial setbacks were progressively overcome by successive waves of pro-parity legislative reforms.

As early as 2001, a clause inspired by the parity reform and stating that "trade unions examine the means to achieve a balanced representation of men and women on candidate lists" for the elections of workers representatives was inserted into a new law on égalité professionnelle (gender equality at work),[18] promoted – not coincidentally – by Catherine Génisson, former parity advocate and head of the Observatory for Parity at the time. With no compulsory gender quota, this clause was not challenged – and never really implemented – but it signaled that parity could be applied beyond politics.[19] Another clause in the same bill organized parity not on the list of candidates – as had heretofore been the case – but in the composition of recruitment and promotion committees (juries) presiding over the access of candidates to positions in public service. The idea of encouraging the presence of both sexes in juries was not new: it had been initiated, with no effect whatsoever, as early as 1983.[20] However, the 2001 law took it a step further as it introduced a minimum of one third of the underrepresented sex on committees in order to ensure gender-balance.[21] This attempt to extend parity beyond politics was curbed by the State Council, which affirmed in a 2007 decision that decisions taken by a committee whose

---

[18] Loi n°2001-397, May 9, 2001.
[19] For an analysis of the implementation of this clause, see Odoul-Asorey (2014).
[20] Circulaire, January 24, 1983.
[21] Percentage fixed by art. 3 of the May 3, 2002 Decree.

composition did not comply with the one-third rule were still valid.[22] In other words, the obligation to have one third women on committees for recruitment into public service was in the end no obligation at all.

At the exact same moment that Catherine Génisson was trying to extend parity to the private sector and the public service, in May 2001 a law that introduced parity on the lists of candidates for the High Council of Magistrates (Conseil Supérieur de la Magistrature) was declared unconstitutional by the CC.[23] While the parity constitutional reform had introduced the idea that the law should promote equal access of men and women to elective functions, the CC argued that this principle was not to be applied outside of politics, putting a (temporary) halt on any diffusion of parity beyond politics. These early attempts by the two highest French courts to curtail the diffusion of parity exemplify the dynamics that presided over the development of parity during the 2000s.

The next important attempt to enter the breach created by the 1999 constitutional reform unfolded several years later with a demand for corporate board quotas (CBQ). Mostly sponsored by right-wing women in powerful political positions in the name of pragmatism and economic efficiency, the CBQ reform displayed a very different dynamic from the parity reform. In 2005, the Minister for parity and gender equality at work, right-wing politician Nicole Ameline, proposed a new bill on égalité professionnelle.[24] The bill mentioned women's presence on boards and the need to reach a gender balance within a five-year period, but did not say how this was to be accomplished. Marie-Jo Zimmermann, right-wing MP and head of both the Observatory for Parity and the National Assembly's parliamentary committee for women's rights, was inspired by the 2003 Norwegian CBQ law to propose several amendments to the bill to include a CBQ provision, setting a limit of 80 percent of members of the same sex on corporate boards, as well as on commissions representing workers in the public sector and supervisory boards of public institutions. However, the bill and the law finally adopted (including Zimmermann's 20-percent quotas) did not define any sanction for non-compliance. Despite an agreement reached in the National Assembly and the Senate on the use of a 20-percent

---

[22] Decision Lessourd, June 22, 2007, req. 288.206; see Moniolle (2014).
[23] Decision 2001-445 DC, June 19, 2001.
[24] Projet de loi n°2214, March 24, 2005.

quota,[25] the Constitutional Council struck down the quota provision. Indeed, sixty deputies referred the law to the CC on procedural grounds (they did not mention the quota provision), but the CC decided to examine the quota provision on its own initiative and, unsurprisingly given its historical commitment against quotas, struck down the provision using a narrow interpretation of the 1999 constitutional amendment that excluded from its scope non-political elected functions and mandates.[26]

Both decisions declaring gender quotas unconstitutional, in 2001 and 2006, denote a continuing and proactive opposition from the Constitutional Council. Indeed, in 1998 the State Council, giving legal advice to the Government on the parity constitutional reform, had suggested that it was unnecessary to include in the revision of art. 3 other domains of application than electoral mandate and elective functions. The State Council based its reasoning on the 1946 Preamble of the French Constitution that states that "the law guarantees to woman, in every domain, equal rights to those of man," as well as on the EU Amsterdam Treaty of 1998 which had introduced the possibility of temporary special measures to promote gender equality in the domains of competence of the EU. The State Council then reasoned that since the CC had founded its 1982 decision on the indivisibility of sovereignty and formal equality of candidates for elections, its decision applied only to the realm of political elections. For other spheres of decision-making, EU law and the 1946 Preamble were thought of as sufficient to ensure the constitutionality of gender quota schemes. Hence, the limited scope of the 1999 constitutional reform reflected the belief of the MPs that other domains beyond politics did not necessitate a constitutional revision. Despite these previous legal discussions, the CC opted to narrowly interpret the 1999 revision and discard any reference to EU law.

A constitutional reform was therefore once again needed to implement this new type of quota. The 2008 constitutional revision planned by President Sarkozy to modernize political institutions gave Marie-Jo Zimmermann the window of opportunity she was looking for. She proposed an amendment to art. 3 to enlarge the constitutional commitment to promoting women's equal access to electoral mandate to "social and professional functions." However, the fight was not so easy to win.

[25] Loi n°2006-340, March 23, 2006.
[26] Decision n°2006-533 DC, March 16, 2006.

Indeed, she was opposing her own political party, since the President, under pressure from organized business representatives, had decided he did not want any constitutional revision on the CBQ issue and rather wanted to add a provision on gender equality in the Preamble of the constitution (therefore with no real binding effect).

The battle for the constitutional revision to add social and professional responsibilities to "electoral mandates" and "elective functions" in art. 3 of the Constitution repeated the arguments already rehearsed in 1999 but in a minor mode, since opposition was now concentrated in the right-wing Senate. During the constitutional debates, arguments already developed to oppose political parity at the end of the 1990s in the name of formal equality and meritocracy were again voiced but with very little effect. In 2008, opposition to quotas in the name of a formal and individualist conception of equality was not prevalent and did not exert any leverage in the parliamentary debate. On the contrary, the idea of compulsory measures with specific targets, although many lamented the need to use them, was much more legitimate than it had been a decade earlier and accepted on pragmatic grounds rather than normative ones. Economic efficiency and the benefits from including women's perspective in the management of business were the rationales put forward.

In the end, Zimmermann prevailed in rallying her own political party to her cause. This successful, and more consensual, 2008 constitutional revision added "social and professional responsibilities" to political functions, and transferred this equal access clause to the first section of the constitution, thereby granting it an even greater symbolic power.[27] The revision led the way to the 2011 Coppé-Zimmermann law implementing a two-step quota of 20 percent by 2014 and 40 percent by 2017 for board members of publicly listed companies, as well as unlisted companies which have more than 500 workers and have had average revenues or total assets of more than fifty million euros during the last three consecutive years. It also applies to some state-owned companies.[28] The sanction is quite direct, since boards with member appointments that do not respect the quota are considered null and board members' benefits can be suspended. During the parliamentary debates for the 2011 CBQ law, pragmatism prevailed in arguments both for and against the quotas. While right-wing MPs opposing the reform

[27] Loi constitutionnelle n°2008-724, July 23, 2008.
[28] I detail the implementation of this law below in Section 2.3.

argued that it would put an undue burden on businesses in a time of economic crisis and that women on corporate boards might negatively impact businesses' profits, MPs in favor of CBQ claimed that women's presence would benefit business. For example, a male right-wing MP declared during the parliamentary debates that women:

> [W]ill inspire new motivations, what is more their presence will mark a new phase for the history of entrepreneurship in our country. Maybe it will even be an opportunity for French economic competitiveness.[29]

In a similarly utilitarian vein, the right-wing Minister for work, Xavier Darcos, declared:

> I am convinced that a society which discards the talents and skills of half of its population is less well prepared to address the challenges of the future, to confront necessary changes and to innovate in all domains of economic and social life.[30]

MPs on the left side of the lower chamber and parity advocates also insisted on both economic and equality arguments, stating that women's presence on boards would benefit women in the private sector and in society at large. They noted that twenty years of equal-pay legislation had not brought major change in women's professional lives, which are marked by discrimination and the glass ceiling, and that women's presence in decision-making bodies in the corporate world would bring an end to these disappointments:

> The day when corporate boards with 40 percent women will discuss equal pay on the basis of the gender equality report [annual compulsory report for large firms comparing men and women's position in the organization], the six laws on equal pay that we voted will maybe at last be enforced. To act at the level of the corporate board should give a new impetus to equal pay measures.[31]

Hence, the CBQ law, contrary to the parity laws, is a top-down process, in great part made possible by the institutions created to institutionalize women's rights during the previous decade: the Observatory for Parity and the parliamentary committees for women's rights. It did not draw a lot of media and public attention, nor did women's rights organizations mobilize to impose it. This lack of contentious debate denotes

---

[29] Assemblée Nationale, débats, January 20, 2010, 252.
[30] Assemblée Nationale, débats, January 20, 2010, 239.
[31] Marie Jo Zimmermann, Assemblée Nationale, débats, January 20, 2010, 239.

a relative acceptance of parity's main claim, that is, the necessity of gender balance in decision-making. Still, the continuing resistance from right-wing MPs and senators as well as from the Constitutional Council suggests that while pragmatic reasons prevailed, the normative ambition of parity advocates to redefine gender equality as equal presence and to introduce gender difference in republican universalism had not yet been fulfilled. The law proved quite efficient, although not perfect. In 2017, the year when the law was to be implemented to its fullest, with the 40-percent quota provision finally applicable to companies with over 500 employees and more than fifty million euros in capitalization, a study by the association of women certified public accountants – an organization which openly promotes parity on boards of companies – revealed that the biggest firms (with more than one billion in capitalization) had nominated 34.8 percent women to their boards. That year medium-sized firms (between 150 million and one billion in capitalization) had nominated only 30.6 percent women, and that in smaller firms to which the law still applied, that is with a capitalization between fifty and 150 million, women comprise 28.3 percent of boards.[32]

2.2.3 Fast-Tracking and Stretching the "Parity Reform Matrix"

It should be noted that ironically, each time the CC opposed a gender quota law – 25 percent for municipal elections in 1982 and 20 percent for boards in 2006 – it only delayed the reform: on both occasions, a quota with a higher threshold, and applying to many more domains, was passed. This was also the case after the CBQ 2011 law. Indeed from 2012 to 2014, multiple legislations were passed that extended the "parity reform matrix" to new domains of social life. In 2012, Marie-Jo Zimmermann (then only a deputy) lobbied to impose a 40-percent gender quota for higher public service functions. Her proposal, integrated into the Sauvadet law on public sector employment was successful, implementing a 40-percent quota (to be reached in 2018) not only to the higher public service but also to administrative and supervisory boards of public institutions, high councils, juries and selection committees in public service procedures, thereby overruling the State Council's 2007 jurisprudence.[33] Again, this process was top-down,

---

[32] Available at: www.femmes-experts-comptables.com/wp-content/uploads/2017/06/TELESCOP_AFECA_2017V2.pdf.

[33] Loi n°2012-347, March 12, 2012.

endogenous to the Parliament and the executive bureaucracy, with scarce public debate on the quota measure, little publicity in the media, and no major political opposition to the quota scheme, all of which suggest a broad underlying consensus on the parity principle.

This dynamic of expansion was enhanced by the victory of the Left in the 2012 legislative and presidential elections. Indeed, parity was further institutionally entrenched when Socialist President François Hollande closed down the Observatory for Parity in order to create the Haut Conseil à l'égalité entre les femmes et les hommes (HCEfh; the High Council for Equality between Women and Men) with a broader mission and an increased staff.[34] The HCEfh has been instrumental since its creation in developing parity as a new norm, a "culture," a principle of social organization that should infuse all spheres of social life. In accordance with this mission, the HCEfh was active in mainstreaming gender quotas to other domains. For example, as a consequence of HCEfh lobbying, in 2013 the Fioraso law reforming higher education also included provisions to promote parity in university decision-making bodies and representative bodies.[35] Similarly, the Vallaud-Belkacem law passed on August 4, 2014 lists new domains where parity will thereafter be implemented, such as chambers of commerce, chambers of agriculture and industry, Boards of Directors and Supervisory Boards of public corporations and companies, Boards of Directors of companies whose workforce is more than 250 employees, sports federations, and organizations for the promotion of cultural cooperation.[36] This new implementation of gender quotas way beyond politics or corporate boards did not meet any opposition; on the contrary, parity and gender quotas seem to have become unproblematic. Asked about how the diffusion of gender quotas promoted by HCEfh for the Vallaud-Belkacem law was received in the Parliament, the Secretary General of the HCEfh observed:

> In the political discourse the evolution during debates at the National Assembly is clear, for the last law [2014] nobody batted an eyelid ...

---

[34] Although still very small, the Observatory now has three full-time employees rather than two. Its members are more numerous, having grown from less than forty to over seventy.

[35] Loi n°2013-660, July 22, 2013 relative à l'enseignement supérieur et à la recherche.

[36] Loi n°2014-873. See HCEfh, *Guide to gender parity* (updated February 2016), available at: www.haut-conseil-egalite.gouv.fr/IMG/pdf/hce_parity_leaflet_feb_2016–2.pdf.

> there is always some resistance in the Senate on quotas, they say they agree with the concept of parity because anyway it has become politically incorrect to be against parity ... but they always find ways to try to suppress quotas, but at the National Assembly ... it's now part of the tools. We used to hear that France is indivisible and all this discourse against positive discrimination, temporary special measures ... and we don't hear that anymore, which is funny because it was legally very entrenched and now it's gone.[37]

While this statement may sound overly optimistic, as I detail bellow, it does suggest that the continued lobbying for parity measures during the 2000s did transform the political landscape. While pragmatism prevailed as femocrats and feminist MPs multiplied attempts to extend parity beyond its initial realm, they met with continuing resistance from right-wing MPs and both high courts. Most of these struggles, however, ended with the final victory of parity advocates: their bills were passed, imposing parity as a new, legitimate principle to regulate women's access to decision-making bodies, entrenching the norm that democratic governance demands women's presence.

2.3 PARITY VS. EQUALITY?

Despite what can be defined as the successful adoption of parity as a new legitimate principle that justifies the use of gender quotas for numerous decision-making bodies, both in the public sphere and in the private sphere, two recent decisions from both high courts suggest that administrative and constitutional judges are not eager to adopt parity as a new legal norm that should infuse the gender equality jurisprudence, and that they continue to efficiently inhibit its legal entrenchment. Hence, the French case offers a striking contrast between, on the one hand, an efficient diffusion of parity as a legitimate principle of governance, as a new way to frame equality issues, and as the preferred mechanism to address gender inequalities proposed by femocrats and, on the other hand, the continued resistance to adopting a more substantive legal definition of equality, despite two constitutional revisions encouraging parity.

The will to continue to promote parity as an important principle for democratic governance, and to give it normative content, is evidenced in particular in the proactive lobbying of the HCEfh since its creation.

---

[37] Interview with the Secretary General of the HCEfh, June 2014.

In 2013, the term parity was for the first time included in the body of a legal text: the Fioraso law on higher education and the 2014 Vallaud-Belkaceme equality law mention explicitly in several of their provisions the word parity. This trend mirrors the political will of the HCEfh to see the parity principle more clearly defined and identified as a principle of equal sharing of power and of representation between men and women. Indeed, the HCEfh's impact study on the Vallaud-Belkacem bill proposal aims to "generalize the constitutional objective of parity," and identifies other domains to which quotas could be applied in the future, such as trade unions, NGOs, and political parties.[38] Hence, virtually every public or professional institution or organization has become a potential site of gender quota implementation and the development of what the HCEfh calls a "culture" of parity. To justify its claim that parity is a principle that should be applied to all domains of social, political, and economic life, the HCEfh presents the parity principle as the ideal combination of positive action measures with the republican universalist tradition. Indeed, the HCEfh recognizes that:

> Quotas are legal and legitimate in the name of a coherent republican universalism. Quotas are not preferential measures but corrective and transformative measures that aim at undoing structural barriers which are incompatible with the principle of equality.[39]

However, the HCEfh continues, the term parity should nonetheless be preferred to gender quotas, because of:

1. The commitment to the idea of equality with reference to three centuries of struggle of women for their rights;
2. Women are half of humankind, they cannot be reduced to a category;
3. Gender quotas targets can become a ceiling (rather than a threshold);
4. Gender quotas run the risk of legitimizing women's right to be elected in the name of their differences rather than because they are full citizens.[40]

This list of rationales that mixes together old, principled arguments for parity (women are half of humankind) with practical reasons

---

[38] Impact study, NOR: DFEX1313602L/Bleue-1, July 1, 2014, p. 78.
[39] Haut Conseil à l'Egalité entre les femmes et les hommes, *Avis sur le projet de loi pour l'égalité entre les femmes et les hommes*, Avis n°2013-0912-HCE-007, 49.
[40] Ibid., 49.

(gender quotas might limit women's access to only 30 percent while parity will ensure access to 50 percent) is in a way typical of the tension between principle and pragmatism that has been at the heart of the parity reform dynamics. These rationales indeed reveal the normative ambition of parity: to be enshrined as a new *citizenship right*, for *half of humankind*. However, they also reveal the difficulty, for the HCEfh femocrats, of defining precisely the relationship between parity, gender quotas, and equality. With this fuzzy but consensual narrative, mixing together all the arguments generally mobilized in favor of quotas and defining quota mechanisms and parity as, in fact, complementary and "republican," the HCEfh clearly attempts to make parity a "common referential principle identifiable by all actors and adapted for each sector [of social and economic life]."[41]

However, these attempts at entrenching parity as a new norm have met with direct opposition from both French high courts. While parity has been promoted by its proponents as a "perfect equality," a necessary complement to formal equality that can achieve full gender equality, neither court has found a legal basis for this ambition. On the contrary, they have constantly refused to enshrine parity as a legal principle, suggesting both that parity is somehow contrary to equality and that it is not a constitutional principle.

Despite two constitutional revisions in 1999 and 2008 in order to promote women's and men's equal access to political, social, and professional responsibilities, in 2013 the State Council struck down a decree to ensure parity on candidate lists for the elections in agricultural chambers.[42] This decision came as a surprise to many observers: how could the State Council invalidate a decree that was so clearly in line with the will expressed by the legislature and enshrined in the Constitution since 2008? As Diane Roman and Stéphanie Hennette Vauchez (2013) note, this decision reveals two strategies of resistance to parity on the part of the State Council. First, the State Council presents parity as somewhat at odds with the principle of equality, stating that the constitutional revisions aimed at reconciling "formal equality" and "equal access." Hence, instead of following the reasoning of the legislature and presenting parity as a complement or an improvement to formal equality, the State Council maintains that formal equality remains the unequivocal norm and standard to be applied, with parity

---

[41] Ibid., 51.
[42] Conseil d'Etat, decision n°362280.

constituting some kind of *exception to the rule* rather than a *new norm*. Second, the State Council argued that only the *law* could promote equal access to positions for women and men, hence a governmental decree was not enough. This very limited vision of what the "law" represents, restricting it to legislation, implies a limit on the State's ability to use its power to implement parity.

A second decision, made in 2015 by the Constitutional Council, denotes the same refusal to consider parity as a constitutional principle that should be combined with formal equality when the situation (or the legislature's will) demands it. Indeed, in 2015 a council representing heads of public universities used the question of constitutional priority – QCP, a mechanism introduced by the 2008 constitutional revision to enable actors other than MPs to access the CC – to challenge the legality of a decree implementing the 2013 Fioraso law on higher education. The heads of universities claimed that the obligation to implement a twofold parity inside the academic council of the university – gender parity and status parity with similar numbers of professors and lecturers – was excessive. Feminist legal scholars intervened in the QPC process as external voluntary participants, arguing that gender parity should apply to the academic councils. The CC rejected the QPC, arguing that the state had not exceeded its power in obliging academic councils to implement this twofold parity.

However, the CC seized this opportunity to state that parity is not a constitutional principle that can be used to make a QPC. In other words, while other constitutional principles enshrined in the first section of the constitution, such as secularism, can serve as grounds for a QPC, parity cannot be used. The CC justified this exclusion by arguing that parity is neither a right nor a freedom protected by the Constitution.[43] While indeed parity, similarly to substantive equality clauses in other countries, cannot be an enforceable right but only a legal principle, this decision closes a potential venue to challenge legislation. Indeed, while future legislation expanding parity might well pass – as numerous bills strengthening or expanding parity have already – there will be no future possibility of challenging legislations in front of the CC in the name of improving or implementing the principle of parity in ways that go beyond what the legislature has decided. Moreover, even the prescriptive nature of the parity provision was called into question.

[43] Decision n°2015-465 QPC, April 24, 2015, §14.

The CC insisted that the first section of the Constitution, promoting women's and men's equal access to elected functions and responsibilities, was a "constitutional permission given to the legislature to intervene to devise rules favorable to parity, *if it wishes to do so*"[44] (my emphasis). With this last episode in the parity saga, it becomes clear that while parity is a constitutional principle – and therefore a qualification to a purely formal conception of gender equality – striving, as it does, for equal presence, its scope so far remains limited: it applies only to gender equality, and it is defined more as an exception to formal equality than as a fulfillment of substantive equality. That is, it is defined as a legitimate exception to the rule of formal equality, which the legislature may want to establish in some circumstances. It therefore falls short – so far – of a normative principle that should guide public action in all circumstances in order to reach substantive equality or even equal presence.

2.4 CONCLUSION: TOWARDS A NEW FRENCH GENDER REGIME?

Almost two decades after the principle of parity was admitted, albeit without being named as such, into the French Constitution, it is still a battleground between, on the one hand, feminist political and bureaucratic actors fighting to transform parity into a powerful norm for public policies and, on the other hand, conservative administrative and constitutional judges who resist attempts to transform and improve the principle of formal equality. Although this epic story is not over yet, one must ultimately ask: Did the introduction of parity in the legal order transform the French gender regime?

The ambition of the parity movement was to challenge women's exclusion from republican universalism and to dismantle the French gender regime based on a valorization of women as mothers and workers and their simultaneous exclusion from active citizenship. Indeed, the strong republican commitment in favor of formal equality had for a long time obscured the differential treatment imposed on women because of their sex and impeded the development of a more substantive conception of equality. The French gender model came under attack from feminists in the 1980s as a norm of gender equality began to prevail in employment policies and as women claimed more power in all

---

[44] Commentary on Decision n°2015-465 QPC, April 24, 2015, 13.

spheres of decision-making, including inside political parties and trade unions. Parity is therefore a direct product of various attempts at dismantling a gender order deemed hypocritical: egalitarian in discourse but exclusionary in practice. However, in the domain of employment, for example, resistance to change often prevailed and reforms remained mainly symbolic (Lépinard and Mazur 2009). Time will tell whether the gender equality reforms inspired by parity since 1999 will have a lasting, transformative impact for women and, further, if they will have dismantled the republican gender regime for good. However, the use of gender quotas will at least, by definition, guarantee women's presence in numerous new sites of power: political assemblies, high civil service, hospitals' public service, corporate boards, boards of directors, supervisory boards of governmental agencies, university juries, and elected commissions, and maybe soon trade unions, internal structures of political parties, cultural institutions, and NGOs. This long list suggests that parity has indeed successfully launched a "reform matrix" or a "cultural revolution"[45] with concrete results, especially during the Left's time in power; and it suggests that France does indeed belong with a set of countries, including Belgium and Slovenia in particular, and to some extent Spain, in which gender quotas can be thought of as *transformative equality remedies*. While gender equality cannot be reduced to gender quotas, the latter contribute to challenging mechanisms of exclusion, discrimination, and the rendering invisible of women in many spheres of social life. To that extent, parity has greatly contributed to redefining the contours of women's citizenship in France, and it has altered the political terrain of future public debates over what is and what should be gender equality, introducing elements of substantial equality into the discussion. From this perspective, gender parity in France may exemplify the non-reformist reforms that gender quotas can bring about, as analyzed in the conclusion of this volume.

In order to achieve these transformations of the French gender regime, a novel alliance of women's organizations, female politicians, feminist experts, academics and bureaucrats was created in the early 1990s. While in many countries women's sections of political parties were instrumental in passing gender quota measures, in France the traditional powerlessness of these sections in political parties meant that other actors had to join forces. This broad – while numerically

---

[45] The term was used by the Minister for Women's Rights, N. Vallaud-Belkacem, cited in Prat (2015).

limited – movement was tremendously influential in the public debate despite staunch resistance from the political-elite. They were helped in their mobilization by resources and discourses forged at the EU level (both in the European Commission and in the Council of Europe), and by new femocrat institutions created in the second half of the 1990s. Their struggle paved the way for a new constitutional principle and prepared the ground for the extension of gender quotas to other spheres. Indeed, corporate board quotas and public bodies quotas were adopted in a top-down fashion, mostly thanks to the activism of femocrats inside the state bureaucracy and with no social mobilization on the part of feminists.

What remains striking about the French case are the efforts that were and still are deployed to transform the demand for parity into a republican motto and a new gender equality principle. Similarly striking is the continuing resistance posed to this project by conservative administrative and constitutional courts. While Belgium has witnessed a similar diffusion of gender quotas to many new spheres beyond politics during the same period, there the spread was not confronted by such staunch judicial resistance. The outcome of this struggle is uncertain: the dynamics of the parity reform have shown that resistance often spurs new forms of mobilization, which, under the right political circumstances, can bring further gains. While the battle to enshrine parity as a new equality principle in the legal sphere has been so far only partially victorious, the pragmatic gains have been numerous. However, it should be noted that those gains have been restricted to women only: the transformation of the French gender regime has not brought about a wider challenge to French republicanism and its exclusion of other groups, such as racial minorities (Ducoulombier 2002; Lépinard 2013). This lapse may be the most problematic of parity's ambivalent achievements.

References

Baudino, Claudie. 2005. "Gendering the Republican System: Debates on Women's Political Representation in France." In *State Feminism and Political Representation*, edited by Joni Lovenduski, 85–105. Cambridge: Cambridge University Press.

Bender, Anne-Françoise, Rey Dang, and Marie José Scotto. 2016. "Les profils des femmes membres des conseils d'administration en France." *Travail, genre et sociétés* 2016/1 (35): 67–85.

Bereni, Laure. 2015. *La bataille pour la parité. Mobilisations pour la féminisation du pouvoir*. Paris: Economica.

Bereni, Laure, and Éléonore Lépinard. 2004. "'Les femmes ne sont pas une catégorie': les stratégies de légitimation de la parité en France." *Revue française de science politique* 54 (1): 71–98.

Chaperon, Sylvie. 2012. "The Difficult Struggle for Women's Political Rights in France." In *The Struggle for Female Suffrage in Europe: Voting to Become Citizens*, edited by Blanca Rodriguez Ruiz, and Ruth Rubio-Marín, 305–20. Leiden: Brill.

Commaille, Jacques. 1993. *Les stratégies des femmes. Travail, famille et politique*. Paris: La Découverte.

Dahlerup, Drude, and Lenita Freidenvall. 2005. "Quotas as a 'Fast Track' to Equal Representation for Women: Why Scandinavia is No Longer the Model." *International Feminist Journal of Politics* 7 (1): 26–48.

Ducoulombier, Audrey. 2002. "Parity is About 'Race': French Republican Citizenship and the French Caribbean." *Modern & Contemporary France* 10 (1): 75–87.

Edel, Frédéric. 2013. "Les instruments juridiques de l'égal accès des femmes et des hommes aux emplois publics: depuis le droit à l'égalité jusqu'aux politiques d'égalité." *Revue française d'administration publique* 145: 109–35.

Fraisse, Geneviève. 2001. *La controverse des sexes*. Paris: PUF.

Gaspard, Françoise. 1996. "Parité: quelles stratégies politiques?" *Projets féministes* 4–5: 231–37.

Gaspard, Françoise, Claude Servan-Schreiber, and Anne Le Gall. 1992. *Au pouvoir citoyennes! Liberté, égalité, parité*. Paris: Seuil.

Guillaume, Cécile, Sophie Pochic, and Rachel Silvera. 2015. "Dans les syndicats: du volontarisme à la contrainte légale." *Travail, genre et sociétés* 2015/2 (34): 193–8.

Jacquemart, Alban, Fanny Le Mancq, and Sophie Pochic. 2016. "Femmes hautes fonctionnaires en France. L'avènement d'une égalité élitiste." *Travail, genre et sociétés* 2016/1 (35): 27–45.

Jenson, Jane. 1986. "Gender and Reproduction: Or, Babies and the State." *Studies in Political Economy*. 20: 9–46.

Jenson, Jane, and Mariette Sineau. 1994. "The Same or Different? An Unending Dilemma for French Women." In *Women and Politics Worldwide*, edited by B. J. Nelson and N. Chowdhury, 243–60. New Haven: Yale University Press.

Lemercier, Élise. 2015. "À l'université: les dessous d'un consensus apparent." *Travail, genre et sociétés* 2015/2 (34): 175–80.

Lépinard, Éléonore. 2007. *L'égalité introuvable. La parité, les féministes et la République*. Paris: Presses de Sciences Po.

———. 2013. "For Women Only? Gender Quotas and Intersectionality in France." *Politics & Gender* 9 (3): 276–98.

———. 2016. "From breaking the rule to making the rules: The adoption, entrenchment and diffusion of gender quotas in France." *Politics, Groups and Identities* 4 (2): 231–45.

Lépinard, Éléonore, and Amy G. Mazur. 2009. "Republican Universalism Faces the Feminist Challenge: The Continuing Struggle for Gender Equality." In *The French Fifth Republic at Fifty. Beyond Stereotypes*, edited by Sylvain Brouard, Andrew M. Appleton, and Amy G. Mazur, 247–66. New York: Palgrave.

Mazur, Amy G. 1995. *Gender Bias and the State: Symbolic Reform at Work in Fifth Republic France*. Pittsburgh: University of Pittsburgh Press.

Moniolle, Carole. 2014. "La représentativité des sexes dans les jurys de concours de la fonction publique." In *La loi et le genre*, edited by Stéphanie Hennette-Vauchez, Marc Pichard, and Diane Roman, 561–82. Paris: Editions du CNRS.

Murray, Rainbow. 2010. *Parties, Gender Quotas and Candidate Selection in France*. Basingstoke: Palgrave Macmillan.

Odoul-Asorey, Isabel. 2014. "Le Droit à l'assaut des effets de genre, dans le champ de la représentation collective des salaries." In *La loi et le genre*, edited by Stéphanie Hennette-Vauchez, Marc Pichard, and Diane Roman, 525–39. Paris: Editions du CNRS.

Opello, Katherine A.R. 2006. *Gender Quotas, Parity Reform and Political Parties in France*. Lanham, MD: Lexington Books.

Prat, Reine. 2015. "Art et culture ... et que rien ne change!" *Travail, genre et sociétés* 34: 187–91.

Rodriguez Ruiz, Blanca, and Ruth Rubio-Marín. 2008. "The Gender of Representation. On Democracy, Equality and Parity." *International Journal of Constitutional Law* 6 (2): 287–316.

2009. "Constitutional Justification of Parity Democracy." *Alabama Law Review* 60 (5): 1171–96.

Roman, Diane and Stéphanie Hennette-Vauchez. 2013. "Note, sous Conseil d'État, Assemblée, 7 mai 2013." *Revue française de droit administratif* 2013: 882.

Rosenblum, Darren. 2006. "Parity/Disparity. Electoral Gender Equality on the Tightrope of Liberal Constitutional Traditions." *University of California Davis Law Review* 39: 1119–89.

Scott, Joan W. 2005. *Parité! Sexual Equality and the Crisis of French Universalism*. Chicago: Chicago University Press.

Siim, Birte. 2000. *Gender and Citizenship. Politics and Agency in France, Britain and Denmark*. Cambridge: Cambridge University Press.

Southwell, Priscilla L. 2013. "Gender parity thwarted? The effect of electoral reform on Senate and European Parliamentary elections in France, 1999–2011." *French Politics* 11 (2): 169–81.

Southwell, Priscilla L. 2014. "How to become a députée – Lean to the Left: Party differences and gender parity in the 2012 National Assembly Elections." *French Politics* 12 (4): 348–56.

Verge, Tània, and Aurélia Troupel. 2011. "Unequals among equals: Party strategic discrimination and quota laws." *French Politics* 9 (3): 260–81.

Viennot, Eliane. 1994. "Parité: les féministes entre défis politiques et révolution culturelle." *Nouvelles Questions Féministes* 15 (4): 76–7.

Vogel-Polsky, Eliane. 1996. "Genre et droit, les enjeux de la parité." *Cahiers du GEDISST* 17: 9–28.

CHAPTER THREE

THE ROLE OF GENDER QUOTAS IN ESTABLISHING THE SLOVENE CITIZENSHIP MODEL

From Gender Blind to Gender Sensitive

Milica Antić Gaber and Irena Selišnik

3.1 THE SLOVENE CONTEXT: CONTINUITIES AND DISCONTINUITIES OF WOMEN'S MOVEMENT HISTORY FROM THE RIGHT TO VOTE TO THE DEMOCRATIC TRANSITION

The history of the women's and feminist movements in Slovenia starts in Carniola, as this was the most important Slovenian region in the Habsurg Empire, and in fact in Carniola the Slovene population enjoyed more rights than in any other region. The women's movement was considered quite moderate at that time. After the First World War, when Slovene territory became part of the Kingdom of Yugoslavia, the women's movement hoped that women's right to vote would be implemented. Yet in spite of all of the activities for legal changes that would improve the situation of women in the newly formed Yugoslavia after the First World War, changes did not take place (Selišnik 2011, 21–39; 2012).

During the Second World War women were a very active part of the anti-fascist front. In socialist Yugoslavia, the majority of the pioneers for women's rights had previous experiences of social organizing in the state-wide Anti-Fascist Women's Front (AFŽ), which was subsequently abolished in the 1950s. After the war, a state feminism was born, supported by important women in the Communist Party (Jeraj 2005), rather than a grassroots women's organization as formed in other countries. Under the leadership of vanguard women, the Communist party started to implement reforms to improve the position of women

in the field of social rights, in family relations, and concerning reproductive rights. Slovene legislative reforms, for example regarding rape
and abortion, were among the most advanced for the time, not only
in Yugoslavia but more broadly (Antić Gaber, Rožman, and Selišnik
2009, 136). In the late 1970s, a new wave of feminism appeared as a self-
conscious and self-defined movement of the intellectual elite in civil
society. Yugoslav feminists discussed issues of socialist theory and practice, and disputed many diverse theoretical and empirical aspects of
the institutionalized women's emancipation project (Zarkov 2000, 2).[1]

An important milestone for change was of course Slovene independence in 1991. At the beginning of the 1990s gender equality was
not considered an important political question in the political project of the new nation-state, as other questions took priority on the
national agenda – an argument that has been used in many cases to
delay the improvement of women's political and other rights. It is not
surprising, however, that systemic changes in the political institutions
in the first years of the transition period were mostly concerned with
the sovereignty of the Slovene nation, the structuring of political pluralism, and the rule of law. However, a few feminist scholars, feminist activists in centre-left and left-wing parties,[2] and small feminist
NGOs supported prioritizing policies for gender equality and emphasized anti-discrimination measures for women. Their efforts resulted
in the establishment of the Parliamentary Commission for Women's
Politics in 1991 and the Governmental Office for Women's Politics in
1992. The Governmental Office for Women's Politics was at first a consultative body connected directly to the Prime Minister's office which
supported progressive measures, reviewed and proposed changes to
new legislation, and prepared national documents concerning gender
equality. The Office was a quite visible institution that worked more or
less independently on gender issues and especially in the 1990s served

---

[1] See, for example, a large debate on the position of women and family in society in
"Družbeni položaj žene i razvoj porodice u socialističkom samoupravnom društvu"
(the social status of women and families in the development of socialist self-managing
society), Komunist, Ljubljana 1979.
[2] In Slovenia the main centrist political party was for almost a decade the LDS (Liberal
Democratic Party), the conservative, right-wing parties were the SLS (Slovene
People's Party), SKD (Christian Democratic Party), and SDS (Slovene Democratic
Party), while the left-wing political party, which supported social democratic principles, was the SD (Social Democrats). While these parties have often changed their
names and acronyms, their ideological orientations have stayed the same.

as a watchdog for women's rights (Antić Gaber and Gortnar 2004). One important role of the Office changed in 2001 when it was renamed the Office for Equal Opportunities. In 2012, the Office was abolished and its functions subsumed into the Ministry for Labour, Family, and Social Affairs. Only after the 2014 elections did the ministry emphasize the importance of equal opportunity, adding it to its name to become the Ministry of Labour, Family, Social Affairs, and Equal Opportunities.

3.2 TRANSFORMATION OF THE CITIZENSHIP MODEL AND GENDER REGIME

Women gained the legal (constitutional) right to vote in Slovenia and Yugoslavia after the Second World War in 1946, as the new communist/socialist regime had been established on the principle of class equality. The citizenship model was based on a simplified notion of equality: the basic principle was connected to a distributive model, according to which every citizen is entitled to the same basic social rights (this was widely known as an ideology of the "same stomachs"). According to this model each citizen should have a right to work and in this way to con-tribute to the welfare of the whole community, and as a reward have the same social and political rights (Jalušič 1999). We could therefore say that the focus was on one part of Marshall's famous triad of citizen-ship – social citizenship (Marshall 1950), while the other two – civil and political citizenship (and in particular, political pluralism) – were not treated as seriously.

When one looks at the citizenship model through the gender lens, at first glance the expectation of the work contribution from both women and men was equal in the sense that both were expected to take part in socialist production, and that they were therefore both expected to be educated to prepare them for entering the sphere of work. This model is not that of the male breadwinner developed in the West but rather that of "two adult working partners" in the family (Javornik 2012; Jogan 1990, 2001). Despite this equitable expectation, this model did not lead to the real equality of women and men in sharing work and care obligations in both private and public life. On the contrary, women were the ones predominantly responsible for the domestic sphere and therefore doubly burdened (Corrin 1992), while men were predom-inantly responsible for public sphere activities and also for political decision-making. Despite the general belief that women did have a high share in political bodies, a careful analysis shows that in the highest political bodies – in which the most important political decisions were made – women's share was, until the 1980s, quite low (Vrečko A. and Antić Gaber 2011). Returning to Marshall's triad, thus, the political part of the citizenship rights of women was poorly developed and reserved for the party elites (in which men were overrepresented). It is possible therefore to conclude that the citizenship model of that time was class sensitive but gender blind.

The dual-earner model, as it was developed in the communist/socialist era in many if not all countries in this political bloc, is well known (Pascall and Lewis 2004), but has some country-specific variations, as one element or another of the political or social system had more or less impact in different countries. The gender regime that can be identified in socialist Slovenia in the late second half of the twentieth century was in fact highly similar to that in Scandinavia (Ferge 1997a). Women's educational level was high; women had the right to abortion on demand; the procedure for divorce was not complicated and costly; the state provided kindergartens that were well developed and accessible; women were most often employed full time and the gender pay gap was small – thus the so-called social dimension of citizenship was quite developed. But on the other hand, gender relations in private life stayed more or less unchanged (in Slovenia as elsewhere in the region), maintaining traditional gender roles according to which it is the women's role to care about children and family, in addition to their full time employment (Antić Gaber 2015; Ferge 1997a; Jogan 1986). Women's employment was of secondary importance and women's wages were frequently treated as only an addition to their husband's wage (Jogan 1986, 27). Ultimately, even in the framework of "socialist democracy" women were "socially emancipated but politically marginalized" (Jalušič 1999).

This situation changed in the late 1980s (referred to among public intellectuals at the time as "the best times of our lives"), when the new political regime, political pluralism, and the rise of conservativism were foreseen, bringing concerns that some of the rights gained for women during the socialist past might be endangered. Krook, Lovenduski and Squires identify three broad models of political citizenship: the liberal, republican, and consociational/corporatist models that "generate distinct political logics that influence the prospects and outcomes of quota campaigns" (2009, 196). An analysis of the Slovene citizenship model that has been outlined since the beginning of 1990s shows that it cannot entirely fit into one of these types but has elements of all three models, as other researchers have similarly concluded in the study of welfare state regimes in Central and Eastern European countries (Auth 2010, 35; Klenner and Leiber 2010, 11). The Slovene model contains the notion of universal citizenship while recognizing the special position of two national minorities (Italian and Hungarian), but at the same time the rights of other social groups are overlooked; it is based on the revival of individual rights (understandably, as this area was neglected throughout the period of state socialism/communism), and much less, if any, concern is given to the rights of social groups – the so-called third generation of human rights. Nevertheless, in the field of social rights the political regime has incorporated negotiations with social partners (such as trade unions and employers' organizations). This stress on universal citizenship and individual rights in particular hindered the process of establishing gender quotas in political parties, particularly in the 1990s and, later, in the electoral laws implemented at the beginning of the twenty-first century.

On the other hand, it is obvious that in recent decades changes to the gender regime in some important fields have occurred that have brought visibility and recognition to the problem of so few women being in important positions in politics. As the statistical data show, in the last few decades women have outperformed men in educational attainment, they have made substantial breakthroughs in several professions (education, law, journalism, and medicine) that have been identified as those which facilitate women's entrance into politics (Cairney 2007; Kenworthy and Malami 1999; Podreka and Antić Gaber 2015), and they have widened the pool of women eligible to be recruited into politics (Matland and Montgomery 2003; Norris and Lovenduski 1993); but still women have remained underrepresented – not only at the highest levels but also in local politics. It is therefore clear that while some shifts in the gender regime in some institutions have been made, these still did not bring a decisive transformation of the gender regime in the field of politics – and it has become obvious that this transformation will not happen without the full engagement of several important social and political actors.

3.3 MOBILIZATION FOR PARTY QUOTAS AND THE FAILURE TO PASS LEGISLATED QUOTAS

In the 1990s, despite the fact that the share of women in parliamentary politics and in the executive branch was very low – it varied from 7.8 (1996) to 12.3 (1992) per cent in the National Assembly (NA), from 3 (1997) to 10 (1993) per cent in the government, and from 10.6 (1994) to 11.7 per cent (1998) at the local level – little support for special measures or gender quotas in politics was observed. In fact, almost everyone resisted the idea of quotas whether based on sex, age, or ideological orientation. Only a few feminist scholars, feminist activists in centre-left (LDS) and left-wing parties (ZLSD),[3] and small feminist NGOs supported them. As was mentioned before, at the end of the 1980s some circles of women (mostly from academia) active in civil society feared that some of the rights gained for women under socialism would be endangered if women were not present in politics in general and in particular in the highest political decision-making bodies. This fear led the above mentioned circles of women from centre-left and left-wing parties to submit proposals for special parliamentary and governmental bodies to monitor women's rights, and to draft new laws for the improvement of women's position in society and internal party quotas.

3.3.1 Women Forerunners for Gender Quotas in Centre and Left-Wing Parties

In fact, at the beginning of the 1990s the only women's circles to show real disappointment with the position of women in politics in general and specifically in their parties were those of the two centre and left-wing parties (LDS and ZLSD). As a result these parties initiated internal debate concerning the incorporation of gender quotas into their party statutes, in a similar process as that started elsewhere in Europe in the 1980s (Lilliefeldt 2012, 197). This was an enthusiastic period of enormous change for Slovene society and its economic and political system. Amongst other changes, this period saw the growth of new parties and the transformation of the old socio-political organizations from the socialist era (Fink-Hafner 1997). Among the latter, the LDS developed from the previous Socialist Youth Organization, which influenced its membership in many ways. Its members were mostly young, educated, and critical men and women imagining the future Slovenia as open to Europe, supporting libertarian and liberal values, and at least in a part sensitive to gender equality (Crnović and Antić Gaber 2011, 307). As mentioned above, in 1990 a few women, vocal

---

[3] From 1993 until 2005, the party was known as the United List of Social Democrats (Združena lista socialnih demokratov, ZLSD). Since 2005 the party's name has been the Social Democrats (SD).

on issues of gender equality, succeeded in putting a requirement for a 30 per cent gender quota into their party programme for the next election (Antić Gaber 1998, 213). Experience quickly showed that this quota was understood by the leaders and highest party bodies more as a distant goal rather than an immediate obligation, leading the same group to propose making the quota obligatory four years later. But they were only half successful, as their proposal was adopted only for the nomination process (up to the party council's nomination stage), which at election day resulted in less than 20 per cent female candidates on the electoral lists for the national election. As the situation and the understanding of quotas in the party evolved, the women's circle developed a more specific proposal for quotas in 1998, in which: "neither gender could have less than one-third of the candidates on the party list for the national election" (Antić and Lokar 2006, 150; Antić Gaber 1998, 214). This shift can be attributed in part to the awareness among a few highly influential party members (female and male) of the necessity to move from verbal support of the principle of gender equality to more binding concrete measures. But this progression was not without interruption, as in 2000 the party lowered the quota to 25 per cent with the provision to increase it by three percentage points in each subsequent election until reaching the final objective of 40 per cent of each gender on the lists for national election (Antić and Lokar 2006).

Women in the ZLSD were more successful in their inner party regulations for gender equality. The ZLSD's origins can be traced back to the League of Communists. In 1992, this left-orientated party merged with smaller, extra-parliamentary centre-left and left-wing parties. Before the general election in 1996, its Women's Forum persuaded the party to introduce a 40 per cent obligatory party gender quota for the National Assembly elections, which did result in 40 per cent female candidates on the electoral lists, but many female candidates were put in unfavourable electoral districts with small or no chance to be elected. Due to very poor party results in that election its highest party bodies decided to make quota provisions non-obligatory for the next election.

These developments in internal party policies were possible due to the fact that women in the two parties became organized and formed strong women's groups inside their parties. While the efforts made by the women's organizations in the parties demonstrated that persistent actions are needed to raise the proportion of women parliamentarians, they also evidenced the need for additional changes to achieve a decisive impact on the percentage of women in politics. In Slovenia, too, it became evident that conditions within the party (especially its organization) are important, as well as party ideology and candidate selection processes (Lilliefeldt 2012, 198).

In Slovenia, both parties that supported internal quotas came from the centre-left of the political spectrum, as has been the case in some other countries (Murray, Krook, and Opello 2009, 15). Women in the ZLSD established their own section – the Women's forum (Ženski forum) – as mentioned before, and their counterparts in the LDS formed their women's faction in 1992 (Minerva), which was then transformed in 1995 into the Women's Net (Ženska mreža) (Kozmik 1999). Both had among their members several strong and renowned female politicians that had either held important positions in the party in the past or had experience in politics in general that enabled them to confront their male colleagues in the leading party positions with demands to consider women in politics seriously and to take some action at the party level to include women's perspective in politics. In their claims, they pointed to the fact that the transition era had been generally orientated against the broadening of women's rights. It is also important to underline that these women's groups had contacts with their sister women's and parties' organizations in Europe, and especially Scandinavian countries,[4] which helped them with the know-how for women's empowerment programmes (for example, a "Women Can do it" toolkit), and they were also supported by feminist scholars who researched feminist movements in Europe and were informed about new mechanisms to increase gender presence and representation in politics and their effectiveness (Bahovec 2005).

However, to understand why soft party quotas did not become a general solution for Slovenia we have to look closely at the parties' behaviour. Political parties were a very new political actor in post-socialist Slovenia. Their main orientation was towards freedom of choice and

---

[4] In LDS there was already an active women's section, the Women's Network, which had at that time established some connections with women in the left-wing Scandinavian parties. The ZLSD was part of Socialist International Women (SIW), which had strongly recommended that all SIW member parties establish women's organizations and set gender targets or employ a quota. Women belonging to the ZLSD party therefore used the recommendations of the SIW, as well as the example of quotas introduced by the Nordic social democratic parties, to persuade their male colleagues that the quota for women employed in the one-party system would yield totally different results in a democratic multiparty system. So the 30 per cent target remained on the books (Lokar 2005, 119).

competition along ideological lines. Due to the Slovene proportional representation (PR) electoral system it is very difficult to get a majority in the parliament, so the parties are very careful when selecting candidates. Internal party structures were weak; many parties were centralized with men in the leading positions; candidates were often not chosen by primaries or other transparent process, and the parties' valued most candidates' electability and past political experience. It is well established that such criteria don't work in favour of women (Fink-Hafner, Krašovec, Deželan, and Topolinjak 2011, 202). Besides the aforementioned women's sections, women's groups in other political parties were weak. Parties did not care much or even at all about the representation of specific social groups.

These two cases explained above show how difficult it was to introduce binding quotas for elections in Slovenia as internal party regulations. The fact that there was no contagion effect (Matland and Studlar 1996), as these party regulations were not taken up by any other parties, weakened the possibilities for women in the two pioneering parties to develop further ideas of gender equity in politics. Yet at the same time, dissatisfaction with the low presence of women in politics among politically engaged women grew and the view that obligatory institutional or legal provisions were needed increased.

3.3.2 The Interconnection of the "Rigid Law Interpretation" and Partitocracy Contra Gender Quotas

Frustration with the situation led these women's circles in left-wing parties to draft several proposals to introduce positive gender equity measures in the 1994 Law on Political Parties, including a provision that would legally bind political parties to ensure equal representation of women and men on their electoral candidate lists, proposing a 40 per cent quota for candidates of each sex on the lists. The provision was advanced by the Parliamentary Commission for Women's Politics,[5] with the explanation that the majority of political parties in western democracies had introduced gender quotas as effective measures to narrow the gap in the political representation of women and

---

[5] The 17 February 1994 Parliamentary Commission for Women's Politics accepted the statement, calling the government to "examine the possibility" of including a 40 per cent gender quota.

men, and that Slovenia, as a democratic state, should follow suit.[6] In the parliamentary discussion, the government and the majority of MPs opposed the proposal with the argument that "political parties could not find enough women," while the Parliamentary Legislative and Legal Service opposed the proposal, alleging that it was in contradiction to the Constitution, but without further explanation. Thus the proposal was not adopted.[7] Instead of a firm gender quota, the Law on Political Parties only stipulated that "the party shall define in its statute a method of ensuring equal opportunities in nominating candidates for the elections" (for more detail, see Antić Gaber 1998 and Antić Gaber and Gortnar 2004).

Two years later, an analysis proposed by the Commission for Women's Politics and undertaken by the Office for Equal Opportunities showed very little progress in parties' policies on equal opportunities[8] – in fact, as the report showed, most only repeated general statements about equality in their documents.[9] These findings boosted new concern for how to improve the situation of women in politics. One proposal made was to bind parties to explicitly state their equal opportunity measures in their party statutes. The proposal also envisaged financial stimulus for the parties that succeeded in increasing the share of women in their parliamentary groups by 10 per cent.[10] The other proposal that arose was to formulate a new measure for gender quotas for the Law on Political Parties. Both of these proposals were put forward in 1996, the former by the female MP from LDS and the latter by a mixed male-female group of deputies from ZLSD.[11] The new quota proposal would establish an obligatory one-third quota for each gender for the party candidate lists in the next election for the National Assembly (1996), increasing by five percentage points for

---

[6] The proposal of 24 March 1994, first signed by Vika Potočnik (LDS), the Chair of the Commission.

[7] Minutes of the 24th session of the National Assembly (1992–6), 27 September 1994, Stenographic Record, available at: www.dz-rs.si/wps/portal/Home/deloDZ/seje/evidenca?mandat=I&type=sz&uid=D08B61F4166AADE3C1257832004838E4.

[8] Report on the work of the NA Commission for Women's Politics in the period 1993–6, Ljubljana, 1996; Minutes of the 22nd session of the Commission for Women's Politics, 1996.

[9] Report on the work of the NA Commission for Women's Politics in the period 1993–6, Ljubljana, 1996.

[10] Minutes of the 22nd session of the Commission for Women's Politics, 1996.

[11] First signed by Mateja Kožuh-Novak.

each following election until full equality was reached. Neither of the proposals obtained support in Parliament.

The negative opinion given by the government to both proposals was based on the argument that they "violate human rights and fundamental freedoms, namely equality before the law, freedoms of assembly and association, limit voting rights, and violate the existing law that regulates the electoral system."[12] It is interesting enough to mention that the government also stated that – in the case that a parliamentary party submits a list which does not include the required gender quota – they "are not convinced that it is necessary to demand that the list should be complemented ... and even less that such a list should be rejected." The negative opinion of the Parliamentary Legislative and Legal Service among other things stressed that the proposed material did not fit into the law but into the political parties' rules. The law experts who informed this opinion justified their position by stating that "in Slovenia there is a complete formal and de facto equality of women and men" guaranteed by the Constitution and that the law would then interfere with this "de facto equality." The argument was that the "law would cause more confusion and damage than improvement."[13] It should be stressed that at the time, the opinion of law experts was something that was highly esteemed and extremely rigidly followed by the state officials, lawmakers, and politicians.[14]

There was not much discussion in the NA about these proposals. Only a few proponents and opponents discussed the issue and then the opponents outvoted the proposal (Gortnar 2004). The opposing argumentation from MPs from right-wing parties accused one party (the ZLSD) of trying to impose these measures regulating candidate lists on the others by force. But ultimately the strongest argument against the introduction of gender quotas was that this kind of solution (positive discrimination measures) would contradict the Slovene Constitution, which guarantees equality before the law.[15]

---

[12] Opinion of the Government on the proposal of the draft law amending the Law on Political Parties, 15 February 1996.

[13] Minutes of the 38th session of the NA (1992–6), 12 March 1996, Stenographic Record. Available at: www.dz-rs.si/wps/portal/Home/deloDZ/seje/evidenca?mandat= I&type=sz&uid=A418C2BEBDBE5DD1C1257832004838F6.

[14] Interview of the author (Antić Gaber) with one of the senior politicians at the time.

[15] One must remember that this was a period of institution-building in the newly independent state, in which the Constitution was one of the strongest institutions, with its second clause stating that Slovenia is a legal and social state. Legality, law, and

As in the previous two attempts, these proposals came from the parties of the left (socialist) or centre-left, and therefore they encountered blanket ideological opposition. There was increased hope for the success of a new proposal put forward in 1998 by ten deputies from different parties, for the first time including a deputy from the conservative party (SLS). This coalition was at least partly the result of the proactive approach of the Office for Women's Politics, which had hosted several debates on women's quotas in politics with the aim of gathering women from different political parties and uniting them around this common goal.[16] In addition, the Parliamentary Commission for Equal Opportunity organized a discussion on the issue in which experts from the fields of law, social science, and political science, as well as representatives of women's sections in the parliamentary political parties debated possible ways of improving the situation.[17] On the basis of this discussion, the Commission decided to reopen the question of including a mandatory stipulation in the fifth paragraph of Clause 19 of the Law on Political Parties which would establish that the "party has to define in its statutes a method of ensuring equal opportunities in nominating candidates for the election," thus making parties include explicit measures in their party constitutions to ensure equal opportunities for women and men in their candidate lists. The government again opposed this proposal, with the argumentation that both passive and active voting rights were already established for women and men equally, and the state should not intervene in inner party regulations and the autonomous will of the parties. This opposition was largely supported by the majority of the MPs across a variety of parties.[18]

---

the Constitution were understood as some of the strongest pillars of the new state. At this time almost no law professional in Slovenia would support a special measure for gender equality (from a personal interview of author Antić Gaber with Lev Kreft, vice president of the NA 1992–6). Article 14 of the Constitution states: "In Slovenia everyone shall be guaranteed equal human rights and fundamental freedoms irrespective of national origin, race, sex, language, religion, political, or other conviction, material standing, birth, education, social status, or any other personal circumstance. All are equal before the law."

[16] Personal interview of author Antić Gaber with the director of the Office for Women's Politics at the time, Vera Kozmik.

[17] Transcription of the expert consultation of the NA Commission for Equal Opportunity Policies, 12 May 1998.

[18] Minutes of the 24th session of the Committee for Interior and Justice, Records from 6 September 1998. Available at: www.dz-rs.si/wps/portal/

The most common arguments used against the introduction of any strong measures to improve the position of women in politics – whether binding gender quotas or extra financial support for the parties to improve their percentage of elected female MPs – referred to the notions of pressure and force. MPs were almost unanimously against the interference of the state in inner party regulations. In the parliamentary debate, for example, one MP stated: "We support women, absolutely, but truly, those who come should come voluntarily, if they are able to, but not forced."[19] Similar argumentation can be found among MPs from almost all the parties, in spite of gender and ideological differences (with the exception of the ZLSD and some LDS MPs who supported gender equality and financial rewards for the accomplishment of set targets, but not binding quotas). Some female deputies who did not support the measure explained that they did not want to be put on the lists (or elected) just because they were women, but rather because they had proved themselves to be good and capable.

Apart from that, among many politicians in the 1990s in right-wing parties (and their supporters), gender quotas came to be associated with the socialist past (also due to the fact that the proposal for legally binding quotas came from the Communist successor party, the ZLSD), as they believed that the Communist Party had introduced some version of quotas for women for decision-making bodies in the 1970s in preparation for the first United Nations (UN) World Conference on Women in Mexico (1975). Those quotas never became legislation as they were only informal rules or targets in the process of the preparation of candidate lists and they did not apply to the highest political positions (Lokar 2005, 118). However, the effects of these informal quotas are apparent when taking a closer look at the share of women in the highest representative posts (delegates in the Slovene National Assembly), where the share of women reached its peak in 1978 with 28 per cent and then fell to 24 per cent in the last election under socialist rule, while in all other periods their share was much lower (Vrečko A. and Antić Gaber 2011, 89).

Home/deloDZ/seje/evidenca?mandat=II&type=magdt&uid=90B471C07685E2 1FC125669600272566. Portal DZ - Izbrani dokument

[19] Minutes of the 38th session of the NA, 28 February 1996, Stenographic Records. Available at: www.dz-rs.si/wps/portal/Home/deloDZ/seje/evidenca?mandat=I&type= sz&uid=A418C2BEBDBE5DD1C1257832004838F6.

Precisely because gender quotas had been associated with the social-ist past, with a "forced emancipation of women" and "forced political activities" which were neither genuine nor effective, a variety of politi-cal actors and the wider public[20] rejected gender quotas and considered them an undemocratic tool on a slippery slope towards the loss of "free choice."[21] In fact, many new political actors (particularly parties) didn't want to have any connection with the old regime (Antić Gaber and Gortnar 2004). Furthermore, if we take into account the data from a 1995 public-opinion survey showing that 46 per cent of the Slovene population thought that "men are better political leaders" (Toš 1999, 529), we can better understand why the political culture expressed no worries about the absence of women in politics. At the same time there was a strong belief that political pluralism per se would bring all the positive and necessary changes with respect to political representation.

To summarize, the positive arguments heard in the public discussion of gender quotas in the 1990s were: the slow progress of the share of women present in politics; the loss of potential for society that it represented; the lack of effort by parties to change this situation; a resulting undemocratic, unrepresentative, and less legitimate political system; the need for radical measures to improve a radical situation; the ability of the law to try to improve equality in the public sphere, which it cannot do in private life; and to bring more equity to society. The arguments against included: the free will of the parties, their difference from one another, and the impor-tance of that difference; the freedom of internal party rules from state and legal interference; the idea that such interference is undemocratic and a relic of the socialist past; the concern that quotas will harm women's ability to win positions by merit; and the unconstitutionality of quotas as breaking with formal equality (in Article 14 of the Slovene Constitution), and as creating inequality for men and women in their passive suffrage rights (in Article 43 which states, "The right to vote shall be universal and equal. Every citizen who has attained the age of eighteen years has the

[20] RTV Slovenia held a public poll on their web page from 28 June to 1 July 2005 with the question: "Would you support the women's quota for the next election?" Out of 835 respondents, a majority of 58 per cent (483) answered no, while 44 per cent (352) answered yes, for partial results, see www.rtvslo.si/slovenija/visje-zenske-kvote-le-postopno/39092; and for final results, see www.dijaski.net/gradivo/soc_ref_zenske_v_slovenski_politiki_01?r=1.

[21] Minutes of the 38th session of the NA, 19 April 1996, Stenographic Records. Available at: www.dz-rs.si/wps/portal/Home/deloDZ/seje/evidenca?mandat=1&type=sz&uid=A418C2BEBDBE5DD1C1257832004838F6.

right to vote and be elected"). This opposing discourse was based on a spe-cific understanding of equality between women and men – in its essence formal equality, equality de jure, as in their opinion women and men are already equal – that is stated in the Constitution. It also argued that using gender quotas could be understood as accepting that women and men are not equal (and therefore don't have equal chances). Those opposing gen-der quotas also problematized the result – of erasing difference between parties if all parties are obliged to have the same share of candidates of each sex on their candidate lists, which then would limit the voters' pos-sibility to cast their vote according to their preference.

These arguments show a clear focus on competition and difference, based on the liberal citizenship model according to which individual-ism and equality of opportunity are understood as the highest prior-ities, and not on equality of results. The opposition also resisted any intervention of the state in parties' candidate selection processes. It is in this respect telling that the same MPs accepted guaranteed political representation of two ethnic minorities (Italian and Hungarian) but refused to see gender as a category deserving of group representation (Krook, Lovenduski, and Squires 2009, 788). Their justification was based on the fact that these groups are recognized as autochthonous national communities, guaranteeing their special rights.

3.4 LEGISLATED QUOTA ADOPTION: FACTORS, ACTORS, AND PROCESSES

There are at least three important interconnected elements that influ-enced the later activities to introduce gender quotas in politics in Slovenia and their remarkable success: recognition of the need for a wider coalition based on initiatives from civil society; the importance of the state and its democratic image; and the pressure of external fac-tors in the process of integration into the European Union.

After almost a decade of trials and failures to introduce gender quotas, and the acknowledgement that the bi-polar division (socialist left and conservative right) of the Slovene political field was still strong, the small left-oriented circles recognized that they could not do much on their own; the introduction of gender quotas would not be possible without wider (political) support. It was also evident that they could not expect changes through the goodwill of (men in) political parties, as the share of women in political decision-making bodies at all levels in the previous decade had not changed at all – by the beginning of the 2000s, there were only

13 per cent women in the National Assembly and in local politics. More and more women in different parties became aware that only widening (political) support for quotas could compete against the strong opposition from powerful party leaderships in almost all of the parties and the strong aversion to interference in parties' and voters' "freedom of choice." It was also obvious that the support of male allies was very important, although not in the way it can be found in some party policies in Western democracies (according to Krook, Lovenduski, and Squires [2009]). Instead the aim was to shift the goal of improved women's presence in politics from a women-only question to a common social goal.

It took some time for women on both sides of the ideological spectrum to become aware that they would have to build a strong women's coalition across parties (which will be detailed further in the following section) and could not only count on the support of their male party colleagues, as they proved to be unanimously disinclined to support gender quotas in politics across all parties. Women in the different parties thus gradually recognized that through common activities they could all gain something.

3.4.1 Coalition for Establishing a Balanced Representation of Women and Men in Public Life

On 20 February 2001, a group of women (mostly from the left wing) met and decided to form a group of allies – a Coalition for Establishing a Balanced Representation of Women and Men in Public Life.[22] They invited women and men of goodwill from different NGOs, governmental organizations, political parties, women's groups within political parties, trade unions, and other organizations in civil society to join them. The coalition soon gathered important female party figures and women from right-wing parties, followed by some prominent male politicians from left-wing parties and eventually also from right-wing parties. The coalition thus joined individuals not only from the left but also from the right of the ideological spectrum and not only women but men as well, notably some high-ranking political leaders and opinion makers.

---

[22] "Already in October there were 145 of us and in 2006 we had 270 members from different places in Slovenia," states a leaflet published by Ženski lobi Slovenije. The leaflet was published under the name *Odločajmo skupaj* (Let's make a decision together) as a supplement of the *Delo* newspaper on 7 March 2009. See https://5050campaign.files.wordpress.com/2009/03/zenski-lobi-2009-2702-1.pdf.

Over the next two years it seemed that there was no major political party leader who would publicly not support the need for gender equality in politics, although not everyone would directly call for gender quotas. These individuals from almost the entire ideological spectrum in Slovene society, gathered in the Coalition, committed to acting individually and together as an organized pressure group to work towards balanced representation of women and men in public life. The coalition recognized that one of the ways to reach this goal was through changes to the laws that influence parties' electoral behaviour, and called for a guaranteed equal share of female and male candidates for local and national elections (Bahovec 2005, 128). The coalition continued to gain supporters in various sectors and organized a wide scope of activities including round tables, public confrontations, and appeals to public opinion, and gradually important political actors who strongly opposed gender quotas began to soften their resistance.[23]

3.4.1.1 The State as an Important Political Actor and Parliamentary Procedure on the Proposed Change to the Constitution

Two important lessons led this process forward: first, recognition that several attempts to establish obligatory measures for gender equality policies in political parties had not been successful and therefore the soft method or incremental track (Dahlerup and Freidenvall 2005) was not adequate for Slovenia, and second, acknowledgement that the state, through its laws, remained the most important political actor for introducing firm quotas and sanctioning political parties, to transcend the problem of disproportionate representation.

As explained above, in the previous attempts to introduce gender quotas into the Law on Political Parties, one of the strongest opposing arguments was that this would contradict the Slovene Constitution (that guarantees gender equality). To avoid this conflict, different case studies were carefully analyzed and brought to the attention of the wider public and even more so to legal experts. Especially powerful were the

---

[23] Some left-wing media also supported this idea by publishing articles, interviews, and analysis of elections from which it was obvious that something more abiding had to be put in the law. One of the largest daily newspapers, Delo, also published the Coalition's supplement before the European Parliament (EP) election with the demand for a "zip list" for the election, and with supportive statements from prominent public and political personae. Ženski lobi Slovenije Leaflet, Odločajmo skupaj, 7 March 2009. See http://5050campaign.files.wordpress.com/2009/03/zenski-lobi-2009-2702-1.pdf.

cases of France and Belgium, the two Western European countries that at that time had introduced quotas in their legislation. The French case was especially relevant to the Slovene environment. Rodríguez-Ruiz and Rubio-Marín have pointed out (2009, 1174) that in France the way to electoral gender quotas was opened in 1999 after the amendment of the French Constitution to allow affirmative action. To avoid what happened in France (i.e. the unconstitutionality of the first quota law), the Slovene political elite decided to amend the Constitution first and then introduce legislated quotas. In France the concept of parity was accepted, while Slovene political elites rejected parity or the zipper system as too "radical" as "political parties are not inclined to these kind of solutions."[24] Yet it seems that ideological factors and beliefs were similar in France and in Slovenia, as in both cases the male elite had made pragmatic calculations about an "escape clause" through the construction of candidate lists which would preserve male domination (Murray, Krook, and Opello 2009, 4).

The proposal to change the Constitution was put forward on 30 November 2001 by seventy-three (of ninety) MPs, moving to add a new paragraph which would state: "The law shall provide the measures for encouraging the equal opportunity of men and women in standing for election to state authorities and local community authorities," and therefore beginning parliamentary and wider public debate.

Proponents of the proposal signalled its importance for the breadth and quality of decision-making and hence the quality of social development. They referred to basic European legal acts and documents, soft laws and directives from 1975 on, such as the Amsterdam Treaty, which obliges European Union (EU) member states to fight against gender discrimination and states that the objectives and activities of its members have to be focused at the elimination of inequalities and the promotion of equality between men and women. They also built their argument on Article 26 of the International Convention on Civil and Political Rights, which distinguishes between differentiation and discrimination. They adopted the position that not "every differential treatment is understood as discrimination," thus "the measure, which is needed to correct discrimination, is in fact a legitimate example of

---

[24] 1095-III The Report on changing the law to Election for European Parliament. Available at: www.dz-rs.si/wps/portal/Home/deloDZ/zakonodaja/izbranZakonAkt?uid=C12565D400354E68C1256E38005AA0E2&db=kon_zak&mandat=III&tip=doc.

differentiation that in purpose is to correct in equalities." They also considered it to be the task of government to take positive measures designed to ensure the positive enjoyment of rights.[25]

Analysing these explanations for the introduction of special measures, it is evident that the proponents based their argument on the idea of basic equity, saying that women represent the majority of the population and a significant part of the workforce, while their share in political decision-making was extremely low and ranked Slovenia on the lowest level among European countries. It is obvious that this kind of argumentation is based on the strategy of inclusion founded in ideals of equality, equity, gender-neutral citizenship, and the representation of ideas (Squires 1999). They also refer to the effectiveness of these special measures in other European countries such as France and Belgium, where the proportion of women in decision-making increased soon after these measures had been introduced, and Scandinavia, where the presence of women in parliament is the highest in Europe due to similar policies.

After the proposal to change the Constitution had been put to the NA, there were two events that were important for a successful outcome: the establishment of a special group of external experts to the Constitutional Committee in the Parliament;[26] and a public discussion to which experts from different fields and civil society were invited, organized by the same committee in 2002.

The expert group's report on the proposal, which was confirmed and accepted by the Constitutional Committee,[27] leaned on two international documents. First, the UN Convention on the Elimination of All Forms of Discrimination against Women, particularly Article 4, which states, "State Parties shall adopt temporary special measures, which aim to accelerate de facto equality between women and men and that this will not be considered discrimination as defined by the present Convention." The report explained that this provision

---

[25] The proposal to initiate the procedure for amending the Constitution of the Republic of Slovenia, 7 April 2004. Available at: www.dz-rs.si/wps/portal/Home/deloDZ/zakonodaja/izbranZakonAkt?uid=C12565E2005ED694C1256B170052D BAE&db=kon_akt&mandat=III&tip=doc.

[26] This group included legal expert Alenka Šelih and sociologist Tanja Rener.

[27] The Report of Expert Group to Initiate Procedures to Change Article 44 of the Constitution of the Republic of Slovenia. Available at: www.dz-rs.si/wps/portal/Home/deloDZ/zakonodaja/izbranZakonAkt?uid=C12565E2005ED694C1256C5 B004AB981&db=kon_akt&mandat=III&tip=doc.

specifically enables the adoption of special measures to achieve de facto equality between men and women, and establishes that those measures taken are not to be considered discrimination. Second, the report used Recommendation 1413 (1999) of the Parliamentary Assembly of the Council of Europe on equal representation in political life. The Recommendation invites national delegations to propose to their parliaments the adoption of special measures to correct the underrepresentation of women in political life.

The report's conclusion was that the "necessity of amendments to the Constitution in relation to the provision of equal access to elected office in the managing of public affairs which is reflected in the disproportionate underrepresentation of half of the population in the elected representative bodies, representing a particular form of discrimination which is potentially a violation of one of the fundamental human rights."[28] It also stated that a constitutional amendment was necessary for the introduction of such measures aimed at eradicating this situation because regulation at the legislative level might contradict the then Constitution. The report added, the "adoption of measures for differential treatment of women and men does not constitute a discriminatory regulation, since it only seeks equal opportunities for both and it is therefore in essence a solution that implies the elimination of discrimination and constitutes a legitimate differentiation." The report was very strict in saying that the "adoption of the law shall be defined as obligatory and cannot be left to the party's discretion."

This report marked the beginning of a new phase, as never before had the parliamentary body given such open support to the proposal of a special measure to eliminate gender inequality in politics. This wind of change was evidenced also in the acceptance of the Law on Equal Opportunities for Women and Men in 2002, presented by the Office for Equal Opportunities as a "must" from the EU perspective. The law included a special article on political parties stating that they should adopt a plan for gender-balanced representation.[29] However, there were still a few political parties that expressed opposition to the amendment

---

[28] The Report of Expert Group to Initiate Procedures to Change Article 44 of the Constitution of the Republic of Slovenia. Available at: www.dz-rs.si/wps/portal/ Home/deloDZ/zakonodaja/izbranZakonAkt?uid=C12565E2005ED694C1256C5 B004AB981&db=kon_akt&mandat=III&tip=doc.

[29] Law on Equal Opportunities for Women and Men. Available at: www.pisrs.si/Pis .web/pregledPredpisa?id=ZAKO3418#.

proposal in 2002 and 2003.[30] The conservative and catholic-oriented Nova Slovenia (NSi) continued to argue that the "equality of men and women is guaranteed in the Constitution and in European Convention," and that the changes in the constitution would therefore make positive discrimination possible, for "which there is no need."[31]

The public discussion in the Parliament a month later brought up already known reservations among law experts and political parties and few new insights into the process. Yet we must add that the majority of the discussants (male and female, experts, politicians, NGO activists, etc.) supported the proposed change of the Constitution. Only a few legal experts still had significant reservations about this change. One of the legal experts in the discussion still maintained that in regard to equal opportunities in the candidacy process, Articles 14 and 43 of the Constitution already provided for the equality of women and men, and he warned that if the proposed changes to Article 43 were accepted it could lead to a conflict with Article 14.[32] Another law expert asked "are females really under-privileged?," therefore raising the question of the "legitimacy of such proposal and the real need for such norms." He argued that in many fields "the proportion of women is significant and comparable to the structure of the population." He therefore concluded that it seemed that the justification of need for such norms is "highly inadequate" and the "necessity of change highly

---

[30] The NSi (Predlogi stališč poslanske skupine Nove Slovenije do osnutkov ustavnih zakonov [NSi – Poslanska skupina Nove Slovenije] / The Position of Nova Slovenija on the Constitution Laws. Available at: www.dz-rs.si/wps/portal/Home/deloDZ/zakonodaja/izbranZakonAkt?uid=C12565E2005ED694C1256E01003CDF8D&db=kon_akt&mandat=III&tip=doc), for example, was against such changes, while ZLSD and DESUS supported it. To see the views of the other political parties, published as Stališče politične stranke, see (analysis): www.pisrs.si/Pis.web/pregledPredpisa?id=USTZ22.

[31] See 365-III Predlog za začetek postopka za spremembo Ustave Republike Slovenije z osnutkom ustavnega zakona / The Proposal to start the process to change the Constitution of RS with the draft of the Constitutional Law. Available at: www.dz-rs.si/wps/portal/Home/deloDZ/zakonodaja/izbranZakonAkt?uid=C12565E2005ED694C1256E01003CDF8D&db=kon_akt&mandat=III&tip=doc.

[32] Recording of hearings for the main parts "Promoting equal opportunities for candidacy of men and women," 28 October 2002 [30 – Constitutional Commission]. Available at: www.dz-rs.si/wps/portal/Home/deloDZ/zakonodaja/izbranZakonAkt?uid=C12565E2005ED694C1256C70002ACEB0&db=kon_akt&mandat=III&tip=doc.

relative." He criticized the proposal as an unnecessary intrusion of political messages into constitutional affairs.[33]

But by a year later (in 2004) there was no political party left that opposed the proposal to change the Constitution nor the proposal to incorporate gender quotas into the laws on election at all three levels (European, national, and local). The constitutional change was unanimously adopted in June 2004[34] shortly followed by the first European Parliament election in Slovenia. The new paragraph in Article 43 of the Constitution reads: "The law shall provide the measures for encouraging the equal opportunity of men and women in standing for election to state authorities and local community authorities."[35] This new article thus provided the important basis for legislative changes, among others for the introduction of gender quotas in the laws on elections.[36]

3.4.2 EU Enlargement Process and the Democratic Image of the New State

In the 1990s and in the beginning of the 2000s, Slovenia was (with a short interruption) governed by wide centre-liberal coalition and in the process of the integration to the EU. As 2004 approached (the year for Slovenia to join the EU), high-level-politicians became more concerned with showing Slovenia as a democratic and successful new post-socialist state oriented towards progressive changes and pro-European goals in their political institutions. It is obvious from the time frame in which gender quotas were adopted in Slovene legislation that the accession process to the EU definitely played an important although indirect role through the additional pressure on national politicians to do something about the low presence of women in politics.

---

[33] Recording of hearings for the main parts "Promoting equal opportunities for candidacy of men and women," 28 October 2002 [30 – Constitutional Commission]. Available at: http://www.dz-rs.si/wps/portal/Home/deloDZ/zakonodaja/izbran ZakonAkt?uid=C12565E2005ED694C1256C70002ACEB0&db=kon_akt& mandat=III&tip=doc.

[34] The required majority for a change to the Constitution is two-thirds of all members of the NA (ninety members). The changes were accepted, with seventy members for and none against the change.

[35] See Constitutional Act Amending Article 68 of The Constitution of the Republic of Slovenia (Uzs68). Available at: www.us-rs.si/en/about-the-court/legal-basis/ constitution/constitutional-acts-amending-the-constitution-of-t/.

[36] The first to be amended was the law on election to the EP in the same year, followed by the law on election to local communities (2005) and the law on election to the NA (2006).

The masculinization of Slovene politics was especially evident when Slovenia's parliamentary delegations started to occupy their seats in the EP. An all male delegation at the time when the average of women in the EP was 30 per cent and the most advanced countries (such as Sweden, Finland, and France) had 40 per cent women or more among their country MEPs was especially telling. It was obvious that the masculine image of the political field was not something that would bring Slovenia any advantage in the EU.[37]

This situation influenced the way the Slovene political elite (among them state officials and law experts) involved in the quota process started to "understand" gender quotas. The supportive argumentation of the expert group and the Constitutional Committee came just before the election for the EP, and even before the constitutional reform was completed, an amendment to the Law on the Elections to the European Parliament (March 2004) introduced a 40 per cent gender quota for candidate lists. When this reform was accepted the Legislative and Legal Service warned that the change could be unconstitutional since the constitutional reform was still in progress. Yet the MPs disregarded this argument and subordinated their voting to the European warning that an all-male Slovene delegation in the European Parliament would not look good.[38] This first quota immediately proved how legislated quotas on party lists are effective in the PR system as 42.8 per cent female MEPs (three out of seven) were elected in the first election to the European Parliament in Slovenia.

Therefore one of the important reasons why the Slovene establishment receded from opposing gender quotas was concern for the image of Slovene democracy in Europe. If in Slovenia nothing was done to improve the representation of women, the image of the Slovene success story could have been endangered. The fact that Slovenia is perceived (and perceives itself) as a "success story" was very important for the self-esteem of the whole country and all citizens, not only the

---

[37] See Slovenian Press Agency (2003) V Evropskem parlamentu za večje število poslank. Available at: www.sta.si/747323/v-evropskem-parlamentu-za-vecje-stevilo-poslank.

[38] Slovenian Press Agency (2004) DZ(34/2): Ženske kvote ustavno sporne? Available at: www.sta.si/810520/dz-34-2-zenske-kvote-ustavno-sporne. In: Predlogi zakonov – konec postopka – Izbran predlog zakona. 1095-III Zakon o spremembah in dopolnitvah zakona o volitvah poslancev iz Republike Slovenije v Evropski parlament / The Report on changing the law to Election for European Parliament. Available at: www.dz-rs.si/wps/portal/Home/deloDZ/zakonodaja/izbranZakonAkt?uid=C1256 5D400354E68C1256E38005AA0E2&db=kon_zak&mandat=III&tip=doc.

government (Antić Gaber and Gortnar 2004, 11). Slovene political elites therefore would rather try to meet expectations and follow the recommendations of international bodies in order to stay in line with other modern democracies in Europe, than risk to being labelled as backward. In other words, the emerging awareness that "something has to be done" does not appear totally as a result of a genuine commitment to gender equality, even though a long bottom-up tradition of actors for change had existed in civil society since the 1990s (Mencin Čeplak 2011). Until the end, formal institutional politics overlooked those initiatives.

Following the constitutional amendment two more electoral laws introduced gender quotas, but in different ways. The first added a gender quota to the Law on Local Elections in 2005, a year before the next local election. The law provided that lists of candidates for the election to municipal councils would have to be drawn up in such a way as to ensure that each gender accounted for at least 40 per cent of all candidates listed, and that the candidates in the first half of the lists had to alternate by sex (Clause 70a). The act provided for a transition period until 2014, when 40 per cent representation of each sex would become compulsory. The regulation deliberately started with a very low (20 per cent) gender quota in the 2006 election, followed by a 30 per cent quota for the election in 2010. In addition, during this transitional period, a partial waiver is permitted by which it would be sufficient for the candidates in the upper half of the list to be arranged in such a way that at least each third candidate is of the other sex (transitional provision). The second was the Law on the Election of the National Assembly, changed in 2006 to include a 35 per cent quota (starting with a 25 per cent quota for women candidates on the voting ballot for the following election). The law also stipulated that if the district electoral commission found that the list of candidates did not comply with this act, the commission should dismiss it (clause 56).[39] Due to the specificity of the Slovene electoral law for election to the NA, it is not possible to mandate the placement of candidates within the list.

Finally, even during this period of acceptance of quotas, the debates in the national Parliament showed a continued conception of quotas as unsuccessful and "undemocratic" mechanisms. However, the party

[39] National Assembly Elections Act. Available at: www.pisrs.si/Pis.web/pregled Predpisa?id=ZAKO185#.

gatekeepers were already aware of how to outsmart the constitutional amendment through the electoral system by placing women candidates in non-elective constituencies.[40]

3.5 CONCLUSION

To summarize, the adoption of legislative gender quotas in Slovenia is definitely the result of a complex political and social situation in the transition period, a period of transformation for many fields of society. To add to this complexity, there was an interplay of both top-down and bottom-up strategies. It was precisely this combination of internal and external pressures that led to the winning combination and final success for gender quotas. The bottom-up process started at the end of the 1980s and the beginning of the 1990s in feminist circles, among women active in feminist NGOs (although they were neither large nor strong), followed in the mid-1990s by women in women's groups within the political parties. It all started with a demand for more women in politics and for a Ministry for Women, as an institution that would defend women's rights, which was later established as Governmental Office for Women's Politics (Mencin Čeplak 2011, 116), followed by the demand for a fair share of women in the leading positions in the party bodies of the centre-left and left-wing parties (LDS, ZLSD), echoed a few years later by prominent female politicians in more traditional political parties (SLS).

In Slovenia now gender quotas are a politically acceptable measure; they have almost no significant opposition. Interestingly, if not surprisingly, the lack of opposition can be also noted in Catholic/conservative media,[41] and even in political parties which a decade ago had had strong reservations and concerns regarding gender quotas, especially in politics. One of the most prominent conservative leaders Alojz Peterle (conservative MEP), for example, has argued for "better representation of discriminated groups and for balanced participation of men and women in society."[42] The other most important opponent party in

---

[40] Minutes of the 18th session of the NA, 21 June 2006, Stenographic Records. Available at: www.dz-rs.si/wps/portal/Home/deloDZ/seje/evidenca?mandat=IV&ty pe=sz&uid=B8481E23C7AF6FE7C125719B0037A948.

[41] Are gender quotas in politics stimulation? Radio Ognjišče. Available at: http://radio .ognjisce.si/sl/124/slovenija/6117/.

[42] Women's Lobby of Slovenia. Let's make a decision together. *Delo*, 2009.

the 1990s – SDS – through their MEP has supported quotas not only in politics but also in the economy.[43] Suggestions for implementing gender quotas in the field of the economy (for example in management boards, as suggested by Commissioner Reding) have no serious opposition in Slovene politics, as we can see from the rare discussions that are initiated by the Ministry for Labour, Family, Social Affairs, and Equal Opportunities. New measures will be based on a proposed directive of the European Parliament and of the Council on improving the gender balance among non-executive directors of companies listed on stock exchanges and related measures. The basis for such directives to be implemented in Slovenia is found in the "Decree regulating the criteria for implementation of the principle of balanced representation of women and men," adopted by the Slovenian government in 2004 for the bodies of the government and nominated government representatives.[44] The most recent data from 2012 shows that through implementation of the Decree the representation of women in working bodies has been increasing, and that the average representation of women in government bodies and in public institutions has exceeded the gender balanced representation threshold of at least 40 per cent representation of both sexes. However, women remain unequally represented in appointments to public agencies and funds, as there were only 31 per cent women present in agencies, and 37 per cent in funds.[45] The government's proposed directive on improving the gender balance among non-executive directors of companies was supported by public opinion, the economic sector, the Parliamentary Committee for European Affairs, and the Committee for Labour, Family, Social Affairs, and Disability. Even though the proposal met with strong

[43] Women's Lobby of Slovenia. Let's make a decision together. *Delo*, 2009.

[44] The Decree lays down the procedure for ensuring the balanced representation of women and men in the composition of working bodies and in appointing and/ or nominating government representatives. Working bodies (such as committees and commissions) are set up by the Government and consist of a president, a deputy president and an appropriate number of members, nominated by the Government. Resolutions are passed by the majority vote of those present at a session. There are three permanent ones: the Committee for State Order and Public Affairs, the Committee for the Economy, and the Commission for Personnel and Administrative Affairs.

[45] Report of the High Commissioner on the role of the public service as an essential component of good governance in the promotion and protection of human rights – good practices in Slovenia. Available at: www.ohchr.org/Documents/Issues/Development/GoodGovernance/Corruption/SLOVENIA.pdf.

opposition from the UK, the Netherlands, and Estonia, the Slovene Ministry for Labour, Family, Social Affairs, and Equal Opportunities promised to prepare legislation by the end of 2015 which would be the basis for a higher presence of women in leadership of companies (Lorenčič 2015), although it has not as of yet been passed as it is still in the first draft phase.

As in France, in Slovenia it seems that gender quotas as a political mechanism have become unproblematic (Lépinard 2016). However, as the structural changes need time, how they influence changes to the existing gender regime remains to be seen in the near future. For the moment, we can say that the introduction of legislative gender quotas in politics and the promise to accept the same logic in the field of the economy, at least at the level of national politics, seems to be a departure from the individualistic liberal citizenship model that was spread in the beginning of the 1990s. The introduction of legal gender quotas in politics with strong sanctions is also a departure from equality of opportunity to equality of results, where the responsibility to achieve the set goal (i.e. 40 per cent women) rests neither with the individual candidates nor with the political parties, but with state institutions (i.e. state electoral committees). The conviction that in politics, as well as in the economy, women and men have to have a fair share is also a sign of change in the gender regime. This could in the near future lead to a more egalitarian one in which women and men will have the same chance of being involved in both spheres (public and private) and of engaging equally in politics.

References
Antić Gaber, Milica. 1998. *Ženske v parlamentu [Women in Parliament]*. Ljubljana: Znanstveno in publicistično središče.
——— 2015. "The structuring of Slovenian society and gender as the structured and the structuring structure." In *Gender structuring of contemporary Slovenia*, vol. 9, edited by Antić Gaber, Milica, 9–22. Frankfurt am Main: Peter Lang GmbH.
Antić Gaber, Milica, Sara Rožman, and Irena Selišnik. 2009. "Zagotavljanje enakih pravic moških in žensk." In *Brez spopada: kultur, spolov, generacij*, edited by Veronika Tašner, et al., 129–42. Ljubljana: Pedagoška fakulteta.
Antić Gaber, Milica, and Maruša Gortnar. 2004. "Gender quotas in Slovenia: A short analysis of failures and hopes." *European political science* 3 (3): 73–9. Available at: http://iknowpolitics.org/sites/default/files/gender_quotas_in_slovenia_090924.pdf.

Antić Gaber, Milica, and Sonja Lokar. 2006. "The Balkans: From total rejection to gradual acceptance of gender quotas." In *Women, quotas and politics*, edited by Drude Dahlerup, 138–67. London: Routledge.

Auth, Diana. 2010. "Welfare states and gender in Central and Eastern Europe: The current state of research and prospective research." In *Welfare states and gender inequality in Central and Eastern Europe: continuity and post-socialist transformation in the EU member states*, edited by Christina Klenner and Simone Leiber, 33–56. Brussels: ETUI.

Bahovec, Eva, ed. 2005. *Gender and governance: The civic and political participation and representation of women in Central and Eastern Europe: Slovenia*. Ljubljana: Faculty of Arts.

Cairney, Paul. 2007. "The professionalization of MPs. Refining the 'Politics-Facilitating' Explanation." *Parliamentary Affairs*. 6 (2): 212–33.

Corrin, Chris. 1992. *Superwomen and the Double Burden, Women's experience of change in Central and Eastern Europe and the former Soviet Union*. London: Scarlet Press.

Crnović, Deja, and Milica Antić Gaber. 2011. "Viktorija Potočnik, poslanka, županja in prva direktorica Urada za enake možnosti." In *Ženske na robovih politike [Women on the fringes of politics]*, edited by Milica Antić Gaber, 297–312. Ljubljana: Sophia.

Dahlerup, Drude, and Lenita Freidenvall. 2005. "Quotas as a 'fast track' to equal representation for women: Why Scandinavia is no longer the model." *International Feminist Journal of Politics* 7 (1): 26–48.

Ferge, Zsuzsa. 1997a. "The changed welfare paradigm: The individualization of the social." *Social Policy and Administration* 31 (1): 20–44.

Fink-Hafner, Danica. 1997. "Development of a party system." *In making a new nation: The formation of Slovenia*, edited by Danica Fink-Hafner and John R. Robbins, 135–55. Aldershot, England: Dartmouth.

Fink-Hafner, Danica, Alenka Krašovec, Tomaž Deželan, and Simona Topolinjak. 2011. "Politične stranke in ženske v času tranzicije [Political parties and women in times of transition]." In *Ženske na robovih politike [Women on the fringes of politics]*, edited by Milica Antić Gaber, 187–208. Ljubljana: Sophia.

Gortnar, Maruša. 2004. "Razprave o kvotah v slovenskem parlamentu: Obravnave Zakona o političnih strankah in Zakona o enakih možnostih žensk in moških." *Teorija in praksa* 41 (5–6).

Jalušič, Vlasta. 1999. "Women in post-socialist Slovenia: socially adapted, politically marginalized." In *Gender politics in the Western Balkans: Women and society in Yugoslavia and the Yugoslav successor states*, edited by Sabrina P. Ramet, 109–30. Pennsylvania: The Pennsylvania State University.

Javornik, Jana. 2012. "State socialism. Dismantling the male-breadwinner family model in Central and Eastern Europe?" Working paper 14/2012.

Department of Sociology, Umeå, Sweden. Available at: www.soc.umu
.se/digitalAssets/111/111121_14_2012_javornik.pdf

Jeraj, Mateja. 2005. *Slovenke na prehodu v socializem*. Ljubljana: Arhiv
Republike Slovenije.

Jogan, Maca. 1986. *Ženska, cerkev in družina*. Ljubljana: Delavska enotnost.

——— 1990. *Družbena konstrukcija hierarhije med spoloma*. Ljubljana: Fakulteta za
sociologijo, politične vede in novinarstvo.

——— 2001. *Seksizem v vsakdanjem življenju*. Ljubljana: Fakulteta za družbene vede.

Kenworthy, Len, and Melissa Malami. 1999. "Gender inequality in political
representation: A worldwide comparative analysis." *Social Forces* 78 (1):
253–69.

Klenner, Christina, and Simone Leiber, eds. 2010. *Welfare states and gender
inequality in Central and Eastern Europe: Continuity and post-socialist transformation in the EU member states*. Brussels: ETUI.

Kozmik, Vera. 1999. "Ženske v politki – kje smo in kaj lahko storimo." In
Ženske, politika, demokracija: za večjo prisotnost žensk v politiki, edited by
Milica G. Antić and Jasna Jeram. Ljubljana: Urad za žensko politiko.

Krook, Mona Lena, Joni Lovenduski, and Judith Squires. 2009. "Gender quotas and models of political citizenship." *British Journal of Political Science*
39 (35): 781–803. doi:10.1017/S0007123409990123.

Lépinard, Éléonore. 2016. "From breaking the rule to making the rules: the
adoption, entrenchment, and diffusion of gender quotas in France."
Politics, Groups, and Identities 4 (2): 231–45. First published online 12
Oct 2015.

Lilliefeldt, Emelie. 2012. "Party and gender in Western Europe revisited: A
fuzzy-set qualitative comparative analysis of gender-balanced parliamentary parties." *Party Politics* 18 (2): 193–214.

Lokar, Sonja. 2005. "A short history of quotas in Slovenia." In *The implementation of quotas: European experiences*, edited by Julie Ballingto and
Francesca Binda, 118–24. Stockholm: International IDEA.

Lorenčič, Aleksander. 2015. "Ženske v gospodarstvu po osamosvojitvi
Slovenije." In *Žensko delo: Delo žensk v zgodovinski prespektivi*, edited by
Mojca Šorn, Nina Vodopivec and Žarko Lazarević, 57–67. Ljubljana:
Inštitut za novejšo zgodovino.

Marshall, Thomas H. 1950. *Citizenship and social class*. New York: Cambridge
University Press.

Matland, Richard E., and Kathleen A. Montgomery, eds. 2003. *Women's access
to political power in post-communist Europe*. Oxford: Oxford University
Press.

Matland, Richard E., and Donley T. Studlar. 1996. "The contagion of women
candidates in single-member district and proportional representation electoral systems: Canada and Norway." *The Journal of Politics* 58 (3): 707–33.

Mencin Čeplak, Metka. 2011. "Politična emancipacija Zveze socijalistične mladine Slovenije in ženska politika." In Ženske na robovih politike, edited by Milica Antić Gaber, 105–24. Ljubljana: Sophia.

Murray, Rainbow, Mona Lena Krook, and Katherine A. R. Opello. 2009. Elite bias, not voter bias: Gender quotas and candidate performance in France. Paper presented at the first European Conference on Politics and Gender, Belfast, 21–3 January 2009.

Norris, Pippa, and Joni Lovenduski. 1993. Gender and party politics. London: Sage.

Pascall, Gillian, and Jane Lewis. 2004. "Emerging gender regimes and policies for gender equality in a wider Europe." Journal of Social Policy 33 (3): 373–94.

Podreka, Jasna, and Milica Antić Gaber. 2015. "Paid work, prestige professions and politics." In Gender structuring of contemporary Slovenia, edited by Milica G. Antić, 103–35. Frankfurt am Main: Peter Lang GmbH.

Rodríguez-Ruiz, Blanca, and Ruth Rubio-Marín. 2009. "Constitutional justification of parity democracy." Alabama Law Review 60 (5): 1171. Available at: www.law.ua.edu/pubs/lrarticles/Volume%2060/Issue%205/rodriguez .pdf.

Selišnik, Irena. 2011. "Volilna pravica kot sumljiva institucija ali kako se je spremenilo pojmovanje politike." In Ženske na robovih politike, edited by Milica Antić Gaber, 21–40. Ljubljana: Sophia.

Squires, Judith. 1999. Gender in political theory. Cambridge: Polity Press.

Toš, Niko, ed. 1999. Vrednote v prehodu II. Slovensko javno mnenje 1990–1998 [Values in transition II] Ljubljana: Fakulteta za družbene vede, IDV CJMMK.

Vrečko A., Lea, and Milica Antić Gaber. 2011. "Mesto in položaj žensk v slovenskih skupščinah in vladah." In Ženske na robovih politike, edited by Milica Antić Gaber, 83–103. Ljubljana: Sophia.

Zarkov, Dubravka. 2000. "Feminism and the disintegration of Yugoslavia: On the politics of gender and ethnicity." Paper. Available at: https://repub .eur.nl/pub/23361.

Sources

283-III Stališče PS ZLSD 08.01.2003 [PS ZLSD] / position PS ULSD 01/08/2003 [PS ULSD]

365-III Predlogi stališč poslanske skupine Nove Slovenije do osnutkov ustavnih zakonov, 27 November 2003 / Position PS NSi to the proposal to initiate the procedure for amending the Constitution of the Republic of Slovenia to the draft constitutional Law 27 November 2003 [NSi – New Slovenia group]

365-III Zapis javne predstavitve mnenj za vsebinsko zaokroženi sklop "Spodbujanje enakih možnosti kandidiranja moških in žensk" 28 October 2002 [30 – Ustavna komisija]

701-III Stališče poslanske skupine DeSus 23 December 2003 [PS DeSus] / position of DeSUS deputy group to proposals for the initiation of procedures for constitutional amendments, 24 November 2003 [DeSUS – group of the Democratic party of pensioners]

Constitutional Act Amending Article 68 of the Constitution of the Republic of Slovenia

Availableat:www.dijaski.net/gradivo/soc_ref_zenske_v_slovenski_politiki_01?r=1

Available at: www.rtvslo.si/slovenija/visje-zenske-kvote-le-postopno/39092

Law on Equal Opportunities for Women and Men

National Assembly Elections Act

Magnetogram strokovnega posveta Komisije DZ RS za politiko enakih možnosti 1998. Državni zbor, 12 May 1998 / Transcription of the expert consultation of Comission DZ RS for politics on equal opportunity 1998.

Poročilo o delu Komisije državnega zbora RS za žensko politiko za obdobje 1993–6. Ljubljana 1996 / Report on the work of the NA Commission for Women's Politics in the period 1993–6. Ljubljana, 1996.

Poročilo Strokovne skupine k predlogu za začetek postopka za spremembo 44. člena Ustave Republike Slovenije (Spodbujanje enakih možnosti kandidiranja moških in žensk na volitvah), 18 September 2002 [Dr Alenka Šelih, članica Strokovne skupine]/Report of the Expert group to the proposal to initiate the procedure for amending Article 44 of the Constitution of the Republic of Slovenia (Promoting equal opportunities for men and women stand elections), 18 September 2002 [Dr Alenka Šelih, State Expert Group]

The Proposal to Initiate the Procedure for Amending the Constitution of the Republic of Slovenia

Recording of hearings for the main parts "Promoting equal opportunities for men and women stand," 28 October 2002

Slovenian Press Agency (2003) V Evropskem parlamentu za večje število poslank. Available at: www.sta.si/747323/v-evropskem-parlamentu-za-vecje-stevilo-poslank

Slovenian Press Agency (2004) DZ(34/2): Ženske kvote ustavno sporne? Available at: www.sta.si/810520/dz-34-2-zenske-kvote-ustavno-sporne

Zapisniki sej državnega zbora / Stenographic Records of National Assembely

Zapisniki sej odbora za notranjo politico in pravosodje / Transcriptions of the Sessions of the Committee for Internal Affairs and Legislation

1095-III POROČILO k predlogu zakona o spremembah in dopolnitvah zakona o volitvah poslancev iz Republike Slovenije v Evropski parlament (ZVPEP-A) / Report on Changing the Law for Election to the European Parilament

365-III Zapis javne predstavitve mnenj za vsebinsko zaokroženi sklop "Spodbujanje enakih možnosti kandidiranja moških in žensk" 28.10.2002 / Recording of hearings for the main parts, "Promoting equal opportunities for men and women stand," 28 October 2002 [30 – Constitutional Commission]

365-III Predlog za začetek postopka za spremembo Ustave Republike Slovenije z osnutkom ustavnega zakona / The Proposal to start the process to change the Constitution of RS with the draft of the Constitutional Law. Ženski lobi Slovenije. Leaflet *Odločajmo skupaj*, supplement to the *Delo* newspaper, 3 July 2009. See: https://5050campaign.files.wordpress.com/2009/03/zenski-lobi-2009–2702–1.pdf

CHAPTER FOUR

GENDER QUOTAS IN SPAIN

Broad Coverage, Uneven Treatment

Tània Verge and Emanuela Lombardo

Spain is one of the few countries where all three types of quota – namely electoral, public administration and corporate boards – have been adopted, though they present large dissimilarities with regard to the parity criteria in use, the timing of application and the measures for incentivizing compliance or sanctioning non-compliance. The Spanish case is intriguing since all these quotas stem from a broader gender equality plan that went well beyond increasing women's presence in positions of power. However, immediate and strong measures were only applied to the electoral sphere, which explains why the gender outcomes produced by quotas for corporate boards and public administration bodies lag behind those of electoral gender quotas.

Legislative quotas were introduced in Spain after party quotas had been in use for almost three decades by left-wing political parties, thereby complementing the gradual progress of women's numerical representation in political institutions (Verge 2013). Party positions on gender quotas in Spain align with general developments across Western European countries, with the Left being the main advocate and the Right the main detractor, in opposition to the country's past in regard to women's suffrage. In the context of the Second Republic (1931–6) – abruptly interrupted by a military coup and the subsequent civil war and authoritarian regime – left-wing parties were initially reluctant to grant women the right to vote, whereas right-wing parties were generally supportive. This tendency reflected parties' strategic calculations based on expectations about women's (allegedly more conservative) political behaviour. Eventually, in 1931 women's enfranchisement received the support of socialist, conservative and regionalist parties (Aguado 2012; Rubio-Marín 2014).

In examining gender quota adoption in Spain, at the macro level of analysis we take into account the gender regime of the country, the political and discursive contexts opening or closing opportunities to gender advocates and the influence of the European Union. At the meso level, we review the institutional configurations that interact in processes of quota adoption (Krook 2009). We identify the enabling and constraining factors for each type of quota. The analysis of the underlying formal and informal rules and practices also helps us identify resistances to changes promoted by gender initiatives (Lombardo and Mergaert 2013). The chapter is organized as follows. The first section introduces the theoretical framework that informs the chapter. The next three sections explore the institutional configurations and the enabling actors for each type of quota. The last section concludes by signalling the differential sequences followed by quota reforms and discussing the implications of quota adoption for the Spanish gender regime.

4.1   MACRO- AND MESO-LEVEL FACTORS IN QUOTA ADOPTION: GENDER REGIMES, INTERNATIONAL INFLUENCES AND INSTITUTIONAL CONFIGURATIONS

Several macro-level factors underpin quota adoption processes. First, the concept of "gender regimes" allows us to understand gender inequality as a system of 'inter-related gendered social relations and gendered institutions' (Walby 2009, 301) that produces specific norms and representations of gender relations and equality, distinct constitutional and legal regulations of gender equality that feed favourable or opposing discourses on gender quotas (see Lépinard and Rubio in this volume). Second, women's political representation and more specifically gender quota adoption are also dependent on the political and discursive context that creates opportunities for feminist advocates to make gender equality claims resonate within existing political institutions (Ferree 2012). Critical actors (Celis 2006), such as women within political parties, have a crucial role in devising strategies to put these claims on the agenda (Caul Kittilson 2006; Freidenvall 2013), as well as femocrats and women's policy agencies (Lovenduski 2005). Third, international pressure and diffusion processes are also relevant. In the case of the

European Union (EU), although legally binding directives on gender quotas have not yet been adopted, the endorsement of positive actions in the Treaties and the development of soft policy measures on women's political representation have contributed to promoting social learning on this issue in the member states (Beveridge 2012). Since the 1990s, the EU has promoted gender equality action programmes, produced reports, created a database on women in decision-making, and convened conferences on parity democracy, such as Athens 1992, Rome 1996 or Paris 1999 (Lombardo 2008). Furthermore, Europeanization entails not only the downloading of EU legislation at the member state level and the discursive usage of the EU by national actors to legitimize gender change, but also the horizontal cross-loading or policy transfer through learning from other member states (Howell 2004).

On the other hand, at the meso level of analysis, as Krook (2009) argues, quota reforms may require multiple attempts to be adopted or effectively implemented since they interact with previous institutions, namely with systemic, normative and practical institutions. We borrow this feminist institutionalist approach originally applied to the study of electoral gender quotas and expand it to corporate and public administration quotas. At the political level, the *systemic institutions* shaping political recruitment involve the formal features of political competition. In the adoption phase, in multi-party systems, parties are more likely to respond to the innovations of their competitors, such as the adoption of party quotas (Matland and Studlar 1996). Proportional representation (PR) systems facilitate women's representation and produce a better fit with quotas, as they are inspired by norms of group participation, whereas majoritarian systems prioritize individuals over groups (Krook 2009, 790). The larger district magnitude within PR systems also facilitates the inclusion of members of traditionally underrepresented groups in party lists (Norris 2004). At the economic level, companies do not compete in the same markets and there is a low visibility of their governing boards, thus making "contagion effects" potentially weaker. Yet, while the internal functioning of firms is largely left to self-regulation instruments (e.g. Corporate Governance Codes), most states impose certain legal requisites such as transparency in the election of board members and the inclusion of (some) independent members. Thus, the higher the state intervention in the regulation of boards in a given country, the stronger the fit we might expect for gender quotas (Engelstad and Teigen 2012). As regards public administration, national legislation on the composition of governing bodies and advisory boards as well as on recruitment of employees may promote or hinder women's presence in such bodies, depending on the existence or not of positive actions and the extent of transparency of data and appointment proceedings.

Regarding *normative institutions*, ideational factors affect both adoption and implementation. These include existing conceptions of equality (opportunities vs. outcomes; formal vs. substantive) and representation (politics of ideas vs. politics of presence) that operate in the three types of quotas. Gender quotas are more easily adopted when legislation (constitution, electoral law etc.), party ideology – typically left-wing ideology – or mass beliefs support equality of results and place value on representatives' characteristics (Caul Kittilson 2006; Dahlerup 2007). In the economic sphere, conceptions of state involvement in the economy may affect whether corporate boards are the targets of quotas or not. Where acceptance of state intervention in the economy is widespread, gender quotas will be considered more legitimate than where beliefs about private business freedom prevail (Tienari et al 2009; Casey, Skibnes, and Pringle 2011; Fagan, González, and Gómez 2012). As to conceptions of equality, equality of opportunities and meritocracy (expertise, efficiency, best-fit) prevail over notions of equality of results and the politics of presence. The latter are usually viewed with reluctance by business actors, who may be more convinced by productivity arguments for the economic benefits of women's inclusion and higher diversity on corporate boards: e.g. risk management in investments, broader reach of consumption habits etc. (Teigen 2012, 135).

Last, political parties determine the formal and informal practices or *practical institutions* that ultimately rule over candidate selection and implementation of gender equality norms. Individual traits (resources and motivations) influence the "supply" of candidates from different groups, but candidate selection practices are also shaped by the "demands" of party selectorates (Lovenduski and Norris 1993). Gender norms in the definition of the "ideal candidate" (Chapman 1993; Kenny 2013) are coupled with a strong gender imbalance in party selectorates (Niven 1998). Men in top positions tend to be supportive of in-group candidates (men) at the expense of out-group candidates (women). Recruitment processes in corporate boards are also shaped by gender norms and stereotypes in the assessment of curriculums and by the pervasiveness of male-dominated business networks and opaque and endogamic practices that exclude women and show a preference for homogeneous boards (Castaño et al. 2009; Mateos, Gimeno, and Escot

TABLE 4.1   Institutional configurations of gender quotas (by type)

	Electoral quotas	Corporate board quotas	Public administration quotas
Systemic institutions	• Electoral rules • Party competition	• Self-regulation code prevails although most states also impose some regulation of corporate boards • Companies do not compete in the same markets and low visibility of corporate boards • Structure of firm ownership • Degree of state intervention in the economy	• National legislation on composition of public administration governing bodies and advisory boards • National legislation on recruitment of employees • Transparency
Normative institutions	• Conceptions of equality: equality of results and politics of presence defended by a variety of actors	• Conceptions of equality: equality of opportunity and meritocracy (expertise) prevail • Conceptions of state involvement in the economy	• Ideational norms of the party in government in regard to equality
Practical institutions	• In-group effects and local male monopolies • Informal networks • The ideal (male) candidate	• Opacity and endogamy • Informal networks • The ideal (male) candidate	• Political will of the party in government • Public visibility

Source: Author's own elaboration.

2010). Since the election of the members of corporate boards reflects in a proportional manner the participation in capital, the size of the board is crucial: the greater the number of posts for stakeholders, the more room for diversity there is (see Bianco, Ciavarella, and Signoretti

2011), which correlates with firm size (Hillman, Shropshire, and Cannella 2007; Miller and Triana 2009). For their part, public administration quotas are subject to the political will of the party in government, which is related to its conception of equality. Government's public visibility of data on parity in public administrations, which is currently low, favours accountability and public debate.

4.2 ELECTORAL QUOTAS: STRONG REGULATION AND SUCCESSFUL IMPLEMENTATION

The institutional configuration for the adoption of electoral gender quotas provided by the 2007 Equality Law presented a highly harmonizing sequence (Verge 2013).[1] Left-wing political parties had already adopted voluntary quotas in the late 1980s, for both electoral lists and party executive boards, due to lobbying by party feminist activists with strong ties with the women's movement and with party feminists from other European parties where quotas had already been passed,[2] as well as with the Socialist International Women (Threlfall 2005; Valiente 2005; Verge 2006). Emulation is easier among countries that share historical ties (Krook 2006, 316), which may favour a cross-loading of quota measures. In the Spanish case, among the Social Democratic party family, the French *Parti Socialiste* was the most influential. In 1979 it invited sister parties to the launch of its quota campaign for the European elections, thereby inspiring Spanish feminists to fight for a similar measure in their own parties.

In 1982, the PSC, the Spanish Socialist Workers' Party (PSOE) in the region of Catalonia, introduced a quota of 12 per cent of party and elected offices for women – proportional to the party's female membership at the time. Party feminists, supported by the party leader, convinced (male) conference delegates (there was only one woman) to have a floor vote on the quota proposal, arguing it did not stand a good chance of passing but it would constitute a great opportunity to raise the party's awareness about equal representation. Surprisingly, the quota was backed by 52 per cent of the delegates. In 1987, male mid-level

---

[1] Organic Law 3/2007 (March 22), on the Effective Equality between Women and Men.
[2] At the time, the women's movement was split into two positions: whereas some feminists "rejected mainstream politics altogether," other feminists joined political parties with a view to engendering state action and made women's political representation a top priority (Valiente 2005, 180–2).

cadres, headed by the very same secretary of the organization, opposed raising the quota to 25 per cent; therefore, it was only updated to reflect the increase in women's membership (15 per cent). In the mid-1980s the women's caucuses in both the Communist Party (PCE) and the PSOE lobbied their respective party leaders and launched intra-party campaigns to implement a quota. The women's policy agency (the Woman's Institute, created in 1983) also pushed demands for women's political representation into the PSOE debate on quotas thanks to the double membership of some influential women in relevant positions of the Women's Institute, in the party executive, and/or in the feminist movement (Valiente 2005, 181). Both the PSOE and the PCE introduced a 25 per cent quota for women in 1987 and 1988, respectively. The United Left (IU) party introduced the same quota in 1989.

The PR electoral system, coupled with closed party lists, allowed these self-reformed parties to significantly increase the proportion of female candidates as well as the levels of elected women MPs. This shift occurred especially once the quotas had been effectively enforced by the party leadership in winnable positions on party lists – easier for the PSOE than for the IU due to its larger seat share in all political institutions. In 1997, the concerted efforts of party feminists and women's organizations[3] along with international calls for gender equality in representation – such as the Athens European Summit of Women in Power (1992), the UN Beijing Platform of Action (1995), the EU IV Plan of Action on Equality of Opportunities (1996–2000) and Socialist International Women – pushed left-wing parties to assume a gender-neutral quota which stipulates that each sex shall be represented at a proportion no lower than 40 per cent or more than 60 per cent.[4] Indeed, there was a conceptual shift from "quotas" to "parity democracy" that encompassed a "new social contract" requiring new foundational terms regarding work-life balance, waged labour and, most crucially, power' (Verge 2006). Parity was also presented by the PSOE as a mechanism of internal democratization,

---

[3] These included the Federation of Progressive Women and the Spanish Committee of the European Women's Lobby, close to the PSOE; and the Dolores Ibárruri Foundation and the Forum of Feminist Politics, close to the IU).

[4] PSOE party feminists were highly influential in these events. In 1995, socialist women within the Woman's Institute and the Ministry for Social Affairs engaged in the preparation of the United Nations Women's Conference (1995) that set the Beijing Platform for Action. It was also during the Spanish Presidency of the EU in 1995 that the IV Plan of Action on Equality of Opportunities came into effect (Jenson and Valiente 2003; Verge 2012).

which contributed to making this reform largely accepted within the party (Threlfall 2005, 154). The other Spanish parties adopted similar measures in the following decade and even the Popular Party (*Partido Popular*, PP), which strongly rejects quotas, adopted a vague goal for gender balance (Verge 2006). Feminists in leftist political parties and the women's policy agency, the Woman's Institute, continued to struggle for parity between the 1990s and the 2000s (Valiente 2005). This struggle paved the way for normative-legal reform.

Between 1996 and 2003, inspired by other European countries such as France and Italy, and with the support of the Spanish Committee of the European Women's Lobby, the IU and the PSOE submitted several bills on women's political representation, whose constitutionality had previously been discussed with law experts[5] to avoid the fate quota laws had experienced in France and Italy – i.e. annulment by their respective constitutional courts (Jenson and Valiente 2003, 91). These bills were blocked by the PP's majority in the lower house (Verge 2008). The frame analysis of official policy documents finds a highly polarized discourse between the PSOE, clearly in favour of electoral gender quotas, and the PP, vocally against them. The PP's objection to quotas was built on individual responsibility and the denial of structural obstacles to women's equal political representation. The party used three main arguments: (i) quotas are humiliating for women; (ii) only the most qualified individuals should be promoted; and (iii) curtailing parties' freedom of election through such legally-binding measures would be unconstitutional. Indeed, during PP's tenure in central office (1996–2004), the Woman's Institute did not support electoral gender quotas but rather softer measures and preferred the term "balanced participation" – employed in the 1995 EU Resolution on decision-making[6] – to avoid using the increasingly widespread concept of "parity democracy" (Valiente 2005, 190). Conversely, the PSOE defended electoral gender quotas as a means to improve the quality and fairness of the political system. Indeed, women's political equality was conceived of as an indispensable condition for democracy and for social progress. Gender experts and women's organizations put forward broad alternative framings that

---

[5] See El País, "El PSOE renuncia a promover la paridad legal antes de junio" (27 December 1998); El País "No al 'feminismo de salón' y sí al de hechos" (7 March 1999); and Peces-Barba (1999).

[6] See Council Resolution of 27 March 1995 on the balanced participation of men and women in decision-making, OJ C168 4 July 1995.

problematized male domination of power positions, gender-biased polit-ical practices and the persistence of patriarchal structures hindering women's political representation, but these framings remained rather marginal in political debates (Verge 2006; Lombardo 2008).

The blockade against quotas at the central level led PSOE party feminists to seek normative reform at the regional level. In 2002, the PSOE-led regional governments in Castile-La Mancha and Balearic Islands adopted legislative quotas for the election of their respec-tive regional parliaments.[7] The PP also boycotted these normative reforms by appealing to the Constitutional Court, which suspended their implementation in practice. No judgment was ever issued on these statutory regional quotas due to the bottleneck of cases in the Constitutional Court, and after winning the 2004 general elections, the PSOE withdrew their pending appeals. In 2005, two more regions passed statutory electoral quotas, Andalusia and the Basque Country.[8] All these regional laws introduced "zipping," in which men and women candidates must alternate throughout the list, except the Basque law, which established a minimum proportion of 50 per cent for women candidates (Alonso and Verge 2015, 251).

Progress towards gender equality in politics was made again in 2007 when the PSOE government passed Organic Law 3/2007 for the Effective Equality of Women and Men, widely known as the Equality Law, with the sole abstention of the PP motivated by the introduction of quotas, despite the fact that the law deliberately used the expression "principle of balanced presence" that the PP had promoted in substitu-tion for parity in the mid-1990s (Valiente 2005, 190). This terminol-ogy shift sought to "sweeten the pill" of quotas to attract PP's positive vote. The principle of balanced presence reforms the electoral law by mandating party lists, for all elections, to include a minimum of 40 per cent and a maximum of 60 per cent of either sex, a proportion to be also respected in each stretch of five candidates. Non-compliance entails the withdrawal of party lists.

Despite the lack of extensive debate on the constitutionality of quo-tas by the early 2000s and the existence of a certain degree of comfort

---

[7] Castille-La Mancha: Law 11/2002 (17 June), which modified the region's electoral law; Balearic Islands: Law 6/2002 (21 June), which modified the regions' electoral law.

[8] Andalusia: Law 5/2005 (8 April), which modified the region's electoral law; Basque Country: Law 4/2005 (18 February), which modified the region's electoral law.

with the notion of gender quotas, as shown by the fact that 75 per cent of Spaniards considered this measure beneficial for decreasing women's discrimination in public office (Centro de Investigaciones Sociológicas 2007), the PP lodged a new appeal before the Constitutional Court which was genuinely tricky. To discredit quotas, the PP presented an all-women list in a small village (Garachico, Canary Islands) where the party expected to obtain no seats at all. The provincial electoral court invalidated this list since it exceeded the maximum of 60 per cent for either sex established by the Equality Law. PP's appeal to the Constitutional Court sustained that quotas offended several sections of the Constitution, such as article 6 (political parties), article 22 (the right of association), article 23 (electoral participation) and articles 9 and 14 (equality). Plaintiffs also referred to the French and Italian experiences and defended arguments similar to those invoked in the late 1990s, namely: the distinction of candidates by sex harms the unity of the electoral body; the restriction on candidates' eligibility violates the right to active and passive suffrage; parties' freedom is hampered; and candidates' merits are neglected (Verge 2012, 402).

The plenary of the Constitutional Court[9] rejected this appeal in 2008.[10] The Court argued that the Constitution explicitly grants not only formal equality via article 14 but also substantive equality via article 9.2 (see Rodríguez Ruiz and Rubio-Marín 2008). Indeed, article 9.2 urges public authorities "to remove the obstacles hindering citizen's political participation and to promote and facilitate the conditions so that its exercise is effective." Thus, the Spanish constitutional

---

[9] Four of the judges are nominated by the lower house, four by the upper house, two by the central government, and two by the General Council of the Judiciary – the governing body of the Spanish Judiciary. Members serve a nine-year term. The plenary was composed of ten male judges and two female judges, one of which held the presidency of the Court at the time. Women's presence in the Constitutional Court was at around 16–18 per cent in the period 2001–15 (Instituto de la Mujer 2016).

[10] Sentence 12/2008 (29 January 2008), available at:www.tribunalconstitucional.es/es/jurisprudencia/Paginas/Sentencia.aspx?cod=15691, accessed 30 November 2015. Thereafter, the case that had motivated the appeal, the Garachico all-women electoral ticket, was also brought by the women candidates before the European Court of Human Rights (ECHR), which declared it inadmissible due to its being manifestly ill-founded (*Méndez Pérez and others v. Spain*, No. 35473/08, 4 October 2011). The ECHR argued that an all-men list would also have been withdrawn by the Spanish electoral authorities, thus discrimination did not operate, and reminded that the goal of the Spanish Equality Law was simply to guarantee a balanced participation of women and men in elective functions.

model endorses substantive equality. The main arguments used by the Constitutional Court to uphold the statutory quota were that quotas did not breach the principle of equality but rather granted equality, and that the Equality Law did not discriminate against men because minimum and maximum proportions applied equally to women and men. The Court stated that quotas were reasonable and proportionate with the aim pursued – that of making political equality effective for both sexes. Quotas were not considered to violate the unity of the electoral body because candidates, the Court sustained, irrespective of their sex, represent the whole electorate during their mandate. This position stands in clear opposition to the ruling of the French Constitutional Council in 1982 (see Lépinard 2013).

Further arguments in support of substantive equality and democracy put forward by the Court included reference to the obstacles traditionally faced by women in politics as a legitimate reason to require parties to ensure the balanced participation of both sexes. Likewise, since women constitute half the population, the increase of their presence in public office was argued to support the democratic principle requiring the "closest identity between elected representatives and the represented" in regards to, as the Court reminded, the "only criterion (sex) that universally divides society into two groups with equilibrated proportions." A final reason given by the Court was that the law could limit parties' freedom, as already happens with other legal ineligibility causes, because it is citizens, not parties, who enjoy the rights of passive and active suffrage (Verge 2012, 403–4). Similar arguments were made in response to the constitutional appeals lodged by the PP against the Basque and Andalusian regional quota reforms. Yet, whereas the Andalusian zipping quota was fully supported by the Court given that the nationwide Equality Law allows for more generous measures for women's representation than those it endorses, in the case of the Basque law, the Court argued that the "minimum" of 50 per cent of positions in party lists for women was constitutional as long as men obtained at least 40 per cent of the positions in the lists, as the nationwide Equality Law guarantees to both sexes (Alonso and Verge 2015, 252).[11]

---

[11] Basque quotas, Sentence 13/2009 (19 January 2009), available at: www.tribunal-constitucional.es/es/jurisprudencia/Paginas/Sentencia.aspx?cod=15877, accessed 30 November 2015. Andalusian quotas, Sentence 40/2011 (31 March 2011), available at: www.tribunalconstitucional.es/es/jurisprudencia/Paginas/Sentencia.aspx-?cod=16307, accessed 30 November 2015.

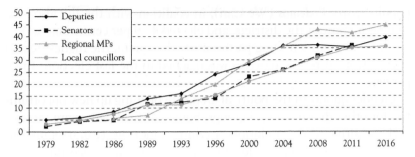

Figure 4.1 Percentage of women in public office, 1979–2016
Source: Author's own elaboration based on Verge (2012) and Instituto de la Mujer (2016).

The implementation of both party and legislative quotas has been eased by the fact that elections at all levels of government are held under proportional representation (D'Hondt system) using closed and blocked party lists, with the exception of the upper house. As shown in Figure 4.1, gender balance has been reached in most regional parliaments since 2007. Significant increases have also been observed in local councils and the upper house, whereas stagnation prevailed in the lower house in the two first post-legislative quota elections – mainly due to the pervasive gender-biased allocation of safe positions and the sharp electoral losses suffered by the PSOE. Overall, the legislative electoral quota consolidated the incremental progress initiated through party quotas in the late 1980s (Verge 2013).

Further advances in the field of electoral gender quotas are limited to left-wing political parties. The IU has used a zipping system, whereby women and men alternate throughout the party lists, since 2008, and the PSOE also adopted this quota reform in 2013. In both parties the aim of this reform is to prevent district-level parties from allocating the lion's share of top positions on party lists to men. For example, in the 2011 elections, PSOE female candidates occupied position number one in 38 per cent of party lists and in the 2015 elections the percentage increased to 50 per cent. While PSOE's seat share shrank in both elections, the negative electoral swing only diminished the party women's representation in 2011 (from 42.3 per cent in 2008 to 38.2 per cent in 2011). In 2016, the party elected 42.3 per cent women. The PSOE has also pledged to reform the quota law to make zipping compulsory for all parties upon returning to central government. The new left-wing populist party *Podemos* (We Can), in coalition with the IU, also used zipping in most of the districts, and elected 47.9 per cent women. As a result of all main left-wing parties using this quota, the highest record ever of women representatives was reached in the last elections (39.4 per cent).

Gender quotas in the political arena are opening up new opportunities for other disadvantaged groups. Some political parties are increasingly sensitive to the inclusion of ethnic minorities (e.g. migrants) in their candidate tickets for local elections, especially since the extension of active suffrage in 2011 to non-EU citizens. For example, the PSOE aims at including candidates from ethnic and sexual minorities as well as citizens with functional diversity. This inclusion is currently a goal, but with weaker status than the mandatory gender proportions (PSOE 2013). Indeed, the percentage of migrant candidates is still very low, and they tend to be located in unwinnable positions (Pérez-Nievas et al. 2014, 51).

4.3 CORPORATE BOARDS QUOTAS: SOFT REGULATION AND POOR IMPLEMENTATION

Women's presence in the economic sphere has experienced a slow and rather marginal growth. Positive action affecting corporate boards was initially introduced in 2006, under the initiative of the recently elected PSOE government, when the Stock Market's National Committee, a supervisory governmental agency, elaborated a new industry self-regulation instrument: the Unified Good Governance Code (Comisión Nacional del Mercado de Valores 2006), known as the Conthe Code, for voluntary application by companies. One of the most contested parts of the Code concerned "gender diversity" in corporate boards, although it followed the "comply or explain principle," whereby listed companies had to either comply with the Code in practice or justify any failure to do so, in accordance with article 116 of the Securities Market Law (de Anca 2008, 97). Recommendation 15 of the Code required companies with few or no women on their board to explain the underlying reasons and undertake actions to correct the situation, paying special attention to the obstacles faced by women in recruitment processes. This can be defined as a "soft quota" or "soft law" since improvement in women's representation was left to the willingness of individual firms and their managers (Fagan, González, and Gómez 2012; Lombardo 2012).

The Conthe Code and the Equality Law were drafted in parallel. Although no specific stimulus was acknowledged, the Norwegian legislation adopted in 2003 may have partially inspired the inclusion of women's representation in the Code by the Socialist government (González and Martínez 2012, 172), which intended to impose further measures through the 2007 Equality Law. The Equality law gave public limited companies and listed firms eight years (until 2015) to achieve gender equality in their boards – that is, the principle of gender balance, with representation of both sexes between a minimum of 40 per cent and a maximum of 60 per cent (article 75). Despite being a statutory measure, its strength was watered down by the absence of sanctions for non-compliant companies. Instead, companies who have distinguished themselves in the promotion of equality will receive a governmental "equality award" and be prioritized in government contracts. Lower preference in the granting of government contracts is a weak sanction compared to nullifying boards' decisions, as in Belgium, or suspension of board members' compensation or dissolution of the board, as in Norway or France (see Piscopo and Clark Muntean 2013).

This measure triggered public debate before and after its adoption. The PSOE defended the measure on grounds of justice and equality. For example, The Minister of Labour considered that the measure addressed "democratic justice, cultural transformation and societal advancement, and economic fair play," highlighting gendered recruitment processes and stereotypes as the locus of discrimination against women (González and Martínez 2012, 175). Gender biases and sexist attitudes privilege the "traditional male stereotype" and undervalue and discriminate against women and male candidates who do not fit the "stereotype of the aggressive, competitive, masculine and improvising Latin male" (González and Martínez 2012, 179). Besides the government (including femocrats of the national Women's Institute) and left-wing parties, support for quotas for corporate boards only came from feminist organizations not related to the economic field, such as the Women Lawyers' Association *Themis* and the Federation of Progressive Women, who have traditionally been strong advocates of gender quotas and engaged in public debates on parity. Their arguments emphasized the legality of quotas and their relevance for removing the barriers women face in selection processes (Comisión Mixta de los Derechos de la Mujer y de la Igualdad de Oportunidades 2006). In a sector such as private business, where notions of equality of opportunities, individual merit and non-regulation of companies' freedom of activity predominate, equality advocates did not constitute a critical mass and cross-sectional alliances to promote gender quotas were not established. Employers' organizations strongly opposed the quota provision as well, mainly on the grounds of the infringement of meritocracy. Similarly, around half of senior executive women disagreed with quotas because they believed their merits would be called into question (González and Martínez 2012, 174). Businesswomen's organizations were also against the introduction of quotas (Comisión Mixta de los Derechos de la Mujer y de la Igualdad de Oportunidades 2006), which attributed women's underrepresentation in corporate boards to supply factors – gender differences in qualifications, availability and willingness to integrate into corporate boards – rather than to demand factors – obstacles of the recruitment process and demands of the selectors (Consejo Económico y Social de España 2006, 17). For its part, the PP saw quotas as a restriction of companies' freedom.

In the face of strong resistance to the 2007 statutory provisions, from 2008 onwards the PSOE government chose a less confrontational approach with the business community by putting emphasis on even softer measures. In 2010, the Objective 15 programme was launched, including sensitizing measures for companies to work in partnership with the government towards the implementation of Recommendation 15 of the Conthe Code (González and Martínez 2012). The PP government elected in 2011 continued this soft approach. The use of such voluntary measures has only led to small and slow increases in the proportion of women on corporate boards, as Figure 4.2 shows for the Spanish case. While Del Brío and Del Brío (2009) attribute the increase in the share of women in Spanish boards from 3.6 per cent to 6.0 per cent in the period 2004–7 to the Conthe Code, this was partly due to the Code's recommendation to increase the presence of independent members in boards (Gonzáléz and Martínez 2012, 189). Indeed, Spanish firms have been depicted as traditionally recruiting board members based on surnames, friendship and family links through opaque procedures (usually by a president of the board or a significant shareholder), showing high rates of localism, endogamy and concentration of ownership, a low degree of rotation, and a high concentration of board posts in the hands of a few people (Mateos, Gimeno, and Escot 2010). With an

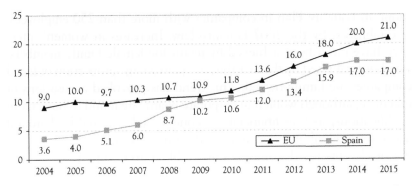

Figure 4.2 Women in publicly listed companies covered by the 2007 Law, 2004–15 (by per cent)
Source: Author's own elaboration based on IESE (2014: 11), Mateos, Escot, and Gimeno (2006), and EIGE (2017).

average annual increase of 0.8 percentage points between 2004 and 2007 and an average annual increase of 1.7 percentage points thereafter, progress was too slow to meet the target of 40 per cent women in boards by 2015. In 2015, women only represented 17 per cent of corporate members of the publicly listed companies, below the EU-28 average of 21 per cent.

Although publicly owned firms or companies with state participation showed better performance, with 29.5 per cent women in their corporate boards, positive action has also had a moderate impact, with a 16.6 per cent increase in the 2008–14 period (Informa 2014, 10). This slow rate of increase comes as no surprise since the Equality Law defined no sanction, thus the feminization of public companies' boards fundamentally depends on the political will of the government with the capacity to make the appointments.

On average, companies sold on the stock exchange (IBEX-35) have 2.23 women board members, where the average board has 13.4 members. Notwithstanding this, soft quotas have managed to reduce the number of firms with no women whatsoever on their boards. In 2004, over 60 per cent of these companies had all-male boards, whereas in 2010 this had shrunk to 29 per cent. Only four companies count over 25 per cent women on their boards (IESE 2014). However, when all publicly listed companies are considered (those covered by the 40–60 legal provision included in article 75), 58 per cent of them still have no women on their boards (Informa 2014, 11). Diversity policies have been advanced in larger Spanish firms due to the obligation to adopt an Equality Plan in companies with more than 250 employees, as established by the 2007 Equality Law. Increases in women's presence have often been achieved by recruiting female family members, which is facilitated by the fact that in Spain a large proportion of listed companies are family-owned. This trend has provoked accusations of tokenism, although women in corporate boards are found to have more qualifications, such as financial or economic educational background and international experience, than their male board peers. Moreover, the newly appointed women are more likely to occupy less powerful positions, mostly non-executive (independent) directors (González and Martínez 2012, 192–6). These practices show how gender biases underpin companies' interpretation and implementation of equality rules.

Despite the fact that Spanish corporate boards fell short of meeting a gender-balanced composition by 2015, the PP government further shifted away from any hard regulatory approach. The new Law for Capital Firms passed in 2014 (Law 31/2014), rather than referring to the gender quotas of the Equality Law, included instead a recommendation for adopting measures to include more women in boards with the aim of achieving a more balanced representation. Firms' selection committees will have to set their own targets for the underrepresented sex in corporate boards, elaborate instructions on how to achieve this target and report on its progress, following the principle of "comply or explain." Similarly, the new Unified Good Governance Code drafted by the National Committee of Value Market included in its Recommendation 14 a target of 30 per cent – a very weak interpretation of parity – and extended the deadline for implementation to 2020 (Comisión Nacional del Mercado de Valores 2015). Likewise, the current nationwide Equal Opportunities Plan (2013–16) emphasizes sensitizing measures under a "framework of collaboration with companies" volunteering to meet a gender-balanced representation in their boards. Women's underrepresentation is framed in this plan as due to women's lack of training, rather than due to organizational (male) resistance to women's presence in boards. Accordingly, the measures proposed include women's training in management skills, the establishment of networks of managerial positions, mentoring programmes and exchange of best practices. This shift is in line with the business community's liberal and individual-centred ideology. The Objective

15 programme is still in place, but no activities have been organized since 2011. Thus, in the field of corporate quotas Spain has moved away from European and international developments and recommendations.

Whereas the PP government has shifted policy measures on gender diversity in boards from "demand" arguments (the gender biases corporate selectorates might sustain) back to "supply" arguments (the characteristics of aspirant women), female economic actors have moved in the opposite direction. On the one hand, businesswomen have organized to challenge the charge of a low supply of suitable female candidates. In 2014, the Federation of Executive Women (*Federación de Mujeres Directivas, Ejecutivas, Profesionales y Empresarias*, FEDEPE) signed an agreement with the Spanish Employers Association to promote qualified women into decision-making positions in companies and employers' organizations (see also de Anca, 2008, 103). In 2006, the same organization had already launched an open directory of women candidates for corporate boards (Díaz García and González Moreno 2012, 59). Similar initiatives are taking place elsewhere in Spain. In Catalonia, the Women, Business and Economy Observatory (*Observatori Dona, Economia i Empresa*, ODEE), located within the Chamber of Commerce of Barcelona, has also set up an open directory of businesswomen and designed a map of the relevant competencies required to lead a business, thus challenging the traditional opacity in the definition of merit and the gender bias in how it is often defined. On the other hand, businesswomen's organizations do now defend stronger quotas for corporate boards, as debates on the most recent regional equality laws have shown.[12] This trend also reflects a change in levels of opposition to quotas among executive women: while half of them rejected the measure in 2007, the percentage had decreased to 37 per cent in 2014 (Adecco 2014).

---

[12] In the hearings before the Committee on Citizens' Rights of the Catalan Parliament drafting the Catalan Equality Law businesswomen urged for the introduction of measures to make parity effective in corporate boards. Available at: www.parlament.cat/web/canal-parlament/sequencia/videos/index .html?p_cp1=7420346&p_cp3=7420651.

4.4   PUBLIC ADMINISTRATION QUOTAS: SUBJECT TO POLITICAL WILL

The 2007 Equality Law also required the government to "pay attention" to the principle of gender-balanced presence (the 40/60 gender-neutral proportion) in public administration bodies, advisory boards and committees for the selection of personnel and assessment of merits (articles 52–4). This reform of systemic institutions was exclusively promoted by the PSOE government and the femocrats who drafted the law. The women's movement did not target public administration boards and advisory committees in their demands for parity, and international pressure has also been low in this field. Like in the case of corporate quotas, despite the statutory character, a soft approach prevailed with no obligation and no sanction defined in case of non-compliance. This approach means that at the level of practical institutions, compliance of these bodies and boards within the public administration fundamentally rests upon the willingness of the government in power, which is inevitably affected by the latter's normative position on quotas.

With regards to ministries, at the central level, parity cabinets with an equal number of female and male ministers were appointed from 2004 until 2011 under PSOE's rule. Subsequent PP governments (2011–15), with 31 per cent female ministers, included a much higher percentage of women than former conservative governments although they did not apply parity. Within ministries, level 1 (highest level of non-political positions, namely sub-secretaries and general secretaries) and level 2 (second level of non-political positions, namely director generals and general technical secretaries) administrators still fall short of parity, as shown in Table 4.2. Again, these positions were more feminized under PSOE governments than under PP governments. Monitoring mechanisms for parity in appointments at the central politico-administrative level could only be found in the Spanish Ministry of Economy and Finances (renamed in 2011 as Ministry of Finance and Public Administrations) and the Ministry of Employment, both of which publish an annual report on the implementation of gender equality policies in their respective administration.

At the regional level, eleven governments reached parity in 2008, seven more than in 2003. The conservative hegemony in the 2011 regional elections reduced the number of parity cabinets to seven. In 2015, the highest record has been achieved, with thirteen parity cabinets. On average, the presence of women ministers has increased from

TABLE 4.2   Women's presence in national and regional government
(by per cent)

	Central government			Regional governments
	Ministers	Level 1 administrators	Level 2 administrators	Ministers (average)
2003	25	11	13	20
2004	50	26	27	29
2008	53	63	38	40
2011	31	57	35	34
2015	31	35	31	44

Source: Author's own elaboration based on EIGE (2017) and Instituto de la Mujer (2016).

20 per cent in 2003 to 44 per cent in 2015, as shown in Table 4.2. Parity cabinets are more common where the PSOE leads the regional cabinet (Alonso and Verge 2015, 252) or where regional equality laws mandate parity to be fulfilled at the executive level: Basque Country, Andalusia, Extremadura and Galicia (Diz Otero and Lois González 2015).

The general retrenchment in Spanish gender equality institutions and policies brought by the PP government has also been detrimental to progress in women's representation within public administration and other politically appointed bodies. For example, as shown in Table 4.3, in the Central Bank women councillors increased from 25 per cent in 2008 to 44 per cent in 2011 but have since then decreased to 25–30 per cent. In the Economic and Social Council women represented 15 per cent of members in 2007, 23 per cent in 2010 and 18 per cent in 2015. Women's representation in other bodies, like the Central Electoral Board and the Council of State show stagnation, with the exception of the Court of Audit and the General Council of the Judiciary where parity has been recently reached.

The limited data available on advisory boards also point at significant progress right after the adoption of the Equality Law but stagnation later on. The Ministry of Economy 2011 report about the implementation of the Equality Law concerning advisory boards claimed that the 40–60 principle was generally applied for the Ministry's representatives in advisory boards, with 42 per cent women and 58 per cent men. Yet, regarding board members with responsibilities as presidents or deputy-presidents, women's presence shrank to 36 per cent (Ministerio de

TABLE 4.3   Women's presence in national public bodies (by per cent)

	2008	2009	2010	2011	2012	2013	2015
Central Bank	25.0	25.0	25.0	44.4	25.0	28.6	30.0
Council of State	6.9	19.2	17.9	19.2	23.3	21.9	23.3
General Council of the Judiciary	28.6	33.3	35.0	33.3	35.0	33.3	42.9
Court of Audit	6.7	7.1	7.1	7.1	6.7	41.7	41.7
Central Electoral Board	7.1	7.7	15.4	8.3	14.3	14.3	14.3
Economic and Social Council	13.6	17.2	23.0	21.3	25.0	19.7	23.0

Source: Instituto de la Mujer (2016).

Economía y Hacienda 2011). Ministerial reports on the Equality Law also claim that committees for the selection of public administration personnel have taken into account the balanced presence of women and men (Ministerio de Trabajo 2011; Ministerio de Economía y Hacienda 2011). This criterion has also affected universities, according to the 14/2011 Law on Science, Technology and Innovation adopted under the socialist government, which mandates that gender balance must be met in the composition of selection committees for permanent professorship positions. The Women and Science Unit, located within the Ministry of Economy and Competition, promoted this reform, inspired by EU activities of the Helsinki Group on Gender in Research and Innovation.

4.5   CONCLUSION

In Spain the broad coverage of the three types of quotas has been matched by an uneven treatment, with a harder approach for electoral than for public administration and corporate board quotas. How to account for this difference? While in the case of quotas in politics we mainly find enabling factors and actors that led to a harmonizing sequence of quota adoption and good fit across systemic, normative and practical institutions, in the case of corporate boards the interaction of quotas with the institutional configuration in the economic field has produced conflict and yielded as a result a highly disjointed sequence. Public administration quotas show a mixed picture, with embryonic progress at the level of systemic institutions and dependence on political will for the remaining institutions. The sequential pattern of quota reforms in politics began with (left-wing) parties pursuing self-reform in their recruitment practices by adopting party quotas, to proceed subsequently with normative-legal reform(s). Critical actors within parties, namely party feminists, with support from the Woman's Institute, placed the issue on the agenda, and developed strategic action and discourse based on the politics of presence and equality of results. For this purpose, they used other European countries, parties, EU policies and conferences on women and decision-making and transnational women's organizations as a source of inspiration and legitimacy. Electoral rules of proportional representation with closed and blocked lists facilitated the implementation of party quotas. When the statutory quota was adopted through the 3/2007 law, the main resistance to gender quotas came from the Popular Party, whose unconstitutionality appeal based on formal individual equality of opportunities and the autonomy of political parties was rejected by the Constitutional Court on the grounds that substantive equality is a constitutionally entrenched principle. The tough sanction imposed on non-compliant parties (i.e. the withdrawal of party lists) secured an effective implementation of the gender-balanced principle.

In sharp contrast, in the case of quotas in corporate boards, the prevalence of self-regulation at the systemic level coupled with normative institutions that prioritize liberal notions of freedom of economic activity as well as individual merit and ability have produced a heavily disjointed sequence. Whereas Europeanization acted as a cross-loading factor that enabled political actors to learn from other European countries' and parties' experiences, in the case of quotas in corporate boards the Norwegian example was inspirational but not determining. Nor did the European Commission's proposed Directive have any particular impact. The quota introduced by the PSOE government in 2007 as part of a broader equality plan failed to address informal gender-biased practices of recruitment. The law included an eight-year implementation period and no sanctions for noncompliance, only incentives, in response to the widespread opposition from the business community. In this case, the right-wing PP won the discursive battle by framing lack of diversity in boards as a matter of low supply of qualified women. In sum, most of the enabling factors that exercised pressure in favour of gender quotas in politics were weak or missing in the economic sector and, thus, could not counteract the strong oppositional factors and actors.

It is yet to be seen if the recent mobilization of businesswomen in favour of hard quotas will succeed in challenging the male-biased discourse of "merit" that puts women's talents to ongoing test, while men's capacities are left unquestioned.

Public administration quotas have not reached the public debate yet. At the level of systemic institutions, the 40–60 principle included in the Equality Law was not coupled with sanctions. Unlike in the case of electoral quotas, no critical actors pushed for them and they received little attention from femocrats drafting the Equality Law, who devoted their energies to the battle of electoral quotas. Pressure from the EU was also low, with the small exception of women in the science sector. As a result of the absence of debate and pressure, the measures adopted were weaker for this type of quota than for electoral ones, making their implementation subject to political will. Normative and practical institutions vary depending on the ideology of the party in government, which shapes the political will of the key selectors within the cabinet. Thus, gender outcomes depend on the political will of the party leading the government and gains are not necessarily maintained. The lack of transparency in the implementation of these quotas, shown by the scarce available data (only two Ministries reporting on parity), further contributes to the low level of public attention to public administration quotas.

Concerning the extent to which gender quotas have affected the gender regime in Spain (see Lépinard and Rubio in this volume), we conclude the following: (i) Spain presents a legal narrative framed more by equality than by difference, shaped by the double membership of women in feminist groups and left political parties, and international – especially EU – influence since the transition to democracy. In opposition to difference feminism, which suggests the need for feminists to distance themselves from state institutions – which are seen as intrinsically patriarchal – egalitarian feminism encourages feminists to enter state institutions. Spanish egalitarian feminism is evidenced in the creation of the Woman's Institute in 1983 at the central level and from the mid-eighties at the regional level (Lombardo 2004; Valiente 2005; Bustelo 2014). This equality narrative has promoted state regulation of gender equality, including quotas. (ii) The Spanish Constitution endorses both formal and substantive equality (Rodríguez Ruiz and Rubio-Marín 2008), supporting the adoption of gender equality policies in a variety of areas and through strategies of equal opportunities, positive actions and gender mainstreaming (Lombardo 2004;

Bustelo 2014). A broad understanding of substantive gender equality was reflected in the 2007 Equality Law. By addressing not only quotas, but also gender equality in employment and paternity leave and gender biases in education, the law was a step forward both in parity democracy and in attempts to redefine gender relations. Provisions on quotas included in the law further developed the constitutional endorsement of substantive equality. (iii) Discourses supporting gender quotas in the electoral arena have become rather hegemonic, while discourses on equality of opportunities and meritocracy still undercut advances in quotas for corporate boards, and a debate on quotas in public administration is still pending. Yet, the Spanish party system is undergoing changes that might affect existing opportunities and resistances to gender equality. Only time will tell whether the shift towards substantive equality and parity signalled by both quotas and the broader gender equality plan envisioned in the Equality Law will effectively secure women's presence in positions of power and challenge unequal gender relations in Spain.

ACKNOWLEDGEMENTS

The authors wish to thank the editors for their helpful comments. Emanuela Lombardo acknowledges the *Ministerio de Economía y Competitividad* for funding the Evanpolge research project (Ref: FEM2012–33117).

References

Adecco (2014). *VI Encuesta Adecco a Mujeres Directivas.* Available at: www .adecco.es/_data/NotasPrensa/pdf/629.pdf. Accessed 7 January 2016.

Aguado, Ana. 2012. "Constructing Women's Citizenship: The Conquest of Suffrage and Women's Political Rights in Spain." In *The Struggle for Female Suffrage in Europe: Voting to Become Citizens*, edited by Blanca Rodríguez-Ruiz and Ruth Rubio-Marín, 289–303. Leiden-Boston: Brill.

Alonso, Alba, and Tània Verge. 2015. "El impacto de la distribución territorial del poder sobre las políticas de igualdad en España." *Revista Española de Ciencia Política* 39: 239–61.

Beveridge, Fiona. 2012. "'Going Soft'? Analysing the Contribution of Soft and Hard Measures in EU Gender Law and Policy." In *The Europeanization of Gender Equality Policies: A Discursive-Sociological Approach*, edited by Emanuela Lombardo and Maxime Forest, 28–48. Basingstoke: Palgrave.

Bianco, Magda, Angela Ciavarella, and Rossella Signoretti. 2011. *Women on boards in Italy.* CONSOB Study n. 70, October 2011. Available at:

www.consob.it/main/consob/pubblicazioni/studi_analisi/quaderni_finanza/qdf70.htm.

Bustelo, Maria. 2014. "Three Decades of State Feminism and Gender Equality Policies in Multi-Governed Spain." *Sex Roles* 74 (3): 107–20.

Casey, Catherine, Renate Skibnes, and Judith K. Pringle. 2011. "Gender Equality and Corporate Governance." *Gender, Work, and Organization* 18 (6): 613–30.

Castaño, Cecilia, Joaquina Laffarga Briones, Carlos Iglesias Fernández, Pilar de Fuentes Ruiz, Juan Martín Fernández, Raquel Llorente Heras, María José Charlo Molina, Yolanda Giner Manso, Susana Vázquez Cupeiro, Miriam Núñez Torrado, and José Luís Martínez Cantos. 2009. *Mujeres y Poder Empresarial en España*. Madrid: Instituto de la Mujer, Estudios n. 108.

Caul Kittilson, Miki. 2006. *Challenging Parties, Changing Parliaments. Women and Elected Office in Contemporary Western Europe*. Columbus, OH: The Ohio State University Press.

Celis, Karen. 2006. "Substantive Representation of Women and the Impact of Descriptive Representation. Case: The Belgian Lower House 1900–1979." *Journal of Women, Politics and Policy* 28 (2): 85–114.

Centro de Investigaciones Sociológicas (CIS). 2007. *Barómetro Septiembre 2007*. Study number 2732. Madrid.

Chapman, Jennifer. 1993. *Politics, Feminism and the Reformation of Gender*. London: Routledge.

Comisión Mixta de los Derechos de la Mujer y de la Igualdad de Oportunidades (CM). 2006. "Comparecencias para informar en materia de igualdad efectiva entre mujeres y hombres." Sesiones 16-17-18. *Diario de Sesiones de las Cortes Generales*, 76-78-79. 16, 24, 25 October.

Comisión Nacional del Mercado de Valores. (2006). *Código Unificado de Buen Gobierno de las Sociedades Cotizadas*. Madrid: CNMV.

Comisión Nacional del Mercado de Valores. (2015). *Código de buen gobierno de las sociedades cotizadas*. Madrid/Barcelona: CNMV.

Consejo Económico y Social de España (CES). (2006). *Dictamen sobre el anteproyecto de ley orgánica de igualdad entre mujeres y hombres*. Dictamen 8/2006. Madrid: CES.

Dahlerup, Drude. 2007. "Electoral Gender Quotas: Between Equality of Opportunity and Equality of Result." *Representation* 43 (2): 73–92.

de Anca, Celia. 2008. "Women on Corporate Boards of Directors in Spanish Listed Companies." In *Women on Corporate Boards of Directors*, edited by Susan Vinnicombe, Val Singh, Ronald J. Burke, Diana Bilimoria, and Morten Huse. Northampton, MA: Edward Elgar Publishing, 96–107.

Del Brío, Esther, and Inmaculada Del Brío. 2009. "Los consejos de administración en las sociedades cotizadas: avanzando en femenino." *Revista de Estudios Empresariales* 1: 102–18.

Díaz García, María, and Ángela González Moreno. 2012. "La cuota de mujeres en los consejos de administración: ¿2015 una utopía?" *Boletín Económico de ICE N° 3027* (June): 53–61.

Diz Otero, Isabel, and Marta Lois González. 2015. "El impacto de las cuotas sobre los ejecutivos autonómicos: presencia y características de la elite gubernamental autonómica." In *Igualdad de género y no discriminación en España: evolución, problemas, perspectivas*, edited by MariaCaterina La Barbera and Marta Cruells López. Madrid: Centro de Estudios Políticos y Constitucionales, 157–182.

El País. 1998. "El PSOE renuncia a promover la paridad legal antes de junio." 27 December.

El País. 1999, "No al "feminismo de salón" y sí al de hechos." 7 March.

Engelstad, Frederik, and Mari Teigen. 2012. "Gender and Varieties of Economic Power – the Significance of Family and State." *Comparative Social Research* 29: xi–xxi.

Fagan, Colette, Maria C. González, and Silvia Gómez. 2012. *Women on Corporate Boards and in Top Management*. London: Palgrave Macmillan UK.

Ferree, Myra Marx. 2012. *Varieties of Feminism. German Gender Politics in Global Perspective*. Stanford: Stanford University Press.

Freidenvall, Lenita. 2013. "Step by Step – Women's Inroads to Parliamentary Politics." In *Breaking Male Dominance in Old Democracies*, edited by Drude Dahlerup and Monique Leyenaar. Oxford: Oxford University Press.

González, Maria C., and Lara Martínez. 2012. "Spain on the Norwegian Pathway: Towards a Gender-Balanced Presence of Women on Corporate Boards." In *Women on Corporate Boards and in Top Management*, edited by Colette Fagan, Maria C. González, and Silvia Gómez, 169–97. Basingstoke: Palgrave.

Hillman, Amy J., Christine Shropshire, and Albert A. Cannella. 2007. "Organizational Predictors of Women on Corporate Boards." *Academy of Management Journal* 50 (4): 941–52.

Howell, Kerry E. 2004. "Developing Conceptualisations of Europeanization: Synthesising Methodological Approaches." *Queen's Papers on Europeanization* 3/2004.

Informa. 2014. *Las mujeres en los consejos de administración y organismos de decisión de las empresas españolas*. Alcobendas, Madrid: Informa D&B, S.A. Available at: www.paridad.eu/docs/10_06_40_330_Estudio_Mujeres_en_Consejos_de_Administracion_2012.pdf. Accessed 15 May 2014.

Instituto de la Mujer. 2016. *Mujeres en Cifras*. Madrid: Ministerio de Sanidad, Servicios Sociales e Igualdad.

IESE. 2014. *Las mujeres en los Consejos del IBEX-35*. Barcelona: Inforpress-IESE. Available at: www.iese.edu/research/pdfs/ST-0332.pdf. Accessed 15 May 2014.

Jenson, Jane, and Celia Valiente. 2003. "Comparing Two Movements for Gender Parity. France and Spain." In *Women's Movements Facing the Reconfigured State*, edited by Lee Ann Banaszak, Karen Beckwith, and Dieter Rucht, 69–93. Cambridge: Cambridge University Press.

Kenny, Meryl. 2013. *Gender and Political Recruitment: Theorizing Institutional Change*. Basingstoke: Palgrave Macmillan.

Krook, Mona L. 2006. "Reforming Representation: The Diffusion of Candidate Ggender Quotas Worldwide." *Politics & Gender* 2 (3): 303–27.

2009. *Quotas for Women in Politics: Gender and Candidate Selection Reform Worldwide*. New York: Oxford University Press.

Lépinard, Éléonore. 2013. "For Women Only? Gender Quotas and Intersectionality in France." *Politics & Gender* 9 (3): 276–98.

Lombardo, Emanuela. 2004. *La europeización de la política española de igualdad de género*. Valencia: Tirant lo Blanch.

2008. "Gender Inequality in Politics. Policy Frames in Spain and the European Union." *International Feminist Journal of Politics* 10 (1): 78–96.

2012. "Gender quotas in corporate boards: Italy and Spain." Note for *Gender quotas in management boards*, by Jo Armstrong and Sylvia Walby. Briefing note for the European Parliament, Policy Department C: Citizens' Rights and Constitutional Affairs, PE 462.429.

Lombardo, Emanuela, and Lut Mergaert. 2013. "Gender Mainstreaming and Resistance to Gender Training. A Framework for Studying Implementation." *NORA Nordic Journal of Feminist and Gender Research* 21 (4): 296–311.

Lovenduski, Joni. 2005. *State Feminism and Political Representation*. Cambridge: Cambridge University Press.

Lovenduski, Joni, and Pippa Norris. 1993. *Gender and Party Politics*. Thousand Oaks: Sage.

Matland, Richard E., and Donley T. Studlar. 1996. "The Contagion of Women Candidates in Single-Member District and Proportional Representation Electoral Systems: Canada and Norway." *Journal of Politics* 58: 707–33.

Mateos, Ruth, Lorenzo Escot, and Ricardo Gimeno. 2006. "Análisis de la presencia de la mujer en los consejos de administración de las mil mayores empresas españolas." *Documento de Trabajo num. 263/2006*. Madrid: Fundación de las Cajas de Ahorros.

Mateos, Ruth, Ricardo Gimeno, and Lorenzo Escot. 2010. "Discriminación en consejos de administración: análisis e implicaciones económicas." *Revista de Economía Aplicada* 53 (XVIII): 131–62.

Miller Toyah, and María del Carmen Triana. 2009. "Demographic Diversity in the Boardroom: Mediators of the Board Diversity–Firm Performance Relationship." *Journal of Management Studies* 46 (5): 755–86.

Ministerio de Economía y Hacienda. 2011. "Informe sobre la aplicación de políticas de igualdad." Available at: www.minhap.gob.es/Documentacion/Publico/PortalVarios/Gestión%20del%20Portal/Igualdad%20de%20

género/IGUALDAD%202011%20INFORME%20DEFINITIVO%20
ECONOMIA%20Y%20HACIENDA%20CO.pdf. Accessed 18 July 2014.
Ministerio de Trabajo. 2011. "Informe sobre la aplicación del principio de
igualdad de trato entre mujeres y hombres en el ministerio de empleo y
seguridad social." Available at: www.empleo.gob.es/es/igualdad/documen
tos/informe-politicas-igualdad-meyss2011.pdf. Accessed 18 July 2014.
Niven, David. 1998. "Party Elites and Women Candidates: The Shape of
Bias." *Women and Politics* 19 (2): 57–80.
Norris, Pippa. 2004. *Electoral Engineering: Voting Rules and Political Behavior.*
New York: Cambridge University Press.
Peces-Barba, Gregorio. 1999. "La cuota femenina en las candidaturas elector-
ales." *El País.* 1 July: 14.
Pérez-Nievas, Santiago, Cristina Daniela Vintila, Laura Morales, and Marta
Paradés. 2014. *La representación política de los inmigrantes en elecciones
municipales. Un análisis empírico. Colección Opiniones y Actitudes* no. 72.
Madrid: Centro de Investigaciones Sociológicas.
Piscopo, Jennifer, and Susan Clark Muntean. 2013. "Getting Women on
Board: A cross-country comparison of corporate quotas in the European
Union." Paper presented at the 3rd European Conference on Politics and
Gender, Barcelona, 21–3 March.
PSOE. 2013. *Conferencia Política.* Madrid: PSOE, Secretaría de Organización.
Available at: https://www.psoe.es/media-content/2016/04/resoluciones-
201310-Conferencia-Politica.pdf. Accessed 2 April 2018.
Rodríguez Ruiz, Blanca, and Ruth Rubio-Marín. 2008. "The Gender of
Representation: On Democracy, Equality, and Parity." *International
Journal of Constitutional Law (I*CON)* 6 (2): 287–316.
Rubio-Marín, Ruth. 2014. "The achievement of female suffrage in Europe: On
women's citizenship." *International Journal of Constitutional Law (I*CON)*
12 (1): 4–34.
Teigen, Mari. 2012. "Gender Quotas on Corporate Boards: On the Diffusion
of a Distinct National Policy Reform." *Comparative Social Research* 29:
115–46.
Threlfall, Monica. 2005. "Towards parity representation in party politics."
In *Gendering Spanish Democracy*, edited by Monica Threlfall, Christine
Cousins and Celia Valiente, 125–61. New York: Routledge.
Tienari, Janne, Charlotte Holgersson, Susan Meriläinen, and Pia Höök.
2009. "Gender, Management, and Market Discourse: The Case of
Gender Quotas in the Swedish and Finnish Media." *Gender, Work, and
Organization* 16 (4): 501–21.
Valiente, Celia. 2005. "The Women's Movement, Gender Equality Agencies,
and Central-State Debates on Political Representation in Spain (1983–
2003)." In *State Feminism and Political Representation*, edited by Joni
Lovenduski, 174–94. Cambridge: Cambridge University Press.

Verge, Tània. 2006. "Mujer y partidos políticos en España: Las estrategias de los partidos y su impacto institucional, 1978–2004." *Revista Española de Investigaciones Sociológicas* 115 (6): 165–96.

———. 2008. "Cuotas voluntarias y legales en España. La paridad a examen." *Revista Española de Investigaciones Sociológicas* 123: 123–50.

———. 2012. "Institutionalising Gender Equality in Spain: Incremental Steps from Party to Electoral Gender Quotas." *West European Politics* 35 (2): 395–414.

———. 2013. "Regulating Gender Equality in Political Office in Southern Europe: The Cases of Greece, Portugal and Spain." *Representation* 49 (4): 439–52.

Walby, Sylvia. 2009. *Globalization and Inequalities: Complexity and Contested Modernities.* London: Sage.

PART II

GENDER QUOTAS AS SYMBOLIC EQUALITY REMEDIES

CHAPTER FIVE

THE PROTRACTED STRUGGLE FOR GENDER QUOTAS IN GREEK POLITICS

Constitutional Reform and Feminist Mobilization in the EU Context

Dia Anagnostou

Greece did not escape the European trend of gender quota reform. In the course of the first decade of the 2000s, legislation was passed to address the low levels of women's representation in the elected bodies of the local government and in the national parliament. Despite the fact that Greek women had gained full suffrage in the early 1950s and despite a vibrant feminist movement that emerged after the transition to democracy in 1974, female representation in political institutions remained dismally low – at 6.3 percent in the Greek Parliament in the mid-1990s. In the 1980s, such low representation was already of concern to at least some of the female Members of Parliament (MPs). While in the early part of that decade the idea of quotas to redress the problem was absent from public discussions and statements on the issue ("H Ellinida stin Politiki" 1982), it did gain at least some currency towards the end of the 1980s. By the early 2000s, when the constitutional barriers were cleared, gender-balancing rules in the form of a minimum 33 percent quota of each sex were introduced in public administration, in local politics, and subsequently in national politics.

Until the second half of the 1980s, gender quotas were highly controversial among the heterogeneous and rather fragmented – not least by political parties – Greek feminist movement (Anagnostou 1991). Objections were especially strongly raised by autonomous and radical feminist groups. For instance, the Non-aligned Women's Movement (Adesmefti Kinisi Gynaikon), and the magazine *Dini*, declared "No to quotas, because we are not a minority, because we are not up for a bargain." Nonetheless, several women's organizations, independent from but also connected to political parties, for the first time set the specific goal of addressing women's underrepresentation and limited participation in politics. They came together in 1988 to form the Coordinating Committee of Women's Organizations and Women's Sections of Political Parties, (Pantelidou-Malouta 2014, 104). In response to that initiative, in the 1990s, Greece's largest political parties adopted voluntary quotas to promote women's participation in their internal organs and decision-making bodies in proportion to women's party membership (Pantelidou-Malouta 2014, 83).[1]

This chapter explores the adoption of gender balancing quotas in Greece and traces the processes of feminist mobilization that has developed in pursuit of this goal since the 1980s. The feminist claims underlying gender quota reform in Greece were homegrown, and spiraled out of the women's movement that flourished in the aftermath of the country's democratic transition. Yet, the struggle for gender quotas has been long and protracted, and it has been waged as much in the political as in the constitutional and judicial arenas. Attempts in the 1990s to introduce gender quotas came up against established constitutional principles. Greece's Constitution, which was adopted in 1975 following the fall of the military regime, introduced the principle of equality between men and women, but it did so in a legal system and a society where inequalities between the sexes were in practice both institutionalized and abundant. Partly for this reason, the Constitution also incorporated a clause that allowed for the differential treatment of the sexes for compelling reasons and as prescribed by law.

Even with this clause permitting differential treatment, attempts to legislate quotas in the early 1990s were struck down as a divergence from the principle of sex equality, and thus unconstitutional. This decision made it clear that, as in other countries (i.e. Portugal, France, and Italy, but unlike Spain; see Mateo Diaz and Millns [2004, 291]), the road to quotas would have to be cleared of juridical and constitutional barriers, specifically shaped by a formal conception of sex equality that saw positive measures as discriminatory and thus illegitimate. The first part of this chapter describes how the constitutional

---

[1] As early as 1993, the center-right party, New Democracy (ND), had committed to including at least 20 percent women in all its party organs, which it would later increase to 30 percent. See Gerapetritis (2006, 557).

and juridical parameters obstructed the adoption of gender quotas until a 2001 constitutional amendment specifically declared the legitimacy of positive measures and their congruity with the equality principle. The second part of this chapter explores the social and political mobilization dynamics that shaped the feminist struggle for a constitutional amendment. The third part of this chapter unravels the contested and contradictory process of legislating gender quotas in the Greek public administration (in 2000), gender candidate quotas for elections at the local and municipal level (in 2001), and later on for elections for the national parliament (2008). This study is based on empirical research of legal and policy documents, review of twenty-five Greek high court cases, secondary literature, and ten interviews with feminist activists, lawyers, and officials from gender equality state agencies.

The analysis in this chapter concedes with a large scholarship on the subject that shows the crucial role of mobilization by women's organizations, female politicians, and equality agency officials in successfully pushing for gender quota reform (Krook 2007; Meier 2012; Śledzińska-Simon and Bodnar 2013). In the first phase, from the late 1980s through the 1990s, the domestic struggle for gender quotas in Greece cannot be understood independently from the relevant international and European Community developments. In fact, the processes of domestic mobilization in Greece should be seen as an integral part of a broader and partly interrelated transnational movement that fought for a similar cause in other European countries during the same period.

In the second phase, after 2000, the battle for gender quota reform was a domestic process pursued by an alliance of women's organizations, female parliamentarians, politicians across political parties, and the state agency General Secretariat for Gender Equality. It must be noted that the feminist demand for legislating gender quotas overwhelmingly developed its discourse and justification in relation to competing conceptions of equality and to the persistent patterns of women's acute underrepresentation and limited participation in politics. Some academics (i.e. law professors and political scientists, such as Papadopoulou (2006) and Pantelidou-Malouta (2014) have elaborated on the different understandings of citizenship and democracy that the quest for women's political representation posits. However, these different ideas about citizenship and democracy have been virtually absent from the explicit discourse advanced by feminist and women's organizations and activists in their public campaigns.

5.1 OVERCOMING LEGAL AND CONSTITUTIONAL BARRIERS TO POSITIVE MEASURES AND GENDER QUOTAS

Political rights were gradually extended to women in Greece over the course of the twentieth century. In the interwar period, women were granted limited voting rights (only to those who were literate and educated) at the local level. Subsequently, the period of resistance against the Nazis and the civil war saw the active political participation of large numbers of women, an experience that transformed the narrowly conceived gender roles of the prewar period (Hart 1996). After the end of the civil war, in the newly established political system women attained full suffrage rights equal with men in 1952. This reform was approved in parliament by a very narrow majority, arguably under pressure from the Allied forces and the UN conventions that had been signed at the time (Samiou 2012).[2]

A few decades later, the country's 1974 democratic constitution (following the end of a military dictatorship 1967–74) introduced for the first time a sex equality provision stating, "Greek men and women have equal rights and equal duties" (Art. 4 para. 2).[3] This was included alongside the general equality clause in the first paragraph of the same Art. 4, which had been carried forward from the 1952 postwar constitution.[4] Until 1974, Greek courts had interpreted that general equality principle in such a way that it did not challenge existing inequalities between men and women: equal treatment was understood to apply to persons who were similar, while those who were not similar ought to be treated differently (Manesis 1983, 14).

The newly introduced 1974 constitutional principle of sex equality (Art. 4 para. 2) went against a host of laws and regulations that were at the time part of the Greek legal system. In view of this contradiction between the constitution's principled commitment and legal-social reality, Art. 116 para. 1 included a transitional clause stating that "rules that are contrary to Art. 4 para. 2 continue to be in effect until they are annulled by law, at the latest until 31 December 1982."

[2] In 1953, the first female Member of Parliament was elected.
[3] The 1975 constitution also stipulated that "all workers, irrespective of sex or other distinctions, shall be entitled to equal pay for work of equal value" (Art. 22 para. 1). *The Constitution of Greece, as revised by the parliamentary resolution of 6 April 2001 of the VIIth Revisionary Parliament.*
[4] Art. 4 para. 1 states, "All Greeks are equal before the law."

At the same time, Art. 116 included a second paragraph that allowed for derogations from the sex equality principle for compelling reasons and as provided for by statute (para. 2).[5] Interestingly, while this clause was included along with the transitional clauses of the 1974 Constitution, it was not temporary but in fact pronounced a rule applicable for an undefined time frame and of unlimited scope (Manesis 1983, 16).

The contestation surrounding the specific formulation of these newly introduced provisions pertaining to sex equality during the development of the 1974 Constitution was significant. Both the insertion of the principle of equality between women and men and the establishment of a seven-year transitional period for the annulment of all laws that were contrary to sex equality, were victories for women's organizations that had pressured for these goals. In fact, as a direct result of the latter, fourteen laws were subsequently modified or abrogated, foremost among them being the reform of family law (Yotopoulos-Marangopoulos 2002).

On the other hand, by allowing for derogations from sex equality, para. 2 of Art. 116 was from the perspective of the women's organizations a regrettable settlement, as it allowed patriarchal prejudice to creep anew into the democratic constitutional order (Yotopoulos-Marangopoulos 2002, 22). The provision was the result of a last-minute compromise reached between feminists who supported the sex equality clause and members of the constitutional assembly who opposed it (Yotopoulos-Marangopoulos 1998, 774). This latter group advocated the need for permissible derogations from sex equality on the grounds that blind application of the sex equality principle without regard to the existing differences between women and men would lead to the deterioration of women's position (Manesis 1983, 17). Theoretically, para. 2 of Art. 116 – possibly a unique provision at the time among national constitutions in Europe – could also be seen as a basis for justifying positive action measures. In reality though, it became a central impediment in the judicial advancement of equality between men and women.

Throughout the 1980s and 1990s, para. 2 of Art. 116 was invoked by decision-makers and courts to justify the perpetuation of old inequalities and the appearance of new ones. In particular, it was frequently

---

[5] Art. 116 para. 2 states, "Derogations from Art. 4 para. 2, are permitted only for compelling reasons and in conditions specifically provided for by law."

invoked to legitimate as exceptions from the equality principle restrictive quotas that limited the number of women who could be recruited into male dominated employment sectors, such as military or police corps and academies. Within the broad scope of permissible divergences from equality allowed for, high court judges accepted such restrictive measures to preserve the gendered nature of particular kinds of professions and employment. For instance, they referred to "intrinsically female" traits, such as caring for others, in order to justify restricting the number of men allowed to enter the Officer's Academy for Nurse Training (Scholi Aksiomatikon Nosileftikis, SAN).[6] At the same time, Greek judges referred to the superior physical abilities of men in order to limit women's entry into the police and military academies, without reference to actual conditions of work (Anagnostou 2013, 139–40). By the same token, Greek government policy unconcernedly continued to employ restrictive quotas overwhelmingly to the disadvantage of women.[7]

Not only did the provision for permissible derogations from sex equality not become a basis for legitimating positive action measures, but it was actually interpreted in such a way as to disallow such measures on the grounds that they were against the principle of gender equality. This very provision became the stumbling block to an early and timid attempt to introduce a gender quota in public administration. In the early 1990s, a statute for the first time instituted a form of affirmative action for women, requiring that at least one woman be present in service councils (ypiresiaka symvoulia) in the public administration, as long as she possessed the necessary qualifications. Service councils are bodies within the different entities and departments of the public administration formed internally by employees, and at the time significantly lacked women's participation. They have a decision-making or consultative role in personnel matters (i.e. such as transfer or secondment of staff members to other administrative departments or public agencies).

Existing studies on the background and politics surrounding that early quota provision hardly reference how and why it was inserted

---

[6] *Council of State*, Section C, case no. 870/1995.

[7] A 1997 Ministerial Order introduced the new restrictive quota for entry into the various military academies, mainly targeting women and only in one case targeting men (in the SAN). *Efimeris tis Kyverniseos tis Ellinikis Dimokratias* [Government Gazette] 2 (292), 10 April 1997.

into a law on the organization, operation and personnel of the public administration (Art. 29, Law 2085/1992) passed in October 1992 under a center-right government led by the political party New Democracy.[8] However, it can, with a fair degree of certainty, be seen as a product of pressure by female MPs from across political parties. As of the late 1980s, female MPs had started to coordinate their action to promote women in politics, as already mentioned in the introductory section. It was far less controversial to push for a quota – and a very "soft" one, mandating only one woman – in the public administration service councils, than in politics.[9] In 1992, the Greek section of the European experts' network on "Women in Decision-Making Centers" was also established and supported the female MPs' initiative (Pantelidou-Malouta 2014, 82–3).

The passage of that early 1992 gender quota provision must have also been influenced by the mobilization initiatives by the European Commission (EC). Less than a month after its passage, the Athens conference on "Women and Political Power" was held under the auspices of the European Commission. In that conference, attended by women who were members of national and European parliaments and ministers from different member states, the Greek Commissioner at the time, a woman – Vaso Papandreou, inaugurated the EC campaign aimed at promoting women's participation in politics. The confer-ence produced a "Declaration" signed by twenty prominent European female politicians, stating that "democracy imposes parity in the rep-resentation and in the administration of the nations," considered a turning point in the feminist movement for parity in France (Bereni 2007, 196). The fact that the passage of the 1992 Greek law took place contemporaneously with the Athens conference and the launching of the EC campaign on the subject, under the lead of Papandreou as com-missioner, suggests that the two were not entirely coincidental. About ten years later, Papandreou, then Minister of Internal Affairs, would again introduce a gender quota to promote women's participation in the administrative service councils.

---

[8] Law 2085/1992 on "Regulation of issues related to the organization, operation and personnel of the public administration," *Efymeris tis Kyverniseos* [Government Gazette], 1 (170), 20 October 1992.

[9] For an overview of how the quota laws in relation to service councils evolved, see the explanatory report for the bill "Regulation of issues related to the Ministry of Internal Affairs, Public Administration and Decentralization," Athens, 18 August 2000.

However, Art. 29 of Law 2085/1992, providing for at least one qualified woman in administrative service councils, was short-lived. In 1995, the Council of State (CoS) – Greece's supreme administrative court, which also engages in incidental constitutional review *in concreto*[10] – struck down the provision as unconstitutional.[11] The decision came in response to a petition by a male public sector employee who claimed that a decision issued against him by the service council in his department was null and void on the grounds that the council's composition was illegitimate. The sixth section of the CoS did not deem positive measures as prima facie unconstitutional. Arguably it could not have done so, because positive action measures had already been incorporated in the Greek legal order via the ratification of the UN Convention on the Elimination of All Forms of Discrimination against Women (CEDAW).[12] Furthermore, positive action measures had been introduced into Greek Labor Law since the 1980s, with Law 1414/1984, which sought to implement the equal pay provisions contained in the EC's Treaty of Rome and in the respective EC Directive.[13] In regards to professional training and employment, Law 1414/1984 (Art. 10 para. 2) provided that measures adopted in favor of one sex are not discriminatory if they contribute to dismantling inequality and to reinstituting equality of opportunities (Gerapetritis 2006, 542).

Despite the domestic incorporation of positive action via the transposition of international and EC law, the 6th section of the CoS still found the gender quota in the administrative service councils to be "an unjustified deviation from the constitutional principle of gender

---

[10] The CoS reviews statutory provisions in the context of deciding a specific case. See Spiliotopoulos (1983, 463).

[11] Greece lacks a constitutional court. Instead, it has a diffused system of judicial review that in principle allows all courts to engage in constitutional review of fundamental rights. However, the practice of lower courts following the decisions of the high courts, and the fact that individual challenges to executive acts are made directly before the CoS, have resulted in the concentration of judicial review in higher courts (Iliopoulos-Strangas and Koutnatzis 2011, 546).

[12] Art. 4 of the CEDAW accepts the adoption of temporary special measures to accelerate de facto equality between men and women. The CEDAW was ratified and incorporated in the Greek legal order with Law 1342/1983 (Kapotas 2005, 18).

[13] Council Directive 75/117/EEC of 10 February 1975 on the approximation of the laws of the Member States relating to the application of the principle of equal pay for men and women.

equality."[14] Paradoxically, it relied on para. 2 of Art. 116, which allowed for divergences from the equality principle if there are compelling reasons and as provided by law. The CoS 6th section claimed that there were no "compelling reasons" to justify the need for such differential treatment in favor of women as there was no clear evidence to suggest that the underrepresentation of women in the service councils was due to discrimination (Kapotas 2005, 18). Because the issue was considered important, the case was referred to the CoS plenum for a final judgment.

By the mid-1990s, even before the final judgment of the CoS, it had become crystal clear that far from being an ally, Art. 116 para. 2 of the Greek Constitution was actually a major adversary in the feminists' struggle for positive measures and quotas. It subverted gender equality by establishing a ground for restrictive quotas (mostly) against women as permissible divergences from sex equality. It also locked lawyers, judges, and feminists into a discourse and argumentation narrowly structured by the binary of equality versus difference. In fact, as Alice Yotopoulos-Marangopoulos (1998a, 90–1) aptly stated, Art. 116 para. 2 made for gender equality *minus*: it was invoked by Greek courts to water down and lessen the force of the formal sex equality clause in the Greek constitution (Art. 4 para. 2). Art. 116 para. 2 carried all the baggage of the pre-1974 patriarchal order, in which biological and functional differences were seen to necessitate or legitimate different roles, duties, and rights between men and women. Since it did not serve as a basis for positive measures – on the contrary, it could be invoked to strike down any kind of quota as unconstitutional – it would have to be altogether eliminated.

The CoS plenum issued its final decision on the constitutionality of a gender quota in administrative service councils in May 1998. In its final decision, in which the judges were substantially divided, the CoS took a notable turn in its jurisprudence on positive measures: it reversed the 6th section judgment and pronounced the constitutionality of the requirement to include at least one qualified woman in the service councils.[15] The majority of the plenum's judges for the first time argued that Art. 4 paras.1 and 2 of the Constitution prescribed not merely a formal, but a substantive notion of equality.

---

[14] CoS 6th section decision no. 6275/1995 (Yotopoulos-Marangopoulos 1998, 786–7).
[15] A total of fourteen decisions were issued by the CoS on 8 May 1998 (case no. 1933 and nos. 1917–29). See Yotopoulos-Marangopoulos (2000).

By also invoking the EC directive 76/207, the UN CEDAW, as well as the EC recommendation 96/694/EC on the balanced participation of men and women in decision-making bodies, the CoS advanced the view that positive measures (in favor of women) are not a divergence from equality; on the contrary, they may be appropriate and necessary in order to reduce existing disparities (such as the underrepresentation of women in the higher levels of public administration) until real equality is achieved.[16] In a phrase that hinted at the European Court of Justice's (ECJ) decision in the Kalanke case, the CoS stated that "in practice, discrimination against a category of persons is so intense that the strict application of the equality principle amounts to equality in appearance, while in reality it entrenches and reproduces an existing situation of inequality."[17] Even though the 1992 service council quota provision had already been abolished in 1994,[18] the CoS Plenum final decision in 1998 would prove to be crucial at the turn of the decade when a constitutional revision process was underway, and as quota reform regained momentum.

Perhaps not so surprisingly, the 1998 CoS plenum decision on the gender quota in service councils was issued on the same day as another decision concerning quotas that limited the number of women (to a maximum of ten percent) accepted into police academies. In that decision, the CoS for the first time deemed as prima facie unconstitutional restrictive quotas for women's entry into various male-dominated professions such as the police, military corps, firefighters, border control officers, etc. Referencing Art. 116 para. 2, the court conceded that while divergences from gender equality may be permitted, they are permissible not only if provided for by law, but if they are justified on the basis of common experience and of specific and appropriate criteria, which citizens and courts can review in order to verify the legitimacy of a particular divergence. The CoS plenum specifically stated that *apart from positive measures*, any other divergence from the principle of sex equality must be scrutinized as described above.[19]

---

[16] CoS decision 1933/1998 has been subject to numerous analyses and legal commentaries. Indicatively, see Gerapetritis (2006).

[17] CoS plenum, case no. 1933/1998.

[18] Law 2085/1992 (Art. 29) had already been abolished with Law 2190/1994, Art. 38 para. 10.

[19] CoS plenum, cases no. 1917–1929/1998. These cases had been referred to the Plenary Session of the CoS, following the CoS section judgment 5646/1996.

It is interesting and significant that the country's high administrative court took a turn in its jurisprudence in regard to positive action and to restrictive quotas simultaneously; it shows that the court in its deliberations thought of the two issues as interconnected in order to clearly distinguish between legitimate and non-legitimate divergences from the gender equality principle. Art. 116 para. 2 of the constitution was the target and the problem in both of cases: in the preceding decade, it had been applied and interpreted both to justify discriminatory treatment of women and to obstruct affirmative action measures favoring women.

The landmark 1998 cases cannot be understood independently from the cumulative influence of the EC/European Union (EU) gender equality legislation on the Greek high court judges, which became more substantial and formative over the course of the 1990s (Iliopoulos-Strangas and Koutnatzis 2011, 561). They were the "culmination of Greek jurisprudence, by which the gender equality constitutional norms have been interpreted and applied in the light of and in conjunction with Community law and international human rights treaties" (Koukoulis-Spiliotopoulos 2006, 659). Even though positive measures were not required by EU law, they were incorporated into a Council recommendation[20] and the Amsterdam Treaty recognized them as legitimate (modified Art. 119, now Art. 141) (Stratighaki 2006, 285).

5.2 FEMINIST MOBILIZATION IN PURSUIT OF A CONSTITUTIONAL AMENDMENT

The 1998 landmark decisions of the CoS described above did not originate in strategically targeted litigation, but once the respective petitions came up for judicial review they presented an opportunity for an intervention. Relevant academic articles and legal commentaries at the time by law professors and leading activists on quotas, such as Alice Yotopoulos-Marangopoulos, were influential in providing arguments in support of positive measures. The writings of Yotopoulos-Marangopoulos and her analyses of positive measures and substantive equality were well known among the legal and juridical

---

[20] Council of the EU recommendation of 13 December 1984 concerning the promotion of positive measures on behalf of women. 84/635/EEC, EU L 331, 19 December 1984.

community in Greece. She had strongly criticized the initial CoS 6th section judgment in 1995 that had pronounced unconstitutional the first quota law requiring the presence of at least one woman in the service councils (Yotopoulos-Marangopoulos 1998a, 92). Yotopoulos-Marangopoulos was the president (in fact, its longest-serving president, for over twenty-five years) of the Hellenic League of Women's Rights (HLWR, or the League), the oldest feminist association in Greece, which had been very active in the Greek suffragette movement in the decades prior to the 1950s. Since its creation in the 1920s, the HLWR had an international orientation, having been a member of the International Alliance of Women since the early part of the twentieth century and later gaining United Nations consultative status. Yotopoulos-Marangopoulos had a lifelong record of activism and involvement in gender equality issues, particularly in relation to the UN system, and for a long time she had written on the subject of substantive equality and quotas.

The failure of the first 1992 gender quota law to pass the CoS sparked interest in and activism around positive action, certainly by the HLWR. It also instilled the conviction that gender quotas would not be accepted in Greece unless the constitution (and Art. 116 para. 2 in particular) was amended. Since the mid-1990s, a process of broad constitutional reform was already underway. At this point the HLWR saw the constitutional reform process as a unique opportunity to push for an amendment. In the mid-1990s, the HLWR launched a well-coordinated campaign of informational and political activities to convince academics, members of the parliament's constitutional committee, and others about the need to endorse positive measures. It did so as the final decision by the CoS plenum on the 1992 service councils' quota law was pending.

The HLWR campaign for a constitutional amendment appealed to a substantive notion of gender equality, criticizing the hollowness of formal equality before the law in a social context where institutionalized and deeply entrenched inequalities persisted. It rallied the support of a broad coalition of organizations, supporters, and activists: law professors and other academics, female members of the Greek Parliament such as Anna Psarouda-Benaki and Vaso Papandreou, the General Secretariat for Gender Equality (the state agency established in 1985 to promote equality between men and women), and a large number of independent feminist organizations. Some of the leading figures in this campaign were well-versed and highly active in developments in EC/EU law, such as Sofia Koukouli-Spiliotopoulou, a professional lawyer, an expert of the European Commission, a member of European networks of collaboration coordinated by the European Women's Lobby (EWL), as well as vice president of the European Women's Lawyers Association (Stratighaki 2006, 280, 283). They had also been followed closely the gender equality cases that were adjudicated by Greece's high courts.

In December 1997, the HLWR organized a public discussion event where it launched its proposal for a constitutional amendment, presenting its position and arguments in support of (1) the elimination of the constitutional provision that allowed for divergences from sex equality, and (2) the specific acceptance of positive measures that could contribute to the realization of substantive equality (Koukoulis-Spiliotopoulos 2001, 522). The above HLWR proposal was provisionally accepted by a comfortable majority of Greek MPs in May and June 1998, who voted to include Art. 116 in the list of constitutional provisions under revision (Yotopoulos-Marangopoulos 1998c, 1577). When the CoS's final decision that declared positive measures to be in accord with the sex equality principle – indeed necessary for substantive equality to be achieved – was announced in May 1998, it gave a major boost to the HLWR-led campaign in pursuit of a constitutional amendment.

In October 2000, the HLWR, together with the General Secretariat for Equality, organized another public discussion event, in which representatives from the different political parties, parliamentarians, and members of the parliament's constitutional reform committee participated. The proposal of the HLWR was signed by twenty-two women's organizations that supported the constitutional amendment that would legitimize positive measures.[21] The ability of the HLWR to build this coalition was instrumental in convincing a sufficiently large number of members (fifty-eight MPs across political parties led by female MP Anna Benaki-Psarouda) of the constitutional assembly to endorse its proposal.[22] In December 2000, the League's proposed amendment was adopted nearly verbatim by the Parliament's constitutional reform committee, which explicitly referred to the 1998 shift in the CoS case law. The amendment was voted through by an overwhelming parliamentary majority (275 out of 280 votes) and it was incorporated in the reformed constitution (Koukoulis-Spiliotopoulos 2006, 664).

---

[21] For an account of the activities and initiatives that the campaign involved, see Yotopoulos-Marangopoulos (1998b; 2000).

[22] Interview, Sophia Koukoulis-Spiliotopoulos, Athens, 16 November 2010.

The strategic decision of the broad alliance of women's and feminist organizations in Greece to place constitutional and legal reform towards positive measures at the top of the Greek feminist agenda cannot be understood outside of the international and European transnational influences and contacts. The feminist campaign for a constitutional amendment in Greece unfolded contemporaneously with initiatives and reforms towards substantive equality across different member states in the 1990s and early 2000s (Papadopoulou 2006, 254). It did so at a time when the controversy around positive measures at the EU level reached a peak (in the period between 1995 and 1998), with the ECJ decisions in the Kalanke and Marschall cases (Cox 1998, 127–9). As its advocacy and awareness-raising activities peaked in 2000, the HLWR stressed to judges, lawyers, and parliamentarians that a "constitutional tradition common to the EU member states had formed" and that a growing number of national constitutions were guaranteeing substantive equality and incorporating positive action provisions (Koukoulis-Spiliotopoulos 2006, 662–6).

The feminist campaign for constitutional reform resulted in a major victory for the HLWR-led coalition, leading to a constitutional acceptance of substantive equality that is far-reaching and possibly unique in Europe. The amended constitution than entered into force in 2001 abolished the embattled Art. 116 para. 2, which had allowed for derogations from the principle of sex equality. It replaced it with another provision stating, "positive measures for promoting equality between men and women do not constitute discrimination on grounds of sex." It added, "the state shall take measures to eliminate inequalities to the detriment of women that exist in practice" (Art. 116 para. 2). It has been debated among Greek constitutionalists whether the amended Art. 116 para. 2 imposes an obligation upon the state to institute positive measures as a form of remedial action for past or ongoing injustices (Gerapetritis 2006, 550); however, there is no evidence showing that the 2001 constitutional amendment forms a basis for individuals to claim affirmative action by the state as a justiciable right.

In view of the amended Art. 116 para. 2 of the constitution, the CoS ruled out any divergence from the equality principle, except in the form of positive measures that aim to restore "real equality" between men and women.[23] Feminists expected that the change would lead to

---

[23] See the important judgment of the CoS plenary court, case no. 365/2006, which declared restrictive quotas in the employment of women as border control officers

the elimination of restrictive quotas that limited women's access to male-dominated employment sectors. In practice, it did not put an end to such differential treatment. However, the amended Art. 116 was interpreted by the majority of judges in the CoS as requiring the legislature to justify on the basis of specific, objective, and verifiable criteria any provision that imposes a restrictive quota for women seeking employment as police and military officers, coast guards, and firefighters, among others. Moreover, since at least the mid-2000s, the majority of CoS judges has come to believe that the amended Art. 116 para. 2 no longer tolerates any divergences from sex equality other than positive measures (Gerapetritis 2006, 559). The juridical interpretation in regard to restrictive quotas remains divided and unsettled to this day, although the former view still prevails.

Notably, the scope of the amended Art. 116 provision, which legitimates positive action and views it as consistent with – indeed conducive to – sex equality, is not limited to a particular sphere (i.e. politics, as in France for instance) but is broad, potentially forming the basis for positive action measures across different sectors, areas of activity, and social groups (Gerapetritis 2006, 549). Taking into account the amended Art. 116 para. 2, Law 3304/2005 (adopted to transpose the EC directives 2000/43/EC of 29 June 2000) and Law 2000/78/EC of 27 November 2000 stated that special measures aimed at disadvantages emanating from racial or ethnic descent, religious or other belief, disability, age, or sexual orientation are not discriminatory.[24] Furthermore, Law 3769/2009, which was adopted in conformity with the EC antidiscrimination directive 2004/103/EC, gave further recognition to positive action in Greece. It stated that "special measures can be instituted for preventing or counteracting disadvantages related to gender, in order to ensure in practice full equality between women and men."[25] The next section explores the policy effects of the 2001 constitutional amendment for quota reform in Greece.

(a maximum of 10 percent of spots to be filled by women) unconstitutional and contrary to the principle of gender equality.

[24] Law 3304/2004, "Implementation of the principle of equal treatment regardless of race, ethnic origin, religious and other convictions, disability, age or sexual orientation," Art. 6 and 12, Government Gazette 16/A, 27 January 2005.

[25] Law 3769/2009, Art. 5, Government Gazette 105, 1 July 2009. This Law implements equal treatment between men and women regarding access to goods and services, in accordance with Directive 2004/113/EC of 13 December 2004.

5.3 THE ROAD TO EXPANDING, BUT HALF-HEARTED, QUOTA REFORMS

The 2001 constitutional amendment of Art. 116 paved the way for the adoption of gender quotas, which had been the main motive behind the feminist campaign for constitutional reform. The first quota law was adopted in September 2000, a few months before the constitutional reform was completed (in December).[26] In view of women's persistent underrepresentation, the socialist government of the Panhellenic Socialist Movement (PASOK), and specifically the state agency the General Secretariat of Gender Equality, introduced a provision that reinstated a gender quota in the administrative service councils, requiring that at least one third of positions be filled by each sex (Pantelidou-Malouta 2014, 105).

The 2000 quota provision applied to service councils in a wide section of the public administration that included all public organization and local government entities. It is somewhat unclear why a one-third quota was chosen, although it may be that it was considered to be in line with the principle of proportionality, as the legal experts of the Greek Parliament noted in the introductory report to the 2000 draft law.[27] Anything close to 50 percent would have most likely been politically controversial and unfeasible, considering the reactions from within political parties to even the one-third quota.

The service councils were directly chosen as the venue for the first attempt to reintroduce a gender quota due to the fact that the CoS plenum had eventually in 1998 accepted the constitutionality of a gender quota in the service councils. The 1998 CoS decision was used to justify the gender quota at a time when the constitutional reform process was still underway, with an uncertain outcome. In fact, the parliament's legal experts in support of the bill relied heavily on the 1998 CoS decision to argue that when social prejudice has led to profound discrimination against a particular category of persons, the strict principle of equality can only lead to a superficial equality that in practice maintains and reproduces an unequal situation. In such a situation, positive measures are a necessary, even if temporary means until substantive

---

[26] Law 2893/2000, Art. 6, Government Gazette 196, 12 September 2000.

[27] See the explanatory report accompanying the respective bill on "Regulation of issues related to the Ministry of Internal Affairs, Public Administration and Decentralization," Legal Department of the Greek Parliament, Athens, 18 August 2000.

equality is achieved. Reference was also made to EEC law[28] and to the decision in Badeck vs. Germany (C-158/97, 28 March 2000), in which the ECJ and the Court of Justice of the European Union (CJEU) found a gender quota law introduced in the public administration of the state of Hesse in Germany to be in line with EU law on sex equality.[29]

Following the entry into force of the amended constitution of 2001, existing initiatives and proposals for the adoption of a gender quota gained fresh momentum that soon led to reform. A broad alliance had been advocating gender quotas in politics. It included the HLWR-led coalition, the Political League of Women (Politikos Syndesmos Gynaikon, PLW), and the women's state agency, the General Secretariat of Gender Equality. The PLW had been established in 1998 by forty female politicians from all political parties (right, socialist, left, and center) with the goal of increasing women's presence in political decision-making. It developed its activities for the first time in advance of the 1998 national elections to support women candidates and engage in information campaigns, and it has often been similarly activated in pre-election periods since then (Pantelidou-Malouta 2014, 105). In 1999, MP Maria Damanaki from the parliamentary group Coalition of the Left (SYN, the predecessor to Syriza) had submitted a draft law proposing the application of quotas or proportional representation of women in a wide cross-section of the public administration, but also in political life on the local level.[30] The bill gained traction in the aftermath of the 2001 constitutional reform and the increased activism around the issue that ensued. The decision to first pursue the quota in local (rather than national) politics should be understood as a strategic one, premised on a possibly accurate reasoning that it would be easier to get it passed through political parties in the Greek parliament.

The discussion of this quota bill in the Greek Parliament revealed significant disagreements from across the political spectrum, both

---

[28] They specifically referred to Council Directive 76/207/EEC of 9 February 1976 on the implementation of the principle of equal treatment for men and women regarding access to employment, vocational training and promotion, and working conditions.

[29] See the explanatory report for the bill on "Regulation of issues related to the Ministry of Internal Affairs, Public Administration and Decentralization."

[30] See Maria Damanaki, "Gia tin proothisi tis isotitas ton fylon – protasi nomou apo tin koinovouleftiki omada tou Synaspismou" [For the promotion of gender equality – draft law from the parliamentary group of SYN], 8 November 1999, available at www.syn.gr/gr/keimeno.php?id=4654.

from the governing Socialist party and from the opposition parties. Objections were raised on the grounds that the gender quota would introduce coercion into political participation, that political parties would pursue only token inclusion of women in their lists in order to meet the numerical quota target, and that their underrepresentation could not be redressed with such measures but with social change.[31] Such objections had not been voiced in regard to the gender quota in service councils in the public administration where voting rights and political participation were not at stake.

Nonetheless, the 2001 quota law requiring at least one third of candidates from each sex in the party ballots for local and regional elections passed with the support of MPs, who saw it as an act of compliance with the amended Art. 116 para. 2 of the 2001 Constitution. Its passage was, critically, supported by the Minister of Internal Affairs at the time, Vaso Papandreou – formerly the Greek Commissioner in the European Commission (1987–92) – who brought the provision into Parliament (Yotopoulos-Marangopoulos 2000). In view of the very low levels of women's representation in elected local and regional councils, the 2001 law was described as a continuation of the quota reform in the service councils.[32] The legal argumentation in support of the quota reform also made reference to European Community "soft" law on the balanced participation of men and women in decision-making[33] and the EU's Framework Strategy on Gender Equality (2001–5). Within the next decade, quota provisions of one third extended to a few other sectors of the state administration, such as research councils and evaluation committees in the area of research and technology,[34] as well as in service councils in the high echelons of public administration.[35]

The 2001 law defined a minimum quota (of at least one third of each sex) for candidates in local elections. The one-third quota was again selected instead of a percentage closer to 50 percent, according to Pantelidou-Malouta (2014, 111), because the more moderate demand was more likely to be accepted politically. The one-third

---

[31] For an overview of the arguments and counter-arguments in the parliamentary discussion, see Pikramenos (2005).

[32] Law 2910/2001, Art. 75 para. 2.

[33] Recommendation 96/694/EC. See Koukoulis-Spiliotopoulos (2006, 698).

[34] Law 3653/2008, Art. 57.

[35] Law 3839/2010, Art. 2.

quota was applied in an open-list proportional representation electoral system, and therefore did not include any placement mandate for candidates from the underrepresented sex to be placed in winnable positions. Furthermore, it was applied to the whole list of party candidates, which could include as many as double the number of the members who would be elected in the municipal or local council. Already diluting its potential to increase the number of women elected was the modification made only a year after its adoption, by the Socialist government, specifying that the one-third gender quota applied to the total number of electoral candidates included in the party lists for all local councils in the country, rather than for each local council separately.[36] This modification was justified as a response to concerns voiced by local party organizations on the eve of the 2002 elections that there were not enough women to fill the one-third quota in a number of municipalities and communes.

At the same time, the 2001 quota law included a rigorous sanction in the form of non-acceptance and non-registration by the first instance court (protodikeio) of those party ballots that did not meet the mandated quota, which would prevent them from participating in the elections. This sanction made it particularly unpalatable to political parties, in spite of its lax design. However, apparently party slates fielded in a number of electoral areas in the 2002 elections did not quite comply with it. Furthermore, a number of male candidates who lost the 2002 municipal and local elections challenged the constitutionality of the gender quota in court.

Local administrative courts from different areas in Greece issued contradictory decisions regarding the quota law, yet the CoS upheld its constitutionality in ten judgments issued in 2003.[37] The CoS reviewed several aspects of the quota law. The main argument that it advanced was that the quota law restricts but does not negate the right of Greek citizens to participate in political life (as guaranteed by Art. 5 para. 1 of the Constitution). The restrictions imposed were seen as legitimate on the basis of Art. 116 para. 2, which allows for positive measures, including in the sphere of politics. The gender quota law was also considered to be in line with the legislators' role to decide about and regulate the electoral system (Art. 54 para. 1 of the Constitution), and

---

[36] This clarification was provided with Law 3051/2002 in view of the October 2002 elections for municipal and local councils.

[37] See CoS decisions 2831-4/2003, 3027-8/2003, 3185/2003, and 3187-9/2003.

with the aim of pursuing substantive equality between men and women in elected office at the municipal and local level – particularly in view of the persistent and entrenched inequalities based on sex.[38] As the one-third quota law defines a minimum threshold for female candidates, the restrictions, according to the CoS are "soft" and proportionate to the aim pursued. The CoS also confirmed the legitimacy of the sanctions imposed, namely the non-registration of the party candidate list and the annulment of those elected if the non-fulfilment of the quota was verified after the election.[39]

Notwithstanding the firm stance of the CoS regarding the constitutionality of gender quotas, the expansion of quotas beyond the service councils and candidates for local and municipal level elections has been slow, limited, and half-hearted. A new campaign involving the same actors – the HLWR and other women's organizations, the General Secretariat for Gender Equality, and women MPs – pressured for and succeeded in legislating candidate gender quotas for national parliament elections in 2008.[40] With their support, twenty-nine women MPs from different political parties submitted a provision requiring at least one third of candidates of each sex in the political parties' ballots for each constituency.

However, the provision that was ultimately included in the electoral law that was passed in January 2008 under the center-right government of New Democracy provided for a one-third quota for each party's candidates *across the country*. This issue was subject to significant debate in parliament, with MPs from the Socialist and the Left parties strongly disagreeing with New Democracy on this formulation [the Communist Party and the right-wing party, People's Orthodox Rally (Laikos Orthodoksos Synagermos in Greek), voted against the provision].[41] The fact that the quota applied to the number of party candidates in the entire country meant that more women candidates would be included in towns and urban centers and fewer

---

[38] CoS case nos. 2831, 2832, 2833/2003; also CoS case no. 3185/2003. See Kapotas (2010, 32–3).

[39] For an overview of the arguments and counter-arguments in the parliamentary discussion, see Pikramenos (2005).

[40] See the draft provision submitted by Alice Yotopoulos-Marangopoulos as president of the Marangopoulos Foundation on 23 October 2007, and which was signed by twenty-four women's organizations.

[41] See discussion in the national assembly of draft law 3636/2008, *Proceedings of the Hellenic Parliament*, 23 January 2008.

in small towns and the provinces, in effect weakening the potential for more female candidates to be elected.[42] The same watered-down formulation had already been used to modify the gender quota for local politics (introduced with Law 2910/2001, Art. 75 § 1). According to the amended provision that was adopted in 2006, the one-third candidate quota was to be applied to the *total number* of a party's candidates running for election in the municipal council, the communes' council, and the local councils of municipalities and communes, rather than to a party's list of candidates for each of these elected bodies separately.[43]

This account of the Greek quota reform following the 2001 constitutional reform reveals a number of aspects that have weakened or undermined the quotas' potential to promote women's participation in politics. Despite the fact that gender quotas in politics have enjoyed some level of cross-party support, predominantly among female MPs, they have also been undermined by ongoing and pervasive (even if not openly expressed) cross-party resistance, especially among male candidates whose reelection has been threatened. Such opposition has not led to a full-blown negation of quotas but rather to a weak (and progressively weakened) institutional design, coupled with persistent reluctance to implement them, alongside a system of sanctions that renders control and verification of their application time-consuming and generally difficult.

The profound concern about male candidate posts being lost due to the quota became evident in 2010. That year, a major reform of local and regional government structures known by the name of "Kallikratis" merged a large number of communes into a smaller number of municipalities, and therefore greatly reduced the total number of elected positions at the local and municipal level in the country.[44] The new law introduced by the Socialist government at the time carried on the one-third gender quota and also extended it to regional councils, which transformed from state-appointed into popularly elected bodies. However, it also reformulated the quota provision to determine the

---

[42] Law 3636/2008, Art. 3. See Koukoulis-Spiliotopoulos (2008); Yotopoulos-Marangopoulos (2007).

[43] Law 3463/2006, Art. 34 § 3.

[44] Law 3852/2010, "New Architecture of Self-Government and Decentralized Administration – the Kallikratis Program." The gender quota was reinserted in this law in Art. 18 para. 3.

number of female candidates to be placed in the ballot as one third of the total number of the elected positions in each body (rather than as one third of the total number of candidates on the ballot, which is much higher). In effect, the Kallikratis reform significantly reduced the number of women being recruited as candidates in the ballots fielded by parties for local, municipal, and regional elections, even as it extended the quota to the regional level. The network of women's organizations under the aegis of HLWR vocally protested to the Minister of Internal Affairs Ragousis and asked the government to reinstate the earlier provision, but to no avail.[45]

Gender quotas have often been conflated with the idea of parity, and used interchangeably with it. It was for the first time in 2009 that parity (in Greek, isarithmi ekprosopisi, literally "equal numbers representation") was advocated in Greece in the frame of a campaign organized by feminist organizations and the PLW in the preelection period for the European Parliament elections. They did so on behalf of the European Women's Lobby (EWL) that advocated 50–50 representation and the so-called "zipper system" in the ballots of political parties. Greek feminist organizations and the PLW organized at least two events to promote the demand for parity, urging Greek political parties to include 50 percent women in their ballots and the zipper system. Only Syriza and the socialist PASOK applied this principle in their ballots for the 2009 European Parliament elections (Panaretou 2009, 4). Since then (2009–10), a number of female politicians and feminists, primarily from the Left, but also from the Center-Right, have advocated for parity as a goal, aiming at 50 percent representation of women in political structures.[46] Female politicians have expressed support for parity as a next step of, rather than as an alternative to, the existing quota system, which has thus far not managed to increase women's participation in politics beyond a minimal level.

---

[45] Letter sent to Mr. Ragousis, 8 October 2010, in author's possession.

[46] Indicatively, see Papadopoulos, "H aristera h tha einai feministiki h den tha yparxei," *Avgi*, 14 April 2009. Speaking in 2009 on behalf of the Women's Network of Syriza (Dyktio Gynaikon SYRIZA), Rena Dourou (presently the Regional Governor for Attika) advocated parity ("isarithmi ekprosopisi" in Greek) of the sexes in centers and structures of decision-making power. See also the position expressed by Katerina Papakosta, female MP with the New Democracy party (center-right), on her personal website, www.katerinapapakosta.gr/index.php/interviews/825-qq28.

5.4 CONCLUSION

In the 1990s, the mobilization around gender quotas and constitutional reform in Greece grew, drawing momentum and arguments from related processes of mobilization in Europe as well as from EC law. Since the 2001 constitutional reform, the legislating of gender quotas in politics has largely taken place as an instrumental but half-hearted concession by the country's main political parties. They did so under pressure from a coalition of women's organizations under the aegis of the HLWR, together with female parliamentarians and politicians, and supported by the state agency General Secretariat for Gender Equality. While these actors have monitored the implementation of the quota provisions by political parties, ongoing resistance and attempts to circumscribe their implementation have undermined the effectiveness of the provisions.

Substantive equality and the promoting of women's participation and representation in decision-making bodies remain central goals in the agenda of the General Secretariat. Under its aegis, a lawmaking committee completed in 2012 a draft text on substantive equality between the sexes, intended to form the basis for a draft law. This text contains an amended provision that increases the gender quota for local and national elections from 33 to 40 percent.[47] A number of projects funded by the European Commission have also focused on how to expand women's participation in decision-making.

Overall, the political momentum for further gender quota reform seems to have subsided somewhat. The issue of and discussion around gender quotas is mainly reactivated in pre-election periods. It has remained predominantly a concern of female parliamentarians, a number of women's organizations, and the General Secretariat, without diffusion or awareness of its implications for representation and democracy among a broader array of stakeholders and segments of society. The decline of political momentum has taken place in the context of the economic and political crisis in Greece since 2010, during which quota reform seems to have been relegated to the back burner.

---

[47] See "Draft law for the substantive equality of the sexes" (Schedio nomou gia tin ousiastiki isotita ton fylon), General Secretariat of Gender Equality, available at: www.isotita.gr/wp-content/uploads/2017/04/Nomosxedio-Isotita.pdf (accessed 30 August 2017).

At the same time, and despite the limited effectiveness of the established gender quotas, there has been a change in terms of understanding the gender regime. The idea of separate spheres, to which men and women belong and have different functions, and which must be accommodated through formal equality understood in the Aristotelian sense, enjoys much less currency now than it did in the past. Instead, the dominant discursive and policy frame is shaped by the notion of substantive equality that legitimates state action to ensure equal opportunities but also seeks to incorporate women into the public sphere of politics. At the same time, the idea of gender parity as a new desirable democratic threshold has only superficially permeated Greek public discourse around gender equality. In the limited references to parity by female politicians and feminists, it is not regarded as an idea distinctive from quotas. Neither is it elaborated in connection with ideas about democracy and citizenship, besides some general references to the democratic deficit stemming from the substantive exclusion of 50 percent of the population.

Pantelidou-Malouta (2014, 113) confirms that parity has been increasingly raised as a goal in Greek politics over the past couple of years, "without, however, the ideological legitimation that it had in France, based on the substantive differentiation of gender as a social subject. By contrast [here in Greece the demand] is advanced as a higher and fairer quota, at times of temporary character, against women's exclusion." She adds that parity "is the only legitimate way of promoting the demand [of balanced representation of the sexes] from the point of view of democratic theory" (ibid.). While the implications of gender parity as a democratic goal are thus discussed in academic writing, they have not permeated public discourse or policy initiatives. The predominant frame of gender equality in the public and policy-related discourse is largely shaped by the idea of substantive equality, such as in the title of the draft text prepared by the General Secretariat.

In the past few years there has been some discussion about increasing women's participation in the management boards of companies, mainly among associations representing private companies, and largely in response to the respective EC initiative.[48] Yet, the issue of a

---

[48] See for instance the event organized in 2012 by the Greek Association of Enterprise Management, and the Greek Council for Corporate Governance, covered in Christina Damoulianou, "Neoi kanones gia simmetochi gynaikon sta D.S. ton

gender quota, even in publicly owned companies, has not been raised by women's movements, parliamentarians or the General Secretariat for Gender Equality. The draft text on substantive equality mentioned above rewards enterprises in the private sector that promote the balanced participation of women in their management bodies, as well as among all categories of employees.[49]

In sum, since their adoption in the early 2000s, gender quotas in politics have progressively contributed to increasing, albeit far from dramatically, women's presence in national and local politics in Greece. A trend of upward progression had already been underway well before the quota reform at the national level. Women's presence in the national parliament increased from 6 percent in 1996 to 22 percent in 2015. However, achieving real, substantive gender equality in politics is not feasible through quotas, but requires a deeper commitment by political actors, as well as systematic feminist engagement and mobilization.

References
Anagnostou, Dia. 2013. "Gender Constitutional Reform, Positive Measures and Transnational Dynamics in Greece and the EU: From formal to substantive equality?" *Canadian Journal of Law and Society* 28 (1): 133–50.
1991. "The Feminist Movement in Greece After 1974: Feminism and Politics, Issues and Strategies," unpublished paper (with the author).
Bereni, Laure. 2007. "French Feminists Renegotiate Republican Universalism: The Gender Parity Campaign." *French Politics* 5: 191–209.
Cox, Katherine. 1998. "Positive Action in the EU: From *Kalanke to Marschall*." *Columbia Journal of Gender and Law* 8 (1): 101–42.
Gerapetritis, Yorgos. 2006. "Ta thetika metra sto syntagma: to taksidi pros tin ousiastiki isotita" [Positive measures in the Constitution: the journey towards substantive equality]. In *Pente Chronia meta ti Syntagmatiki Anatheorisi tou 2001* [Five Years After the 2001 Constitutional Reform], edited by Ksenophon Kontiadis, 541–71. Athens: Sakkoulas.
"H Ellinida stin Politiki" [The Greek woman in politics]. 1982. *O Agonas tis Gynaikas* 15 (July–September).
Hart, Janet. 1996. *New Voices in the Nation – Women and the Greek Resistance 1941–1964.* Ithaca: Cornell University Press.

---

eisigmenon" [New rules for women's participation in the administrative boards of the companies in the stock market], *Kathimerini*, 26 October 2013.
[49] Draft text of law-making committee for substantive equality of the sexes.

Iliopoulos-Strangas, J. and S.-I. Koutnatzis. 2011. "Greece." In *Constitutional Courts as Positive Legislators*, edited by Allan-Randolph Brewer Carías. Cambridge: Cambridge University Press, 539–571.

Kapotas, Panagiotis. 2005. "Gender Equality and Positive Measures for Women in Greece." Paper for the 2nd London School of Economics PhD Symposium on Modern Greece: Current Social Science, 10 June.

Kapotas, Panos. 2010. "Gender Quotas in Politics: The Greek System in the light of EU law." *European Law Journal* 16 (1): 29–46.

Koukoulis-Spiliotopoulos, Sophia. 2001. "H tropopoiisi tou arthrou 116 § 2 tou syntagmatos – apo tin tipiki stin ousiastiki isotita ton fylon" [The reform of Art. 116(2) of the constitution – from formal to substantive gender equality]. *Dikaiomata tou Anthropou* 10: 509–28.

———. 2006. "Greece: From Formal to Substantive Gender Equality – The leading role of the jurisprudence and the contribution of women's NGOs." In *Essays in Honour of Alice Yiotopoulos-Marangopoulos*, edited by A. Manganas, 659–700. Athens: Nomiki Vivliothiki/Bruylant.

———. 2008. "Greece." *European Gender Equality Law Review* 2: 57–9.

Krook, Mona Lena. 2007. "National Solution or Model from Abroad? Analyzing International Influences on the Parity Movement in France." *French Politics* 5: 3–19.

Manesis, Aristovoulos. 1983. "H syntagmatiki kathierosi tis isonomias metaksy andron kai gynaikon." [The constitutional acceptance of equality between men and women]. *Dikaio kai Politiki* 4.

Mateo Diaz, Mercedes, and Susan Millns. 2004. "Parity, Power and Representative Politics: The Elusive Pursuit of Gender Equality in Europe." *Feminist Legal Studies* 12: 279–302.

Meier, Petra. 2012. "From Laggard to Leader: Explaining the Belgian Gender Quotas and Parity Clause." *West European Politics* 35 (2): 362–79.

Panaretou, Soula. 2009. "H panevropaiki ekstratia tou Evropaikou Lobby Gynaikon gia tis Evroekloges 2009, kai h proothisi tis stin Ellada" [The pan-European campaign of the EWL for the 2009 European Parliament elections and its promotion in Greece]. *Agon tis Gynaikas* 86.

Pantelidou-Malouta, Maro. 2014. *Domes Politikis Ekousias* [Structures of Political Power]. Athens: KETHI.

Papadopoulou, Lina. 2006. "Gynaikeia simmetochi kai dimokrateia: oi pos-ostoseis ypo to phos tis syntagmatikis kai politikis theorias" [Women's participation and democracy: Quotas in the light of constitutional and political theory]. *Dikaiomata tou Anthropou* 32: 219–74.

Pikramenos, Michalis. 2005. "H posostosi fylou stiw ekloges ton OTA kai h nomologia tou Symvouliou tis Epikrateias" [The gender quota in local government elections and the jurisprudence of the Council of State]. Unpublished paper.

Samiou, Demetra. 2012. "So Difficult to be Considered as Citizens: The History of Women's Suffrage in Greece, 1864–2001." In *The Struggle for Female Suffrage in Europe – Voting to Become Citizen*, edited by Blanca Rodriguez Ruiz, Ruth Rubio-Marín, 439–52. Leiden: Brill.

Śledzińska-Simon, Anna, and Adam Bodnar. 2013. "Gender Equality from Beneath: Electoral Gender Quotas in Poland." *Canadian Journal of Law and Society* 28 (1): 151–68.

Spiliotopoulos, E. 1983. "Judicial Review of Legislative Acts in Greece." *Temple Law Quarterly* 56: 463–502.

Stratighaki, Maria. 2006. "Politikes gia tin isotita ton fylon stin Ellada" [Policies for gender equality in Greece]. In *Evropaiki Oloklirosi kai Ellada*, edited by Napoleon Maravegias and Theodoros Sakellaropoulos, 279–300. Athens: Dionikos.

Yotopoulos-Marangopoulos, Alice. 1998a. *Affirmative Action: Towards Effective Gender Equality*. Athens: Sakkoulas/Bruylant.

1998b. "Dipli Niki – Vouli kai Symvoulio tis Epikrateias apodechontai ousiastiki isotita kai thetika metra yper ton gynaikon" [Double victory – Parliament and CoS accept substantive equality and positive measures in favor of women]. *Agonas tis Gynaikas* 65: 1–3.

1998c. "Oikoumeniki Diakiriksi Dikaiomaton tou Anthropou kai Ousiastiki Isotita" [Universal Declaration of Human Rights and Substantive Equality]. *Nomiko Vima* 46: 1572–8.

1998. "Historiki strofi tou StE pros pragmatiki isotita: Scholio stis apofaseis tis olomeleias tou StE 1933/1998 kai 1917–1929/1998" [The historical turn of the Council of State towards substantive equality: Comment on the decisions of the CoS plenum 1933/1998 and 1917–1929/1998]. *To Syntagma* 4: 773–87.

2000. "Pros statheropoiisi mias sovaris kataktisis – h ousiastiki isotita sto neo syntagma" [Towards ensuring a major achievement – substantive equality in the new constitution]. *Agonas tis Gynaikas* 69.

2002. "Kataktontas tin politiki isotita" [Gaining political equality]. Gynaika kai Politiki – 50 chronia gynaikeias psifou [Women and Politics – Fifty Years of female vote], special issue of *Kathimerini* (15 December): 22–3.

2007. "Protasi diataksis kai aitiologiki ekthesi gia ti simetochi ton gynaikon toulachiston kata to 1/3 sta psifodeltia ton vouleftikon eklogon" [Proposal and explanatory report for the participation of at least one third women in party candidate lists for parliamentary elections]. Athens, 23 October 2007.

ANNEX

TABLE 5.1   Greek quota legislation

Law	Title	Quota	Level targeted	Sanctions
Law 2085/1992, Art. 29	Regulation of issues related to the organization, operation and personnel of Public Administration	At least one woman in every service council	Service Councils in public administration	None
Law 2839/2000, Art. 6 § 1	Regulation of issues of the Ministry of Interior, Public Administration, Decentralization	One third of appointed members must be of each sex	Service Councils, collective bodies appointed by the public administration and local government	None
Law 2910/2001, Art. 75 § 1	Entry and stay of foreigners and other provisions	One third of candidates must be of each sex	Political party candidates in elections for municipal councils and for local councils	Non-registration of the party's candidate list
Law 3463/2006, Art. 34 § 3	Code of Municipalities and Communes	One third of candidates must be of each sex	Political party candidates in elections for municipal and commune councils, as well as local councils	Non-registration of the party's candidate list
Law 3636/2008, Art. 3; and Presidential Decree 26/2012, Art. 34 §6	Amendment of Law 3231/2004 "Election of MPs"; Legislation for the election of MPs	One third of candidates must be of each sex	Political party candidates in national elections	

(cont.)

TABLE 5.1   (*cont.*)

Law	Title	Quota	Level targeted	Sanctions
Law 3653/2008, Art. 57	Institutional frame for research and technology	One third of members must be of each sex	National Council for Research and Technology, sector-specific research councils, and evaluation committees for research project proposals	
Law 3839/2010, Art. 2	Selection of managers and directors of administrative units on basis of objective and meritocratic criteria	One third must be of each sex	Service councils at high and mid-level public administration	
Law 3852/2010, Art. 8 § 3, and Art. 120 § 3	New Architecture of Self-Govt. and Decentralized Administration	One third of candidates must be of each sex	Political party candidates in elections for municipal and regional councils	Non-registration of the party's candidate list
Law 4255/2014, Art. 3 § 3	Election of Members of European Parliament and other provisions	One third of candidates must be of each sex	Political party candidates or candidates of political party coalitions	

Source: Table compiled by author on the basis of information provided by the General Secretariat for Gender Equality, available at www.isotita.gr/index.php/docs/c104/?theme=print

CHAPTER SIX

EPPUR SI MUOVE

The Tortuous Adoption and Implementation of Gender Quotas in Conservative Italy

Alessia Donà

In Italy, the road to increase female representation in elected bodies has been bumpy. Legislative quotas were first introduced for both local and national elections in the early 1990s and subsequently nullified by the Constitutional Court in 1995. The 2000s witnessed pro-electoral-quota constitutional amendments and a shift in the Court's interpretative frame, while the Berlusconi centre-right governments (IV 2001–6; V 2008–11) took an ambiguous position towards gender quotas, adopting them in some domains (European Parliament (EP) elections; corporate board composition) and resisting in others (national and local elections). After the fall of Berlusconi in 2011, the phase of the technocratic government (Monti 2011–13) and the start of the grand coalition governments (Letta 2013–14, Renzi 2014–16, Gentiloni 2016–present), Italy is experiencing a "wave" of quota legislation, adopted for municipal elections in 2012, European elections in 2014, national elections in 2015 and 2017, and regional elections in 2016.

This chapter focuses on the interplay between the institutions of the Parliament, the government, and the Constitutional Court, and on the role of the women's movement and the Women's Policy Agencies (WPAs) in a context of increasingly complex multilevel influences arising from the European Union (EU) and other international organizations. The following questions will be addressed: when equal gender representation has moved onto the agenda, how has it been addressed; what discourses and rhetorics have been predominant; what actors or group of actors have acted in favour of or against the adoption of promotional measures for a more gender-balanced representation; what conditions and processes have facilitated the adoption of gender quotas? And finally, has the adoption of gender quotas challenged the dominant conception of female Italian citizenship and the broader conservative gender regime? To answer these questions, I conducted research using data from official records, government declarations and speeches, parliamentary debates and reports, and wider media coverage. The argument advanced here is that despite the introduction of significant legal measures to increase the presence of women in politics, in many other domains (rigid labour market organization, discriminatory educational system, poor family service, diffuse male violence) conditions still persist that negatively affect the capacity of women to act as full citizens, as evidenced by rankings in the 2016 Global Gender Gap Report. These mixed results might be explained through the different attitude of the Italian political elite towards the EU and its policies for gender equality, alternating between the Euroenthusiasm of the centre-left coalition and Euroscepticism of the centre-right coalition.

The chapter is organized to cover the period from the early 1990s onwards and it is divided into four chronological sections: the fall of the First Republic in the early 1990s; the period of alternation between centre-right and centre-left government (1996–2011), and of the government of experts led by Mario Monti (2011–13); and finally, the phase of the grand coalition governments (2013–present), with special attention paid to the two-year period of the government headed by Matteo Renzi (February 2014–December 2016), during which significant reforms were approved. In each of these sections, the main legislative initiatives, political debates, decisions, or other relevant political events will be considered. The conclusion will outline the main results.

6.1 THE COLLAPSE OF THE ITALIAN *PARTITOCRAZIA* AND THE ELECTORAL REFORMS

In the early 1990s, the old party system and its governing parties (Christian Democracy Party, Socialist Party, Social Democratic Party, Republican Party, and Liberal Party) abruptly collapsed due to the investigation of the Milan prosecutors into large-scale political corruption and the diffuse practice of illegal financing of parties (Cotta 2015). The decline of the traditional party actors opened a window of opportunity for the mobilization of new actors.

6.1.1 The 1993 and 1995 Electoral Legislation with Gender Measures

Electoral reform was considered the best way to transform the Italian consensual democracy towards a competitive logic of functioning based on political alternation (Fabbrini 2009). Specifically, between 1993 and 1995, three laws were adopted which modified the existing electoral systems for the appointment of representatives at the local and national levels (Guadagnini 2005). These laws were:

(1) Law no. 81 of 25 March 1993, concerning the election of mayors, presidents of provincial governments, and members of the municipal and provincial councils. This law established that neither sex could account for more than two-thirds of the candidates listed for election to municipal and provincial councils. Thus, this measure (list quota) ensured that political parties would include women in their candidate lists, but did not guarantee that women would be elected (since the voters could freely express their candidate preferences).

(2) Law no. 277 of 4 August 1993, "New regulations for the election of the Chamber of Deputies," which stated that 75 per cent of seats were to be assigned with a uninominal (first-past-the-post) electoral system and 25 per cent with a proportional one. The law established that for the 155 (out of 630) proportionally elected seats in the Chamber of Deputies, the candidate lists should be composed of both sexes in alternating order (zipping) in a frozen (*bloccate*) list, where the voters do not vote for individuals but rather for parties, and the seats are distributed according to the votes received by the parties (where the candidates at the top of the list are more likely to be elected).

(3) Law no. 43 of 23 February 1995, which applied the same rule as Law no. 81 to the election of regional councillors.

The measures introduced by these laws prescribed two different ways to promote an increase of female representation in elected offices: by fixing a certain minimum proportion of women on the party candidate lists (30 per cent in local elections), and by imposing an alternating order for female and male candidates in the party lists for national elections. These measures were the results of coordinated pressure from women in parliament and women in WPAs. In a context of political and economic crisis, and a consequent loss of legitimacy by the male political leadership, space opened up for the activity and influence of previously marginal actors. Among them, two eminent female politicians were able to build a cross-political alliance in favour of electoral gender quotas: Tina Anselmi (Christian Democracy Party), then president of the National Commission for Equality and Equal Opportunities,[1] and Livia Turco (Democrats of the Left, former Italian Communist Party), a deputy and active campaigner for the rights of women. During the debate on these measures, the WPA strategically used the EU guidelines and directives, as they had previously in pushing for legislation to remove obstacles to women's access to the workplace.[2]

However, the consensus on these measures was not unanimous. During the parliamentary debate, a split opened between the centre (Christian Democracy Party) and left-wing parties (Democrats of the Left, Rifondazione Comunista), traditionally close to the feminist movement and its claims, and the extreme-right-wing party (Italian Social Movement, MSI-AN), which viewed gender quotas as a system resembling that of protecting an endangered species. Exponents of the business world expressed their position against quotas to media, underlining the idea that women must progress on the basis of their own abilities and not through a regime of special protection by law. Their opposition fuelled a dominant cultural stance contrary to any system promoting the greater presence of women in politics. Nonetheless, the provisions for national and regional elections were finally approved, for many reasons including the weakness of the policy subsystems, the majoritarian view that gender provisions would not be considered compulsory, and the general expectation that the Constitutional Court would certainly reject the measure (which in fact happened).

The women's movement's involvement was minimal, and the movement remained fragmented during the political debate, similarly to the lack of alliance between women's associations during the period of struggle for female suffrage (Mancini 2012). To understand this

[1] The Commission was set up in 1984 as part of the Prime Minister's Office, with the task of providing assistance and guidance on activities to be carried out to achieve gender equality in all sectors. The composition includes representatives of the parties, social partners, women's associations, and other members of society. It was supposed to be the arena to channel the demands of civil society (Guadagnini and Donà 2007).

[2] In 1991 (Law no. 125/1991) and 1992 (Law no. 215/1992), the Parliament enacted two laws with the goal of creating spaces for women in a variety of workplaces by adopting various promotional measures (*azioni positive*) and a national fund for promoting female entrepreneurs (see Donà 2011).

situation, we must recall that from the late 1960s to the present day the women's movement has been characterized by the conflict between emancipation and liberation: "Emancipation means working from within existing systems and trying to change them, whereas liberation implies a complete overthrow of the status quo" (Pojmann 2005, 74). This cleavage emerged again in the case of gender quotas. The feminist autonomous groups and cultural centres of difference feminism – though uninterested in politics – opposed the quota system on the grounds that it ratified the weakness of women (as they would be seen as requiring special measures to enter into male institutions) and their subordination to men (whose support was ultimately needed for quotas to be approved). By contrast, the more politically integrated part of the movement – closer to the parties on the left – was in favour of the greater representation of women within political institutions but was divided on how to achieve it (Guadagnini 2005). Because of these internal divisions, the issue of female political representation did not enter the public agenda but remained largely a matter for "insiders" (i.e. women in the institutions and femocrats).

The media contributed to the marginalization of the issue of equal representation and moreover associated a negative connotation with the quota system. They described it as a corporative measure, a dispute among the few women with seats in parliament, and in general an issue marginal to the more important debate on the electoral reform intended to establish a new model of democracy. Finally, of note is the absence of a cultural debate (in the media and in academia) informing the public about the reasons for the adoption of promotional measures in parliament and furnishing a more comparative and international account of equal representation (Guadagnini 2003). Consequently, the quotas came into effect without adequate public knowledge and without substantial political and civil legitimacy.

6.1.2   The 1995 Ruling of the Constitutional Court

In September 1995 a ruling by the Constitutional Court[3] declared that the measures introduced for increasing female political representation were unconstitutional. The Court at that time was composed of twelve men and no women. Only in 1996 was the first woman nominated as a

---

[3] Italian Constitutional Court, Judgment no. 422/1995, 12 September 1995, accessed 20 July 2016, available at: www.cortecostituzionale.it.

member of the Court by the President of the Republic (as of February 2018, the Court counts three women out of fourteen members).

The case was started by the elector Giovanni Maio, according to whom Law no. 81/1993 was violated when only one woman was included in the party list for the town council election of Baranello (a small village in Molise, with a population below 15,000 inhabitants), while art. 5, para. 2 of that law prescribed a candidate list with at most two-thirds of the same sex. The case was referred to the Constitutional Court when the Council of State (Consiglio di Stato) raised doubts about whether the law was legitimate according to art. 3 ("All citizens have equal social dignity and are equal in front of the law, without distinction of sex, race, language, religion, public opinion, personal, and social condition. It is the task of the Republic to remove all obstacles of an economic or social nature that in any way restrict the liberty and equality of citizens, preventing the full development of the person and the effective participation of all workers in the political, economic and social organization of the country") and art. 51 ("All citizens of one or the other sex have access to public offices and to elective mandates under equal conditions, according to the rules established by law") of the Constitution.

The Constitutional Court, taking a formalistic interpretation of the constitutional articles, declared art. 5, para. 2 of Law no. 81/1993 unconstitutional and extended this interpretation to the provisions of Law no. 277/1993 and 43/1995, thus cancelling all of the electoral quotas introduced in that period. In the Court's view, art. 51 of the Constitution, which provides for equal access by women and men to public and elective offices, had an absolute value, meaning that equality does not permit any gender consideration or differentiation in politics. In this judgment, the Court emphasized that the political rights of every citizen are absolute rights that cannot be limited in favour of citizens belonging to a disadvantaged group (Palici di Suni 2012). The Court specified that affirmative actions and special measures are admissible only in the economic realm (as ruled in Judgment no. 109/1993), not in the political realm. According to the Court's interpretation, the kind of quotas introduced did not aim to remove the obstacles that impede women from reaching political position but give these results directly to them (Judgment no. 422/1995, § 6). The Constitutional Court states: "Any differentiation on grounds of sex cannot but be discriminatory, in that it diminishes for some citizens the concrete content of a fundamental right in favour of other citizens belonging to a

group deemed disadvantaged" (§ 6). However, the Court did not analyse the substantial differences between the quota for candidate lists
and the alternate seating of women and men on the lists but considered
them as interchangeable measures and declared both unconstitutional.
The Court concluded by suggesting that although they are unconstitutional when introduced by law, electoral quotas may be voluntarily
adopted by political parties, associations, or groups that participate in
the elections (§ 7).[4]

6.2 THE QUOTA DEBATE DURING THE PERIOD OF POLITICAL ALTERNATION

The period 1994–2011 was characterized by the alternation in government between centre-left and centre-right coalitions. A right-wing
coalition composed by the new party Forza Italia (Go Italy; Raniolo
2006), Northern League, and MSI-AN won the elections in 1994 and
ruled until 1996 (due to Berlusconi's resignation). During that time a
new right-wing feminism emerged, since the women elected in Forza
Italia were not part of the Italian feminist movement and stood against
any measure that promoted them simply as women instead of as women
with merits.

In the April 1996 elections, won by the centre-left coalition, the
number of women elected decreased after the abolition of the quotas: the Chamber of Deputies dropped from 15.1 per cent women in
1994 to 11.3 per cent, and the same declining trend was registered
for the local-level elections. However, the creation of the Ministry for
Equal Opportunities in 1996 and the appointment of ministers with
experience in the women's movement (such as Anna Finocchiaro in
1996 and Laura Balbo in 1998) opened points of access and influence
to national policymaking. Moreover, a closer collaboration between
the government and the EU was established in transposing directives,
as well as increased reference to EU discourse and frame guidelines
when promoting legal domestic changes in a traditionally conservative context (Donà 2011; Lombardo and Sangiuliano 2009). During
this period, a major constitutional reform concerning the reallocation

---

[4] After the sentence, a small group of jurists reacted against the decision of the
Constitutional Court (Carlassarre 1997; Beccalli 1999). However, the discussion
remained confined to a few specialized journals and books, without opening a great
public debate.

of competences between the national and local authorities took place (Constitutional Law no. 3/2001; see below for more details). The subsequent victory of a centre-right coalition in the May 2001 general election, and the following change in government, meant the paralysis of Italian state feminism, the exclusion of women's organizations from policymaking (Guadagnini and Donà 2007), and the adoption of a more sceptical attitude towards the EU (Carbone 2009). The centre-right government attempted to reform the Constitution but with results well below their expectations. Finally, a short-lived centre-left government (2006–8), followed by the return of the centre-right coalition (2008–11) meant that for most of the decade 2001–10 Silvio Berlusconi was Prime Minister, with a significant impact on Italian legislation and culture, maintaining Italy as a right-wing, conservative country (Donovan and Gilbert 2015), prioritizing national interest over that of the EU (Carbone 2009).

Despite the lack of public attention, but thanks to the EU's persisting influence, the issue of increasing the presence of women in politics remained on the agenda, leading to an amendment to Constitution during this period of political alternation. We now turn to examine how this happened, who promoted it, and with what effects.

6.2.1 The 2001 Constitutional Amendments

During the 1996–2001 left-wing governments, the WPAs increased their visibility and operated in a coordinated way to promote balanced representation of men and women in elective offices, supported on this issue by part of the women's movement. After the 1995 decision by the Constitutional Court, a debate influenced by international milestones (1995 UN Beijing Platform for Action and 1997 EU Amsterdam Treaty) emerged among women in the institutions (WPAs members and politicians), urging the modification of the Constitution in order to make possible the introduction of affirmative action by law. In Italy, any constitutional amendment must be adopted by both the lower and upper chambers of the Parliament, twice, with an interval between the votes of no less than three months. An absolute majority is required (art. 138 of the Constitution), and if requested by one-fifth of the members of a House or 500,000 voters or five Regional Councils, the constitutional amendments shall be approved by a popular referendum – except when the amendment has been approved in the second voting by each of the Houses by a majority of two thirds of the members, the referendum shall not be held. Usually the popular referendum is an instrument for opposition parties to contest and nullify the constitutional amendments approved by the governing majority in Parliament.

The National Commission for Equality and Equal Opportunities, chaired by Silvia Costa (Christian Democracy Party), intervened in the ongoing debate on the transformation of the Italian unitary state leading to the adoption in 2001 of the constitutional reform on devolution (Law no. 2/2001 and no. 3/2001) (Guadagnini and Donà 2007). These laws modified Title V (arts. 114–33) of the Constitution to arrange the relationship and the division of competences between the national government and the regions towards a more federal state-like system. This reform put Italy in line with the process of devolution and federalization that was taking place in many countries across Europe (Baldi 2007). The modifications made to art. 117 also recognized regional-level positive measures for gender-balanced representation as legitimate (Law no. 3/2001 of 18 October 2001. The new wording of art. 117, para. 7 stated that "regional laws have to remove all obstacles which prevent the full equality of men and women in social, cultural, and economic life, and promote equal access of men and women to elective offices"; Carlassare 2002). The reform was carried forward by the centre-left government, but not with an overwhelming majority. The centre-right parties (Forza Italia and the Northern League) opposed the constitutional reform because they considered that it did not devolve enough power and would fail to deliver effective fiscal and political autonomy for the regions and the second chamber, for territorial representation. However, the popular referendum, held in autumn 2001 during Berlusconi's second government (after winning the elections in May 2001), had a positive outcome (64.2 per cent approved the motion to change the Constitution, of the 34 per cent of eligible voters who turned out for the referendum).

As of 2017, the distribution of powers between the regions and the central state established in the 2001 structural reform remains in place despite centre-right attempts at counter-reforms (Cotta and Verzichelli 2016). During the 2001 constitutional revision processes, the substantial anti-institutionalism of Italian feminism remained unchallenged and no claims were put forward by women's organizations. Cultural transformation remained the main area of interest and commitment during the post-First Republic period (Campus 2015), and the majority of the women's movement remained at the margins and politically invisible. The 2001 reform instituted a paradox at the constitutional level: while it legitimated possible measures for affirmative action at the regional level, at the level of central government the situation remained unchanged.

6.2.2 The 2003 Constitutional Revision and 2005 Electoral Reform

The constitutional reform was extended to the central level two years later, when in 2003 a modification of art. 51 of the Constitution was approved by a large majority (Law no. 1/2003 of 12 June 2003). The sentence added to article 51 specified: "For this purpose the Republic adopts specific measures in order to promote equal opportunities for women and men." The constitutional change was initiated by centre-left women MPs during the left-wing government and later approved under the centre-right government headed by Berlusconi (2001–6) when the Minister for Equal opportunities, Stefania Prestigiacomo, a Sicilian woman with no connection with the women's movement, successfully invoked a cross-party alliance of women MPs. The main frame dominating the debate referred to the declining number of elected women and the need to adopt affirmative actions to neutralize the negative impact of the semi-majoritarian electoral system introduced in 1993. The influences of other European countries where female representation rose during the 1990s (and especially that of France, where the Constitution was amended in 1999), together with the recommendations and guidelines on equal representation adopted by international institutions (United Nations declarations, European Union Charter of Fundamental Rights, Council of Europe conventions), figured in the arguments in favour of the constitutional amendment (Guadagnini 2005).

Also, on this occasion the reform was enacted without any public debate. Once again, the women's movement was fragmented: on one side was the integrated movement (elected women, femocrats, women activists, experts, and associations) which participated in the debate; on the other was the "difference feminism" movement, closer to the left, which kept out of the discussion, giving low priority to the issue (Guadagnini 2005). The only women to apply pressure and to act to raise awareness were those in parliament, who formed alliances across parties.

When the time came to implement the constitutional reform by approving an electoral law on gender quotas, strong resistance emerged from the parties, as shown by the negative ending of the 2005 debate on electoral reform which replaced the semi-majoritarian system with a proportional system and a majority premium (Law no. 270/2005), but without the adoption of a gender quota (Regalia 2015). During the debate, many MPs belonging to both rightist and leftist parties contended that women had no need of quotas and therefore opposed their adoption, while other members continued to consider quotas unconstitutional, despite the reform of art. 51 (Donà 2007).

In late 2005, Minister Prestigiacomo – in opposition to her own party – presented a legislative initiative for the introduction of a quota system in candidate party lists, but she was unable to mobilize support from women's associations and the end of the legislative session in April 2006 quickly stopped its progress. Consensus and alliance between women in the movement and women in politics – the most important factor for the adoption of gender quotas (Krook 2009; Lovenduski 2008) – was lacking. During the centre-right coalition government, the WPA system was restructured and weakened (the National Commission was transferred under the control of the minister and became less independent), most of the legislation passed was inspired by a conservative and repressive approach, and the EU was under attack in Italy for its highly bureaucratic procedures and distance from citizens.

The absence of civil society support (Della Porta 2003) and the emerging scepticism towards the EU, together with the lack of a majoritarian political consensus to undertake substantive reform, may be the explanatory factors behind the Italian difficulties in introducing a gender quota system at the national level. The contradictory sequence of constitutional reforms – with first the amendments relative to the regions and then the national amendment – reflected a weakness of political will (Palici di Suni 2012). As we have seen, the first constitutional reform was approved by a centre-left government and the second by a centre-right one. Both governments needed to appear committed to an improved gender balance in politics (in front of European partners, EU institutions, and international obligations like the Convention on the Elimination of All Forms of Discrimination Against Women [CEDAW]). So we may define the 2003 constitutional reform as a case of symbolic reform, "which occurs when policy designed to address certain social problems fails to effectively solve these problems. Often, before symbolic policies are even formalized, decision-makers, more interested in image making than problem solving, design policy statements with no teeth" (Mazur 1996, 2). Moreover, the approval came not after wide-ranging domestic debate, but mainly through a desire to emulate neighbouring countries (France) and an absorption of EU and international indications. Interestingly, in the same period, quotas were adopted for the 2004 EP elections, and some of the twenty regions decided to implement their own quota system, as we will explore below.

6.2.3 The 2004 Legislation for EP Elections

While the Parliament resisted the introduction of a quota system for the national elections, paradoxically, on 8 April 2004, it approved legislation for the EP elections that established a two-thirds quota in the party candidate lists valid for the elections of 2006 and 2010.[5] However, it is not so surprising that Italian MPs voted in favour of a gender quota for the EP elections, which are traditionally considered second-order elections, since a seat in the EP is less powerful than a seat in the national parliament. During the debate, while the centre-left women and the WPA demanded equal presence (50/50), as the EP recommended, the then Minister for Equal Opportunities, Prestigiacomo – supported by the centre-right women – favoured the 30 per cent quota system that was finally adopted. The use by feminist activists and by the WPA of arguments relating to the European discourse on gender equality in decision-making (MacRae 2012) played an important role in pressuring members of parliament to vote for the legislation, but the goal of gender parity remained distant. As an effect of the quota, female representation doubled in the following two electoral rounds from 11 per cent in 2006 to 22 per cent in 2010. The legislation was renewed and strengthened in 2014 for the EP elections of 25 May 2014 (Law no. 65/2014; see below for details).

6.2.4 Government vs. Regions: The Decisive Role of the Constitutional Court

If the central government was reluctant to approve electoral quotas for national elections, to the contrary almost all twenty regions (except four: Basilicata, Liguria, Molise, and Piemonte) decided to implement gender quotas, as legitimated by the 2001 constitutional revisions. This path of local governments acting as front-runners for national legislation echoes the progression by which the Italian regions recognized local voting rights of women well in advance of national recognition (Mancini 2012). The measures adopted included list party quotas

---

[5] Law no. 90/2004 "Norme in materia di elezioni dei membri del Parlamento europeo e altre disposizioni inerenti ad elezioni da svolgersi nell'anno 2004."

varying from 30 per cent (Sicily, Val d'Aosta in 2005) to 40 per cent (Friuli Venezia Giulia in 2007) and/or the "double gender preference" (*doppia preferenza di genere*) system (in which the voter may express two preferences only for candidates of different sexes). Both these measures were contested for supposed unconstitutionality by the centre-right government then in power, who appealed twice to the Constitutional Court (via review *principaliter*, used for issues related to the constitutionality of legislation that can be raised only before special constitutional courts; Cappelletti 1971). In both cases, the Court ruled in favour of the regions.

These two rulings of the Constitutional Court (no. 49/2003 on the 2002 Valle d'Aosta electoral legislation and no. 4/2010 on the 2009 Campania electoral legislation) shaped the judicial interpretation of affirmative action measures and the prosecution of the gender quota debate. The two promotional measures declared legitimate by these judgments (i.e. the list quota and the *doppia preferenza di genere*) afterwards expanded into the electoral legislation for municipal (Law no. 215/2012), European (Law no. 65/2014), national (Law no. 52/2015), and regional (Law no. 20/2016) elections.

In Judgment no. 49/2003,[6] the Court declared the constitutionality of the electoral rules of the Valle d'Aosta region, which required the presence of both sexes (without establishing a proportion) on every electoral list of candidates, meaning that a list composed of only male (or only female) candidates would be declared invalid (Brunelli 2003). According to the government, which challenged the law, such measures would jeopardize the electoral rights of citizens of both sexes and would diminish the absolute political rights of every citizen as stated under arts. 3 and 51 of the Constitution and affirmed by the Constitutional Court's ruling no. 422/1995. Here the Court's interpretation differs from the 1995 decision, and the Court itself recognizes the change of perspective. The decision is framed "in light of a constitutional frame of reference that has evolved with respect to the one current at the time of the 1995 pronouncement, in particular after the 2001 constitutional revision by laws 2 and 3/2001 and the ongoing 2003 debate on the art. 51 reformulation" (Judgment no. 49/2003, § 4), and continues:

> The revised constitutional frame explicitly recognizes the goal of gender balance and declares admissible the introduction by law of measures

---

[6] Italian Constitutional Court, Judgment no. 49/2003, 13 February 2003, accessed 20 July 2016, available at: www.cortecostituzionale.it.

that promote equal access to public offices. In light of this frame, the Constitutional Court declared admissible the promotional measure adopted in Valle d'Aosta because the legal obligation to include both sexes in the electoral list of candidates affects only the list and those in charge of preparing the list [the parties]. (§ 3.1)

In the reasoning of the Court, the measure introduced expresses the intent to facilitate political representation of citizens and to realize an "effective gender balance between men and women, given the uncontroversial fact that elected assemblies are characterized by a gender imbalance, where women are underrepresented" (§ 4). As the Court clearly explains, by imposing an obligation, the Valle d'Aosta legal disposition reduces the freedom of the parties to prepare candidate lists "without a direct limitation of the fundamental rights of the citizens" (§ 3.1), since belonging to one sex or another is neither the criterion to be elected nor to be selected as a candidate. In sum, when the legal obligation affects the pre-electoral phase of party list formation (under control of the parties), the passive and active electoral rights of citizens remain unaltered; the vote decides who wins, while the party list measure aims to remove an obstacle against female participation in the party selection process (Califano 2003).

With this judgment, the Court declared legitimate any measure that uses gender neutral wording, does not specifically advantage women, and therefore respects the formal principle of equality: "The measure refers to candidates of both sexes, and does not imply a differentiated treatment in favour of citizens belonging to a disadvantaged group" (§ 4.1). Moreover, according to the Court, the measure introduced in Valle d'Aosta is a minimal attempt ("by prohibiting the total exclusion of candidates of one sex from the party list") to remove discrimination against one sex in candidate selection, while other more effective measures will be required in the Italian case in general (§ 4.1). The Court also cited the international obligations for more gender-balanced representation signed by Italy, such as the 1979 CEDAW and the 2000 European Charter of Fundamental Rights, thus underlining the broader frame of reference for its interpretative role, beyond the Italian Constitution (§ 4).

During the IV Berlusconi government (2006–11), the Campania region introduced Law no. 4/2009, instituting both a two-thirds quota in electoral lists and a new measure, *doppia preferenza di genere* (double gender preferences), innovative for Italy and for Europe (Califano 2010). In this case the elector may express two preferences for two candidates of different sexes. Again the right-wing government challenged the regional law on the grounds that it unconstitutionally limited the electoral rights of citizens under arts. 3 and 51 of the Constitution, but in Judgment no. 4/2010,[7] the Constitutional Court confirmed the legitimacy of the measure adopted to promote equal access to representation on the basis that norms such as those subject to judicial scrutiny could only furnish voters with further possibilities of choice, without affecting the electoral result" (Judgment no. 4/2010, § 3.3). The Court further argued that "the uncertainty of the result demonstrates that the censured norm envisages, not a constrictive mechanism, but solely a promotional one, in the spirit of the constitutional and statutory provisions" (§ 4). Coherent with the constitutional framework and the previous judgment, the Court (re)affirmed that all norms that are gender neutral and are merely promotional in the candidate selection stage do not violate the Constitution. Moreover, the Court denounced the persisting female underrepresentation in elected councils, citing the cultural, economic, and social factors that impede real and effective equal opportunities between men and women, despite the principle of formal equality for election.

6.3 GENDER QUOTAS FOR BOARD COMPOSITION AND LOCAL ELECTIONS (2011–13)

The financial, political, and sexual scandals surrounding the figure of Berlusconi and his declining international reputation, together with the severe economic crisis, led President Napolitano to replace him as prime minister in November 2011 with Mario Monti, a university professor and former European Commissioner. The Monti government, composed of experts and sustained by a unanimous political consensus, approved several reforms in the areas of the labour market, pensions, and public finance control to steer Italy through its debt crisis (Giannetti 2013). During the Monti government, two measures to increase the presence of the underrepresented sex in board membership and the municipal councils were introduced.

6.3.1 The 2012 Implementation of Quotas in the Economic Sector

The Italian law on gender quotas in the economic sector, introduced by Law no. 120/2011 after a tortuous passage through parliament during

---

[7] Italian Constitutional Court, Judgment no. 4/2010, 14 January 2010, accessed 20 July 2016, available at: www.cortecostituzionale.it.

the Berlusconi IV government (Donà 2013), established a phased application of the provision, beginning with a 20 per cent quota for the first board mandate and a 30 per cent gender quota from the second renewal of a company board's mandate. The provision applies to three renewals of boards of directors. The law became effective one year later, in August 2012, after the enactment of executive decrees by the Monti government. In the event that a company disregards the gender quota requirement, a letter of caution is issued for the first mandate in non-compliance, which may be followed in a second case of non-compliance by a fine ranging from 10,000 to 1 million euros. If the non-compliance continues in subsequent mandates, the board of directors will be dissolved. The supervisory authority in the case of listed companies is Consob (the Antitrust Agency), and in the case of state-controlled companies is the prime minister or the minister appointed for equal opportunities, with the support of the Department for Equal Opportunities.

The law was interpreted as a success for the mobilization and alliance among (left- and right-wing) women in parliament, women in the feminist movement, and women managers in industry (Saraceno 2012). In order to understand what facilitated women's cross-party alliance, we must recall that in February 2011 women had taken the streets across Italy under the leadership of the movement *Se non ora quando?* (SNOQ; "If not now, when?"), whose founding committee consisted of Italian women from different backgrounds, such as film-makers, journalists, academics, economists, and politicians. Their objective was to react against Berlusconi's scandals and to denounce the diffused representation of women as sexual objects in television, newspapers, and advertising. This cohesiveness among new and old feminist groups facilitated the introduction of corporate quotas in a country with a persistent vertical segregation in the labour market.

The variety of voices supporting gender quota legislation included leading (male) representatives of the economic system and economists, the press industry (almost unanimously), the Ministers for Equal Opportunity in office, and a cross-party alliance of women in parliament (in fact the law is also named "Mosca and Golfo Law," after the two women proponents from the Democratic Party [Partito Democratico, PD] and the Freedom Party [Popolo delle Libertà, PDL]). The Berlusconi right-wing government, close to the positions of Confindustria (the major organization of employers, that at the time was headed by a woman, Emma Marcegaglia), sought to obstruct the bill by proposing amendments to water down the quota. The bill thus provoked a political and institutional clash between government and parliament whose outcome was a victory of the parliament over the government. The women proponents of the bill were able to invoke a paradigm driven by economic efficiency and utility to build a new discourse on the issues of gender quotas involving many segments of society and not only women's associations. It was also accompanied by lively public and academic debate promoting the increasing presence of the so-called "woman factor" (*Fattore Donna*) in the economy as a driver of economic growth (Casarico and Profeta 2010; Ferrera 2006). This argument proved effective in neutralizing resistance and obstacles against the measure's approval, in a country undergoing severe economic crisis.

6.3.2   The 2012 Legislation for Municipal Elections

Also during 2012, quota systems were approved for the election of local councils and executives. Law no. 215/2012 of 23 November 2012 introduced provisions intended to *gradually* promote gender balance in the local administrations. The bill was promoted by a cross-party coalition of women of the PD and PDL in 2010 during the Berlusconi IV government, and supported by the Minister for Equal Opportunities Mara Carfagna. It took two years for the bill to be approved, and despite a majoritarian consensus across the parties, opinion against these promotional measures persisted during the parliamentary debate.

The law first modified the legislation on municipal council elections. For municipalities with more than 5,000 inhabitants, the law established two measures: the "list quota" (neither of the two sexes may represent more than two-thirds of the candidates on electoral lists; however, only in municipalities with more than 15,000 inhabitants does the failure to respect the quota entail annulment of the list) and the introduction of the "double gender preference," allowing the voter to express two preferences, provided that the preferences are for candidates of different sexes; if not, the second preference is annulled. For all municipalities with up to 15,000 inhabitants, however, the lists of candidates must at least ensure the representation of both sexes.

Second, the mayor and the president of the province must appoint an executive in compliance with the principle of equal opportunities for women and men, ensuring the presence of both sexes (but without a specific gender quota target, until Law no. 56/2014 – see below). Moreover, municipal and provincial statutes must establish rules that "guarantee" – and no longer simply "promote" – the presence of both sexes in the executive and in the non-elected collegial bodies of the municipality and province, as well as of the agencies and institutions dependent on them. In sum, local bodies composed of men only may be declared invalid by the court. Since the introduction of the law, there has been a significant growth of female representation in municipal bodies at the level of both councils and executives.[8]

The provisions concerning the local executive composition were reinforced by a disposal contained by the subsequent Law no. 56/2014 of 26 April 2014 (also known as Delrio Law, named after the government undersecretary in the Renzi cabinet) which introduces important changes in the Italian local government organization and reforms the roles and functions of metropolitan cities and provinces. Art. 1, para. 137 of this law prescribes that "the local executives of municipalities with more than 3,000 inhabitants should include at least 40% representation of each of the two sexes." This means that today, in forming a local government, the mayor is obliged to respect arts. 3 and 51 of the Constitution, the provisions on equal opportunities of Law 267/2000, art. 6 (*Testo Unico degli Enti Locali*) and Law no. 215/2012, and finally the target of 40 per cent introduced by Law no. 56/2014. To enforce these measures, a crucial role was played by the regional administrative courts, such as courts of first instance, and the Council of State, as a court of second instance. In the last ten years, the administrative jurisprudence has recognized the direct applicability of art. 51 of the Constitution, and the compulsory nature of the municipal statutes requiring the promotion of gender equal representation in the composition of local executives (Adamo 2011, 2016). The administrative case law established: the direct and immediate applicability of the norms on equal opportunities; the court jurisdiction on the administrative acts of the mayor, specifically the acts by which the assessors are appointed; and the capacity of women's associations, common citizens, gender equality advisors, and municipal councillors to start a litigation in the case of local executive composition in breach of the principle of gender equal representation (Amato 2011). In the face of a situation where – despite these norms – executives composed of men only

---

[8] Federico De Lucia and Giuseppe Martelli, "Doppia preferenza: raddoppiano le donne nei consigli comunali," Centro Italiano Studi Elettorali, 13 June 2013, accessed 10 February 2016, available at http://cise.luiss.it/cise/2013/06/13/doppia-preferenza-raddoppiano-le-donne-nei-consigli-comunali/.

persist, many petitions filed by the regional gender equality advisors are pending in the regional administrative courts.

6.4 THE QUOTA DEBATE DURING THE GRAND COALITION YEARS

The results of the February 2013 national elections did not bring a clear political majority (D'Alimonte 2013). After a period of political stalemate, first, on March 2013, Enrico Letta (vice-secretary of the PD), then, on February 2014, Matteo Renzi (secretary of the PD since December 2013), and finally, on December 2016, Paolo Gentiloni (PD Foreign Affairs minister during the previous Renzi government) were nominated to form a grand coalition government consisting of the PD, PDL (which after a few months was split between Forza Italia in opposition to and the New Centre Right in favour of the grand coalition), and other minor parties. The Renzi government's activities are examined in this paragraph in the light of its relatively long duration and consequent capacity to promote reforms across policy sectors. After the resignation of Prime Minister Renzi due to the negative result of the constitutional referendum held on 4 December 2016, the institutional crisis was resolved with the appointment of Paolo Gentiloni as the new prime minister, with the specific task of bringing policy continuity and guaranteeing, without more turmoil, the natural end of the parliamentary term in 2018.

The renewed, younger, and more gender balanced parliament (with 31 per cent women, the highest percentage of women members in the history of the republic) affected the government composition, with a significant number of women (from 30 per cent in the Letta government to 50 per cent in the Renzi government, then declined again to 30 per cent in the Gentiloni government), and a significant reduction in the average age of ministers. A new generation of politicians in favour of European integration (Brunazzo and della Sala 2016) acceded to decision-making positions through both election and appointment – a possible explanatory factor behind the impressive wave of gender quota legislation introduced in the last few years, despite the institutional weakening of the WPA, which remained without a political guide from 2013 until May 2016, when Maria Elena Boschi (already serving as Minister for Constitutional Reforms and Relations with the Parliament) was nominated Minister for Equal Opportunities, and the position of head of Department for Equal Opportunities was filled in

January 2017, after years of vacancy. Specifically, during the Renzi government, three electoral laws (described below) with gender quota provisions have been introduced: for the EP, the national elections , and regional elections.

6.4.1   Law No. 65/2014, 22 April 2014, for EP Elections
In early 2014, there was the need to renew the gender disposition of Law no. 90/2004 for the incumbent EP elections, with the aim of introducing more stringent measures to promote female representation in the European legislative branch, since Italy was among the countries with the lowest number of women MEPs (23 per cent), below the European average (29 per cent). The debate started in January 2014 in the Senate, and then continued in the Chamber of Deputies in March:[9] the timeline was strict since the elections were planned for May 2014. The parliament approved Law no. 65/2014 on 22 April 2014, prescribing (from the 2019 EP election onwards) the following measures: the paritarian composition of electoral lists and the triple gender preference. The former mandates that in the party list composition no more than half of the candidates should be of the same sex, otherwise the list shall be declared inadmissible; moreover, the first two candidates in the list must be of different sexes. The latter determines that the elector may express up to three preferences, which should be for candidates of different sexes. If the voter expresses three preferences, two might be for male or female candidates, but the third must be for a candidate of a different sex. If the voter expresses only two preferences for candidates of the same sex, the second preference is annulled; and if all three preferences are for candidates of the same sex, both the second and the third preference are annulled.

The paritarian quota list was the biggest step taken and it was inspired by the EP resolution of 4 July 2013 on improving the practical arrangements for the holding of the European elections in 2014, which "calls on the Member States and the political parties to press for a higher proportion of women on the lists of candidates and, as far as possible, to encourage the drafting of lists that ensure equal representation."[10] The influence of EU discourse on Italian MPs proved to be crucial in the adoption of a 50 per cent gender quota in the composition of candidate

[9]   See "Atto Senato n. 1224," available at: www.senato.it/leg/17/BGT/Schede/Ddliter/comm/43706_comm.htm.
[10]   European Parliament 2013/2102(INI), 4 July 2013.

lists. The incremental approach to reaching gender balance was here abandoned, albeit in the case of the second-order EP elections legislation. Once again, the feminist movement remained on the margins, while indifference prevailed in public opinion and in media coverage, as the PD rapporteur Doris Lo Moro lamented.[11]

Despite the political decision to postpone the gender parity quotas to the 2019 elections, because the candidate list preparation had already begun, and because of the need to maintain the PD–New Centre Right–Forza Italia agreement on the other electoral reform, Italicum (see below), the results of the 2014 European elections recorded a doubling of female representation (40 per cent of the seventy-three seats allocated to Italy were won by women, compared with a European average of 30 per cent).

6.4.2 The Electoral Legislation for National Elections: From Renzi's Italicum to Gentiloni's Rosatellum

Due to the decision on 4 December 2013 of the Constitutional Court,[12] which ruled as unconstitutional major parts of the 2005 electoral law, and after the uncertain results of the 2013 general elections, the issue of electoral reforms moved up the political agenda. During Renzi government, the parliamentary and political debate was monopolized by a proposal of a new electoral law for the election of the Chamber of Deputies resulted from the January 2014 agreement between the PD and Forza Italia. The original text of the Italicum stated that 50 per cent of the candidates on an electoral list should be women, without requiring the genders to alternate in the list. During the first reading in the Chamber of the Deputies, the alternating order was presented as an amendment by an alliance of women MPs of the centre-right and centre-left, but during the floor voting on 10 March 2014 it was rejected through a secret ballot by members of Forza Italia and a minority of the PD (one hundred deputies), to which were added the votes of the Five Star Movement (M5S), a party openly against the quotas.

---

[11] Susanna Turco, "Quote rosa alle Europee, legge col trucco nessuna parità di genere nel voto 2014," *L'Espresso*, 20 March 2014, http://espresso.repubblica.it/palazzo/2014/03/20/news/quote-rosa-alle-europee-legge-col-trucco-nessuna-parita-di-genere-nel-voto-2014-1.157864.

[12] Italian Constitutional Court, Judgment no. 1/2014, 4 December 2013.

The Italicum was parked in the Senate because of political opposition against the constitutional reform aiming to abolish the Senate.[13] In this context, the government decided to take the initiative with a new electoral reform proposal. The new Italicum included a premium for winning parties (but not coalitions) to ensure a majority, a share of seats assigned with the preference vote, a minimum of 40 per cent of votes required to secure the premium in the first round, and a minimum of 3 per cent of votes to win a seat. Thus, the party who led after the first ballot with at least 40 per cent of votes would get 54 per cent of seats in the Chamber. If no party reached 40 per cent, the two most-voted lists would go to the run-off round and the winner would receive 54 per cent of seats. The text of Italicum included clauses to encourage the presence of women in parliament: a party list composition quota (no more than 50 per cent of candidates of the same sex); alternating order (the same sex should not be listed consecutively more than twice); a quota for head-of-list candidates (no more than 60 per cent of candidates of the same sex); together with double gender preferences. Renzi's programme was based on implementing a package of reforms (in public administration, schools, and the labour market) to make the country more competitive, and the goal of gender parity was part of this process of modernization; thus his commitment to getting the Italicum approved despite widespread opposition. The bill was discussed and approved in the Senate on 27 January 2015. The revised text was passed for a second reading by the Chamber, and in order to avoid parliamentary delay the Renzi government called a confidence vote on the reform, whereby it was approved on 4 May. The law – no. 52/2015 of 6 May 2015 – came into force in July 2016, but in January 2017 the Constitutional Court declared the unconstitutionality of some parts of the new electoral legislation and modified them accordingly.[14] After the Judgment of the Court, what remained of the Italicum

---

[13] The constitutional reform proposed redesigning the Italian parliamentary system towards a differentiated bicameralism, where the upper house Senate would be abolished as an elected chamber, and would have no ability to veto legislation. For Renzi the reform was a crucial passage towards modernizing Italian democracy. It was approved in April 2016 (see the Chamber site, available at: www.camera.it/leg17/465?tema=riforme_costituzionali_ed_elettorali), but then it was rejected by a large majority in a popular referendum held on 4 December 2016. After the referendum defeat, Renzi resigned as prime minister.

[14] Italian Constitutional Court, Judgment no. 35/2017, 25 January 2017, accessed 20 February 2018, available at: www.cortecostituzionale.it

was a proportional electoral system (without runoff voting procedure), with untouched gender electoral quotas for party list composition.

The two Constitutional Court's judgments in 2013 and 2017 established that the electoral system in place for Senate elections was the proportional Consultellum[15] of 2013, while the system for the Chamber was the modified Italicum, potentially majoritarian, but proportional in practice.

Under the appeal of the President of the Republic Sergio Mattarella on April 2017 and the full support of the Renzi's successor, Paolo Gentiloni, the remaining months of the legislature were mainly dedicated to design a new legislation to make the electoral systems for the two chambers homogeneous for the forthcoming 2018 national elections. With a confidence vote called by Gentiloni government to avoid parliamentary delay, the electoral reform was approved on 26 October 2017 by PD with the support of Forza Italia and the Northern League, whereas Five Star Movement and leftist parties strongly opposed it. The new electoral Law no. 165/2017, called *Rosatellum* after the name of Ettore Rosato, the Democratic Party parliamentary leader who proposed it, introduced a mixed system. For both the Chambers around a third of the seats are allocated using a first past the post electoral system, while the remainder are allocated using a proportional method, with one round of voting. Finally, in order to gain the seats by proportional representation, parties need to win at least 3 per cent of the vote in both houses, while coalitions need at least 10 per cent of the vote. It means that any party or coalition will likely need more than 40 per cent support to win enough seats to govern. For promoting female representation, the law establishes that for the proportionally elected seats the candidate lists should be composed of both sexes in alternating order in a frozen list; and for the uninominal elected seats neither sex could account more than 60 per cent of the candidates listed.

In late December 2017 president Sergio Mattarella dissolved the parliament to put the country on track for general elections of 4 March 2018. At the time of writing (February 2018), the electoral results appear unpredictable due to the high abstention and electoral volatility registered among voters by the pools.

---

[15] Consultellum refers to a pure proportional system with an 8 per cent threshold, which is derived from 2013 ruling by the constitutional court that declared illegitimate the electoral law approved in 2005.

6.4.3   The 2016 Legislation for Regional Elections

Facing a situation where female councillors represented only 17.7 per cent of the total regional councillors in 2015, and with the aim of establishing a common general framework for regional elections, Law no. 20/2016 was approved on 3 February 2016 to integrate the general principles according to which the regions make their electoral legislation.[16] The law also obliges the regions to adopt affirmative measures to promote equal opportunities between men and women for access to the regional council. The law prescribes that in cases where regional legislation establishes party list competitions with the expression of preference, in the party list neither sex can account for more than 60 per cent of the total candidates, and the elector may express two preferences only if for two candidates of different sexes. In cases where regional legislation establishes party list competition without preference voting, there must be an alternating order between candidates of different sexes, and candidates of one sex cannot account for more than 60 per cent of the total candidates. In cases where the regional legislation establishes uninominal constituencies, the candidate party list must respect the two-thirds gender quota.

The bill, proposed by a PD woman senator but sustained by a cross-party alliance (PD, Forza Italia, and New Centre Right), was approved in September 2015 in the Senate and then approved without amendments by the Chamber on 3 February 2016. For the PD female parliamentarians the law has represented another step towards full citizenship between men and women in Italy, that – according to them – will enhance the quality of Italian democracy (*"verso un paese civile e moderno"*).[17] Due to easy access and diffusion of EU and other international rankings (Global Gender Gap Reports, UN index, etc.), it has become evident how distant Italy is from other EU (and non-EU) countries in terms of pursuing the goal of gender equality and guaranteeing human rights more generally (Amnesty International 2016). During the Renzi government, whose mission was to reform Italy, the winning rhetoric presented legislation as a means to modernize Italy and reduce the gap with other EU countries. In the case of the introduction of electoral gender quotas for regions, women MPs used this rhetoric successfully.

---

[16] Parliamentary debate, Chamber of Deputies, available at: www.camera.it/leg17/126?tab=1&leg=17&idDocumento=3297&sede=&tipo=.

[17] See the PD forum, available at: www.partitodemocratico.it/donne/parita-di-genere-nei-consigli-regionali-via-libera-definitivo/.

As in preceding debates on gender quotas, the women's movement was absent, public opinion was indifferent, and media coverage was minimal, but at this time no evident resistance against the gender quota emerged. It might be that, like France (Lépinard 2016), Italy first struggled against gender quotas but that by twenty years after their first introduction gender quotas had become the recognized legitimate and undisputed instrument to promote an increasing gender balance in institutions.

6.5 CONCLUSION

This chapter provides a historical overview of Italian gender quotas mostly supported by women in the institutions, rather than by women in society, and with selective and fluctuating attention by the media and public opinion. Especially in the period after 2014, during the Renzi government (2014–16), which was more open to the European and international discourses on gender equality and aware of the necessity to modernize the country, Italy experienced a process of gender quota strengthening and diffusion.

However, Italy remains a conservative regime, where traditional conceptions of the role of women in society remain dominant and unchallenged and gender quotas have been introduced as symbolic equality remedies. Italian women suffered exclusion from citizenship for a long time (Mancini 2012), and despite the recognition of universal suffrage and formal equality they still experience discrimination in many sectors (Rossi-Doria 1996; Alesso 2012), especially in the labour market, where female participation is among the lowest in Europe.[18] The United Nations, and in particular the CEDAW Committee, has periodically informed Italy of the inadequacy of its measures to improve participation by women in the country's political, social, economic, and cultural life (Donà 2018).

High-minded principles have been established, but the cross-party political consensus among women in parliament is not enough to turn those principles into effective measures and to redefine democracy with the discourse of gender parity, for many reasons. First, Italy lacks

[18] International Monetary Fund, "Italy," Country Report No. 16/223, accessed 2 August 2016, available at: www.imf.org/external/pubs/ft/scr/2016/cr16223.pdf. See also the European Commission (2013) and European Parliament (2014) country reports on gender equality.

a cohesive women's movement attentive to multi-level dynamics and present in international arenas, or able to channel external pressures to induce the national government to undertake domestic reforms; moreover, Italian feminists as a whole opposed gender quotas in politics for a long time and these measures are still contested by many feminist groups. The legislation by itself is not sufficient for ensuring gender equality when there are no societal actors ready to mobilize and use those legal instruments, nor a widespread culture of equality. Second, Italy has experienced a process of gradual political and institutional weakening of the WPA structure (leading to a period of paralysis during the Renzi government),[19] a structure which has traditionally been key in supporting women's rights, promoting cultural change by framing the new discourse on parity, and articulating demands using international and European norms. In this scenario, the women in national parliament able to build cross-party alliances emerged as key players in promoting measures for gender equality and convincing a male elite of the effectiveness of these measures, by using different kinds of rhetoric over the years (from the importance of gender balance in decision-making, to the goal of making Italy a more competitive and modern country). At regional and provincial levels, the gender equality advisors (*consigliere di parità*) are active in litigating cases in front of administrative courts to dissolve the local executives composed without ensuring gender quota targeting of 40 per cent. The gender equality advisors, figures introduced since 1991 to supervise compliance with the law on equality in the labour market, are now bringing actions before the court for cases concerning discrimination against women both at the workplace and in the municipal politics. The National Network of Equality Advisors is the structure wherein local activities are coordinated, and the exchange of information and best practices is ensured.

All the legal changes that have occurred in the last two decades have moved Italy beyond the absolute principle of formal equality and towards the objective of substantive or de facto equality between men and women. In this respect, the approval of the 2001 and 2003 constitutional amendments represented a turning point, after which the

---

[19] *Huffington Post*, 31 January 2016, "Palazzo Chigi: dalle droghe, alle pari opportunità alle adozioni, dipartimenti vuoti senza referenti politici," accessed 20 October 2016, available at: www.huffingtonpost.it/2016/01/28/politiche-antidroga_n_9097422 .html.

state and the regions were allowed to introduce measures to promote gender equality in politics. The Constitutional Court played a crucial role in consolidating the shift from formal to substantial equality, overcoming its initial rejection of gender quota measures which were in the end introduced for EP, national, regional and municipal elections. Noticeably, these legal transformations in search of substantive equality for women in politics were mostly driven by the political elite, without a meaningful public debate and the involvement of civil society. The only exception to this pattern was the adoption of corporate board quotas in 2011 where strong support from media and civil society coalesced in a period of feminist movement revival in the context of the economic crisis. More recently, what Éléonore Lépinard and Ruth Rubio Marín call the juridification of the struggle around gender quotas in their conclusion to this volume, has been translated at the local level due to the litigation strategy of the gender equality advisors in the regional administrative courts.

The main rhetoric displayed in favour of gender quotas in politics and in the economic domain is one that links the introduction of these measures with Italy following the example of more modern Western European countries. In the end, though, none of these measures have succeeded in sufficiently transforming the symbolic position of women who, in Italian culture, are still primarily seen through their role as caregivers in the family structure. The influence of the Catholic Church and the weak secularity of the Italian state are the main factors explaining the resistance against taking "all appropriate measures to modify or abolish existing laws, regulations, customs and practices which constitute discrimination against women," as prescribed by the CEDAW convention. It remains to be seen whether the pressure to further "modernize" Italy under the influence of the EU and other European countries might contribute to the overall reform of the Italian conservative gender regime by addressing remaining inequalities across interconnected domains. Two weeks before Italian general elections, the three main blocks (PD and its minor allies; Forza Italia with the Northern League and Brothers of Italy; and M5S) are campaigning with heated debates on immigration, security and economy, while the pools tell us that the result will be a stalemate. The uncertainty of the current political situation makes any sensible predictions about the possibility of Italy moving towards a transformative scenario very difficult.

References

Adamo, Ugo. 2011. "La promozione del principio di pari opportunità nella composizione delle giunte negli enti territoriali alla luce della più recente giurisprudenza amministrativa." *AIC Associazione italiana dei costituzionalisti* 2: 913–34.

———. 2016. "La composizione delle giunte comunali alla luce della l. n. 56 del 2014 e della (più recente) giurisprudenza amministrativa." *Rivista di diritto delle autonomie territoriali* 3: 420–38.

Alesso, Ileana. 2012. *Il quinto stato*. Milano: Franco Angeli.

Amato, Alfredo. 2011. "Focus sulla giurisprudenza amministrativa in materia di pari opportunità nell'accesso agli uffici pubblici e alle cariche elettive." *Istituzioni del federalismo* 4: 913–34.

Amnesty International. 2016. "Report 2015/16. The State of the World's Human Rights." February. www.amnesty.org/en/latest/research/2016/02/annual-report-201516/.

Baldi, Brunetta. 2007. *Stato e territorio. Federalismo e decentralismo nelle democrazie contemporanee*. Roma-Bari: Laterza.

Beccalli, Bianca, ed. 1999. *Donne in quota. E' giusto riservare posti alle donne nel lavoro e nella politica?* Milano: Feltrinelli.

Brunazzo, Marco, and Vincent della Sala, 2016. "'Adesso le cose sono cambiate': Matteo Renzi e l'Unione Europea." *Rivista italiana di politiche pubbliche* 1: 115–34.

Brunelli, Giuditta. 2003. "Un overruling in tema di norme elettorali antidiscriminatorie." *Le Regioni* 5: 902–17.

Califano, Licia. 2003. "Corte e Parlamento in sintonia sulle 'pari opportunità.'" *Quaderni Costituzionali* 2: 366–67.

———. 2010. "L'assenso 'coerente' della Consulta alla prefenza di genere." *Quaderni Costituzionali* 2: 404–06.

Campus, Donatella. 2015. "Women in politics." In *The Oxford Handbook of Italian Politics*, edited by Erik Jones and Gianfranco Pasquino. Oxford: Oxford University Press.

Cappelletti, Mauro. 1971. *Judicial Review in the Contemporary World*. New York: Bobbs-Merrill Co., Inc.

Carbone, Maurizio. 2009. "Italy in the European Union, between Prodi and Berlusconi." *The International Spectator* 3: 97–115.

Carlassare, Lorenza. 1997. "La rappresentanza femminile: principi formali ed effettività." In *Genere e democrazia. La cittadinanza delle donne a cinquant'anni dal voto*, edited by Franca Bimbi and Alisa Del Re, 81–92. Turin: Rosenberg & Sellier.

———. 2002. "L'integrazione della rappresentanza: un obbligo per le Regioni." In *La rappresentanza democratica nelle scelte elettorali delle Regioni*, edited by Lorenza Carlassare, Alessandro Di Blasi, and Marco Giampieretti, 1–59. Padova: CEDAM.

Casarico, Alessandra, and Paola Profeta. 2010. *Donne in attesa*. Milan: Egea.

Cotta, Maurizio. 2015. "Partitocracy." In *The Oxford Handbook of Italian Politics*, edited by Erik Jones and Gianfranco Pasquino. Oxford: Oxford University Press.

Cotta, Maurizio, and Luca Verzichelli. 2016. *Il sistema politico italiano*. Bologna: Il Mulino.

D'Alimonte, Roberto. 2013. "The Italian elections of February 2013: The end of the Second Republic?" *Contemporary Italian Politics* 5: 113–29.

Della Porta, Donatella. 2003. "The women's movement, the left and the state: Continuities and changes in the Italian case." In *Women's Movements Facing the Reconfigured State*, edited by Lee Ann Banaszak, Karen Beckwith, and Dieter Rucht, 48–68. Cambridge: Cambridge University Press.

Donà, Alessia. 2007. "La partecipazione e la rappresentanza femminile nel sistema politico italiano." In *Donne, diritti e democrazia*, edited by Giovanna Fiume. Rome: XL Edizioni.

2011. "Using the EU to promote gender equality policy in a traditional context: Reconciliation of work and family life in Italy." In *The Europeanisation of Gender Equality Policies*, edited by Maxime Forest and Emanuela Lombardo, 99–120. London: Palgrave.

2013. "The Italian political debate on promoting women in economic decision making: The making of law 120/2011." Paper prepared for the *3rd European Conference on Politics and Gender*, Univesitat Pompeu Fabra, Barcelona, Spain, 21–3 March.

2018 (forthcoming). "How do international norms matter? The impact of the Convention on the Elimination of all Forms of Discrimination Against Women in Italy." *Italian Political Science Review*. https://doi.org/10.1017/ipo.2017.28

Donovan, Mark, and Mark Gilbert. 2015. "Silvio Berlusconi and Romano Prodi." In *The Oxford Handbook of Italian Politics*, edited by Erik Jones and Gianfranco Pasquino. Oxford: Oxford University Press.

European Commission. 2013. "The current situation of gender equality in Italy – Country Profile 2013." http://ec.europa.eu/justice/gender-equality/files/epo_campaign/131203_country_profile_italy.pdf.

European Parliament. 2014. *The Policy on Gender Equality in Italy*. In-depth Analysis for the FEEM Committee, PE 493.052. www.europarl.europa.eu/RegData/etudes/note/join/2014/493052/IPOL-FEMM.

Fabbrini, Sergio. 2009. "The transformation of Italian democracy." *Bulletin of Italian Politics* 1 (1): 29–47.

Ferrera, Maurizio. 2006. *Il fattore D*. Milano: Mondadori.

Giannetti, Daniela. 2013. "Mario Monti's technocratic government." In *Italian Politics. Technocrats in Office*, edited by Aldo di Virgilio and Claudio M. Radaelli. New York: Berghahn.

Guadagnini, Marila. 2003. "Introduzione." In *Da elettrici ad elette*, edited by Marila Guadagnini. Torino: Celid.

——. 2005. "Gendering the debate on political representation in Italy: A difficult challenge." In *State Feminism and Political Representation*, edited by Joni Lovenduski, 130–52. Cambridge: Cambridge University Press.

Guadagnini, Marila, and Alessia Donà. 2007. "Women's policy machinery in Italy between European pressures and domestic constraints." In *Changing State Feminism*, edited by Joyce Outshoorn and Johanna Kantola, 165–81. London: Palgrave.

Krook, Mona Lena. 2009. *Quotas for Women in Politics*. New York: Oxford University Press.

Lépinard, Éléonore. 2016. "From breaking the rule to making the rules: The adoption, entrenchment, and diffusion of gender quotas in France." *Politics, Groups, and Identities* 4 (2): 231–45.

Lombardo, Emanuela, and Maria Sangiuliano. 2009. "Gender and employment in the Italian policy debates 1995–2007: The construction of 'non employed' gendered subjects." *Women's Studies International Forum* 32 (6): 445–52.

Lovenduski, Joni. 2008. "State feminism and women's movements." *West European Politics* 31 (1): 169–94.

MacRae, Heather. 2012. "Double-speak: The European Union and gender parity." *West European Politics* 35 (2): 301–18.

Mancini, Susanna. 2012. "From the struggle for suffrage to the construction of a fragile gender citizenship: Italy 1861–2009." In *The Struggle for Female Suffrage in Europe*, edited by Blanca Rodriguez-Ruiz and Ruth Rubio-Marín. Leiden: Brill.

Mazur, Amy. 1996. *Gender Bias and the State: Symbolic Reform at Work in Fifth Republic France*. Pittsburgh, PA: Pittsburgh University Press.

Palici di Suni, Elisabetta. 2012. "Gender parity and quotas in Italy: A convoluted reform process." *West European Politics* 35 (2): 380–94.

Pojmann, Wendy. 2005. "Emancipation or liberation?: Women's associations and the Italian movement." *Historian* 67 (1): 73–96.

Raniolo, Francesco. 2006. "Forza Italia: A leader with a party." *South European Society and Politics* 11 (3–4): 439–55.

Regalia, Marta. 2015. "Electoral systems." In *The Oxford Handbook of Italian Politics*, edited by Erik Jones and Gianfranco Pasquino. Oxford: Oxford University Press.

Rossi-Doria, Anna. 1996. *Diventare cittadine. Il voto alle donne in Italia*. Firenze: Giunti.

Saraceno, Chiara. 2012. "La protesta delle donne: un successo con molte ombre." In *Politica in Italia. I fatti dell'anno e le interpretazioni. Edizione 2012*, edited by Anna Bosco and Duncan McDonnell, 219–34. Bologna: Il Mulino.

CHAPTER SEVEN

FROM ELECTORAL TO CORPORATE BOARD QUOTAS

The Case of Portugal

Ana Espírito-Santo

In Portugal, a so-called Parity Law[1] was approved in August 2006. According to that law, all lists presented for local, legislative, and European elections must guarantee a minimum representation of 33.3 per cent for each sex. Parties that do not respect this minimum are fined. The approval of that law places Portugal within a global trend for the adoption of such measures. This trend has intensified greatly over the last fifteen years, and at the moment, more than one hundred countries have gender quotas for political office (Franceschet, Krook, and Piscopo 2012, 3). Although political gender quotas are the oldest and by far the most common ones, two further generations (Holli 2011) or groups (Meier 2013) of gender quotas have recently appeared in several countries: gender quotas for advisory boards and for boards of publicly listed and state-owned companies. Up until very recently, these two additional types of quotas were not present in Portugal, and quotas were synonymous with electoral gender quotas. However, in August 2017, a law aiming to achieve a more equilibrated representation of women and men in the administrative and fiscal organs of listed and state-owned companies was adopted.[2]

This chapter has two main objectives. The first is to analyse the role, interactions, synergies, and alliances of the most important (f)actors

---

[1] Organic Law 3/2006, available at: https://dre.pt/application/dir/pdf1sdip/2006/08/16000/58965897.PDF (accessed in January 2016).

[2] Law 62/2017, available at: https://dre.pt/web/guest/pesquisa/-/search/107791612/details/normal?l=1 (accessed in July 2017).

that made the adoption of gender quotas in Portugal possible both at the political and economic levels. This part of the paper follows the conceptual model provided by Krook (2009), who identifies three categories of potential actors in quota campaigns in the literature: (1) civil society actors such as women's movements and women's sections inside political parties; (2) state actors such as national leaders and courts; and (3) international and transnational actors such as international organisations and transnational non-governmental organisations (NGOs) (Krook, 2009, 20). Nevertheless, this chapter gives special emphasis to three crucial (f)actors that have often been overlooked in the gender quota literature (see the chapter "Introduction"): namely the legal and constitutional preconditions, the national gender equality agencies, and the role of European institutions and other international actors. The second main objective of this chapter is to explore how gender quotas challenge and transform the political gender regime in Portugal, and in particular the way democracy and equality are conceived.

In order to reach these two objectives, both document-analysis and interviews were used, including two different sets of interviews with Portuguese MPs. The first set was conducted in 2005, just one year before the adoption of the electoral quota law, whereas the second set was conducted in 2014/15.[3] Furthermore, several documents were analysed and some specialists were contacted by email. All referenced materials appear in footnotes, where appropriate.

This chapter is organised as follows: Section 7.1 sequentially describes the progression of events leading up to the adoption of the Parity Law in 2006. Section 7.2 analyses the role that the most important mobilising (f)actors played in the adoption of electoral quotas. Section 7.3 pursues the same goal, but for the business sector. Section 7.4 reflects on how gender quotas might have transformed the national narrative and discourses, while the last section, Section 7.5, summarises the main conclusions.

7.1 FROM PARTY QUOTAS TO ELECTORAL QUOTAS: A TIMELINE

As in many other countries, voluntary party quotas were first implemented in Portugal by left-wing parties. The first party to adopt them

---

[3] Within the project *Mulh(j)er e Poder* (PTDC/IVC-CPO/4088/2012) that was coordinated by Nina Wiesewomeier at the Institute for Social Sciences in Lisbon.

was the Socialist Party (PS) in 1988, assuming a 25 per cent quota for both sexes. However, although the PS officially adopted party quotas, they remained dormant as the party did not comply with them for another decade. In contrast with other countries (Caul 2001; Meier 2004), in Portugal there was no diffusion effect, i.e. no other parties adopted their own internal quotas until decades later. In 1999, a new political party was founded in Portugal, the Left Bloc (BE). It is an extreme-left libertarian political party that managed to get into parliament (2/230 MPs) in the first legislative elections in which it participated, in the year that it was founded.[4] The BE has always been a party very committed to gender equality; it identifies as feminist,[5] and it has often aimed at and accomplished a relatively gender equilibrated parliamentary group. Nevertheless, it has never had party quotas as such (i.e. applied to electoral candidates) defined in its statutes, although since 2003 the BE's statutes have mentioned that the main party organs should observe the parity criterion.

The awakening of the PS to gender equality issues started to take place in the beginning of the 1990s. In 1992, António Guterres – who is known as someone very committed to gender equality[6] – was elected leader of the PS. His tight connection with the Socialist International (SI) and his international connections in general might explain at least part of his commitment. In fact, in the 1992 party Congress where he was elected for the first time, he put forward a motion identifying the under-representation of women in political power as a problem that should be solved.[7] In 1994, three female Portuguese MEPs from different parties organised a symbolic moment, the Parity Parliament, which was sponsored by the EU (Bettencourt and Silva Pereira 1995; Cabrera, Martins and Flores 2011). Within this initiative, 115 former and current female members of Parliament invited the same number of male partners to sit with them in a Parity Parliament gathered to debate the situation of women, citizenship, and parity democracy.[8] Guterres, who took part in the event, presented a proposal suggesting that the candidates' lists should include one woman for every four

---

[4] Earlier in the same year (1999), it had run for the European elections but did not manage to elect any MEPs.

[5] Personal interview with BE MP Helena Pinto (2005).

[6] According to several interviewers, both in 2005 and 2014.

[7] Motion "Mudar para Ganhar," António Guterres, X PS Congress, 1992, 10.

[8] More information available at: www.db-decision.de/CoRe/Portugal.htm (accessed in December 2016).

positions (Cabrera, Martins and Flores 2011, 89). The first legislative elections during Guterres' leadership took place in 1995, a year marked by an intensification of the PS party strategy concerning women's representation. From that year onwards, the PS officially defined itself as a party engaged in increasing women's election by defending (for the first time in an electoral programme) constitutional and legislative measures to promote an equilibrium between men's and women's access to political positions.[9]

The PS won the elections, Guterres became prime minister, and soon after, in 1997, the fourth revision of the Constitution took place (see Section 7.2.1, "The legal and constitutional preconditions"). In the following year (1998), the PS attempted to introduce a gender quota law for the first time, which was rejected in Parliament. Between 1998 and 2006, several bills were proposed by both the PS and the BE (for a timeline overview of those bills please see Table 7.1 in Appendix). These are the only two political parties that have pushed for the passage of the Parity Law in Portugal. The three remaining parties with parliamentary representation – the Communist Party (PCP), the centre-right, liberal Social Democratic Party (PSD), and the right-wing, conservative Democratic Social Centre (CDS) Party – are all against quotas. The PCP is against quotas on the grounds that they do not help solve the source of the problem, which the Communists feel is a socio-economic one; they argue that "quotas are only favourable to middle class or upper-middle class women."[10] Furthermore, the PCP is also usually against any state interference in the internal organisation of parties. The CDS' three main reasons for opposing quotas are: that they are humiliating for women, that they lead women without aptitude to be elected, and that their party does not need quotas to allocate women to very high political positions.[11] Finally, although the PSD official position has always been against quotas, it is a very heterogeneous party on this matter (see Section 7.3, "Gender quotas in the economic sphere"). Therefore, there are some people within the party who totally oppose quotas on the basis of the arguments presented by the CDS, whereas many others (mostly women) see them as the only

---

[9] PS Party Manifesto, legislative elections, 1995, 1–5.
[10] PCP MP, Odete Santos at CERC debates: *24.ª reunião*, 18 September 1996.
[11] Personal interview with CDS politicians, Maria José Nogueira Pinto, Mariana Cascais, and Teresa Caeiro (2005).

solution to solving the problem of unequal numbers of women and men among politicians.[12]

It was only in 2006, when the PS had a majority in Parliament, that its bill and three bills from the BE (see Table 7.1 in Appendix) passed on their general principles in the Assembly of the Republic. While the Socialists targeted all three different types of elections (local, legislative, and European) in one bill, the BE opted to dedicate one bill to each type of election, hence the four very similar but separate bills. These bills all proposed the adoption of a 33.3 per cent minimum representation for each sex.

7.2 MAIN (F)ACTORS FOR THE ADOPTION OF ELECTORAL GENDER QUOTAS

7.2.1 The Legal and Constitutional Preconditions

The fourth revision of the Portuguese Constitution took place in 1997.[13] This revision is of major importance for the purpose of this chapter because it contained the introduction/alteration of two paragraphs that particularly target equality between women and men. First, a paragraph (h), "To promote equality between men and women," was added to article 9° (*Fundamental tasks of the State*); and secondly article 109 (*Citizens' participation in politics*)[14] was substantially changed. Instead of "citizens," the article began referring expressly to "men and women." In addition, a new phrase was added. Its text since the revision has been: "The direct and active participation in political life by *men and women* is a condition for and a fundamental instrument in the consolidation of the democratic system, and the *law must promote both equality in the exercise of civic and political rights and the absence of gender-based discrimination in access to political office*" (new sections included in italic).

These changes were a stepping-stone. There is consensus among several constitutionalists that any quota measure would have been considered unconstitutional before the 1997 revision (Miranda 1998, 44; Moreira 1998, 48). This argument is mainly based on article 13° (*Principle of equality*), according to which, "no one may be privileged,

---

[12] Several personal interviews with PSD MPs and ex-MPs (2005).

[13] So far, the Portuguese Constitution (which originated in 1976) has been revised seven times: 1982, 1989, 1992, 1997, 2001, 2004, and 2005.

[14] Article 109 corresponded to article 112 before this revision.

favoured, prejudiced, deprived of any right, or exempted from any duty for reasons of ancestry, sex …" This article prevents the adoption of any legal measures that privilege women or any other group (Moreira 1998, 48). Another argument for unconstitutionality before the revision could have been based on the unity and indivisibility of the electoral body – an argument also used in France in 1982 to render a quota system unconstitutional (Moreira 1998, 59). In fact, up until 1997, the articles that included the word "citizens" did so without any reference to sex. As the Portuguese Constitution now stands, "citizenship has a sex," since article 109° specifically mentions men and women (Moreira 1998, 59).

Both quoted constitutionalists agree that quotas are not necessarily the only measure allowed by the current Constitution; there is some room for the legislature to choose the manner and form of reaching the gender equality prescribed in article 109°, but they also agree that adopting no measures at all could be considered unconstitutional (Miranda 1998, 46; Moreira 1998, 50–1, 55).

Revisions of the Portuguese Constitution "require passage by a majority of two-thirds of the Members of the Assembly of the Republic in full exercise of their office" (article 286°); hence, they can never be brought about by a single party. Therefore, this revision was only possible because the PS and the PSD negotiated to find some consensus and, at a later stage, presented a common proposal for revision, which included the two paragraphs referred to above, targeting equality between women and men. It is important to emphasise that this revision was vast and deep, as it included 192 changes in total and comprised the modification of the numbering of more than 150 articles.[15] The major topics of the revision – which received considerable media exposure – included the autonomy of the regions, electoral system reform (mainly concerning the number of MPs and the introduction of uninominal districts), and the political rights of emigrants (Magalhães 1999, 64). Hence, the amendments to the articles related to gender equality were only a small part of that revision and did not get any media attention, as they were considered minor issues.[16] It is likely that the PS convinced the PSD – which officially opposes quotas –

---

[15] Available at: www.publico.pt/espaco-publico/jornal/acabar-com-o-frenesim-consti tucional-e-debater-a-europa-173194 (accessed in January 2016).

[16] Personal interview with PS MP José Magalhães (2015).

to include those changes as part of the broader common proposal, possibly compromising in other areas.

The process of revision of the Constitution was initiated by the CDS in January 1996 (Magalhães 1999, 56). All other parties and, for the first time, some civic associations presented their own proposals shortly thereafter. The revision was conducted over almost two years (from the beginning of 1996 to September 1997), and therefore each of the proposals was debated and voted on several times. The most informative debate took place within the respective Legislative Committee, the Occasional Committee for the Revision of the Constitution (referred to from now onwards as CERC). The CERC debate as well as the debate in the Plenary on both changes are analysed below.[17] The two changes mentioned above were initially suggested by two different political parties.

The addition of Paragraph (h) to article 9, making reference to the equality between men and women as a new goal to be promoted by the state, was included in a proposal by the Green Party (Os Verdes or PEV).[18] The PEV is a very small party that, since the end of the 1980s, has systematically run for legislative elections in coalition with the PCP. However, once elected, their parliamentary groups work independently. As a result of their agreement with the PCP, the PEV has always managed to elect two MPs, and one of these has often been a woman.

The first time this proposal was discussed in the CERC, all parties that were present (the PEV was absent) pronounced themselves against it, including the PS.[19] The Socialist MP Elisa Damião argued that the new paragraph compromised the right to be different. She also said "the inequalities that should be emphasised are the economic, social, and cultural ones. The remaining differences between women and men should be embraced."[20]

However, as mentioned above, in the following months, the PS and the PSD negotiated among themselves in order to present one single proposal for the revision of many articles. One of the changes included in this common proposal was the addition of the paragraph

---

[17] All documents consulted and mentioned in this section can be found on the CD-ROM attached to Magalhães 1999.
[18] Proposta de Revisão Constitucional n° 10/VII, 4 April 1996.
[19] CERC debates: 17.ª reunião, 4 September 1996.
[20] CERC debates: 17.ª reunião, 4 September 1996.

that the PEV had proposed to article 9°, simply changing the order of the words "men" and "women" – in the Greens' proposal the word "women" came first. This "new" proposal was debated and voted on in the CERC in April 1997, but the content of the debate is unavailable.[21] Later on (in July 1997)[22] the change was discussed for the last time in the Plenary and only the CDS (MP Maria José Nogueira Pinto) stood against it. In this party's opinion, adding the paragraph to article 9° implied treating women as if they were a minority, which they are not. One day later, the change was submitted for final voting in the Plenary and passed with the support of all parties (PS, PSD, PCP, and PEV) except for the CDS, which voted against it.[23]

The change to article 109° – introducing the promotion of gender equality in the political realm as the state's responsibility – was suggested by the PS.[24] The first debate about this change (on 18 September 1996, in the CERC) was conducted in relation to quotas. Even if the PS MP, Elisa Damião, did not mention quotas at all when she presented the proposal for the change,[25] almost all of the following interventions from the other parties brought them systematically back to the centre of the debate. For instance, PSD MP Luís Marques Guedes asked the PS whether the intention of the change was to force the legislature to approve any legislation establishing gender quotas for the composition of candidates' lists for political positions. And at a certain point, another PS MP, Alberto Martins, recognised that the PS's intention with the constitutional change was indeed to enable positive discrimination: "what we intend is to open up the possibility that the State, the law, enables some measures of positive discrimination in order to stimulate women's political participation and to guarantee the conditions that allow them to participate in greater accordance with their rights, since the reality has not permitted that to happen."

The President of the Committee (PS MP Vital Moreira) mentioned the risk that quotas might be declared unconstitutional. Later on, the

---

[21] CERC debates: 75.ª reunião, 11 April 1997.

[22] Plenary debates: Diário da Assembleia da República, I série, n° 94, 16 July 1997.

[23] Plenary debates: Diário da Assembleia da República, n° 95, 17 July 1997.

[24] Proposta de Revisão Constitucional n° 3/VII, 29 February 1996.

[25] CERC debates: 24.ª reunião, 18 September 1996. In her short intervention, Damião argued that the justification for the change in the Constitution was to guarantee a bigger democratisation of the political system.

same anticipation of unconstitutionality was recognised by PS MP Alberto Martins as a reason for suggesting the constitutional change: "obviously, when this question was discussed, many of us believed that, without a constitutional validation, quotas could hardly be applied without the risk of unconstitutionality."

Everybody, including the PS MPs, recognised that the words chosen by the PS for their proposal were not ideal.[26] The original proposal read: "the law will ensure nondiscrimination based on sex for access to political positions, aiming at a fair equilibrium in the participation of men and women." When the PS's proposal was revived and presented as part of the aforementioned agreement between the PS and the PSD, the text – which consisted of the current article 109° (see the text in Section 7.2.1 "The Legal and Constitutional Preconditions") – was very different to the original. This revised proposal was much influenced by the proposal of the Portuguese Association of the Women Lawyers (Moreira 1998, 51).[27] It clearly mentions "equality," whereas the original sentence referred to a "fair equilibrium," and it imposes gender equality as the state's responsibility, while the only duty of the state in the original version was only to ensure nondiscrimination. The revised version is more assertive and ambitious.

The new proposal was debated in the CERC in June 1997.[28] This debate was much less lively than the first one. When PS MP José Magalhães presented the proposal for change, he mentioned that this proposal did not identify and did not want to interfere with the famous polemical issue of gender quotas. Indeed, contrary to the first debate, this time the change was not discussed in relation to quotas.

The last debate on this change took place in the Plenary in July 1997.[29] Here, the PS and PSD equated the change to a new conception of democracy, defending the idea that there is no real democracy if there is an inequality of power between women and men. Expressions such as "it is indispensable to 'democratise democracy'" were used. The PSD MP Maria Eduarda Azevedo went even further by describing parity democracy as the only real democracy: "the real democracy is not

---

[26] CERC debates: 24.ª reunião, 18 September 1996.
[27] Projecto apresentado pela Associação Portuguesa Mulheres Juristas and CERC debates: 102.ª reunião, 5 de June 1997.
[28] Projecto apresentado pela Associação Portuguesa de Mulheres Juristas and CERC debates: 102.ª reunião, 5 June 1997.
[29] Plenary debates: Diário da Assembleia da República, n° 99, 23 July 1997.

only representative and pluralist but also paritarian." No measures to reach such a parity democracy were mentioned.

The change was put to the final vote in the Plenary on 24 July 1997 and passed with the support of all parties (PS, PSD, PCP, and PEV) except for the CDS, which abstained from the vote.[30] It is surprising that the PCP voted favourably, since it has always been against gen-der quotas, as has previously been mentioned. It only voted favoura-bly because it did not associate the new article with quotas, but with an effective commitment to the end of any kind of discrimination against women.[31]

7.2.2 Revision of the Constitution and Adoption of the Parity Law

As the description above suggests, there remains some uncertainty about whether or not the revision of the Constitution, in particular the change to article 109° that was proposed by the PS, was made specifically because it had been anticipated that without it, a bill proposing a quota law would be declared unconstitutional. However, several facts demonstrate that this was indeed the case. The first is the evidence of the timeline as described in the previous section: in 1995 the PS began to include gender equality in politics as part of its political agenda, namely on its manifesto for the legislative elections; in 1996/7 it fought for the approval of a substantive change to arti-cle 109° of the Constitution and in 1998, it introduced its first bill related to quotas.

The second fact is the explicit written and oral (see above) refer-ences to the need to revise the Constitution before quotas could be adopted. One of these written references was made in the PS mani-festo for the 1995 legislative elections,[32] while another appeared in the exposition of motives of the bill that the PS introduced in 1998: "Until 1997, a law calling for positive discrimination for women's access to State organs might have been considered unconstitutional."

Why then did the debates on the change to article 109° not always mention quotas? Three answers are plausible. The first is for strategic reasons: after the failure to convince the other parties of

---

[30] Plenary debates: *Diário da Assembleia da República*, n° 100, 24 July 1997.
[31] PCP MP Luís Sá at Plenary debates: *Diário da Assembleia da República*, n° 99, 23 July 1997.
[32] PS Party Manifesto, legislative elections, 1995, 1–6.

the virtues of the change to article 109° the first time it was debated, the strategy adopted later on – and agreed with the PSD – might have been to avoid such a controversial topic. The second answer is that the PS is also a heterogeneous party concerning quotas. Even today, there are some people who oppose the measure (Verge and Espírito-Santo 2016) and therefore, depending on the MP who is conducting the debate, slightly different attitudes are observable. Yet another possible answer is that the PS has tried to follow the example of France; that is, to rhetorically distinguish between gender quotas and parity in order to avoid the negative connotation of quotas (see Chapter 2).

When the bill that eventually became the Parity Law was approved in parliament, it was sent (following the normal legislative process) to the president of the Republic for enactment (Aníbal Cavaco Silva, affiliated with the PSD). Opposition parties tried to persuade the president nevertheless to ask the Constitutional Court to study the constitutionality of the law. In the opinion of those parties, two related constitutional provisions had been violated. The first was the fact that the bill did not impose a time frame (i.e. it was *forever*), which is at odds with article 109°, and the second is that the idea of parity (i.e. perceived as the division of the democracy between women and men) violates the aforementioned equality principle of article 13°.[33]

The president decided not to ask the Constitutional Court to study the constitutionality of the law, but vetoed it in June 2006. The main reason presented to justify the veto was that the sanctions included in the bill (i.e. the outright rejection of non-compliant party lists) were considered excessive: "In his opinion, draconian punishment mechanisms would threaten both the freedom of the parties and the dignity of the women elected" (Baum and Espírito-Santo 2012, 329).[34] Although the president did not choose to clearly articulate the reasons for the veto as constitutional violations, he did mention that in this case the aim did not justify the means, mainly since

---

[33] Report of the Legislative Committee of Constitutional Issues, Rights, Freedoms, and Guarantees: *Diário da Assembleia da República*, II série A N.°93/X/1, 11 March 2006, 25–6.

[34] *Diário da Assembleia da República*, II série A No.120/X/1, 14 June 2006, 2–3.

the means clashed with some political and constitutional values that deserved to be preserved.[35]

Therefore, the bill was sent back to the Assembly and amended. The main amendments were: the imposition of fines on parties with non-compliant lists instead of the initial outright rejection of such lists and the insertion of an article requiring that the Parity Law be re-assessed in five years' time based on its impact on gender balance in Portuguese electoral politics. The bill passed again, although this time only with the support of the PS. The BE decided not to sign on to the amended bill due to the less stringent sanctions.

7.2.3 The National Gender Equality Agency and the NGO Section

In the late twentieth century, women's policy agencies (WPAs) were created in several countries to take responsibility for the demands of women's movement activists (Lovenduski 2005; Mazur and Stetson 1995). As Lovenduski (2005, 1) describes: "These vary in scope, size, resources, stability, and location. They appeared at different times in different countries but are now part of the political landscape. Their existence is, at least in symbolic terms, an acknowledgement of women's demands for representation."

In Portugal, the most important WPA has gone through several transformations. Since 2007, it has operated under the name Commission for Citizenship and Gender Equality (CIG).[36] Since the 1970s, the Commission has contained an advisory board with two sections, the Interministerial Section and the NGO Section, where associations of women participate. The number of participating associations has been increasing significantly: whereas in 1975 it had twelve associations, by 2007 the number had increased to fifty-four (Monteiro and Ferreira 2012, 16). Furthermore, between 1991 and 2002 (when important reforms happened), those organisations received annual subsidies and were also given a meeting room in the CIG's headquarters (Monteiro and Ferreira 2012, 16).[37]

---

[35] *Diário da Assembleia da República*, II série A No.120/X/1, 14 June 2006, 2–3.

[36] Available at: www.cig.gov.pt (accessed in January 2016), Law Decree 164/2007 of 3 May.

[37] In 2002, reforms led to an increasing distance between the Commission and NGOs. The relationship between them began to follow more rules and became more formal. In 2005, for example, the room that the NGOs used to have in the Commission

Monteiro and Ferreira (2012, 17) argue that in the second half of the 1970s, the Commission played an important role, since it participated in the process of decision-making several times and it had influence in the legislative content, i.e. in the quality of policy implementation. However, from the 1980s onwards, as the Commission gradually became more institutionalised as a part of the state's bureaucracy it also became more of a task performer than a proponent of policies (Monteiro and Ferreira 2012, 21). Therefore, the role of the Commission has become mostly *marginal* and *formative* (Monteiro and Ferreira 2012, 17). It is *marginal* in that, when the Commission tries to intervene in a certain political agenda (and actually does so through internal discussions, elaborating proposals, etc.), it does not manage to participate in the decision-making process because the system excludes it. It is *formative* in that the Commission's main goal is to increase the consciousness of both public opinion and political agents. In recent decades, although the Commission and its network of organisations have tried in various ways to influence decision-making, their role has been blocked and limited by exogenous factors, namely by the political system (Monteiro and Ferreira 2012, 17).

Concerning the adoption of the Parity Law, the persistence of the Portuguese WPA and in particular its NGO Section, must be high-lighted (Monteiro 2011). Monteiro (2011, 47) argues that the symbolic action of the WPA was decisive in promoting the importance of gender quotas among political agents, mainly because there was great consensus among all women's associations present in the NGO Section. Nevertheless, the same author mentions at least two crucial points that illustrate the limits of the Commission's role in this agenda. First, the fact that it was only called on to participate in parliamentary debates on gender quotas in 1997–8 and not afterwards, i.e. it was not part of the decision-making process (Monteiro 2011, 41). Second, its influence in drafting legislative content was also limited, as can be seen by the fact that the law refers to a 33 per cent minimum presence of each sex, when the Commission had a clear preference for a real parity (50 per cent) (Monteiro 2011, 38).

Aside from their official connections to the Portuguese women's policy agency, some NGOs – in particular, *União de Mulheres Alternativa e Resposta* (UMAR), the Portuguese Platform for Women's

headquarters was taken away from them, which symbolically and physically implied the end of a close relationship (Monteiro and Ferreira 2012, 22).

Rights (PPDM), and the Portuguese Network of Young People for Gender Equality (REDE) – organised individual actions in favour of the adoption of the 2006 Parity Law. For instance, several NGOs sent protest statements to the media and to parliamentarian parties when the President vetoed the parity bill in June 2006 (namely PPDM and UMAR).[38] Similarly, REDE organised the mentoring project "From woman to woman" in 2006 and in 2009, which aimed to contribute to increasing the participation of young women in decision-making processes.[39] On 8 March 2006, UMAR, together with some public figures, distributed a little bag – a "kit for parity" filled with symbolic objects – among the MPs in Parliament.[40] Finally, in 2009 the PPDM managed the 50/50 campaign in Portugal, launched by the European Women's Lobby (Baum and Espírito-Santo 2009).[41]

The role of the NGOs in the adoption of the Parity Law is hard to assess; their work is mainly invisible – Portugal has a comparatively weak civil society, and in particular, women's/feminist associations have the lowest levels of membership among adults (Fernandes 2012, 3). Furthermore, politicians do not mention NGOs when asked about what motivated them to pursue this agenda. However, since the feminist NGOs have always been the most progressive voices in Portugal concerning equality between women and men, and since they have been very persistent following the parity agenda, they were/are a source of inspiration to some politicians.

7.2.4 European Institutions and Other International Actors

According to Krook (2009, 17), "the actors that are most often overlooked are international organisations and transnational networks." And yet, these actors played a determinant role in the case of Portugal in several ways. In general, it can be said that the "European directives and recommendations create a framework in which national policies

---

[38] Available at: http://plataformamulheres.org.pt/docs/PPDM-Lei-paridade.pdf and www.umarfeminismos.org/index.php?option=com_content&view=article&id=144:nota-de-protesto-da-umar-ao-veto-presidencial-a-lei-da-paridade&catid=15:noticias-e-comunicados (accessed in December 2016).

[39] Available at: http://redejovensigualdade.org.pt/dmpm1/novidades.html (accessed in December 2016).

[40] Available at: www.casacomum.org/cc/visualizador?pasta=10092.004.018.017 (accessed in December 2016).

[41] Available at: http://plataformamulheres.org.pt/spot-nao-ha-democracia-europeia-moderna-sem-igualdade-entre-mulheres-e-homens (accessed in December 2016).

and legislation must be elaborated" (Ferreira 2011, 181). However, political parties and other actors are differently affected by international trends.

The introduction of the party quota in the PS in the 1980s is largely seen as the result of the personal initiative of the secretary-general at the time, Vítor Constâncio, who was driven by some key female figures within his party and was inspired by events in other European countries, particularly Norway.[42] Furthermore, the SI was crucial in the PS's decision to pursue this agenda,[43] and might have been a determining factor in Guterres' position on this matter. The type of contact this organisation generates among the many social democratic parties that usually favour quotas has played at least some role in the way the party has evolved on this issue. Subsequently, in 2003, the PS party quota was enlarged to one third of positions in party organs and electoral lists for either sex following a call from the Socialist International Women urging affiliated parties to introduce or expand quota provisions (Verge 2013, 445).

Turning to international organisations, Portugal has primarily been affected by three: the United Nations, the European Union, and the Council of Europe (Santos, 2011). In fact, the evolution of the positions of both the PS and the BE regarding the election of women closely followed the developments within those three organisations (Baum and Espírito-Santo 2012, 330–2). This influence can be confirmed through an analysis of the parties' strategies and, more directly, through the references to international recommendations and guidelines contained in the electoral programmes and the majority of bills presented by both parties between 1988 and 2006. The latter references seem to work as a legitimation or justification strategy.

Transnational factors are also relevant in their capacity to be transversal to almost all actors involved in the process of the adoption of gender quotas. In fact, they seem to also be very inspiring for women's associations (NGOs) that are organised in international and European platforms.

7.2.5 Women within Political Parties

Krook (2009, 21) states that "Evidence from many cases indicates that efforts to nominate more female candidates rarely occur in the absence of women's mobilization," and Portugal is not an exception. It seems

---

[42] Personal interview with Vitor Constâncio (2005).
[43] Several personal interviews with PS MPs (2005).

plausible that a crucial role was played by (some) women within political parties, irrespective of these individuals' membership in women's sections.[44] As BE MP Helena Pinto has said: "To this day within the BE, it is mainly women who push for feminist issues. And, depending on the specific issue, it might not be all women, but just some of them, even within the BE."[45] Socialist and Communist MPs interviewed made similar statements.

The influence of women, both organised and not, is hard to prove due to its indirect character and the fact that most initiatives are carried out by men. An illustrative example of the difficulty in identifying relevant actors is the PS's adoption of a party quota in 1988. Although PS leader Constâncio stated that he was the one who had thought of the idea,[46] this seems improbable, considering that PS member Maria Belo had put forward a motion officially raising the issue for the very first time during the 1986 Congress.[47] In addition, two members of the Socialist women's section at that time, Maria do Carmo Romão[48] and Ana Coucello,[49] assert that Romão had the original idea. According to Coucello, Constâncio simply pledged to support the measure, but he did ultimately fulfil this promise.

Most Portuguese parties have an internal women's section. However, the women's sections tend to have a rather weak role. This is even the case within the PS – one of the most important parties for the passage of the Parity Law – whose women's section is neither particularly renowned nor especially influential within the party (Monteiro 2011), since the most powerful women in the party prefer not to play an active role in it.[50] Furthermore, the section's strength and position (more feminist or more conservative) varies a lot depending on who is the president. When the PS introduced the proposal that eventually became the Parity Law in 2006, the president of the women's section was Manuela Augusto (2005–11), who describes herself as someone who is *for the female condition* instead of *for gender equality.*[51] It is

---

[44] Several personal interviews with PS and PCP MPs (2005).
[45] Personal interview (2005).
[46] Personal interview with Vitor Constâncio (2005).
[47] Motion "O Partido Socialista e as Mulheres," Maria Belo, VI PS Congress, 1986.
[48] Personal interview (2005).
[49] Email exchange with Ana Coucello in 2016.
[50] Several personal interviews with PS MPs (2014).
[51] Personal interview with PS MP Catarina Marcelino (2014).

understandable, then, that the women's section did not play a deter-minant role at that moment.

In summary, it is likely that transnational actors, along with some influential women within parties, are the (f)actors that matter the most for convincing party leaders – the most visible face of all proposals – to be more proactive in gender equality issues. The revision of the Constitution was also crucial. Based on the fact that the opposing par-ties still raised issues of unconstitutionality when the 2006 bills were introduced, it is easy to imagine what would have happened had the revision of the Constitution not taken place.

7.3 GENDER QUOTAS IN THE ECONOMIC SPHERE

Until very recently, only a few tentative steps had been taken in order to reach a more gender-balanced distribution of the highest positions in the economic sphere. In 2012, the first measure with some bind-ing pressure was accomplished through a Resolution of the Council of Ministers[52] (Casaca 2014, 194). That resolution "determined [it] compulsory" for all state-owned companies to implement internal equality plans aimed at: (a) reaching a *de facto* equality between women and men in the way they are treated and in the opportunities they have; (b) eliminating all kinds of discrimination; and (c) facil-itating the reconciliation between professional, family, and personal lives. This resolution was not very efficacious, not only because it only compelled the companies to implement internal equality plans (i.e. it failed to dictate how demanding the objectives established in those plans should be) but also because it imposed no sanctions on non-compliant companies, which are crucial to the efficacy of any measure of this kind. A few other resolutions in this area were approved during the term of the previous centre-right government (a coalition of PSD and CDS; 2011–15). The most important of those was signed in March 2015,[53] which mandated some govern-ment officials to compel all listed companies to commit to reach-ing a minimum of 30 per cent of the under-represented sex on their administrative boards until 2018. Although thirteen listed companies

[52] RCM n° 19/2012, available at: www.cite.gov.pt/pt/destaques/complementosDestqs/RCM_19_2012.pdf (accessed in January 2015).
[53] RCM n° 11-A/2015, available at: https://dre.pt/home/-/dre/66689598/details/maxi mized?p_auth=jMmNC35f (accessed in July 2017).

(70 per cent of their total number) committed to that goal, the results proved rather small.[54]

Nevertheless, in 2017, a formal gender quota law was approved in Portugal. In January 2017, the centre-left government (PS[55]; 2015–19) introduced a bill in the Assembly of the Republic proposing gender quotas for listed and publicly-owned companies.[56] When presenting the bill, two main arguments were emphasised by the PS. The first was the justice argument, which is that women are similarly or more qualified than men, and that their participation is indispensable to a more balanced and fair society. The second argument was that of fulfilling a duty – a constitutional duty – to comply with European directives and to follow the best practices of other countries (Germany, France, and Italy).[57]

After having suffered several changes, the bill was put to a final vote in the Plenary on 23 June 2017 and passed with the support of some parties (PS, BE, PEV, and PAN – People, Animals, Nature; and seven CDS MPs). The PSD and a few CDS MPs abstained from the vote, while the PCP and the remaining CDS MPs (six in total) voted against the bill. The new law applies to both state-owned and listed companies, but on different terms. Concerning the former, from 2018 onwards, each administrative and fiscal board shall not have less than 33.3 per cent of members of either sex. In cases of noncompliance, the designations are considered invalid and new ones have to be proposed within ninety days. As for listed companies, the minimum is 20 per cent, which will rise to 33.3 per cent from 2020 onwards. The sanctions for private companies that fail to comply with the law boil down to: public exposure if the noncompliance is not corrected within ninety days and a fine (with no minimum value specified) if it is not corrected within 360 days.

The bill initially proposed by the Socialist government was more ambitious than the final draft, particularly with regards to the sanctions

[54] Available at: http://expresso.sapo.pt/politica/2017-06-23-Empresas-prometeram-nomear-mais-mulheres-mas-nao-cumpriram (accessed in July 2017).

[55] The current PS government is a minority government (86/230 MPs), supported by the PCP-PEV (17/230) and the BE (19/230).

[56] In February 2017, the Left Block introduced a similar – though more ambitious – bill, but later decided to give it up and to support the PS bill. For more details on these bills, please see Table 7.1 in Appendix.

[57] Plenary debates: *Diário da Assembleia da República*, I série, n° 99, 17 February 2017, 29–37, available at: http://debates.parlamento.pt/catalogo/r3/dar/01/13/02/052/2017-02-17/29?pgs=29-37&org=PLC (accessed in July 2017).

to be applied to listed companies. A compromise was adopted in order to increase the probability of passing the law. Since the PCP was against the measure, the PS was forced to negotiate with the CDS. The CDS proposals of changes to the original bill sought to address companies' demands, which were clearly opposed to the law. The CDS legislative reports clearly stated several objections, mainly concerning the fines which would, in their opinion, make an already fragile economy even more fragile.[58] Therefore, in the last draft of the bill, the fines for listed companies were significantly reduced – hypothetically to the symbolic amount of one euro.[59] Aside from a few exceptions, opinions on the bill were favourable both inside and outside of parliament.[60]

The PCP position was to be expected, considering that the party had voted against the electoral gender quotas in 2006 on the same grounds. According to the Communists, corporate gender quotas deal solely with a symbolic dimension of women's representation, since they only affect an elite group, while the major structural problems remain unsolved (salary inequality, career progression, parental leave, etc.).[61] More surprising is the CDS position, which had voted against the Parity Law (in 2006). This time it decided to give a free vote to its MPs, thus enabling the passage of the law. The main person responsible for the CDS position on this matter was its female party leader, Assunção Cristas, who was a critical actor in this process as she managed to convince some CDS MPs to vote favourably. The CDS is a conservative party which traditionally does not talk about gender equality and is usually against quotas. By contrast, Cristas was publicly in favour of gender quotas and considered this law to be very connected to natality and work–family policies, which are preferred themes of the CDS.[62] Cristas was trying

---

58 Report of the *Associação de Empresas Eminentes de Valores Cotados em Mercado* and of the *Comissão de Mercado de Valores Mobiliários*, available at: www.parlamento .pt/ActividadeParlamentar/Paginas/DetalheIniciativa.aspx?BID=40919 (accessed in July 2017).

59 Available at: www.jornaldenegocios.pt/economia/detalhe/aprovacao-de-quotas-nas-empresas-tremida-ate-ao-fim (accessed in July 2017).

60 Available at: www.publico.pt/2017/02/14/sociedade/noticia/mais-de-100-personali dades-e-50-organizacoes-subscrevem-carta-aberta-em-defesa-da-paridade-nas-empresas-1761996 (accessed in July 2017).

61 See note 52.

62 Available at: http://expresso.sapo.pt/politica/2017-06-25-Assuncao-Cristas-Fiquei-muito-feliz-por-ver-o-CDS-viabilizar-a-lei-das-quotas (accessed in July 2017).

to attract another kind of electorate to her party, although not without criticism from within its own ranks.

A similar situation had occurred during the previous government (2011–15), when the Secretary of State of Parliamentary Affairs and Equality, Teresa Morais of the PSD, was probably the most instrumental person in terms of passing the aforementioned Resolutions of the Council of Ministers. She was the government spokesperson to the media every time a measure was made public, and declared herself profoundly committed to gender equality issues.[63] She also took a clear stand in favour of gender quotas, going against her party, which had always been officially against them. However, as previously mentioned, the PSD is a heterogeneous party on this matter. In fact, although the party abstained from the final vote on the bill that eventually became law in 2017, the current president of the Republic, Marcelo Rebelo de Sousa, affiliated with the PSD, promulgated the law enthusiastically[64] – in sharp contrast to his predecessor (Cavaco Silva) who had vetoed the Parity Law in June 2006.

The centre-left government that pushed the corporate board quotas CBQ had also been working with another critical actor, the Secretary of State for Citizenship and Equality, Catarina Marcelino, who offers one important difference. Compared to Morais and Cristas, Marcelino – who appeared profoundly committed to gender equality[65] – is not at odds with her party's position.

Three other actors were very important to this process. Besides the CIG – mentioned above – another WPA, the Commission for Equality in Labour and Employment (CITE),[66] intervened. CITE specialises in fighting discrimination and promoting equality, specifically in labour, employment, and vocational training. Although CITE did not argue directly in favour of gender quotas in the economic sphere, it did call attention to the lack of women on administrative boards of companies and championed a promotional campaign aimed at raising awareness in different actors in order to change this trend.[67] When

---

[63] Personal interview with Teresa Morais (2005).

[64] Available at: www.jornaldenegocios.pt/economia/seguranca-social/detalhe/sera-um-dia-feliz-para-marcelo-quando-der-luz-verde-as-quotas-nas-empresas (accessed in July 2017).

[65] Personal interview with PS MP Catarina Marcelino (2014).

[66] Available at: www.cite.gov.pt/en/about_us.html (accessed in January 2016).

[67] Available at: http://cite.gov.pt/pt/acite/mulheres_conselhos.html (accessed in January 2016).

asked by the Assembly of the Republic to give their formal assent to the legislative bill, both CIG and CITE were in favour.

The EU appears as a very relevant factor, not only to the gender quotas law recently passed, but also to all the other documents approved since 2012. References to this international actor are made in many public interventions and also in the content of the resolutions and bills presented by both the current and previous governments. The EU influence was particularly visible in the first actions undertaken by the previous government (spearheaded by Teresa Morais), which clearly followed the challenge launched in May 2011 by the vice president of the European Commission, Viviane Reding, for European companies to adopt self-regulatory measures to promote the equilibrium between women and men on their administrative boards (Casaca 2014, 186). In fact in 2012 Teresa Morais contacted the twenty biggest Portuguese companies to propose the goal laid out by Reding. Only four of them then responded, and negatively. This anecdote shows not only the influence of EU incentives on national policy-making but also the pervasive resistance of the business elite to the principle of gender quotas.

Throughout the whole process until the adoption of the gender quota law for companies, no constitutional provisions were called into question, neither in the official documents nor in the Assembly of the Republic legislative debates and public discourses. The exposition of motives of the 2017 PS bill begins with a reminder of Paragraph (h) of article 9° of the Constitution, which states that the promotion of equality between women and men is one of the fundamental tasks of the state. Then, the text proceeds with a description of the legislative framework for the current bill that started with the adoption of the Parity Law in 2006. This beginning seems to aim to immediately rule out any possibility of considering the bill unconstitutional, even if nobody in the PS expected such a bill to face constitutional issues.[68] In fact, the bill progressed as the party expected. The report that the Legislative Committee of Constitutional Issues, Rights, Freedoms, and Guarantees – which was the committee responsible for the discussion of the bill – issued in February 2017 clearly confirms its constitutionality.[69]

---

[68] Personal interview with PS MP José Magalhães (2015) and email exchange with constitutionalist Vital Moreira (2016).

[69] Report of the Committee, available at: www.parlamento.pt/ActividadeParlamentar/Paginas/DetalheIniciativa.aspx?BID=40919 (accessed in July 2017).

7.4 GENDER REGIME AND DISCOURSES

The biggest transformations in the national gender narrative occurred during the long process leading up to the adoption of the Parity Law. A significant change was marked by the introduction of the word "parity" as a qualifier of the term "democracy" in the political agenda. The expression "parity democracy" appeared for the first time in a party manifesto in Portugal in 1991, in the PS manifesto for the legislative elections.[70] However, the PS commitment to parity has not been straightforward from that moment onwards. In fact, it took more than ten years for the PS to use the expression "parity democracy" again in a party manifesto.[71] Even if the PS (headed by the aforementioned António Guterres) started adopting an identity as a party committed to gender equality in politics during the 1990s, it chose another narrative, marked by expressions such as "positive discrimination of the least represented sex." The change in the conception of equality within the PS is visible in the bills introduced by the party concerning the political sphere (Table 7.1 in Appendix). While the 1998 PS bill emphasises "equality of opportunities for citizens of either sex" – with the word "parity" totally absent – all bills that the PS introduced from the year 2000 onwards have the word "parity" in their titles. The approval of a Parity Law in France in June 2000 might have motivated for the use of this expression in Portugal. In fact, the example of France is mentioned in the 2000 PS bill. The bill also states that "parity has a philosophical inspiration which differs from quotas, since parity considers the duality of humanity – i.e. the existence of male and female citizens – as its guiding principle." The same idea is further developed by a PS MP: "for a long time, the equality issues were discussed from the point of view of the poor women who require special measures ... and that is not at all the party's position ... The equality between women and men is an essential issue – which is in itself a condition – which defines the development of societies."[72]

The BE shares the same vision of gender equality,[73] as the word "parity" also appears in all of the bills introduced by this party concerning political representation. Since these are the only two parties that have been pursuing an agenda of gender equality in politics in

---

[70] PS Party Manifesto, legislative elections, 1991, 175.
[71] PS Party Manifesto, legislative elections, 2002, 146.
[72] Personal interview with PS MP Sónia Fertuzinhos (2005).
[73] Personal interview with BE MP Helena Pinto (2005).

an active way, it could be said that this agenda in Portugal has been characterised by a gendered conception of democracy. Having said that, two factors raise a note of caution regarding this portrayal. First, by no means do all political parties share this vision of democracy, not even on the left wing. The second factor is that even the parties that pursue this agenda in Portugal operationalise parity in a soft way, i.e. not following the more commonly used 50/50 measure, but instead using a quota of at least 33 per cent for either sex.[74] This number is referred to in the exposition of motives of the 2006 PS bill (while the BE's bills have similar arguments) as the "parity threshold – a value above which it is possible to have an effective representation of the whole of humanity and an expression of its both masculine and feminine sides." Furthermore, after the law's implementation, gender equality in politics once again vanished from the political agenda, suggesting that the main actors are satisfied with the 33 per cent representation threshold. Only a few NGOs are still engaged in achieving an increase in the threshold (50/50).[75] This lack of interest is visible not only in the absence of discourses on the issue but also in the way the law has been implemented. Although compliance with the law has been quite successfully achieved,[76] political parties only comply with its minimum requirements – very seldom do the lists surpass the 33 per cent minimum requirement for women's inclusion. This minimum effort is true even for the Socialist party. In contrast to Spain, in Portugal the statutory quota blurred the differences between parties with different commitments to gender-balanced representation (Verge and Espírito-Santo 2016).

While gender equality in politics has vanished from the political agenda, recent years have been marked – although not that intensely – by the debate on corporate gender quotas. Although it is too soon to analyse its implementation or what gender transformations it might provoke, it is curious to see that the word "parity" has been avoided both in the official documents and in the debates, even though the Parity Law marked the legislative framework of this law (as stated in the exposition of motives of the PS 2017 bill).

---

[74] 2006 bills from both the PS and the BE.

[75] For example: http://plataformamulheres.org.pt/wp-content/ficheiros/2016/04/Pp DM-Argumentario-afinal-o-que-e-a-democracia-paritaria.pdf (accessed in January 2015).

[76] Apart from local elections, where a few problems remain.

The word is mentioned only once throughout the PS bill – and not in the title (in fact the bill has no title) – and it is not mentioned at all in the final law. Expressions such as "equilibrated representation between women and men" or "equality between genders" have been used much more often.

7.5   CONCLUSION

This chapter has focused on the process of gender quota adoption in Portugal. It has mainly tackled electoral quotas, but has also looked at the very recent steps towards gender quotas in the business sector. The situation in each sphere is very different. There have been party quotas since the 1980s and statutory electoral quotas since 2006, whereas the first measure with binding pressure related to the economic sphere passed in 2017. This chapter had two objectives. The first was to analyse the role, the interactions, synergies, and alliances of the most important (f)actors that pursue the adoption of gender quotas in Portugal, both in the political and the economic spheres. The second main objective of this chapter was to explore how gender quotas challenge and transform the political gender regime in Portugal.

Concerning the first objective, as argued in Krook (2009), in the case of Portugal, we observe that gender quotas are the result of multiple groups of actors. In both spheres, some key women within political parties determined events, although there is a crucial difference between them. Whereas women activists mainly remained in the background in the case of the electoral quotas, they gave a face to the measures within the economic sphere in each of the governments that have so far been involved in quotas for companies. The fact that two parties that officially oppose quotas either introduced legislation in that direction or contributed to enabling a related law shows that the simple presence of a key actor might tip the balance of ideology. Since the women's section in the PS is rather weak and not necessarily feminist,[77] being part of this organisation does not increase the likelihood of being a crucial actor in the pursuit of this agenda. But several women within the PS were very committed and were crucial to the passage of both the corporate and the electoral gender quotas laws.

---

[77] In May 2016, a feminist woman (Elza Pais) was elected President of the Women's Section and she has promised to take gender equality more seriously.

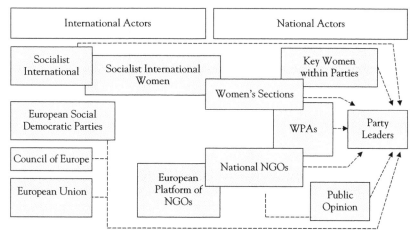

Figure 7.1 Synergies between the most important (f)actors for the adoption of gender quotas

The second determinant mobilising actor that applies to the measures adopted in both spheres is the presence of European and international actors. Besides the more or less direct influence that these actors might have on the parties and party leaders, their role is even more fundamental because they also intervene indirectly, i.e. through other actors. Figure 7.1 consists of an attempt to schematise the synergies between the most important (f)actors in Portugal. While some international actors, such as the SI, other European social democratic parties, the Council of Europe, or the European Union are likely to influence party leaders directly, these and other international entities (such as the SI women's section or the European Women's Lobby) are also important for setting the agenda of certain national actors, such as the parties' women's sections, the WPA, and the NGOs. These national actors then, with more or less success and relatively directly, try to impact party leaders. Accordingly, the international actors assume a crucial double role here.

Furthermore, it is important to emphasise the synergies that arise between some national actors that might improve their likelihood of being successful. These synergies are only possible because there are some structures (and there were even more before the WPA was reformed, i.e. when the Parity Law was adopted) that enable the NGOs, the parties' women sections, and the WPA to come together.

Concerning the second objective, there are two critical moments to consider. The first occurs with the revision of the Constitution in 1997, when equality was first endorsed in a substantive way. Up until 1997, the Constitution clearly privileged a formal conception of equality, i.e. an equality based on equal treatment preventing discrimination or privileges based on factors such as race, sex, etc. There were very few exceptions, including e.g. protection measures at work for pregnant and postpartum women (Moreira 1998, 49). However, from the fourth revision onwards, it has been part of a select group of constitutions that enable affirmative actions in favour of women's participation in the political sphere (Miranda 1998, 43) and in the economic sphere, implying a clear shift towards a substantive equality. The passing of quota legislation enhanced the entrenchment of substantive equality even further.

The second decisive moment happened when the political sphere began to view democracy in a paritarian way and to use this view as the main basis for the adoption of electoral quotas. While other motives are also presented – namely (a) the contribution to the improvement of the democratic system, (b) the question of justice (the equal rights argument), and (c) the idea that women's and men's different views of the world (due to historical and cultural reasons) complement each other (the differential framings argument)[78] – parity remains the structural backdrop that ultimately justifies the adoption of such artificial measures in the political sphere.[79] There has been an evolution from a discourse on affirmative action (bills introduced until the year 2000 by the PS) to a paritarian logic, implying a renewed conception of democracy. However, not all intervening actors agree with this vision – it is mostly the parties that have proposed the Parity Law that stand for it – and even these defend a soft parity, i.e. parity with a minimal representation threshold. In fact, as mentioned before, almost no one in Portugal seems to be currently engaged in a real parity. Furthermore, the paritarian conception of democracy remains a discourse for political actors; it is not reflected in broader society, which continues to be

[78] The first two motives are present in both the PS and the BE 2006 bills, whereas the latter motive does not appear in the BE's bill.

[79] Since a debate about gender quotas in the economic sphere is only just beginning, it is hard to identify the main rationale behind it. However, the grounds of justice and equality seem to justify it.

rather indifferent to this topic.[80] Probably because of this, the paritarian lexicon was not used during the debate on gender quotas in the economic sphere that took place in 2017.

While gender-balanced representative bodies are welcomed and a significant absence of women in powerful organs is often criticised, gender equality is not (yet) seen as a democratic requirement. Nevertheless, discourses against gender quotas – grounded on merit – are becoming progressively less common. In fact, the debate about corporate gender quotas enjoyed a certain consensus.

References

Baum, Michael, and Ana Espírito-Santo. 2009. "As Causas para a Adopção da Lei da Paridade em Portugal." In *Representação Política: O Caso Português em Perspectiva Comparada*, edited by André Freire and José Manuel Leite Viegas. Lisbon: Sextante.

——— 2012. "Portugal's 2006 Quota/Parity Law: An Analysis of the Causes for Its Adoption." *West European Politics* 35: 319–42.

Bettencourt, Ana Maria, and Maria Margarida Silva Pereira. 1995. *Mulheres Políticas – as suas causas*. Lisbon: Quetzal Editores.

Cabrera, Ana, Carla Martins, and Teresa Mendes Flores. 2011. "Representações Mediáticas das Deputadas Portuguesas: o «caso» do Parlamento Paritário." *Brazilian Journalism Research* 7 (11): 75–93.

Casaca, Sara Falcão. 2014. "A Igualdade entre Mulheres e Homens e a Tomada de Decisão na Esfera Económica: o Longo Percurso dos Instrumentos Normativos." *Revista do Centro de Estudos Judiciários* 1: 173–99.

Caul, Miki. 2001. "Quotas: A Cross National Analysis." *The Journal of Politics* 63 (4): 1214–29.

Fernandes, Tiago. 2012. "Civil Society after Dictatorship: A Comparison of Portugal and Spain, 1970–1990." Working paper 384. The Helen Kellogg Institute for International Studies. Available at: https://kellogg.nd.edu/publications/workingpapers/WPS/384.pdf.

Ferreira, Virgínia. 2011. "Engendering Portugal: Social Change, State Politics and Women's Social Mobilization." In *Contemporary Portugal – Politics, Society and Culture*, 2nd edn, edited by António Costa Pinto, 153–92. New York: Columbia University Press.

Franceschet, Susan, Mona Lena Krook, and Jennifer M. Piscopo. 2012. *The Impact of Gender Quotas*. New York: Oxford University Press.

---

[80] Recently in Parliament, the BE has recommended the alteration of the name of the Portuguese identity card from "Citizen Card" (which in Portuguese assumes the male version *Cartão do Cidadão*) to the neutral expression "Citizenship Card." This recommendation did not get any support in Parliament and became a public joke.

Holli, Anne Maria. 2011. "Transforming local politics? The impact of gender quotas in Finland." In *Women and Representation in Local Government: International Case Studies*, edited by Barbara Pini and Paula McDonald, 142–58. London and New York: Routledge.

Krook, Mona Lena. 2009. *Quotas for Women in Politics: Gender and Candidate Selection Reform Worldwide*. New York: Oxford University Press.

Lovenduski, Joni. 2005. "Introduction: State Feminism and the Political Representation of Women. In *State Feminism and Political Representation*, edited by Joni Lovenduski, 1–19. Cambridge: Cambridge University Press.

Magalhães, José. 1999. *Dicionário da revisão constitucional*. Lisbon: Editorial Notícias (includes a CD-ROM).

Mazur, Amy, and Dorothy McBride Stetson (eds.). 1995. *Comparative State Feminism*. London: SAGE Publications.

Meier, Petra. 2004. "The Mutual Contagion Effect of Legal and Party Quotas: A Belgian Perspective." *Party Politics* 10 (5): 583–600.

——— 2013. "Quotas, Quotas Everywhere: From Party Regulations to Gender Quotas for Corporate Management Boards. Another Case of Contagion." *Representation* 49: 453–66.

Miranda, Jorge. 1998. "Igualdade e participação política da mulher." In *Democracia com mais Cidadania*, edited by Vitalino Canas, 37–46. Lisbon: Imprensa Nacional.

Monteiro, Rosa. 2011. "A Política de Quotas em Portugal: O papel dos partidos políticos e do feminismo de Estado." *Revista Crítica de Ciências Sociais* 92: 31–50.

Monteiro, Rosa, and Virgínia Ferreira. 2012. "Metamorfoses das relações entre o Estado e os movimentos de mulheres em Portugal: entre a institucionalização e a autonomia." *ex aequo* 25: 13–27.

Moreira, Vital. 2005. "Participação Política das Mulheres: do sufragismo à paridade." In *Direitos Humanos das Mulheres*, edited by Anabela Miranda Rodrigues et al., 61–92. Coimbra: Coimbra Editora.

Santos, Maria Helena. 2011. *Do défice de cidadania à paridade política: Testemunhos de deputadas e deputados*. Porto: Edições Afrontamento.

Verge, Tània. 2013. "Regulating Gender Equality in Political Office in Southern Europe: The Cases of Greece, Portugal and Spain." *Representation* 49: 439–52.

Verge, Tània, and Ana Espírito-Santo. 2016. "Interactions between Party and Legislative Quotas: Candidate Selection and Quota Compliance in Portugal and Spain." *Government and Opposition* 51 (3): 416–39.

APPENDIX

TABLE 7.1   Timeline of the bills introduced by the PS and the BE related to gender quotas

Electoral:

1998 (PS): *Proposta de Lei 194/VII, DAR II série A No.68/VII/3*, 9 July 1998

2000 (PS): *Proposta de Lei 40/VIII, DAR II série A No.59/VIII/1*, 15 July 2000

2001 (BE): *Projecto de Lei 388/VIII, DAR II série A No.38/VIII/2*, 3 March 2001

2003 (PS): *Projecto de Lei 251/IX, DAR II série A No.76/IX/1*, 13 March 2003

2003 (BE): *Projecto de Lei 324/IX, DAR II série A No.110/IX/1*, 4 July 2003

2006 (BE): *Projectos de Lei 221/X, 222/X, and 223/X, DAR II série A No.93/X/1*, 11 March 2006

2006 (PS): *Projecto de Lei 224/X, DAR II série A No.93/X/1*, 11 March 2006

Corporate:

2015 (PS): *Projecto de Lei 1016/XII/4, DAR II série A N.º155/XII/4*, 25 June 2015*

2017 (PS): *Proposta de Lei 52/XIII, DAR II série A N.º54/XIII/2*, 18 January 2017

2017 (BE): *Projeto de Lei 406/XIII, DAR II série A N.º68/XIII/2*, 10 February 2017

*This bill expired without being subject to any debate or vote.

CHAPTER EIGHT

GENDER QUOTAS AND WOMEN'S SOLIDARITY AS A CHALLENGE TO THE GENDER REGIME IN POLAND

*Anna Śledzińska-Simon**

8.1 INTRODUCTION

The adoption of electoral gender quota law and soft quota rules for corporate boards and academia in Poland poses a challenge to the gender regime built upon the Romanticist national tradition which glorified Polish women as mothers and custodians of family values and confined them to the domestic sphere.[1] After the democratic transition of 1989, this tradition was legitimized by the government and the Catholic Church, which became an informal veto-player in the Polish political scene. Although in the new social contract enshrined in the Constitution of 1997, women and men have guarantees of equal rights in all aspects of life, including politics, the constitutional interpretation of substantive equality emphasized the remedial and compensatory function of positive measures and preserved the image of women as

---

* I am grateful to Ruth Rubio-Marín, Éléonore Lépinard, Adam Czarnota and Wojciech Sadurski for their valuable comments to the earlier draft of this chapter. The usual disclaimer applies. This chapter develops views presented in: Anna Śledzińska-Simon, Adam Bodnar, "Between symbolism and incrementalism: moving forward with the gender equality project in Poland," Working Paper, EUI Law 2015/30.

[1] Janion (2009). Janion noted that "[t]he modern concept of the nation and emerging nationalism underpinned the stereotype of masculinity, a mythology of a male community."

needful of special protection in the social and economic sphere, rather than promoting the concept of equal citizenship, autonomy or parity democracy. Instead the focus of the constitutional jurisprudence on the reproductive role of women reinforced the sexual contract and the traditional understanding of gender roles and gender relationships.

The adoption of the gender quota law proposed as a citizens' legislative initiative[2] was the first success of a new women's movement arising from anger and frustration about the marginalization and instrumentalization of women's issues by all successive post-1989 governments. In the process of collecting signatures under this initiative, Polish women showed unprecedented solidarity, which gave a start to a new movement promoting gender equality at local and regional levels. In this process women defined themselves as political subjects and claimed their right to be present in politics.

However, the quota law turned out to be only a partial victory. Although the implementation of the law significantly increased the number of female candidates in the electoral lists and led to a gradual change in women's representation in law-making bodies, it did not affect the outcome of political process, in particular after political parties inimical to gender equality and minority rights dominated the Parliament. Yet, women's solidarity has not faded away and instead showed its strength during the recent organization of mass protests against the government's support for the abortion ban. The mobilization around the quota law was thus a first challenge to the gender regime in Poland and an attempt to delegitimize the normative framework and the existing structures of power. In this process, it also became evident that in absence of legislative rules mandating gender parity or quotas in corporate boards, academia or the judiciary, these institutions are not going to change gender imbalance on a voluntary basis.

In sum, the adoption of gender quotas in Poland is an impressive example of legal and political mobilization in a gender regime that was not deeply committed to gender equality in practice, and persisted with a traditional public–private divide. While the relatively high proportion of Polish women in the labour market could be explained by a dual-breadwinner model of family inherited from the Communist

---

[2] Pursuant to Article 118(2) of the Constitution of Poland, any group of at least 100,000 citizens who have the right to vote in elections may propose a bill to the Lower Chamber of Parliament.

period,[3] their underrepresentation in politics clearly showed a missing commitment to egalitarian values and participatory citizenship. Hence, the adoption of legislative gender quotas was understood as a symbolic embrace of gender equality and was designed to have a limited impact on electoral results. Although gender quotas have not been introduced or voluntarily accepted in other domains, the social movement established to support gender equality had a truly transformative potential for Polish society. Emerging as a bottom-up initiative, the new social movement provided the quota legislation sufficient legitimacy that accounts for the subsequent lack of constitutional challenges to the law.

In the long run, the women's movement turned out to be the only social force capable of resisting oppressive laws under the government of the Law and Justice Party, which not only questioned the existing constitutional order, by official acts in blatant disregard to the letter of the Constitution and its established interpretations, but also objected to abiding by laws adopted in the European Union and disregarded the European Commission recommendations issued in the Rule of Law Framework.[4] It thus appears that gender quotas in a regime lacking strong egalitarian political and civic traditions are likely to be hijacked by political forces which fear that gender equality will transform the existing power relations and social roles. These forces not only openly oppose so-called gender ideology[5] but also challenge the very concept of liberal constitutionalism.

8.2 CLAIMING THE RIGHT TO BE PRESENT IN POLITICS AND PUBLIC LIFE

The adoption of gender quota law in Poland is the result of social mobilization against the denial or underestimation of women's role in national history and public life by each successive government since the transition to democracy in Poland in 1989. Although the electoral

---

[3] As of 2011 the general participation rate of women in the Polish labour market equals 53.1 percent and is lower than the EU average (58.5 percent). See *The current situation of equality in Poland – the country profile* (2012), available at: http://ec.europa .eu/justice/gender-equality/files/epo_campaign/country_profile_poland_en.pdf.

[4] See Recommendation of 26 July 2017 regarding the rule of law in Poland complementary to Commission Recommendations (EU) 2016/1374 and (EU) 2017/146, Brussels, 26 July 2017 C (2017) 5320 final.

[5] See Szulc (2016).

quota law was successfully passed in 2010, the idea of granting political privileges to women has been long contested by political parties
and constitutional experts. While many right-wing political leaders
declared that the position of women in politics should be improved
by other than legislative means, the center and left-wing political parties were more sympathetic to gender equality claims, yet often placed
women on the "unelectable" positions on electoral lists.[6]

The concept of the gender quota was for the first time proposed in
1996 in a bill on the equal status of men and women, and presented as
an initiative of the Parliamentary Group of Women.[7] The sponsors of
the bill argued that the existing laws did not guarantee actual equality
between men and women and did not prevent gender discrimination.
They also noted that the legal system did not provide women with
effective remedies against discrimination or mechanisms for enforcement of their legal rights.[8] The bill was reintroduced in 1998 after a
number of amendments, but rejected due to insufficient political support.[9] The voting took place after Electoral Action "Solidarity" won
elections in 1997, and the new government did not consider gender
equality as a political priority.[10]

---

[6] In constituencies that are traditionally dominated by another political party even
being placed in an electable position does not guarantee electoral success.

[7] The Parliamentary Group of Women was established in 1991 as a cross-party alliance of female MPs and acted to integrate Polish women's organizations and lobby
groups. Between 1993 and 1997 the Group participated in the constitution-making
process and proposed provisions concerning equal rights of men and women that
were eventually accepted in the final text of the Constitution of 1997 (Article 33).
The impact of the Group on the legislative work was, however, often limited due to
tight party discipline on ideologically important matters.

[8] The bill on the equal status of women and men was prepared by two university
professors – Małgorzata Fuszara and Eleonora Zielińska. It set as a goal a gradual
increase of women's representation from 30 to 40 percent in all collective organs
appointed or nominated by organs public authority and on lists of candidates for
collective elective organs.

[9] The concept of gender quota law was later proposed by Olga Krzyżanowska, an MP
of the Union of Liberty, in the bill amending the electoral law in 2001, but the Sejm
rejected this amendment. The bill on the equal status reappeared as the Senate's
initiative in 2002, but was again rejected in 2005.

[10] In 1999 Sejm rejected the bill with 212 votes against, 177 for and nineteen abstain-
ing. The government party, Electoral Action "Solidarity," almost entirely voted
against the bill. While the Liberty Union and the Polish Peasants' Party split in the
voting, the entire Social Democratic Alliance supported the bill.

In the early parliamentary debates on the equal status of men and women, three different positions were represented by the main political parties. The view represented by Electoral Action "Solidarity" emphasized that gender discrimination was not an actual problem in Poland, and that the position of women in the society was the result of their different role. Against this "separate but equal" approach the Liberty Union called for the improvement of equal opportunities of women in Poland but distanced itself from the Communist vision of equal rights and mandatory participation of women in public or professional life. The third approach, represented by the Social Democratic Alliance, promoted a vision of full emancipation and explicitly relied on the Beijing Platform for Action, international human standards and feminist postulates of gender parity.[11]

At the same time, public opinion agreed that the representation of women in decision-making positions needed to be improved, but opposed legislative reforms concerning the election system. In 1999 only 21 percent of respondents supported legislative gender quotas, while 63 percent contested them.[12] Still, in 2001 the main political parties – the Social Democratic Alliance, the Liberty Union and the Labor Union – voluntarily adopted the 30-percent rule on their candidate lists.[13] Notably, the Green party had gender parity as a voluntary party rule from its inception, but has never won seats in the Parliament.

In this political context, gender parity has become a long-term strategy for Polish feminists.[14] However, the success of the project depended not only on the concerted efforts of female politicians and activists, women's organizations (including the Polish Party of Women) and caucuses (the Parliamentary Group of Women), as well as the Ombudsman and the Government Plenipotentiary for Equal Treatment, but also on extraordinary circumstances. In fact, the introduction of electoral gender quotas was a concession given to women in the course of the early

---

[11] Bator (1999).

[12] Opinion poll, "Udział kobiet w życiu publicznym – prawne gwarancje równości," CBOS (BS/26/97), Warszawa 1997.

[13] Druciarek (2012).

[14] The concept of gender parity (50/50) was promoted by feminists (e.g. Agnieszka Graff, Kinga Dunin and Magdalena Środa) and female politicians mainly related to the Social Democratic Alliance. The gender electoral parity law was later promoted by the Office of the Government Plenipotentiary for the Equal Status of Women and Men, led by Izabela Jaruga-Nowacka (2001–4) and Magdalena Środa (2004–5).

presidential campaign.[15] In April 2010, the main presidential candidate, Bronisław Komorowski, promised to support gender quotas in exchange for support of female voters. This promise was duly kept after his election in recognition of a new women's movement that proposed a citizens' bill introducing gender parity to the electoral law.[16]

The new social movement emerged after the organization of the first Congress of Women in June 2009. The Congress of Women was convened in reaction to the official celebration of the twenty-fifth anniversary of "Solidarity" and the twentieth anniversary of democratic transformation in Poland. It was a symbolic act of solidarity with women whose role in overthrowing Communism in Poland had been demeaned in official presentations. The Congress was intended to emphasize the presence of women in Polish history and public life, but also to discuss current problems regarding women's rights. The first Congress of Women gathered several hundred participants who debated the feminization of poverty, unemployment, reproductive health and domestic violence, and the execution of alimony dues. They drew up a list of demands, which included gender parity in decision-making bodies.

The first Congress of Women was a transformative moment for Polish women, who collectively claimed the right to be present in public life and politics. Women in the Congress understood that any social change needs to be sustained through legal reforms, which require not only popular support, but also support of institutionalized actors – policy-makers, courts, law-enforcement, etc. However, they have also realized that women should not exclusively rely on institutionalized politics but undertake direct actions and initiatives that remedy the unprincipled approach to women's issues taken by the government, political parties and leaders. The Congress gave a start to a women's solidarity pact against the instrumentalization of women's issues in politics and law.

After the success of the first assemblage, the Congress was transformed into an association,[17] and consecutive women's congresses were

---

[15] The electoral campaign took place amidst a national tragedy after a plane crash which killed a number of key government officials, including the President of the Republic, Lech Kaczyński.

[16] Śledzińska-Simon and Bodnar (2013).

[17] The aim of the Association is to "to build ties and solidarity among women, based on knowledge of their economic, cultural and educational heritage, on the memory of their historical achievements and hopes concerning an equal society of the future."

held annually in Warsaw to address recent challenges to women's rights. Moreover, the model of a congress of women has spread to other cities and regions. Since 2009 the Congress of Women has been attracting diverse women's groups and organizations, as well as politicians, public figures, entrepreneurs, journalists, academics and individuals – women and men – who share a belief in equal rights and *de facto* gender equality. While the first Congress was inspired by feminists, it was oriented towards all women and gathered participants of different social, economic and religious backgrounds. In this way, the Congress provided a discursive forum for all Polish women to express their diverse voices and needs.[18] Still, the Congress was not publicly supported by women related to ideologically conservative circles, including the currently ruling Law and Justice Party.

Over time, the Congress of Women has become an important actor in the Polish political scene. It has not come to be a political party, but appointed the Shadow Cabinet of Women[19] and the Political Council – an internal body to promote female candidates in elections. While many women affiliated to the Congress aspire to decision-making positions and offices, they do also realize that equal representation is difficult to attain. Therefore, the Congress has launched national and regional programs in the field of education, culture, health and care, as well as professional and personal development to strengthen the position of women outside the domestic sphere. In this way, the Congress implements a strategy of enhancing the economic and social opportunities of women that in a long run may help to narrow the gender gap in the area of political representation.

The adoption of electoral gender quota law in Poland should thus be seen as the consequence of women's mobilization around a new social movement. This new social movement evolved from a feminist critique into a social practice that has made an incremental change in the political life.[20] Although the number of women in elective bodies has

---

[18] This pluralism of women's voices means in this context that many women share conservative beliefs about the model of family with feminist views on women's role in public life. Kułakowska and Łuksza (2015). In the autobiography of the First Lady, the authors attempt to reinterpret the Polish twentieth-century history "by dismantling its male-oriented perspective with restored feminine 'little narratives'." Danuta Wałęsa is an example of a unique post-socialist feminine sensibility, combining conservative ideology with a feminist voice about her public role.

[19] See www.kongreskobiet.pl/pl-PL/text/o_nas/Gabinet_Cieni.

[20] Chełstowska et al. (2015).

not yet reached 30 percent, since 2011 the number of female candidates participating in elections has doubled, and women have gained greater visibility in electoral campaigns. It is also noteworthy that in the 2015 parliamentary elections, the three main political parties nominated women as candidates for the Prime Minister's office.

The recent Prime Minister, Beata Szydło, is the third female head of government in Poland. Although it is a commonly held belief that she executes the political will of a *de facto* head of the government, Jarosław Kaczyński, rather than speaking in her own right,[21] the independence of her leadership may be a question of time. The example of Ewa Kopacz, who was the first Speaker of the Sejm and the second female Prime Minister, shows that women in positions of power learn to emancipate from male dominance when the opportunity arises.[22]

8.3   THE WORLD WITHOUT WOMEN

The World Without Women (*Świat bez kobiet*) is the title of a book written by Agnieszka Graff in 2001 which describes the marginalization of women and women's issues in Poland during the first decade of democratic transformation.[23] Educated on the "second wave" feminist literature, Graff noticed that problems of women's rights protection and gender equality have their origin in a low representation of women in decision-making processes. She was among several women in the Congress who publicly demanded the introduction of gender parity – the 50-percent rule – on electoral lists.

For a large part of Polish history, Polish women remained invisible in the political arena. Their rights and interests were usually subservient to the national struggle for independence. Even Polish women who had fought for national independence did not have an equal share in the victory and power. Needless to say, their participation in the government after 1918, 1945 and 1989 was purely symbolic.[24] Between 1919 and 1939, only 1.9 percent of deputies in the Lower Chamber and 3.8 percent of the Senate were women, whereas between 1945 and 1989

[21] Buras (2016) ("Kaczyński is the *de facto* ruler of the country today, with Prime Minister Beata Szydło and President Andrzej Duda is doing little more than obediently enforcing his ideas").

[22] Ewa Kopacz as the successor of Donald Tusk was ranked by Forbes as the world's fortieth most powerful woman in 2015.

[23] Graff (2001).

[24] Fuszara (2009, 2010).

female deputies never had more than 23 percent of seats in the unicameral Parliament. Today, the lower house – the Sejm – is 27-percent women. Still, in elections based on majority voting, the number of elected women does not grow. In 2015, women held only 13 percent of seats in the Senate.[25]

Although Polish women had already gained voting rights by 1919, the trajectory of their movement was different from the Western counterparts. In the nineteenth century, women's groups did not seek universal suffrage and emancipation, but rather the preservation of tradition and culture.[26] The traditional understanding of gender roles in society was strongly influenced by the Catholic Church, which played an important role in the national struggle for independence. Notably, the patriarchal model of family persisted through the interwar and Communist periods. Although the Communist government officially endorsed feminist ideology and promoted gender equality in employment through access of women to certain professions and institutionalized care, the Communist party leaders never allowed women to enter the world of politics with full rights. Moreover, the economic emancipation of women did not contribute to a sharing of domestic obligations by men.

Thus, it shall come as no surprise that the early years of democratic transition in Poland were characterized by a social aversion to feminism.[27] Additionally, neoliberal reforms introduced in the 1990s only deepened the existing inequalities between men and women, manifesting themselves as a gender pay gap or the relegation of women to low-paid positions and industrial sectors. It is also noticeable that patterns of systemic gender discrimination have been engrained in the law and reinforced by state institutions.

According to Ewa Łętowska, the former judge of the Constitutional Tribunal and the first Ombudsman (Ombudswoman) in Poland, the state pension system petrified the status of women as carers. Clearly, different treatment of men and women with regard to the pensionable age and early retirement pushed women out of the labour market and

---

[25] Between 2011 and 2015 the Sejm was 23-percent women and the Senate 13 percent. Senators in Poland are chosen in single-mandate electoral districts by majority voting. In 2015 only 14 percent of candidates for senators were women and 13 percent won a seat.

[26] Fuszara (2012).

[27] Rubio-Marín (2014).

made them bear the financial consequences of this situation. In addition, women also had to carry out state obligations towards the needy (including children and the elderly) because of the shortage of institutional care. This double jeopardy was not regarded as a disadvantage by the Constitutional Tribunal, which upheld different pensionable ages for men and women as consistent with the principle of gender equality.[28] Notably, in this case the full adjudicating panel was comprised of eight men and for women, while all three dissenters were women.[29]

The absence of women in Polish politics was both symbolic and real, due to their underrepresentation in decision-making bodies. Only a few women from amongst the leaders of the anti-Communist opposition were invited to the 1989 Round Table Talks and occupied positions of power after the democratic change.[30] Moreover, in the 1990s women's issues were addressed mostly by newly established civil society organizations, which remained weak and divided.[31] Women's organizations could not form one front against a coalition of the state (government) and the Catholic Church, which took advantage of the historical role it had played during Communism to secure its influence over legislation, specifically in areas concerning the place of religion in public life, but also in terms of abortion, reproductive rights and sex education.[32] The government made this concession in exchange for the support of the Episcopate to Polish accession to the European Union (the so-called "abortion compromise"). In this way, a new social contract – between laymen in power and the clergy – was made in Poland, the result of which was that women were subjected to rules that restricted their choices and expanded protection for conscientious objectors.[33]

---

[28] Judgment of 15 July 2010, Case no. K 63/09 (women's pensionable age).

[29] The Constitutional Tribunal found that a gradual equalization of the pensionable age for men and women was consistent with the Constitution (judgment of 7 May 2013, Case K 43/12), but signalled that the pension reform should be accompanied by effective and comprehensive employment and family policy, supporting the activation of certain socially vulnerable categories, as well as the family responsibilities of working persons towards children and the elderly (decision of 17 July 2014, Case no. S 3/14).

[30] Penn (2005).

[31] Fuszara (2006); Czerwińska and Piotrowska (2009).

[32] The lack of consensus regarding the status of human embryos prevented the ratification of the Oviedo Convention for the Protection of Human Rights and Dignity of the Human Being with regard to the Application of Biology and Medicine.

[33] Notably, the Constitutional Tribunal played an important role in maintaining this status quo. In 1997 the Tribunal struck down a provision in the abortion law that

In 2009, women in the Congress declared that twenty years of democratic transformation had not improved their situation. On the contrary, they found themselves adversely affected by neoliberal changes and deprived of many of the social benefits and much of the institutional support they had previously enjoyed. The first Congress of Women enabled them to talk publicly about their problems and claim their rights, some of which – like the execution of alimony dues – were raised in public debate for the first time ever.

8.4 THE IMPACT OF EU LAW ON GENDER EQUALITY

The important impulse for the mobilization of Polish women came from global processes of constitutionalization beyond the state, and specifically from European integration. After 1990, women's organizations entered new institutional relations with international and European organizations, including women's groups and NGOs, and addressees of their programmes.[34] Although integration with the European Union did not lead to the consolidation of the Polish women's movement at the European level in the form of a national umbrella representation in the European Women Lobby, it helped to establish a support network outside the state.[35] It was also in the process of Polish negotiations with the EU that the government established the Office for Equal Status of Men and Women, in 2001. Still, the history of the Office shows that it has always been subject to the political whims of the current government.[36]

permitted termination of pregnancy on social grounds (judgment of 26 May 1996, Case no. K 26/96). This decision was called "the most outrageous case, of all constitutional courts [cases] in CEE, of judicial usurpation of the law-making power." Sadurski (2005). More recently, the Tribunal found the law on medical professions unconstitutional because it excluded the use of the conscience clause by doctors in other than life-saving emergency situations (judgement of 7 October 2015, Case no. K 12/14). In both decisions women's autonomy has a lower status than the right to life of a fetus and freedom of conscience. See also Ostrowski (2010).

[34] Choluj and Neususs (2004); Fuszara et al. (2008).
[35] Grabowska and Regulska (2007).
[36] The Office of the Government Plenipotentiary for Equal Status of Men and Women embodies the story of other weak and dysfunctional women's policies agencies in the region. Not only were its names and competences constantly changed, but it was eradicated altogether between 2005 and 2007. Bego (2015). Still, the Office was actively involved in promotion of women's rights during the terms of Izabela Jaruga-Nowacka (2001–4), Magdalena Środa (2004–5), Agnieszka Kozłowska-Rajewicz

The accession of Poland to the European Union and the availability of EU funds have had a significant impact on the institutional strategies of Polish women's organizations, and strengthened their watchdog role in monitoring government policies and activities. Relying on European Union law and the standards of human rights protection adopted in the Council of Europe, women's organizations in Poland could more effectively exercise their control over the government.[37] Yet, the expectation that the transposition of EU anti-discrimination directives into the Polish legal system would harmonize the equality standard at the national level and also raise public awareness about gender equality could be only partially fulfilled.[38] Although EU law could be seen as a source of the re-legitimization of gender equality guaranteed in the Polish Constitution, it has not become a "living" principle endorsed by state institutions. Rather the implementation of EU directives was only a matter of formal compliance with treaty obligations.[39]

In practice, the impact of the EU on gender equality in Poland is limited to the areas of employment and social protection.[40] Likewise, the implementation of gender mainstreaming in government policies is limited to equal opportunities for men and women in public administration and the labour market. While the availability of EU funds created a "demand" for projects aimed at the professional activation of women, gender mainstreaming has not actually changed the structure of the labour market or the common practice of denying women the status of full-time employees. Moreover, the focus on gender mainstreaming accentuated gender equality rather than the unequal position of

---

(2011–14) and Małgorzata Fuszara (2014–15). In 2016, the new Plenipotentiaries for Equal Treatment and Civil Society appointed by the Law and Justice Party distanced itself from promoting so-called "gender ideology."

[37] Grabowska (2014).

[38] Opinion Poll "Równouprawnienie płci?" CBOS (BS/31/13), Warszawa 2013.

[39] The poor quality of this legislation makes its application practically impossible. So is the case of the Act of 3 December 2010 on the implementation of some of the provisions of the European Union with regard to equal treatment; *Journal of Laws* 2010 No. 257, Item 1700.

[40] In comparison with other vulnerable groups in Poland, women are relatively better protected in the area of employment. See the 7th and 8th Periodic Reports of the Government of the Republic of Poland for the period of 2002–10 and the Alternative Report on the implementation of the Convention on the Elimination of All Forms of Discrimination Against Women, submitted to the UN Committee on the Elimination of Discrimination Against Women.

women in public policies.[41] Whereas the shift from "women" to "gender" and "rights" to "opportunities" enabled the inclusion of gender equality in policy-making, it also disabled any serious debate about other areas of inequality between men and women, such as reproductive rights, gender-based violence and violence against women.[42]

In consequence, the piecemeal nature of EU anti-discrimination directives actually reinforced the stereotype that women need protection in economic and social life, rather than helping to shift the paradigm from equality to the full enfranchisement model.[43] This understanding of women's position in fact permeated the dominant interpretation of substantive equality enshrined in the Constitution. The Constitutional Tribunal consistently held that laws granting special or privileged economic or social rights to women are justified by biological differences and aim to compensate their role as caregivers.[44] In this vein, the constitutional jurisprudence maintained the image of women as biologically determined and in need of special protection rather than promoting equal citizens' rights in all areas of life.[45] In the end, neither integration with EU nor the implementation of EU law could challenge the culturally entrenched model of power relations or discharge the existing "sexual contract."[46]

8.5 THE ADOPTION OF LEGISLATIVE GENDER QUOTAS

The gender quota law was introduced as an amendment to the Electoral Code in 2011,[47] and requires that electoral lists in all types of elections based on proportional voting have at least 35 percent of either gender among their candidates. The bill originally proposing electoral gender parity was exchanged for a 35-percent gender quota during the presidential campaign. While the coalition of organizations supporting

---

[41] Rutkowska (2008)

[42] Grabowska (2014).

[43] Rodríguez Ruiz and Rubio-Marín (2008).

[44] Judgments of 3 March 1987, Case no. P 2/87 (limits to medical schools); of 24 October 1998, Case no. K 6/89 (pensions for coal miners and their families); of 29 September 1997, Case no. K 15/97 (early pensions in civil service); and of 4 November 2013, Case no. K 63/07 (pensionable age for men and women).

[45] Dębska (2014).

[46] Pateman (1988).

[47] Act of 5 January 2011, Electoral Code, Journal of Laws 2011 No. 21, Item 112.

the bill believed that only gender parity could make a difference in political representation, the ruling party that supported the main presidential candidate agreed only to threshold quotas. Yet, in contrast to other countries with legislative electoral gender quotas, the Polish law was proposed as a popular initiative backed by very strong democratic support. This could be one of the reasons why the electoral quota system has not been challenged before the Constitutional Tribunal, even though other disputed provisions of the Electoral Code have been eventually struck down as unconstitutional and even though many constitutional experts insisted on quotas being contrary to the constitution.[48]

In Poland, gender quota law could be passed without a constitutional amendment because the Constitution guarantees not only the principle of equal treatment and non-discrimination (Article 32), but also the equal rights of men and women in all spheres of life (Article 33). Still, the introduction of a system of electoral gender quotas raised serious constitutional doubts. First, the literal meaning of Article 33 does not suggest that there is an obligation to implement *de facto* equality between men and women. Second, it has been accepted in the legal doctrine that compensatory privilege (positive discrimination) is permissible to benefit weaker social groups like women, but it needs to be applied differently in relation to social rights and differently (more restrictively) in relation to personal and political rights. In particular, due to the categorical nature of equality in the electoral process, some scholars doubted whether the aim of achieving *de facto* gender equality could be used to justify what they argue was a "limitation of passive electoral rights."[49]

The voices of experts who emphasized that gender parity or quotas were not only in line with the substantive equality enshrined in Article 33 of the Constitution, but also consistent with the Convention on Elimination of All Forms of Discrimination Against Women were almost unnoticed in the academic debate.[50] Notably, all these experts were commissioned either by the Plenipotentiary for Equal Treatment or the Congress of Women.[51] Characteristically, experts commissioned by the Sejm Bureau of Research were very critical of the gender quota

---

[48] Judgment of the Constitutional Court of 14 July 2011, Case no. K 9/11.
[49] Garlicki (2003); Urbaniak (2011).
[50] Wieruszewski and Sękowska-Kozłowska (2010).
[51] Adam Bodnar, Anna Śledzińska-Simon and Wiktor Osiatyński were in favour of electoral gender quota as temporary positive measures.

bill. They contended that quotas violate the principle of equal treatment and non-discrimination, the principle of free and equal elections, political pluralism and the internal autonomy of political parties.[52] In this view, electoral gender quotas constrain freedom of voting because voters need to take gender into account, in addition to their political and personal preferences.[53] Still, because there was no need to introduce the concept of substantive equality between men and women in political life in the Constitution, the quota law could eventually be passed. Furthermore, in contrast to Spain, in Poland the electoral quota law has not been subject to constitutional review.[54]

In 2010, the parity bill was sponsored by the Congress of Women and proposed by the European women's network and politicians like the EU Parliament head, Jerzy Buzek, the EU Commissioner, Danuta Hübner and foreign experts such as Drude Dahlerup. Yet, the concept of gender quotas was recognized by Polish political leaders only in the course of the presidential elections. Therefore, it was not a paradigm shift but political opportunism, because female support was necessary for a victory. Nevertheless, the Polish case shows that state law is not an "autopoietic" system, immune to social dynamics, but is open to underground pressures and compromise between the ruling class and the demands of the class seeking emancipation.[55] While the right-wing political parties ideologically contested both electoral gender parity and quotas, the left-wing parties supported the bill in order to increase their popularity and attract women voters.

Notably, a statistical Pole was much more supportive of positive measures favouring women's participation in politics than a statistical politician. In 2009, according to some data, 70 percent of women and 52 percent of men were in favour of gender parity.[56] Yet, the opinion polls showed more moderate social support for promoting women's opportunities in politics by legislative means (56 percent of respondents were in favour of and 29 percent against the gender parity law).[57] In consecutive years, the level of support has slightly decreased, probably because the

---

[52] Skotnicki (2010); Szmyt (2010).

[53] Banaszak (2009).

[54] Judgment of the Spanish Constitutional Court of 28 January 2008, Case no. 12/2008, upholding the law on the effective equality between men and women.

[55] Broumas (2015).

[56] Fuszara (2008).

[57] Opinion Poll, "Parytety prawną gwarancją większego udziału kobiet w polityce," CBOS (BS/130/2010), Warszawa 2010.

feeling of solidarity with and among women in the historical momentum of the first Women's Congress has melted away. According to an opinion poll conducted in January and February 2013, a significant part of society was in favour of increasing the number of women in the decision-making positions in the government (47 percent), foundations and social organizations (47 percent), political parties (46 percent), public administration (42 percent) and companies and enterprises (45 percent). The respondents underscored the fact that the under-representation of women in public life was related to women's greater engagement in household duties (59 percent) and male dominance in the public sphere (43 percent). Every third respondent considered it fair that the law should define a percentage of places reserved for women on the electoral lists, but the majority of respondents (59 percent) were against such a rule. However, respondents who were in favour of electoral gender quotas opted for a 40-percent quota for women.[58]

8.6 THE IMPACT OF ELECTORAL GENDER QUOTAS

Up to the time of writing, the 35-percent gender quota rule applied to the 2011 and 2015 elections of the Lower House of the Parliament and to the 2014 elections of the European Parliament and local government. Overall, the number of female candidates has grown significantly, reaching around 44 percent in 2014 and 42 percent in 2015, but the increase of women representatives was rather modest. In 2007 there were 1,428 female candidates (23 percent of all candidates) running in the parliamentary elections (for the Lower House of Parliament) and ninety-four women (21 percent of all deputies) were successful. In 2011, there were 3,064 female candidates and only 110 women won a seat (24 percent). Thus, in the 2011 elections the number of female had candidates grown by 100 percent, but the number of female deputies by only 3 percent.[59] In contrast, in the outcome of 2015 elections, women occupied 27 percent of seats in the Lower House for the first time.[60] In 2009, among fifty deputies to the European Parliament, eleven were women, and in 2014 this proportion was fifty-one to twelve. Such is the case even though women occupied between

---

[58] Opinion Poll "Kobiety w życiu publicznym," CBOS (BS/34/2013), Warszawa 2013.
[59] Flis (2014).
[60] See also Republic of Poland, Parliamentary Elections 25 October 2015, OSCE/ODIHR Election Assessment Mission Report, Warsaw 2016.

40 and 50 percent of the lists, showing that the occupation of positions by women increased by one half from 2009 to 2014.[61]

The insignificant growth of women's representation in legislative bodies is frequently related to the composition of the list rather than the actual number of women on the lists. It is therefore the lack of a placement mandate which makes electoral gender quota ineffective.[62] According to the leading Polish expert in election systems, Jarosław Flis, gender quotas work only on the level of selection of the candidates and not on the level of election of the deputies. In his opinion, male politicians "agreed" upon the introduction of the quota law because they anticipated that the 35-percent rule would not endanger their leadership.[63] Flis observes that political preferences in Poland are territorially and ideologically intertwined, while gender is only one (and often the least significant) factor for voters supporting big political parties. Therefore, gender quotas do not make a significant difference to the outcome of voting in an open-list electoral system combined with the practice of composing lists with double the number of candidates than the actual number of mandates to be shared. The outcome of voting also depends on the size of electoral districts and the number of political parties taking part in the elections. In this context, successful female candidates need not only to associate with strong political parties, but also to have an already recognizable name.

Other analysts of electoral gender quotas in Poland maintain that a visible position on the list does not guarantee electoral success.[64] Instead, a list subsumes recognizable names. It is thus argued that the introduction of the zipper system or gender parity in Poland should be combined with electable positions corresponding to the number of mandates that a given political party forming a separate electoral committee has won in the previous election and soft-law mechanisms promoting political opportunities for women before the electoral run. For the time being, the process of composing electoral lists by political parties remains nontransparent and unaffected by changes in the electoral law.

---

[61] Data on election statistics, Państwowa Komisja Wyborcza, available at: http://wybory2011.pkw.gov.pl/kom/pl/statystyka.html.

[62] Some parties, like the Civic Platform, introduced internal rules, placing at least one woman among the first three positions on the lists and at least two among the first five.

[63] Flis (2014).

[64] Niżyńska (2011).

8.7 INTRODUCING A ZIPPER SYSTEM

In 2013 two independent proposals introducing a zipper system[65] and a zipper system combined with the gender parity rule were drafted to remedy the lack of a significant change regarding gender balance in politics pursuant to the 35 percent quota law.[66] Both the Congress of Women and the left-wing oriented party – *Twój Ruch* - sponsoring the parity bill argued that it would help to increase the number of female deputies and overcome the resistance of political incumbents who would be potentially affected by such changes. Remarkably, the zipper quota system was prepared by members of the government party as the realization of a promise given by the former Prime Minister, Donald Tusk, during the annual conference of the Congress of Women in 2012. This gesture signalled a formal recognition of their key postulations.

The two bills were later merged in a joint proposal that maintained a 35-percent electoral gender quota and a zipper requiring that female and male candidates to appear alternatively on the electoral lists, up to the tenth place.[67] The purpose of these bills was to prevent the practice of placing women on non-electable positions. Yet again all five opinions on the joint proposal commissioned by the Sejm Bureau of Research found the zipper system "unnecessary," "discriminatory" and "unconstitutional."[68] According to experts, the zipper system amounts to an unconstitutional derogation from the principle of equal treatment, violates passive electoral rights, the principle of political pluralism and the internal autonomy of political parties. They argued that the

---

[65] A zipper system mandates political parties to alternate female and male candidates on candidate lists. The bill (no. 1151) was introduced by the Parliamentary Group of Women on 24 January 2013 and required that the first two places on the electoral list registered for the elections of the Sejm, the European Parliament and the law-making organs of local self-government at the provincial and regional level are based on the principle of gender parity. The rule should apply to any two consecutive places until the 35-percent gender quota requirement is satisfied.

[66] The zipper system was also recommended by regional and international organizations analyzing the political situation of women in Poland – OSCE/ODIHR (Election Assessment Mission Reports of 2011 and 2015) and CEDAW (CEDAW/C/POL/CO/7-8).

[67] The zipper quota bill was withdrawn from the voting order by the sponsor because it turned out that the alternation of men and female candidates up to the tenth place on the list would in fact result in gender parity in situations when there are less than ten places on the electoral list. Another constitutional problem with the zipper system would appear in case of death of a candidate. Jabłoński (2014).

[68] Chmaj (2014).

zipper system is likely to promote female candidates on the basis of their gender rather than on their merit. In particular, it was contended that the proposed legislation was not justified by any urgent social need and was to be considered unnecessary.[69] Notably, none of the commissioned opinions took into account the debates on the importance of rank-order rules in quota legislation systems in other European countries.[70]

For some experts, the abstract principle of equality requires not equality in a share of the places, but the availability of every place on the electoral list for a person of either gender. They held that the zipper parity or quota system was too rigid because it significantly restricted the electoral process. In this context, it was emphasized that the electoral quota system should leave the decision about the position of a particular candidate on the electoral list to the electoral committees (of political parties, coalitions of political parties or voters). It was also argued that the zipper could be introduced as a voluntary rather than mandatory rule. Therefore, experts recommended that gender quality should achieved through the self-regulation of political parties, greater individualization of the electoral systems and financial incentives for political parties promoting female candidates.[71]

The critics of the bill also repeated that legal measures might not compensate for the unequal opportunities of female candidates, which result from the social and cultural inequality of women. Relying on the shared conviction that electoral success depends not on the place on the list but on the electoral campaign, they argued that the zipper system lacked a rational connection between the aims and the means. It was thus emphasized that any project aimed at the advancement of the political representation of women should more specifically explain the relationship between the low number of women in politics and voters' preferences. Yet, the same argument could be used to support the zipper system – as the only means available to change the negative attitudes of conservative parties towards female candidates.[72]

The above-mentioned arguments were informed by formal equality rhetoric and focussed on the question of whether the zipper parity or quota system was a constitutional means to advance *de facto* equality between men and women in politics. Characteristically, most experts

---

[69] Chmaj (2011).
[70] Freidenvall and Dahlerup (2013).
[71] Muszyński (2014).
[72] Matland (2003).

disapproved of positive measures as applied to political participation even if they generally approve of preferential treatment of women "justified" by biological differences in the area of social and economic rights. Another frequently mentioned argument against preferences for female candidates posited that gender-based legislation might raise the expectations of other groups (national, ethnic or social origin, age, religion, sexual orientation, residence, economic status, profession etc.) of challenging their insufficient representation in the decision-making processes. In sum, there has been a consensus between legal experts commissioned by the Sejm Bureau of Research on the nature of political representation. Their rejection of the descriptive representation model could be perhaps explained by negative sentiments towards the concept of "corporationist" representation that was officially endorsed as the Communist state doctrine. Yet in Poland there were no written rules according to which the outcome of elections would reflect the structure of the society.[73]

8.8 GENDER QUOTAS IN ACADEMIA AND CORPORATE BOARDS

The promotion of gender equality by means of gender quotas has also reached academia and the corporate world, but progress in these areas has been very slow. The Law on Higher Education includes a statutory requirement for gender quotas with respect to the membership in the Polish Accreditation Committee (*Państwowa Komisja Akredytacyjna –* PAC).[74] The PAC is an independent authority, appointed by the Minister of Higher Education and Science, which evaluates the quality of higher education in Poland. Pursuant to the Law on Higher Education, the number of female members of the PAC should constitute at least

---

[73] According to Article 1 of the 1952 Constitution, the subject of power was the "working class of town and country." Between 1947 and 1989, parliamentary elections were neither free nor democratic but organized as a form of plebiscite for the Communist Party, which had a final say on who was placed on the party lists. This practice subverted the electoral law that entitled political organizations, unions, cooperatives, the Association of Peasants' Self-Help, the Association of Polish Youth, and other mass social organizations of the working people to nominate candidates for deputies.

[74] Act of 27 July 2005 – Law on Higher Education, Journal of Laws, No. 164, item 1365.

30 percent.[75] This means that the Minister of Higher Education and Science should take gender into account when appointing a person as a member of the PAC.

Moreover, there is also a statutory requirement to respect the principle of gender parity in the appointment of members of the General Council of Science and Higher Education (*Rada Główna Nauki i Szkolnictwa Wyższego* – the Council).[76] The Council is an advisory body, representing different academic institutions and based in the Ministry of Higher Education and Science. However, the principle of gender parity is not a mandatory rule but rather a general guideline that should be taken into consideration in the appointment process. In fact, a mandatory rule would not work in this context since the realization of gender parity would require coordination between different institutions electing the members of the Council. Therefore, the Law on Higher Education includes just a recommendation that the appointing institutions should consider the principle of gender parity.

There is no doubt that the adoption of positive measures in the appointment of members of collective advisory or control bodies in the area of higher education and science is the result of gender mainstreaming, promoted as the key mechanism of gender equality at the EU level. Yet, careful analysis of the academic reality shows a strong preference for scholars holding at least a second academic degree (the post-doctoral degree of a titular professorship) in decision-making bodies at universities. Although the number of women with a second academic degree has been steadily growing, a balanced gender representation in academia cannot be achieved simply by statutory regulation. Hence, there is a pressing need for institutional responses to help women to advance their academic careers. For example, some research programmes envision different age limits for female applicants when they indicate family responsibilities.[77]

Another problem related to gender equality in academia is the participation of women in scientific conferences and seminars where panellists are only or mostly men. In reaction, many scholars protest

---

[75] Article 48 Section 4 of the Law on Higher Education.

[76] Article 46 Section 3 of the Law on Higher Education. During the 2014–17 term the Council counted thirty-two members, including eight women.

[77] Przybylska-Maszner and Trosiak (2011).

against this practice and refuse to participate in such events.[78] Several protests concerning the organization of conferences and seminars presenting only the male perspective, started a public discussion about the low visibility of female researchers. In consequence, more conference conveners observe gender balance in conference programmes. This approach has gradually become a part of academic best practice.

Since the release of the draft directive on corporate gender quotas by the European Commission and the proposal to introduce gender quotas attracted the attention of Western media and literature,[79] the debate on enhancing the gender balance of corporate boards in Poland has not been very serious. A proposal to introduce the 30-percent gender quota in the corporate boards of state-controlled companies until 2013 and 40-percent until 2014 was debated in the Parliament with regard to the principle of subsidiarity in the framework of the Early Warning Mechanism.[80] Notably, both Chambers of Parliament declared that the proposal of the European Commission was contrary to the principle of subsidiarity. This position was also taken by the majority of legal experts commissioned by the Sejm Bureau of Research,[81] but not those who were commissioned by the Office of the Government Plenipotentiary for Equal Treatment.

Still, the Third Congress of Women put forward a 40-percent gender quota in listed companies as one of its key aims in 2011. The Ministry of Economy also started a debate on corporate quotas in 2013, but it later affirmed that the introduction of gender quotas in business would not take place if there was no support from the side of business.[82] Notably, the Ministry did not propose that companies should adopt new training

---

[78] See the Facebook page "I don't go to panels in which only men participate," available at: www.facebook.com/NieChodzeNaPaneleWKtorychWystepujaTylkoMezczyzni.

[79] Proposal for a Directive of the European Parliament and of the Council on improving the gender balance among non-executive directors of companies listed on stock exchanges and related measures, 14 November 2012, COM (2012) 614 final.

[80] The Early Warning Mechanism is provided in Article 6 of the Protocol on the Application of the Principle of Subsidiarity and Proportionality following the Treaty of Lisbon. It grants national parliaments the power to assess whether a proposed EU legislation is compatible with the principle of subsidiarity. In this context the principle of subsidiarity implies that EU legislation shall not be adopted as long as the same legislative objectives could be effectively achieved by the Member States.

[81] See Zeszyty Prawnicze BAS No. 1(37) (2013), 7–105.

[82] Corporate quotas were promoted by the Ombudsman, the Plenipotentiary for Equal Treatment, the Congress of Women and some groups of Polish businesswomen like the Foundation of Business Female Leaders.

strategies enhancing professional opportunities for women in corporate management. In the accompanying debate it was typically argued that the number of women qualified to hold managerial posts was not sufficient and that therefore women who were not as qualified as men would be promoted to such positions. At the same time, it was emphasized that the corporate world functions on the basis of freedom of economic activity and protection of the property interests of shareholders and that the appointment of members of corporate boards should not endanger these principles.

Despite the criticism of corporate gender quotas, in 2013 the Minister of the State Treasury issued a document indicating "good practice" with regard to equal representation of men and women in the supervisory boards of the State Treasury-owned companies.[83] According to this document, the Ministry of the State Treasury would aim to achieve 30-percent representation of women working in publicly trading companies in which the Ministry had shares or in other key companies until 2015. After the government change in 2015 the prospects of developing any official gender quota agenda by the Ministry or any state-owned companies are very low. The current rate of women's participation in supervisory boards of State Treasury-controlled companies is 17.2 percent. "Good practice" suggested that the Ministry used the right to vote in general assemblies of state-owned companies to elect new candidates to supervisory boards by taking into account not only their qualifications, but also the need to achieve proper gender representation. The implementation of these standards was monitored by the Ombudsman who also recommended "exporting" them to other companies, including those which are privately owned and trading in the Warsaw Stock Exchange (WSE).[84]

According to Rule 9 of "Good Practice for Publicly Traded Companies" at the WSE, all publicly listed companies should observe a balanced representation of men and women in management and supervisory boards. However, this rule is only part of the "comply or explain" mechanism. In fact, the boards of the majority of companies

---

[83] "Good practice" statement of 8 March 2013, available at: www.msp.gov.pl/pl/media/aktualnosci/25131,Dobre-praktyki-w-zakresie-zapewnienia-zrownowazonego-udzialu-kobiet-i-mezczyzn-w.html.

[84] Letter by Ombudswoman to the Minister of State Treasury of 30 December 2013, RPO-712795-I/12/KWŻ, available at: www.sprawy-generalne.brpo.gov.pl/pdf/2012/09/712795/1778455.pdf

are predominantly male, with only a small percentage of women.[85] Therefore, it seems that the only way to change the situation is through legislative provisions or stronger corporate governance rules. The latter solution requires a deeper public understanding of the issue. Although some corporations change their internal policies and voluntarily accept the Diversity Card,[86] without strong legislative requirements no significant change is likely to occur with regard to the representation of women in business.

8.9   WOMEN BEYOND THE STATE

While the government change in 2015 took a radical turn towards conservative ideology, promoting a traditional family model and the reproductive, family-oriented role of women, the impact of electoral gender quota law has been limited to the realization of the right to be present in the public life rather than the realization of a particular outcome of electoral or political processes.[87] In this respect, the numerical change in representation has not essentially challenged the culturally entrenched model of gender relations and male dominance. However, the increased presence of women in public life has enabled new forms of

---

[85] According to a study prepared by the Warsaw Stock Exchange in cooperation with the Capital Markets' Institute (*Instytut Rynku Kapitałowego*) in 2012, women constituted 12.2 percent of members of management boards and 15.7 percent of members of supervisory boards. These proportions did not change much between 2012 and 2015. In 2015, there was no single woman in the corporate boards of the 312 publicly-traded companies at the WSE. Sirocka (2016).

[86] The Diversity Card is a voluntary commitment of a corporation to follow various diversity rules in its operation. This international initiative started in Poland in 2012 and is supported by numerous governmental institutions. See more at http://kartaroznorodnosci.pl/pl/en.

[87] Since the 2015 election, left-wing parties have not been represented in Parliament. This situation invites a new research agenda on the presence of right-wing women in politics. A stunning example of their passivity towards violations of women's rights was the governing party's unanimous vote passing a bill that introduced an abortion ban even in cases of rape or incest and subjected women to criminal liability – with 230 votes cast in the first reading, including those of fifty-four women. The bill was sponsored by a citizens' initiative that gathered over 450,000 signatures and was initially endorsed by the ruling majority and the Catholic Church. After mass street protests organized by women against the bill on 3 October 2016, the government withdrew its support and rejected the proposal in the second reading.

women's public engagement which go beyond political representation and therefore avoid the classical problem of feminist essentialism.[88]

For the time being, partnership with the state has become an uncertain strategy for the realization of gender equality. While women and women's organizations continue to represent their interests at the state level, they also take advantage of new global opportunities and seek allies in international and European organizations and bodies. The flight to supranational and sub-national levels is thus the most natural response to the institutionalized politics. It indicates a process of alienation from the state which leads women towards other fora that provide greater self-actualization.

In this process, women focus on activities and initiatives that do not require state authorization. It is thus a process of emancipation from the state, whereby women do not reject the state altogether, but expand a sphere of autonomy not dominated by the state. Although they formally accept the limits of law and the state power, their movement simultaneously de-constitutionalizes the state through the attempt to transgress from the constituted to the constituent power. As a result, the monolith of the state's legal monopoly is challenged by new societal norms and practices that call the existing normative framework and structures of power into question.

The adoption of quota legislation in Poland needs to be perceived as an attempt by the women's movement to formulate new paradigms of social coexistence and to promote a vision of egalitarian, participatory and democratic governance within the state.[89] Although the principles of gender equality, liberty and solidarity are formally recognized in the Constitution, Polish women have not substantially benefited from their realization by any government in power after 1989. Notwithstanding a noticeable trend towards including women experts as well as some feminist demands in official policies, women's voices have not been taken seriously and policy outcomes have remained beyond the reach of women's organizations save in exceptional circumstances when they have coincided with the goals of political leadership.[90]

The emergence of the women's movement is thus the result of dissatisfaction with formal constitutionalism, which replicates the existing

---

[88] Butler (1988).
[89] Still, the Congress has not concretized this vision in a political manifesto or a comprehensive plan of action.
[90] Jovenduski and Guardagnini (2010).

power structures. The movement emerges both as an experience and a social practice. In this regard, it provides women with a strong feeling of identity in contrast to an identity built on legal rights that remain largely ineffective. Like the Solidarity movement in 1980s,[91] women's solidarity in Poland embodies not only a struggle for freedom, democracy and basic rights, but also the actual exercise of freedom, democracy and rights.

For the first time in the history, Polish women are creating their own regime outside the spheres of law and institutionalized politics. In this regime of gender equality, freedom and solidarity, women have established their own institutions – like the Shadow Government of Women, the Congress of Women and regional congresses – which derive their power not from a written constitution or laws, but from actions and practices. Although the above institutions imitate state institutions, their aim is to transform social reality.[92] Moreover, through these new forms of collective work, women experience citizenship in the public realm and leave behind the mantle of intimate citizenship which confined them to the private sphere.[93]

The women's world emerged in opposition to the political–legal regime after all state institutions had proven hostile to women's claims. Characteristically, in this process of emancipation from the state created a constitutional moment that released the latent constituent power and a moment of the self-reflection conditional for emancipation. As long as this power is not formalized in political institutions but emerges through the spontaneous and organized presence and participation of individual women and their groups it enables not only a plurality of voices, but also dissent. It also enjoys strong legitimacy because of its

---

[91] Foucault (2002).

[92] The main points of concern for the Congress of Women are: equal of opportunities for women in public life (gender parity and quotas); prevention of violence against women; a balance between the caretaking and professional work of men and women; the political, civic and social activation of women; access to healthcare for women and protection of their patients' rights (including reproductive rights); the professional activation of women; combating negative gender stereotypes in education and media; promotion of cultural activity of women; and improving the situation of rural women. See www.kongreskobiet.pl/pl-PL/text/o_nas/nasze_cele.

[93] The concept of "intimate citizenship" refers to the fact that certain groups within the political community, who formally enjoy the status of equal citizens, actually face inequality and marginalization based on their gender or choices in private life that do not conform to the prevailing constitutional and political preferences. Plummer (2003).

bottom-up nature, decentralization and focus on the individual. In this way, women constitute themselves as independent subjects outside the state. Yet, from a statist perspective they remain Nietzschean subjects behind actions.

The current transformation of the gender regime in Poland proves that the emancipation of women seems to be possible only outside the structures of power that deem women invisible as subjects or construe them as inferior to men.[94] As noted by Ernesto Laclau, the concept of representation implies hegemonic relations and structural inequality, which explains the impossibility of identification.[95] Hence, the solution for the problem of identification could be perhaps found in the stage of pre-representation where women may identify not in relation to men, but as independent and autonomous beings. Only then might they construe their own identity not as a normative ideal, but as an empirical reality. And only then might they challenge legal institutions that once "constituted" them as subjects and also claimed to represent them. In this pre-representation stage, persons of either gender who stand against gender inequality and the instrumentalization of women in politics may create their own emotional and intellectual community.[96] Only then, it seems, is the symbolic – cultural – transformation of the gender regime and the political emancipation of women a viable possibility.

References

Banaszak, Bogusław. 2009. *Konstytucja Rzeczypospolitej Polskiej. Komentarz.* Warsaw: Wydawnictwo C.H. Beck.

Bator, Joanna. 1999. *Wizerunek kobiety w polskiej debacie politycznej. Perspektywa feministyczna.* Warsaw: Instytut Spraw Publicznych.

Bego, Ingrid. 2015. *Gender Equality Policy in the European Union. A Fast Track to Parity for New Member States.* Houndsmills: Palgrave Macmillan.

Broumas, Antonios. 2015. "Movements, Constitutability, Commons: Towards a Ius Communis." *Law Critique* 12: 11–26.

---

[94] Butler (1990). Laclau (1994, 2001). Hence, the solution for this paradox could be perhaps found in direct participation in the stage of pre-representation.

[95] Laclau (1994, 2001).

[96] The rapid development of such communities can be observed on Internet fora where women share their personal experiences or seek the advice of other women. Lidia Rodak from the University of Katowice calls the phenomenon of "sisterhood" a fourth wave of feminism based on the community of sisters.

Buras, Piotr. 2016. "Where is Poland headed?" Commentary. European Council of Foreign Relations. 16 January.

Butler, Judith. 1988. "Performative Acts and Gender Constitution: An Essay in Phenomenology and Feminist Theory." *Theatre Journal* 4 (40): 519–31.

1990. *Gender Trouble*. London: Routledge.

Chełstowska, Agata, Małgorzata Drucianek, Aleksandra Niżyńska, and Natalia Skoczylas. 2015. *Udział kobiet w wyborach parlamentarnych 2015. Wyniki monitoringu Obserwatorium Równości Płci*. Warsaw: Instytut Spraw Publicznych.

Chmaj, Marek. 2011. "Parytet płci w kodeksie wyborczym." In *Kodeks wyborczy. Wstępna ocena*, edited by Krzysztof Skotnicki. Warsaw: Wydawnictwo Sejmowe.

2014. "Opinia prawna w przedmiocie: oceny zgodności poselskiego projektu ustawy o zmianie ustawy – Kodeks wyborczy z dnia 5 stycznia 2011 r. (druk nr 1146) oraz poselskiego projektu ustawy o zmianie ustawy – Kodeks wyborczy (druk nr 1151) z Konstytucją Rzeczypospolitej Polskiej." 13 January. http://orka.sejm.gov.pl/rexdomk7.nsf/Opdodr?OpenPage&nr=1151.

Choluj, Bożena, and Claudia Neususs. 2004. "EU Enlargement in 2004: East-West Priorities and Perspectives from Women Inside and Outside the EU." Discussion Paper 7. www.frauenakademie.de/dokument/img/gender_equality_enlargedEU.pdf.

Czerwińska, Alicja, and Joanna Piotrowska. 2009. "*20 lat zmian - raport. Kobiety w Polsce w okresie transformacji 1989-2009*." Warsaw: Foundation Feminoteka.

Dębska, Hanna. 2014. *Władza, Symbol, Państwo*. Warsaw: Wydawnictwo Sejmowe.

Druciarek, Małgorzata, Małgorzata Fuszara, Aleksandra Niżyńska, and Jarosław Zbieranek. 2012. *Women on the Polish Political Scene*. Warsaw: Instytut Spraw Publicznych.

Flis, Jarosław. 2014. "Opinia prawna w przedmiocie: oceny zgodności poselskiego projektu ustawy o zmianie ustawy – Kodeks wyborczy z dnia 5 stycznia 2011 r. (druk nr 1146) oraz poselskiego projektu ustawy o zmianie ustawy – Kodeks wyborczy (druk nr 1151) z Konstytucją Rzeczypospolitej Polskiej." 13 January. Available at: http://orka.sejm.gov.pl/rexdomk7.nsf/Opdodr?OpenPage&nr=1151.

Foucault, Michel. 2002. "The Moral and Social Experience of the Poles Can No Longer Be Obliterated." In *The essential works of Michel Foucault, 1954-1984*. Vol. 3, Power, 465–73. New York: The New Press.

Freidenvall, Lenita, and Drude Dahlerup. 2013. "Electoral Gender Quotas and their Implementation in Europe." *Study for the European Parliament*, Update. Brussels: European Parliament.

Fuszara, Małgorzata. 2006. *Kobiety w Polityce*. Warsaw: Trio.

2008. "Poland: One Step Forward, One Step Back. A Polish Dance Around the Quota System." In *Electoral Gender Quota Systems and Their Implementation in Europe*, edited by Drude Dahlerup and Lenita Freidenvall, 72–82. Brussels: European Parliament.

2009. "Kobiety w polityce dwudziestolecia (1989–2009)." In *Kobiety dla Polski, Polska dla Kobiet, 20 lat transformacji*, Raport, edited by Małgorzata Fuszara, 187. Warsaw: Kongres Kobiet Polskich.

2010. "Participation of Women in Public Life and Women's Rights in Poland." In *Democracy in Poland 1989–2009. Challenges for the Future*, edited by Jacek Kucharczyk and Jarosław Zbieranek, 89–100. Warsaw: Institute of Public Affairs.

2012. "Polish Women's Fight for Suffrage." In *The Struggle for Female Suffrage in Europe: Voting to Become Citizens*, edited by Blanca Rodríguez-Ruiz and Ruth Rubio-Marín, 143–57. Leiden: Brill.

Fuszara, Małgorzata, Joanna Grabowska, Joanna Mizielinska, and Joanna Regulska. 2008. *Współpraca czy Konflikt? Państwo, Unia Europejska i Kobiety*. Warsaw: Wydawnictwa Akademickie i Profesjonalne.

Garlicki, Lech. 2003. "Komentarz do art. 33." In *Konstytucja Rzeczypospolitej Polskiej. Komentarz*, vol. III, edited by Lech Garlicki, 10–12. Warsaw: Sejmu.

Grabowska, Magdalena. 2014. *Unia Europejska Oczami Kobiet: Polityka Rządu, Równość płci i Polskie Organizacje Kobiece*. Raport. Warsaw: Heinrich Böll Stiftung.

Grabowska, Magdalena, and Joanna Regulska. 2007. "New Geographies of Women's Subjectivities in Poland." In *Global Babel: Interdisciplinarity, Transnationalism and the Discourses of Globalization*, edited by Margueritte Murphy and Samir Dayal, Newcastle, UK: Cambridge Scholars Publishing.

Graff, Agnieszka. 2001. *Świat bez kobiet*. Warsaw: Wydawnictwo WAB.

Jabłoński, M. 2014. "Opinia prawna w przedmiocie: oceny zgodności posel-skiego projektu ustawy o zmianie ustawy – Kodeks wyborczy z dnia 5 stycznia 2011 r. (druk nr 1146) oraz poselskiego projektu ustawy o zmianie ustawy – Kodeks wyborczy (druk nr 1151) z Konstytucją Rzeczypospolitej Polskiej." 13 January. Available at: http://orka.sejm.gov.pl/rexdomk7.nsf/Opdodr?OpenPage&nr=1151.

Janion, Maria. 2009. "Solidarity – a Great Collective Obligation of Women." [*Solidarność – wielki zbiorowy obowiązek kobiet*] Keynote speech, Congress of Women, Warsaw, June 20–1.

Jovenduski, Joni, and Marila Guardagnini. 2010. "Political Representation." In *The Politics of State Feminism. Innovation in Comparative Research*, edited by Dorothy E. McBride, and Amy G. Mazur. Philadelphia: Temple University Press.

Kułakowska, Katarzyna, and Agata Łuksza. 2015. "The Voice of Poland. The Case of Danuta Wałęsa." Special Issue: Mediating Post-Socialist Femininities. *Feminist Media Studies* 15 (1): 53–73.

Laclau, Ernesto. 1994. "Minding the Gap: The Subjects of Politics." In *The Making of Political Identities*, edited by Ernesto Laclau. London: Verso.

2001. "Democracy and the Question of Power." *Constellations* 8 (8): 3–14.

Matland, R. 2003. "Zwiększanie uczestnictwa politycznego kobiet: nominacja do ciał ustawodawczych a systemy wyborcze," translated by P. Rogala. In *Aktorzy życia publicznego. Płeć jako czynnik różnicujący*, edited by Renata Siemieńska. Warsaw: Wydawnictwo Naukowe Scholar.

Muszyński, Mariusz. 2014. "Opinia prawna w przedmiocie: oceny zgodności poselskiego projektu ustawy o zmianie ustawy – Kodeks wyborczy z dnia 5 stycznia 2011 r. (druk nr 1146) oraz poselskiego projektu ustawy o zmianie ustawy – Kodeks wyborczy (druk nr 1151) z Konstytucją Rzeczypospolitej Polskiej." 13 January. Available at: http://orka.sejm.gov.pl/rexdomk7.nsf/Opdodr?OpenPage&nr=1151.

Niżyńska, Anna. 2011. *Kandydatki w wyborach samorządowych w 2010*. Warsaw: Instytut Spraw Publicznych.

Ostrowski, Adam, ed. 2010. *Kościół, państwo i polityka płci. Raport*. Warsaw: Heinrich Böll Stiftung.

Pateman, Carole. 1988. *The Sexual Contract*. Cambridge: Polity Press.

Penn, Shana. 2005. *Solidarity's Secret. The Women who Defeated Communism in Poland*. Ann Arbor: University of Michigan Press.

Plummer, Kenneth. 2003. *Intimate Citizenship: Private Decisions and Public Dialogues*. Wash–Chesham: University of Washington Press.

Przybylska-Maszner, Beata, and Cezary Trosiak. 2011. "Uwarunkowania awansu zawodowego kobiet na polskich uczelniach." *Przegląd Politologiczny* 3: 167–83. http://wnpid.amu.edu.pl/images/stories/pp/pp-3-2011/167-184.pdf.

Rodríguez Ruiz, Blanca, and Ruth Rubio-Marín. 2008. "The Gender of Representation: on Democracy, Equality and Parity." *International Journal of Constitutional Law* 6: 287.

Rubio-Marín, Ruth. 2014. "The Achievement of Female Suffrage in Europe: On Women's Citizenship." *International Journal of Constitutional Law* 12 (1): 4–34.

Rutkowska, Ewa. 2008. "Gender Mainstreaming in Poland: A Case Study." In *Gender Mainstreaming. How Can We Successfully Use Its Political Potential*, edited by Agnieszka Grzybek, 87–120. Warsaw: Heinrich Böll Foundation.

Sadurski, Wojciech. 2005. *Rights Before Courts. A Study of Constitutional Courts in Postcommunist States of Central and Eastern Europe*. Dordrecht, Netherlands: Springer.

Sirocka, Anna. 2016. *"Kobiety we władzach spółek giełdowych w Polsce 2016."* Warsaw: Fundacja Liderek Biznesu.

Skotnicki, Krzysztof. 2010. "Opinia w sprawie wprowadzenia parytetu płci na listach wyborczych." *Przegląd Sejmowy* 3: 129.

Szmyt, Andrzej. 2010. "Opinia w sprawie wprowadzenia parytetu płci na listach wyborczych." *Przegląd Sejmowy* 3: 137.

Szulc, Łukasz. 2016. "The New Polish Government and 'Gender Ideology'." Notches Blog. http://notchesblog.com/2016/04/28/the-new-polish-government-and-gender-ideology/

Śledzińska-Simon, Anna, and Adam Bodnar. 2013. "Gender Equality from Beneath: Electoral Gender Quotas in Poland." *Canadian Journal of Law and Society* 28 (2): 1–18.

2015. "Between Symbolism and Incrementalism: Moving Forward with the Gender Equality Project in Poland." EUI Law Working Paper 2015/30. http://cadmus.eui.eu/handle/1814/35981.

Urbaniak, Krzysztof. 2011. "Parytety, kwoty a Konstytucja RP." *Państwo i Prawo* 2: 67–78.

Wieruszewski, Roman, and Katarzyna Sękowska-Kozłowska. 2010. "Opinia w sprawie wprowadzenia parytetu płci na listach wyborczych." *Przegląd Sejmowy* 3: 14.

PART III

GENDER QUOTAS AS CORRECTIVE EQUALITY REMEDIES

CHAPTER NINE

QUOTA CONTAGION IN GERMANY

Diffusion, Derailment, and the Quest
for Parity Democracy

*Sabine Lang**

Germany was an early adopter of quotas for women in political parties
and public administrations (Kolinsky 1991; Lemke 2001; Davidson-
Schmich 2006; Von Wahl 2006). Since the Green Party entered Federal
Parliament in 1987 with a zippered female–male list system, most political parties have established some form of quota in their party statutes
(Davidson-Schmich 2016, 28f.) – the exception remaining the Liberal
Party and the new right-wing nationalist Alternative für Deutschland.
In a parallel mobilization since the mid-1980s, feminist insiders in
state (Länder) public administrations pushed, together with women's
movement activists, for equality plans with quotas in sub-national public administration (Schiek et al. 2002). Even though these measures
initially were controversial, several decisions by the European Court
of Justice (ECJ) as well as an amendment to the German Basic Law in
1994 helped mainstream the notion that positive action in general, and
quotas under certain conditions, are appropriate strategies to advance
gender equality (Ebert 2012). In public administration, the mainstreaming of soft and hard gender quota plans that include decision quotas has
given advocates much needed leverage to advance a gender equality
agenda. Third and most recently, quotas were introduced in 2015 for

* I am deeply grateful to Eléonore Lépinard, Ruth Rubio-Marín, and the participants
of the EUI workshop on gender quotas, September 2014, for their close reading,
helpful comments, and challenging questions.

corporate boards of private businesses (CBQ) as well as for all public boards from the local to the state and federal level. This latest push for corporate board quotas gained increasing public support after attempts to entice voluntary compliance of the business sector did not result in stronger representation of women. Taken together, these areas of quota adoption seem to indicate that the German gender regime was an early and insistent champion of gender equality. However, this assessment is misleading. Quotas in the German context are perceived by activists as the only way to counter the legacy of a masculinist gender regime based on a "separate but equal" citizenship model. Only in the aftermath of German unification did differential frames give way to stronger egalitarian notions of women's citizenship. However, as the 2018 federal elections show, when women's representation in the German Bundestag went down almost six percent to 30.9 percent, gender equality has a long way to go in Germany.

In their mobilization for quotas, feminist insiders in parties and in public administration acted jointly with women's movement activists to upend Germany's traditionally strong male-breadwinner orientation with its undercurrent of a gendered separation of public and private spheres, long upheld by legal provisions, economic incentives, and social conventions. German feminists fought an array of legal stipulations that had discriminatory content or implications, such as a provision in the Civil Code, removed only in 1977, that formally allowed women to take up employment only if their husband consented. Also until 1977, women were required to take their husband's name at marriage and were obliged by a civil statute to do the housework (Berghahn 2011, 5). Protective legislation, such as that which prohibited women from working night shifts and provides tax incentives for mothers to stay home with young children, solidified a culture of protectionist difference. It was primarily Christian Conservatives who promoted this difference approach to women's rights, but it had supporters in trade unions and among Social Democrats as well. Arguably the most effective challenge to the difference approach to gender equality came on the heels of German unification. Amending its Basic Law in 1994, Germany formally shifted to a substantive equality model by declaring positive action measures constitutional and affirming a more activist state approach to equality of treatment and results. The first argument of this chapter, therefore, is that the scope and depth of quota diffusion is a result of Germany historically lagging in gender equality, and, more specifically, it is a political response to a historically salient male bread-winner society.

A second theme I investigate is the derailment of quota implementation. Whereas adoption has been mainstreamed across most parties
and the public sector, implementation is often haphazard. In one of the
largest and richest of the German Länder, electoral regulations have not
been made compatible with parties' voluntary party quota stipulations
(Ahrens et al. 2016). Across quota arenas, there is evidence of a uneven
enforcement (Holtkamp and Schnittke 2008; Holtkamp, Wichmann,
and Schnittke 2009) Papier and Heidbach 2014 in previous citation.
(Papier and Heidebach 2014). A lack of sanctions compounds quota
derailment. The initiative to diffuse quotas into the business sector,
however, has rekindled public debate about the instrument's necessity
and effectiveness. In a representative survey in 2014, 48 percent of
German women supported a mandatory quota for corporate boards.[1]
Broad coalitions of professional women now advocate for the use of
quotas in a range of employment sectors, indicating that quotas over
the past three decades might have become a more widely *accepted* and
also more *routinized* answer to underrepresentation of women in the
German gender regime.[2]

The argument put forward here is that quota contagion has hol-
lowed out the traditional German gender regime, which was based
on an "equal but different" ideology and corresponding social, political, and economic practices (MacRae 2006). Both unification and
Europeanization posed major challenges to difference-based gender
equality (Lang 2017). Since the 1990s, quotas have not only spread
across domains. They have also strategically unified actors across
party lines, particularly party women who historically tended to be
bound by strict ideological divisions. Germany has not adopted legislative quotas. When we consider, however, the overall trajectory of
the country, it is indeed part of the gender quota revolution that the
editors of this volume identify (see Lépinard and Rubio-Marín's introduction). German quota institutionalization and contagion is the
political answer to – as well as a reflection of – the country's legacy
as a conservative welfare state with a deep-seated male breadwinner
model based on a politics of gender difference. Progressive activists

---

[1] "Mehrheit der Frauen fühlt sich im Job benachteiligt," in *Frankfurter Allgemeine Zeitung*
October 19, 2014, available at: www.faz.net/aktuell/wirtschaft/yougov-umfrage-drei-
viertel-aller-deutschen-frauen-fuehlen-sich-im-job-benachteiligt-13217539.html
(accessed October 9, 2016).

[2] This echoes Éléonore Lépinard's assessment of quotas in the French case (2015).

in parties and in state offices realized that without formalized rules for descriptive women's representation, German civic culture was not easily prone to gender-sensitive transformation. Thus, and inadvertently, Germany became in effect a pioneer for affirmative action measures for women, and the controversial policies it generated for quotas in public administrations became the basis for European Union (EU)-level case law (Lépinard and Rubio-Marin's introduction to this volume). The focus on institutionalizing substantive equality via legal means is still strong: Now it shows in the increasing mobilization for a parity law that would force broader revisions of electoral regulations and an orientation towards equality of results. Proponents of such a law advocate 50-percent quotas for women in all electoral bodies of representative democracy, from districts to the federal level of parliament. The quest for a parity law, however, stands in stark contrast to lingering incrementalism in equality policies and active or passive resistance against quotas.

In theoretical terms, the German case is anchored in two literatures. One is the extensive research on constitutional gender equality and quota diffusion, highlighting contagion within and across states and spheres of influence.[3] A second theoretical anchor for the German quota system is federalism. In federalist states, access of women's movement actors to state agencies stimulates experimentation and innovation (Lang 2010; Lang and Sauer 2013). The federal structure in Germany allowed feminist insiders in subnational Länder offices to explore quotas in public administration and as part of contractual compliance for state contracts much earlier than on the national level. In effect, it was subnational governments that paved the way for quotas in public administration on the national level, in state-subsidized institutions, and on corporate boards.

In the following sections, I will unpack diffusion, derailment, and the quest for parity democracy in relation to quotas in parties, in public administration, as well as on corporate boards. I argue that post-unification politics and EU-level influences served as catalysts for changing the German gender regime from a difference-based equal opportunity orientation towards a stronger parity focus.

---

[3] See Baines and Rubio-Marín 2005; Dahlerup 2007; Meir 200, 2008; Krook 2009; Krook, Lovenduski, and Squires 2009 and also in particular the chapters on France and Belgium in this volume.

9.1 PARTIES: VOLUNTARY LIST QUOTAS
AND THE GERMAN ELECTORAL SYSTEM

Party quotas have been debated in Germany for more than a century. As early as 1908, and in tandem with increasing mobilization to gain suffrage, Social Democratic women demanded specific actions to ensure the participation of women in all party functions according to their membership percentage. Thus, strong women's sections within the SPD were not only key to gaining suffrage in 1918; they were equally central to the demands for stronger representation in the party (Sacksofsky 2012). Party statutes historically included only the obligatory mention of democratic representation of women, without specific proactive measures that would help achieve that goal. While the SPD had 19 percent female membership upon the founding of the Federal Republic in 1949, women held only 9.5 percent of the SPD's parliamentary seats. This ratio worsened during the 1950s and 1960s, reflecting a pervasive male breadwinner society and case law by the German Constitutional Court that was based on the "separate but equal" doctrine (Berghahn 2011; Rodriguez-Ruiz and Sacksofsky 2005). In 1972 the Social Democratic Parliamentary caucus of the Federal Parliament had only 5.4 percent female members (Wettig-Danielmeier 2008; Wettig-Danielmeier and Oerder 2012, 22). It was former Chancellor Willy Brandt who pushed the idea of establishing a quota for women in parliamentary bodies that matched the percentages of female party members (Wettig-Danielmeier and Oerder 2012, 21). The vast majority of men, but also women, in the party were initially skeptical. According to the former head of the Association of Social Democratic Women (ASF), at the time party women were convinced that their party program was sufficient to ensure that women would advance through the ranks, and that the male members simply had to be convinced to give women a chance (Wettig-Danielmeier and Oerder 2012, 23). Historically, quotas were perceived as undermining individual achievement and SPD women articulated a trope that still is present in the German gender regime: Women should demand respect on the basis of individual competency and reject the quota crutch as a patronizing strategy.

While the ASF sought to convince men rather than legislate equality, the newly founded Green Party entered Federal Parliament in 1983. Since the Greens saw themselves as the party of 1970s social movements, including the women's movement, gender equality was a key Green concept. Feminist party members with ties to autonomous groups initiated a Women's Statute in 1986. With this statute, the Greens established zippered candidate lists in which every uneven seat on all lists from local to national-level elections, as well as for party functions, had to be filled with a woman. After the 1986 elections, the Greens were the only party sending more women than men into the Federal Parliament (Lemke 2001). The party also instituted a system of two party leaders with the stipulation that at least one be a woman, as well as a dual leadership for the parliamentary party caucus.

Afraid of losing women voters to the Greens, the SPD voted in 1988 with a two-thirds majority of party delegates to adopt quotas as a binding principle. At the time, women made up 27 percent of party members. Setting a 33-percent goal quota for both elections and party offices, the party congress introduced this quota as a temporary measure, set to expire after twenty-five years. Raising the bar, the SPD moved in 1996 towards establishing a 40-percent quota for both genders in candidate selection and parity in all elective party offices (Wettig-Danielmeier and Oerder 2012, 21f.). In 2004, the ASF succeeded in turning the quota from a temporary measure into a fixed gender parity objective for the party.

Drawing on Murray, Krook, and Opello's framework for analyzing the institutionalization of quotas (2012, 25), the German case exhibits a confluence of all three of the authors' possible explanations for instituting party quotas: German parties adopted quotas in order to *attract women voters* (see also Davidson-Schmich 2006; Kittilson 2006; Meier 2004). *Ideological incentives* were particularly dominant in the Green Party, with their focus on social inclusion of underrepresented constituencies. Yet one can also detect a somewhat *strategic element* in quota adoption, in particular as Social Democrats were pressured by a more leftist party to sharpen their equality profile. All three motives, however, needed institutional and civic anchoring. Without strong women's party organizations as well as a women's movement articulating the large gender gap in representation, quotas might not have passed muster in party headquarters. Hence, it was a combination of internal party rationales and women's mobilization that led to early adoption of quotas.

With the SPD and the Greens courting women voters, the conservative Christian Democratic Union (CDU) was pressured by its own women's organization to address the underrepresentation of women within the party (Kolinsky 1991). In 1985, an entire party congress was devoted to women's issues (Wiliarty 2010, 24). A controversial party meeting in 1988 refused to use the term "quota", but instead created a voluntary "quorum" of 33 percent of party list seats and party office seats to go to women (Lemke 2001). As in the SPD, it was the Women's Union within the CDU that pushed for the quorum.[4] By contrast, their Bavarian-based ally, the Christian Social Union (CSU), refused all formal equality measures and instead added a paragraph to the party statute stipulating in the most general terms that "women have to be considered" as candidates (Lemke 2001). The principled stance of the CSU against quotas was somewhat ironic, since the party had actually instituted a minimum for inner-party representation of women (one woman in every elected and appointed party office) as early as 1946 (Werner 2010, 96). The rationales of the opponents of formal quotas in both conservative parties centered on the notion that women would not be perceived as competent if elected by way of quotas and that a quota would undercut democratic choice by promoting women over men (Poleschner 2010, 44). For both parties, it proved difficult to shed the women's "3K" image (Kinder, Küche, Kirche – children, kitchen, church) that had been reconstituted as conservative gender ideology after the end of Nazism. It was overwhelmingly due to the perceived need to capture more female voters that the Women's Union and Chancellor Kohl mobilized for the quorum (Wiliarty 2010, 130f). The liberal Free Democratic Party (FDP), historically just as averse to quota regulations as the CSU, was confronted with demands from its women's caucus in 2013 to institute a quota for party offices. FDP women argued that it was clear that voluntary regulations were not working to advance more women in the party, pointing to the 13.3 percent women on the FDP's advisory board and 10 percent women on the executive board (Opitz 2013). The party congress, however, voted against a quota.

It was the advent of the former East German Socialist party (PDS) – and its later iteration as The Left (Die Linke) – onto the national political stage that solidified women's representation with a 50-percent quota. The PDS acted strategically to position itself in Western politics by making gender equality one of its key demands. With a visible dearth of political representation among women in the former

---

[4] "What really helped us [on participation] was the Greens getting into the Bundestag with lots of women. The SPD also had a quota early and they had more women" (Renate Diemers, leader in the Women's Union, in Wiliarty 2010, 124).

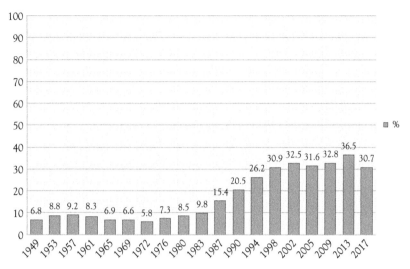

Figure 9.1 Proportion of women in German Bundestag, 1949–2017 (by percent)
Source: Der Bundeswahlleiter 2017, Frauen im Deutschen Bundestag. Wiesbaden.

Federal Republic, and with the intention to sever ties with the former male-dominated Socialist Unity Party (SED) of East Germany,
the makeover of the PDS included establishing a 50-percent quota for
party lists as well as candidates and party offices. This pushed the total
number of women in parliament to 20.5 percent after the elections of
1990, then further, to 26.2 percent, in 1994 and 30.9 percent in 1998.
Arguably, German unification contributed to an increased presence of
women in politics in the 1990s (Lang 2007 and 2017) (Figure 9.1).

Yet despite consensus among the major parties that quotas were
necessary to break up traditional male party structures and a gendered
selection bias, women parliamentarians could not cut through a glass
ceiling of roughly 33 percent in the decade between 1998 and 2009
(Fuchs 2006; Fonseca and Espirito-Santo 2008; Hoecker and Scheele
2008; Davidson-Schmich 2010; Davidson-Schmich and Kürschner
2011). It was the election of 2013 that gave equal representation
another push, increasing parliamentary representation of women by
roughly 4 percent, from 32.8 percent to 36.9 percent (Giebler and
Spittler 2014). The most likely explanation for this increase is an
indirect contagion effect of Angela Merkel's second successful term
as Chancellor. Merkel paved the way for women in her party as well
as in others to enter candidacies (Mushaben 2014 and 2017). Even
though she was historically opposed to quotas, she admitted during her

tenure, "without the quorum ... I would not have made it" (Lau 2007). This success, however, was short-lived. In the federal elections of 2017, the number of women in parliament fell again by almost 6 percent from 36.5 to 30.7 percent. Three parties are responsible for this substantial downturn in women's representation: The right-wing nationalist Alternative for Germany (AfD) entered parliament with 12.6 percent of the vote, but only 10.6 percent of their seats went to women. The Liberals, who received 10.7 percent of the vote, featured 22.5 percent women in their caucus. Lastly, Chancellor Merkel's own caucus has only 20 percent women. If the center and left parties' would not have sent 58 percent women (the Greens), 54 percent women (The Left) and 42 percent women (Social Democrats) into parliament, thus balancing out the low numbers in the center-right and right-wing parties, women's parliamentary representation in Germany in 2018 would look much like in the early 1990s.

The question remains if voluntary quota commitments are sufficient to achieve equal representation. Some see the electoral system as the culprit. Germany's mixed electoral system is an instructive case for the different impact of proportional and first-past-the-post systems on women's representation (Kaiser and Hennl 2008; Fortin-Rittberger and Eder 2013). Historically, almost twice as many women were elected by way of the proportional party list vote as opposed to the first-past-the-post direct candidate vote (Davidson-Schmich 2014, 87). And even though this gap is narrowing nationally, some subnational electoral regulations give preference to the first-past-the-post provisions of the electoral process and thus diminish the impact that the voluntary party quota can have. Yet electoral regulations are not set in stone; they are based on political decisions (Kenny 2013; Verge and De La Fuente 2014). Derailment of quotas can simply take the form of deciding on specific regulations. An instructive case of subnational derailment is the German election to the European Parliament of May 2014. All parties, aside from the conservative CDU, operated with national candidate lists. The ninety Social Democratic, twenty-six Green, and twenty Linke (Left) candidates were zipped alternately along the gender dimension.[5] The CDU, by contrast, decided not to organize candidate selection nationally. Left to their own devices, subnational Länder

---

[5] "Die deutschen Kandidatinnen und Kandidaten für die Europawahl," *Europawahl 2014*, available at: www.europawahl-bw.de/kandidaten.html (accessed September 11, 2016).

TABLE 9.1   Christian Democratic Union candidates for EU Parliament election in Germany, May 2014

State	Male candidates	Female candidates
Baden-Wuerttemberg	9	1
Bavaria	7	5
Berlin	2	1
Brandenburg	3	0
Bremen	2	1
Hamburg	3	1
Hessen	6	3
Mecklenburg-Vorpommern	2	0
Lower Saxony	5	3
North Rhine-Westphalia	9	4
Rhineland-Palate	3	2
Saarland	2	1
Saxony	3	1
Saxony-Anhalt	2	0
Schleswig-Holstein	3	1
Thuringia	3	2

Source: CDU Brussels, "Kandidaten von CDU und CSU für die Europawahl 2014." Compiled by the author.

CDU chapters missed the 33-percent quorum by ten percentage points – only 23.4 percent of candidates were women (Table 9.1).[6]

The conservatives in the rich southern state of Baden-Württemberg nominated nine men and one woman. In the former East German states of Brandenburg, Mecklenburg-Vorpommern, and Saxony-Anhalt, the CDU presented no female candidates at all. However, derailment is not only a prerogative of conservative parties. In the local council elections of May 2014 in Baden-Württemberg, a state where the Green Party has governed since 2011, roughly 25 percent women were voted

---

[6] "Kandidaten von CDU und CSU für die Europawahl 2014," CDU Kreisverband, available at: www.cdu-bruessel.org/index.php?ka=1&ska=1&idn=212 (accessed January 8, 2014).

into local councils, exposing subnational first-past-the-post elections as particularly resistant to quota implementation.

Compliance and sanctions (Dahlerup 2006; Dahlerup and Freidenvall 2008; Freidenvall and Micheletti 2013; Geissel 2013; Verge and De la Fuente 2014; Davidson-Schmich 2016) are issues of rising concern among German feminist politicians and gender advocates, and strong German federalism adds complexity to the perceived need for monitoring compliance more effectively. Whereas federalism generally is considered to be women-friendly as it allows for experimentation and more direct influence of women's equality actors (Lang and Sauer 2013), quota advocates face particular challenges in addressing derailments that appear on multiple levels of the German political system. An obvious obstacle to implementation is the mismatch of party statutes and different electoral laws on the federal and subnational levels that inhibit parties' control of direct candidate selection. However, inner-party regulations can be equally harmful. In Chancellor Merkel's conservative party, the 33-percent soft quota is only applied during the first round of election for public or inner-party office. If this quota is not met during the first round, this round is disqualified and electoral aspirants enter into a new round of elections without a quota stipulation. "Aussitzen" or "sitting out" the quota round is thus a proven strategy to circumvent the quorum stipulation. Some SPD members also resist quotas. An essay by a male party executive in 2011 titled "Why 25 years of women's quotas are enough" (Funken 2011) argues that when the SPD established the quota in 1988, it did so on the basis of a twenty-five-year limit. Ten years before this deadline, a party convention voted it down because not enough progress had been achieved. The fact that the party leadership decided in 2013 to also institute an obligatory quota for direct candidacies is seen by some as one more step in the wrong direction. Scores of men – Funken and others allege – have since left the party, and only their departure has increased the relative percentage of female party members. In effect, the quota is being blamed for voter disenchantment.

Debates on how to counter quota derailment take place simultaneously within Länder administrations, across Länder parties, and on the federal ministerial level. On the Länder level, quota advocates from within parties and women's groups push for a change of electoral regulations in particularly resistant states such as Baden-Württemberg. Center-left party women and advocates from women's policy agencies

289

(WPAs) and women's groups have floated the idea of a German parity law modeled after the French law (Deutscher Juristinnenbund 2014; Laskowski 2011, 2014). To orchestrate visibility for their demands, these quota advocates look beyond German borders and invoke the gender policies of other European and non-European countries. As early as 2011, the Women's Council of Rhineland-Palatinate pointedly asked, "What do Belgium, France, Spain, Poland or Senegal have that we don't have?" (Landesfrauenbeirat 2011, 3), underscoring their demand for a change to German electoral laws and requiring legally binding quotas for electoral lists.

With the push for a parity law modeled on France, quota advocates capitalize on changing framings of gender equality in Germany. Since unification and with increasing Europeanization, difference feminism has lost out as the major paradigm for equality aspirations, and new generations in particular reject traditional frames of complementarity. A growing consensus emerges around state intervention being essential for orchestrating parity. Even feminist political scientists, however, question the feasibility of instituting a parity law.[7] As it would involve curbing party autonomy and possibly a constitutional revision, momentum for such a law is only building slowly. Instead, calls for stricter internal party enforcement of quotas are becoming louder. The Social Democratic Women's Organization has long demanded that lack of compliance be sanctioned with the withdrawal of party funds (ASF 2008, 21). Others argue that party office seats should remain open until a woman is selected in cases of underrepresentation (Schlote 2013, 31).

However, as women's mobilization for effective quotas is on the rise, so is resistance within parties and among a growing number of antifeminist activists. Whereas until recently more subversive and passive forms of contestation were employed to undermine voluntary party quotas, there is now stronger vocal opposition. The expanding acceptability of antifeminist rhetoric can be traced in part to the rise

---

[7] Interview with Professor Birgit Meyer for FrauenMatchtPolitik, Helene Weber Kolleg, April 2014, available at: http://frauen-macht-politik.de/aktuelles/archiv-schwerpunktthemen/schwerpunktthemaparite0/interview-liberte-egalite-parite .html. The Conservative Party of Chancellor Angela Merkel opposes a 50-percent quota in principle. The Social Democrats, as the second largest party in Parliament, are split in regard to a parity law, with opponents arguing that it would interfere with paragraph 21 of the German Basic Law that guarantees freedom of parties.

of the new right-wing nationalist party AfD. The AfD steers a strict anti-quota course.[8] It frames its opposition in terms of massive discrimination against men in political and economic arenas, a renewal of meritocracy, and women's choice to be stay-at-home mothers. The AfD runs on an antifeminist platform and has, amongst other initiatives, initiated a campaign exhibiting a young AfD member stating: "I am not a feminist because I will' achieve my goals through effort and not through a quota."[9] In their campaign rhetoric preparing for the 2017 federal elections, the Liberals as well have solidified their anti-quota position.

Beyond the AfD and the Liberals, a number of antifeminist blogs invoke the "threat" that a parity law seems to pose. The youth organization of the CDU demands an end to the quorum, arguing that it has failed to provide adequate results.[10] Critics of established quotas argue for a quota-lite, favoring a cascade model based on party membership. With women traditionally exhibiting much lower party membership than men, this would substantially reduce the number of women candidates. The Social Democrats, who operate with a 40-percent quota, have only 31.5 percent female party members. Both the Green Party and the Left Party have a 50-percent quota, but only 37.8 percent and 37.7 percent female party members, respectively (Niedermayer 2013).

These critiques, however, do not reflect majority opinion; they might be seen in fact as a reaction to an overall political culture that has learned to embrace or at least live with quotas. Public debate is galvanized not by "whether," but by "under what conditions" quotas are effective, why the mainstreaming of quotas has induced little compliance, how to implement policies "with teeth" (i.e. more effective sanctions), and how to push a parity law that would elevate descriptive representation by way of a legislative quota. German gender advocates have profited from quota contagion among parties, and they find support in increased demands for a quota in other sectors of society. This

---

[8] See for example Alternative für Deutschland, "Grundsatzprogramm 2016," p. 51, available at: www.alternativefuer.de/wp-content/uploads/sites/7/2016/05/2016-06-27_afd-grundsatzprogramm_web-version.pdf (accessed June 1, 2016).

[9] Junge Alternative für Deutschland 2012. "Gegen die Frauenquote." February 11, available at: www.facebook.com/media/set/?set=a.220581474799061.1073741835 .109330799257463&type=1&stream_ref=10.

[10] "Junge Union kämpft gegen Frauenquote," Die Welt, October 15, 2012, available at: www.welt.de/regionales/hamburg/article109147205/Junge-Union-kaempft-gegen-Frauenquote.html.

acceptance signals a radical departure from a German gender regime that historically seemed enshrined in a "different but equal" doctrine and strong divisions between a masculinist public sphere and the private realm of women.

9.2 QUOTAS IN PUBLIC ADMINISTRATION

Gender quotas in Germany's public administration were not the result of public mobilization, but of inner-administrative and parliamentary pressure by feminist government insiders. Women's activists' political and professional decision in the late 1970s to advance gender equality from within the state fuelled a speedy institutionalization of women's policy infrastructure (Ferree 2012, 128ff; Lang and Sauer 2013). State and local offices for women's equality, as well as ministerial portfolios that included women's affairs, spread across subnational administrations and were later also established at the national level. Women's underrepresentation in public administration was one of their early targets.

The Northern German city-state of Hamburg was the first to advance positive action for women – just as it had been the first to grant women free association in 1902 (Sacksofsky 2012, 131). When Hamburg established its advancement plan for women in 1984,[11] it already included language for preferential treatment for women in hiring and promotion in cases of equal qualification with men. The plan received support from Ernst Benda, the former head of the Federal Constitutional Court, who argued in 1986 that the state had the responsibility to ensure substantive equality and not just to grant equal opportunities through equal rights, and therefore had some leeway under Art. 3 of the Basic Law to implement gender equality (Benda 1986). The first comprehensive women's equality law took effect 1989 in North Rhine-Westphalia, combining a decision quota with a goal quota of 50 percent for women employees.[12] The left-leaning city-states of Berlin, Bremen, and Hamburg followed in the early 1990s with similar combined decision and goal quota regulations. Particularly noteworthy for

---

[11] Richtlinie zur Förderung von Frauen of January 1, 1984, Hamburg.

[12] Gesetz zur Förderung der beruflichen Chancen von Frauen im öffentlichen Dienst NRW FFG, October 31, 1989. A decision quota stipulates that, in cases of equal qualification, preference will be given to underrepresented women. A goal quota is generally based on an affirmative action plan and sets goals for representation on a particular job level (see Rodriguez-Ruiz and Sacksofsky 2005, 157).

the time is paragraph 9 of the Hamburg Law of 1991. It did not define qualification merely as job-related performance, but also asked public employers to consider skills and experiences from family work in their employment decision.[13]

Within a decade, between 1989 and 1998, all sixteen states in unified Germany established women's or gender equality laws with some stipulations attempting to ensure substantive equality of women on all levels of public administration.[14] They relied on decision and goal quotas at a time when a substantial body of German legal texts were still trying to prove positive discrimination to be unconstitutional (see Weingärtner 1988, 14). Benda's path-breaking expertise helped mobilize feminist activists and femocrat insiders to demand a stronger constitutional commitment to equality in the German Basic Law. The opportunity for constitutional change presented itself with German unification in 1990.

Art. 3 section 2 of the German Basic Law states that men and women have equal rights.[15] After unification, and with pressure from a cross-party coalition of women parliamentarians and in particular former East German women politicians (see Limbach and Eckertz-Hoefer 1993), the article was amended in 1994 to include a stronger equality mandate for the state. Even though German feminist constitutional scholars such as Vera Slupik and Heide Pfarr had demanded amending Art. 3 section 2 well before the wall fell (Lang 2017), it was the Unification Treaty that provided an opening for revision. Several initiatives formed to strengthen constitutional women's rights. Feminist party insiders ensured that the Joint Constitutional Commission took up the issue between 1991 and 1993. The debates in the Commission

---

[13] "In assessing qualification, skills and experiences that are acquired by way of family work shall be considered" ("Bei der Bewertung der Qualifikation sind auch durch Familienarbeit erworbene Fähigkeiten und Erfahrungen einzubeziehen" [my translation]). Gesetz zur Gleichstellung von Frauen und Männern im hamburgischen öffentlichen Dienst, Paragraph 9, March 19, 1991, available at: www.jura.uni-hamburg.de/media/ueber-die-fakultaet/gremien-und-beauftragte/hamburger-gleich stellungsgesetz.pdf.

[14] 1989: North-Rhine Westphalia; 1990: Bremen, Berlin; 1991: Hamburg; 1993: Hessen; 1994: Brandenburg, Mecklenburg-Vorpommern, Lower Saxony, Saxony, Saxony-Anhalt, Schleswig Holstein; 1995: Baden-Württemberg, Rhineland-Palatinate; 1996: Bavaria, Saarland; 1998: Thuringia (Gützkow et al. 2003, 29–30).

[15] "Männer und Frauen sind gleichberechtigt," Revised Basic Law for the Federal Republic of Germany, Federal Law Gazette Part III, classification number 100–1, as last amended by the Act of July 21, 2010 (Federal Law Gazette I, p. 944).

were accompanied by scientific recommendations from experts in constitutional law, democratic theory, and gender (Limbach and Eckertz-Hoefer 1993). Feminist scholars Ute Gerhard and Andrea Maihofer advocated for a citizenship model based on the recognition of difference, attempting at the same time to avoid traditional hierarchies in which women lose out (Maihofer 1998, 157). This approach, however, did not succeed, given the general resistance against a politics of difference that had historically kept women successfully in the private sphere. In the end, the Constitutional Commission settled on a revision of Art. 3.2 that reads "Men and women shall have equal rights. The state shall promote the actual implementation of equal rights for women and men and take steps to eliminate disadvantages that now exist."[16] Thus, unification provided the political opportunity to solidify Germany's pivot towards substantive equality. At the same time, the constitutional compromise indicated that lawmakers were not willing to decide "how much inequality" was legitimate in order to reach parity (Wilde 2001, 153).

Along similar lines, the German Federal Constitutional Court in the 1990s refrained from issuing a generalized ruling on quotas. It ruled in several cases, however, that de facto disadvantages usually faced by women could be compensated by advantageous regulations, according to the equality norm of Article 3.2 (Battis 2008). The most important guidelines for quotas in the German citizenship regime actually came from the ECJ. Up to 2005, the ECJ decided four cases on gender quotas, three of them put forward by Germany. All three became landmarks for German quota law. In the Kalanke case, a male job applicant sued the state of Bremen over its positive action law for women in underrepresented parts of its public administration.[17] The law stipulated preferential hiring or promotion of equally qualified women when underrepresented at a particular employment level. The ECJ ruled in 1995 that the strict equal opportunity law in the state of Bremen violated European law because it gave automatic preference to women in cases of equal qualification – an automatism that the Court argued discriminated against men[18] (see also Donahue 1998, 731). The ECJ ruled that quota laws needed hardship clauses and that each individual decision required evaluation of the specific circumstances of the applicants.

[16] Ibid.
[17] *Kalanke v. Freie Hansestadt Bremen*, Case C-450/93; 1995 ECR I-3078.
[18] Ibid.

As the first decision by the ECJ on quota regulations in an EU-member state, the Kalanke case was widely scrutinized. German and European women's rights advocates deplored this ruling as initiating a backlash against positive action plans in general and quotas in particular.[19]

In 1997, a second German case involving quotas in public administration reached the ECJ, this time concerning the North Rhine-Westphalian positive action plan. In the Marschall case,[20] a male job candidate protested against preferential treatment of a female applicant. In this ruling however, the ECJ did not reject quotas, arguing that as long as the decision to advance a woman is made on a single-case basis (*Einzelfallprüfung*) and considers the merits of each individual candidate, quotas are legal.[21] Since the North Rhine-Westphalian positive action plan included such a single-case provision, the Court upheld lower-court decisions and confirmed that equal employment policies could entail active preferential treatment, including quotas. The Marschall case has since become the litmus test for positive action plans and quota regulations across Germany and the EU. In a third German case in 2000, the ECJ upheld the legality of decision quotas, goal quotas, and fixed quotas for training positions in the Hesse Statute.[22] The Court argued that since the Statute did not give unconditional preferential treatment to women and utilized fixed quotas only for very limited purposes, it operated within European Law. The ECJ decisions thus solidly shifted the grounds of the German quota debate. Following the subnational levels of administration, the Federal Equality Law (Bundesgleichstellungsgesetz) of 2009 also established decision quotas for women in federal public administration (BMFSFJ 2011, 9).[23] In effect, the ECJ's social opening clause, condoning quotas if social context factors of equally qualified applicants were taken into account, has created the opening for quota activists to lobby more broadly. In 2015, the "Law on Equal Participation of Women and Men

---

[19] E.g. "Gender War," *Focus Magazine* 43 (1995).

[20] *Marschall* v. *Land Nordrhein-Westfalen*, Case – C-409/95; ECR I-6363, 1997.

[21] Ibid.

[22] *Badeck* v. *Hessische Ministerpräsident*, Case C-158/97; 2000 ECR I-1875. See also note 13.

[23] Gesetz zur Durchsetzung der Gleichberechtigung von Frauen und Männern (2. Gleichberechtigungsgesetz; 2. GleiBG) 1994, BGBL I, p. 1406. Amended in 2009 BGBL I, p. 160.

in Private-Sector and Public-Sector Management Positions"[24] stipulated a goal quota of 30 percent for women in leadership positions of
the German public administration.

Federal quota legislation for public administration has made a difference. Overall, the number of women in leadership positions of the
federal administration increased to 33 percent in 2016 (Statistisches
Bundesamt 2016). If one breaks down the category of "leadership position" and focuses on the most prestigious and influential administrative
offices, the picture is somewhat less rosy: In 2009, only 3 percent of
Deputy State Secretaries in Federal Ministries were women and only
14 percent of Administrative Unit Directors were female (BMFSFJ
2014, 32). In 2016, these numbers had increased to 20 percent and 28
percent, respectively (Statistisches Bundesamt 2016, 8), thus still not
reaching the 30-percent quota. At the same time, critics argue that
the quota should actually be more like 40 percent in order to approach
parity. A recent legal report on the practices of implementing quota
regulations commissioned by North Rhine-Westphalia (Papier and
Heidebach 2014) argues that public offices have adapted to the current
policies by simply not letting cases of equal qualification materialize.
In the day-to-day practices of public administrative hiring, the criteria
for jobs and advancement are micro-adjusted to the degree that cases
of equal qualification between male and female applicants are systematically avoided. Thus, mirroring the quota derailment in the political
sector, inner-institutional practices still undercut formal advancement
policies. The Papier and Heidebach Report suggests that legal language
concerning sanctions for non-compliance be firmed up, but also –
without giving specific direction – that alternative ways for women's
advancement be considered (2014, 52). Despite these criticisms, quotas diffuse into other sectors of German society.

9.3   QUOTAS ON CORPORATE AND PUBLIC SECTOR
BOARDS

Women in higher office in German businesses are far and few between.
According to a study by the German Institute for Economic Research,
in 2012 women held only 4 percent of CEO positions and 13 percent

---

[24] Gesetz für die gleichberechtigte Teilhabe von Frauen und Männern an
Führungspositionen in der Privatwirtschaft und im öffentlichen Dienst, 24. April
2015, "FüpoTeiG"; BGBl. I, 642.

of corporate board seats in the top 200 German companies (Holst and Schimeta 2013).[25] The issue had been simmering in German public debate since the early 2000s, but both the social democratic Schröder government and conservative Chancellor Merkel have resisted more than cosmetic regulations, sidelining mobilization by the Social Democratic Women's Organization and women's business associations. Instead, they relied on a "flexi quota" – in essence a voluntary program by business for business to advance women, which has proved inconsequential.

When in 2012 the EU Commission proposed a 40-percent quota for the underrepresented sex in non-executive board member positions by 2020 (European Commission 2012), Chancellor Merkel ordered the Berlin representation in Brussels in blunt language to "immediately – and on diplomatic levels – promote the German position" and ensure the "rejection of the proposed guidelines."[26] Whereas the European Parliament voted in support of the initiative, the Merkel government was able to stop the directive in the Council, arguing that the measure was too rigid and would impede economic growth. As in the case of the public administration quotas, federalism saved the day, as it took the German subnational Land-level to advance the issue. In a strong showing of trans-party alliance, on September 21, 2012 the Parliamentary Chamber of Länder governments, the Bundesrat, with the support of two conservative Länder Governors, proposed a federal law based on a Hamburg initiative that would require 20-percent women on corporate boards by 2018 and 40-percent by 2023.[27] The Bundesrat initiative included fines for noncompliance, such as tax increases, as well as the threat of public disclosure to shame companies into compliance. A trans-party women's alliance formed in reaction to public advocacy by quota critics, most importantly from several German business associations as well as liberal and conservative politicians, who insisted on free markets and independent corporate governance. Supporters of the

[25] In 2010, the German telecommunications company Deutsche Telekom was the first listed corporation in Germany to voluntarily introduce a binding 30-percent quota to be achieved by 2015.

[26] "Germany to Lobby against EU Gender Quota," *Der Spiegel*, March 6, 2013, available at: www.spiegel.de/international/europe/germany-to-lobby-against-eu-gender-quota-a-887174.html (accessed April 12, 2013).

[27] Bundesrat 2012. Gesetzesantrag der Freien und Hansestadt Hamburg: Gesetz zur gleichberechtigten Teilhabe von Frauen und Männern in Führungsgremien DS 330/12; May 29, 2012.

law argued that the business sector had had plenty of time to increase substantive representation of women on a voluntary basis, to no avail.[28] Party quotas and public 'administration quotas had helped normalize the notion that positive action including quotas is necessary if voluntary action fails. Even though the liberal-conservative majority in the federal parliament rejected the initiative in April 2013, the conservative party remained openly divided on the issue. This uncertainty served as a catalyst for many conservative women to articulate support for the CBQ, which traditionally they would have been reluctant to voice under disciplinary rules in the German party caucus state.

Several factors coalesced to create a perfect public storm for the CBQ to travel onto the public agenda. Firstly, two conservative Länder Governors did shun party discipline and voted for the social democratic initiative. Secondly, even within Merkel's coalition, there existed dissent: The influential conservative female Labor Minister (and former Women's Minister) Ursula von der Leyen positioned herself against the Women's Minister from her own party and advocated publicly for quotas while the Women's Minister rejected them. And, thirdly, her reaction to the EU directive threatened to stigmatize Merkel as a backward-looking veto power in the European Union. Women's organizations across the country weighed in and the media, though they exploited the sensationalist character of "the quota wars" and the quota "battle with Brussels,"[29] also advanced substantive debate. The proponents of the CBQ invoked discrimination within a still male-dominated business sector and the fact that voluntary commitments to raise the number of women had failed. Opponents used the liberal tropes of individual achievement and women's choice to argue that the quota had no place in the business world. Chancellor Merkel found herself between a rock and a hard place. She had to find a way to appease the quota supporters while forcing them to reject the quota law that was on the table. Trying to buy time, she brokered a compromise that entailed writing mandatory quotas for business into the party program for the 2013 election and a quota of 40 percent to take effect in 2020.

---

[28] One of the conservative party "dissident" governors supporting the quota was Annegret Kramp-Karrenbauer, then Governor of Saarland and since 2018 General Secretary of the CDU, in taz – Die tageszeitung February 2, 2011.

[29] Jabeen Bhatti. "The Quota Wars. Norway introduced affirmative action for women in the boardroom six years ago. Other European countries are following suit. But does it work?" In *German Times* 2011 and. "Germany to Lobby against EU Gender Quota," In: *Der Spiegel*, March 6, 2013.

When the *New York Times* commented that "in a rare political setback for the world's most powerful woman, Chancellor Angela Merkel on Thursday found herself forced to give in to a rebellious bloc in her own party,"[30] it left unmentioned the combined force of the Länder initiative, EU signals, and cabinet support by the Labor Minister, which had provided the bedrock for this success. Even if the Merkel government could fend off mandatory quotas before the election in 2013, it was forced to give in to their own women's lobby and establish quotas for 2020 in case of business inertia. What the *New York Times* called a "rebellious bloc" was in fact a broad spectrum of conservative women, led by the Labor Minister, who later became the first female Defense Minister of Germany.

After the federal elections in fall 2013, the quota issue became part of the Grand Coalition negotiations between the Social Democrats and the Conservatives. Merkel was pushed by the conservative women's organization to give in to SPD demands for an immediate quota law for corporate and public boards. The SPD-led Ministries of Justice and Women drafted a law that was adopted by Parliament in March 2015 and went into effect in 2016.[31] Companies registered on the German stock exchange are now required to have at least 30 percent women on their corporate and public boards. In case of non-compliance, an "empty chair" policy is enforced until a given seat is filled with the underrepresented gender. Additionally, about 3,500 large businesses will have to submit plans for promoting more women into top corporate positions. Even though this first German CBQ law is being hailed as a step in the right direction, it has its limits: It only applies to about a hundred large firms 'in Germany that are publicly traded and, because they fall under codetermination regulations, are fully accountable to the state (Pütz and Weckes 2014). Thus, in the wake of the 2017 federal elections, seventeen large German women's NGOs demanded that the 30-percent quota be extended to those 3,500 large businesses that at this point only have to submit advancement plans.[32]

---

[30] Melissa Eddy, "Merkel Concedes on Quotas for Women," *New York Times*, April 18, 2013, available at: www.nytimes.com/2013/04/19/business/global/merkel-concedes-on-quotas-for-women.html (accessed March 12, 2016).

[31] Gesetz für die gleichberechtigte Teilhabe von Frauen und Männern an Führungspositionen in der Privatwirtschaft und im öffentlichen Dienst, 2015, Bgbl. I-642. April 30, 2015.

[32] Berliner Erklärung von 17 Frauenverbänden, September 2017, available at: www.berlinererklaerung.de (accessed April 10, 2017).

These limits notwithstanding, the quota law for corporate and public boards is a success for German quota advocates. Policy learning took place among Länder WPAs who were frustrated with the slow pace of advancing women in business. They used the developing EU initiative as rationale for moving away from conservative laissez-faire politics. The fact that governors of conservative Länder were willing to depart from their party line showcases the ability of federal structures to advance innovative bottom-up policies against the explicit policy direction of a strong federal Chancellor. Having an ally in the cabinet (the Labor Minister) and support from women's organizations facilitated the original dissent in 2013. The multilevel agenda setting from the EU Commission, the German Bundesrat, and conservative party "dissidents," all within a few months, effectively coalesced to produce policy change. If the EU had not introduced its own draft law around the same time, Länder WPAs could not have cited urgency of action in convincing their Länder governors to support a national initiative. Thus, supranational combined with subnational pressure was decisive in creating momentum for quotas in the German corporate sector.

9.4   CONCLUSION

Since their inception three decades ago, quota policies have permeated German politics, public administration, and as of late corporate and public boards, signaling a major shift in the historically conservative gender regime. Hoping to capitalize on higher quota acceptance by the German public, women activists increasingly demand quotas for other sectors of the labor market where the glass ceiling seems particularly unbreakable. Women journalists have recently founded the initiative ProQuote, women movie directors demand quotas in the German Public Movie Sponsoring Agency, and women medical doctors have founded the initiative ProQuote: Medizin to demand equal representation in top-level posts of these professions.[33] Women's Ministers from the Länder support these initiatives (GFMK 2012).

---

[33] "Frauenquote in den Medien," ProQuote, available at: www.pro-quote.de (accessed May 5, 2016); "mehr Frauen an die Spitze," ProQuote-Medizin, available at: www.pro-quote-medizin.de (accessed May 5, 2016).

Quotas have become part of a political architecture that has replaced the traditional male breadwinner model with a gender regime now increasingly focused on substantive equality. The path from women's quotas to gender quotas and from voluntary flexi quotas to decision and goal quotas within positive action plans was paved by femocrat insiders in parties and public administration, facilitated by post-unification constitutional change, and shaped by ECJ rulings. EU initiatives have also played a central role in the recent push to establish quotas on corporate and public boards. Beyond the EU, the openings created by subnational federal administrations on the Länder level have generated momentum for quotas and positive action plans. The German case thus illustrates quota diffusion based on feminist insider commitment, competitive voter orientation of parties, subnational WPA policy experimentation as well as transnational influences from the EU.

However, the German quota story is not one of linear progress. The 2017 elections resulting in a 6-percent decrease of women's representation in federal parliament indicate that voluntary party quotas are just that – voluntary, therefore volatile, and highly dependent on center-left parties' commitment and presence in elected office. Voters of the two parties with an explicit anti-quota position (AfD and the Liberals) were mostly male and garnered a combined vote of 23.3 percent. The electoral results thus speak to the overall contentious political and cultural environment in which quotas live. What Éléonore Lépinard and Ruth Rubio-Marín call "corrective equality remedies" (see Lépinard and Rubio-Marín's conclusion in this volume) signifies in the German case a still-uneasy combination of voluntary quotas (parties) combined with a limited, mostly 30-percent oriented gender quota, as well as uneven enforcement options in public administration and the private sector. The transformative potential of quotas is thus not fully realized.

Critique and derailment of existing regulations and resistance against expanding the quota architecture will most likely increase in the coming years. The main voice in the anti-quota mobilization, the right-wing nationalist and Eurosceptic AfD, as of 2017 has not just been newly elected to the federal Bundestag, but also has representatives in thirteen Länder parliaments. The AfD has announced that it will make fighting the "excesses" of gender equality and in particular quota policies a focus in parliament.

In response to derailment and anti-quota mobilizations, there is an emerging debate among feminist activists, Land-level WPAs and left-leaning party women to emulate France's parity law and replace voluntary party quotas with legally binding quotas (Laskowski 2014). Here, as in many other cases in this volume, the coordination of women's activists inside and outside of political parties is a central factor in advancing the quota cause (see Lépinard and Rubio-Marín's conclusion in this volume). Whereas the feasibility of a parity law is questionable under current political conditions, the very fact that it is discussed is an indicator of how substantially the German gender regime has changed, as well as of the role of quotas in facilitating and sustaining this change. Just as suffrage in 1918 was not only the end of a long struggle but also the beginning of women's demands for stronger civic, social, and political rights, so establishing a quota architecture over the past thirty years was only the beginning of a substantive transformation that, however painstakingly slowly, is uprooting Germany's patriarchal legacy.

References

Ahrens, Petra, Katja Chmilewski, Sabine Lang, and Birgit Sauer. 2016. "Why the Fine Print Matters. Electoral Systems and Regulatory Policies for Implementing Party Quotas in Germany and Austria." Paper for the ECPR Joint Sessions, Pisa, April.

ASF – Arbeitsgemeinschaft Sozialdemokratischer Frauen. 2008. 18. Proceedings of Federal Conference, Kassel.

Baines, Beverley and Ruth Rubio Marconstitutional gender equalityn, eds. 2005. *The Gender of Constitutional Jurisprudence*. New York: Cambridge University Press.

Battis, Ulrich. 2008. "Chancengleichheit – nicht Ergebnisgleichheit." *Forschung & Lehre*. Available at: www.forschung-und-lehre.de/word press/?p=536. Accessed April 15, 2016.

Benda, Ernst. 1986. "Notwendigkeit und Möglichkeit positiver Aktionen zugunsten von Frauen im öffentlichen Dienst." *Expertise Commissioned by the Women's Equality Office*, Hamburg.

Berghahn, Sabine. 2011. "Der Ritt auf der Schnecke. Rechtliche Gleichstellung in der Bundesrepublik Deutschland." Available at: www.fu-berlin.de/sites/gpo/pol_sys/gleichstellung/Der_Ritt_auf_der_Schnecke/Ritt-Schnecke-Vollständig.pdf. Accessed April 6, 2016.

BMFSFJ. 2011. "Erster Gleichstellungsbericht." Drucksache 17/6240. Berlin: Bundesministerium für Familie, Senioren, Frauen und Jugend.

BMFSFJ 2014. *"Statistischer Datenreport: Durchführung von vorbereitenden statistischen Analysen und Auswertungen zur Umsetzung des*

Bundesgleichstellungsgesetzes." Berlin: Bundesministerium für Familie, Senioren, Frauen und Jugend.

Dahlerup, Drude, ed. 2006. *Women, Quotas and Politics.* New York: Routledge.

2007. "Electoral Gender Quotas: Between Equality of Opportunity and Equality of Result." *Representation* 43 (2): 73–92.

Dahlerup, Drude, and Lenita Freidenvall. 2008. "*Electoral Gender Quota Systems and Their Implementation in Europe.*" Brussels: European Parliament PE 408.309.

Davidson-Schmich, Louise. 2006. "Implementation of Political Party Gender Quotas: Evidence from the German Länder 1990–2000." *Party Politics* 12: 211–32.

2010. "Gender Quota Compliance and Contagion in the 2009 Bundestag Election." In *Between Left and Right: The 2009 Bundestag Elections and the Transformation of the German Party System*, edited by Eric Langenbacher, 151–72. New York: Berghahn Books.

2014. "Closing the Gap. Gender and Constituency Candidate Nomination in the 2013 Bundestag Election." *German Politics and Society* 32 (20): 86–105.

2016. *Gender Quotas and Democratic Participation. Recruiting Candidates for Elective Offices in Germany.* Ann Arbor: University of Michigan Press.

Davidson-Schmich, Louise K., and Isabelle Kürschner. 2011. "Stößt die Frauenquote an ihre Grenzen? Eine Untersuchung der Bundestagswahl 2009." *Zeitschrift für Parlamentsfragen* 42 (1): 25–34.

Deutscher Juristinnenbund. 2014. "Editorial." *Zeitschrift des Deutschen Juristinnenbunds* 27 (3): II.

Donahue, Ann. 1998. "The Kalanke Ruling: Gender Equality on the European Labor Market." *Northwestern Journal of International Law and Business* 18 (3): 730–57.

Ebert, Berit. 2012. *Gleichstellung und Gender in der Jurisdiktion des Gerichtshofes der Europäischen Union. Eine Analyse unter Berücksichtigung kontemporärer Gerechtigkeitstheorien.* Berlin: Logos Verlag.

European Commission. 2012. "Proposal for a Directive of the European Parliament and of the Council on improving the gender balance among non-executive directors of companies listed on stock exchanges and related measures." COM (2012) 614. Available at: http://eurlex.europa.eu/LexUriServ/LexUriServ.do?uri=COM:2012:0614:FIN:en:PDF. Accessed April 13, 2013.

Ferree, Myra Marx. 2012. *Varieties of Feminism. German Gender Politics in Global Perspective.* Stanford: Stanford University Press.

Fonseca, Sara Claro da, and Ana Espírito-Santo. 2008. "Quotenfrauen – Kandidatinnen, Listen-und Direktmandate im deutschen Wahlsystem." *WZB-Mitteilungen*, Heft 120, Berlin.

Fortin-Rittberger, Jessica, and Christina Eder. 2013. "Towards a Gender-Equal Bundestag? The Impact of Electoral Rules on Women's Representation." *West European Politics* 36 (5): 969–85.

Freidenvall, Lenita, and Michele Micheletti, eds. 2013. *Comparisons, Quotas, and Critical Change: In Honor of Drude Dahlerup*. Stockholm: Stockholm University Department of Political Science.

Funken, Klaus. 2011. "25 Jahre Frauenquote sind genug." *Nachdenkseiten*. Available at www.nachdenkseiten.de/upload/pdf/110614_funken_25_Jahre_frauenquote_sind_genug_korrigiert.pdf. Accessed September 16 2016.

Fuchs, Gesine. 2006. "Politische Partizipation von Frauen in Deutschland." In *Politische Partizipation zwischen Konvention und Protest*, edited by Beate Hoecker, 235–60. Opladen: Budrich.

Geissel, Brigitte. 2013. "Successful Quota Rules in a Gendered Society – Germany." In *Breaking Male Dominance in Old Democracies*, edited by Drude Dahlerup and Monique Leyenaar, 197–216. London: Oxford University Press.

GFMK. 2012. 22. Konferenz der Gleichstellungs-und Frauenministerinnen 2012, Stellungnahme zu den Beschlüssen der 22. Konferenz der Gleichstellungs-und. Frauenministerinnen. Nürnberg.

Giebler, Heike, and Marcus Spittler. 2014. "Review of the Bundestagselection 2013: FDP Out – Women In?" *Wissenschafts-Zentrum Berlin für Sozialforschung: Democracy Blog*. Available at: democracy.blog.wzb.eu/author/gieblerspittler/. Accessed July 13, 2014.

Gützkow, Frauke, Robert Horak and Doreen Lindner. 2003. *Landesgleichstellungsgesetze im Vergleich*. Frankfurt a.M.: GEW Publ.

Hoecker, Beate, and Alexandra Scheele. 2008. "Feminisierung der Politik? Neue Entwicklungen und alte Muster der Repräsentation." *Femina Politica* 2 (8): 9–20.

Holst, Elke and Julia Schimeta. 2013. "Frauenanteil in Topgremien grosser Unternehmen in Deutschland nimmt geringfügig zu." In *DIW Wochenbericht 3: Managerinnen-Barometer*. Berlin: Deutsches Institut für Wirtschaft 3–14.

Holtkamp, Lars, and Sonja Schnittke. 2008. "Erklärungsmodelle für die Unterrepräsentation von Frauen." *Femina Politica* 2 (8): 53–64.

Holtkamp, Lars, Elke Wichmann, and Sonja Schnittke. 2009. *Unterrepräsentanz von Frauen in der Kommunalpolitik. A Study for the Heinrich-Böll-Foundation*. Berlin: Heinrich-Böll-Stiftung.

Kaiser, Andre, and Annika Hennl. 2008. "Wahlsysteme und Frauenrepräsentation. Ein Vergleich der deutschen Landesparlamente." *Zeitschrift für Politikwissenschaft* 2 (8): 167–84.

Kenny, Meryl. 2013. *Gender and Political Recruitment. Theorizing Institutional Change*. Basingstoke: Palgrave.

Kittilson, Miki. 2006. *Challenging Parties, Changing Parliaments*. Columbus: Ohio State University Press.

Kolinsky, Eva. 1991. "Political Participation and Parliamentary Careers: Women's Quotas in West Germany." *West European Politics* 14: 56–72.

Krook, Mona Lena. 2009. *Quotas for Women in Politics*. New York: Oxford University Press.

Krook, Mona Lena, Joni Lovenduski, and Judith Squires. 2009. "Gender Quotas and Models of Political Citizenship." *British Journal of Political Science* 39: 781–803.

Landesfrauenbeirat, Rheinland-Pfalz. 2011. *Faire Aussichten? Geschlechterquoten bei Wahlen zu (Kommunal) Parlamenten*. Mainz: Landesfrauenbeirat Rheinland-Pfalz.

Lang, Sabine. 2007. "Gender Governance in Post-Unification Germany: Between Institutionalization, Deregulation, and Privatisation." In *Changing State Feminism*, edited by Johanna Kantola and Joyce Outshoorn, 171–98. Basingstoke: Palgrave Macmillan.

2010. "Gendering Federalism – Federalizing Gender: Women's Policy Agencies and Policies in German Multilevel Governance." *German Studies Review* 33 (3): 517–30.

2017. "Gender Equality in Post-Unification Germany: Between GDR Legacies and EU-Level Pressures." *German Politics* 4: 556–73.

Lang, Sabine, and Birgit Sauer. 2013. "Does Federalism Impact Gender Architectures? The Case of Women's Policy Agencies in Germany and Austria." *Publius – The Journal of Federalism* 43 (1): 68–89.

Laskowski, Silke. 2011. "Zur Verfassungsmässigkeit gesetzlicher Paritéregelungen für die Kommunal-und Landtagswahlen in Thüringen." Gutachten für Bündnis 90/Die Grünen, Landtagsfraktion.

2014. "Nur die gesetzliche Quote wird Chancengleichheit bringen." *Heinrich-Böll Stiftung*. Berlin. Available at: www.boell.de/de/2013/12/05/nur-die-gesetzliche-quote-wird-chancengleichheit-bringen. Accessed September 15, 2016.

Lau, Miriam. 2007. "Quorum, Quote, Krippenplätze." *Die Welt*. June 3. Available at: www.welt.de/politik/article749201/Quorum-Quote-Krippenplätze-100-Jahre-Frauenbewegung.html. Accessed May 13, 2016.

Lemke, Christiane. 2001. "Changing the Rules of the Game: The Role of Law and the Effects of Party Reforms on Gender Parity in Germany." In *Has Liberalism Failed Women? Assuring Equal Representation in Europe and the United States*, edited by Jytte Klausen and Charles S. Meier, 123–42. London: Palgrave.

Lépinard, Éléonore. 2015. "From Breaking the Rule to Making the Rules: The Adoption, Entrenchement, and Diffusion of Gender Quotas in France." *Politics, Groups, and Identities* 4 (2): 231–45.

Limbach, Jutta, and Marion Eckertz-Hoefer. 1993. *Frauenrecht im Grundgesetz des geeinten Deutschland*. Baden-Baden: Nomos.

MacRae, Heather. 2006. "Rescaling Gender Relations: The Influence of European Directives on the German Gender Regime." *Social Politics* 13 (4): 522–50.

Maihofer, Andrea. 1998. "Gleichheit und/oder Differenz? Zum Verlauf einer Debatte." In *Geschlechterverhältnisse im Kontext politischer Transformation*, edited by Eva Kreisky and Birgit Sauer, 155–76. Wiesbaden: Westdeutscher Verlag.

Meier, Petra. 2000. "The Evidence of Being Present: Guarantees of Representation and the Belgian Example." *Acta Politica: International Journal of Political Science* 35 (1): 64–85.

——. 2004. "The Mutual Contagion Effect of Legal and Party Quotas: A Belgian Perspective." *Party Politics* 10 (5): 583–600.

——. 2008. "A Gender Gap Not Closed by Quotas: The Renegotiation of the Public Sphere." *International Feminist Journal of Politics* 10 (3): 329–47.

Murray, Rainbow, Mona Lena Krook, and Katherine A. R. Opello. 2012. "Why Are Gender Quotas Adopted? Party Pragmatism and Parity in France." *Political Research Quarterly* 65 (3): 529–43.

Mushaben, Joyce. 2014. "The Best of Times – the Worst of Times. Angela Merkel, the Grand Coalition, and Majority Rule in Germany." Unpublished paper, Council of European Studies.

——. 2017. *Becoming Madam Chancellor. Angela Merkel and the Berlin Republic*. New York: Cambridge University Press.

Niedermayer, Oskar. 2013. "Parteimitglieder seit 1990." Arbeitshefte aus dem Otto-Stammer-Zentrum No. 30. Berlin.

Opitz, Olaf. 2013. "Die Männerpartei FDP entdeckt plötzlich ihr Frauenproblem." *Focus Magazin*. July 21. Available at: www.focus .de/politik/deutschland/bundestagswahl-2013/tid-32447/liberale-diskutieren-frauenquote-die-maennerpartei-fdp-entdeckt-ploetzlich-ihr-frauenproblem_aid_1048692.html. Accessed February 15, 2016.

Papier, Hans-Jürgen, and Martin Heidebach. 2014. "Rechtsgutachten zur Frage der Zulässigkeit von Zielquoten für Frauen im öffentlichen Dienst sowie zur Verankerung von Sanktionen bei Nichteinhaltung. Im Auftrag des Landes Nordrhein Westfalen." Düsseldorf.

Poleschner, Katrin. 2010. "Gegen die Frauenquote – Für eine echte Frauenförderung in der CSU." In *Frauen in der Politik*, edited by Isabelle Kürschner, 41–6. Materials of Hanns Seidel Stiftung No. 70. Munich: Hanns-Seidel-Stiftung.

Pütz, Lasse, and Marion Weckes. 2014. "Geschlechterquote." *Auswertung zur Mitbestimmungsförderung*. Düsseldorf: Hans-Böckler-Stiftung. Available at: www.boeckler.de/pdf/mbf_pb_geschlechterquote_puetz-weckes_20140414.pdf. Accessed February 3, 2016.

Rodriguez-Ruiz, Blanca, and Ruth Rubio-Marín. 2012. "On Parity, Interdependence, and Parity Democracy." In *Feminist Constitutionalism. Global Perspectives*, edited by Beverly Baines, Daphne Barak-Erez, and Tsvi Kahana, 188–203. New York: Cambridge University Press.

Rodriguez-Ruiz, Blanca, and Ute Sacksofsky. 2005. "Gender in the German Constitution." In *The Gender of Constitutional Jurisprudence*, edited by Beverley Baines and Ruth Rubio-Marín, 149–73. New York: Cambridge University Press.

Sacksofsky, Ute. 2012. "Winning Women's Vote in Germany." In *The Struggle for Female Suffrage in Europe*, edited by Blanca Rodriguez-Ruiz, and Ruth Rubio-Marin, 127–42. Leiden: Brill.

Schiek, Dagmar, Heike Dieball, Ingo Horstkötter, Lore Seidel, Ulrike M. Vieten, and Sibylle Wankel, eds. 2002. *Frauengleichstellungsgesetze des Bundes und der Länder. Kommentar für die Praxis zum Bundesgleichstellungsgesetz und den Gleichstellungsgesetzen, Gleichberechtigungsgesetzen und Frauenförderungsgesetzen der Länder*. 2nd revised edn. Frankfurt: Bund Verlag.

Schlote, Sara. 2013. *Ursachen für die Unterrepräsentanz von Frauen in der Kommunalpolitik*. Berlin: WZB.

Statistisches Bundesamt. 2016. *Gleichstellungsindex 2016*. Berlin: BMFSFJ Publ.

Verge, Tania, and Maria De La Fuente. 2014. "Playing with Different Cards: Party Politics, Gender Quotas, and Women's Empowerment." *International Political Science Review* 35 (1): 67–79.

Von Wahl, Angelika. 2006. "Gender Equality in Germany." *West European Politics* 3 (6): 461–88.

Weingärtner, Dr. 1988. *Die Quotierung zugunsten von Frauen in Organen der politischen Willensbildung im Inland und im europäischen Ausland*. FB III. Bonn: Wissenschaftlicher Dienst des Deutschen Bundestags.

Wettig-Danielmeier, Inge. 2008. "20 Jahre Quote." In *90 Jahre Frauenwahlrecht!*, edited by Elke Ferner, 93–105. Berlin: Vorwärts Buch.

Wettig-Danielmeier, Inge, and Katharina Oerder. 2012. *Feminismus – und morgen? Gleichstellung jetzt*. Berlin: Vorwärts Buch.

Wiliarty, Sarah. 2010. *CDU and the Politics of Gender in Germany*. Cambridge: Cambridge University Press.

Werner, Melanie. 2010. *Gesetzesrecht und Satzungsrecht bei der Kandidatenaufstellung politischer Parteien*. Osnabrueck: Universitätsverlag.

Wilde, Gabriele. 2001. *Das Geschlecht des Rechtsstaats*. Frankfurt: Campus.

CHAPTER TEN

THE AUSTRIAN PARADOX

The Challenges of Transforming a Conservative Gender Regime

Nora Gresch and Birgit Sauer

In recent debates and speeches especially of conservative Austrian politicians, "gender equality" seems to have advanced into a crucial and defining core value of Austrian identity and principle of Austria's democracy.[1] The draw to allude to gender equality as a defining principle and the verve with which it is done is remarkable, since Austria is usually described as having institutionalized a "conservative-institutional" (Langan and Ostner 1991, 310–12), "conservative-corporatistic, marriage-centered" (Dackweiler 2003, 194), or "strong breadwinner" welfare-state system (Lewis and Ostner 1994, 19–25) that prioritizes social services depending on the husband's income and is reluctant to set incentives for social care services outside the family or for men to engage in care activities (Allhutter 2003, 114). According to these analyses, the Austrian welfare-state regime does not sufficiently support the institutionalization of equal opportunities for women in comparison to the possibilities available for men.

Nevertheless, Austria started to introduce measures for enhancing women's participation and representation in political life and equal opportunities in the workforce relatively early. The equal status of men and women before the law was stated in article 7 of the constitution in 1920 and the ratification of the Convention on Equal Pay of Male and Female Workers for Equal Work was incorporated into national law in the 1950s. Also, due to ratifications of the

---

[1] We want to thank Anna Gius for her valuable research work for this chapter.

European Social Charter and the International Pact for Economic and Cultural Rights of the UN, Austria implemented its first equal opportunity law for the private sector (Gleichbehandlungsgesetz)[2] in 1979 (Feigl et al. 2006, 18). A programme for the advancement of women in public service (Frauenförderprogramm) came into force in 1981 (Pelinka and Rosenberger 2003, 217). The first quota regulation of a political party was introduced by the Social Democratic Party (Sozialdemokratische Partei Österreichs, or SPÖ) in 1985 and the first quota regulation within Austria's legal corpus came into force in 1993 with the Federal Equal Treatment Act for the Public Services (Bundes-Gleichbehandlungsgesetz). Moreover, in 1998 the government amended article 7 of the constitution, stating that all citizens are equal before the law, with the following paragraph (article 7.2): "The federation, provinces and municipalities profess to de facto equality of man and woman. Measures fostering de facto equality of women and men especially to end existing inequalities are permissible."

Focusing on this paradoxical situation of having implemented a "conservative-corporatistic" welfare state and gender regime on the one hand and a "differentiated and broad-ranging corpus of gender equality legislation" (Gresch and Sauer 2015, 36) on the other, we will critically explore Austrian gender quota policies from the perspective of substantive equality and gender democracy. Gender quota claims inherently entail the potential to deepen democracy and transform societies towards more substantive justice and equality (Lépinard 2014, 1). Thus, by focusing on gender quota policies we will approach the question of whether these regulations can foster substantive equality or if their implementation within the Austrian "conservative-corporatistic" gender regime has moulded them into symbolic measures that do not really deepen democracy.

Accordingly, we will first lay out the topography of gender quota policies and their debate as well as the participation of women in political decision-making bodies to draw the contours of the Austrian paradox. Second, we will analyze the most influential explanatory factors by describing the specific institutionalization of political decision-making processes with a focus on court decisions, and we will explore how crucial legislation for ensuring women's participation in public decision bodies has been adopted. These factors, we contend, might be described as the Austrian gender regime. With the analytical concept of gender regime,

---

[2] BGBl Nr. 1979/108.

we would like to address three dimensions: first, the reciprocal power relations inscribed in the institutional context of decision-making processes, encompassing the political architecture, gender equality institutions, and legislation, as well as welfare state regulations (Galligan 2015; Lewis and Ostner 1994); second, the dominant meaning of gender and gender equality – the frames of the country's dominant gender equality discourse – including the values and narratives of gender relations that are ingrained within and shape the institutions as a *gender narrative* (Pfau-Effinger 2005); and third, practices of doing politics, i.e. the processes of negotiating, agenda-setting, and implementing quota regulations and gender equality measures, including the actors participating in these processes. The concept of gender regime stresses the importance of the relationships between elements and, of course, delineates the field of inquiry to the area of gender (Walby 2004, 5).

Our exploration will distinguish the debates and controversies around specific moments: the achievement of women's suffrage rights, the institutionalization of gender equality machinery, the introduction of gender quota regulation in the Federal Equal Treatment Act for the Public Services, and the amendment of the constitution regarding the commitment to de facto equality. In conclusion, we will argue for a stronger theorization of the concept of gender regime to more deeply and precisely understand the specific workings of power relations within a society that support gender inequalities and to assess continuities and discontinuities in women's political empowerment. It is thus our argument that a conservative gender regime with elements fostering a corporatist, male breadwinner model and a dominant gender difference narrative is unlikely to implement gender quota regulations as transformative measures, but will try to integrate and shape them accordingly, framing the meaning of the quota regulations to support the conservative logic of the gender regime (see also conclusion by Lépinard and Rubio-Marín in this volume).

10.1 THE FISSURED TOPOGRAPHY OF AUSTRIA'S GENDER QUOTA POLICIES AND THEIR CONTESTATIONS

To approach our question of to what extent gender quota policies can exercise their leverage in regards to substantive equality in Austria, in this section we will describe the current topography of gender quota policies, first for electoral politics and second for public administration.

10.1.1 Party Quotas and Women's Representation: An Unfinished Challenge?

The share of female members of Austria's federal parliament varied between 5 and 6 per cent until the 1970s, rose to 10 per cent in 1979, and made its biggest leap between the elections of 1986 and 1990 from 11 to 20 per cent. In the 2002 elections the percentage of women in parliament passed the 30 per cent threshold for the first time (at 34 per cent), then falling to 27 per cent in 2008, rising to 33 per cent after the 2013 elections,[3] and finally decreasing after internal changes within parties to 30.6 per cent in 2016.[4] The same pattern can be traced in the representation of women in the composition of cabinets. The first female minister was Grete Rehor from the Christian-conservative Austrian People's Party (Österreichische Volkspartei or ÖVP) in 1966 (Steininger 2006, 253). The period of governments led by the social-democratic SPÖ from 1970 to 1994 raised women's participation in ministerial offices to over 20 per cent (Geisberger 2010, 363–4). During the conservative-right government of the ÖVP-FPÖ coalition women holding ministerial office increased to 31 per cent in 2002, with Susanne Riess-Passer from the Freedom Party (Freiheitliche Partei Österreichs or FPÖ) as the first woman to be vice-chancellor of the Second Republic. The highest representation of women within a cabinet, at 40 per cent, was achieved in the government of the SPÖ-led coalition under Chancellor Gusenbauer in 2007 (Geisberger 2010, 363–4). The percentage of female cabinet members after the elections in 2013 and changes in the cabinet in 2016 fell to 21.4.

Scrutinizing the presence of women in the second chamber, the Bundesrat (Federal Council), representing the governments of the nine provinces, women's participation has wavered from 20 per cent since the 1980s to 29.5 per cent after the 2006 elections[5] and is currently

---

[3] "Entwicklung des Frauenanteils im Nationalrat," Republik Österreich Parlament, available at: www.parlament.gv.at/SERV/STAT/PERSSTAT/FRAUENANTEIL/entwicklung_frauenanteil_NR.shtml. Accessed 27 April 2016.

[4] "Frauenanteil im Nationalrat," Republik Österreich Parlament, available at: www.parlament.gv.at/SERV/STAT/PERSSTAT/FRAUENANTEIL/frauenanteil_NR.shtml. Accessed 27 April 2016.

[5] "Entwicklung des Frauenanteils im Nationalrat," Republik Österreich Parlament, available at: www.parlament.gv.at/SERV/STAT/PERSSTAT/FRAUENANTEIL/entwicklung_frauenanteil_BR.shtml. Accessed 27 April 2016.

at 31.1 per cent.[6] The representation of women in the governments of the provinces presently ranges between 0 per cent in Upper Austria and 50 per cent in Tyrol, showing an average women's participation of 29 per cent.[7] As of 2016, only two women have been governors of Austrian provinces: Gabi Burgstaller (SPÖ) was president of Salzburg from 2004 to 2013 and Waltraud Klasnic (ÖVP) was governor of Styria from 1996 until 2005 (Geisberger 2010, 365). Moreover, the participation of women is traditionally lowest at the communal level (Pelinka and Rosenberger 2003, 214): 6.6 per cent of Austria's municipalities are currently governed by women (Zögernitz 2016, 5).

As there are no legislative quotas or reserved seats within the parliamentary system, Austria can be described as a country with voluntary "political party quotas" (Dahlerup and Freidenvall 2005, 36). As early as 1985, the SPÖ was the first party to introduce a voluntary 25 per cent quota for women on candidate lists and for appointed offices. This resolution required some effort by the party's women's section: it was adopted only after all female delegates threatened to leave the party convention if the proposal was rejected, since the rhetoric of equality and equal treatment as party principles had not resulted in changes regarding the composition of party organs and representative offices (Niederkofler 2013, 96–7).[8] The amendment of the 25 per cent quota to a voluntary 40 per cent quota in 1993 was vehemently argued for by the then president of the women's section and Austrian Women's Minister Johanna Dohnal, by framing the dominance of men within decision-making positions as an unjustified men's quota that contradicted the socialist principle of equality. Hence, she called for a change of men's expectations concerning their unwarranted entitlements (Niederkofler 2013, 98–104). However, the regulations did not include any sanctions if the quotas were not met. The requirement that all lists alternate between women and men was introduced in 2010. But interestingly, the word "quota" is not mentioned in the

---

[6] "Entwicklung des Frauenanteils im Bundesrat," Republik Österreich Parlament, available at: www.parlament.gv.at/SERV/STAT/PERSSTAT/FRAUENANTEIL/frauenanteil_BR.shtml. Accessed 27 April 2016.

[7] "Österreich brachte weniger Frauen in die Politik," available at: http://derstandard.at/2000032273916/. Accessed 27 April 2016.

[8] There is only a little research about the struggle over quotas in the SPÖ (Niederkofler 2013) but none about the struggle – years later in the 1990s – in the conservative ÖVP.

party programme.[9] In 2004, the party met its voluntary quota of 40 per cent in the executive committee of the party (Bundesparteivorstand), but the number fell slightly again afterwards (Geisberger 2010, 368). Furthermore, there has been no female president of the party so far and the alternating nomination of candidates is not fulfilled in every province. Thus, some provinces do not dispatch women into the SPÖ-fraction of the federal parliament (Nationalrat) (Geisberger 2010, 369), which led to a share of 32.7 per cent female members of parliament from the SPÖ in the 2013–17 legislative period.[10] Due to the decrease of women in parliament, sanctions for not meeting the quota have been discussed regularly during recent years. The topic came back to the fore in 2014, when the SPÖ was immersed in intense discussions regarding who would succeed the deceased former president of the parliament, Barbara Prammer, as a member of parliament, since appointing the subsequent listed male candidate would reduce the share of women in the SPÖ fraction. After appealing to the party's internal jury, the male candidate was given the mandate although the decision was against the quota regulation of the party. Due to protest against this decision, especially from the women's fraction, the party convention adopted new enforcement regulations in 2014: Candidate lists that do not fulfil the quota are invalid and will be rejected. If the party's executive committee of the province will not change the list, the executive committee of the federal party has to finalize the candidate list and submit it to the federal party council.[11]

The Christian-conservative ÖVP introduced a 30 per cent quota for women in its political programme in 1995. Nevertheless, the number of women in the federal parliament as well as in the executive committee of the party has been decreasing since 2002 and the quota regulation has not been met, garnering strong criticism by the women's organization of the party (Geisberger 2010, 368). In 2016, 27.5 per cent of the members of the ÖVP-fraction in parliament were women.[12]

---

[9] Andrea Brunner, SPÖ, "Informationen zur Frauenquote," email response to authors, 14 March 2014.

[10] "Frauenanteil im Nationalrat," available at: www.parlament.gv.at/SERV/STAT/PERSSTAT/FRAUENANTEIL/frauenanteil_NR.shtml. Accessed 27 April 2016.

[11] "Die neue Quotenregelung der SPÖ," available at: http://derstandard.at/2000007815415/Die-neue-Quotenregelung-der-SPOe. Accessed 28 January 2015.

[12] "Frauenanteil im Nationalrat," available at: www.parlament.gv.at/SERV/STAT/PERSSTAT/FRAUENANTEIL/frauenanteil_NR.shtml. Accessed 27 April 2016.

Following the party statutes, only the chairwoman of the women's organization of the party is a mandatory member of the executive committee of the ÖVP (Geisberger 2010). The women's organization of the party adopted the proposal to introduce the alternating principle for all party lists unanimously during its convention in 2014.[13] Although the party convention did not support this claim, the ÖVP introduced in its new party programme a 40 per cent quota for all committees as well as the alternating principle for candidate lists, but only for lists pertaining to federal and provincial elections. Moreover, the ÖVP introduced a mandatory "preference option" for internal elections, which contradicts the alternating principle since the "preference principle" usually favours the election of men. Sanctions for not fulfilling the quota were not introduced.[14]

The right-wing FPÖ, the third-strongest party in Austria's parliament, is against "coercive quota for women" and proclaims that "women do not want to be 'quota women' and do not need quotas if they are successful ... Within the FPÖ, women and men are absolutely of equal value (*gleichwertig*) and are also treated in this way. Equal treatment is thus not necessary."[15] In 2016 the percentage of women in the FPÖ fraction is 16.2 per cent.[16] But in comparison to the other traditional Austrian parties of the Second Republic, FPÖ women hold representative offices more frequently. In 1988, Heide Schmidt became the first female secretary general of the party and in 1993 its first president (Bundesparteivorsitzende). In 2000, Susanne Riess-Passer was elected as the first vice-chancellor of Austria and was also the president of the FPÖ. Ursula Haubner took over the presidency in 2004. It is important to mention that at that time Jörg Haider was very influential in nominating candidates as well as in determining the alignment of the programme of the party (Geisberger 2010, 370). Therefore, we contend that the women in the FPÖ were less a sign of gender democracy than of party autocracy.

---

[13] "Frauenquote. Wenn es etwas besseres gibt, her damit," available at: http://derstandard.at/2000006723108/Frauenquote-Wenn-es-etwas-besseres-gibt-her-damit. Accessed 28 January 2015.

[14] "Schwarzer Vorstand erteilte neuen Grundsätzen seinen Segen," available at: http://derstandard.at/20000014542290/Schwarzer-Vorstand-erteilte-neuen-Grundsaetzen-seinen-Segen. Accessed 15 December 2015.

[15] Susanne Rosenkranz, FPÖ, "Frauenquote," email response to authors, 9 April 2014.

[16] "Frauenanteil im Nationalrat," available at: www.parlament.gv.at/SERV/STAT/PERSSTAT/FRAUENANTEIL/frauenanteil_NR.html. Accessed 27 April 2016.

The Green Party established a 50 per cent quota in 1987 for all elected organs and party functions and today is the only party in Austria that exceeds its own quota. In 2016, 54.2 per cent of Green Party members in federal parliament were female. From 2008 until May 2017, Eva Glawischnig was the head of the party followed by Ingrid Felipe after Eva Glawischnig resigned due to internal party conflicts. After the elections in October 2017, the Green Party is not present in the federal parliament anymore. Since then, the party is led by Werner Kogler on an interim basis. Women held representative offices early on in the Green Party. In 1986, Freda Meissner-Blau was the first president of the Green fraction in the Nationalrat and thus the first woman in this position in Austria's history of parliamentarian government (Geisberger 2010, 371). She was also the first woman to run for the office of president, in 1986. Madeleine Petrovic was president of the Green Party from 1994 until 1996. Moreover, in 1994, the Green Party amended its statutes to ensure that its quota regulations really enforced the advancement of women: If a man is in the first position on a candidate list, the next two following spots must be filled by women, since the 50 per cent quota would be in danger if only three candidates were elected. This regulation is only applicable to women (Geisberger 2010).

The remaining parties currently present in the National Council are the liberal-conservative Team Stronach, founded by the Austrian-Canadian multi-millionaire Frank Stronach, and the liberal-progressive NEOS, which consists of a union of the party Liberal Forum (Liberales Forum or LIF) and the party New Austria (Das Neue Österreich). Both parties participated for the first time in the election to the Nationalrat in 2013. Team Stronach is against a quota regulation for women in general: "A women's quota is nothing more than an instrument of socialist economic planning. Team Stronach would never agree to such an infringement of the free will of companies and employers concerning decisions. The stronger presence of women in leading offices must be achieved without coercive measures like a women's quotas but through the awareness and responsibility of both sexes to each other."[17] However, in 2016 Team Stronach is the party with the second highest percentage of women – 50 per cent – in

---

[17] Julia Zednik, Team Stronach, "Frauenquote," email response to authors, 24 March 2014.

parliament, after the Green party.[18] Furthermore, the party academy, the youth organization, and the party organizations in the provinces of Vienna, Lower Austria, and Styria are led by women, while only one man works in the federal coordinating office (Bundesgeschäftsstelle) of the party.[19] Since the party was founded recently, analyses concerning its impact in regards to Austria's political landscape as well as women's politics are still open.

Women make up 11.11 per cent[20] of the NEOS fraction in parliament in 2016 and the party is in internal discussions about whether a women's quota will be implemented in the future to advance the representation of women in the party.[21] Interestingly, in regards to the recruitment process of its candidates, NEOS has implemented a very unique system for Austria's party system: All citizens are allowed to apply for candidacy and introduce themselves and their vision and goals at a public hearing. As a next step, all residents who are interested, independent of their origin and also of their party affiliation, can vote for a candidate electronically. The third step is the vote by the executive committee of NEOS and the last step is the final vote by the member council of the party.[22] Nonetheless, until now this system has brought only 11 per cent women into the federal parliament.

Thus, looking at the parliamentary system concerning quota regulations, some of the parties do implement voluntary quota regulations, but with the exception of the SPÖ there are no sanctions if the self-imposed quota is not met. This situation represents the paradoxical structure of gender equality policies in Austria. On the one hand, fractions of the parties and especially the women's sections have strongly advocated and fought for women's quotas in the SPÖ and the ÖVP, leading to the introduction of quota regulations. On the other hand, parties have not introduced instruments like sanctions or bonus incentives to ensure the implementation of their quota regulations.

Regarding the introduction of quota regulations within the SPÖ and the ÖVP, the decisions for their adoption occurred at a time when those parties faced severe challenges due to election losses and

[18] "Frauenanteil im Nationalrat," available at: www.parlament.gv.at/SERV/STAT/PERSSTAT/FRAUENANTEIL/frauenanteil_NR.shtml. Accessed 27 April 2016.

[19] Zednik, "Frauenquote," 24 March 2014.

[20] "Frauenanteil im Nationalrat," available at: www.parlament.gv.at/SERV/STAT/PERSSTAT/FRAUENANTEIL/frauenanteil_NR.shtml. Accessed 27 April 2016.

[21] Heike Fleischmann, NEOS, "Frauenquote bei NEOS," 2 May 2014.

[22] Fleischmann, "Frauenquote bei NEOS," 2 May 2014.

the newly emerging Green Party in the 1980s. The adoption of party quotas within these parties – the most influential parties in Austria – thus supports the thesis of "party pragmatism" (Murray, Krook, and Opello 2012, 530) as the most crucial factor in the adoption of gender quotas and could be interpreted as a "pragmatic compromise" (541). By contrast, the implementation and realization of gender equality in the Green Party can be seen as a founding ideological principle of the party. Nevertheless, nearly thirty years after the first quota regulations were introduced in Austria's party statutes, a 30 per cent participation of women in public offices seems to be the magic limit that is hard to overcome.

10.1.2 Gender Equality in Administrative Office: The Role of Courts

Although Austria has not adopted legislative quotas for political elections, it has implemented quota regulations within its state administration and in 1998 amended its constitution to ensure the enforcement of de facto gender equality or "equality of results" (Dahlerup and Freidenvall 2005, 30–1). After pressure by the Women's Minister Johanna Dohnal, in 1993 the government passed the first Federal Equal Treatment Act for the Public Services, explicitly stating that each unit of a ministerial department must create affirmative action plans if the percentage of women in the department is below 40 per cent.[23] The quota was raised in 2010 to 45 per cent and in 2012 to 50 per cent.[24] As said previously, the amendment of article 7 of the country's constitution specifically permits measures fostering de facto equality to end existing inequalities, namely quotas. On the basis of this law, the University Law was amended in 2009 and 2015, now stipulating that the percentage of women in university organs and committees must be at least 50 per cent, with the possibility of intervention by the university's working group for questions pertaining to equal treatment (Arbeitskreis für Gleichbehandlungsfragen) if the quota is not addressed.[25] In 2010, a 45 per cent women's quota was introduced for all positions of the Austrian public broadcasting agency (ORF), except

---

[23] Bundesgesetz über die Gleichbehandlung von Frauen und Männern und die Förderung von Frauen im Bereich des Bundes (Bundes-Gleichbehandlungsgesetz – B-GBG), BGBl Nr. 100/1993.

[24] BGBl Nr. 140/2011.

[25] BGBl Nr. 81/2009 and BGBl Nr. 21/2015.

the positions in committees and the managing board.[26] In July 2011 the cabinet decided to introduce a quota of 35 per cent for women pertaining to all supervisory boards of state-owned enterprises where the state is the majority shareowner until 2018, which was a demand from the women's fraction of the SPÖ and the Green Party and strongly advocated for by the then Minister for Women, Gabriele Heinisch-Hosek. If this corporate board quota for state-owned firms is not achieved in 2018, further measures will be established.[27] As of March 2017, the speakers of the cabinet reported that with the end of 2016, five years after its introduction, 55 per cent of the respective companies had fulfilled the 35 per cent quota (thirty-one out of fifty-six companies).[28] Thus, the parties of the then ruling coalition, the SPÖ and ÖVP, introduced a bill for a mandatory 30 per cent quota regulation for corporate boards for all stock listed companies and for companies with more than 1,000 employees as of January 2018. Following the German legal model (see also Lang in this volume), if the quota is not met, the election of the board is not valid and the mandate remains open.[29] Intriguingly, the introduction of the quota was not met with strong resistance at this point in time. In 2011, when the then EU Justice commissioner, Vivian Reding, launched the campaign to promote women's presence on corporate boards (see the introduction to this volume), 80 per cent of Austria's companies were strictly against the introduction of legal quota regulations.[30] Nevertheless, §87.2a of the Austrian Stock Corporation Act (Aktiengesetz) also stated, before the introduction of the quota regulation, that the composition of boards should take into account diversity according to gender, age, and the country of citizenship. Also, the Austrian Corporate Code (Unternehmensgesetzbuch) as well as the Corporate Governance Codex of 2015 urges companies

[26] BGBl Nr. 50/2010.
[27] "Aufsichtsräte: Regierung einigt sich auf eine Frauenquote," available at: http://diestandard.at/1297820484932/Aufsichtsraete-Regierung-einigt-sich-auf-eine-Frauenquote. Accessed 27 April 2016.
[28] "Ministerrat: Frauenanteil in Aufsichtsratsgremien staatsnaher Unternehmen auf 40,3 Prozent gestiegen," available at: www.bka.gv.at/-/ministerrat-frauenanteil-in-aufsichtsratsgremien-staatsnaher-unternehmen-auf-40-3-prozent-gestiegen. Accessed 13 July 2017.
[29] "Verpflichende Frauenquote im Aufsichtsrat ab 2018," available at: www.salzburg.com/nachrichten/oesterreich/politik/sn/artikel/verpflichtende-frauenquote-im-aufsichtsrat-ab-2018-251449/. Accessed 13 July 2017.
[30] "Eine Frage der Quote," available at: http://diepresse.com/home/wirtschaft/economist/5165039/Eine-Frage-der-Quote. Accessed 13 July 2017.

to report on their measures to include women in their boards ("Frauen. Management. Report" 2016, 15–16).

Interestingly, the legal decisions responding to contestations of the quota regulations of both the Federal Equal Treatment Act for the Public Services and the University Law mirror and manifest the same paradoxical approach in regards to substantive equality. On the one hand, the decisions endorse the legal quota regulations and the approach of substantive equality that implies, amongst other things, the concept of "equality of results" through the means of quota regulations. On the other hand, the decisions do not foster or strengthen the implementation of the quota regulations. In a first important case in 2001, the Highest Court of the Republic (Oberster Gerichtshof or OGH) dismissed the complaint of a plaintiff who claimed to have been twice unlawfully passed over for a judgeship at the High Court of the Vienna province (Oberlandesgericht Wien) due to the quota regulation of the Federal Equal Treatment Act. He argued that this quota regulation in fact contradicted European Community Law, as well as the rule of law, because women would not be treated equally but would receive extreme preference, since they were not obliged to fulfil the same criteria as equally qualified men.[31] In its decision, the OGH focused on the question of whether the Federal Equal Treatment Act would contradict the European Community directive 76/207/EWG from 1976 that deals with equal treatment of men and women in regards to the access to occupation, occupational training, and promotion. In its argumentation, the national court referred to the judgment of the European Court,[32] which states that female candidates should not automatically and necessarily be preferred and that the personal situations of all candidates have to be taken into account.[33] Also, criteria like age or date of last promotion need only be taken into account if those pertain to the suitability and performance of the candidates.[34] The OGH, referring to another decision of the European Court,[35] also stressed that the plaintiff's complaint of having a weaker prospect for his career development than his female competitors was a consequence

---

[31] OGH 1Ob80/00x, 30 January 2001, p. 2.
[32] Decisions of 28 March 2000, Rs C-158/97 Badeck and 6 July 2000, Rs C-407/98 Abrahamsson.
[33] Rs C-158/97 Badeck.
[34] Rs C-407/98 Abrahamsson.
[35] 25 October 1988, Rs C-312/86 – Commission/France, Slg 1988, 6315 Rn 15.

of the EU directive, which aimed to reduce or abolish the actual inequality of men and women in the foreseeable future.[36] While this case confirmed the lawfulness of gender quota mechanisms, a subsequent case struck a less positive note.

In 2010, the OGH again made a decision relevant to the implementation of quota regulation.[37] The court stated that the employment of a male candidate for a position as university assistant would have been "unlawful" only if the decision was made without justified reason. But in the eyes of the Court, the female candidate who was not chosen for the job did not experience discriminatory treatment on the basis of her gender since any other person in a similar situation irrespective of his/her gender would have experienced similar treatment, and thus her claim for compensation on the basis of discrimination was unjustified with regards to §11b paragraph 2 B-GlBG. In other words, the non-implementation of the affirmative action policy was not judged as discrimination, and the female plaintiff was not considered as having experienced sex discrimination. Thus, if a public institution can justify a reason for not preferring a woman in the case of equal qualification, the quota regulation (and the aim of increasing the participation of women) is not seen as prior and the decision remains without sanction.

In 2013, a group of professors of the University of Linz submitted a complaint to the Austrian Constitutional Court (Bundesverfassungsgericht) against the decision of the election commission of the university which had rejected a candidate list for the upcoming election of the senate without the then required 40 per cent quota of female candidates. The group of professors claimed that the rejection would infringe upon: (1) articles 20, 21, and 23 of the Basic Rights Charter of the European Union – stipulating that all people are equal, emphasizing the equality of women and men, especially regarding employment and work, and prohibiting discrimination on the basis of gender; (2) article 3 of the Basic State Law (StGG) – ensuring that public offices are equally accessible for all citizens; and (3) article 7 of the constitution, since the quota regulation of the University Law did not treat men and women equally (Hauer 2014, 81–3). The Constitutional Court stated in its decision that article 7, paragraph 2 of the constitution empowers actions towards "positive discrimination" in situations where gender

---

[36] OGH 1Ob80/00x, 30 January 2001, p. 8.
[37] OGH 8 ObA 35/10w, 2 November 2010.

relations do not correspond to equal ratios (Hauer 2014, 86).[38] The Constitutional Court thus interprets article 7, paragraph 2 as a directive to implement regulations fostering actual "equality of results." But the Constitutional Court also explained that the quota regulation for candidate lists for university bodies does not imply the regulation of candidates' positions (Hauer 2014, 89). Furthermore, the Constitutional Court argued that the arbitration commission of a university can – after an objection from the university's working group for questions regarding equal treatment (Arbeitskreis für Gleichbehandlung) and if there are not enough women from a certain area available or if women do not want to participate in this way – decide to justify not fulfilling the quota regulation (Hauer 2014, 86–8). Again, this judgment shows the paradoxical implementation of quota regulations, on the one hand stressing the importance of working towards substantive equality, but on the other hand legitimizing the evasion of quota regulations.

Having described the topography of gender quota policies in Austria and their low leverage for engendering substantive gender equality, we will now explore more profoundly explanatory factors which constitute the Austrian gender regime by analyzing, first, the specific institutionalization of political decision-making processes in Austria and, second, the process by which legislation for ensuring women's political and public representation has been adopted.

10.2 THE GENDER-BIASED INSTITUTIONALIZATION OF POLITICAL DECISION-MAKING PROCESSES

For the Austrian gender regime, the particular institutionalization of a "neo-corporatist" political system is crucial for analyzing policy and decision-making processes (Tálos 2006, 425). Being structured as a federal republic, Austria has two chambers of parliament – the Nationalrat (National Council) as the directly elected first chamber of parliament and the Bundesrat (Federal Council) as the second chamber of parliament, representing the governments of the nine Austrian provinces. The Nationalrat is the primary legislative body. The Bundesrat is rather weak and usually only has the right to make objections to decisions of the Nationalrat, which the Nationalrat can ignore (Fallend 2006, 1032–3).

---

[38] 12 March 2014, B 803/2013.

The Austrian version of neo-corporatism institutionalizes private sector professional interests as public corporations. The respective private as well as public professional organizations – the "social partners" – are highly centralized bodies and legally entitled to be included in processes of policy implementation as well as policy drafting (Fink 2006, 443–4): The major social partners are the Austrian Trade Union Association (Österreichischer Gewerkschaftsbund or ÖGB), the Chamber of Labour (Bundesarbeiterkammer), the Chamber of Commerce (Wirtschaftskammer), and the Chamber of Agriculture (Landwirtschaftskammer).

In addition, Austria's neo-corporatist structure is embedded within two different functional networks (Tálos 2006, 430–1): A vertical network encompasses institutionalized interactions as well as advocacy for common interests and close cooperation between the social partners and the parties. This network structures and intensifies the main ideological cleavages in Austrian politics: on the one hand the ties between the Christian-conservative ÖVP and the Conference of Presidents of the Chamber of Agriculture and the Chamber of Commerce, and on the other hand the connections between the Chamber of Labour, the Austrian Trade Union Association (ÖGB), and the SPÖ (Tálos 2006, 430). A horizontal network consists of institutionalized as well as informal interactions between the social partners, and, occasionally, between the social partners and the government (Tálos 2006, 431). Due to these informal networks, the corporatist system has always included "informal or hidden quotas" since a certain number of seats of the SPÖ and ÖVP contingent "have been traditionally reserved for prominent members of the social partnership organisations" (Köpl 2005, 35).

From the perspective of gender democracy, Austria's "corporate corporatism" (Neyer 1996, 88–92) is literally "manned" (Appelt 1995, 612). The androcentric structure is one factor for the exclusion of women's issues from political deliberation as well as of women from political decision-making processes. However, at the end of the 1970s, conflicts within the social partnership associations diminished their influence in political processes (Tálos 2006, 436). This shift provided an opportunity structure at the turn of the 1980s, wherein women-specific issues could be raised and the institutionalization process of the gender equality policy field could be established.

Since the turn of the century, the social partners' leverage within policy drafting processes has declined even more due to national,

European, and international pressures on national policy making. The conservative-populist coalition of ÖVP and FPÖ (2000–6), for instance, refrained from including the social partners during policy drafting on a broad range of issues, preferring instead the opinions of experts from outside the social partner networks (Tálos 2006, 440). Looking at the representation and inclusion of women within this neo-corporatist system, the ÖGB is the only organization that has introduced a quota regulation through an amendment of its statutes in 2007, resulting from a long-standing demand of the women's organization of the ÖGB. This "relational quota" regulation determines that the percentage of women within the organs of the association has to adequately correspond to the ratio of female members (Geisberger 2010, 373). While the quota regulation was achieved in the executive committee in 2008, its implementation has not been realized within the individual trade unions (Geisberger 2010, 374). Before the amendment, the statutes (established in 1979) already declared that one of the vice-presidents must be the representative of the ÖGB women's organization. But to this date, no woman has been president of the ÖGB. The Union of Private Employees, Print, Journalism, and Paper (Gewerkschaft der Privatangestellten, Druck, Journalismus, Papier) is the only union to have had a female president – Eleonore Hostasch, from 1989 until 1994 (Geisberger 2010, 373–4). Hostasch has also been the only female president of the Chamber of Labour, from 1994 until 1997. The representation of women in the organs and committees of the remaining social partner organizations varies between 0 and 25 per cent, reaching 25 per cent only in the executive committee of the Chamber of Commerce in 2008. In addition, the Chamber has had one female Secretary General. In the different sections of the Chamber of Commerce, women's participation remains sparse (375).

10.3 DEBATING WOMEN'S POLITICAL PARTICIPATION IN THE AUSTRIAN GENDER REGIME

In this section, we will discuss the processes regulating women's political participation and at the same time point out those features of the Austrian gender regime which are important for the adoption and implementation of gender equality measures and which show some path dependency in the Austrian political system.

10.3.1 The Achievement of Women's Suffrage

In March 1911, 20,000 men and women participating in the first International Women's Day demonstration in Vienna marched to the parliament and sang suffrage songs (Bader-Zaar 2012, 192). This action came five years after women in Finland had been enfranchised and seven years before women were given the right to vote in Austria. This visible manifestation of the claim for women's suffrage can be described as a late, but fulminating realization of the fact that nearly all the rights and possibilities for political participation for women in the Hapsburg Monarchy and especially in the German-speaking part had actually been successively taken away in the evolving nation-states.

After the liberal revolution of 1848, several provinces had entitled both women and men with the right to vote if they paid a certain amount of tax (Bader-Zaar 2006, 108). But with the introduction of the Austrian Association Law of 1867, women were prohibited from becoming members of or founding political associations (Sauer 2008). The beginning of parliamentary representation via direct election in 1873 shifted towards a census-based suffrage: Female landowners, but also female teachers, nuns, and public servants – independent of their tax revenue – possessed the right to vote, however women could not be elected for an open position (Sauer 2008). Thus, in response to the electoral reform of 1889, which disenfranchised this group of women, female teachers in particular called for protest and launched the first campaign for women's suffrage and the abolishment of the prohibition of organizing in associations (Bader-Zaar 2012, 193; Sauer 2008, 32).

It was also during this decade that women in Austria began to organize systematically to raise awareness of women's issues. But in Austria, the women's movement was split from its start. A first strand comprised the liberal-conservative women with an often middle-class and Catholic background who focused primarily on issues of education and social welfare for women and families (Sauer 2008, 36ff.). The other strand of the developing women's movement comprised the socialist female workers' movement, which as part of the Social Democratic Party (SPÖ) centred its interest on the improvement of working conditions for women as well as the working and living conditions of all workers (Bader-Zaar 2012, 194). Although the claim for universal suffrage rights for men and women was included in the early SPÖ party programme as a result of the campaign of the socialist women's movement, the party leader, Viktor Adler, announced that the achievement of women's suffrage should be of secondary status within the party priorities – and the female workers' movement submitted to the party's ruling, especially during the phase when equal suffrage for men was discussed in parliament (Bader-Zaar 2012, 194–5). The result was that all women lost the right to vote when equal universal male suffrage was introduced in 1907. Only the Social Democratic Labour Party of Austria (Sozialdemokratische Arbeiterpartei Österreichs or SDAPÖ), founded in 1889, demanded the same rights for men and women who worked and even included the claim for universal suffrage rights for men and women in its articles in 1892.

The main argument voiced by suffragists of both the liberal and socialist strands of the Austrian women's movement emphasized the "natural" or "inherent" qualities and values of women – like morality, devotion, care, and motherliness – that were necessary to realize a more just and better society. Another important argument concerned the "complementarity" of the qualities of men and women in political life (Bader-Zaar 2012, 199). Thus, for the evolving gender-regime in Austria, the "difference approach" and the exclusion of women from the institutionalization of political decision-making structures have been crucial determinants. Hence, the leverage for obtaining women's political rights was weakened not only by the exclusion of women from the developing institutionalization and democratization of political decision-making structures, but also by a frayed women's movement that mobilized frames not of equality but rather of difference.

10.3.2 Struggles for Political Representation in the 1980s: Changing the Meaning of Gender Equality

When Chancellor Bruno Kreisky announced the cabinet members after the SPÖ had won the majority of votes in the federal parliament election in 1979, the proposed cabinet included only one female minister and one female state-secretary, although Kreisky had claimed to support the demands of the women's movement in his campaign (Köpl 2005, 22–3). Activists from the so-called "autonomous women's movement" and especially the women's organization within the SPÖ started to protest against the scandalous underrepresentation of women in the new cabinet as well as the federal parliament and framed their claim primarily as an issue of justice: Although women were well included within the party organization, they were not allowed to hold decision-making positions within the party (Köpl 2005, 23). After discussions within the party, two state secretariats in charge of women's policies were established (against the opposition of some party officials): one pertaining to the "issues of women in the labour market" at the Ministry for Social Affairs (Staatssekretariat für Angelegenheiten der berufstätigen Frauen, headed by Franziska Faist) and the other pertaining to "general women's issues" at the Federal Chancellery (Staatssekretariat für allgemeine Frauenfragen, headed by Johanna Dohnal) (Tertinegg and Sauer 2007, 5–6). Although state secretaries are members of the cabinet they do not have the right to vote within the cabinet; they are assigned to a ministry and its respective hierarchical structure, and cannot act or initiate policy proposals independently. Nevertheless, the appointment of two state secretaries marked the beginning of the institutionalization and recognition of women's policy as an independent policy field in Austria (Tertinegg and Sauer 2007, 6), although in a "paternalistic political model" (Kreisky 1998, 29).

After the SPÖ lost its majority in the elections of 1983 and entered into a coalition with the at this point liberal-rightist FPÖ, the state secretariat for "issues of women in the labour market" was abolished. It took until the election of 1990 for the state-secretary of "general women's issues" to be transferred into the Federal Ministry of Women's Affairs with their own administrative staff and budget, as well as the right to veto decisions in the cabinet (Tertinegg and Sauer 2007, 6–7). The state secretary for general women's issues at that time, Johanna Dohnal, became the first Austrian Minister for Women's Affairs.

An emerging state feminism and a growing and visible women's movement in the 1970s were important actors for demanding the institutional representation of women's issues. The Austrian women's movement started with meetings and discussion groups initiated by women in the SPÖ and supported by femocrats in government and in the administration. This mobilization triggered the motivation to initiate independent women's groups like the Platform of Independent Women (Aktion Unabhänginger Frauen or AUF) or women artists, who addressed questions of women's public invisibility and abortion. For the AUF, the battle against the criminalization of abortion was the initial unifying motivation (Dick 1991, 8–10; Geiger and Hacker 1989, 13–18). This group viewed the emancipation of women as part of the class struggle for a socialist society. Therefore, the aim of including and attracting female workers was an explicit goal of the organization, since the majority of the AUF members were well-educated, middle-class women (Dick 1991, 13; Geiger and Hacker 1989, 32).

One of the main arguments made by these participants in the women's movement for increasing the number of women in political offices and especially in legislative bodies was that women and especially mothers have different life experiences to men, which are necessary to prioritize certain important societal issues on the political agenda, like violence against women, social welfare for women, environmental protection, child abuse, and reconciliation of work and family (Köpl 2005, 23–4). Thus, the "difference approach" was also crucial for determining the meaning and importance of women's political recognition and intelligibility in the struggles of the women's movement.

10.3.3 Transforming the Male State: Gender Quotas in Public Bodies

Within Austria's legislative body, the Federal Equal Treatment Act for the Public Services of 1993 was the first law entailing a concrete quota regulation, which, as described above, stipulates that ministerial units must create affirmative action plans if the share of women employed dips below 40 per cent (amended to 45 per cent in 2010 and 50 per cent in 2012).[39] The initiative for implementing this law came from the then Minister of Women's Affairs, Johanna Dohnal, who drafted and negotiated the policy proposals of the so-called equal treatment package entailing several measures and proposals concerning welfare policies and social issues[40] – with the addendum that she would use her veto in the cabinet regarding a mandatory amendment of the pension law if the equal treatment package were not passed (Köpl 2005, 27).

Although Dohnal could bargain on the basis of her position as minister, she nonetheless had to negotiate the policy proposals within the neo-corporatist structure of Austria's political decision-making institutions. But for the drafting and implementation process of this law, female politicians of the major parties, the SPÖ and ÖVP, as well as female members of parliament from the Green Party and trade union representatives allied to support the policy proposal (Köpl 2005, 31). Furthermore, the social partnership organizations from the labour sector

---

[39] Bundesgesetz über die Gleichbehandlung von Frauen und Männern und die Förderung von Frauen im Bereich des Bundes (Bundes-Gleichbehandlungsgesetz – B-GBG), BGBl 100/1993.

[40] The first steps to Dohnal's policy proposals were scientific studies on the situation of women; in the case of this law, the feminist political scientist Eva Kreisky conducted the first study on the representation of women in public service in order to gather gender segregated data (Niederkofler 2013).

sent women as their representatives for the pre-parliamentary negotiations. Thus, the arguments of the policy draft's opponents – such
as primarily high-ranking civil servants and the male dominated civil
servant's trade union (Gewerkschaft Öffentlicher Dienst), as well as
members of the FPÖ – that the nomination of equal treatment officers
in departments would not be necessary, the proposed measurements
would erode the competence of experience, and preferential treatment
of women would be equal to reverse discrimination, were not convincing enough against the proponents' major claim to strive for de facto
equality between men and women (Köpl 2005, 28–31).

At this point, the most influential frame used in the debates on wom-
en's representation in state office was the "equality approach" brought
forward by femocrats and, again, by Dohnal as Women's Minister,
which posited that the low representation of women in public service
showed a lack of equal opportunities for women (Köpl 2005, 30–1).
Female actors from different women's and social partnership organizations joined forces to build up political leverage for the policy proposal.
Only the initial demand that the burden of proof regarding discrimination claims should be shifted to the federal ministries and agencies
was not included in the final law proposal due to the missing support
of women from the ÖVP and the members of the civil servant trade
union (Köpl 2005, 31). The law was passed with the stipulation that
the state institutions only need to explain not having discriminated
against women in cases of conflict (Köpl 2005, 29–31). After the government passed the Federal Equal Treatment Act, the provinces also
had to adopt their own Equal Treatment Laws for the Public Services in
order to implement the quota. The nine provinces implemented their
laws at quite different paces (Tertinegg and Sauer 2007, 16).

10.3.4 Changing the Constitutional Meaning of Gender Equality

When the SPÖ/ÖVP coalition launched their first austerity programmes during the mid-1990s due to the international recession and
the costs of joining the EU in 1995, Johanna Dohnal (then Minister for
Women's Affairs) and movement activists mobilized to form a women's
party, since the austerity programmes targeted primarily social welfare
programmes that concerned services for women (Kogoj 1998, 253–56).
Although the women's party never materialized, the idea attracted
much media attention and stimulated a debate on Austrian women's
current social situation as well as their poor political representation.
Within this context, the chairwoman of the Green fraction, Madeleine

Petrovic, initiated a private member's bill in 1996 to make 15 per cent of the public subsidies to political parties "contingent upon the number of female representatives being proportional to their presence in the population" (Köpl 2005, 33). The first parliamentary debate on this bill was held in 1996 and members of the SPÖ and ÖVP as well as Minister of Women's Affairs Helga Konrad supported the motion (Köpl 2005, 35). There was an apparent consensus on the importance of increasing women's participation in politics, but the opponents of the bill – including members of the FPÖ and the liberal party, Liberales Forum (LIF), but also members of the SPÖ and ÖVP – criticized the bill as a coercive measure that would contradict the principle of individual commitment and initiative that should govern the recruitment process. The argument that quota regulations would conflict with prioritizing qualifications was one of the major arguments against the bill (Köpl 2005, 34). The argument that Austrian parties had utterly failed to increase the number of women in representative positions so far was of crucial concern for the proponents of the bill (Köpl 2005, 33). Furthermore, proponents argued for the importance of women in politics, stressing that women would "not only bring different experiences and perspectives to their jobs but will also change legislative style" (Köpl 2005, 35), stating that they would be less aggressive and favour a more consensus-based, harmonious, and cooperative style of working and communicating instead of being commanding and controlling (Köpl 2005, 33–5).

The "difference approach" is here again an important frame within the Austrian gender regime for arguing for equal rights in gender related policy discussions, with almost an essentializing and stereotypical attitude towards women's capabilities and behaviour. After the first parliamentary debate on the bill, it was assigned to the Equal Treatment Committee of the National Council (Gleichbehandlungsausschuss des Nationalrats), which in 1999 recommended the rejection of the bill with a majority of MPs of all parties except the Green Party (Köpl 2005, 35).[41]

---

[41] The Equal Treatment Committee of the Austrian parliament cannot be considered a femocrat institution. Its task – similar to other parliamentary committees – is to discuss and decide on all bills and directives that deal with equal treatment of men and women, due to ethnicity, religion, age, and sexual orientation. All parties in parliament are represented in all committees. In 2016, the Equal Treatment Committee included eight members from the SPÖ and ÖVP, six from the FPÖ, four from the

Reacting to the austerity politics of the mid-1990s, in 1996 a group of female academics, journalists, feminist activists, and left-ist politicians organized, in the association Autonomous Women's Platform (Unabhängiges Frauenforum, or UFF), to launch a people's referendum on women's issues,[42] the so-called women's referendum (Frauenvolksbegehren) of 1997 (Dackweiler 2003, 146–7; Rosenberger 1998a). The proclaimed aim of this people's initiative was to push for implementing legal measures fostering substantive gender equality in Austria by demanding that equal treatment be anchored within the constitution, as the preamble of the referendum, and stipulating eleven further legal measures.[43] The eleven points targeted the following three dimensions: (1) the non-discriminatory access of women to labour-centred social security systems, for example by treating part-time and minor employment as equal to full employment with regards to social and labour law provisions; (2) the improvement of work and life reconciliation, for example by establishing more public child-care institutions; and (3) the improvement of equal opportunities for access to the labour market for women, for example by giving public funding only to those companies or projects that can guarantee the inclusion of women at all hierarchical levels according to women's percentage in the population (Dackweiler 2003, 147). Moreover, the initiators of the UFF wanted to provide a different forum than the established women's organizations in the parties for engaging with and participating in the political debate, namely through an independent and inclusive platform for women's claims. Central to the aim of constituting an inclusive organization was the intention to raise awareness concerning the restriction of women's rights (Rosenberger 1998a, 207). Their focus was thus much wider than their specific policy goals of questioning the gender bias of the social security arrangement and the masculinist

Green Party, and one from NEOSNEOS and Team Stronach. See www.parlament.gv.at/PAKT/VHG/XXV/A-GL/A-GL_00001_00367/.

[42] Article 41 of the Austrian constitution stipulates four ways of submitting law proposals: to the National Council as proposals of its members; to the Federal Council or a third of the members of the Federal Council, as proposals of the government; and as a people's referendum, if the referendum is signed by 100,000 people eligible to vote or by a sixth of the people eligible to vote in three provinces respectively. The National Council only has to deal with the issues of the referendum and can decide whether the issues are relevant for further implementation or not.

[43] See "Volksbegehren. Frauen-Volksbegehren," available at: www.parlament.gv.at/PAKT/VHG/XX/I/I_00716/fname_139596.pdf. Accessed 10 September 2016.

norm of work-life structure, engaging rather with the conditions of women's situation in general.

The women's referendum attracted significant media attention and was signed up for by 11.2 per cent of people eligible to vote, making it one of the most successful people's initiatives in Austrian history, supported by a broad range of women's organizations, as well as gender equality representatives and femocrats (Dackweiler 2003, 146–50; Rosenberger 1998b, 242–4;). In contrast to its success, the government did not follow suit with an implementation plan, leading to demonstrations against the government's inaction. The demands of the women's referendum were finally assigned to the Equal Treatment Committee of the National Council, whose members then developed three concrete proposals to be voted on: (1) to amend the constitution by including the paragraph that "the Federation, provinces and municipalities subscribe or profess to the de-facto equality of men and women. Measures to promote factual equality of women and men, particularly by eliminating actually existing inequalities are admissible," and to state that official titles can express the sex of the office holder;[44] (2) to amend the maternity protection law (Mutterschutzgesetz) and the parental leave vacation law (Eltern-Karenzurlaubsgesetz) to allow for minor employment during the phase of leave;[45] and (3) to amend the labour relations law (Arbeitsverfassungsgesetz) to ensure that the worker's council of a business has the right to debate measures of affirmative action and work – life balance with the management.[46] All three proposals of the Equal Treatment Committee were passed by the National Council.

When the parliamentary debate was held, almost a year after the referendum had been submitted, media attention and interest in the claims of the women's platform was again high, supported by the

---

[44] "Bericht und Antrag des Gleichbehandlungsausschusses betreffend den Entwurf eines Bundesverfassungsgesetzes, mit dem das Bundes-Verfassungsgesetz (B-VG) geändert wird," available at www.parlament.gv.at/PAKT/VHG/XX/I/I_01114/fname_140005.pdf. Accessed 10 September 2016.

[45] "Bericht und Antrag des Gleichbehandlungsausschusses betreffend den Entwurf eines Bundesgesetzes, mit dem das Mutterschutzgesetz 1979 und das Eltern-Karenzurlaubsgesetz geändert werden," available at: www.parlament.gv.at/PAKT/VHG/XX/I/I_01116/fname_140003.pdf. Accessed 10 September 2016.

[46] "Bericht und Antrag des Gleichbehandlungsausschusses betreffend den Entwurf eines Bundesgesetzes, mit dem das Arbeitsverfassungsgesetz geändert wird," available at: www.parlament.gv.at/PAKT/VHG/XX/I/I_01115/fname_140004.pdf. Accessed 10 September 2016.

fact that during the same period two women were campaigning to be elected president of the republic, Gertraud Knoll (SPÖ) and Heide Schmidt (LIF). However, prominent women from the UFF were split along party lines concerning support for the female candidates. During the parliamentary debate, both candidates were present with their respective supporters from the UFF platform, sitting in different boxes of the visitors' gallery in the plenary hall ("Eine Kandidatin auf der Galerie. Turbulenzen um Frauen im Plenum" 1998). Eventually, the debate concerning the demands of the women's referendum was scheduled for 2:00 p.m. But due to the strategic intervention of an urgent motion by members of the of FPÖ regarding the question of whether Austria should begin negotiations for joining NATO, the debate was interrupted and postponed for four hours, finally taking place between 7:00 and 11:00 p.m. – an inconvenient time for media coverage.

Nonetheless, during the debate all parties declared themselves in support of women's policies, emphasizing their different initiatives and proposals to support women and advance gender equality. The main points of discussion during the debate were repeated remarks concerning the importance of improving the balance of work and family and the critique of having missed the opportunity to achieve farther-reaching results for the advancement of women, expressed particularly by the MPs of the SPÖ and the Green Party, since the amendment to the constitution was the only substantial result – besides the inclusion of minor occupations in the social security system – of the demands of the women's referendum.[47]

The formulation of the amendment to the constitution was a major subject of discussion during the debate, since the text suggested by the Equal Treatment Committee of the National Council – which stated "that the federation, provinces and municipalities profess to de facto equality of man and woman and that measures fostering de facto equality to end existing inequalities are permissible" – is a declaration and not a commitment. On the one hand, some MPs remarked that a constitution is not the right place for a commitment, while on the other, MPs – particularly from the Green Party – stressed that this formulation would express a non-commitment to the advancement of women.[48]

---

[47] Stenographic protocol of the 116th session of the National Council of the Republic of Austria, XX legislative period, held 16 and 17 April 1998, available at: www .parlament.gv.at/PAKT/VHG/XX/NRSITZ/NRSITZ_00116/.

[48] Ibid., Doris Kammerlander, Green Party, 169.

Interestingly, the term "quota" was mentioned only once in regard to the discussed amendment, by Willi Brauneder from the FPÖ. He remarked that it would be damaging to interpret the "measures" as quota regulations, since quotas would introduce a collective equality principle in opposition to the individual equality principle, which is of prime concern in constitutional rights.[49] Shortly before voting, Madeleine Petrovic, from the Green Party, tried to lure the SPÖ women out of coalition party discipline, since most members of the SPÖ – and especially female MPs – criticized the recommendations of the Equal Treatment Committee as too limited and disappointing. Petrovic attempted to frame the issues at hand as an opportunity for creating a coalition-free space for women's issues.[50] But the SPÖ/ÖVP coalition voted for the proposal and only the oppositional parties – the Green Party, FPÖ, and LIF – voted against. Thus, the amendment to the constitution was the only concrete result of the women's referendum to be implemented, although since it was not a commitment, no sanctions or measurements are provided to achieve equal treatment.

After the debate in the Nationalrat, the two major representatives of the UFF women's platform left the association and the platform dissolved ("Frontfrauen verlassen nun Frauenfront" 1998). The UFF had initiated an impressive political agenda concerning women's political representation and equal participation, but it was also criticized by autonomous feminists for focusing only on questions relating to equality rights and reconciling work and family. These feminists claimed that by looking only at issues that target (presumably) "most women" and specifically well-educated women from mainstream society, gendered power relations and the situations of women of different social, economic, and family status, as well as of different ethnic origins were completely ignored (Dackweiler 2003, 150–2).

10.4 THE REVERBERATIONS OF AUSTRIA'S CONSERVATIVE GENDER REGIME: CONCLUSIONS

Having analyzed the different debates concerning the implementation of legal and institutional measures pertaining to women's representation in Austria, we can conclude that Austria's legislative and institutional bodies incorporate several quota regulations as well as

---

[49] Ibid., Willi Brauneder, FPÖ, 203.
[50] Ibid., Madeleine Petrovich, Green Party, 209–10.

measurements or directives to include women in political decision-making positions. Quota regulations for party election lists are voluntary commitments of the respective parties, set down in the parties' statutes or programmes. The Federal Equal Treatment Law for Public Services includes target quota regulations, while the University Law has, since 2009, contained binding quotas for all committees and university organs. Nonetheless, women in Austria's decision-making bodies are still vastly underrepresented. Gender equality institutions such as the Women's Ministry were deprived of power at the turn of the century, when the right-wing conservative government dissolved the Ministry in the year 2000. Although the Women's Ministry was re-established in 2003, gender equality issues have been added to ministries such as Education or, since 2016, to Health. Hence, Austrian quota regulation in party politics and state administration functions as symbolic politics, implemented weakly and targeting mainly white, middle-class women, while ignoring migrant and poorly educated women. Overall, women remain 'outsiders within' the Austrian political system. Austrian quota regulations have not proved to be transformative measures for its gender regime and gendered power relations, as in other countries described in this volume, and can be described as "corrective equality remedies" (see conclusion by Lépinard and Rubio-Marín in this volume).

In conclusion, we suggest that to understand the political leverage of quota regulations – and not only in Austria – it is fruitful to include an analysis of the effects of the country's gender regime. The question of institutional change and why Austria has passed gender quota regulations at all might be answered with a claim of "institutional isomorphism" (Mackay, Monro, and Waylen 2009, 258) in a twofold way: With respect to voluntary party quotas, Germany has been serving as an institutional model for Austria on the one hand (see Lang in this volume). Although the Austrian SPÖ introduced a voluntary quota earlier than the German SPD, Austrian social democrats introduced the alternating system only in 2010. Moreover, Norway's quota measurements for corporate boards put pressure on Austrian legislation. On the other hand, the country's political system – namely the neo-corporatist system of social partnership – already implied "quasi" quota regulations on electoral lists. Hence, the Austrian introduction of voluntary gender quotas on party candidate lists might be seen as institutional layering (Waylen 2014, 7–8), as quotas for social partners on party candidate lists have a long, although informal, tradition in Austria, whereby the SPÖ reserves positions for union functionaries and the ÖVP for functionaries from the Chamber of Commerce. Another important factor for the introduction of quotas has been the mobilization of the women's movement since the mid-1970s in coalition with the SPÖ women's section and social democratic femocrats. Eventually, a changing societal structure and hence, changing opportunity structures – such as the educational progress of women, their (partial) integration into the labour market, and their emancipation as voters – has led to the discovery of women as voters and a relative openness of parties to pass quota measures. A final factor was the framing of modernity by the women's movement and social democratic women, who claimed that Austria was falling behind "modern Europe" without significant representation of women in parties and in the executive.

The weak implementation of quota regulation might again be explained by the institutional setting of social partnership, which is characterized by a thick network of male bonding. This network successfully enfolds strategies that restrict the implementation of quota regulations as transformative measures on different levels of the legislative and the executive. Additionally, throughout the different phases of institutionalizing women's political representation, the political actors have developed and reiterated a dominant meaning of gender and gender relations based on the "difference approach" (Gresch and Sauer 2015). The "difference frame" is rooted in longstanding notions of family and women as mothers, and institutionalized in Austria's political citizenship narrative, its ethno-cultural citizenship model, and the principle of jus sanguinis, which traditionally gives women the role of "bearers of the nation." This framing feeds into the conservative Austrian gender regime, which perceives women mainly as mothers and, hence, as part of the private sphere of the family but not as members of the public sphere of politics, which represents a precondition for achieving "public parity" (see conclusion by Lépinard and Rubio-Marín in this volume).

10.5 LIST OF E-MAIL RESPONSES

Brunner, Andrea. SPÖ. "Informationen zur Frauenquote." 14 March 2014.
Fleischmann, Heike. NEOS. "Frauenquote bei NEOS." 2 May 2014.
Rosenkranz, Susanne. FPÖ. "Frauenquote." 9 April 2014.
Zednik, Julia. Team Stronach. "Frauenquote." 24 March 2014.

References

Allhutter, Doris. 2003. *Europäische Chancengleichheit von Frauen und Männern im österreichischen Recht.* Linz: Trauner Verlag.

Appelt, Erna. 1995. "Frauen und Fraueninteressen im korporatistischen System Österreichs." In *Bericht über die Situation der Frauen in Österreich*, edited by Bundesministerium für Frauenangelegenheiten/Bundeskanzleramt, 610–14. Wien: Bundeskanzleramt.

Bader-Zaar, Birgitta. 2006. "'Wir streben nicht blindlings das Wahlrecht an, sondern in klarer Erkenntnis, dass das Wahlrecht Macht ist.' Zur Geschichte des Frauenwahlrechts in der österreichischen Reichshälfte der Habsburgermonarchie." In *Mit Macht zur Wahl. 100 Jahre Frauenwahlrecht in Europa. Band 1 – Geschichtlicher Teil*, edited by Bettina Bab, 108–17. Bonn: Frauenmuseum.

———. 2012. "Gaining the Vote in a World in Transition: Female Suffrage in Austria." In *The Struggle for Female Suffrage in Europe*, edited by Blanca Rodríguez-Ruiz and Ruth Rubio-Marín, 192–203. Leiden: Brill.

Dackweiler, Regina-Maria. 2003. *Wohlfahrtsstaatliche Geschlechterpolitik am Beispiel Österreichs.* Opladen: Leske und Budrich.

Dahlerup, Drude, and Lenita Freidenvall. 2005. "Quotas as a 'Fast Track' to Equal Representation for Women." *International Feminist Journal of Politics* 7 (1): 26–48.

Dick, Hildegund. 1991. "Die autonome Frauenbewegung in Wien. Entstehung, Entfaltung und Differenzierung von 1972 bis Anfang der 80er Jahre." PhD Thesis, Universität Wien.

"Eine Kandidatin auf der Galerie. Turbulenzen um Frauen im Plenum." 1998. Die Presse. 17 April. Innenpolitik, 7.

Fallend, Franz. 2006. "Bund-Länder-Beziehungen." In *Politik in Österreich. Das Handbuch*, edited by Herbert Dachs et al., 1024–40. Wien: Manz.

Feigl, Susanne, Angelika Kartusch, Karin Lukas, and Birgit Weyss (2006), *Ihr gutes Recht. Gleichbehandlung und Gleichstellung von Frauen und Männern in der Privatwirtschaft*, Wien: Bundesministerium für Gesundheit und Frauen.

Fink, Marcel. 2006. "Unternehmerverbände." In *Politik in Österreich. Das Handbuch*, edited by Herbert Dachs et al., 443–61. Wien: Manz.

"Frauen.Management.Report: Frauen in Geschäftsführung und Aufsichtsrat in den Top 200 und börsennotierten Unternehmen." 2016. Wien: Arbeiterkammer.

"Frontfrauen verlassen nun Frauenfront." 1998. Die Presse. 23 April. Innenpolitik, 8.

Galligan, Yvonne. 2015. "States of democracy. An overview." In *States of Democracy. Gender and politics in the European Union*, edited by Yvonne Galligan, 1–14. London: Routledge.

Geiger, Brigitte, and Hannah Hacker. 1989. *Donauwalzer/Damenwahl*. Wien: Promedia Verlag.

Geisberger, Tamara. 2010. "Repräsentation und Partizipation von Frauen in Politik und Wirtschaft." In *Bericht über die Situation der Frauen in Österreich*, edited by Bundesministerium für Frauen und Öffentlichen Dienst im Bundeskanzleramt, 351–86. Wien: Bundeskanzleramt.

Gresch, Nora, and Birgit Sauer. 2015. "Topographies of Gender Democracy in Austria." In *States of Democracy. Gender and politics in the European Union*, edited by Yvonne Galligan, 33–49. London: Routledge.

Hauer, Andreas. 2014. "Die Frauenquote bei Senatswahlen. Anmerkungen zu VfGH 12.3.2014, B 803/2013." *Zeitschrift für Hochschulrecht* 13 (4): 81–9.

Kogoj, Traude. 1998. *Lauter Frauen. Hintergründe und Perspektiven des Frauenvolksbegehrens*. Wien: Turia & Kant.

Köpl, Regina. 2005. "Gendering Political Representation: Debates and Controversies in Austria." In *State Feminism and Political Representation*, edited by Joni Lovenduski and Claudie Baudino, 20–40. Cambridge: Cambridge University Press.

Kreisky, Eva. 1998. "Man hält die Demokratie nur am Leben, indem man sie in Bewegung hält. Bruno Kreisky und die neuen politischen Bewegungen." In *Bruno Kreisky. Seine Zeit und mehr*, edited by Stiftung Bruno Kreisky Archiv, 15–33. Innsbruck: Studienverlag.

Langan, Mary, and Ilona Ostner. 1991. "Geschlechterpolitiken im Wohlfahrtsstaat. Aspekte im internationalen Vergleich." *Kritische Justiz*, 3: 302–17.

Lépinard, Elénore. 2014. Gender quotas and transformative politics. RSCAS Policy Paper 2014/06, Robert Schuman Centre for Advanced Studies, European University Institute, Fiesole.

Lewis, Jane, and Ilona Ostner. 1994. *Gender and the Evolution of European Social Policies*. Bremen: University of Bremen Centre for Policy Research.

Mackay, Fiona, Surya Monro, and Georgina Waylen. 2009. "The Feminist Potential of Sociological Institutionalism." *Politics & Gender* 5 (2): 253–62.

Murray, Rainbow, Mona Lena Krook, and Katherine A.R. Opello. 2012. "Why Are Gender Quotas Adopted? Party Pragmatism and Parity in France." *Political Research Quarterly* 65 (3): 529–43.

Neyer, Gerda. 1996. "Korporatismus und Verbände. Garanten für die Stabilität eines sexistischen Systems?" In *Der halbierte Staat. Grundlagen feministischer Politikwissenschaft*, edited by Teresa Kulawik and Birgit Sauer, 82–104. Frankfurt: Campus.

Niederkofler, Heidi. 2013. "Von der Hälfte des Himmels, oder: Die Geduld der Frauen ist die Macht der Männer. Geschlechterdemokratie und Quotendiskussion in der SPÖ." In *Johanna Dohnal. Ein Politisches*

Lesebuch, edited by Maria Mesner and Heidi Niederkofler, 89–104. Wien: Mandelbaum Verlag.

Pelinka, Anton, and Sieglinde Rosenberger. 2003. *Österreichische Politik*. Wien: Facultas.

Pfau-Effinger, Birgit. 2005. "Wandel der Geschlechterkultur und Geschlechterpolitiken in konservativen Wohlfahrtsstaaten – Deutschland, Österreich und Schweiz." 1–10. Available at: www.fu-berlin.de/sites/gpo/tagungen/Kulturelle_Hegemonie_und_Geschlecht_als Herausforderung/Birgit_PfauEffinger__Wandel_der_Geschlechterkultur_und_Geschlechterpolitiken_in_konservativen_Wohlfahrtsstaten___Deutschland___sterreich_und_Schweiz/wandel_geschl_Pfau_effinger.pdf.

Rosenberger, Sieglinde K. 1998a. "Alles was Recht ist? Eine politikwissenschaftliche Einschätzung des Frauen-Volksbegehrens." In *Lauter Frauen*, edited by Traude Kogoj, 202–26. Wien: Turia & Kant.

———. 1998b. "Von der 'AUF' zum 'UFF.' Eine Analyse der 'Dritten Frauenbewegung'." In *Lauter Frauen*, edited by Traude Kogoj, 241–525. Wien: Turia & Kant.

Sauer, Birgit. 2008. "Möglichkeitsstrukturen, Ressourcen und frames. Die Erringung des Frauenwahlrechts in Österreich." In *Frau und Nation*, edited by Johanna Laakso, 25–50. Wien: LIT.

Schwelle, Dagmar. 1998. "Gleichstellung kommt in die Bundesverfassung. Rechte der Frauen: Ball wieder bei der Regierung." Die Presse, Inland, 14 April, 6.

Steininger, Barbara. 2006. "Frauen im Regierungssystem." In *Politik in Österreich. Das Handbuch*, edited by Herbert Dachs et al., 247–64. Wien: Manz.

Tálos, Emmerich. 2006. "Sozialpartnerschaft. Austrokorporatismus am Ende?" In *Politik in Österreich. Das Handbuch*, edited by Herbert Dachs et al., 425–42. Wien: Manz.

Tertinegg, Karin, and Birgit Sauer. 2007. "Issue Histories: Austria: Series of Timelines of Policy Debates." QUING Project: Quality in Gender and Equality Policies. Institute for Human Sciences [IWM], Wien. Available at: www.quing.eu/files/results/ih_austria.pdf.

Walby, Sylvia. 2004. "The European Union and Gender Equality: Emergent Varieties of Gender Regime." *Social Politics* 11 (1): 4–29.

Waylen, Georgina. 2014. Understanding Institutional Change from a Gender Perspective. Working Papers in Gender and Institutional Change, No. 1, December. Available at: www.manchester.ac.uk/uic.

Zögernitz, Werner. 2016. Frauen in der Spitzenpolitik in Österreich. Wien: Institut für Parlamentarismus und Demokratiefragen. Available at: www.parlamentarismus.at/fileadmin/Inhaltsdateien/IfPD/Dateien/2016_OE-_4_-_vom_24_02_2016.pdf.

PART IV

GENDER QUOTAS AS ACCESSORY EQUALITY MEASURES

CHAPTER ELEVEN

THE "NATURAL" PROLONGATION OF THE NORWEGIAN GENDER EQUALITY POLICY INSTITUTION

Mari Teigen

Norway was the first country to propose (1999), adopt (2003), and implement (2008) gender quotas for corporate boards, and thus became an
initiator of the later wave of corporate board quotas that has swept across
Europe and other parts of the world (Armstrong and Walby 2012; Fagan,
Gonzalez Menendez, and Gomez Ansón 2012; Teigen 2012b; Terjesen
et al. 2015). This diffusion of gender quotas for corporate boards, which
for most countries occurred after the break of the financial crisis in 2007,
addresses questions about the importance of the gendering of economic
decision-making (Walby 2015, 7). Global trends of deregulation in the
1980s and 1990s have been claimed to be a major cause of the financial, and then economic, crisis (Walby 2015). Hence, the economic
crisis provided a new and serious frame for debating the need for regulation to advance gender parity in many countries – as highlighted by
Lépinard and Marín in the concluding chapter of this book, but this was
not the case in Norway. Indeed, the adoption of corporate board quotas
in Norway can be understood partly as a break, and partly as a continuity
of the institutionalization of gender equality policies in the country.

This chapter proposes to investigate the particular aspects of the institutionalization of gender equality policy in Norway, and how and why
the scope of gender quota measures expanded from politics to economic
decision-making in this country. Gender quota measures have been an
important and integrated part of gender equality policies in Norway (Teigen
2012a). Quota schemes have been introduced as voluntary measures in a
majority of the political parties, with the exception of the Conservative
Party and the Progress Party. The Gender Equality Act has since 1981

341

regulated gender parity through gender quotas in publicly appointed boards, councils, and committees (public committees),[1] mandating at least 40 percent of each gender since 1988. Legislative gender quotas for corporate boards were finally introduced in the company legislation in 2003.

Hence, the introduction of gender quotas for corporate boards can be understood in continuity with a legacy of gender quotas as central part of the institutionalization of Norwegian gender equality policy. The persistent male dominance in economic decision-making, as well as an apparent lack of will within economic life to take action, constitutes an important context for why policymakers have regarded state imposed gender quotas as a relevant solution to the problem. Simultaneously, corporate board quotas constitute a break through long-established borders around state intervention into the autonomy of economic life.

This chapter scrutinizes the adoption of gender quotas in different domains in Norway, and more particularly, why and how gender quotas for corporate boards first occurred in Norway. The main question addressed concerns the conditions and processes that have enabled the introduction of corporate board quotas in Norway. Particular emphasis is placed on the institutionalization of Norwegian gender equality policy and its strategic choice in favor of gender quota procedures. While this chapter proposes to give a comprehensive picture of the conditions and processes that led to the first adoption of corporate board quotas, I also speculate in the concluding section of this chapter about how we can understand the diffusion of gender quota policies from party politics to the economy – and discuss whether the irresistible rise of gender quotas in both politics and the economy in Europe is caused by a shift toward a gender parity governance model, where legislative regulations of gender parity constitute a measure to counteract challenges of legitimacy and democratic deficit within decision-making assemblies. Similarly, Lépinard and Rubio-Marín maintain in the concluding chapter of this book that gender parity is part of a constitutional shift where gender parity has become essential for democratic legitimacy.

The chapter commences with an outline of the institutionalization of core aspects of gender equality policies in Norway. The scope

---

[1] I use the term gender parity in this chapter although gender balance ('kjønnsbalanse' in Norwegian) is the most commonly used term in the national gender equality policy debate, as well as in policy documents and in the "Act relating to Gender Equality" (Chapter 3, section 13). Gender parity/balance is generally understood as meaning a gender composition where at least 40 percent of each gender is represented.

of gender quota policies – voluntary and legislated measures – is particularly scrutinized. I then provide a brief description of the legislation that regulates gender parity on corporate boards and show how the legislation has produced changes in the gender composition of those boards. The importance of a legacy of imposing gender quota policies is further elaborated by including the significance of the Norwegian tradition of industrial democracy and nation-specific adjustments to deregulation of the economy in the 1980s and onwards. The following section aims to present an analysis of the role of political agency in the making of gender quotas for corporate boards in Norway. Finally, investigating the important role of the media in the political process that led to the introduction of gender quotas for corporate boards, I present an analysis of the main arguments for and against gender quotas for corporate boards in the media debate and the consultation around the quota proposal.

11.1 THE INSTITUTIONALIZATION OF GENDER EQUALITY POLICIES IN NORWAY

Participation is central to how citizenship has been understood in Norway and the other Scandinavian countries. Norway gained universal suffrage relatively early, in 1913, after New Zealand (1893), Australia (1902), and Finland (1905). Denmark followed two years after Norway in 1915; Sweden in 1921. Women's right to vote had little consequence for the political inclusion of women in the years to follow, however. Major transformations have characterized the post-World War II gendering of citizenship in Norway in terms of social, economic, and political citizenship (Skjeie and Siim 2000, 347).

Women's economic and social citizenship developed from the early 1970s onwards through the shift of the male breadwinner model into a universal breadwinner/universal carer model. The Norwegian Gender Equality Act,[2] which came into force in 1979, prohibited discrimination on the basis of gender (section 5) and provided for positive differential treatment to promote gender equality between men and women (section 7), thus sanctioning a substantive conception of equality. This early and explicit provision in favor of positive differential treatment is an important reason why gender equality policies

---

[2] "The Act relating to Gender Equality," Ministry of Children and Equality, published April 20, 2007, available at: www.regjeringen.no/en/dokumenter/the-act-relating-to-gender-equality-the-/id454568/ (Accessed August 2017).

in Norway have emphasized gender quotas and positive action policies. The dual approach, anti-discrimination and positive action, was the result of a push from "below" by the women's movement, and in particular feminist legal scholars (Dahl 1985; Skjeie 1992). In connection with the 200-year anniversary of Norway's constitution in 2014, the constitution was reformed. As a part of the reform, prohibition of discrimination was included in a new Article 98: "All people are equal under the law. No human must be subject to unfair or disproportionate differential treatment." The Norwegian Constitution does not include a specific clause on the right to gender equality.[3] The Convention on the Elimination of All Forms of Discrimination against Women (CEDAW) convention was ratified by Norway in 1981, and from 2005 was incorporated in the Norwegian Gender Equality Act. From 2009 the incorporation in the Gender Equality Act was repealed, and it was then incorporated in Human Rights legislation, which means that the CEDAW convention has priority in cases of conflict with Norwegian legislation.

Norwegian welfare-state policy has been oriented towards gender equality through generous parental leave schemes and sponsored childcare policies established from the 1970s onwards, and these policies have been regarded as crucial woman-friendly policies (Hernes 1987). The generous leave schemes and the extensive childcare facilities have facilitated reconciliation between family and work by promoting women's participation in the labor market as well as promoting men's participation in the family and care for children. Concerning parental leave, the "daddy-quota" has probably contributed to fathers' changing and increased participation in the family.[4]

Women's political citizenship developed in the same period through a steep increase in women's participation and representation in political decision-making bodies. Gender quota policies have been established in Norway to promote and regulate gender parity in decision-making assemblies: imposed by the state for public commissions, they have been adopted voluntarily by a majority of the political parties. The representation of women in the national parliaments developed steadily throughout the 1970s and 1980s, reaching about 30 percent in Norway in 1985; it did not rise above 40 percent until 2009, however, and has stayed at this

---

[3] Available at: www.stortinget.no/en/In-English/About-the-Storting/The-Constitution./ (Accessed August 2017).

[4] In 1993 the "daddy-quota" was introduced as part of the parental leave scheme – four of the total forty-two weeks were reserved for the father. From july 2018, 14 of forty-nine weeks are reserved to the father.

level since (Dahlerup 2011, 67). In fact, the institutionalization of equality (Krizsan, Skjeie, and Squires 2012) in Norway emphasizes a tradition of privileging gender above other equality strands, as well as privileging some policies above others, i.e. gender quotas above gender mainstreaming. Since 1981 the Gender Equality Act has stated that both genders should be represented on public committees, and since 1988 the Act has specified the demand for gender parity to at least 40 percent of each gender in state appointed commissions, etc.; the same regulation has been included in the Municipal Act since 1992 for municipal commissions.[5]

Table 11.1 provides an overview of the main types of gender quota procedures applied in Norway:

TABLE 11.1   Main types of gender quota procedures in Norway

Fields	Types	Adopted	Procedures
Politics	Voluntary party quota	Liberal Party 1974; Socialist Left Party 1975; Labor Party 1983; Center Party 1989; Christian Democratic Party 1993	Quotas (at least 40% of each gender) regulate party election lists and internal bodies[a]
Public commissions	Legislated gender quotas	1981, first regulation of gender composition in the Gender Equality Act; 1988, specification of 40% of each gender; 1992, same formulation included in the Local Government Act	Minimum of 40% of each gender should be represented in publicly appointed boards, councils, and committees
Corporate boards	Legislated gender quotas	Adopted 2003. Implementation for state-owned, inter-municipal companies, 2004; for new public limited companies, 2006; for all PLCs, 2008	Minimum of 40% of each gender should be represented in specified company boards

[a]The Liberal Party only applies gender quotas to internal bodies.

[5] Public commissions constitute a central part of the Norwegian corporatist system. The coporatist system consists of structural arrangements for expertise exchange, involvement, and negotiations between the state/municipalities and the social partners and other key civil society organizations. Public commissions play a particularly significant role in policy preparation in Norway and Finland (Woldendorp 2011).

Gender quotas have been voluntarily adopted by a majority of the political parties. Five of the major Norwegian political parties adopted such measures from the mid-1970s onwards. The Conservative Party and the right-wing Progress Party have no such regulations, neither has the relatively new Green Party. Party quotas also imply a "zipper system," where candidates of each sex alternate on the election lists, as well as demands for at least 40 percent of each gender in internal party bodies. National legislation to regulate gender parity in the electoral system was discussed by the Election legislation committee in 2001 (NOU 2001), but dismissed on the basis that this would contravene with parties' autonomy in the nomination process. Whether or not gender parity in elected political bodies should be legislated was again discussed by the Equality commission (NOU 2012: 15). The majority recommended that gender representation rules should be included in Norwegian election legislation, but the recommendation was not seriously discussed by the government. The general view appears to be that the relative gender balance in elected political bodies in Norway means that there is not really a need for national legislation to regulate gender parity. This can be interpreted in line with what Drude Dahlerup has called the saturation theory: that as soon as the representation of women increases above 30 percent, this is considered enough, because women are present and can make their voices heard (Dahlerup 2011).

The adoption of party quotas implies that male-dominated decision-making bodies have to accept policies apparently against their own self-interest (Murray, Krook, and Opello 2012). Explanations of why gender quotas are introduced have emphasized party competition to capture women's votes, national models of inclusion, legitimacy, response to external pressure, or even that gender quotas could be in the self-interest of men, because men find women candidates easier to defeat (Murray, Krook, and Opello 2012). A study of women's increased integration into Norwegian party politics, to some extent due to the introduction of gender quotas, emphasizes party competition as a central mechanism that has worked to the advantage of women (Skjeie 1991). Skjeie argues that the problem of male abdication is not necessarily perceived by individual male politicians as a threat to their position, because their position is most of all dependent on support for their party in the electorate (Skjeie 1991, 99).

Gender quota policies have been more strongly emphasized in Norway compared to the other Scandinavian countries, as procedures to promote gender equality progress. Although quota policies can be understood to be in line with the strong ideals of participation and equality, which characterize Scandinavian social democracy, such procedures nonetheless often meet with resistance and are portrayed as anti-egalitarian, even in Nordic countries. However, gender quotas have met with the least opposition in Norway, and the scope of areas for their implementation has been the widest compared to other Scandinavian countries. Voluntary party gender quotas similar to those in Norway (see Table 11.1) emerged later in the 1990s in Sweden; none of the Danish political parties currently apply gender quota regulations.[6] Comparatively, gender mainstreaming has been more strongly emphasized in Sweden than in the other Scandinavian countries, while Denmark has been characterized as the "deviant case" with a less active, moderate institutionalization of gender equality policies (Borchorst et al. 2012).

Critical for the institutionalization of gender quotas in Norway was Prime Minister Gro Harlem Brundtland's second government in 1986, which set a standard – that has not subsequently been surpassed – of at least 40-percent women in the cabinet, as well as completing the revision of the Gender Equality Act requiring at least 40 percent of each gender in all publicly appointed boards. Politically the possibility of regulating the gender composition of different political decision-making fora had already emerged in the 1970s, and the establishment of Norwegian gender quota policies was the result of classic state-feminist dynamics: the introduction of gender quota procedures was justified and pushed through on a broad front by many women and some men in the political parties, in the central public administration, by feminist researchers, journalists, women's movement activists, etc. The introduction of gender quotas for corporate boards expanded the scope of quota policies from political life to the economy and will be scrutinized in closer detail below.

11.2 GENDER QUOTAS FOR CORPORATE BOARDS

For about twenty-five years the only legislated gender quota procedure in Norway applied to public committees. In 2003 the Norwegian parliament adopted gender quotas for corporate boards, including the boards of public limited companies (PLCs), inter-municipal companies,

---

[6] "Quota Database," The Quota Project, available at: www.quotaproject.org/ (Accessed August 2017).

and state-owned companies. Legislated corporate board quotas were expanded to include cooperative companies and municipal companies in respectively 2008 and 2009 (Teigen 2015). The numerous, but mostly small- and medium-sized private limited companies are not subject to gender quota legislation. Expansion of the scope of the legislation to include these companies, especially the largest of them, has been discussed but has not been pursued by the right-wing government that came to power in 2013.

The following analysis of the introduction of gender quotas for corporate boards in Norway is based on empirical analyses of all relevant policy documents as well as other types of information, e.g. the media coverage of the issue in the main Norwegian newspapers. The most important documents are: (1) Consultation proposal on the revision of the Gender Equality Act from the Ministry of Children and Family Affairs, 1999,[7] (2) White paper "Proposal no. 77 on reforms to the Gender Equality Act (2000–2001)" from the Ministry of Children and Family Affairs,[8] (3) Consultation proposal on gender representation in public limited companies, state limited companies, and state businesses, and proposal to change the Companies Act and some other Acts,[9] and (4) White paper "Proposal no. 97 on reforms to Company legislation on gender representation in company boards (2002–2003)" from the Ministry of Children and Family Affairs.[10] The analysis in this chapter is

---

[7] "Consultation: Proposal for revising the Gender Equality Act," Ministry of Children and Family Affairs (Høring: Forslag til endringer i likestillingsloven, Barne- og familiedepartementet), published 1999.

[8] "Proposal no. 77 on reforms to the Gender Equality Act (2000–2001)," Ministry of Children and Family Affairs (Ot.prp. 77 [2000–1], Om lov om endringer i likestillingsloven mv., Barne- og familiedepartementet), published 2001, available at: www.regjeringen.no/nb/dep/bld/dok/regpubl/otprp/20002001/otprp-nr-77-2000-2001-.html?id=123306 (Accessed August 2017).

[9] "Consultation: gender representation on boards of public limited companies, state limited companies and state companies etc. – proposal to change Public Limited the Companies' Act and specific other acts," Ministry of Children and Family Affairs (Høring: Kjønnsrepresentasjon i styret i allmennaksjeselskaper, statsaksjeselskaper og statsforetak, m.v. – forslag til endringer i allmennaksjeloven og i enkelte andre lover, Barne- og familiedepartementet), published 2001, available at: www.regjeringen.no/en/dokumentarkiv/Regjeringen-Stoltenberg-I/bfd/Horinger/2001/Horing-kjonnsrepresentasjon-i-styrer.html?id=421560 (Accessed August 2017).

[10] "Proposal no. 97 on reforms to Company legislation on gender representation in company boards (2002–2003)," Ministry of Children and Family Affairs (Ot.prp. 97 [2002–3], Om lov om endringer i lov 13. juni 1997 nr. 44 om aksjeselskaper, lov 13. juni 1997 nr. 45 om allmennaksjeselskaper og i enkelte andre lover [likestilling i

also based on in-depth analysis of the first stages of the political process, provided in Evenrud (2010), Engelstad (2011), Sørensen (2011), and Teigen (2002, 2015), as well as in Cvijanovic's (2009) analysis of the media debate on the issue of gender quotas for corporate boards. Central aspects of deregulation policies were described in the government-commissioned report on the privatization of public enterprises.[11]

Legislated gender quotas for corporate boards are regulated through company legislation. For public limited companies, the criteria for gender representation on the boards is set in the Norwegian Public Limited Liability Companies Act in its articles 6–11a, "Demand for representation of both genders on the board."[12] Parallel formulations apply for the other types of companies subjected to the gender quota ruling. The rules established are formulated as follows: (1) Where there are two or three members of the board, both genders should be represented. (2) Where there are four or five members of the board, both genders should be represented by at least two members. (3) Where there are six to eight members of the board, both genders should be represented by at least three members. (4) Where there are nine or more members of the board, the membership should comprise at least 40-percent men and 40-percent women. (5) Rules (1) to (4) also apply for the election of deputy members.

The legislation adopted in 2003 was formulated as "threat" legislation: if the companies had not voluntarily reached the gender demands by July 2005, the legislation would be effected. Although the representation of women increased between 2003 and 2005, the target of at least 40-percent women was far from being reached in public limited company boards. Thus, in late autumn 2005 the government decided to implement the legislation for all new companies, starting in 2006, and for all PLCs from 2008. One main reason for the

styrer i statsaksjeselskaper, statsforetak, allmennaksjeselskaper mv.], Barne- og familiedepartementet), published 2003, available at: www.regjeringen.no/en/dep/bld/dok/regpubl/otprp/20022003/otprp-nr-97-2002-2003-.html?id=127203 (Accessed August 2017).

[11] "Should public sector be exposed to competition? – A mapping of national and international experiences," Bør offentlig sektor eksponeres for konkurranse? – En gjennomgang av nasjonale og internasjonale erfaringer, Arbeids- og Administrasjonsdepartementet) (NOU 2000: 19), available at: www.regjeringen.no/no/dokumenter/nou-2000-19/id117394/ (Accessed August 2017).

[12] The rules regarding representation of both sexes are to be applied separately to employee-elected and shareholder-elected representatives in order to ensure independent election processes.

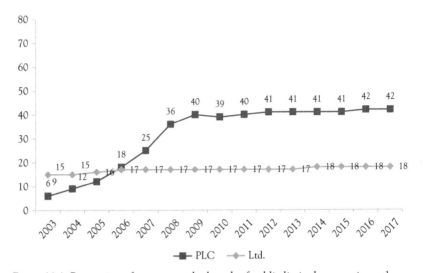

Figure 11.1 Proportion of women on the boards of public limited companies and limited liability companies, Norway, 2003–17
Source: Statistics Norway, available at: www.ssb.no/virksomheter-foretak-og-regnskap/statistikker/styre/aar

effective implementation of gender quotas for corporate boards is the rather tough sanctions that were implemented for breach of the law. The Company Act applies identical sanctions for breaches of any of its rules, beginning with warnings and fees and including forced dissolution as the final step. The business register that is established to ensure compliance with the law reports on companies to ensure that they follow the gender quota ruling or that they comply with it after dialogue with the register.

Figure 11.1 shows the change in the presence of women on the boards of public limited companies subject to gender quota legislation, and the presence of women in the boards of private limited companies not subject to gender quota legislation. The representation of women in public limited company boards made a quick leap after the "threat" legislation (2003–5) became actual legislation (2005), and continued to rise until full implementation (2008). The figures also indicate, however, that the quota legislation did not have ripple effects to company boards not subject to gender quota legislation, and the underrepresentation of women in private limited company boards has remained steady. Further, a study of the relationship between the gender composition in corporate boards and senior management indicates that quotas for corporate boards have not yet led to more gender parity in senior management groups of companies with gender balanced company boards (Halrynjo, Teigen, and Nadim 2015).

In sum, the introduction of gender quotas for corporate boards appears to be a continuation of a decades-long tradition of Norwegian gender equality policy. However, until the implementation of corporate board quotas, Norwegian gender equality policy had been limited by clear boundaries concerning legitimate state interventions. From this perspective, gender quotas for corporate boards constitute an incursion of legitimate state interventions into economic life – breaking with the borders of non-interference with property rights and freedom of business. The tradition of Norwegian gender equality policy was certainly important for why corporate board quotas were initiated and then introduced. But other contextual factors have intervened: Particularly important is the regulation of an employee's right to be represented on company boards. Another important factor is how the deregulation of the economy in Norway, and in particular the liberalization of state-owned enterprises, was discussed in light of its gendered effects at this moment.

11.2.1 Employee Representation on Corporate Boards

The company legislation's regulation of employees' right to representation on company boards constitutes an important factor in the story of corporate board quota adoption in Norway. The owners' autonomy to choose all board members has been restricted since the revision of the Companies Act in 1972, which gave employees in companies with more than fifty employees the right to elect up to one-third of the board members. In companies with more than 200 employees, the company was obligated to set up an enterprise assembly, where one-third of the members were elected by employees and two-thirds by shareholders (Engelstad 2015; Hagen 2015). Employees' right to boardroom representation can be considered an essential aspect of the institutionalization of industrial democracy in Norway.

Employee representation on company boards expresses the fact that board members' mandate should be wider than just serving the interests of the shareholders of the company. In the consultation document for the preparation of a revision of the Gender Equality Act, an enlargement of industrial democracy was in fact presented as a reason for introducing gender quotas for corporate boards:

> In Norway the content of democracy is constantly evolving. How we conceptualize democracy is changing through practice, and demands for and implementation of democratic arrangements are arising for more

new areas. This was the reasoning behind the introduction of industrial democracy at that time. It could be relevant to draw a line between the development of industrial democracy and gender representation in company boards. Although there was disagreement about the introduction of industrial democracy, it is today granted and fully accepted that employees should be represented in company boards.[13]

In other words, the argument is based on drawing a parallel between employee representation and gender representation, and through this comparison pointing to the fact that restrictions to the autonomy of owners in the composition of company boards already exist.

11.2.2 Deregulation Meets the Institutionalization of Gender Equality Policies

Another factor important for the political process leading to the adoption of gender quotas for corporate boards concerns the consequences of the deregulation of the economy. Heavy deregulation of publicly owned businesses was effectuated in Norway from the 1980s onwards (Engelstad et al. 2003; Stjernø 2005). An unintended effect of deregulation was that the scope of the existing gender quotas for public commissions in the Norwegian Gender Equality Act was narrowed, because deregulated companies were no longer recognized as being subject to regulations applying to public companies. The main idea behind processes of deregulation was that the competitive situation should be equal irrespective of type of ownership. On this basis the government argued in its consultation document of 1999 and in its proposal to parliament in 2002 that if regulation of the gender composition of boards were limited to state companies it would change the conditions for competition between private and public owned companies.

> The government wishes to grant all companies equal conditions to compete, irrespective of whether they are public or private companies. Rules of minimum representation of both genders in the boards of private enterprises will give private enterprises equal conditions for competition as for public enterprises.[14]

While important parts of Norwegian gender equality policies have been oriented towards state control, rules, and regulations, policies

---

[13] "Consultation: Proposal for revising the Gender Equality Act" (1999), 58, my translation.

[14] Ibid.

of deregulation have been developed based on the necessity to reduce government regulation and power over business and industry (Derthick and Quirck 1985).[15] In this light, deregulation and gender equality policies appear to be inherently contradictory. Thus, to justify expansion instead of confinement of the scope of gender quota legislation as a salient solution, the government evoked the principle of equal competition. In addition, the fact that the Norwegian state is a prominent owner and actor in economic life, and in particular among the listed companies registered on the Oslo Stock Exchange, has strengthened the legitimacy for the state to take action. About one-third of the values on the Oslo Stock Exchange are publicly, mainly state-, owned.[16]

Moreover, as the debate on corporate board quotas arose, there were simultaneously other movements in the direction of expansion of the field of gender equality legislation. Until the revision of the Gender Equality Act in 2002, the duty to make active, targeted, and systematic efforts to promote gender equality had been restricted to public authorities; after the revision, employer and employee organizations were also included.[17] Hence, at the turn of the millennium, mandatory gender quotas for corporate boards and the expanded duty to make active equality efforts can be interpreted as an expression of movements in the border area between the state and political life, and the economic field.

11.2.3 The Media's Agenda-Setting Role

The political process that developed the innovative idea that the gender composition of corporate boards could be regulated through legislation was boosted by persistent media attention. The debate about women in management was particularly high on the public agenda throughout the 1990s in Norway, as well as in most of the industrialized world. However, to some extent the debate hit Norway particularly hard, as it interfered with a national self-image of being particularly successful in affairs of gender equality. The relatively low number of women in top

---

[15] According to Vogel, considerable confusion exists over the term "deregulation." Deregulation can be described as "the reduction and elimination of government regulations" and liberalization as "the introduction of more competition within a market" (Vogel 1996, 3).

[16] "Ownership Structure of Listed Companies," Oslo VPS (Eierfordeling i børsnoterte selskap, Oslo VPS), available at: http://vpsinfo.manamind.com/sectorstats/index .do?l=no (Accessed August 31, 2016).

[17] "The Act relating to Gender Equality," chapter 3, sections 12 and 14.

positions was considered a paradox in the context of the gender equal-ity achievements of the country. At the turn of the millennium, par-allel power and elite studies in all the Scandinavian countries showed that women were especially poorly represented in top management in those countries (Niskanen 2011; Teigen and Wängnerud 2009), and in fact there are indications that the representation of women in top management in business and industry is higher in many European countries and the United States than in the Scandinavian countries (Bekhouche et al. 2015; Birkelund and Sandnes 2003). However, a comparison of the 200 biggest companies in Norway and the United States documents great similarities in persistent male-dominance in top management groups.[18] The poor representation of women in senior positions, combined with a lack of will of business to adopt initiatives promoting gender equality (Skjeie and Teigen 2003) led gender parity in boardrooms to become a pressing political issue. Consequently, the long-established and generally accepted claim for self-regulation of pri-vate businesses was challenged by a growing claim for state regulation and governance of gender parity. From the mid-1990s a debate emerged over whether the gender parity of corporate boards could be regulated in the Gender Equality Act in the same manner as it was for public boards and commissions.

11.2.4 Main Arguments in the Debate

Analysis of the media debate (Cvijanovic 2009) and the responses from organizations and other actors to government proposals on gender quotas for corporate boards (Engelstad 2012; Evenrud 2010; Sørensen 2011; Teigen 2002) provides a picture of the main actors in the debate. The central arguments in the public debate represented a wide range of opinions, revolving around three classic types of argument in gender quota debates: justice, utility, and democracy.

The Justice Argument: The proponents of gender quotas for corporate boards argued that gender parity in economic decision-making posi-tions concern issues of justice, often without specifying when and why "justice" is relevant in this context. It was argued that justice would be a matter of redistribution of resources, and that gender quotas would comprise a necessary tool to achieve gender equality. The strong male

---

[18] CORE Norwegian Gender Balance Scorecard 2017. Available at: www.samfunns forskning.no/core/english/publications/core-norwegian-gender-balance-scorecard/ (Accessed 19 February 2018).

dominance in Norwegian corporate boards and in economic decision-making in general was then posited as unacceptable and as a possible indication of unfair treatment of women.

The main counterargument based on justice maintained that regulation of the gender composition of company boards would not be fair. Recruitment to corporate boards should not be based on the gender of candidates, but on the owners' right to select the candidates they find most suitable. Gender quota regulations were argued to be illegitimate, unequal treatment and discrimination against men.

The Utility Argument: Arguments about utility and profitability were particularly central as arguments in favor of gender quotas for corporate boards. This argument claimed that since the total talent potential of a population is distributed fairly evenly between men and women, male dominance in corporate boards indicates an underutilization of women's skills. This argument used the rhetoric of business life and thus appeared more unassailable.

The main counterarguments based on utility claimed that corporate board quotas would lead to less competent women replacing more competent men. This argument was grounded on the opinion that not enough women have relevant experience, and that the recruitment of qualified women would have to start earlier and further down the organizational hierarchy to create a pool of well-qualified women. A related argument has been that the gender quota legislation would lead foreign investors to be less inclined to invest in Norwegian companies, with the consequence that Norwegian companies would lose their competitive advantage. The debate on the effects of gender quotas for business performance is ongoing. Some analysis finds a negative effect (Ahern and Dittmar 2012), while others find a non-effect or a moderate positive effect for the poorest-performing companies (Dale-Olsen, Schøne, and Verner 2013).

The Democracy Argument: The government also argued that gender parity in economic decision-making was crucial for Norwegian democracy, and in particular emphasized the importance of equal rights to participation in the boards of the biggest and most influential companies, where the state was often a major owner. In addition they argued that regulation of the gender composition of corporate boards implied an enlargement of industrial democracy. The democracy argument was general – in the sense that democracy is used to create a link between gender parity in political decision-making, and gender parity in economic decision-making – but specific in the sense that it drew on arguments concerned with industrial democracy, especially the company

355

legislation mandating employee representation in company boards, as described previously. In the arguments for gender quotas for corporate boards, employee representation and gender parity were positioned as arrangements that would strengthen industrial democracy.

The main counterargument concerned with democracy held that gender quota regulations would be at odds with the principles of shareholders democracy. Gender quota regulations, it was argued, would hinder owners' democratic rights to recruit the candidates they found the most suitable, and interfere with the election process. As the owners invested and risked their own money they should therefore have the right to decide who they wanted to represent them on the board.

The main voices against gender quotas for corporate boards were from corporate managers and owners and representatives of employer's organizations, while the supporters included mostly politicians, high-ranking civil servants, and representatives connected to the gender equality machinery. The supporting politicians came from a broad spectrum of political parties, mainly the Norwegian Labor Party, the Conservative Party, and the Christian Democratic Party. Opposing politicians were few, but mainly represented the Progress Party and the Conservative Party.

The women's organizations did not take an active part either in the public debate or in the consultation process. This lapse reflects the general weakening of civil society organizations and women's organizations in particular. In addition, corporate board quotas probably appeared too elitist and narrow an issue to fit into the agenda of the main women's organizations.

11.2.5 The Role of Political Agency in the Introduction of Gender Quotas for Corporate Boards

The first initiative to introduce a gender quota regulation for corporate boards[19] was announced in the consultation audit regarding a major revision of the Gender Equality Act in 1999.[20] The revision of the Gender Equality Act was proposed by the minority government

---

[19] The motion was made to expand the functioning sphere of Article 21 of the Gender Equality Act to include all company boards, but it required only a 25-percent minimum of each gender, not 40 percent, as was the case for publicly appointed boards ("Consultation: Proposal for revising the Gender Equality Act," Ministry of Children and Family Affairs, published in 1999).

[20] The main reason for this revision was to adapt Norwegian gender equality legislation to Norway's European Economic Area obligations.

coalition constituted by the Liberal Party, the Center Party, and the Christian Democratic Party. The minister in charge was Valgerd Svarstad Haugland, from the Christian Democratic Party, in the Ministry of Children and Family Affairs. The gender quota motion was withdrawn, however, due to the need for legal clarification of whether a gender quota regulation for corporate boards should be based in the Gender Equality Act or the Companies Act.

After the change of government in 2000, a new motion was sent out for consultation by the Labor Party government in 2001.[21] Some important changes can be seen in this proposal, compared to the white paper from 1999. First the proposal was now included in the Companies Act, and not in the Gender Equality Act. Second, while the 1999 proposal included all companies irrespective of company type or size, the new proposal restricted regulation of the gender composition to state-owned, inter-municipal, and public limited companies. Third, the gender quota was expanded from the original proposal of "at least 25 percent of each of the genders" to "at least 40 percent of each gender." This 2001 motion was finally presented to parliament in 2003 – after another change of government – by the new conservative-centerist government coalition,[22] as "Proposal to parliament no. 97 (2002–2003)."[23] When the new gender quota law was passed in parliament it received broad political support; all parties except for the Progress Party voted in favor of its adoption. The main argument of the Progress Party against the gender quota legislation was based on a rejection of gender quota measures in principle.

---

[21] "Consultation – gender representation on boards," Ministry of Children and Family Affairs (Høring: Kjønnsrepresentasjon i styret i allmennaksjeselskaper, statsaksjeselskaper og statsforetak, m.v. – forslag til endringer i allmennaksjeloven og i enkelte andre lover, Barne- og familiedepartementet), published 2001, available at: www.regjeringen.no/en/dokumentarkiv/Regjeringen-Stoltenberg-I/bfd/Horinger/2001/Horing-kjonnsrepresentasjon-i-styrer.html?id=421560 (Accessed August 2017).

[22] A center-conservative government coalition composed of the Conservative Party, the Liberal Party, and the Christian Democratic Party.

[23] "Proposal no. 97 on reforms to Company legislation on gender representation in company boards (2002–2003)," published in 2003; "Government proposal on the revision of the Companies Act," Ministry of Trade and Industry (Ot.prp. nr 97 [2002–3]. Om lov om endringer i lov 13. juni 1997 nr. 44 om aksjeselskaper, lov 13. juni 1997 nr. 45 om allmennaksjeselskaper og i enkelte andre lover [likestilling i styrer i statsaksjeselskaper, statsforetak, allmennaksjeselskaper mv.]. Oslo: Næringsdepartementet.)

In the process leading up to the adoption of gender quotas for corporate boards, the political agency displayed by critical institutional and political actors became particularly important at two moments. The first critical moment occurred during the preparation of the 1999 proposal. At that time, the persistent male-dominance in senior management was a very hot issue on the public agenda, and it became salient as the revision of the Gender Equality Act approached. The first record of gender quotas for corporate boards as a legal possibility can be found in a letter from the Gender Equality Ombudsperson, Anne Lise Ryel, in connection with the preparation of the Gender Equality Act revision. However, it is surprising that the ideas was picked up and included in the revision by Minister Haugland from the Christian Democratic Party. The Christian Democratic Party is acknowledged as being more concerned with traditional family values than with gender equality. A comparison of the programs of the political parties, however, has shown that women and management actually has been one of the Christian Democratic Party's main gender equality issues (Vik 2012). Moreover, Minister Haugland could have had personal motives for becoming involved with a matter of gender equality, because at that particular point in time she had acquired a reputation of being anti-gender equality due to her central position and responsibility for introducing the cash-for-care reform – a core issue of the Christian Democratic Party and one that represented their emphasis on traditional family values.[24] The intense and heated debate surrounding the cash-for-care initiative, which came into force in 1998, argued in part that the arrangement symbolized a backlash against the Norwegian gender equality project (Ellingsæter 2006). Thus, the proposal of corporate board quotas presented an opportunity for Minister Haugland to strengthen and confirm her authority in relation to gender equality.[25] Nonetheless, the fact that the first political initiative for corporate board quotas came from a relatively unexpected source did probably influence later proceedings.

In between the initial phase and the final adoption, the legislation was by and large prepared in silence. The Labor Party continued the political and legal assessment process, and left its mark by changing

---

[24] The cash benefit reform provided all families with children between one and three years old with a monthly allowance, similar to the cost of the per-child state day care subsidies.

[25] The same applies for her successor, Laila Dåvøy (Minister of Children and Family Affairs from 2001–5), also from the Christian Democratic Party.

the quota from 25- to 40-percent representation of each gender. This adjustment harmonized the new gender quota initiative with the main direction of the Norwegian gender quota tradition.

The second critical moment came as the quota legislation was about to be adopted in 2003. At this point in time there still existed internal disagreement among the representatives of the Conservative Party within the center-conservative coalition government in power which had to be overcome before the government could present the quota regulation proposal to parliament. This final phase was hailed as of paramount importance by the international press,[26] especially the actions of the Minister of Trade and Industry, Ansgar Gabrielsen, from the Conservative Party. Shortly before the proposed law was to be discussed by the government, Gabrielsen gave an interview to the (then) largest Norwegian newspaper, claiming that he was "sick and tired of male dominance in business life" and arguing that quota legislation was necessary to make change happen.[27] This statement was an unexpected and vigorous support from a male politician from the Conservative Party who enjoyed high esteem within the business sector. The uncertainty at the time regarding whether the gender quota law would be passed in parliament rested on the heavy opposition against the corporate board quota legislation from within the economic sector. The Conservative Party has a strong tradition of being attentive to the opinions of the business sector, but Gabrielsen's sudden initiative in favor of the quota law in the final phase of the political process, and his clear opinion about the problems of male dominance in Norwegian economic life were decisive in tipping a divided government in favor of the quota legislation (see Magma 2010).

Many have speculated about his motives. He himself argues that he was convinced that more women would be "good for business" (Magma 2010). Whatever his motivation, his role contributed to creating a basis for broad majority support of the gender quota proposal. The fact that a progressive gender equality reform was proposed by a center-conservative government coalition constituted a breach with established "divisions of labor" within Norwegian politics, in which politics

---

[26] See i.e. *The Economist*, March 13, 2010; *Time Magazine*, April 26, 2010; *Der Spiegel*, July 8, 2010.

[27] "Sick and tired of male dominance in business life" (Møkk lei 'Gutteklubben grei'), VG Nyheter, February 22, 2002, available at: www.vg.no/nyheter/innenriks/artikkel .php?artid=3024189 (Accessed August 2017).

of gender equality have been dominated by the left-wing parties, while the interests, rights, and self-regulation of economic life have been the concern of the right-wing parties. Thus, it was sensational that gender quotas for corporate boards were initiated by a centerist government and then introduced by a center-conservative government. Many of the political actors who are normally skeptical of regulations and gender equality initiatives may have become somewhat confused and more hesitant to oppose than they otherwise would have been if the law reform had been issued by the Labor Party – generally acknowledged for being pro-regulation and pro-gender quotas.

11.3   CONCLUSION

The meaning of full "participation" for women has changed from simply the right to vote and hold political office to women's equal participation with men in political decision-making (Krook and True 2012), as witnessed by the last couple of decades' spread of political gender quotas around the world (see Dahlerup and Freidenvall 2005; Franceschet and Piscopo 2013; Krook 2008, 2009). In recent years the scope of gender quotas has further spread from the spheres of political decision-making to economic decision-making as well. Illustrating, as maintained by Lépinard and Marín in the introduction to this volume, that women's underrepresentation in every domain of authority is being addressed.

In Norway, women gained suffrage in 1913, however with limited consequences for the inclusion of women in the years that followed. In Norway, as in the other Scandinavian countries, the breakthrough for women's participation in political decision-making emerged in the 1970s, and voluntary party gender quotas strengthened this process. The parties that have voluntarily adopted gender quotas are generally characterized by a more equal representation of men and women than those who have not adopted quotas. A gender parity norm in decision-making assemblies is further confirmed by the legislation regulating the gender composition in public commissions, etc., in the Gender Equality Act.

In this chapter I have claimed that the way gender equality policy has been institutionalized in Norway, with its emphasis on gender quota measures, was crucial for the expansion of gender quotas from politics and public commissions to the economy, along with a strong tradition of industrial democracy, and in particular employees' right to be represented on company boards. Processes of economic deregulation and liberalization then shaped a critical moment for addressing the scope of the quota legislation: Should its scope narrow following the logic of deregulation or enlarge to level the playing field for a wider spectrum of businesses? Finally, although these factors were important, the commitment of individual politicians and their will to act was pivotal. All of these factors in combination paved the way for the adoption of gender quotas for corporate boards as a "natural" prolongation of the institutionalization of gender equality policy in Norway.

One main perspective on gender parity posits that parity in political decision-making concerns fundamental issues of justice and democracy, while gender parity in economic decision-making primarily concerns issues of anti-discrimination and individuals' career opportunities – the right to an interesting job (Phillips 1995, 64–5). In post-economic crisis times, maintaining a clear distinction between the spheres of politics and the economy appears less feasible – even risky and unsustainable. Ongoing social changes, connected to neoliberalism and deregulation, have interfered with and altered the characteristics of these social spheres. In this context, many have emphasized the crucial intertwinement of economic and political decision-making (Stiglitz 2010; Walby 2015). New debates are emerging that scrutinize economic decision-making, asking questions about what characterizes the economic power elite – descriptively and substantively – and whether they are the only ones or the right ones to manage such responsibility in the interests of a sustainable society. These questions need to be analyzed in the context of the evolving gender equality framework in Europe and other parts of the world, where the ambitions and visions for gender equality may be shaping a paradigm wherein women's full citizenship includes gender parity in all spheres of power (Rubio-Marín 2014). A broad set of factors, treated in detail in this chapter, paved the way for gender quotas for corporate boards in Norway, where the institutionalization of gender equality policy, combined with a strong commitment to industrial democracy, offered a discursive opportunity to refute the public/private divide. Simultaneously, the Norwegian gender quota reform for corporate boards hit a nerve in many European countries concerned with the legitimacy of male-dominance in decision-making and the interrelationship between economic and political decision-making, as evidenced by the proliferation of corporate board quotas on the public agenda in numerous countries in the following years, as well as the many debates on alternative approaches to changing the male dominance of economic decision-making.

References

Ahern, Kenneth R., and Amy K. Dittmar. 2012. "The Changing of the Boards: The Value Effect of Massive Exogenous Shock." *Quarterly Journal of Economics* 127 (1): 137–97.

Armstrong, Jo, and Sylvia Walby. 2012. *Gender Quotas in Management Boards*. Note. Directorate-General for Internal Policies, Policy Department, Citizen's Rights and Constitutional Affairs. Available at: www .europarl.europa.eu/document/activities/cont/201202/20120216AT-T38420/20120216ATT38420EN.pdf.

Bekhouche, Yasmina, Ricardo Hausmann, Laura D'Andrea Tyson, and Saadia Zahidi. 2015. *The Global Gender Gap Report 2015*. Geneva: World Economic Forum. Available at: http://reports.weforum.org/ global-gender-gap-report-2015/.

Birkelund, Gunn E., and Toril Sandnes. 2003. "Paradoxes of Welfare States and Equal Opportunities: Gender and Managerial Power in Norway and the USA." *Comparative Social Research* 21: 203–42.

Borchorst, Anette, Lenita Freidenvall, Johanna Kantola, Liza Reisel, and Mari Teigen. 2012. "Institutionalizing intersectionality in the Nordic Countries? Anti-Discrimination and Equality in Denmark, Finland, Norway and Sweden." In *Institutionalizing Intersectionality? The Changing Nature of European Equality Regimes*, edited by Andrea Kriszan, Hege Skjeie, and Judith Squires. Basingstoke: Palgrave Macmillan. pp. 59–88.

Cvijanovic, Anette. 2009. Rettferdig og rimelig? – om kjønnskvotering i styrene i allmennaksjeselskap. Masteroppgave i politikk og samfunnsendring. Fakultet for samfunnsvitenskap, Høgskolen i Bodø.

Dahl, Tove Stang. 1985. *Kvinnerett I*. Oslo: Universitetsforlaget.

Dahlerup, Drude. 2011. "Women in Nordic Politics – A Continuing Success Story?" In *Gender and Power in the Nordic Countries. With Focus on Politics and Business*, edited by Kirsti Niskanen. Oslo: NIKK-publication. pp. 59–86 Available at: www.nikk.no/wp-content/uploads/NIKKpub2011_ broschyr_K%C3%B8n-og-magt_Gender-Power.pdf (Accessed August 2017).

Dahlerup, Drude, and Lenita Freidenvall. 2005. "Quotas as a 'Fast Track' to Equal Representation for Women. Why Scandinavia is No Longer the Model." *International Feminist Journal of Politics* 7 (1): 1–22.

Dale-Olsen, Harald, Pål Schøne, and Mette Verner. 2013. "Diversity among Norwegian Boards of Directors: Does a Quota for Women Improve Firm Performance?" *Feminist Economics* 19 (4): 110–35. doi: 10.1080/13545701.2013.830188

Derthick, Martha, and Paul J. Quirk. 1985. *The Politics of Deregulation*. Washington D.C.: The Brookings Institution.

Ellingsæter, Anne Lise. 2006. "The Norwegian Child Care Regime and Its Paradoxes." In *Politicising Parenthood in Scandinavia*, edited by Anne Lise Ellingsæter and Arnlaug Leira. Bristol: Policy Press. pp. 121–44

Engelstad, Fredrik. 2012. "Limits to State Intervention into the Private Sector Economy: Aspects of Property Rights in Social Democratic Societies." In *Firms, Boards and Gender Quotas: Comparative Perspectives*, edited by Fredrik Engelstad and Mari Teigen. Bingley: Emerald. pp. 235–65.

———. 2015. "Property Rights, Governance and Power Balances." In *Cooperation and Conflict the Nordic Way. Work, Welfare and Institutional Change in Scandinavia*, edited by Fredrik Engelstad and Anniken Hagelund. De Gruyter Open. Berlin, Boston: Sciendo Migration. pp. 36–55. Retrieved 19 February 2018, from https://degruyter.com/view/product/462497.

Engelstad, Fredrik, Espen Ekberg, Trygve Gulbrandsen, and Jon Vatnaland. 2003. *Næringslivet mellom marked og politikk*. Oslo: Gyldendal forlag.

Evenrud, Marte. 2010. *Politisk diskurs forut for innføringen av lov om representasjon av begge kjønn I styrene til allmennaksjeselskap. Masteroppgave*. Oslo: University of Oslo.

Fagan, Colette, Maria C. Gonzalez Menendez, and Silvia Gomez Ansón. 2012. *Women on Corporate Boards and in Top Management. European Trends and Policy*. London: Palgrave.

Franceschet, Susan, and Jennifer Piscopo. 2013. "Equality, Democracy and the Broadening and Deepening of Gender Quotas." *Politics & Gender* 9 (3): 310–16.

Hagen, Inger Marie. 2015. "Participation and Co-Determination. Why Some Arrangement Fail and Other Prevail." In *Cooperation and Conflict the Nordic Way. Work, Welfare and Institutional Change in Scandinavia*, edited by Fredrik Engelstad and Anniken Hagelund. De Gruyter Open. Berlin, Boston: Sciendo Migration. pp. 77–95. Retrieved 19 February 2018, from https://degruyter.com/view/product/462497.

Halrynjo, Sigtona, Mari Teigen, and Marjan Nadim. 2015. "Kvinner og menn i toppledelsen." In *Virkninger av kjønnskvotering i norsk næringsliv*, edited by Mari Teigen. Oslo: Gyldendal akademisk. pp. 6–176.

Hernes, Helga. 1987. *Welfare State and Woman Power. Essays in State Feminism*. Oslo: Norwegian University Press.

Krizsan, Andrea, Hege Skjeie, and Judith Squires. 2012. "Institutionalizing Intersectionality: A Theoretical Framework." In *Institutionalizing Intersectionality: The Changing Nature of European Equality Regimes*, edited by Andrea Krizsan, Hege Skjeie, and Judith Squires. Basingstoke: Palgrave Macmillan. pp. 1–32.

Krook, Mona L. 2008. "Quota Laws for Women in Politics: Implications for Female Practice." *Social Politics* 15 (3): 345–68.

2009. *Quotas for Women in Politics: Gender and Candidate Selection Reform Worldwide*. New York: Oxford University Press.

Krook, Mona Lena, and Jacqui True. 2012. "Rethinking the life cycles of international norms: The United Nations and the global promotion of gender equality." *European Journal of International Relations*: 18 (1): 103–27. doi: 10.1177/1354066110380963

Magma. 2010. "Da kvoteringsloven kom til verden: En politisk styrtfødsel. Intervju med Ansgar Gabrielsen i tidsskriftet Magma" [Interview with Ansgar Gabrielsen in the scientific management journal, Magma]. *Magma* 7: 15–19.

Murray, Rainbow, Mona Lena Krook, and Katherine A. R. Opello. 2012. "Why Are Gender Quotas Adopted? Party Pragmatism and Parity in France." *Political Research Quarterly* 65 (3): 529–43.

Niskanen, Kirsti, ed. 2011. *Gender and Power in the Nordic Countries – With Focus on Politics and Business*. Oslo: NIKK-publication 2011, Vol. 1. Available at: www.nikk.no/wp-content/uploads/NIKKpub2011_broschyr_K%C3%B8n-og-magt_Gender-Power.pdf (Accessed August 2017).

NOU. 2000. *Bør offentlig sektor eksponeres for konkurranse? – En gjennomgang av nasjonale og internasjonale erfaringer*. Norwegian Official Report 19.

2001. *Velgere, valgordning, valgte*. Norwegian Official Report 3.

2012. *Politikk for likestilling*. Norwegian Official Report 15.

Phillips, Anne. 1995. *The Politics of Presence*. Oxford: Clarendon Press.

Rubio-Marín, Ruth. 2014. "The Achievement of Female Suffrage in Europe: On Women's Citizenship." *I:CON* 12 (1): 4–34.

Skjeie, Hege. 1991. "The Uneven Advance of Norwegian Women." *New Left Review* 187: 79–102.

1992. *Den politiske betydningen av kjønn. En studie av norsk top-politikk*. ISF-rapport 92:11. Oslo: Institutt for samfunnsforskning.

Skjeie, Hege, and Birte Siim. 2000. "Scandinavian Feminist Debates on Citizenship." *International Political Science Review* 21 (4): 345–60.

Skjeie, Hege, and Mari Teigen. 2003. *Menn i mellom. Mannsdominans og likestillingspolitikk*. Oslo: Gyldendal Akademisk.

Stjernø, Steinar. 2005. *Solidarity in Europe: The History of an Idea*. Cambridge: Cambridge University Press.

Stiglitz, Joseph. 2010. *Freefall: Free Markets and the Sinking of the Global Economy*. London: Penguin.

Sørensen, Siri Øyslebø. 2011. "Statsfeminismens møte med næringslivet. Bakgrunnen og gjennombruddet for kjønnskvotering i bedriftsstyrer som politisk reform." *Tidsskrift for kjønnsforskning* 35 (2): 102–19.

Teigen, Mari. 2002. "Kvotering til styreverv – Mellom offentlig og privat handlefrihet." *Tidsskrift for samfunnsforskning* 43 (1): 73–104.

2012a. "Gender Quotas for Corporate Boards in Norway – Innovative Gender Equality Policy." In *Women on Corporate Boards and in Top*

Management: European Trends and Policy, edited by Colette Fagan, Maria C. Gonzalez Menendez, and Silvia Gomez Ansón. London: Palgrave. pp. 70–90.

2012b. "Gender Quotas in Corporate Boards – On the Diffusion of a Distinct National Policy Reform." In *Firms, Boards and Gender Quotas: Comparative Perspectives*, edited by Fredrik Engelstad and Mari Teigen. Bingley: Emerald. pp. 115–46.

2015. "The Making of Gender Quotas for Corporate Boards in Norway." In *Cooperation and Conflict the Nordic Way. Work, Welfare and Institutional Change in Scandinavia*, edited by Fredrik Engelstad and Anniken Hagelund. De Gruyter Open. Berlin, Boston: Sciendo Migration. pp. 96–117. Retrieved 19 February 2018, from https://www.degruyter.com/view/product/462497.

Teigen, Mari, and Lena Wängnerud. 2009. "Tracing Gender Equality Cultures: Elite Perceptions of Gender Equality in Norway and Sweden." *Politics and Gender* 5: 21–44.

Terjesen, Siri, Ruth Aguilera, and Ruth Lorenz. 2015. "Legislating a Woman's Seat on the Board: Institutional Factors Driving Gender Quotas for Boards of Directors." *Journal of Business Ethics* 128 (2): 233–51.

Vik, Malin Lenita. 2012. *Kjønnslikhet, kvinneulikhet, og mangfold – «velment og forent» eller på tvers og tverke? En komparativ studie av norsk likestillingspolitikk 1981–2013*. Masteroppgave, Institutt for statsvitenskap, Universitetet i Oslo.

Vogel, Steven K. 1996. *Freer Markets, More Rules. Regulatory Reform in Advanced Industrial Countries*. Ithaca, NY: Cornell University Press.

Walby, Sylvia. 2015. *Crisis*. Cambridge: Polity Press.

Woldendorp, Jaap. 2011. "Corporatism in Small North-West European Countries 1970–2006: Business as Usual, Decline or a New Phenomenon." Working Paper Series 30 (February), Department of Political Science, VU University Amsterdam.

CHAPTER TWELVE

GENDER EQUALITY WITHOUT LEGISLATED QUOTAS IN SWEDEN

Lenita Freidenvall

Sweden is often highlighted in research and among policy-makers as the undisputed forerunner worldwide regarding women's political representation. Gender balance (*jämn könsfördelning*) in the national parliament, as well as in regional and local elected assemblies, happened as early as 1994, and at a time when the international average in these bodies had barely passed the 10 percent threshold. As of 2018, almost all of the political parties in Sweden – left and right – embrace the ideal of gender balance in elected decision-making bodies, and the current parliament, elected in 2014, consists of 44 percent women and 56 percent men. Despite the fact that Sweden, together with the other Nordic countries, has long been recognised for its high political representation of women, no legislated gender quotas have been enacted. While legislated quotas were discussed in the late 1980s, primarily in relation to the proposals made in a State Commission of Inquiry, political parties greeted them with scepticism. In order to achieve gender balance in elected bodies, political parties instead adopted special measures ranging from targets and recommendations to voluntary party quotas.

While gender balance in all decision-making bodies, not only in politics, has been an outspoken goal of the Swedish government since the mid-1980s, not all sectors have reached this goal. In particular the business sector has deviated markedly from the positive development of women's and men's equal access to power and influence. While gender balance on the boards of public (state-owned) companies was achieved in the early 2000s, the gender composition of the boards of private companies has been less balanced. As in the political sector, legislated company board quotas have been regarded with scepticism, and voluntary codes of conduct have been the preferred strategy to increase the number of women. Thus, while gender balance in all aspects of decision-making (from the government to sports clubs) is one of the major objectives of Swedish gender equality politics and an undisputed principle in Swedish society, the success of this objective varies in different sectors, and the means of achieving it have been subject to much debate (Dahlerup and Freidenvall 2008).

This chapter analyses the adoption of special measures in Sweden, including party quotas and corporate governance codes, and provides an assessment of the factors that facilitate or hinder increases in the proportion of women decision-makers in the political and economic sectors. By applying feminist institutional theory, particularly Mona Lena Krook's (2009) distinction between systemic, practical, and normative institutions, the dynamics of institutional configurations facilitating or hindering change will be investigated. Drawing on Melanie Hughes and Pamela Paxton's (2008) research, forces for change as well as forces for resistance in the adoption of special measures to redress gender imbalances in decision-making bodies will also be discussed. This chapter argues that the interplay of institutions in the political sector operated in a mutually reinforcing way, thereby constituting a good fit, while the interaction of institutions in the economic sector functioned in a conflicting way, thus constituting a poorer fit. In addition, it claims that women's movement organisations (working both within and outside of the political parties) represented critical actors in implementing party quotas in Sweden. Such coordinated efforts did not exist in the corporate sector. There, the forces of resistance were much stronger than the forces for change, thereby hindering the introduction of a compulsory legislated corporate gender quota.

The paper is organised as follows. Section 12.2 gives a background to the Swedish model of gender equality and outlines the key features of feminist institutionalism. Sections 12.3 and 12.4 analyse the adoption and rejection of special measures (including party quotas, corporate governance codes, and compulsory quotas) to increase the share of women in elected bodies and on company boards, respectively. In these sections, the national preconditions, processes of adoption of special measures, and transnational/European influences will be addressed, including an assessment of the actors mobilising for gender quotas and those resisting change. Section 12.5 discusses institutional change pertaining to the development of the two sectors, politics and business. Finally, Section 12.6 concludes by highlighting the importance of actors pushing for change as the key enabling factor.

12.1 SETTING THE STAGE: THE SWEDISH MODEL OF GENDER EQUALITY AND KEY FEATURES OF FEMINIST INSTITUTIONALISM

A key characteristic of the Swedish model of gender equality is its close connection to the social democratic welfare state ideology and its egalitarian ideology of social citizenship (Bergqvist et al. 1999; Hernes 1987; Sainsbury 1996). The social democratic welfare state ideology – sometimes called the Swedish Model – generally refers to the economic and social policies that developed in Sweden after WWII, including a combination of free market social democracy with a comprehensive welfare state and collective bargaining at the national level. This system of governance generally includes support for a universalist welfare state enhancing individual autonomy and social mobility, a corporatist system involving a tripartite arrangement of social partners negotiating wages and labour market policies, and a commitment to private ownership, free markets and trade. In recent years, as in other countries, neoliberal principles including privatisation and de-regulation have increasingly been integrated into the structures and processes of Swedish governance, making the Swedish model less persistent.

In its promotion of a socially egalitarian citizenship model, based on notions of solidarity and redistributive justice, the Swedish social democratic welfare state has to a great extent been based on universalism. In contrast to the male breadwinner model accepted in many other countries, a dual-income earner model has been formed in Sweden. In this model, which is closely related to the labour market, Swedish women and men are seen as independent and self-supporting individuals. Key policies instituted have therefore included the abolition of joint taxation (and the introduction of individual taxation in 1971) and progressive reforms such as the introduction of publicly financed day care for children in the 1970s and gender neutral parental leave in 1974.

In Sweden, gender equality policies have to a large extent been initiated "from above" in line with the politics of state feminism (Hernes 1987) and substantive equality was constitutionally enshrined already in 1976 (chapter 2 article 13 Instrument of Government). An evident example of early gender equality policies is the adoption of the Gender Equality Act in 1979 and the Gender Equality Ombudsman in 1980 to oversee proper compliance with the law. Initially, the purpose of the Gender Equality Act was to combat discrimination and promote equal rights regardless of sex in working life. The act stipulated, among other things, that discrimination against applicants or employees is prohibited with regard to labour market policy activities, but that this prohibition would not prevent measures that contribute to efforts to promote equality between women and men. It also stipulated that employers are to conduct "goal-oriented work" to actively promote equal rights and opportunities in working life regardless of sex. Thus, active measures to promote gender equality in working life have long been legally protected in Sweden.[1] The major reason for introducing affirmative action – such as these active measures – in the Instrument of Government was to avoid any norm conflicts between the constitution and the Gender Equality Act (Equal Opportunities Act), which had an affirmative action agenda to promote gender equality.[2] The adoption of the Gender Equality Act, in turn, was promoted by the new centre-right/liberal government elected in 1976, after forty-four consecutive years of a social democratic government in Sweden.

The ideal of gender balance in all decision-making bodies, not only in elected political bodies, has been an outspoken goal of the Swedish government since the mid-1980s.[3] In 1987, a set of targets to achieve gender balance in public boards and committees and in state commissions of inquiry was adopted. According to this decision, government bodies and bodies appointed by the government should be comprised of 30 percent women in 1992, 40 percent women in 1995, and 50 women by 1998.[4] Although these targets functioned as

---

[1] In 2009, the Gender Equality Act was amalgamated with other acts against discrimination into the Anti-Discrimination Act. Likewise, the Gender Equality Ombudsman and other Equality Ombudsmen were merged into the Anti-Discrimination Ombudsman. See Borchorst et al. (2012).

[2] Government bill 1975/76:209.

[3] Government bill 1993/94:147, Committee Report 1993/94:AU17, Rskr. 1993/94:290.

[4] Ibid. The first goal – 30-percent women by 1992 in the boards and committees of government agencies and committees – was achieved the same year and the result was reported in the 1992 Budget Bill (1992/93:100, appendix 12, p. 337 f.). Also the second goal – 40-percent women by 1995 – was achieved that year (in fact, 42-percent women) and reported in the Government report Jämställdhetspolitiken [Gender Equality Politics] (Report 1996/97:41, appendix 2, Committee Report 1996/97:AU8, Parliament Report 1996/97:155). The third and last goal – 50-percent women – was

recommendations and did not comprise any sanctions for non-compliance, they have successfully provided the government with a clear objective to be reached. Since 1988, the nomination of candidates to be part of public boards and committees has been reported to the Division of Gender Equality within the Government Offices. The Division, and ultimately the Gender Equality Minister, scrutinises the nomination of candidates before the government decides on the final composition of the boards and committees. Furthermore, since 1988, the representation of women and men in public boards and committees has been reported annually in an appendix to the Budget Bill. More broadly, since 1994 women's and men's equal access to power and influence in all sectors of society, including politics, business, public administration, and academia, has been one of the major objectives of Swedish gender equality policy.[5] The ideal of gender balance in decision-making has thus spread from politics to other arenas and sectors of public life. Gender balance has been defined as a minimum representation of 40 percent of either sex, which implies that gender balance exists when the representation of women is within the 40–60 percent interval.

While gender balance in decision-making bodies has been a major objective of Swedish gender equality policies since the 1990s, legislated quotas have been resisted. Rather, various kinds of soft laws and other special measures have been the preferred strategy to reach equal representation of women and men in decision-making bodies. The adoption of measures has generally followed an incremental, path-dependent track to equal representation, as this chapter will show.

Two attempts to introduce quotas other than in politics and on corporate boards need to be mentioned. In 1995, the academic sector was subjected to gender quotas, when the Minister of Education Carl Tham in the Social Democratic Government decided to implement a measure to increase the proportion of women academics. Thirty full professors and a number of graduate and research assistant positions were subject to a new type of open, competition-based recruitment procedure, so-called earmarking. The procedure favoured minority candidates (in this case women) in cases where applicants had comparable qualifications (Dahlerup and Freidenvall 2008; Törnqvist 2006). The system of

achieved in 2015 (51-percent women) and reported in the 2016 Budget Bill (2016/17:100, appendix 3).

[5] Government bill 1993/94:147, Committee Report 1993/94:AU17, Rskr. 1993/94:290.

earmarking was ended as a result of a decision by the European Court of Justice in 2003 in the Abrahamsson and Andersson v Fogelqvist case, as a contravention of the EU Equal Treatment Directive 8 Article 141(4). In this case Mr Andersson was slightly better qualified than his three female competitors for a position as Professor of Hydrospheric Science at the University of Gothenburg. The position, however, was offered to one of the women applicants, Ms Destouni. When she turned down the offer, Ms Fogelqvist was offered the job. Ms Abrahamsson argued that she was better qualified than Ms Fogelqvist, but less qualified than Mr Andersson. The European Court of Justice ruled that this form of positive discrimination was unlawful because it overrode consideration of applicant's individual merits. A rule which required an underrepresented group to be promoted (here women) over the other (here men) was justified if the two candidates were equally qualified and the assessment was based on an objective assessment of their personal situation, which did not happen in this case.[6]

Another example is the attempt to apply a system of reserved seats in academia for ethnic minorities. In 2003, Minister for Gender Equality Issues Jens Orback of the Social Democratic Government decided to implement a measure to improve ethnic diversity among law students. Thirty of a total of 300 places at the prestigious School of Law at Uppsala University were reserved for students of minority background (defined as students with foreign-born parents). This effort was also terminated when the Supreme Court of Sweden ruled that Uppsala University was guilty of discrimination against Swedish applicants by using a system where places were reserved for less qualified people with

---

[6] At paragraph 55, the European Court of Justice stated:

"55. ... even though Article 141(4) EC allows the Member States to maintain or adopt measures providing for special advantages intended to prevent or compensate for disadvantages in professional careers in order to ensure full equality between men and women in professional life, it cannot be inferred from this that it allows a selection method of the kind at issue in the main proceedings which appears, on any view, to be disproportionate to the aim pursued.

56. The answer to the first question must therefore be that Article 2(1) and (4) of the Directive and Article 141(4) EC preclude national legislation under which a candidate for a public post who belongs to the underrepresented sex and possesses sufficient qualifications for that post must be chosen in preference to a candidate of the opposite sex who would otherwise have been appointed, where this is necessary to secure the appointment of a candidate of the underrepresented sex and the difference between the respective merits of the candidates is not so great as to give rise to a breach of the requirement of objectivity in making appointments."

an immigrant background. The decision of the court was the final ruling on a case brought by two women (of non-immigrant background) that were not admitted to the course in 2003, despite having better grades than all thirty of the successful applicants of immigrant backgrounds. The Supreme Court ruled that setting quotas is acceptable, but only as long as applicants are treated equally.[7] In this case, it was ruled that the two Swedish-born women had been discriminated against in the application process.

These two cases have often been referred to by quota opponents as illustrative examples of the supposedly discriminatory character of quotas. The cases have, as a consequence, made it difficult for quota proponents to continue pressing for quotas to be adopted. In fact, Göran Lambertz, Justice Ombudsman and a quota proponent, who represented the State in the latter case, argued that the verdict clearly shows that all kinds of quotas, including gender quotas, are to be seen as illegal when seats are reserved for certain groups without taking their individual merits into consideration. The Gender Equality Ombudsman, Claes Borgström, also a proponent of gender quotas, was less negative, arguing that in working life there is a rule permitting exceptions to promote equality between women and men and that its interpretation was not affected by this ruling. Borgström pointed out, however, that even if positive action is permitted in the workplace, it may only occur when two candidates have equal qualifications.

This chapter is based on the notion that institutions – the formal and informal "rules of the game" – shape political life. In line with Helmke and Levitsky (2004, 727), formal institutions are defined as the "rules and procedures that are created, communicated, and enforced through channels that are widely accepted as official," and informal institutions are defined as "socially shared rules, usually unwritten, that are created, communicated, and enforced outside of officially sanctioned channels," Institutions, be they formal or informal, are also gendered. A key aspect of feminist institutionalism, therefore, involves analysing the gendered character of institutions and their gendering effects. As pointed out by Mackay (2011, 183), institutions interact to shape political outcomes. They may interact in complementary or contradictory ways, and the institutional configurations and their effects may be gender neutral but also gender biased. Thus, an important notion

---

[7] Högsta Domstolen, NJA 2006, nr. 84, available at: www.notisum.se/rnp/domar/hd/HD006683.htm.

when analysing institutional reform and change is that institutions are complex, and they may work in facilitating as well as obstructive ways. Informal "rules-in-use" may complement and reinforce formal institutions. They may substitute the regulative framework when there are no formal institutions available. However, they may also provide alternative rules when formal rules are not wanted and do not resonate well with the context for application (Mackay 2011, 184).

Following Mona Lena Krook (2009), the effects of quotas are shaped by rules, practices and norms, which can be conceptualised as three broad categories of institutions: systemic, practical, and normative. *Systemic institutions* refers to the formal features of political systems, including, for example, the electoral system, the party system and the existence of oversight bodies. *Practical institutions* constitutes the formal and informal practices shaping candidate selection criteria and selection practices. *Normative institutions*, finally, refers to the formal and informal principles guiding candidate selection, including principles such as equality and representation, but also the values and commitments that inform the actions taken by political actors in candidate selection or, more concretely, in the implementation of quota policies. Based on Krook's conceptualisation of institutions, it is important to address the ways in which quotas interact with existing rules, practices and norms. In analyses of institutional stasis and change, it is essential to explore the interplay between various kinds of institutions and institutional levels; sometimes the institutional configuration constitutes a good fit, sometimes it results in conflict. As this chapter makes clear, Sweden displays both cases.

The theoretical institutional perspective outlined above is complemented by integrating the role of critical actors, such as movements, as agents for change (Hughes and Paxton 2008).

12.2 REGULATIONS IN THE POLITICAL SECTOR IN SWEDEN

Sweden has, together with the other Nordic countries, served as the model for progress in women's political representation (Bergqvist 1994; Freidenvall 2006; Wängnerud 1998; Wide 2006). Since universal and equal suffrage was introduced in 1921, the proportion of women members of parliament (MPs) has gradually increased to its current level of 44 percent, with a take-off phase in the 1970s when the 20 percent threshold was passed for the first time. Gender balance in legislative seats was achieved in 1994, seventy years after the suffrage reform. This pattern of growth has been described as the "incremental track" to equal representation between women and men, in contrast to the "fast track" to equal representation, in which countries have experienced steep increases in women's proportion of legislative seats following the adoption of legislated gender quotas (Dahlerup and Freidenvall 2005; Freidenvall 2013).[8]

One systemic institution that has facilitated this incremental process towards equal representation between women and men in political decision-making is the election system: a proportional representation (PR) system with high district magnitudes and closed electoral lists. Although a system of preferential voting has been introduced, it was introduced only in 1998 (after the increase of women in politics), and has shown little effect on the gender composition of elected bodies (Freidenvall 2007). Another key systemic institution, which follows from the electoral system, is the party system, which has developed from a five-party system in the 1970s to an eight-party system today, facilitating an important arena for partisan competition and contagion effects, as this chapter will show. Two of the main opponents from the left and the right, the Social Democratic Party and the Liberal Party, have been particularly prominent in addressing gender equality matters and promoting measures to achieve gender balance in decision-making bodies. Other facilitating factors often mentioned in research are women's entrance into the labour market in the 1970s and the introduction of welfare state reforms that enabled women to combine professional work with household responsibilities.

One practical institution that has contributed to reaching equal representation between women and men is the adoption of party regulations ranging from voluntary targets and recommendations (soft quotas) to binding party quotas (Freidenvall 2006; Freidenvall, Dahlerup, and Skjeie 2006). These regulations were introduced step-wise in each party, usually first targeting internal party boards and committees and then electoral lists. For example, in 1972 the Liberal Party

---

[8] These two tracks are also associated with different theories of changes; the first assuming that gender balance may take time, but higher levels of women's legislative presence will be achieved as women's education, labour-force participation, and family-friendly policies advance, and the second assuming that gender balance might not inevitably increase over time because of mechanisms of marginalisation and discrimination taking place in candidate selection (Dahlerup and Freidenvall 2005).

(a centre-right party) recommended that internal party boards and committees within the party structure be made up of a minimum of 40 percent of each sex. A few years later, in 1974, this provision was extended to cover the electoral lists as well. In 1984, the party recommended all of its electoral lists be based on the zipper system. Over time, the measures adopted were more far-reaching, in gender balance and in sanctions imposed. For example, in 1972 the Social Democratic Party recommended party districts place "more women" on electoral lists. In 1978, it was recommended that lists reflect the "proportion of female party members," in 1987, a 40-percent minimum target was introduced, and in 1993 gender balance (50 percent) was promoted through the adoption of party quotas based on the zipper system.

While voluntary targets and recommendations (soft quotas) were introduced in the 1970s, binding party quotas were first introduced in the 1980s. The Green Party was the first party to adopt party quotas. In 1981, when it was first established, the Green Party introduced internal gender quotas, stipulating a minimum of 40 percent of each sex on internal boards and committees, as well as a joint male/female chair of the party. This provision was extended in 1987 to entail a minimum of 40 percent of each sex on the party's electoral lists. Like many Green Parties emerging at the time, the Swedish Green Party stressed the need for social justice, including gender equality, in addition to its promotion of ecological sustainability, social responsibility, and grassroots democracy. Later on, the Left Party and the Social Democratic Party followed suit and adopted party quotas in 1987 and 1993, respectively. The Left Party required all electoral lists to consist of a minimum of 50 percent women, based on the argument that female presence and even over-representation (even legislative bodies comprising 100-percent women) in decision-making is justified as long as society is permeated with patriarchal structures and norms. The Social Democratic Party adopted the zipper system, in which men and women candidates are placed alternately on party lists. Thus, the anti-patriarchal stance combined with an increased trend to view gender imbalance as an expression of a flawed democracy, as will be shown later, functioned as key normative institutions.

The adoption of party regulations to achieve gender balance has thus diffused across the party spectrum. In line with their ideologies, left-wing parties adopted party quotas, while parties to the centre and to the right preferred to introduce targets and recommendations (soft quotas). As mentioned previously, the Liberal Party recommended a minimum representation of 40 percent of the underrepresented sex on party lists in 1974, and in 1984 a new recommendation about zipped lists was introduced. In 1987 the Christian Democratic Party introduced a minimum target of 40 percent of the underrepresented sex on party lists and in 1993, the Centre Party and the Moderate Party adopted goals of gender balance on party lists. While political parties to the left and to the right continue to have different positions on party quotas, gender balance in elected bodies is axiomatic at the normative level and most of them nominate an equal number of women and men on electoral lists, i.e. within the 40–60 percent span. Thus, a key effect of the adoption of party quotas can be observed at the discursive level: competition between the parties together with the gender equality debates generated by the measures have forced parties along the entire spectrum to react and take an active stance on issues of representation (Freidenvall, Dahlerup, and Skjeie 2006).

12.2.1 Forces for Change and Forces of Resistance

The primary forces for change were the women's organisations, organised within political parties, in political party women's sections, and in autonomous women's organisations. Despite that fact that the suffrage reform of 1921 formally ended the exclusively male right to legislative representation, and gave women the right to vote and stand for election, gender balanced representation was far from being the case. In 1921, only five women were elected to the Swedish parliament. In the 1920s and 1930s, national women's federations with regional and local women's sections within four of the five parliamentary parties were formed (the exception was the Communist Party) with the aim of mobilising women to vote and recruiting women for party work (Freidenvall 2006; 2013). During the 1940s and 1950s, the national women's federations grew into mass organisations, recruiting and educating thousands of women and supporting women in the nomination process. Despite the pressure they put on party organisations to place more women on electoral lists, parties usually nominated just one or a few women candidates in each constituency; the "obligatory" woman (Karlsson 1996). This obligatory woman was to represent women as a group and to comply with the demands for representation made by the women's federations. The issue of gender quotas sometimes surfaced within the women's federations. For example, as early as 1928 the National Federation of Social Democratic Women (SSKF) proposed that the Social Democratic Party introduce gender quotas so that women would be placed in electable positions on electoral lists, but this proposal was rejected in accordance with the notion that all of the positions on the electoral lists should be based on equal opportunity and thus subject to open competition (Freidenvall 2005). Gender quotas were a controversial issue, even among SSKF members, and an ongoing discussion about their pros and cons started within the organisation.

Women activists were also involved in many campaigns to convince party organisations to place more women on electoral lists. For instance, in 1934, the Fredrika-Bremer Association (FBA) – one of the oldest non-partisan (and liberal) feminist organisations in Sweden – organised a meeting with twenty-five independent women's organisations to discuss women's right to equal representation. In 1938, they established a network – the Committee for Increased Female Representation – to raise awareness on the issue of women's underrepresentation in politics. In the 1940s they launched a series of public campaigns claiming that "Without Women – No Rule by the People." Thus, the complex pattern of alliances inside and outside of parliament that was formed during the suffrage campaign in the beginning of the 1900s continued well into the mid-century.

During the 1970s, the women's movement experienced a renaissance (Freidenvall 2013). The second-wave women's movement mobilised thousands of young women, encouraging women to protest against pornography, prostitution, and violence against women. Even first-wave women's movement organisations were active. For instance, the liberal FBA organised public hearings on a regular basis in which party leaders and government representatives were asked to explain the underrepresentation of women in elected bodies and their efforts to rectify this situation. The FBA even coined the term "the 51 percent minority," questioning why a majority of the population constituted a minority in decision-making. At the same time, the national women's federations within the political parties noted that local party organisations addressed selection criteria such as geography, age, and class in list composition but neglected gender as a category of representation. The federations claimed that the share of women on electoral lists should reflect the share of women in the population, framing women's underrepresentation in political assemblies as a violation of equal rights and as something that contributed to a skewed view of democracy. The framing of women's political representation as citizens' rights had strategic advantages (Sainsbury 2005, 199). It highlighted unity among women, as well as the fact that although they constituted half the citizenry, they were only given a limited share of seats in elected bodies.

The underrepresentation of women was thus framed as a question of a deficiency in Swedish democracy. It was also strategically presented in such a way as to make it difficult to oppose. Hence, "the 51 percent minority" catchphrase became a useful discursive strategy. Women to the left and to the right, both within the political parties and in the autonomous women's movement organisations, thus challenged the traditional male concept of citizenship, arguing that an all-male political assembly was undemocratic and unacceptable (Dahlerup 1998).

The women's federations and sections examined the underrepresentation of women through careful studies, published the results, and pushed to get more women in electable positions on the party lists. They organised numerous activities, including public hearings, roundtables and conferences. In their internal mobilisation for special measures, including party quotas, they often drew on electoral incentives: they were quick to point to the gains made in rival parties in order to push for stronger measures within their own party. Thus, the women's federations were the main actors behind the adoption of special measures within the parties, first pressing parties to adopt voluntary targets and recommendations, and then – in the left-wing parties – also pressing parties to adopt party quotas. They functioned partly as a bridge for women into politics, partly as an arena for cooperation between women party members and members of non-parliamentary women's organisations (Wängnerud 1998). Women in Sweden have therefore adopted two parallel strategies: (a) to work in formal politics and inside the established party structures, learning the rules of the game and collaborating with men, and (b) to establish their own federations and networks with the autonomous women's movement. This double strategy thus consists of two polar aspects: integration and separation (Dahlerup 1988; Sainsbury 1996).

Quotas were often discussed as one possible measure to achieve gender balance. Party elites, often male, viewed quotas as a violation of the principle of equal opportunity and the sovereignty of the party districts to compile their own electoral lists. Unlike in other countries, constitutional arguments were not put forth in the quota debate in Sweden since there is no tradition of referring to the Instrument of Government (which enshrined gender equality in the Swedish Constitution) in political debates. Quotas was a method that not only conflicted with democratic ideas, including the importance of the votes of the electorate, but also with the ideals of gender equality, as policies should aim at improving the situation of both women and men. The women's federations had a more positive stance on quotas, although they were not overly optimistic (Freidenvall 2006). In the view of the SSKF, gender quotas were seen as a necessary evil or a method to be used only as a last resort. On many occasions the SSKF tried to tone down its demands for more women in politics by avoiding the word "quotas" or by reformulating it as "methods of redistribution" (Freidenvall 2005). The SSKF, and party women generally, thus made use of the party ideology to frame their demands for gender quotas within the party. By linking their demands to party ideology, the SSKF claimed that quotas did not violate the principle of equal opportunity and the privilege of the local party organisation to form its own list, rather, quotas could serve as a mechanism to realise the party's ideas about social justice and redistribution. Party women, consequently, were engaged in a discursive strategy to make their claims for quotas fit the practical and normative institutions. In general, however, political parties and women's federations explained women's underrepresentation in politics as an issue of supply: an effect of women's lack of political resources in terms of time, money, and education. Within the women's federations it was also argued that as long as the number of women in politics increased, there was no need for more radical solutions, such as quotas.

12.2.2 Threat as Strategy

While the numbers of women in political assemblies increased in the 1970s and 1980s, the representation of women in boards, committees, and commissions appointed by the Government remained low.[9] Although the process towards gender balance in the executive is different from that in the legislative, the former spilled over into the latter. In the report of a State Commission of Inquiry in 1987, a new discourse on political representation was displayed.[10] It addressed the underrepresentation of women in all spheres of politics as a matter of power and conflict between the sexes, and it advocated compulsory public body quotas as the only strategy that would increase the number of women in committees, commissions, and boards appointed by the government. The Commission of Inquiry was appointed by minister (Social Democratic Party), and chair of the SSKF, Anita Gradin. However,

---

[9] Commissions are regularly appointed by the government on a temporary basis to inquire into a matter and submit recommendations. A committee's terms of reference (kommittédirektiv) define the scope and direction of its inquiry.

[10] SOU 1987:19.

the report concluded that resistance to quotas in Sweden was very strong, and it therefore stopped short of demanding that compulsory public bodies quotas for these positions be introduced. Instead, a series of voluntary measures were suggested, with a full-scale quota system to be enacted in relation to a range of political and policy-making institutions if women's numbers did not rise "naturally."[11] The report was entitled *Varannan Damernas* (every other one for the women), which refers to a countryside dance custom in which women are invited to ask men for every other dance.

Based on the report, the government decided in 1987 to institute a new objective for gender balance on committees, commissions, and boards appointed by the state and a timetable for its implementation (Govt bill. 1987/88): equal representation of women and men on these committees, commissions, and boards was to be achieved by 1998; as a first step in the process, 30-percent representation of women was to be achieved by 1992, and 40-percent representation by 1995. Although the initial proposal for compulsory public body quotas was turned down, the idea of introducing mandatory quotas was definitely on the political agenda. What is more, despite the fact that the proposal targeted public bodies only, it also opened up for a discussion on introducing compulsory quotas in elected bodies, as had been proposed by the SSKF for many years.

In the general election of 1991, women's representation in the Swedish parliament decreased for the first time since 1928. Party elites were surprised by the sudden decrease, from 38 to 34 percent. Although this percentage was high, in fact the highest in the world, it clearly showed that the gradual increase in women's political representation had come to an end. A heated debate took place, and the network *Stödstrumporna* (the Support Stockings) was formed. The network, which consisted mainly of influential female academics and journalists, threatened to establish a Women's Party unless the political parties nominated more women for the next election. Although the decrease in 1991 was primarily a result of the right-wing and populist party New Democracy entering parliament with only three women out of twenty-five places, the 1991 election gave rise to debate, activism, and pressure groups (Freidenvall 2006, 2013).

In response to the threat, and fearing that many party women would switch to the Women's Party unless they gave in to the demands made

[11] SOU 1987:19.

by the SSKF to adopt party quotas, the Social Democratic Party decided in 1993 to adopt the principle of *varannan damernas* on all lists for all elections (a zipper system). Although the principle is a parity quota, stipulating that party districts must put women into every other seat on their party lists, the term *varannan damernas* gave the principle a more sympathetic association with rules for taking turns. It thus fit in well with the idea of gender equality as a harmonious relation between the sexes – not a relation of power and conflict – and of measures that guarantee not only women's but also men's positions in political assemblies. In addition, the term carried positive associations with rural dancehalls (in Swedish, *dansbanor*) and to the political image of the Swedish *"folkhem,"* the idea of Sweden as the home of the people, a narrative of solidarity and equality put forward by the Social Democratic Party in the 1930s to disassociate social democratic politics from the antagonistic class-based politics of earlier times. What is more, the metaphor of every other one for the women also transformed the framing of quotas as a "top-down Stalinist method," or a method that was based on conflicts of interest between women and men, into that of a dance that promoted the free will of two parties (Törnqvist 2006). It was thus framed in terms of ideals that enabled calls for equal representation to resonate with discourses of consensus and equality (Bergqvist 1994; Freidenvall, Dahlerup, and Skjeie 2006). As pointed out by Maud Eduards (2002), gender politics in Sweden have traditionally been consensus oriented; women and men are supposed to collaborate, side-by-side, and neither is to be given special treatment at the expense of the other. Gender equality is perceived as double emancipation, a win-win situation, with benefits for both sexes. The notion of *varannan damernas* fitted well into the normative institutions at the time.

Rival political parties soon followed suit, adopting similar policies. Some parties opted for a policy of strict proportions, while others preferred softer formulations, such as "at least 40 percent of each sex." These policies resulted in the election of 41 percent women in 1994, 43 percent in 1998, 45 percent in 2002, and 47 percent in 2006. In the two last elections to parliament, the proportion of women has decreased, to 45 percent in 2010 and 44 percent in 2014 (See Figure 12.1).[12] Today,

---

[12] The decrease in 2010 can be explained primarily by the election of the populist Sweden Democratic Party, with three women out of twenty places in parliament (15-percent women). The proportion of women elected in the Sweden Democratic party increased to 22 percent in 2014, but continued to be considerably lower than

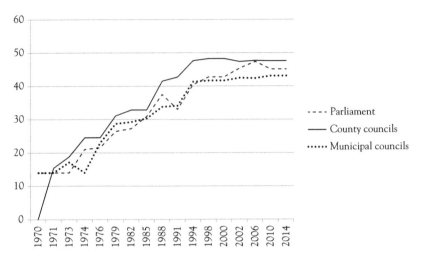

Figure 12.1 Women's representation in elected bodies, 1970–2014 (by percent)

gender balance in parliament, but also in other elected decision-making bodies, is an axiom among all of the parties, with the exception of the populist Sweden Democratic Party. The parties differ, however, in their views on how to achieve the shared goal.

Recent developments in Sweden point to the continued promotion of gender balance in decision-making bodies in politics, although the measures to achieve this goal vary depending on the actors involved. The Alliance parties (centre-right parties), as well as the populist Sweden Democratic Party, seem to continue on their path as opponents of any kind of legislated compulsory quotas, while the three left-wing parties – the Social Democratic Party, the Green Party, and the Left Party – have all continued on their path as party-quota proponents. The latter adopted party quotas for electoral lists in the 1980s and 1990s, and in the 2000s they all submitted motions to parliament proposing the introduction of corporate gender quotas, a topic that will be discussed in the next section.

12.3 REGULATION IN THE ECONOMIC SECTOR IN SWEDEN

Unlike the political sector, the business sector has for a long time stayed out of the political debate on gender equality in Sweden (Freidenvall

in rival parties. In the 2014 election, the proportion of women parliamentarians also decreased in the Liberal Party, from 42 percent to 26 percent.

and Hallonsten 2013). The low proportion of women in decision-making positions in companies, particularly private companies, was considered an internal matter for the business sector, in line with the so-called Swedish model of corporate governance. It was not until the 1990s, when women's political representation was high on the political agenda, that the overwhelming male dominance of the business sector also began to attract attention in public debate. In the ensuing years, several state commissions of inquiry were initiated to analyse the situation.

Discussions on equal representation of women and men in the political sector spilled over to the business sector, particularly regarding the representation of women and men in the boards of state-owned and private owned companies. To redress the underrepresentation of women in state-owned companies was an easy task for the government, since the nomination of candidates to public bodies, including state-owned companies, lies within its control. In 1999, a regulation concerning women's participation in state-owned companies was adopted. The regulation, which represents a key practical institution, mandated the achievement of gender balance on the boards of state-owned companies. As a first step in the process, the share of women on state-owned company boards had to reach 40 percent by 2003.[13] This numbered target implied no sanction for non-compliance. In 2002, women comprised 37 percent of the board members, and in 2003, the objective was reached (43 percent women). Since then, the share of women on state-owned company boards has been reported annually to parliament. In 2017, women comprised 49 percent of the board members of these companies, and 45 percent of the chairs. However, quite to the contrary, the representation of women and men on the boards of privately owned companies – corporate boards – was far from gender balanced.

12.3.1 Forces for Change

Gender Equality Ministers were the key actors in the promotion of gender balance on corporate company boards. In 1993, Deputy Prime Minister and Gender Equality Minister Bengt Westerberg (Liberal Party) in the centre-right coalition government appointed a commission of inquiry to study the possibility of achieving a more equal distribution

---

[13] Government report skr 1999/2000:24.

of male and female managers in business. In the directives for the commission of inquiry, it was clearly stated that the issue of quotas was not to be taken up. The inquiry resulted in the report *Men's Perceptions about Women and Leadership*.[14] It showed that 72 percent of private company boards at that time consisted only of men and that 56 percent of companies had management teams consisting exclusively of men. The report also underscored that key to understanding the Swedish economy was its corporate tradition. The so-called Swedish model of corporate governance can be described as a system based on consensus between large capital owners and the labour movement, both normally led by men, and each comprising important elites in the Swedish business sector. The collaboration between the government and industry has even been labelled "Harpsund democracy,"[15] based on the idea that private owners enjoy considerable autonomy, provided that they take responsibility for their employees and for society in general (Agnblad et al. 2001, 251). The report also noted that a handful of representatives of powerful capitalist networks dominated Swedish industry and commerce. As Heidenrich (2012) has pointed out, the Swedish Stock Exchange continues to be dominated by a few large enterprises. In fact, one family, the Wallenberg family, controls half of the market value on the Stockholm Stock Exchange. Consequently, the absence of strong systemic institutions in Swedish business life at the time contributed to the strengthening and consolidation of the power of deep-rooted and entrenched practical and normative institutions: a strong network of male industrialists, representatives of the social partners, and members of the government at the practical level, as well as the Swedish model of corporate governance at the normative level. Drawing on feminist institutional theory, informal rules of the game provided alternate rules when formal rules were not wanted or did not resonate well with the context in which they were applied (Mackay 2011, 184).

Almost ten years later, in 2002, Deputy Prime Minister and Gender Equality Minister Margareta Winberg in the Social Democratic Government commissioned a follow-up to the 1994 study. This study resulted

---

[14] SOU 1994:3. Mäns föreställningar om kvinnor och chefskap. Stockholm: Socialdepartementet.
[15] "Harpsund" refers to a Government mansion in the outskirts of Stockholm where key government deliberations are held, including, for instance, internal discussions on the budget bill.

in the report *Male Dominance in Transition*.[16] The report concluded that there were indications of an increased awareness of the problem of women's underrepresentation in corporate boards but that male dominance in positions of leadership persisted, even among young executives, indicating that the problem would continue.

Despite the growing attention, the strength of the practical and normative institutions remained; few initiatives to redress the situation were taken, and the share of women on company boards only slowly increased. In 1993, the boards of listed Swedish companies were comprised of 1.4 percent women members, and in 2002 the share of women board members had increased to 5.8 percent (Nilsson 2009). Due to the persistent underrepresentation of women on company boards, particularly in relation to the political sphere, Minister Margareta Winberg in the Social Democratic Government proposed that legislated corporate board quotas be adopted. Similarly to the way in which the *Varannan Damernas* study on women in politics had been used, she utilised the strategy of threat. In 1999, the same year that a regulation concerning women's participation in the boards of state-owned companies was adopted and she was appointed Minister for Gender Equality, she gave listed companies five years to improve the gender balance; otherwise legislated corporate board quotas would be introduced. In 2002, Minister Winberg repeated her demands: unless companies had achieved a 25 percent proportion of women board members by 2004, corporate quotas would be adopted (Fredell 2005). Her arguments were based on equality; women and men are to share power and influence in all sectors of power. She also claimed that women would contribute by improving dialogue, collaboration, and networking in companies. The fact that a bill on corporate gender quotas was presented to the Norwegian parliament in 2002, to take effect in 2005, most likely contributed to making the threat effective. Her proposal of a 25 percent quota, and her argument that it was 'less tough' than the Norwegian 40 percent quotas, signalled that this was an offer to take seriously to avoid more stringent measures. However, there was sizable opposition to quotas, even among women. A survey of 500 women leaders in 2000 showed that 93 percent of the respondents were against the introduction of legislated corporate quotas (Fredell 2005). Businesswomen

---

[16] SOU 2003:16. Mansdominans i förändring. Om ledningsgrupper och styrelser. Stockholm: Utbildningsdepartementet.

claimed that they wanted be selected due to their competence, not their gender.

After Winberg's threat in 2002 to introduce legislated corporate boards quotas, the proportion of women on company boards rapidly increased (Bohman, Bygren, and Edling 2012). In fact, during the years 2002 and 2006, the proportion of women board members tripled, from 5.8 percent to 17.9 percent (Nilsson 2009, 293). Right-wing members of parliament asked the government not to go forward with a legal proposal, based on the argument that quotas would threaten the right of companies to appoint their board members, as stipulated by the Company Act.[17] As alternative solutions they suggested general debates on gender equality in the business sector, together with management and leadership courses for women executives. The powerful Confederation of Employers' Organisations (*Svenskt näringsliv*) emphasized the principle of self-regulation in the composition of company boards and maintained that the proportion of women board members would increase automatically once the share of women in mid-level and high-level positions in the private sector increased (Bohman, Bygren, and Edling 2012). Similar to the incremental track discourse that characterised the framing of women's underrepresentation in politics, the confederation claimed that once women had entered executive positions in greater numbers, they would be eligible for positions as board directors among the pool of individuals with executive experience (Dahlerup and Freidenvall 2005; Freidenvall, Dahlerup, and Skjeie 2006). The social partners, furthermore, were generally in favour of continued self-regulation, in line with the Swedish model of corporate governance. Thus, the strength of the practical and normative institutions held, providing an alternate rule when formal rules – in this case a legislated corporate board quota – were not wanted.

12.3.2 Forces of Resistance

In 2005 the Ministry of Justice of the Social Democratic Government noted in a memorandum that the proportion of women in top management would not increase by itself at the pace needed to reach the goal set by Minister Winberg. As of 2005, the proportion of female board members in listed companies was approximately 18 percent. The Social Democratic government hesitated; the new Gender

---

[17] Aktiebolagslagen (2005: 551), available at: www.riksdagen.se/sv/dokument-lagar/dokument/svensk-forfattningssamling/aktiebolagslag-2005551_sfs-2005-551.

Equality Minister (2003–5), Mona Sahlin, declared that the government intended to present a proposal for legislated corporate board quotas. However, the following Gender Equality Minister of the Social Democratic Government, Jens Orback (2005–6), argued that time was not ripe for the introduction of quotas. In June 2005, however, the Ministry of Justice assigned legal scholar Catarina af Sandeberg to investigate the matter. The many turns taken indicate that the Social Democratic Government was not fully convinced of the urgency of adopting quotas.

In the report of the government investigator, *The Gender Composition on Corporate Boards*, it was suggested that corporate quotas be adopted.[18] Framing the demand as an issue of equal rights and relating it to one of the goals of Swedish gender equality policy – "equal access by women and men to positions of power and influence" – the report proposed that the members of the boards of public limited-liability companies should consist of at least 40 percent of each sex. The rules should take effect for listed companies on 1 January 2008, whereas unlisted public limited-liability companies would not be included until 1 January 2010. Companies that were already formed would have a two-year transition period. Furthermore, state-owned and private limited-liability companies would be subject to the 2008 rules, while municipal companies were excluded from legislation. Failure to comply with the rules would result in a company paying a fine of 150,000 SEK (15,000 Euros) to the *Bolagsverket* (Swedish Companies Registration Office).

The report also concluded that rules that limit the power of the shareholders to elect board members were not legally prohibited by EU regulations (European Convention on Human Rights [ECHR] and European Commission [EC] law). Nor were there any obstacles in the Swedish Instrument of Government (Constitution) or in the Anti-Discrimination legislation. It was also concluded that a restriction of the type at issue could not be considered an "unauthorised" restriction on ownership rights, nor were the suggested rules in conflict with freedom of trade. Thus, the report made it perfectly clear that the proposed rules on the gender distribution of company boards were not in violation of Swedish legislation or of the ECHR.

---

[18] Ds 2006:11. Könsfördelningen i bolagsstyrelser. Stockholm: Justitiedepartementet. When the law proposal was being worked out, the question of statutory corporate quotas in other countries was still in its inception. Only Norway had adopted corporate gender quotas at the time, and was the only country mentioned in the report.

Meanwhile, processes had begun within the business sector to avoid a quota regulation for company boards. In January 2004, representatives of *StyrelseAkademin* (a group of representatives from the private and financial sector) presented codes for board work. Later the same year, a state commission of inquiry (*Förtroendekommissionen*), which included representatives from the business sector, was established to formulate corporate governance codes at the national level. Its final report presented the Swedish Code of Corporate Governance.[19] The Code, which was adopted in 2005, is a set of guidelines for good corporate governance that all stock exchange listed companies are obliged to apply. The code applies to all large companies listed on the Stockholm Stock Exchange and stipulates, among other rules of conduct, a balanced gender distribution on boards. The code is based on the principle of "comply or explain," meaning that a company can deviate from the code without this deviation being seen as violation, however it must explain why the deviation occurred. There is no provision for sanctions against those that breach the code, except for the possible 'ill will' a violation of the code could generate. Since 2005, the Swedish Corporate Governance Board has managed and administrated the Code. The Code has been revised a couple of times, but the stipulation of gender balanced boards has been kept intact. The Code's specific design, based on an idea of self-regulation with no sanctions for non-compliance, fits well with the context in which it was applied, with the threat of legislated corporate board quotas stronger than ever before. In terms of institutional theory, a new practical institution was created: a practical institution that resonated with the persistent resistance towards legislated quotas in the business sector, and among political parties to the right and the centre primarily, and could serve as a necessary complement to the introduction of stronger regulations.

In September 2006, a centre-right coalition won the election and formed a new government (the Alliance government comprising the Moderate Party, the Centre Party, the Liberal Party, and the Christian Democratic Party). The new government declared that corporate quotas were not "a suitable method for improving gender equality in business, since the composition of boards is an issue for the company owners." The Minister for Gender Equality, Nyamko Sabuni (Liberal Party) insisted that merit and competence should be the guiding principle in candidate selection: in an article in the evening paper, *Expressen*,

---

[19] SOU 2004:47.

Sabuni stated, "I want a gender equal society in which women and men are judged on the basis of our competence, abilities and merits, not on the grounds of our sex or colour of our skin" (Sabuni 2008). This quote can be seen as an illustration of the neoliberal turn in Swedish politics. It can also be seen as an attempt by Minister Sabuni, as the first black female minister in Sweden, to show that her ministerial appointment did not have anything to do with gender or ethnicity. The issue of corporate gender quotas thus came to a halt (Nilsson 2009). Rather than proposing quotas, as suggested in the 2006 government investigation, the Alliance government supported the Code as an alternative to legislation, believing that a set of norms for good corporate governance and self-regulation was preferable to legislation. It also proposed a series of initiatives to promote women leaders (Freidenvall and Hallonsten 2013). For instance, a national board programme for women was established in 2009 to promote women to leadership functions. About 200 women were accepted into a mentoring programme and received scholarships for educational purposes. Projects such as the Allbright Foundation and The Battle of the Numbers aim at promoting diversified company boards by presenting concrete examples of how to increase the number of women in leading positions. Generally, the government initiatives focused on the supply side of candidate selection. In a series of parliamentary debates, Gender Equality Minister Maria Arnholm (Liberal Party), who succeeded Sabuni in 2012, reiterated the responsibility of company owners themselves to secure diversity on their company boards and said that both women's and men's competence should be utilised. Arnholm maintained that company boards should "live up to the rule of self-regulation" that is stipulated in the Code of Corporate Governance.[20] She also claimed that the state must lead by good example, making reference to the gender composition of state-owned company boards, in which 49 percent of members were women and 41 percent of the chairs of those boards were women. Occasionally, the Minister of Finance Anders Borg (2006–14, the Moderate Party) warned the Swedish business sector that he would impose quotas, following countries such as Norway, unless they moved quickly to rectify gender imbalances on their boards. At the same time, the Alliance government, which promoted itself as the New Workers' Party, stressed the importance of the Swedish model, reiterating the key role played by the social partners. As a response to these threats

---

[20] Answer to Interpellation 2012/13: 578. Swedish Parliament.

of legislation, as well as the ongoing work to promote more women in leadership functions, the share of women on company boards increased from 18 percent in 2006 to 26 percent in 2014.

12.3.3 Resistance Despite European Pressure

In September 2014, the Alliance government lost the election after eight years in office, and a minority government comprising the Social Democratic Party and the Green Party was installed (2014–18). The government presented itself as the first feminist government in the world. In his Government Address in October 2014, Prime Minister Stefan Löfven of the Social Democratic Party announced that a bill on legislated corporate board quotas would be presented to parliament if the proportion of women on company boards did not exceed 40 percent after the annual shareholders meetings in 2016.

In order to be ready to quickly submit a bill to parliament, a government white paper was prepared within the government offices (Ds 2016:32). In this white paper, which was based on the 2006 white paper, a change of the Company Act was proposed so that at least 40 percent of each gender is represented in the boards of public limited companies and publicly owned enterprises. It was argued that the male domination on company boards must be broken, and that it would be in the interest of companies themselves to make the best use of the competence women have. It was also claimed that gender equal decision-making promotes diversity, which would increase the competitiveness of companies.

Although the proportion of women on company boards increased, from 26 percent in 2014 to 30 percent after the closure of the annual meetings of shareholders in June 2016, the stipulated goal was not reached. As a consequence of this result, the Government announced on 9 September 2016 that it had "lost its patience" and that a bill would shortly be submitted to parliament, stipulating that company boards must comprise at least 40 percent of either sex, in line with the white paper. The proposed law was to enter into force in 2017, but the rules for non-compliance – including a fee of 250,000–5 million SEK (25,000–500,000 Euros) depending the size of the company, would not be enforced until 2019. In January 2017, however, the process came to a halt again. This time, the Swedish Parliament announced, in its reply to a series of motions presented to Parliament, that the government should work to ensure that it was still a question for the shareholders to determine the gender distribution of company boards (Committee

Report 2016/19:CU6). The Government's intention to present a bill on gender quotas was thus stopped by Parliament. The many turns taken illustrate not only the resistance towards gender quotas generally, but also the difficulty minority governments have getting their policy proposals adopted.

The Swedish parliament has previously demonstrated its reluctance towards the adoption of corporate gender quotas. In fact, in a response to the proposal by the European Commission for a new directive on minimum representation of 40 percent of each sex on company boards by 2020,[21] the Swedish parliament has stated that the proposal is in conflict with the principle of subsidiarity.[22] While the parliament has made clear that it welcomes initiatives to achieve an equal distribution of women and men in decision-making positions in the economic sector, it has claimed that the proposal is not attuned to the decision-making role of shareholders in many EU member states and that the goal of achieving a more gender equal distribution of power in decision-making in the business sector is better achieved through national initiatives. This position was reiterated by Parliament in January 2017, declaring in a Committee Report that the government should work within the EU for national self-determination regarding the representation of women and men on the boards of companies in the Swedish Stock Exchange (Committee Report 2016/19:CU6).

In contrast to these numerous policy developments, women's organisations, including the women's sections within the parties, did not consider corporate gender quotas a key issue. Neither has the Feminist Initiative, a feminist party that is represented in several municipal councils and that managed to secure a seat in the European parliament in the 2014 election, put the issue at the top of its agenda.[23]

---

[21] KOM (2012: 614), available at: http://ec.europa.eu/transparency/regdoc/rep/1/2012/SV/1-2012-614-SV-F1-1.Pdf.

[22] Utl. 2012/13:CU14, rskr. 2012/13:138. Swedish Parliament.

[23] The Feminist Initiative is a feminist political party in Sweden. Since its founding in April 2005, the party has put up candidates for elections to the municipal councils, county councils, national parliament, and European parliament. In the 2010 general election, it received four seats in the municipal council of Simrishamn and in the 2014 general election, it gained representation in thirteen municipal councils throughout the country. It also received one seat in the European parliament in 2014. Among its prioritised issues are work and the economy, welfare, security and human rights, and sustainability. One of its major slogans for the 2014 elections was "out with the racists, in with the feminists."

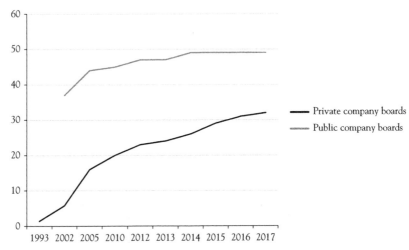

Figure 12.2 Women's representation on company boards, 1993–2015 (by percent)

The issue of corporate quotas has generally been seen as a matter for elite women, and thus not the main interest for women's organisations based on ideas of social justice and redistribution (Figure 12.2).

12.4   COMPARING INSTITUTIONAL CONFIGURATIONS IN THE POLITICAL AND ECONOMIC SECTORS

As noted in the theoretical section of this chapter, it is important to address the ways in which quotas interact with existing rules, practices, and norms in any given context. In analyses of institutional stasis and change, it is essential to investigate the complex dynamics of formal and informal institutions and institutional levels in quota adoption; sometimes the institutional configuration constitutes a good fit, sometimes it results in conflict.

The adoption of party regulations on candidate selection for elected bodies in politics, including targets, recommendations, and party quotas, was facilitated by systemic institutions such as the fact that elections at all levels of government in Sweden are based on proportional representation (PR) with high district magnitudes. Another key systemic institution has been the multi-party system, triggering competition for votes by parties to the left and the right. The adoption of party quotas was also facilitated by the fact that Swedish politics has been dominated by the Social Democratic Party, although liberal parties have also introduced recommendations for gender balanced electoral lists. Practical institutions were also beneficial. Although political parties varied in their adoption of special measures, they were all pressured by female party members and women's organisations to add gender as a selection criterion and to increase the number of women on electoral lists. The quota provisions that were adopted functioned as "high-echelon quotas"; they were introduced in a political situation in which parliamentary representation was already increasing to around 30 percent (Freidenvall, Dahlerup, and Skjeie 2006). Thus, an already strong group of women in the parties took advantage of their positions of power to protect the level of representation against backlash, and the adoption of party quotas supported the incremental track that parties in Sweden have embarked upon since the 1970s. The adoption of party regulations was also facilitated by contagion effects, as mentioned above. Once one party had introduced a new measure to increase the share of women on electoral lists, rival parties followed suit in order not to be punished electorally. In terms of normative institutions, ideals about representation and equality were contested. Over time, the view of women's political representation changed: from the perception that one woman – the "obligatory woman" – was enough to represent women to the notion that women comprise half of the citizenry and should as such be equally represented. While resistance to quotas lingered on, the reframing of quotas – from a system perceived as creating unfair advantages into a system that aims at an equal division and sharing of political power – enabled the adoption of voluntary party quotas. In sum, while systemic and practical institutions have been quite favourable towards equal representation in Sweden, the normative institutions have been more resistant. With the reframing of quotas, the content of institutions has shifted in mutually reinforcing ways.

In relation to the economic sector, systemic institutions such as the Swedish Instrument of Government, the Anti-Discrimination Act, and the Company Act did not pose any formal problems for the adoption of special measures. At the practical level, the practices of owners and shareholders at the annual general meetings, having a key role in discharging and appointing board members, might hinder the adoption of corporate quotas. Despite the Code of Corporate Governance, companies and their nomination committees – the old boys' network – continue to exercise autonomy over review of board performance and nomination of new candidates, since the selection criteria in the Code did not specify how gender balance was to be achieved. Their right to self-determination and autonomy was thus protected. Concerning norms, finally, the principle of self-regulation in directing the composition of boards seems to be a stronger value than gender equality. What is more, diversity rather than gender appeared to be a more important criterion in the selection of board members. Similar to the political sector, however, great resistance to quotas have persisted. Quotas were seen contrary to the rule of equality of opportunity and meritocracy. More importantly, they were seen as a break with the idea of non-interference of the state in the business sector and with the historical free-zone granted by the state to capitalists in matters of private ownership. As stated in the 1990 state report, few demands have been imposed by the state to reduce the power of private companies over the years, and those that have been made have not been successful.[24] In particular, quotas were seen as a break with the Swedish model of governance and the right of the social partners to regulate conditions in the labour market. One main point of conflict was, thus, the struggle between the Swedish state and private companies fighting for autonomy. The promotion of compulsory corporate board quotas endangered the holy alliance between the state and capital – the Harpsund democracy model. The adoption of the Code seemed to be an easy way out of this potential problem.

Compared to the issue of party quotas, neither social democratic nor liberal women's federations lobbied hard to promote legislated corporate board quotas, at least not in a systematic way. Thus, there was no social mobilisation or feminist activism around the issue. The radical feminist analysis (including its analysis of structural discrimination and subordination of women in the business sector) that permeated much of the discussion on gender at the time of quota adoption might have scared off potential quota proponents in the business sector, since it could create an antagonistic climate in the relationship between business and state authorities, a relationship that most politicians respected.[25] Generally, the radicalised discursive climate, the weak state and a relatively strong business community represented factors that hindered change.

[24] SOU 1990:44. Demokrati och makt i Sverige. Maktutredningens huvudrapport. Stockholm: Justitiedepartmentet.
[25] SOU 1987:19.

12.4.1 Discussing Institutional Change

Similar to Norway, the adoption of various rules and regulations can be interpreted as the result of timing and sequencing of events, the specific Swedish gender equality policy institution, and the agency of actors in promoting policy processes.

As for timing and sequencing, the developments pertaining to equal participation of women and men in decision-making bodies in Sweden have to a great extent followed an incremental, path-dependent track. Built on previous rules and regulations and shaped by past legacies, new institutions have emerged step by step, gradually covering new arenas or sectors of society. The institutional innovations that have been made, including party quotas and the Code, have to a large extent been circumscribed, framed within pre-existing institutional and cultural contexts, and nested within an existing institutional structure. Elements of the old thus co-exist with elements of the new. As pointed out by Mona Lena Krook and Fiona MacKay (2011), institutions are "sticky." What is more, while legislated quotas in politics and on company boards have been resisted, the adoption of various kinds of soft law regulations and other special measures in combination with discursive shifts in favour of balanced representation has been instrumental in facilitating an equal representation of women and men in an increasing number of sectors of society.

The adoption of new institutions, such as party quotas and the Code, can be seen as a natural extension of the Swedish gender equality policy institution. The various rules and regulations that have been introduced build on a policy legacy of soft laws and regulations. Gradually they have been extended to be stronger – first promoting simply more women and then gender balance – and to cover more sectors of society. New institutions have emerged through layering, adding new elements to existing institutions (Streeck and Thelen 2005). Thus, although the development can be characterised as incremental and path-dependent, institutional change is possible through endogenous processes of layering.

As for policy agency, institutional change depends on the institutional configuration in combination with the provision of agents and their strategies in promoting change or resistance. In the Swedish context, different kinds of actors have been active in the two policy processes. In politics, women working inside and outside political parties have been successful forces of change, fuelled by the competition between the political parties to be the "best" at gender equality.

In business, quite to the contrary, women's movement actors have been more or less non-existent. Here the centre-right Alliance government and representatives of the business community, as well as the social partners, have been powerful forces of resistance. The success of these agents has also depended on the coalitions they have been able to forge.

The threat by Social Democratic Governments and other actors of imposing compulsory quotas has stimulated the continuous adoption of soft law and other special measures to show that the enactment of legal quotas is not necessary. The policy of publicly reporting the gender composition of decision-making bodies and naming-and-shaming the less successful ones has been an effective way to speed up the process.

12.5 CONCLUSION

Sweden has developed two distinct approaches to gender quotas, with party quotas for elected bodies and corporate governance codes for the business sector. Both are based on the ideal that gender balance in decision-making is the goal, but that it is up to the individual party or company to decide how to achieve and maintain this objective. In general, there has been persistent criticism of legislated measures to redress the underrepresentation of women in politics and business. The dominant legal narrative for gender equality, thus, firmly rejects positive action, but promotes soft laws. In this narrative, matters concerning gender (im)balance in decision-making positions should be solved in line with the Swedish model for gender equality, based on ideals of a consensus-oriented, cooperative, and non-conflictual model of deliberation. The case of regulation in the political sector shows that a good fit between systemic, practical, and normative institutions has facilitated the introduction of party quotas. In fact, while quota adoption was aimed primarily at reforming party selection practices, discussions about these policies intersected in various ways with existing norms and discourses. The content of institutions therefore shifted in mutually reinforcing ways. The case of regulation in the business sector shows that the interplay between institutions has been marked by a poor institutional fit, due to the lack of strong discursive support for gender balanced company boards. Reforming corporate boards via voluntary guidelines, such as the Code, seems to have contributed to a better fit between institutions. The Code provided an alternate rule when formal rules such as legislated quotas were not desirable. Generally it could be argued that legislated quotas failed in both approaches, but while voluntary quotas in politics have been quite efficient due to the fit between normative and practical institutions, a corresponding result in business has been less noticeable, primarily due to the weakness of the normative institutions' resistance towards quotas. In the end, it seems like the women's movement's pressure for change has been the main factor for institutional change in politics, while the collaboration between the Alliance government, the industrialists, and the social partners has been a powerful force of resistance in business. The many turns in Swedish politics pertaining to corporate gender quotas indicate that the discussions will most likely continue.

References

Agnblad, Johan, Erik Berglöf, Peter Högfeldt, and Helena Svancar. 2001. 'Ownership and control in Sweden: Strong Owners, Weak Minorities, and Social Control.' In *The Control of Corporate Europe*, edited by Fabrizio Barca and Marco Becht, 228–58. Oxford: Oxford University Press.

Bergqvist, Christina. 1994. *Mäns makt och kvinnors intressen*. Acta Universitatis Upsaliensis. Uppsala: Uppsala Universitet.

Bergqvist, Christina et al. 1999. *Equal Democracies. Gender and Politics in the Nordic Countries*. Oslo: Scandinavian University Press.

Bohman, Love, Magnus Bygren, and Christofer Edling. 2012. 'Surge under Threat: The Rapid Increase of Women on Swedish Boards of Directors.' In *Women on Corporate Boards and in Top Management: European Trends and Policy*, edited by Colette Fagan, Maria González Menéndez, and Sylvia Gómez Ansón, 91–108. Houndmills, Basingstoke: Palgrave Macmillan.

Borchorst, Anette, Lenita Freidenvall, Johanna Kantola, Liza Reisel, and Mari Teigen. 2012. '"Institutionalizing Intersectionality in the Nordic Countries: Anti-Discrimination and Equality in Denmark, Finland, Norway, and Sweden."' In *Institutionalizing Intersectionality: The Changing Nature of European Equality Regimes*, edited by Andrea Krizsan, Hege Skjeie and Judith Squires, 59–88. Basingstoke, UK: Palgrave Macmillan.

Dahlerup, Drude. 1988. 'From a Small to a Large Minority: Women in Scandinavian Politics.' *Scandinavian Political Studies* 11 (4): 275–98.

1998. *Rødstrømperne. Den danske Rødstrømpebevaegelses udvikling, nytænkning og gennemslag 1970–85*. Copenhagen: Gyldendal.

Dahlerup, Drude, and Lenita Freidenvall. 2005. 'Quotas as a "Fast Track" to Equal Political Representation for Women. Why Scandinavia is No Longer the Model.' *International Feminist Journal of Politics* 7 (1): 26–48.

2008. *Kvotering*. Stockholm: SNS.

Eduards, Maud. 2002. *Förbjuden handling: om kvinnors organisering och feministisk teori*. Malmö: Liber.

Fredell, Åsa. 2005. *Lagstadgad könskvotering i bolagsstyrelser? En analys av den svenska mediadebatten*. Working Paper Series, No 2. The Research Program on Gender Quotas. Stockholm: Stockholm University.

Freidenvall, Lenita. 2005. 'A Discursive Struggle – The Swedish National Federation of Social Democratic Women and Gender Quotas.' *Nordic Journal of Women's Studies* 13 (3): 175–86.

———. 2006. *Vägen till Varannan damernas. Kvinnorepresentation, kandidaturval och kvotering i svensk politik 1970–2002*. Stockholms universitet.

———. 2007. *Regeringsformen ur ett könsperspektiv: en övergripande genomgång*. SOU 2007:67. Stockholm: Fritzes.

———. 2013. 'Sweden: Step by step – Women's Inroads into Parliamentary Politics.' In *Breaking Male Dominance in Old Democracies*, edited by Drude Dahlerup and Monique Leyenaar, 97–123. Oxford: Oxford University Press.

Freidenvall, Lenita, Drude Dahlerup, and Hege Skeije. 2006. 'The Nordic countries. An Incremental Model.' In *Women, Quotas and Politics*, edited by Drude Dahlerup, 55–82. London: Routledge.

Freidenvall, Lenita, and Hanna Hallonsten. 2013. 'Why Not Corporate Gender Quotas in Sweden?' *Representation* 49 (4): 467–85.

Heidenrich, Vibeke. 2012. 'Why Gender Quotas on Company Boards in Norway – and Not in Sweden?' In *Firms, Boards, and Gender Quotas in Comparative Perspectives*, edited by Fredrik Engelstad and Mari Teigen, 147–83. Comparative Social Research 29. Bingley: Emerald.

Helmke, Gretchen, and Steven Levitsky. 2004. 'Informal Institutions and Comparative Politics: A Research Agenda.' *Perspectives on Politics* 2 (4): 725–40.

Hernes, Helga. 1987. *Welfare State and Woman Power. Essays in State Feminism.* Oslo: Norwegian University Press.

Hughes, Melanie, and Pamela Paxton. 2008. 'Continuous Change, Episodes, and Critical Periods: A Framework for Understanding Women's Political Representation over Time.' *Politics & Gender* 4 (2): 233–64.

Karlsson, Gunnel. 1996. *Från broderskap till systerskap. Det socialdemokratiska kvinnoförbundets kamp för inflytande och makt i SAP.* Lund: Arkiv Förlag.

Krook, Mona Lena. 2009. *Quotas for Women in Politics. Gender and Candidate Selection Worldwide.* New York: Oxford University Press.

Krook, Mona Lena, and Fiona Mackay, eds. 2011. *Gender, Politics, and Institutions: Towards a Feminist Institutionalism.* New York: Palgrave.

Mackay, Fiona. 2011. 'Conclusion: Towards institutionalism?' In *Gender, Politics, and Institutions: Towards a Feminist Institutionalism*, edited by Mona Lena Krook and Fiona Mackay, 181–93. Basingstoke, UK: Palgrave Macmillan.

Nilsson, Tomas. 2009. 'Kön och makt I svenskt näringsliv.' In *Kön och Makt I Norden del 1 Landsrapporter*, edited by Kirsti Niskanen and Anita Nyberg. Oslo: Nordic Council of Ministers.

Sabuni, N. 2008. 'Quotas are the Wrong Way to Go.' *Expressen*. 27 October.

Sainsbury, Diane. 1996. *Gender, Equality and Welfare States*. Cambridge: Cambridge University Press.

——— 2005. 'Party Feminism, State Feminism and Women's Representation in Sweden.' In *State Feminism and Political Representation*, edited by Joni Lovenduski, 195–215. Cambridge: Cambridge University Press.

Streeck, Wolfgang, and Kathleen Thelen, eds. 2005. *Beyond Continuity. Institutional Change in Advanced Political Economies*. Oxford: Oxford University Press.

Törnqvist, Maria. 2006. 'Könspolitik på gränsen. Debatterna om varannan damernas och Thamprofessurerna.' Ph.D. Dissertation, Stockholm University.

Wide, Jessika. 2006. 'Kvinnors politiska representation i ett jämförande perspektiv - nationell och lokal nivå.' Ph.D. Dissertation, Umeå Universitet.

Wängnerud, Lena. 1998. 'Politikens andra sida. Om kvinnorepresentation i Sveriges riksdag.' Ph.D. Dissertation, Göteborg studies in politics 53.

CHAPTER THIRTEEN

GENDER EQUALITY WITHOUT GENDER QUOTAS

Dilemmas in the Danish Approach to Gender Equality and Citizenship

Lise Rolandsen Agustín, Birte Siim and Anette Borchorst

This chapter addresses the dilemmas, contradictions and paradoxes in the Danish approach to gender equality and citizenship. Scholars propose that the Danish gender and citizenship model, like in other Scandinavian countries, is premised on public–private cooperation between the state and civil society and on the interplay between women's roles as workers, mothers and citizens (e.g. Hernes 1987; Siim 2000, 156–63). Comparative Nordic research finds that the particular Danish approach to gender and democracy is characterised by a "bottom-up," "movement oriented" model and a weaker institutionalisation compared to the other Nordic countries (Christensen 1999; Borchorst, Christensen and Raum 1999; Borchorst and Siim 2002; Borchorst and Dahlerup 2003). The Danish approach to gender equality has, as in the other Nordic countries, been based upon consensus policies about the goal and disagreements about the means to achieve gender equality (Freidenvall, Dahlerup and Skjeie 2006, 64). In Denmark the consensus dates back to the struggle for voting rights and reform of family legislation in the beginning of the twentieth century (Fiig and Siim 2012). During the 1970s and 1980s gender equality policies were passed with the support of almost all parties (Borchorst 1999). Gender quotas have, however, always been controversial in Denmark, both in relation to elections and in party politics as and in relation to the labour market and public committees. It is also worth noticing that what has been framed as a "daddies quota" in parental leave schemes was abandoned precisely with reference to the resistance against quotas (Borchorst and Freidenvall 2012).[1]

Gender equality policies influence power relations in regard to cit-izenship, democracy and governance.[2] In this chapter, we address the general debate on gender quotas in Denmark and subsequently explore two cases of gender quotas: first in politics (party quotas and electoral quotas) and then in the economic arena. This chapter is primarily concerned with an analysis of Danish discourses and decisions in both areas, taking into account the dynamics between political actors and the political opportunity structures in the two cases.

The Danish approach to gender equality (*ligestilling*) and gender quotas raises theoretical, normative and analytical questions. Like the other Scandinavian countries, Denmark has a strong passion for social and gender equality, but the gender profiles of the three Scandinavian countries have different characteristics (Borchorst, Christensen and Raum 1999). One difference is that legislation concerning the option for adopting gender quotas in the labour market and in public com-mittees and boards is weak and restricted in the Danish case compared to the Norwegian and Swedish legislative approach (Borchorst 1999). Furthermore, unlike Norway and Sweden, no gender quotas exist in political parties. Gender quotas were adopted for a short period by two political parties on the Left, the Socialist People's Party and the Social Democrats, but their use to increase women's representation was aban-doned by both parties' congresses in 1996 (Borchorst and Christensen 2003). Studies of the arguments of political actors indicate that the meaning of gender quotas in politics changed for women within the two parties between the 1970s and the 1990s. In that period, women's political representation increased from a small to a large minority and women on the Left who had previously favoured gender quotas began to argue that they were no longer needed (Christensen 1999, 78–84).[3]

---

[1] The period of leave after birth that is reserved for the mother is not framed as a quota.

[2] Bacchi (2006) has discussed the theoretical arguments for and against electoral quotas for women focusing on equality, representation, citizenship and rights. One important point she makes is that context is crucial when reflecting on these issues. Another is that theoretical interventions need to take into account the diversity of women's voices in relation to class, race, sexuality and physical normalcy (46–7).

[3] The Socialist People's Party (SF) implemented party quotas between 1983 and 1990 and candidate quotas between 1988 and 1990. For more detailed discussions of the arguments for and against gender quotas, see Christensen (1999, 80–1); Borchorst and Christensen (2003, 107–12).

During the last six elections, women's political representation in parliament has been between 37 and 39 per cent. The increase of women's representation to 39 per cent at the general election in 2011 may be attributed to political mobilisation when the Social Democrats regained power after ten years in opposition. In addition, there is a distinct gender gap in voting behaviour, since women tend to support the left-wing parties much more than men do. In the 2000s there was a competition between the social democratic female leader Helle Thorning Schmidt and Anders Fogh Rasmussen, the leader of the Liberal Party. Thorning Schmidt became the first Danish female Prime Minister and formed a government including the female leader of the Social Liberal Party, Margrethe Vestager, as Minister of the Economy.[4] In 2015, a new right-wing government took over with a male prime minister and supported by three right-wing parties, all headed by men. The many strong and successful female leaders of parties on the political Left – as well as on the political Right – is an indication that women play an important role in the political elite.[5]

Compared to other European countries, it is a paradox that in Denmark since 1998 a relatively high female representation has been reached without gender quotas. In addition, it has been reached at a time when previous collective mobilisation in the women's movement and momentum for gender equality policies was decreasing (Christensen 1999). This development thus tends to support the dominant political discourse that gender equality in politics may be achieved without quotas (Freidenvall, Dahlerup and Skjeie 2006). The Danish case illustrates that context matters, and questions gender quotas as a universal strategy for achieving equal representation in politics. It challenges the theoretical arguments for adopting gender quotas as well as the typology of resistance to gender quotas (Krook 2007, 2016) and illustrates that

[4] In all of the eight political parties represented in Parliament about one third of the elected members are women. The Socialist People's Party and the Social Liberal Party both have more than 50 per cent women, while the Danish People's Party has the lowest percentage of women, with only 32 per cent. The Social Democrats, however, has only 36 per cent.

[5] In the internal struggle over leadership in the Social Democratic Party in 2011 Helle Thorning Schmidt became famous for boldly proclaiming: "I can beat Anders Fogh." On the Left, the Social Democrats, the Socialist People's Party, and the Red-Green Alliance both had female leaders in 2011. The previous Minister of Internal Affairs and Economy, Margrethe Vestager, was leader of the Social Liberal Party from 2007 to 2014, after which she became European Commissioner for Competition. On the Right, Pia Kjærsgaard was the founder and long-time leader of the Danish People's Party until she stepped down in 2013 (Meret and Siim 2017).

it may be useful to employ different means to achieve gender equality in different contexts, depending on the particular political cultures and political opportunities in specific arenas. On the analytical level, the Danish case supports the arguments by Nordic scholars that gender quotas in politics may not be the most important factor for women's political representation compared to other factors, especially women's participation in the labour market and women's political mobilisation (Freidenvall, Dahlerup and Skjeie 2006). Quota provisions may play only a limited role in explaining women's high political representation in the Nordic countries compared to institutional, socio-economic, and cultural factors combined with political mobilisation by the women's movement and campaigns launched by political parties.

However, the Danish experience also shows that the voluntary strategy towards a more equal gender balance can work in some political areas, for example in electoral politics, but not in others. Studies of the gender composition of elites within politics, administration, science and private companies confirm that it is difficult to translate the voluntary approach to gender equality from politics to the private business sector and point to variations in institutional barriers as an explanation for the higher hurdles for women in the business elite (Christiansen, Møller and Togeby 2002, 89).

Denmark (along with the other Scandinavian countries) has during some periods been ahead of other European countries regarding women's participation in the labour market and to some extent also regarding gender parity in politics. Having lagged behind many other European countries for some years, the country now performs above the EU average in relation to equal representation in economic decision-making, with a 25.8 per cent share of women on the boards of the largest publicly listed companies, according to the 2015 European Commission Database on women and men in decision-making. With considerable room for improvement, there is agreement about the need for gender balance in company boards but gender quotas have been controversial. In 2012, the social democratic-headed government abandoned its own proposal for quotas, faced with resistance from the liberal opposition and the private companies, deciding to opt for a voluntary strategy instead.[6] Scholars question whether this voluntary approach will have an effect in the economic arena.

---

[6] Despite the fact that gender quotas had been part of the winning 2011 programme of the social democratic-headed government.

On the theoretical and normative level this chapter raises issues about the intersections of citizenship, democracy and gender justice. Gender theory and research has argued that gender quotas would and should be a means to achieve equal rights, gender equality and gender justice.[7] Gender theory has presented diverse arguments for gender quotas based on justice, effective use of resources, and protecting women's interests. Moreover, gender parity in politics can be perceived as one dimension of gender justice, next to redistribution and recognition (Fraser 2013, 164–7). The Danish and Nordic approach to gender equality, citizenship and welfare has been traditionally concerned with class and gender, i.e. with women's roles as mothers and workers as well as with their citizenship roles in terms of participation and representation. The strength of the Nordic approach has been its focus on social rights/redistribution and political participation/representation and it is only recently, following EU directives, that Nordic countries have become concerned with recognition policies in the form of anti-discrimination (see Borchorst and Siim 2008, 213). It may seem paradoxical that despite this focus on social equality, gender equality in economic decision-making has only recently become part of the political agenda in Denmark. The growing emphasis on gender equality and diversity in economic decision-making cannot be explained by the Nordic emphasis on redistribution – social inequalities have been growing in Denmark, and the other Nordic countries, since the 1990s. Rather, the focus on gender equality in economic decision-making is part of another logic of participation and equal representation, which fits with the voluntary regulation approach in political representation that has characterised Nordic countries such as Denmark.

No single institutional logic can explain the Danish approach to gender quotas in both the political and economic arena. Instead, this analysis illustrates that the dynamics between institutions and social actors, the Left/Right dynamic as well as the arguments employed, are different in the two cases, as we now demonstrate.[8]

---

[7] Teigen (2000) and Freidenvall, Dahlerup and Skjeie (2006, 67–70) have summarised the different arguments for and against gender quotas in Nordic debates. During the 1990s, a new discourse and rhetoric of profitability of gender equality within a range of institutions from business to higher education became prominent, arguing for example that quotas are not only beneficial for women's rights but also for industry, for society, and for men.

[8] More qualitative gender research is needed to compare the dynamics of gender equality policies in general and gender quotas in particular in relation to different policies,

13.1   SETTING THE STAGE: THE DANISH GENDER
EQUALITY REGIME AND CITIZENSHIP MODEL

Gender equality has become part of the national Nordic self-understanding. Studies have found that there are both similarities and differences between welfare and gender equality policies in the Nordic countries depending on the different political settings (Bergqvist et al. 1999; Dahlerup 2002; Borchorst and Siim 2008; Borchorst and Freidenvall 2012; Siim and Stoltz 2015). In relation to gender quotas in politics and the economy, there are more differences than similarities between the countries in the region.[9] We underline here two important features of the Danish case: the democratic citizenship regime oriented towards bottom-up and voluntary approaches to gender equality, and the changing Left/Right divide over gender equality issues.

Nordic gender research has previously characterised Danish equality policies as the most "movement-oriented" approach compared to the other Nordic countries, where gender equality policies have to a larger extent been initiated "from above" (Borchorst, Christensen and Raum 1999). The democratic approach to mobilising social and political actors "from below" dates back to the beginning of the twentieth century.[10] Alliances between social movements, social partners and women's groups were important for the adoption of women's right to vote and equal pay, and social reform movements were also crucial to the long tradition for extended public responsibilities for childcare (Christensen and Siim 2001; Borchorst and Siim 2002; Fiig and Siim 2012). Danish democracy and political culture have been characterised by a

---

levels and arenas. The effects of adopting/not adopting gender quotas in different policy areas are complex and difficult to examine. In addition, it is a specific challenge to evaluate the effects of the non-implementation of gender quotas in particular arenas with many different social actors involved.

[9] The Nordic countries have a long tradition of cooperation, for example via the Nordic Council, and in international organisations, for example in the UN. Cross-Nordic inspiration through the feminist and trade union movements and national comparisons by political forces and government agencies have historically played an important role in the development of gender equality policies (Bergqvist et al. 1999; Freidenvall, Dahlerup, and Skjeie 2006; Borchorst and Siim 2008).

[10] Women gained the right to vote in 1915 and at the first elections in 1918 women's representation reached only 2.9 per cent. The percentage of elected women was below 10 per cent until 1966. For an overview of women's representation in parliament since 1918, see www.ft.dk/folketinget/oplysningen/folketingsmedlemmer/kvindeprocenten.aspx.

combination of preference for civil society solutions with strong individualism in family, labour and social policies (Borchorst and Siim 2008). Research suggests that the bottom-up Danish model, based on the mobilisation of social movements and respect for the independence of social dialogue has been perceived as a strength as well as a weakness by political actors (Fiig and Siim 2012). It has proven to be an advantage when there is a strong mobilisation of the women's movement and of social actors within and across the political parties pushing for gender equality policies, as was the case in the struggle for suffrage in the late 1800s and early 1900s, and again in the 1970s and 1980s. Women's political mobilisation gradually faded during the 1980s and since then the Left has generally been weakened and social movements and women's organisations have become increasingly fragmented.

Denmark is characterised by a majoritarian democracy with parliamentarian supremacy, and the courts play a modest role compared to the parliament. Gender equality is not inscribed in the Constitution and the Supreme Court is not influential in shaping policies of gender equality. EU directives on gender equality have emphasised antidiscrimination as a legal approach to reducing gender equality. This court-oriented approach may be the most potent strategy for addressing gender equality, but there are many obstacles to using the judicial route in the Danish context, due to the resistance of politicians and the main social partners, the Danish Confederation of Trade Unions (LO) and the Confederation of Danish Employers (DA) to bypassing parliament and the collective agreements (Borchorst and Rolandsen Agustín 2015).

In line with this citizenship regime, the Danish approach to gender equality in political representation has generally favoured the voluntary method without quotas – premised on the parties' willingness to nominate a large number of women candidates and the citizens' willingness to vote for women – with a fair amount of success, as we detail below (Bergqvist et al. 1999; Dahlerup 2006). Similarly, in terms of increasing the number of female managers and getting more women into publicly appointed committees, the Danish approach (similar to the Icelandic one) favours voluntary methods (Borchorst 1999). The 1976 Equal Treatment Directive, of the then European Economic Community, which opened the door to affirmative action and quotas, was implemented in a weak and restricted way in Denmark.[11]

---

[11] Denmark became member of the European Economic Community in 1973 as the only Nordic country. Sweden and Finland joined in 1995.

Affirmative action in education and employment was only allowed if an exemption had been granted. From 1978 to 2000, the Council of Equal Status had the authority to grant these exemptions and each of the two main social partners that were represented in the Council, together with the women's organisations, could veto the decision. Due to strong resistance from the social partners, few exemptions from the law were granted. Since 2000, the responsible minister as has been able to grant exemptions but the number of initiatives is still very low.

Furthermore, the Danish government did not adopt legislative quotas on the gender composition of public committees and boards from 1985 to 1990, due to strong resistance in parliament. Instead, a weak formulation was adopted, establishing that appointments should include proposals for both women and men. This application contrasts with the Swedish, Finnish and Norwegian legislation on membership of public committees and boards from the late 1970s and early 1980s, which set up a minimum of 40 per cent members of "the underrepresented sex" (Borchorst 1999).

Some studies have also pointed towards the different national opportunity structures as an explanation of the differences in development of gender equality policies between Denmark, Norway and Sweden (Borchorst and Freidenvall 2012). Denmark has a Left/Right divide in gender equality policies, which has until recently been stronger than in Sweden and Norway and has played an important role in the unfolding of gender equality policies since the 1990s. Indeed, since the Second World War, the Social Democratic Party has been a strong supporter of both class and gender equality, with a focus on strengthening women's equal citizenship and equal position in the labour market and in education, including equal pay. During the 1970s and 1980s, there was a relatively high degree of support for gender equality policies across the Left/Right divide, and alliances among women across the dominant political parties. Women in the Social Democratic Party, the Social Liberal Party, and the Conservative Party played an important role in adopting gender equality policies. As stated earlier, the parties also agreed not to adopt quotas for appointments to public committees and boards. The 1990s, however, saw growing resistance to more regulation on gender equality and above all to gender quotas of any kind. The resistance comes from both women and men in liberal, conservative, and populist parties, whose position is based upon strong beliefs in equal rights as equal opportunities, premised on the liberal principles of individual citizens' "free choice." Gender quotas have, however, been controversial in the social democratic party as well, due among other things to the resistance from male unionists. Only during a very short period in the 2000s did the party support gender quotas in company boards. A social democratic-headed government did, however, introduce a fathers' quota in the parental leave provision in 1997 (to reserve some weeks of parental leave for fathers), against the votes of the Right.

The dominant approach to gender equality changed when the liberal-conservative government took office from 2001 to 2011, supported by the Danish People's Party. Gender equality was no longer about equal rights and social justice, but a utilitarian means to economic growth, and the reference group for gender equality was primarily ethnic minority women that were perceived to be oppressed by their culture and religion (Meret and Siim 2013). This change led to abandonment of the fathers' quota by the Right wing government in 2002, at the same time as it expanded the total parental leave to fifty-two weeks (Borchorst and Freidenvall 2012). Earmarking some weeks of the allowance for fathers as a quota was framed as tutelary and as a violation of the free choice of the family. In this way, Denmark has maintained the most gender-biased division of parental leave, since only two weeks immediately after the birth is reserved for the father (together with the mother). The following twelve weeks of the leave are reserved for the mother, and the rest of the leave may be shared between the mother and the father; but it is considered mothers' leave by all parties involved (mothers, fathers, colleagues and employers).

The shift in government after the 2011 elections to a minority government of the Social Democrats, the Social Liberal Party and the Socialist People's Party (the latter left the government in the spring of 2014) was followed by high expectations for a more proactive gender equality policy compared to the policies of the previous liberal-conservative government. The Government Platform document from October 2011, "A Denmark that stands together," includes a section on equality and diversity. As mentioned earlier, the proposals included earmarking part of the parental leave allowance for fathers, and gender quotas within corporations' boards. Both proposals were, however, withdrawn. Instead of gender quotas in corporations, an alternative, softer strategy to increase women's participation in public and private boards was adopted (see below).

After the elections in June 2015, the Liberal Party regained power as a minority government supported by the Danish People's Party – which became the largest 'social-conservative' party – the Liberal

Alliance, and the small conservative party. Since then, the most salient political issues have been immigration and refugees. Gender equality has again become a concern in relation to asylum seekers, for example separating 'child brides' under eighteen years of age from their spouses in asylum centres.[12]

In the following two sections, we analyse the Danish approach to gender equality and gender quotas by looking in more detail at debates, proposals, and policies for gender equality in two cases: (1) gender quotas in representative politics, and (2) gender quotas in corporate boards. The focus is on the institutional logics, key actors and the main arguments set forward.

13.2 THE DANISH APPROACH TO GENDER QUOTAS IN POLITICS

Denmark is an example of a country with high representation of women in politics without gender quotas. Arguably one of the factors behind this situation is the historical strength of the Danish women's movement in all its diversity (Dahlerup 2013, 147). Gender equality (in Danish, *kønsligestilling*) has been a major political goal, but compared to the other Scandinavian countries, Denmark represents an exception, since the country does not implement any gender quotas, voluntary or compulsory, in politics. In the political arena, the debate for and against gender quotas has primarily been a debate between the two political parties that had at one time adopted party quotas: the Social Democratic Party (1983–96) and the Socialist People's Party (1977–96) (Christensen 1999, 78). Both the Social Democrats and the Socialist People's Party abolished gender quotas at their party congresses in 1996, but the process for each was rather different. In the Social Democratic Party, there was resistance to gender quotas from male members, who generally favoured emphasis on class over gender. Here the party congress voted to abolish the internal quota rules against the wishes of the Equality Committee and the Executive Committee (Christensen and Damkjær Knopp 1998, 17). The opposition to gender quotas in the Socialist People's Party was particularly strong among young women arguing that quotas were no longer needed and that gender equality should be the common goal for both women and men (Christensen 1999, 81; Dahlerup 2013, 161).

---

[12] "Denmark to separate 'child bride' asylum seekers from spouses," *International Business Times*, 12 February 2016.

The main arguments against gender quotas in both parties were that equal representation should and could be reached by voluntary democratic means through a mobilisation of women and men within and outside the parties to get more votes for female candidates through the electoral system.[13] While the male resistance to gender quotas within the Social Democratic Party fits neatly within the typology proposed by Krook (2016), the resistance to existing candidate quotas by young female activists within the Socialist People's Party represents arguments that challenge the existing typology of resistance.

There has been widespread consensus in the Danish debate that gender quotas are not an appropriate strategy in politics. Despite the lack of gender quotas, women have in the last five elections made up more than 37 per cent of the elected members of Parliament.[14] At the elections in 2011 the percentage rose to 39.1 per cent but fell again to 37.4 in 2015.[15] It is an apparent paradox that the Danish parliament with 37 per cent female representatives is regarded as gender equal, whereas the Swedish parliament with 45 per cent women is seen as gender unequal (Freidenvall, Dahlerup and Skjeie 2006, 79). Whether gender parity in politics can be said to be successful clearly depends on interpretation. In 2016, three out of eight party leaders in the Danish parliament are women, although there is a Left-Right divide, with women generally dominating the leadership on the Left and men dominating the leadership on the Right.

---

[13] Freidenvall, Dahlerup and Skjeie (2006: 68) state that you can find arguments that women can do without quotas in most countries but that they have greater value in the Nordic countries because of the historical increase in women's representation without quotas. We add that this argument is especially strong in the Danish political culture, where women's representation has increased since 1996 without the use of quotas. Dahlerup emphasises that because of the many active women in the Socialist Peoples' Party during the 1990s, however, the gender-neutral formulations in some cases helped men (Dahlerup 2013, 161).

[14] See www.ft.dk/folketinget/oplysningen/folketingsmedlemmer/kvindeprocenten.aspx.

[15] It is remarkable that in Denmark and the other Nordic countries the number of women elected in local municipalities is lower than in the national assemblies. The first female Minister, Nina Bang, was appointed by the first Social Democratic government in 1924. Since the 1990s women have made up more than 30 per cent of the Ministers in governments on the Left and the Right; in two governments women made up around 40 per cent of the ministers: The social democratic-headed government of Poul Nyrup Rasmussen in 1998 and the Liberal minority government of Lars Løkke Rasmussen in 2008 (Statistics Denmark 2015).

13.3 PROPOSALS FOR GENDER QUOTAS IN ECONOMIC BOARDS

The issue of female representation in decision-making in relation to the private sector has been quite visible on the agenda in Denmark since the 1990s. In general, there is no tradition for legislation on gender equality issues in the private sector (except for antidiscrimination measures) and gender quotas are met with strong resistance. Instead we find a large variety in the goals, strategies and practices that companies employ to stimulate the participation of women on the boards of the largest companies. In 2015, Statistics Denmark published a national survey, which showed that 68 per cent of the respondents did not want to introduce quotas in favour of gender representation in private company boards, as had been done in Norway.[16]

Without gender quota legislation, an increase in the percentage of women on boards has nevertheless been identified over the last decade: according to Nordic Statistics,[17] the share of female board members of larger publicly listed companies rose from 11 per cent in 2003 and 18 per cent in 2009 to 24 per cent in 2014. According to more recent data from the Danish Business Authority,[18] which includes larger listed companies with more than 250 employees, the share rose from 11 per cent in 2005 to 19 per cent in 2015. Taking into account all listed companies, the percentage of women on boards increased from 10 per cent in 2009 to 13 per cent in 2013 (Ministry for Gender Equality 2014).

In the late 1990s, organisations like the Danish Association of Managers and Executives and the Confederation of Danish Industry (DI)[19] contributed to putting the issue of women and leadership in private companies on the agenda. The Danish Association of Managers and Executives argued, amongst other things, that "the private sector

---

[16] "Danskerne er imod kvoter for kvinder i bestyrelser," Statistics Denmark, 11 June 2015. A survey carried out in 2011 by one of the largest trade unions, the Union of Commercial and Clerical Employees (HK), showed that 49 per cent of their female members and 30 per cent of their male members supported quota legislation to enhance gender equality on company boards. This result was an increase from the 22 per cent of female members and 10 per cent of male members who supported legal quota measures in 2009. See www.e-pages.dk/hk/717/.

[17] See norden.org.

[18] Danish Business Authority, "Undersøgelse af kønsfordelingen i visse børsnoterede selskaber," 24 March 2015.

[19] Ritzaus Bureau, "Andelen af danske kvinder i erhvervslivets top er i bund," 29 November 2004.

should, like the public one, hire far more women at leadership level,"[20] although the Association did not support quotas as such.[21]

In 2005, the women's organisation Danish Women's Society made a general assembly statement asking for more equal representation in company boards. It referred to the threat of legal measures in Norway before the adoption of legislation as a way to increase women's representation as well as to studies showing the economic advantages of having more women on boards.[22] The Danish Women's Society encouraged "the Parliament to pick up the thread from Norway and let go of the fear of gender quotas. By now it has been acknowledged everywhere but Denmark that quotas are an efficient tool to regulate inequality."[23] Different associations of businesswomen were also active in the field: together with the network Women on their Way, Karrierekvinder.dk (Career Women) launched a database with female profiles for Danish company boards.[24] However there was no political pressure to improve the gender balance on the boards of private companies and no plans to introduce legislation in the field at the time.[25]

The liberal-conservative government started taking action in the field in the mid-2000s. Their initiatives were based on dialogue and networking with private companies and employer organisations, focusing on female board members as resources, the economic advantages of diversity at a management level, as well as recruitment benefits. The emphasis was clearly on initiatives and goals stemming from the companies themselves. In 2006, the Ministry of Gender Equality and the Confederation of Danish Industry (DI) held a camp for top level managers from large companies in order to produce ideas for new strategies and initiatives in the field, among them an ambassador corps of ten prominent business leaders working to get more women in management and on boards and to influence the public agenda in the field.

---

[20] Ritzaus Bureau, "Ledere ønsker flere kvinder," 6 July 1995.

[21] Ritzaus Bureau, "Andelen af danske kvinder i erhvervslivets top er i bund," 29 November 2004.

[22] Several studies were published in the mid 2000s showing the economic advantages of a more diverse leadership, among them "For the Benefit of the Bottom Line," commissioned by the Minister for Gender Equality in 2005.

[23] Dansk Kvindesamfund, "Kvinder skal lovgives ind i erhvervslivets bestyrelser," 10 April 2005.

[24] Dagbladet URBAN/Ritzaus Bureau, "Kvinder står i kø til bestyrelseslokalet," 8 March 2006.

[25] Information/Ritzaus Bureau, "De gamle hvide mænd," 22 January 2007.

In 2007 the DI launched the database Women on Board, aiming to support companies in finding female board members.

In 2008, the liberal-conservative government introduced a "Charter for More Women in Management" as a policy (not a law) in cooperation with the business sector. The Charter was based on voluntary processes and self-regulation to enhance the number of women in management positions through explicit strategies, goals, human resource policies and mentoring initiatives. No sanctions were included in the Charter and it was criticised for lack of visible results. In 2011, another voluntary measure followed to supplement the Charter, "Operation Chain Reaction on Recommendations for More Women on Boards": companies committed themselves to making targeted efforts in terms of recruitment based on the ideas of economic advantage, increased competencies, and the unexplored female talent pool. The action targeted shareholders in particular, emphasising the need to engage all levels of the recruitment process in order to produce results. Thus, some corporations have already adopted goals and strategies to improve the number of women on their boards, and some have adopted gender quotas voluntarily (Bloksgaard 2014).

In 2008 the Social Democrats followed in the footsteps of the Socialist People's Party by declaring their support for quotas in company boards. This decision was partly a matter of oppositional politics in the late 2000s as the issue had not been high on the Social Democrat agenda until then, provoking in this sense a Left/Right divide on the issue during these years. The liberals and the conservatives were against quotas, arguing that forcible measures should not be used and that companies themselves would know best what measures to be taken and which path to follow. The Social Democratic opposition criticised the voluntary measures of the liberal-conservative government and proposed, on several occasions, a 40 per cent quota for women on boards, inspired by EU initiatives and the Norwegian model (which has played an important role in contemporary debates about gender equality in economic decision-making in Denmark, as a role model for the Centre/Left, and as an example of the road not to take for the Centre/Right).

This support for gender quotas, formulated as gender equality on the boards of private and public corporations, was mentioned as one of the proposals in the 2011 Government Platform of the then newly elected social democratic-led government. However, the proposal was dropped in 2012 after resistance from the private sector: the major employer and business organisations – the DI, the DA, and the Confederation of Danish Enterprise – were not in favour of quotas on the grounds that competence should outweigh gender and that companies should maintain all management rights. The majority of the trade unions nevertheless supported quota measures.

The resistance from the business sector thus seems to have been the main reason why the social democratic government changed its position from mandatory to voluntary gender quotas and dropped the idea of gender quotas on boards, instead proposing a soft law without quotas. Another factor may have been lack of consensus among the three parties of the government coalition, with the Socialist People's Party supporting quotas, the Social Democrats tied up in internal disagreements on the issue, and the Social Liberal Party changing their stance.[26] This situation was combined with resistance against quotas from the general public, as mentioned above. In the parliamentary debate the liberals and the Danish People's Party furthermore speculated as to whether the government anticipated an EU intervention in the field, through the proposed directive, and therefore decided not to introduce unpopular binding quota measures themselves, waiting for the EU to do it through the backdoor.

In any case, the quota proposal of the social democratic-led government was replaced by a law which obliges the 1,100 largest public and private companies to set goals for gender equality on their boards and present policies to stimulate the participation of women in economic decision-making, including plans for recruitment in order to address the levels below top management. The model was based on input from the business sector as well as experiences from other countries. This law was adopted in the parliament in December 2012: it was labelled the "Danish model" and explicitly presented as an alternative to the binding measures of the Directive proposed by the European Commission. The law came into force on 1 April 2013 but its enforcement has been relatively weak.[27]

---

[26] Politiken, "S og SF er uenige om kvindekvoter," 24 April 2012.

[27] With reference to the alleged administrative burden, the current liberal government changed the legal guidelines in 2016 so that companies no longer need to determine new and more ambitious goals once they have reached their initial ones. DR, "Regeringen lemper regler for kvinder i bestyrelser," 7 March 2016.

It is illustrative of Danish political culture that the four centre/right oppositional parties voted against this law:[28] even though the centre/right-wing parties applauded the abandonment of the quota strategy, they still rejected the law, favouring voluntary measures and criticising the administrative and economic burden placed on companies. The strategies of the different political coalitions are largely the same when it comes to the measures proposed; the difference resides in whether companies are forced to implement them or can sign up voluntarily.

The law proposal for the Danish model was scheduled for hearing in June 2012, prior to the parliamentary debates. Only the employer's organisation, the Danish Construction Association, did not want to support the proposed law, due to the administrative burden and the possibility of an economic sanction for noncompliance. Several employer and business organisations (the Confederation of Danish Enterprise, the DI/Confederation of Danish Industry, the Danish Association of Managers and Executives and the Danish Agriculture and Food Council) as well as some companies and universities (Novo Nordisk, IT University and the Technical University of Denmark) expressed their satisfaction with the absence of quota measures in the proposal, citing their support for "talent/competences-before-gender," the companies' right to make their own management decisions, the voluntary character of the proposed measures and/or the need to adapt measures to the reality of each specific company. Several of them also agreed on the need to limit the administrative burden. The Danish Centre for Gender, Equality and Diversity (KVINFO), as well as several trade unions (the Danish Society of Engineers, the FTF/Confederation of Professionals in Denmark and the Danish Association of Lawyers and Economists), expressed positive views, considering the law proposal a "step in the right direction," although some explicitly stated that they would prefer quotas (HK/Union of Commercial and Clerical Employees),[29] and some emphasised the need for more guidance for companies (the LO/Danish Confederation of Trade Unions, the Financial Services Union Denmark and the Danish Institute for Human Rights). The two largest national women's organisations in Denmark, the Women's Council and the Danish Women's Society, agreed that the proposal was a good initiative but that they would both have preferred specific goals and

---

[28] See http://forside.kvinfo.dk/tema/kvinder-og-bestyrelser/danmark.
[29] The union covering the retail sector and administrative staff in both the public and the private sector.

doubted that the model proposed would have significant effect. They suggested that companies should have access to guidance, and that clear sanctions for noncompliance should be introduced, as should demands related to the quality of the tasks that companies are supposed to undertake and the level of ambition in terms of the goals to be defined by the companies. The Danish Women's Society proposed, as an alternative, restricting public contracts only to companies with a balanced gender representation on boards, following the Spanish model.

During the first parliamentary debate on the proposed law, in October 2012, the divide between the social democrat-headed government and the centre/right-wing opposition was clearly marked by the different framings of "intervention" vs. "voluntary measures" (normatively and as a way to enhance the active participation of companies). The spokeswoman for the Liberal Party, Fatma Øktem, criticised the "administrative burden" and "massive bureaucracy" imposed by the law proposal and argued for qualifications before gender.[30] Øktem furthermore argued for additional measures, such as tax deductions for services like private child care and house cleaning, in order to enhance the structural possibilities for women to take up top management positions (in order to "ease the burden for families where the woman *also* wants a top-level position," our italics).[31] The spokeswoman for the Liberal Alliance, also in opposition, Merete Riisager, argued for women's right to choose the life that they want and women's capacity to become top-level mangers "if that's what they want."[32]

Thus the problem is depicted as having three dimensions: women (freedom of choice and their potential lack of ambition), companies (patterns of recruitment) and structures (possibilities in terms of leave, child care, and responsibilities in the household). Only the Red-Green Alliance (far Left) framed a democratic argument, which referred to the importance of having equal representation within the powerful sphere of top management where decisions affecting all citizens are made. This argument was subsequently supported by the Minister of Gender Equality during the debate.

---

[30] Parliamentary debate on law proposal L2 on amendments to the Act on equality between men and women, as well as on law proposal L17 on amendments to the companies Act, 23 October 2012.

[31] Ibid.

[32] Ibid.

The proposal was criticised for being overly bureaucratic, mainly due to the fact that even a 0 per cent goal for female participation in boards would be accepted within the framework of the legal measure. Thus the exercise would potentially be purely symbolic, since a company could set a goal aiming for no female participation whatsoever and still comply with the new measure legally. The governing parties, however, argued that the measure was also a means of spreading information (on company policy and awareness of gender equality) and that "nobody is that unambitious" nor willing to publicly state that they are uninterested in gender equality.[33]

The debate still revolved largely around free choice vs. force and intervention, to such an extent that the spokesman for the Social Democrats, Rasmus Horn Langhoff, claimed that "inflation has somehow hit the word 'force.' Every time someone wants something, every time someone proposes something, every time someone makes some kind of political statement, it is like you are accused of it being force, that it is horrible: 'Oh, how terrible! For God's sake, don't do anything,' everything will somehow happen by itself."[34] His expression of frustration to some extent reflects the general discourse, wherein quotas have almost become a taboo (when discussing actual implementation) and are always met with strong resistance. During the debate, the idea of force was articulated both in relation to women (i.e. not forcing them to become leaders against their wishes and preserving their free choice) and companies (i.e. not forcing them to recruit women against their will and protecting their preferences for qualifications over gender).

Feminist civil society mobilisation on the issue has, in general, not been very visible. A few well-known businesswomen have argued in favour of quotas, based on their own experiences in the field. The Women's Council and the Danish Women's Society both identify equal representation in the economic sphere as one of the key issues in their work. They have a clear stance on the topic, favouring gender quotas as an efficient measure towards equality.[35] However, they have no significant visibility in the public debate on this issue: they have made few press releases over the years – compared to other issues – and run no major campaigns, compared to the ones on political representation (encouraging people to vote for female candidates), for example.

---

[33] Ibid.
[34] Ibid.
[35] See www.danskkvindesamfund.dk/maerkesager/kvinders-repraesentation.html.

The relative importance of gender quotas on company boards, compared to other gender issues like equal pay, parental leave policies, violence against women, or prostitution and trafficking, is thus considered to be low in civil society mobilisation and among the women's movements. Regarding quotas in the political sphere, for instance, they undertook lobbying efforts through hearings (which could be considered a better channel for action than widespread campaigns). Nevertheless, the women's organisations have not been the main partners in dialogue as successive governments have developed initiatives in the field. As described above, professional women's associations and in particular business organisations have been much more influential. Another dimension to the lack of mobilisation in the field could be the perceived relative importance of the issue compared to other gender inequality problems. Already in 2006, Pernille Rosenkrantz-Theil (formerly of the Red-Green Alliance) was arguing that she found it paradoxical that a class-conscious party like the Social Democrats would be more concerned with getting more women on boards than with unequal pay or female unemployment. This argumentation however is not typically found in statements from the women's organisations,[36] although it may affect their priorities.

In conclusion, the resistance against gender quotas in the economic arena primarily came from the liberal opposition, but private corporations played a key role as well. While most parties agreed on the need to make use of all resources and talents, and the potential for enhanced competitiveness as a consequence of greater gender balance, the business sector claimed that the proposal for public regulation of industry was an excessive legal intervention into "the right as employers to decide." In spite of this resistance, both the Liberal Party and the Social Democrats prioritised cooperation and dialogue with the business sector: either by making the measures voluntary and respecting the companies' right to decide for themselves in the phase of implementation (in the case of the former liberal-conservative government); or in the process of preparing the proposed law, which resulted in obligatory measures that were, nevertheless, softer than quotas and therefore more

---

[36] In fact in 2009, Randi Theil Nielsen, chairwoman of the Women's Council, argued against the former Minister for Gender Equality, Inger Støjberg of the Liberal Party, when she said that "gender equality in migrant families is more important than gender quota on boards." Ritzaus Bureau, "Minister: Indvandrerkvinder største problem," 10 October 2009.

acceptable to companies. In 2012, the Minister for Gender Equality at the time, the social-liberal Manu Sareen, argued that through the political debate around the Danish model we "have found the limit at quotas. We have been to the other EU countries and seen what they do, and the committee made a trip to Norway to see what is being done there, and we have found – at least the government has found, and I know that we agree – that the line must be drawn at quotas."[37]

13.4 CONCLUSION

The Danish case raises analytical, theoretical and normative questions about gender quotas as a means to create gender equality. The high representation of women in Danish politics without gender quotas challenges existing typologies and questions whether one size fits all. In the Nordic countries, gender equality has become the general norm while gender quotas have not been the main factor explaining patterns of women's representation (Freidenvall, Dahlerup and Skjeie 2006). The Danish approach to gender equality presents an exception to the general trend towards adoption of gender quotas to increase gender balance and achieve gender equality in the political and economic are-nas (Krook 2007). Gender quotas have generally been controversial in relation to electoral quotas and in party politics, as well as in relation to the labour market and public committees. Gender equality is supported by the main political actors on the Left and Right, including the pop-ulist right-wing Danish People's Party, but there is disagreement about the meaning of gender equality, as well as the means to achieve it.

The electoral quotas adopted by the Social Democrats and the Socialist People's Party between 1986 and 1996 thus present an excep-tion to the general trend, which is explained by the mobilisation of women within the two parties at that time. This case illustrates that Denmark does not fit Krook's (2016) typology of resistance either, since the opposition against gender quotas was in part presented by young women in the Socialist People's Party. Since 1996 there has been consensus on using the voluntary approach to achieve gender equality in politics.

---

[37] Parliamentary debate on law proposal L2 on amendments to the Act on equality between men and women, as well as on law proposal L17 on amendments to the companies Act, 23 October 2012.

The "Charter for More Women in Management" adopted by the liberal-conservative government in 2008 was premised on a voluntary approach, while the Centre/Left opposition proposed a 40 per cent quota for women on boards. When the Centre/Left came to power again in 2011, it adopted a law but without mandatory gender quotas. In this case the resistance against gender quotas came from both the liberal opposition and private companies.

In the Danish context, gender balance in economic life is still contested. It is noteworthy that the success of the voluntary Danish approach until recently has mainly been in relation to political representation, and scholars have questioned whether it is possible to increase women's representation in the economy without gender quotas. Arguably, there is a growing tendency among citizens to regard gender balance in corporations as a democratic issue and among corporations to go beyond the voluntary Danish model introduced by the previous Red-Green government and to introduce measures themselves, possibly to pre-empt or avoid political regulation or new legal gender quotas. It is possible to identify the beginning of a norm shift in this regard, making gender inequality illegitimate. This trend may result in a decentralised, fragmented and unfair or unequal gender model in economic decision-making, which leaves measures to corporations. This model resembles the Danish approach to parental leave, which depends on the willingness of corporations and the strength of unions.

According to Nancy Fraser, a global transformation of the economy is ongoing and markets tend to be dis-embedded from democracy and society (2013, 230). From this perspective, the current problems with political and economic governance, democracy and social justice also represent opportunities to put gender equality on the agenda in relation to participation and representation in political and economic fora, not only at the national but also at the transnational level.

References

Bacchi, Carol. 2006. "Arguing for and Against Quotas. Theoretical Issues." In *Women, Quotas and Politics*, edited by Drude Dahlerup, 32–51. London: Routledge.

Bergqvist, Christina, Anette Borchorst, Ann-Dorte Christensen, Viveca Ramstedt Silén, Nina C. Raum, and Audur Styrkásdóttir, eds. 1999. *Equal Democracies: Gender and Politics in the Nordic Countries*. Oslo: Scandinavian University Press.

Bloksgaard, Lotte. 2014. "Negotiating Leave in Workplace: Leave Practices and Masculinity Constructions among Danish Fathers." In *Fatherhood in the Nordic Welfare States. Comparing Care Policies and Practice*, edited by Guöný Björk Eydal and Tine Rostgaard, 141–61. Bristol: Policy Press.

Borchorst, Anette. 1999. "Gender equality law." In *Equal Democracies: Gender and Politics in the Nordic Countries*, edited by Christina Bergqvist, Anette Borchorst, Ann-Dorte Christensen, Viveca Ramstedt Silén, Nina C. Raum, and Audur Styrkásdóttir, 190–207. Oslo: Scandinavian University Press.

Borchorst, Anette, and Ann-Dorte Christensen. 2003. "Kønskvotering i SF og i forskerstillinger – diskursiv praksis og forandring" [Gender Quotas in the Socialist People's Party and in research positions]. In *Ligestillingspolitik som diskurs og praksis*, edited by Anette Borchorst and Drude Dahlerup, 101–23. Frederiksberg: Forlaget Samfundslitteratur.

Borchorst, Anette, Ann-Dorte Christensen, and Nina Raum. 1999. "Equal Democracies. Conclusions and Perspectives." In *Equal Democracies: Gender and Politics in the Nordic Countries*, edited by Christina Bergqvist, Anette Borchorst, Ann-Dorte Christensen, Viveca Ramstedt Silén, Nina C. Raum and Audur Styrkásdóttir, 277–91. Oslo: Scandinavian University Press.

Borchorst, Anette, and Drude Dahlerup. 2003. *Ligestillingspolitik som diskurs og praksis [Gender Equality Policies as Discourse and Praxis]*. Frederiksberg: Forlaget Samfundslitteratur.

Borchorst, Anette, and Lenita Freidenvall. 2012. "Parental Leave in Denmark and Sweden: Similar and Different." In *Comparisons, Quotas and Critical Change: In Honor of Drude Dahlerup*, edited by Lenita Freidenvall and Michele Micheletti, 38–50. Stockholm: Stockholm University Department of Political Science.

Borchorst, Anette, and Lise Rolandsen Agustín. 2015. "Judicialization and Europeanization: The Danish Equal Pay Case." Unpublished paper.

Borchorst, Anette, and Birte Siim. 2002. "The Women-Friendly Welfare State Revisited." *NORA. The Nordic Journal of Women's Studies* 10 (2): 90–8.

——— 2008. "The Women-Friendly Policies and State Feminism: Theorizing Scandinavian Gender Equality." *Feminist Theory* 9 (2): 207–24.

Christensen, Ann-Dorte. 1999. "Women in Political Parties." In *Equal Democracies. Gender and Politics in the Nordic Countries*, edited by Christina Bergqvist, Anette Borchorst, Ann-Dorte Christensen, Viveca Ramstedt Silén, Nina C. Raum and Audur Styrkásdóttir, 65–87. Oslo: Scandinavian University Press.

Christensen, Ann-Dorte, and Poul Damkjær Knopp. 1998. *Kvinder og politisk repræsentation i Danmark* [Women and Political Representation in Denmark]. GEP's Working Paper 7, Aalborg Universitet, Aalborg. Available at: http://vbn.aau.dk/files/48901621/GEP_Tekstserie_No7.pdf.

Christensen, Ann-Dorte, and Birte Siim. 2001. *Køn, demokrati og modernitet. Mod nye politiske identiteter [Gender, Democracy and Modernity. Towards New Political Identities]*. Copenhagen: Hans Reitzels Forlag.

Christiansen, Peter, Birgit Møller, and Lise Togeby. 2002. "Køn og eliter" [Gender and Elites]. In *Kønsmagt under forandring*, edited by Anette Borchorst, 72–91. Copenhagen: Hans Reitzels Forlag.

Dahlerup, Drude. 2002. "Er ligestillingen opnået? Ligestillingsdebattens forskellighed I Danmark og Sverige." [Has Gender Equality been Achieved? Variations in the Gender Equality Debate in Denmark and Sweden]. In *Kønsmagt under Forandring*, edited by Anette Borchorst, 226–46. Copenhagen: Hans Reitzels Forlag.

———. 2013. "Denmark: High Representation of Women without Gender Quota." In *Breaking Male Dominance in Democracies*, edited by Drude Dahlerup and Monique Leyenaar. Oxford: Oxford University Press.

———, ed. 2006. *Women, Quotas and Politics*, Abindon: Routledge.

Fiig, Christina, and Birte Siim. 2012. "Democratization of Denmark. The Political Inclusion of Women." In *The Struggle for Female Suffrage in Europe. Voting to Become Citizens*, edited by Blanca Rodriquez Ruiz and Ruth Rubio-Marín, 61–77. Leiden: Brill.

Fraser, Nancy. 2013. *Fortunes of Feminism: From State-Managed Capitalism to Neoliberal Crisis*. London: Verso.

Freidenvall, Lenita, Drude Dahlerup, and Hege Skjeie. 2006. "The Nordic Countries an Incremental Model." In *Women, Quotas and Politics*, edited by Drude Dahlerup, 55–82. London: Routledge.

Hernes, Helga Maria. 1987. *Welfare State and Woman Power: Essays in State Feminism*. Oslo: Norwegian University Press.

Krook, Mona Lena. 2007. "Candidate Gender Quotas: A Framework for Analysis." *European Journal of Political Research* 46: 367–94.

———. 2016. "Contesting Gender Quotas: Dynamics of Resistance." *Politics, Groups and Identities* 4 (2): 268–84.

Meret, Susi, and Birte Siim. 2013. "Gender, Populism and Politics of Belonging. Discourses of Right-Wing Populist Parties in Denmark, Norway and Austria." In *Negotiating Gender and Diversity in an Emergent European Public Sphere*, edited by Birte Siim and Monika Mokre, 78–96. London: Palgrave/Macmillan.

———. 2017. "Men's Parties with Women Leaders: A Comparative Study of the Rightwing Populist Leaders Pia Kjaersgaard, Marine Le Pen and Siv Jensen." In *Understanding the Populist Shift*, edited by G. Lazaridis, A. Benveniste, and G. Campani. London: Routledge.

Ministry for Gender Equality. 2014. *Redegørelse/Perspektiv- og handlingsplan 2014*. Copenhagen: Ministry for Gender Equality.

Siim, Birte. 2000. *Gender and Citizenship. Politics and Agency in France, Britain and Denmark*. Singapore: Cambridge University Press.

Siim, Birte, and Pauline Stoltz. 2015. "Particularities of the Nordic: Challenges to Equality Politics in a Globalized World." In *Remapping Gender, Place and Mobility: Global Confluences and Local Particularities in Nordic Peripheries*, edited by Stine Thidemann Faber and Helene Pristed Nielsen, 19–34. London: Routledge.

Statistics Denmark. 2015. *Kvinder og mænd i 100 år – fra lige valgret mod ligestilling.* Copenhagen: Statistics Denmark.

Teigen, Mari. 2000. "The Affirmative Action Controversy." *Nordic Journal of Feminist and Gender Research* 8 (2): 63–77.

CONCLUSION

Assessing the Transformative Potential of Gender Quotas for Gender Equality and Democratic Citizenship

Éléonore Lépinard and Ruth Rubio-Marín

Drawing on the richness of these thirteen cases, our European comparison sheds new light on three important phenomena reshaping women's political inclusion in Europe that we explore in this concluding chapter. First, our comparative investigation helps us delineate patterns of both resistance and adoption among countries as the domains of quotas spread, bringing new insights on the transformative potential of gender quotas in different contexts. In particular, our case studies show in which contexts gender quotas can contribute to erode the public/private divide and reconfigure women's citizenship and conceptions of gender equality, and in which contexts their scope is likely to remain more limited. In order to tease out these differences and explore these dynamic patterns of quota reform, still in the making for most of our case studies, we identify four ideal-type scenarios for gender quota adoption, rejection, and diffusion, suggesting different degrees of transformative potential. For each group of countries, we identify outliers and tease out internal differences. Similarly, we acknowledge the possibility that some of the cases may be currently transitioning from correction or symbolism to transformation (Germany and Italy) or experiencing a slowing down in the agenda with as of yet unclear consequences in terms of typology fit (Spain).

Second, studying the various campaigns for gender quotas in comparative perspective offers a productive site to explore the elaboration of new discourses around gender equality and their translation in the legal realm, given the high juridification of the struggle in most of the countries covered. Third, the various struggles for gender quotas across Europe since the 1970s offer an exceptional opportunity to assess the reconfiguration of women's movements after the second wave of feminism, and in particular to address whether the struggle for gender quotas has become an unexpected heritage of the radical years of the second wave, which spurred new alliances with institutional actors at the national and supranational levels, original cross-party mobilization, and the development of new forms of feminist action. Finally, this broad comparison allows us to assess gender quotas' transformative potential – and its limits – for gender equality and democratic citizenship in Europe.

C.1 UNDERSTANDING THE ADOPTION AND DOMAIN DIFFUSION OF GENDER QUOTAS IN EUROPE: A NEW TYPOLOGY

Regarding those Nordic countries where quotas have been applied, Anne-Maria Holli describes a sequence of adoption/diffusion which a first generation of legislated electoral quotas (LEQs) is followed by Public Bodies Quotas (PBQs) and then Corporate Board Quotas (CBQs) (Holli 2011). However, our cases show that this sequence cannot be generalized across Europe. Indeed, the timing and sequencing of quotas differ greatly across our case studies. While in some countries such as Spain, France, or Slovenia voluntary party quotas – and their persistent inefficiency – led to the adoption of legislated electoral quotas (LEQs); in countries such as Norway, Sweden, and Denmark, the relative effec-tiveness of party quotas made claims for LEQs less legitimate and, finally, unsuccessful. In Denmark, party quotas were even abandoned in the mid-1990s precisely at the time when other European countries were picking up gender quotas for electoral politics. Moreover, some of the countries that did not adopt LEQs were among the first to adopt PBQs and CBQs, starting in the early 1990s, although this was not a general rule. Thus, while Norway invested as early as 1981 in compulsory affirm-ative action to raise the numbers of women in public service decision-making, Denmark and Sweden did not. Other countries like Belgium and Greece started to experiment with public bodies quotas relatively early on, at the beginning of the 1990s, at a time when Italy was passing its first electoral gender quota law, soon to be declared unconstitutional.

These variations across countries in timing and sequencing, as well as in the preferred domains of quota implementation, suggest that the gender quota revolution unfolds differently in different scenarios. We claim that these scenarios, determined by the way quota reform is discussed, contested, adopted, or rejected in the three domains where

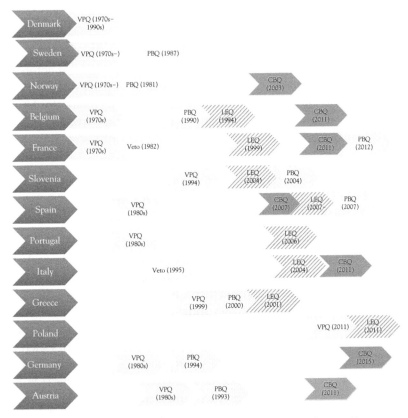

Figure C.1 Sequence of adoption of gender quota mechanisms in thirteen European countries
VPQ: Voluntary party quotas (period of adoption)
PBQ: Public bodies quotas (year of first adoption)
LEQ: Legislated electoral quotas (year of first adoption of law that has not been constitutionally nullified)
CBQ: Corporate board quotas (year of first adoption)
Veto: Constitutional decisions nullifying previous LEQs

quotas have so far been mostly applied, reveal the extent to which gen-der quotas might successfully challenge a country's prevalent gender regime. From the sequence chart described in Figure C.1, we identify four groups of countries, each following a different historical trajectory when it comes to adopting – or rejecting – gender quotas in the three domains. Studies on other countries might expand the number of paths that the quota revolution can take and further enhance and nuance our understanding of the irresistible rise of gender quotas by capturing other dynamic processes that characterize the adoption and diffusion of gender quotas within a country. Ours is an inductive typology, which does not aim to be empirically exhaustive, but rather tries to define the contours of different patterns explaining the scope of gender quotas adoption, the resistance they meet with, and their eventual ability to transform a country's gender regime. The first of the four identified scenarios includes Denmark, Sweden, and Norway. It is characterized by a relative paucity of quota schemes despite an early interest in the question of gender equality in decision-making, attested by the early presence of voluntary party quotas. These countries, especially Denmark and Sweden, illustrate, to various degrees, what we call the *gender quotas as accessory equality measures* scenario – that is, a reluctance to use quotas in the context of a public gender regime where trust is placed in bottom-up processes that spontaneously express already-existing commitments to gender equality. In some cases, like Sweden, these quotas are accessory measures, called "high echelon quotas" to ensure that women's presence does not *decrease*: they act as lower threshold rather than as ambitious goals (Dahlerup and Freidenvall 2005).

The second group includes France, Belgium, Slovenia, and Spain, which are countries characterized by mixed gender regimes with relatively high participation of women in the labor market, but low presence in politics up until the end of the 1990s. Here the quota revolution is unfolding, however at different paces and with different outcomes, and is often linked to the broader of making the democratic system more inclusive and/or disestablishing traditional gender roles. In all these countries, a sequence of diffusion of quotas is shown moving to spheres other than politics, and gender quotas are developed as part of a *transformative equality remedies* strategy.

A third group comprises countries such as Italy, Greece, Portugal, and Poland; countries sharing a mixed or conservative domestic gender regime in which the adoption of gender quota schemes was often particularly protracted, and which continue to display important sites of resistance by male incumbents to the potential for gender regime change brought by quotas. In this group, quotas can be better described as *symbolic equality remedies*, with the possible exception of Italy, which may be fast progressing towards the transformative model in the last few years. Finally, a last group includes Germany and Austria, countries also sharing features of conservative domestic gender regimes but which, contrary to the previous group, adopted PBQs early on, thus confirming their early commitment to substantive gender equality in the employment domain and, at the same time, conditioning the

427

chances of successful domain diffusion, with some domains, such as those of representative or elected positions, turning out to be more impenetrable than others, such as corporate governance. In these countries the early development of gender quota policies has so far not brought about the expected gains for women, and gender quotas remain *corrective equality remedies*.

C.1.1   Gender Quotas as Accessory Equality Measures

Gender quotas in general have, maybe paradoxically, been only weakly endorsed in Nordic countries – and in the case of Denmark strongly rejected. These countries are characterized by a public gender regime based on a dual-breadwinner welfare state and are committed to strong egalitarian values and participatory citizenship. Sweden, Norway, and Denmark in particular have all rejected LEQs, while officially embracing gender equality and women's participation in politics under the pressure of the second wave feminist movement – in fact these countries were among the first to adopt what turned out to be rather successful voluntary party quotas. In these countries with relatively high numbers of women in political representation as early as the 1980s, the debate on women's equal representation and the adoption of voluntary party quotas largely preceded both the international momentum around the Beijing Platform for Action and the European initiatives in this domain, both converging in the mid-1990s. In Sweden, Norway or Denmark, debates about women's political participation and gender quotas revolved around gender equality and equal participation without relying on concepts such as parity democracy or parity governance. Instead, local idioms played an important role, strong traditions of participatory citizenship providing room to claim an equal share of power by women. This is exemplified by the Swedish motto inspired by ancient practices of rural dancing, *Varannan Damernas*: for every other dance the women are the ones to choose their partner; meaning equal participation by turns (Freidenvall 2006, 2013). In other words, in those countries, the legitimacy of the need to share power equally was already rooted in a strong egalitarian political and civil culture, and legislated, as opposed to voluntary, quotas have been perceived as defeating the trust in a bottom-up and consensual democratic tradition over a rights-based, top-down imposition of a purportedly deeper form of democracy.

In fact, the three countries fare very high in terms of women's representation in politics, with Sweden being the first European country in the world ranking with 43.6 percent women MPs (2014), followed by Norway with 39.6 percent (2013), and Denmark at 37.4 percent (2015), meaning that the political elite is not male-dominated anymore. Although they all attach less overall relevance to a rights framework in their majoritarian democratic self-understanding (something which accounts for the relatively low juridification of the quota debate), the three countries still show some variation in the ways in which the notion of substantive gender equality has been legally enshrined and foregrounded in the mobilization of women's rights organizations for gender quotas as well as in Women's Policy Agencies' (WPAs) interest in pushing for quota legislation. These variations explain how, while Sweden and Denmark have so far resisted all forms of legislated quotas, Norway has adopted both PBQ and CBQ.

In Denmark, as Lise Rolandsen Agustín, Birte Siim, and Anette Borchorst detail in their chapter, while women's participation in the labor market is among the highest in Europe, and while political parity (40/60) was reached early on during the 1990s, gender equality is not inscribed in the Constitution, which is old and difficult to amend. Equal rights legislative framings have also failed to come to the foreground despite European influence, and even the EC Equal Treatment Directive from 1976, which legitimized some forms of affirmative action and quotas in the employment domain, was implemented in a weak and restricted way, giving social partners considerable scope to define the parameters of their actions. Voluntary party quotas were adopted for a limited time, until the mid-1990s, and only by two political parties, and the only measure for public bodies consists in a soft rule by which at least one woman and one man should be among the candidates for publicly nominated positions. Moreover, the women's movement has not been very much interested in the gender quota agenda, be it for politics or for corporate boards. Only longstanding organizations such as the Danish Women's Society have advocated for quotas in politics for a while. Contrastingly the younger generation rejects altogether this approach, and the femocrats have not lobbied in this direction either. Indeed, Denmark remains a country that prides itself on refusing gender quotas in the name of its particular understanding of gender equality.

Contrastingly, Mari Teigen shows that in Norway, despite a similar discourse and resistance to gender quotas in the name of a participatory articulation of gender equality, PBQs, and later on CBQs, were put in place under the impetus of a strong gender equality bureaucratic machinery, and as a logical development of the country's commitment to substantive gender equality enshrined into law as early as 1981.

Sweden presents a middle road between these two countries. While the Swedish Constitution (Instrument of Government) enshrined substantive gender equality allowing for affirmative action in 1976 and gender balance, understood as a distribution between 40 and 60 percent of both sexes, has been an outspoken goal of the government since the adoption of the Gender Equality Act in 1979, the general understanding is that this goal is to be reached voluntarily by political parties and institutional actors, as Lenita Freidenvall shows in her chapter. Peculiar to this group of countries is the fact that, while few gender quotas have been adopted, they have been often debated, and each time the threat of a legislated quota has served to force social partners (political parties or corporate boards) to self-regulate and reach gender equality voluntarily. In summary, while the rejection of legislated quotas in the name of the goal of gender equality has overall prevailed – in favor of reaching that goal through consensus and voluntary participation – this has sometimes been overturned by top-down policies involving WPAs and key actors reacting against the slowness of the spontaneous process, but never pressed for by bottom-up mobilization.

C.1.2   Gender Quotas As Transformative Equality Remedies
This path characterizes a set of countries epitomized by Belgium and France, but arguably encompassing also Slovenia and Spain. What characterizes gender quota adoption in this group is that gender quotas are primarily perceived as tools to transform the gender regime in a fundamental way and, in some instances, the country's overall understanding of democratic legitimacy. As a shared point of departure, these five countries are characterized by a mixed gender regime, in which women's participation in the labor market is high, a dual breadwinner model is generally promoted by social policies, but women's participation in politics has been historically low,[1] political parties, mostly on the Left, having proven reluctant to actually implement the voluntary quotas they adopted under the pressure of a minority of feminists within their structures. Spain is a relative outlier, because its gender regime is more conservative and women's exclusion from the political

---

[1] For a detailed description of the Spanish mixed gender regime, see Lombardo (forthcoming). In the case of France, Birte Siim (2000) has characterized this combination of gender friendly social policy and political exclusion of women as a republican citizenship model.

sphere was not so blatant, and because, while the gender quotas revolution was embraced by Zapatero's left-wing government, recent austerity politics are threatening the transformative potential of gender quotas (Lombardo 2017). However, given the scope of its quota reforms, Spain remains part of this group that intentionally uses gender quotas to transform important features of the country's gender regime, democracy, and/or citizenship.

In these countries, the entrenched resistance from the political elites to including women has often been articulated through a rights discourse and a constitutional narrative, putting the emphasis both on formal sex equality and on the autonomy of political parties – the latter discourse proving to be especially appealing in Slovenia given the connection drawn between the former communist regime and quotas. In all except for Spain (where a constitutionally conformist interpretation of the challenged legislation proved sufficient), a process of constitutional reform has accompanied the adoption of quotas, entrenching substantive conceptions of gender equality as a result. To overcome the resistance from male elites in these five countries, we find women organizing inside but also significantly outside political parties, eventually forging cross-partisan alliances using the gender-balanced participation and parity democracy discourses to promote women's inclusion in electoral politics through LEQs and to challenge, most clearly in France, the democratic legitimacy of overwhelmingly male sites of power. These mobilizations were backed up by relatively strong WPAs that lobbied as insiders in the government, sometimes allowing the women leading them to step outside their party lines and facilitate cross-party alliances.

In these four countries, gender quotas were therefore adopted in the context of a project of democratic transformation or renewal and/or as part of a more comprehensive challenge to the gender order. The former is most clearly epitomized by France's transition from a unitary, Republican, universalist model to a parity democracy model, and by Slovenia's embracing of "modern" democracy in the context of EU accession. As for the latter, it is revealing that in two of the countries concerned, France and Spain, gender quotas were included to some extent in broader equality legislation seeking to disestablish gender roles both in the public and in the private sphere.[2] European incentives

---

[2] Spain's organic law on the Real Equality of Women and Men (Organic Law 3/2007, March 22, 2007), which was responsible for introducing for the first time the principle

as well as gender balance representation and parity democracy rhetoric were of particular import in these four countries.

Sharing a mixed gender regime, the adoption of LEQs in these countries came to challenge the exclusion of women from the sphere of institutional politics. The demands for guaranteeing women's access to political decision-making were all the more successful because, in these countries, women had for a long time been part of the workforce, gender equality policies and WPAs existed to support women's participation in the labor market, and women's movements from the 1970s onwards had created abeyance structures that could be, in part, remobilized for the gender quota campaigns. The extent of the transformation of the gender regime that gender quotas have enabled remains of course to be assessed – most of their quota schemes are less than a decade old – however, numbers speak clearly in the realm of democratic representation, with women now comprising high percentages of the lower chambers of these countries, with 39.3 percent in Belgium (2014),[3] 39.1 percent in Spain (2016), 36.7 percent in Slovenia (2014), and 38.8 percent in France (2017).

Once LEQs were adopted, other forms of gender quotas followed suit in a more top-down fashion. Indeed, in this group of countries the diffusion of quotas to other domains is in full swing, showing that, when framed as a remedy to the lack of legitimacy of governance structures and as a tool to design a new overall model of gender relations, the reach of the quota revolution is potentially wider than when framed only as a zero-sum game concerning women's (versus men's) rights and opportunities. Indeed, all four countries have adopted forms of PBQs. Belgium and France have adopted strong CBQs, while Spain, where the parity democracy project has been significantly stalled since the arrival of the conservatives to power in 2011, adopted a soft CBQ with no sanction (under the last socialist regime) that has ultimately

of gender-balanced representation into the Spanish legal order, incorporated measures to facilitate both the reconciliation of work, personal, and family lives and the joint responsibility for domestic tasks and family caretaking. Also, France's Title I of the Comprehensive Gender Equality Statute seeking "professional equality between men and women" contains provisions that lengthen paternity leaves and incentivize fathers to take them.

[3] Spain is the highest non-Nordic European country in the world ranking of women's presence in national parliaments, see "Les femmes dans les parlements nationaux," Union Interparlementaire, available at: www.ipu.org/wmn-f/classif.htm, accessed April 12, 2018.

been abandoned in favor of non-coercive codes of conduct. CBQs are now under discussion in Slovenia. Belgium, France, and Spain have also adopted quotas or gender-balance targets for university decision-making bodies; Belgium for the High Council of Justice and Unions, and France for sports federations, and chambers of agriculture, industry, and commerce. Additionally, although there is significant variation of quota thresholds among both countries and domains, the evolution in time clearly points to the higher goal of equal representation of each sex (as opposed to the minimal representation of the underrepresented sex, i.e. women). This strong dynamic of diffusion suggests that the parity and gender-balanced representation rhetoric – and associated goals, which can be framed in gender neutral terms – can be exported easily to other spheres of decision-making traditionally dominated by men, thus enhancing the transformative potential of gender quotas.

C.1.3   Gender Quotas As Symbolic Equality Remedies

Looking at our set of countries, it appears that, surprisingly, quotas are also likely to be adopted in countries with traditional conservative gender regimes, that is, those which tend to consider women as mothers in charge of social reproduction and hence insist on the separate (and gendered) spheres tradition. However, two groups of conservative countries should be distinguished. The first group comprises Italy, Greece, Portugal, and Poland, four countries that have adopted LEQs but only embraced these policies half-heartedly, which has led quotas to perform a role that is more symbolic than anything else[4] (though this seems to be changing now in Italy and to some extent in Portugal). By symbolic here we mean that while the discourse on gender balance in decision-making or parity democracy might have been adopted, it does not translate into policies that aim at anything that comes close to a 50/50 balance or at transforming conservative gender relations. Cosmetic laws are adopted that water down the promise of equality and do not prevent male-dominated politics as usual.

The four countries in this group share a conservative and domestic gender regime, which tends to assign women to the private sphere, unpaid care work, and the informal economy. In these countries women's participation in the labor market has traditionally been significantly lower than men's participation. And while the historical

---

[4] For a definition of "symbolic reform" as applied to gender equality policies, see Mazur (1996).

433

reasons for the institutionalization and stabilization of this regime differ in each country, the entrenched conservatism with regards to gender roles has not been efficiently challenged by sufficiently strong and cohesive women's movements. Portugal is a bit of an outlier here, with a higher participation of women in the job market. However, this participation is still very much predicated upon a traditional vision of gender roles that is only beginning to be dismantled by pragmatic social policies, and it is vulnerable to setbacks due to austerity policies (Ferreira 2014). While bureaucratic structures in charge of women's rights do exist in the four countries, they too are rather weak so that their ability to advance women's rights is strongly correlated with the government in power. What is striking in these countries is the level of resistance that claims for gender quotas have been met with, including in constitutional terms. Indeed, while resistance exists in all countries where demands for gender quotas are made, the obvious lack of political will from the majority of the male political elites – with only some individual exceptions – in Portugal and Italy, and the very active resistance of these elites in Greece and Poland, have efficiently stalled the process of quota adoption and diffusion and/or limited the ambition of the gender quota reforms. In this group, quotas establish only minimum thresholds that never surpass 35 percent, even though in all of these countries, except Poland, the Constitution was amended to enshrine substantive equality, mainly to allow for the adoption of gender quotas. This lower threshold for female candidates generally means lower numbers of elected women, except for Portugal, which now has 34.8-percent women in its legislative chamber (2015). Contrary to the countries in the previous group, in these four countries, strong resistance from the male-dominated political elite was not initially, nor for a long time afterwards, counterbalanced by sufficiently powerful and united women's movements or by strong and independent WPAs. As a matter of fact, for a long time in these four countries political parties effectively resisted even the adoption of voluntary party quotas (VPQ): in Portugal only the Socialist party adopted a VPQ with a low threshold (25 percent in 1988), and in Greece the PASOK and the New Democracy Party adopted VPQs that were both weak (between 20 and 30 percent) and quite late (1994 and 1999) compared to their European neighbors. Even more laggard, the Italian Democratic Party adopted a VPQ only in 2008, and in Poland some left-leaning parties opted for a 30-percent voluntary quota in 2011.

While actors fighting for LEQs tried to use the European discourses and soft laws in favor of gender-balance in decision-making, their impact was in fact limited. In Portugal, Italy and, to a lesser extent, in Greece, the term parity was finally adopted but, interestingly, has been interpreted as satisfied by 33-percent rather than 50-percent women in decision-making bodies. This watering-down of the European discourse on parity democracy suggests active resistance on the part of power holders. As Dia Anagnostou details, for Greece, while the EU jurisprudence was crucial in enabling a – very limited – form of PBQs in the 1990s, and in opening the door to a more substantive redefinition of gender equality through constitutional revision in 2001, the European narrative on parity democracy was not picked up in the public debate – despite earlier efforts from feminist legal scholars – until the end of the 2000s. In Poland, it finally took a renaissance of women's mobilization and a bill proposed by citizens to circumvent the sustained hostility of male parliamentarians to adopting a quota, and Polish MPs nevertheless managed to decrease the threshold from the initially proposed 50 percent to 35 percent during the legislative process. In Italy, the divisions inside the women's movements meant that only femocrats and key female politicians were in a position to push for gender quota adoption, in a top-down fashion.

In none of these countries do we find diffusion of gender quotas beyond the electoral realm, except for Italy, which adopted corporate board quotas in 2011 and might be gradually transitioning towards the previous typology, i.e. towards a transformative scenario. Even then, the adoption of CBQs in Italy was, as Alessia Donà retraces in her chapter, the result of a right-wing discourse on the *fattore donna*, praising diversity, merging economic efficiency and individual entrepreneurial liberalism with only some hints at gender equality, in the context of a severe economic downturn. In other words, the Italian adoption of CBQs reflects an instrumentalization of gender equality discourse in favor of economic interests rather than the legitimation of gender quotas as a means to challenge power structures that exclude women from decision-making in the name of either equality or parity governance. In 2016, Portugal has taken some steps to announce a debate on CBQ, but the direction towards a diffusion of quotas to other spheres remains to be confirmed by actual measures.

In view of this we can conclude that in these four countries the transformative potential of gender quotas has clearly been limited by male-dominated power structures, weak women's movements, and weak WPAs. The situation is susceptible to change when left-wing governments arrive in power, as has been the case in Italy since 2013, and as women's share in elected politics rises, a phenomenon currently happening in Portugal, Italy, and Poland. At the time of writing, gender quotas remain, however, mostly of a symbolic nature.

C.1.4 Gender Quotas As Corrective Equality Remedies

The second group of conservative countries that have adopted some form of gender quota comprises Germany and Austria. Both countries, characterized by a strong male breadwinner model, have rejected LEQs, in part because, contrary to the previous group, women's political representation did improve through voluntary party quotas, even though parity has by no means been reached or, for the most part, been articulated as the desired end. Based mainly on the substantive equality logic of equal opportunities, these countries have, however, adopted PBQs and CBQs (although limited to publicly owned companies in Austria), contributing to a progressive and piecemeal dismantling of their conservative gender regimes through a system of gradual corrections, rather than a purportedly "revolutionary" and self-conscious moment of overall transformation. The domains of implementation, scope, and the moment of quota adoption in these two countries varies but in both countries gender quotas in public bodies were initially embraced by WPAs in the early 1990s, including at the time in domains such as universities and research in Austria. These processes mostly take place in a top-down fashion as attempts to hollow out the traditional breadwinner model by imposing women's presence in sites of power in the public sphere, one quota at a time, the next always building on the previous one, combining both principled (equality) and strategic (economic efficiency) reasoning. In both Germany and Austria, quota adoption has been a process encouraged by federalism and Land-level experimentation (Lang and Sauer 2013), and accompanied by processes of constitutional reform entrenching substantive gender equality.

Germany exemplifies this type. As Sabine Lang notes in her chapter, although Germany has traditionally been a laggard in gender equality, the early implementation of gender quotas in public bodies in the early 1990s, thanks to the impetus of women's policy agencies, paved the way for the (partial) inclusion of women in the state and federal bureaucracy. It also paved the way for the diffusion of quotas to corporate boards, despite strong and long-lasting resistance from the Christian-democratic party in power. These breaches in the traditional conservative gender regime opened the door to new claims for gender quotas in elite professions such as journalism and medicine. At the same time, the political representation of women, achieved through relatively under-enforced voluntary quotas, remains far from parity, and only recently has the language of parity penetrated the discourse and the possibility of legislating electoral quotas to achieve it been picked up by some critical voices. While the process has not yielded such positive results in Austria, the adoption of PBQs in 1993 and the mobilization of the women's movement to include a substantive equality clause in the Constitution in 1998 contributed to challenging and eroding the conservative breadwinner model, as Nora Gresch and Birgit Sauer detail in their contribution, and women in the two main political parties, the socialist SPÖ and the conservative (ÖVP), have recently started to mobilize for LEQs. In both countries, the fact that PBQs, rather than LEQs, were first adopted, means that the path to gender quotas remained much more contained within bureaucratic and institutional politics. This bureaucratic path has somehow restrained the debate to legal arguments in court cases about positive action for women in public service, rather than articulating gender quotas within a broader framework of democratic renewal following the lead of European institutions.

In summary, in both Germany and Austria, gender quotas have acted as mechanisms seeking the progressive correction of gender inequalities, proceeding domain by domain and often under the leadership of the WPA officially commissioned to ensure women's equality. The process has entailed the explicit articulation of substantive equality as the new constitutional paradigm. As a result, gender quotas are gradually helping overcome the traditional breadwinner family model, which has deep cultural roots. Yet, contrary to those scenarios in which gender quotas have been conceived as tools to enforce a comprehensive and fast-track reform of the country's gender and/or citizenship model, in these countries, legislated gender quotas have so far avoided the central domain of parliamentary representation (where women continue to be underrepresented) and the parity or gender-balanced framing so relevant in other European countries. Only now, and especially in Germany, might there be some signs that this is about to change.

Our comparative perspective on thirteen European countries therefore sheds new light on the adoption and diffusion of gender quotas in Europe. Beyond a broad convergence towards the adoption

437

of gender quotas at the global level, and a dynamic tending towards higher thresholds in some regions of the world, our comparison shows that paths towards the adoption of gender quotas vary, and that the transformations they bring to existing gender regimes and democratic understandings are contrasting. We have delineated here four different scenarios. While not exhaustive, our typology brings new insights into why some countries adopt public bodies quotas rather than electoral quotas first, and the consequences of these institutional trajectories. Our typology shows that while the actors who push for quotas remain the same – women's rights organizations, women's sections in political parties, and WPAs – the lack of one of these forces, such as a mobilized women's movement, can be replaced by strong and active WPAs, or by key insiders, especially female politicians, as much on the right as on the Left. These variations between the paths that countries have followed in adopting – and resisting – quotas explain why in some countries, such as France, Belgium, Spain, and Slovenia, gender quotas are articulated as issues of democracy and governance, leading to a diffusion of gender quotas to many spheres of decision-making, while in other countries gender quotas have remained limited to a bureaucratic approach of contained affirmative action in the public sector or, under EU pressure, to the corporate world, where women's presence in boards has often come to be justified in the name of economic efficiency and in a context of economic crisis.

C.2 THE JURIDIFICATION OF THE STRUGGLE AROUND GENDER QUOTAS: TRANSFORMING THE MEANING OF CONSTITUTIONAL GENDER EQUALITY?

It was not until the turn of the twentieth century, with women's access to suffrage, that political equality between men and women gradually became the constitutional norm. In some cases, the belated recognition of women's political rights triggered constitutional amendments "to write women in."[5] Alternatively, women were simply read into the abstract, generic "male" used by constitutions when crafting rights to political participation, sometimes with the assistance of interpreting courts. Be that as it may, since the end of WWII, and clearly by the

---

[5] This was, for instance, the case with the 19th Amendment to the US Constitution, granting women equal suffrage, passed in 1920.

time the gender quotas movement started to cross the continent, women's equal rights status with men had become a "defining feature" of Europe's democratic constitutionalism. Typically, in European constitutional democracies, the protection of this principle of gender equality was entrusted to the courts though judicial review. It is thus not surprising that, unlike the struggle for suffrage, where law and courts played only a very modest role, the struggle for gender quotas in Europe has been highly juridified, with constitutional rights and principles as well as constitutional courts and experts playing a leading role in the fight for and against gender quotas. From the case studies included in this volume, the only departure from this rule has been that of the Nordic countries' majoritarian democracies which, with the exception of Norway, have remained reluctant to resort to judicial review, constitutional law and courts being granted overall less centrality in public life. In these countries only the direct influence of European law has somewhat increased the role of the judiciary in settling affirmative action-related controversies.

Interestingly, this volume shows that the juridification of the battle around gender quotas – that is, its removal from the political arena and its partial or central placement within the constitutional one – has, in virtually every case, translated into an increase in the hurdles for women's public empowerment. As a starting point we must recall that, in Europe, it was the formal sex equality model that became the defining constitutional gender equality paradigm in postwar constitutionalism. This paradigm rests on two pillars: first, the proclamation of equal rights between men and women, and second, the recognition of the principle of nondiscrimination on several grounds, including sex. To be accurate, this articulation of gender equality coexisted in some constitutional orders with general provisions expressing a vision of substantive equality, by compelling the state to take proactive action to remove societal discrimination and ensure equal opportunities in favor of marginalized groups, clauses which could potentially be read as including women (e.g. Spain's article 9.2 and Italy's article 3.2). However, the enshrining of positive action, parity, quotas, or even substantive equality explicitly targeting women's or sex-based inequalities were nowhere to be found in early post-WWII constitutionalism.

With formal gender equality being the norm, then, the agenda of gender quotas encountered constitutional hurdles of several kinds. Most clearly, for those countries committed primarily to a formal understanding of equality, granting citizens equal political rights while proscribing any type of distinctions on the grounds of sex, the adoption of gender quotas immediately posed a constitutional problem. Both the argument that quotas for women can unduly restrict male candidates' active and passive suffrage rights, and that it can stigmatize women themselves by suggesting that they in fact need special treatment beyond the recognition of equal rights, can be pressed in terms of formal equality. In Italy, for instance, it was claimed that quotas treated women like pandas (i.e. like an endangered species), and in Portugal, President Cavaco Silva vetoed one decree (which later in fact became the quota law that was adopted) for being too harsh in its enforcement mechanisms, arguing that the law as crafted infringed upon women's dignity. In more recent times, with quotas being articulated as 50/50 parity or gender-balanced thresholds that apply equally to both genders, the formal equality challenges have sometimes been rejected (for instance by the Italian and Spanish Constitutional Courts) on the basis that these measures in fact treat men and women equally and are articulated in gender neutral terms.

An overarching commitment to formal notions of gender equality (in connection to rights of political participation) reinforced by the country's espousal of a Republican universalist conception of citizenship, explains the strength of the constitutional resistance in France, not only against the adoption of political quotas but also against any further extension of quotas to other domains, including that of corporate governance. Indeed, France is unique in that almost every attempt to expand parity beyond elective functions during the 2000s was met with resistance by both the Constitutional Council and the *Conseil d'Etat* (the highest administrative Court), even after the first constitutional reform enabling the adoption of political quotas had taken place, precisely because the reform was interpreted as a narrow exception to the dominant norm of formal equality. Thus, the introduction of parity in the lists of candidates for the High Council of Magistrates (*Conseil Supérieur de la Magistrature*) – the main governing body of the judiciary – was declared unconstitutional by the *Conseil Constitutionnel*.[6] Likewise, corporate board quota legislation was struck down before a second constitutional reform was passed in 2008 to enable this specific domain expansion. Contrary to recalcitrant France, in all other

---

[6] Conseil Constitutionnel, Decision 2001-445 DC, June 19, 2001.

countries, once reformed, the Constitution was no longer held to be a valid tool to prevent quota domain expansion.

This book shows that even in those European countries which do not only embrace formal equality in their Constitution but are also committed to substantive equality – with constitutional provisions asking public powers to remove societal obstacles to the meaningful enjoyment of rights – it has not automatically followed that such generic provisions (expressing concern around the inhibiting potential of social inequalities) cover political quotas for women. Rather, quotas have been seen as affecting not only women's (or men's) political or equality rights, but also the country's overall political system of representation. Only in some cases, such as Spain, has a general constitutional clause expressing commitment to substantive equality (article 9.2) been interpreted as providing sufficient constitutional coverage to gender quotas when challenged in front of the Constitutional Court. Yet in other countries, such as Italy, this has not been possible; instead, the Court has attached to formal equality an absolute value in the political domain by underscoring its link to representativeness. In Italy, despite a generic substantive equality clause, the Constitution still had to be amended before electoral gender quotas could be passed. Moreover, depending on the specific way in which quotas are crafted, they can be interpreted as more or less justified departures from formal equality for the purpose of achieving remedial goals. In this regard, sometimes a line is drawn separating measures that validly ensure equal opportunities from those that arguably step beyond the legitimate realm of remedial action to directly seek equal results, something which can be seen as constitutionally problematic (a line drawn by the Constitutional Court in Italy, for instance).

However, the constitutional hurdles for gender quotas lie not only in the possibility of infringing on provisions of equality before the law and active and passive voting rights of male candidates. In almost every country in this volume, opponents and plaintiffs challenging quota legislation have also alleged that gender quotas infringe on the prima facie constitutional claim to freedom of political parties and their immunity from state interference. Not surprisingly, this argument has found great resonance in Eastern European countries from the former socialist bloc, which are particularly sensitive to the question, given their previous authoritarian traditions of repressing political pluralism, whether or not the passage of electoral gender quotas required a prior constitutional amendment (as it did in Slovenia, but not in Poland).

In addressing constitutional challenges against quotas, some national courts have explicitly recalled their international obligations (calling on both hard and soft law) pertaining to the gender-balanced representation of women to favorably interpret their constitutions. This was the case, for instance, in Italy and in Greece. In the latter, the Council of State invoked EC Equality Directive (76/207), but also the CEDAW Convention and EC recommendation 96/694/EC about the balanced participation of men and women in decision-making bodies, to advance the view that positive measures in favor of women were not contrary to equality. Also, as we saw in several countries, including the Nordic ones, when the matter was determined to fall within the competence of EU law – paradigmatically, but not only, when it concerned quotas in the public employment sector – national courts deferred to the judgment of the ECJ, and European, not national, law became the relevant legal parameter for deciding what affirmative action measures were legally permitted when challenged by formal equality claims of male plaintiffs, as illustrated in the chapters on Germany, Austria, and Sweden.

Given the manifold constitutional obstacles that can and have been raised to resist the tide of gender quotas, this book illustrates the rich typology of mechanisms that have been put into place in order to address these hurdles. In a nutshell, we find that the two main mechanisms have been constitutional reform and constitutional interpretation by courts, with the former being the dominant tool expressed in two possible varieties, a pure and a mixed form. Given the level of generality of constitutional provisions (including those concerning equality) and the existence of several constitutional rights and principles relevant to the conversation, the interpretive role of courts has proven essential in some jurisdictions, making constitutional reform unnecessary in some instances (e.g. Spain).

As for constitutional amendment processes, we distinguish three types: "preemptive," "enabling," and "reinforcing" amendments. In some countries (such as Portugal or Slovenia), a constitutional amendment was passed before the adoption of quota legislation (hence, preemptively) in the understanding that, without it, such legislation would not have overcome possible constitutional hurdles. In other countries, the constitutional amendment process was undertaken after intervening constitutional courts had detected otherwise insurmountable constitutional obstacles, thus enabling quota legislation to be enacted (as was the case in France and Italy). Finally, in some cases, constitutional amendment processes were held only to reinforce and strengthen the constitutionality of legislation that had already been declared by the courts through constitutional interpretation (as in Belgium or in Greece – thanks, in the latter case, to a change of doctrine resulting from strategic litigation in front of the Council of State with judicial review powers). In fact, these countries owe the constitutional acceptance of gender quotas to a process that ultimately combined evolutionary constitutional interpretation through the courts with formal constitutional amendments. The exception thus remains the case of Spain, where constitutional interpretation by the Constitutional Court alone was sufficient to overcome formal challenges to the constitutionality of legislation. In addition to this, the book contains examples of constitutional amendments enshrining substantive gender equality that were not a direct response to a specific challenge of (proposed or approved) legislated gender quotas, but a general move towards a new gender equality paradigm (such as in Sweden, Germany, and Austria).

In these amendment processes to enshrine substantive gender equality and/or to enable the passage of legislative quotas, we can distinguish between bottom-up processes (as in Germany, Austria, and Greece) and top-down processes (as in Portugal and Italy, where women's groups either did not engage in the quota struggle actively or did so with very little effect), as well as between a variety of different actors taking the lead. These include mostly political parties (as in Portugal and Italy) and women's groups, sometimes with the assistance of cross-party alliances (as in Germany, where a cross-party alliance of women in parliament was key to the reform of article 3.2GG; Greece, where a wider constitutional reform process in the second half of the 1990s presented an opportunity for feminists to push for positive measures leading to the 2001 constitutional amendment; or Austria, where a popular movement called the women's referendum was crucial for the constitutional amendment). In exceptional cases, the courts themselves proposed the need for constitutional reform, as in France, where the Constitutional Council took the lead in suggesting its need *motu proprio*. This volume clearly shows that, in Europe, constitutional reform processes as well have had a contagion effect, with the French reform affecting those in Belgium and Italy, and the reforms in Austria, Germany, and Portugal affecting that in Greece, where the reform campaign explicitly referred to a constitutional tradition in the making, shared by many EU member states in a growing number of national constitutions guaranteeing substantive equality and incorporating positive action provisions. Not surprisingly, the narrative in support of constitutional amendments in most of these countries included arguments based on international and European laws and policies in support of women's empowerment.

As for the substantive outcome of constitutional reforms, some countries inserted provisions compelling the state to actively take measures to ensure equality between men and women and to eliminate inequalities specifically to the detriment of women, without any specific mention to a concrete domain (e.g. Greece's article 116.2, Germany's article 3.2, or paragraph h of article 9° of the Portuguese Constitution). Other reforms, especially when responding to a direct need to give constitutional coverage to gender quotas, have been more explicit, introducing a clause either enabling or compelling the state or the legislature to take measures to promote equality or equal opportunities for women to stand for elections and to access electoral office (as in Slovenia and Portugal), or to advance equal access by women and men to elective mandates and public office (France and Italy) or to positions of professional and social responsibility (France). Belgium is the exception: it has not only adopted an enabling clause, but also inserted a form of gender quota directly into its Constitution (with article 11 bis, known as the parity provision, requiring the executive to contain members of both sexes, and article 67, mandating, since 2011, no more than two thirds of senate members of the same sex). However, none of the other constitutional reforms set the basis for a subjective entitlement, allowing women to claim an enforceable right to equal representation – and in fact the possibility has been explicitly rejected by the French Constitutional Council in its recent decision on the matter, upholding statutory gender quotas in certain university governance committees.[7]

In general, the overall assessment of the constitutional reforms discussed in this book shows that in most of the European countries in which gender equality is centrally entrenched in the country's constitutional democracy, a process of constitutional transformation has indeed taken place, supporting a renewed conception of women's citizenship. Indeed, in an increasing number of European countries, renewed constitutional standards demand state action to ensure the presence of women in representative institutions and decision-making bodies, not just passive recognition of their abstract entitlement to an equal right to participation. These cases mark a constitutional shift, through amendment and interpretation, towards substantive gender

---

[7] Conseil Constitutionnel, Décision n° 2015-465 QPC, April 24, 2015.

equality and renewed conceptions of democratic legitimacy, making the active participation of women an essential precondition. In some cases the specific placement of the reform is most telling of its symbolic dimension. This is the case in France, where the commitment to gender parity now figures in article 1 of the Constitution, among the fundamental values defining the French Republic.

C.3 PATTERNS OF MOBILIZATION: RECONFIGURATIONS AND ALLIANCES FOR GENDER EQUALITY IN THE TWENTY-FIRST CENTURY

Besides documenting the increasing role of supranational and national courts in many European countries debating gender quotas, the set of cases collected in this volume offers confirmation of the key actors in quota adoption, identified by previous studies, but also new insights. When analyzed from a comparative perspective, these countries reveal new patterns of mobilization for women's rights and women's political participation, in which women's policy agencies play a crucial role.

Indeed, the authors of this volume confirm that women's sections in left-wing political parties (as well as, where women's sections were weak, simply individual women within left-wing parties) have been instrumental in starting the quota revolution by pushing for internal quotas in their parties and, more importantly in terms of impact, for quotas on candidate lists. The historically lukewarm embrace of female suffrage by left-wing political forces, fearing women's conservative or regressive politics, seems to have finally faded – whether or not such forces have then prioritized women's empowerment in national settings (Rubio-Marín 2014, 9–11). Indeed, socialist, social-democratic, and green parties in Austria, Belgium, Denmark, France, Germany, Norway, Spain, and Sweden were among the first to adopt voluntary gender quotas, between the end of the 1970s and the mid-1980s. While quota adoption by political parties signalled the penetration of the feminist second wave into the realm of formal politics, implementation varied greatly from one country to the next, with France and Belgium being examples of failed voluntary party quotas and Norway and Sweden illustrating the potential of these self-imposed tools for bringing more and more women into politics.

Mobilizations inside political parties were often relayed or supported by mobilizations outside political parties, that is, within the autonomous women's movement. Indeed, the coalition between women inside and outside of political parties has proven to be as beneficial as it was in the fight for female suffrage (Rubio-Marín 2014, 12–15). These coalitions formed in different ways across European countries, with autonomous women's organizations pressuring parties through competition, shaming tactics, and, eventually, bypassing them entirely when resistance proved too hard to overcome internally. In France, when feminists within parties were unable to obtain better political representation, they changed tactics and, instead of pursuing internal lobbying, they allied with autonomous women's organizations to get around their parties' fierce opposition to their demands. Once they had succeeded in making the issue politically relevant, they encouraged party competition. In Sweden, as shown by Lenita Freidenvall's chapter, women's organizations went even further and reacted to the decrease in female representation following the 1991 legislative elections by forming a network called *Stödstrumporna* (the Support Stockings) and threatening to create a women's party, a threat which finally proved efficient in convincing traditional political parties to place more women on their lists. In Austria, feminists threatened to create a women's party and then created an autonomous association, *Unabhängiges Frauenforum* (UFF, Autonomous Women's Platform) in 1996 to launch a people's initiative on women's issues, the so-called "women's referendum" that proved crucial in revising the Constitution and enshrining a more substantive conception of equality. In Greece, it was mostly women lawyers who mobilized outside political parties to create momentum in the public sphere to ask for a constitutional revision of the definition of gender equality, a revision that proved instrumental in passing gender quota laws. Hence, in countries where political parties proved responsive to the claims of women inside their ranks, voluntary party quotas proved efficient and women's sections in parties and autonomous women's organizations allied at strategic junctures to ensure compliance. In countries where political parties, including on the Left, proved unwilling to change, the gender quota revolution was delayed and women's autonomous organizations played a much more important role, displacing the debate from inside parties to the public realm, asking for legislated quotas or threatening to take away women's votes by creating women's parties. In those countries where both the commitment of political parties and women's movements were missing, the revolution was, as we have seen, very limited in scope and reach.

While the struggle for women's political representation offered women inside and outside parties an opportunity to form coalitions, public bodies quotas and corporate board quotas offered a different set of opportunities to a different set of actors. Indeed, unlike electoral quotas, for the most part neither type of quota stirred up important public debates or feminist mobilization (even though in some cases women's social movements did take part in the debate, such as in Germany and Italy). To a large extent this difference can be explained by the fact that these struggles were seen as "corporatist" struggles for already privileged women. Instead, these gender quotas were generally the work of bureaucratic insiders and critical feminist actors within executive or the legislative powers. In line with scholarly work showing women's policy agency's increasing – although unstable and variable – power in European countries since the 1990s (McBride and Mazur 2010), our set of cases shows the crucial role played by femocrats and gender equality offices in the conquest of gender quotas. In Norway, Austria, and Germany, none of which had adopted LEQs, emerging state feminist institutions were crucial in pushing, and passing, PBQs as early as the 1990s. In France and Belgium these institutions were instrumental in the diffusion of quotas – from electoral quotas to public bodies and corporate boards – and allowed crucial actors to step outside party lines.

The comparative perspective on the adoption of corporate board quotas shows that they rarely spark mobilization from the traditional actors in the women's movement. Nor is the cause often framed as a matter of equality or equal rights. Rather, CBQs have often been encouraged by businesswomen – increasingly united around this cause in view of the slowness of spontaneous, market- and merit-based progress, which many initially defended – often in the name of women's specific abilities in governance (i.e. risk averse attitudes) or in the name of diversity (the business case for diversity). These arguments are in a spirit typical of the growing business-feminism that has taken shape globally and that foregrounds the notion of general interest over that of justice or rights, something that, once again, may account for its relative success in a short time (Engelstad and Teigen 2012). Also, CBQs have often been the work of critical individual actors, both left- and right-wing ministers for women's rights or MPs invested in bureaucratic organs in charge of gender equality. In France, Marie-Jo Zimmermman, head of the Observatory for Parity, was instrumental in the passing of the corporate board quota law. In Norway, the Gender Equality Ombud, Anne Lise Ryel, launched the idea, which was later picked up and included in the revision of the Norwegian gender equality act by Minister Haugland. In Sweden, as early as 1993, Deputy Prime Minister and Gender Equality Minister Bengt Westerberg (from the Liberal Party) appointed the first commission of inquiry to study the possibility of achieving a more equal distribution of male and female managers in business. In 2002, with no clear change in the numbers of women on boards in sight, Minister Margareta Winberg from the Social Democratic government threatened companies with the adoption of legislated corporate board quotas if they did not comply voluntarily within five years, a threat that proved effective.

The stories of individual critical actors – often, but not always, women – should not obscure the fact that they tend to act as representatives of WPAs, thereby overshadowing the potential of the latter as sites of institutional non-partisan commitment to women's equality. Women's policy agencies indeed provide key actors with important resources – expert reports, statistics, and networks – that are crucial for their claims to be successful. In France, Marie-Jo Zimmerman actively lobbied within her own conservative party to pass a constitutional reform enabling CBQs after the Conseil Constitutionnel had struck down pertinent legislation, while she was head of both the Observatory for parity, a governmental agency in charge of monitoring the implementation of LEQs, and the parliamentary delegation for women's rights. She was therefore a key insider with an important network and resources she could mobilize to lobby her cause and even resist opposing internal party pressure.

In short, corporate board and public bodies quotas offer significantly different paths to quota adoption than legislated electoral quotas, and they show the importance of women's policy agencies and individual femocrat insiders. Yet interconnections abound, and these bureaucratic insiders and key political figures were able to capitalize on previous legal gains – made during the process of adoption of LEQs or PBQs – to press for quota diffusion in other domains. In particular, we find that constitutional reforms explicitly enshrining substantive gender equality (as in Austria, Belgium, and Germany), or preexisting comprehensive equality statutes (like the Norwegian gender equality act), have all facilitated the adoption of gender quotas in public bodies. Once enshrined in law, these foundational legal equality frames have proven crucial for WPAs to promote the diffusion of gender quotas to other domains, illustrating the ways in which further gains can be achieved for women's citizenship in an era of institutionalization of gender equality and feminism. Where strong WPAs do not exist, for example in Greece, the adoption of constitutional amendments that enabled the passing of LEQs has not led to the fast diffusion of gender quotas mechanisms to other domains such as CBQs, as a lack of institutional structures fails to provide key insiders with the needed tools and platform. In short, while the rationales used by actors to push for quotas remain strikingly similar across countries and across domains, combining the usual equality and difference frames as well as principled and pragmatic arguments, the actors who use them differ from one domain to the next.

The various paths to quota adoption reveal the complex picture of women's mobilizations in the twenty-first century. Indeed, we see women's organizations using multilevel governance and transnational networks to pursue their goals, relying on ties to international and European institutions and their legal instruments and policies, and drawing on common framings and narratives as well as on the shared experience and accumulated knowledge of neighboring countries. We see women's policy agencies taking an important role in quota diffusion and sometimes forging alliances with women's organizations that increase the opportunities for passing ambitious gender quota schemes, or even taking the lead where movement mobilization is largely absent, often under the leadership of key individual actors, even if it means settling for less ambitious reforms. While CBQs attest to the emergence and increasing relevance of a form of market-friendly, moderate, or soft feminism that puts the accent on efficiency rather than gender justice[8] (as one would reasonably expect in the private sector and with regards to elite professions), with some rare exceptions, traditional women's rights organizations remain much less interested in the question of women's access to economic power than in women's access to political power. This bias, inherited from the second wave, explains the low mobilization for corporate board quotas, which is largely perceived as an elitist bourgeois agenda of secondary interest for women's struggles. As a consequence, this claim is mainly promoted through EU governance tools (such as the European Strategy for Gender Equality (2016–19)) and WPAs.

[8] Johanna Kantola and Judith Squires (2012) use the concept of "market feminism," while others use the term "business feminism," corporate feminism, or post-feminism to describe this trend within power elite professions and organizations, mostly studied at the global level. See also Elias (2013); Blanchard, Boni-Le Goff, and Rabier (2013).

C.4 QUOTAS AND TRANSFORMATIVE POLITICS: TOWARDS PARITY GOVERNANCE?

The irresistible diffusion of gender quotas from one domain to the next when political circumstances are favorable – that is, from electoral politics to the public administration, the judiciary, universities, or corporate boards – is imposing women's presence in the remaining bastions of patriarchal power. Moreover, the diffusion across countries and domains of gender quotas invites the question of whether a consensus is gradually emerging across Europe around substantive gender equality as the new shared sex equality paradigm or, to go even further, around "parity governance" requiring the equal presence and participation of both genders in decision-making (Rubio-Marín 2012). Whereas in citizenship terms, the former could possibly encompass the adoption of temporary remedial measures to ensure equal opportunities or de facto equality within a liberal egalitarian tradition of citizenship, especially suited to social democratic regimes dominant in Europe, the latter would instead propose an important redefinition of democratic citizenship, making the equal presence of women a new overall requirement for legitimacy. Susan Franceschet and Jennifer Piscopo (2013) have argued that in Latin America, the spread of quotas across domains other than the legislative, the increase in the expected percentages for gender balance (to a ratio of 60/40 and/or 50/50), the permanence of the intended measures, and the shift in the framing narrative (from temporary special measures/affirmative action/minimal thresholds to gender-balanced representation and parity) all suggest that gender quotas have become a tool in the redefinition of democracy with gender parity now seen as a structural precondition for democratic legitimacy. The question is whether something similar can be said of the process in Europe – a process that uniquely includes the diffusion of quotas into corporate governance (not at all widespread in Latin America) and hence, into the private domain of power and governance.

Our set of countries shows a clear and positive shift towards substantive gender equality, with European law rendering the legitimacy of affirmative action to remedy societal discrimination ever more explicit and many European countries joining the trend of constitutional reforms to allow the state to take proactive measures to ensure women's *de facto* equality. This in itself is a significant and important finding. As to the possible convergence towards a parity-governance model the answer is more nuanced. Indeed, the rationale for equal sharing of political power, and the terms parity, parity democracy, and gender-balanced representation – all of which have been advanced by the European institutional machinery – can be found in increasingly more European countries, including Sweden, Norway, Belgium, France, Greece, Italy, Portugal, Poland, Spain, Slovenia, and also, recently, Germany. However, this concept does not always mean the same thing or endorse the same operational tools in every setting. Thus, when it comes to electoral politics, although quotas are generally conceptualized as permanent, not temporary measures, the threshold, far from targeting the 50/50 or 40/60 ratios that gender parity or gender-balanced representation are associated with, in some cases remains at one third (i.e. the traditional minimum threshold) despite the use of a parity or gender-balanced rhetoric. This has been the case in Portugal, Italy, Poland, and Greece, for example. Time will tell whether the difference is in principle or only in strategy, reflective of what might be perceived as different opportunity structures in different scenarios, even if the ultimate objective is a shared one. It also remains to be seen if the pressure from women's movements or WPAs will increase these low thresholds to 50 percent. On the other hand, the domain expansion is indeed a confirmed trend, though it has proceeded at very different speeds, leading to a wide variety of participation thresholds. For spheres other than politics, the majority of countries that implement quotas consider that gender balance now means at least 40-percent women, with exceptions in Belgium, which still implements one-third quotas, and Germany and Austria, which implement 30- or 35-percent quotas for corporate boards.

All in all, these variations suggest that convergence may not be automatic, and that the parity democracy discourse has not, by itself, had the same impact in different arenas of power, neither in terms of domain spread for quota policies nor in terms of target thresholds. Moreover, beyond numbers, the parity democracy discourse and gender quotas in general have not reconfigured the relationship between gender equality, democracy and the public/private dichotomy in the same way across countries. For a long time the political and academic debate on gender quotas has focused on the "critical mass" argument, implying that as more women enter decision-making positions thanks to quotas, their participation would change the rules of the game.[9] Our

---

[9] For examples of studies testing the critical mass argument see Celis (2006) and Franceschet and Piscopo (2008). For a critical discussion of this argument, see Childs and Krook (2008); Lépinard (2014).

comparative perspective shifts the focus away from sheer numbers to the transformation that gender quotas may or may not bring to gendered citizenship. As our typology has meant to suggest, in some countries the transformative potential of gender quotas is more fully engaged than in others, where the adoption of gender quotas does not succeed in challenging the dominant gender regime, whether because of the persistent resistance of political elites, the lack of women's mobilization, the weakness of WPAs, or a combination of all of these factors. These mixed results indicate that, depending on the context, gender quotas can be corrective measures – defined by Nancy Fraser (2003) as remedies which do not challenge the state of power relations among groups or preexisting structures of oppression – or transformative measures, which aim to tackle the root of economic and political inequalities by changing economic, social, and political structures, affecting not only the situation of an exploited class or a dominated group but of everyone in society; i.e. the prevalent gender order.

At face value, gender quotas might appear to be paradigmatic examples of corrective mechanisms: like other affirmative action policies, gender quotas acknowledge existing gender inequalities and how they are embedded in pervasive structures of power but do not address the root cause of the problem behind women's disempowerment, such as job market segregation, gendered citizenship, the gendered division of labor, and the public/private divide. Like many affirmative action policies, gender quotas seem to aim at correcting inequalities at the margins, or rather at the high end of a pyramid of inequalities embedded in social mechanisms that extend way beyond the realm of political representation, corporate boards, or state organs. However, the difference between corrective and transformative measures might not be as clear as it seems. Indeed, Fraser herself suggests the possibility of "nonreformists reforms," that use corrective mechanisms but by doing so alter or transform the grounds upon which future policies will be elaborated (and future social struggles will be fought). These non-reformist reforms, despite their apparently corrective nature, initiate a trajectory of social change.

Following Fraser's insights, we may argue that gender quotas, which appear at first sight to be a purely corrective and reformist tool, may in fact contribute to a more radical social transformation than their current political agenda reveals. Nonetheless, whether a corrective mechanism can become a transformative one heavily depends on *context*.

Quotas are not per se either a corrective mechanism or a transformative tool. Underlying the typology we have described, we sustain the claim that gender quotas have a greater transformative potential when backed by a broad social and political consensus around the need to redefine the gender and/or citizenship model, and when they require parity or gender-balanced representation in all spheres of male domination both in the public and private domain. As the chapters in this volume show, the realization of this consensus of course depends heavily on the preexisting gender regime in each country. It is also important to note, as countries may shift over time from one category to the next, that the dynamic of transformation that characterizes gender quota reforms can rapidly change. Countries in which gender quotas are seen as only corrective measures may, depending on the evolution of the political context, use this tool in a more transformative manner in the future. Moreover, two additional elements, detailed below, can make gender quotas more transformative.

The first element is the way in which gender quotas may or may not validate a substantive conception of equality as equality of outcome in the legal order, going beyond mere constitutional proclamation and paving the way for more positive measures for women. In this sense, the justifications used for gender quotas matter. The fact is that, as remarked by Rolandsen Agustín, Siim, and Borchorst in their chapter, during the 1990s a new discourse and rhetoric of the profitability of gender equality within a range of institutions, from business to higher education, has become prominent, reinforcing the argument that gender quotas are beneficial not only for women's rights but also for industry, for society, and for men. The business case for diversity in company boards is another clear example of this type of justification. While the argument that gender quotas on company boards will increase economic competitiveness might be appealing to the business community and provide instrumental reasons to gain wide support while, at the same time, being less divisive than an argument coined in terms of gender equality and social justice, these rationales can in fact limit the transformative potential of quotas. Indeed, this argument subsumes normative arguments about gender equality beneath pragmatic economic arguments, with the risk that quotas will be delegitimized if they don't deliver economic results (which may likely be the case). The discourse based on expected economic gains makes gender discrimination invisible and creates a normative hierarchy between economic profitability and equality (and therefore a hierarchy between the economic sphere and the political sphere) that does not contribute to subverting gender hierarchies. In other words, there may be instrumental and strategic – and not only principled – considerations among the panoply of arguments put forward to gather consensus around disputed reforms, but some of the arguments deployed may have mid-term political and practical consequences for the reach and the meaning of those very reforms.

The second element to consider is whether gender quotas are indeed coupled with the objective of disestablishing the public/private divide, and the ways in which it has unduly restricted women's equality and men and women's capabilities since its entrenchment in the structure of the modern state. By affirming that the power to decide should be fairly distributed between men and women, the discourses on parity democracy and gender-balanced participation (understood as a 50/50 or a 40/60 distribution respectively) contribute to eroding the traditional association of men with the public sphere and of women with the private sphere. Gender quotas aiming at parity can therefore be seen as providing new social norms for governance and democracy (Rodríguez Ruiz and Rubio-Marín 2008). This link between gender quotas and the disestablishment of the public/private divide is apparent for example in the 2011 Council of Europe's Parliamentary Assembly Resolution 1825, which states that, in order to increase women's participation in decision-making bodies, its member states should not only implement gender quota mechanisms on corporate boards, but also "introduce positive measures to ensure reconciliation of private and working life, in particular as regards parental leave, balanced participation of women and men in family life ..." In this emerging, and still marginal, discourse, gender quotas are only one tool among many – but an important one – to challenge the gendered dimension of the public/private dichotomy (Rosenblum 2009). In fact, quotas indeed are sometimes adopted within legislative frameworks seeking this broader objective – a promising sign, for in the end, "public parity" cannot be achieved without "private parity."

Future prospects for true transformation of citizenship are uncertain. There are some hopeful signs, such as the fact that the gender quota revolution is still very much in the making with the clear and mostly irreversible trend (only contradicted in our set of countries by Denmark) of more and more countries adopting gender quotas (if and when they realize that gender equal representation will not happen spontaneously) in a growing number of domains, with ever-higher thresholds and with an expectation of permanence. The institutionalization of WPAs also suggests that the gender quota revolution might continue to unfold even in the absence of a strong women's movement. Moreover, in the European context, substantive gender equality has increasingly become the new gender equality paradigm, often with explicit constitutional recognition, and male governance, including in the corporate world, has reason to be challenged in view of the dramatic economic downturn.

On the other hand, there are less promising signs. For one, the recent upsurge of extreme right-wing, xenophobic, populist, and sometimes clearly anti-European political forces embracing an explicit anti-gender and anti-quotas agenda is a new phenomenon whose ultimate reach is difficult to predict. Moreover, while the overall deterioration of the living conditions of many Europeans since the financial and economic crisis – only aggravated by austerity policies – can indeed help highlight the importance of gendering economic decision-making and support the spread of corporate board quotas to counter the global trends of deregulation which are partly responsible for the crisis, these conditions can also succeed in lowering the relative political salience of the struggle for women's empowerment. Similarly, the perceived threat of immigrant and refugee flows, and the "more fundamental" challenges to women's equality that those flows are said to bring, may divert the attention away from the forms of domination still affecting the preexisting population of women. More importantly, the prevailing neoliberal/minimal state ethos makes it unlikely that European states will follow (or improve on) the Nordic example by increasing their level of involvement to alleviate care demands traditionally placed on families and hence, on women, and to interfere with spontaneous family arrangements regarding the distribution of care – which have always overburdened women and continue to do so today. In other words, in most European countries we are still far from approaching gender parity in the private domain of care, and the conditions to promote this agenda seem doubtful.

Last but not least, if the comprehensive transformation of citizenship into forms that guarantee greater inclusiveness and equality is the ultimate goal, it must be noted that the struggle for the empowerment of the oppressed and underrepresented, as expressed through the struggle for quotas, has on the whole remained restricted to gender in the countries under scrutiny in this volume. That is, in almost none of our cases did the debate on electoral gender quotas evolve into serious debates for the political inclusion of other minorities, especially ethnic or visible minorities. While in Belgium the preexisting representation of linguistic communities did help the claim for gender quotas, the reverse has not happened in any of the countries we have examined. Only in corporate governance has the discourse of gender quotas been articulated around corporate imperatives for diversity, but with no empirical evidence as yet of concrete measures developing this broader agenda. An expanding field of research examines the relationship between gender quotas and quotas for other minorities and ethnic groups (see Bird 2001; Htun 2004; Krook and O'Brien 2010; Hughes 2011; Lépinard 2013), but the empirical primacy given to gender over other grounds of discrimination remains so far unchallenged, leaving open the question of whether a profound transformation of citizenship can rest on the disestablishment of the gender binary alone.

References

Bird, Karen. 2001. "'Liberté, egalité, fraternité, parité ... and diversité.' The Difficult Question of Ethnic Difference in the French Parity Debate." *Contemporary French Civilization* 25 (2): 271–92.

Blanchard, Soline, Isabel Boni-LeGoff, and Marion Rabier. 2013. "A Priviledged Fight? Women's Movements for Equal Access to Corporate Leadership and Management Positions." *Sociétés Contemporaines* 89 (1): 101–30.

Celis, Karen. 2006. "Substantive Representation of Women and the Impact of Descriptive Representation. Case: the Belgian Lower House 1900–1979." *Journal of Women, Politics and Policy* 28 (2): 85–114.

Childs, Sarah, and Mona Lena Krook. 2008. "Critical Mass Theory and Women's Political Representation." *Political Studies* 56 (3): 725–36.

Dahlerup, Drude, and Lenita Freidenvall. 2005. "Quotas as Fast track to Equal Representation for Women: Why Scandinavia Is No Longer the Model." *International Feminist Journal of Politics* 7 (1): 26–48.

Elias, Juanita. 2013. "Davos Women to the Rescue of Global Capitalism: Postfeminist Politics and Competitiveness Promotion at the World Economic Forum." *International Political Sociology* 7: 152–69.

Engelstad, Fredrik, and Mari Teigen, eds. 2012. *Firms, Boards and Gender Quotas: Comparative Perspective*. Bingley, UK: Emerald.

Ferreira, Virgínia. 2014. "Employment and Austerity: Changing Welfare and Gender Regime in Portugal." In Maria Karamessini and Jill Rubery (orgs.), *Women and Austerity – The Economic Crisis and the Future for Gender Equality*. New York: Routledge: 207–27.

Franceschet, Susan, and Jennifer M. Piscopo. 2008. "Gender Quotas and Women's Substantive Representation: Lessons from Argentina." *Politics & Gender* 4 (3): 393–425.

2013. "Equality, Democracy and the Broadening and Deepening of Gender Quotas." *Politics & Gender* 9 (3): 310–16.

Fraser, Nancy. 2003. "Institutionalizing Democratic Justice: Redistribution, Recognition and Participation." In *Pragmatism, Critique, Judgment: essays for Richard J Bernstein*, edited by Seyla Benhabib and Nancy Fraser (125–48). Cambridge, MA: MIT Press.

Freidenvall, Lenita. 2006. *Vägen till Varannan damernas. Kvinnorepresentation, kandidaturval och kvotering i svensk politik 1970–2002*. Stockholms universitet.

2013. "Sweden: Step by step – Women's Inroads into Parliamentary Politics," in D Dahlerup and M Leyenaar eds. *Breaking Male Dominance in Old Democracies* 97–123 Oxford: Oxford University Press.

Holli, Anne-Maria. 2011. "Transforming local politics? The impact of gender quotas in Finland." In *Women and Representation in Local Government. International Case Studies*, edited by Barbara Pini and Paula McDonald (142–57). New York: Routledge.

Htun, Mala. 2004. "Is Gender Like Ethnicity? The Political Representation of Identity Groups." *Perspectives on Politics* 2: 439–58.

Hughes, Melanie M. 2011. "Intersectionality, Quotas and Minority Women's Political Representation Worldwide." *American Political Science Review* 105 (3): 604–20.

Kantola, Johanna, and Judith Squires. 2012. "From State Feminism to Market Feminism." *International Political Science Review* 30 (4): 382–400.

Krook, Mona Lena, and Diana Z. O'Brien. 2010. "The Politics of Group Representation. Quotas for Women and Minorities Worldwide." *Comparative Politics* 42 (3): 253–72.

Lang, Sabine, and Birgit Sauer. 2013. "Does Federalism Impact Gender Architectures? The Case of Women's Policy Agencies in Germany and Austria," in *Publius – The Journal of Federalism* 43 (1): 68–89.

Lépinard, Éléonore. 2013. "For Women Only? Gender Quotas and Intersectionality in France." *Politics & Gender* 9 (3): 276–98.

2014. "Gender Quotas and Transformative Politics." RCAS Policy Papers 2014/6.

Lombardo, Emanuela. 2017. "The Spanish Gender Regime in the EU Context: Changes and Struggles in the Wake of Austerity Policies." *Gender, Work and Organizations* 24 (1): 20–33.

Mazur, Amy G. 1996. *Gender Bias and the State. Symbolic Reform at Work in Fifth Republic France*. Pittsburgh: University of Pittsburgh Press.

McBride, Dorothy, and Amy G. Mazur. 2010. *The Politics of State Feminism. Innovation in Comparative Research*. Philadelphia: Temple University Press.

Rodríguez Ruiz, Blanca, and Ruth Rubio-Marín. 2008. "The Gender of Representation: On Democracy, Equality and Parity." *International Journal of Constitutional Law* 6 (2): 287–316.

Rosenblum, Darren. 2009. "Feminizing Capital: a Corporate Imperative." *Berkeley Business Law Journal* 6 (1): 55–95.

Rubio-Marín, Ruth. 2012. "A New European Parity-Democracy Sex Equality Model and Why it Won't Fly in the US." *American Journal of Comparative Law* 60 (1): 99–126.

2014. "The Achievement of Female Suffrage in Europe: On Women's Citizenship." *International Journal of Constitutional Law* 12: 4–34.

Siim, Birte. 2000. *Gender and Citizenship. Politics and Agency in France, Britain and Denmark.* Cambridge: Cambridge University Press.

INDEX

CAMBRIDGE STUDIES IN LAW AND SOCIETY

Books in the Series

Diseases of the Will
Mariana Valverde

The Politics of Truth and Reconciliation in South Africa:
Legitimizing the Post-Apartheid State
Richard A. Wilson

Modernism and the Grounds of Law
Peter Fitzpatrick

Unemployment and Government: Genealogies of the Social
William Walters

Autonomy and Ethnicity: Negotiating Competing Claims in Multi-Ethnic
States
Yash Ghai

Constituting Democracy: Law, Globalism and South Africa's Political
Reconstruction
Heinz Klug

The Ritual of Rights in Japan: Law, Society, and Health Policy
Eric A. Feldman

Governing Morals: A Social History of Moral Regulation
Alan Hunt

The Colonies of Law: Colonialism, Zionism and Law in Early Mandate
Palestine
Ronen Shamir

Law and Nature
David Delaney

Social Citizenship and Workfare in the United States and Western
Europe: The Paradox of Inclusion
Joel F. Handler

Law, Anthropology, and the Constitution of the Social: Making Persons
and Things
Edited by Alain Pottage and Martha Mundy

Judicial Review and Bureaucratic Impact: International and
Interdisciplinary Perspectives
Edited by Marc Hertogh and Simon Halliday